Early Greek Myth

Volume Two

Early Greek Myth

A Guide to Literary and Artistic Sources

Volume Two

Timothy Gantz

The Johns Hopkins University Press   *Baltimore and London*

© 1993 The Johns Hopkins University Press
Printed in the United States of America on acid-free paper

The Johns Hopkins University Press
2715 North Charles Street
Baltimore, Maryland 21218-4319
The Johns Hopkins Press Ltd., London

Originally published in a one-volume hardcover edition, 1993
Johns Hopkins Paperbacks edition, in two volumes, 1996
05 04 03 02 01 00 99 98 97 96   5 4 3 2 1

Library of Congress Cataloging-in-Publication Data

Gantz, Timothy.
    Early Greek myth : a guide to literary and artistic sources / Timothy Gantz.
        p.   cm.
    Includes bibliographical references and index.
    ISBN 0-8018-4410-X (hc)
    ISBN 0-8018-5360-5 (v. 1: pbk.: alk. paper)
    ISBN 0-8018-5362-1 (v. 2: pbk.: alk. paper)
    1. Mythology, Greek.   I. Title.
BL782.G34   1993
292.1'3—dc20   92-26010

A catalog record for this book is available from the British Library.

In memoriam
Kyle Meredith Phillips, Jr.

Contents

ix

Contents

xi

Contents

VOLUME TWO

Early Greek Myth

Volume Two

14   Thebes

Kadmos   Most likely when we think of Thebes' earliest history, that is, its founding, we think of Kadmos' trek from Delphi to Boiotia, following the prophesied cow that led him to the city's destined site. As early as the *Iliad,* indeed, the Thebans are called Kadmeioi (the only name the poem ever uses for them), suggesting some awareness of this story. But the *Iliad* never actually mentions Kadmos himself or the founding, and the *Odyssey* names him only once, as the father of Ino (see below). Quite the contrary, *Odyssey* 11, the *Nekuia,* offers a completely different founding legend, that of Antiope who bore to Zeus Amphion and Zethos, builders of the walls of Thebes. The *Ehoiai,* Pherekydes, and Pindar also refer to the efforts of these twins, and thus it seems clear that from some fairly early point in time we have two completely separate foundation myths. Fitting them together obviously posed a problem for mythographers; Pherekydes puts Amphion and Zethos first and then follows with Kadmos (3F41d), but the more usual solution was to suppose Antiope's sons the authors of a refounding of the city during some convenient break in the line of Kadmos. Such an expedient is scarcely what the original stories intended, but since like the mythographers we must begin somewhere, we will follow the lead of this latter arrangement.

In chapter 6 we found, as part of the line of Io from Inachos, quite conflicting traditions about the father of Europa, who is sometimes Agenor and sometimes Phoinix. Presumably Kadmos is always her brother, or at least a relative (why else would he set out to search for her?), but our first actual mention of his lineage is in Pherekydes, where he is the son of Agenor and half-brother of Phoinix (3F21), while our first specific acknowledgment of Europa and Kadmos as sister and brother appears in Hellanikos, if this part of a scholiast's summary does derive from that author (4F51: both siblings are children of Phoinix). To Kadmos' one appearance in the *Odyssey* noted above (as Ino's father: 5.333) we can add that he marries Harmonia at the end of the *Theogony* (937, 975–78: Semele, Ino, and three other children named), and is again Semele's father in *Homeric Hymn* 7. Of his own exploits, however, there is not a word in Hesiod, and he is entirely absent from what remains of the *Ehoiai.* Almost certainly he played a role in Stesichoros' lost *Europeia,* for our one surviving reference says that Athena sowed the dragon's teeth (195 *PMG*). Pausanias also speaks on several occasions of another Europa poem, often ascribed to Eumelos, which must have covered a considerable territory, since Amphion and Zethos are treated, but he never mentions it when discussing Kadmos himself (9.5.8). Of more uncertain origin and date is the remark (by a scholiast) that Mousaios in a *Titanographia* (?) related how Kadmos followed the cow from Delphi (2B1). From these scant crumbs we are, I think, entitled to conclude that the tale of Kadmos' founding of Thebes was probably well known in the seventh and sixth centuries (if not earlier), and has escaped fuller presentation only through chance.

Nevertheless, the full details of the story do not survive before the fifth century and Pherekydes. From three different references we see that the Athenian mythographer must have related most if not all of the familiar events at Thebes preceding the founding: Kadmos slays the dragon with a sword (3F88), whereupon Ares and Athena give him half the teeth (the other half go to Aietes) and he sows the ground with them at Ares' direction (3F22). Armed men then spring up out of the earth, causing Kadmos in fear to throw a stone at them. Thinking to be attacked by each other, they turn to mutual slaughter, until only five—Oudaios, Chthonios, Echion, Pelor, and Hyperenor—remain, and these become the foundation of the city. Such details give us most of the basic story, at least in outline. Pindar, although he mentions Kadmos only in connection with his daughters, does several times name the Spartoi, that is, the sown men (*Py* 9.82–83; *Is* 1.30; 7.10; fr 29 SM), and Aischylos in the *Hepta* calls the Theban defender Melanippos one of these same Spartoi, spared by Ares (*Hepta* 412–13). But the founding seems not to have been dramatized in tragedy—Euripides' *Kadmos* most likely concerned later misfortunes—and our first consecutive account derives from an *Iliad* scholion that claims both Hellanikos and Apollodoros as sources (ΣA *Il* 2.494 = 4F51).[1] Here, suspending for the moment judgment on authorship, we find that after Europa, daughter of Phoinix, has been kidnapped from Sidon, her brother Kadmos is sent out to find her. Failing in this, he goes to Delphi, and is advised not to interfere in the matter of Europa, but rather to make use of the cow-guide and found a city wherever she should stop to rest. He of course follows this advice, and travels through Phokis until he encounters a suitable cow that leads him through all of Boiotia before sinking to the ground. Wishing to sacrifice the cow to Athena, Kadmos sends his men to fetch water from the spring of Aretias, but a dragon guarding the place kills a number of them. Kadmos in his turn kills the dragon, and on Athena's advice sows the teeth, thus producing the earth-born men. The dragon, however, is somehow sacred to Ares, and the god in anger wishes to destroy Kadmos; Zeus intervenes to save him. As a result Kadmos is given Harmonia, daughter of Ares and Aphrodite, to wife, but must first perform menial service for a year as atonement for the dragon's death. All the gods and the Mousai attend the wedding, and each brings to Harmonia a gift.

To this detailed but uncertainly attested account we can add from other scholia the facts (definitely Hellanikian) that Kadmos killed the dragon with a stone (4F96), that he sowed the teeth by the will of Ares, and that five men *alone* (with the same names as in Pherekydes) sprang up out of the ground; thus here there was no combat (4F1). But how much of the *Iliad* 2.494 scholion as a whole might derive from Hellanikos remains uncertain. Apollodoros, the second author cited by that scholion, has in fact the first part of its text in almost the same words (Ap*B* 3.4.1–2), leaving us to suspect that (as often) the scholiast has gone directly to that source for a good deal of his information. But Apollodoros then turns to Pherekydes (whom he names) and other sources for the battle among the Spartoi, a battle not mentioned by the scholiast and explicitly not a part of Hellanikos' version. Since the scholiast has here (if not before) surely utilized a source drawn from Hellanikos, we may well wonder if the subsequent details of his account—Ares' anger, Zeus' intervention, Kadmos' servitude to Ares and marriage to Harmonia—are not likewise derived from that author, even if they also appear (minus Zeus' explicit role) in Apollodoros.[2] Elsewhere in Hellanikos, there is admittedly one small detail seemingly in conflict, namely that Harmonia is a daughter of Elektra and Zeus, rather than Ares and Aphrodite (4F23); but here too we remain uncertain of authorship, since that (unusual) genealogy is in the scholiast source only preceded and followed by references to Hellanikos.

Several plays of Euripides also dealt with pieces of the legend. The prologue to his lost *Phrixos B* (spoken by Ino?) begins with a description of why Kadmos came from Phoinicia to Thebes; alas the quote breaks off before we learn why (fr 819 N[2]). In the *Herakles* we find as in Aischylos the idea that Ares saved a few of the Spartoi to populate Thebes (*HF* 4–7); the same play later suggests that Ares himself sowed the teeth after he had taken them from the dragon's jaws (*HF* 252–53). And in the *Phoinissai* the chorus provides a rapid survey of the major events: Tyrian Kadmos following the cow as the oracle has commanded until it falls to earth and signals the place of settlement; Ares' dragon guarding the spring, and Kadmos slaying it with a rock when he comes for water; then the sowing of the teeth (by Athena's command) and the combat of the resulting warriors (*Pho* 638–44, 657–75). Further on in the drama, Teiresias tells Kreon that his son Menoikeus must die if Thebes is to be saved, and as reason for this cites Ares' continued anger over Kadmos' slaying of the dragon (*Pho* 931–44). Kreon and his sons are the last of the pure line of the Spartoi, the men born of the dragon's teeth, and thus the lot falls to them. Herodotos contributes to all this only the more historical detail that Kadmos stopped at Kalliste/Thera on his journey from Phoinicia, and there left his friend Membliaros and others to colonize the island (Hdt 4.147).

From all these sources we obtain a remarkably consistent tradition; the one major variant is Hellanikos' notion that only five Spartoi were born, and thus that no fight took place. By contrast the combat is clearly recognized in Pherekydes, Aischylos, and Euripides, and the extreme brevity of Aischylos' reference shows that it must be older than his *Hepta*. Still somewhat unclear, however, is Ares' role in the sowing and his response to the death of the dragon. Our summary of Pherekydes shows that there Athena and Ares give Kadmos the teeth together, and Ares directs the sowing. Hellanikos adds that this sowing was by the will of Ares; the attribution in ΣA *Il* 2.494 of it to the advice of Athena might mean (if this is also from Hellanikos) that she conveyed to Kadmos Ares' demands (or proposed to Ares this course of action). But either way the god's participation suggests that the sowing was an atonement for the dragon's death, that is, a way of assuring that Kadmos' new city would not exclude the previous powers inhabiting that site. Puzzling if that is true is the *Iliad* scholia's belief that Ares was angry *after* the sowing and that Zeus had then to intervene. Possibly neither Pherekydes nor Hellanikos included this detail or the subsequent servitude to Ares. But more likely, I think, the scholiast has slightly confused the order of events, and sowing, servitude, and marriage are all part of a single settlement worked out by Athena, if not by Zeus. Euripides' statement in the *Herakles* that Ares himself sows the teeth gives us no real clue to the god's motives; the same is true for Stesichoros, where Athena does the sowing.

In art we have only a little evidence. Our earliest illustration is probably a Lakonian cup of the mid-sixth century now in the Louvre; on it a warrior with helmet, shield, and spear attacks a serpent that has twisted itself around a column of a shrine or fountain house and rears itself up to strike (Louvre E669). Most often this is taken to represent Achilleus at the fountain house where he will ambush Troilos,[3] but without Troilos present it is hard to see how customers would recognize the story, unless a preliminary encounter with a snake was a standard part of the literary tradition. We will see in chapter 16 that a snake does in fact appear with Achilleus in several artistic representations of the ambush, but never as an object of Achilleus' concern. More likely then, our painter intended to show this deed of Kadmos, although in the absence of additional figures (other than animals) our understanding of the story is not much improved. The same must be said for a Red-Figure cup by Apollodoros in Tarquinia where a warrior draws his sword to strike a snake (RC 1123); here, without any fountain house to provide backdrop, even the supposition of a myth is dubious.

More helpful, and clearly showing the story in question, are two vases of the mid-fifth century in New York.[4] On one, a calyx krater near the style of the Niobid Painter, we see Kadmos starting back in alarm, one hand holding a water jug and the other with a stone poised to throw (NY 07.286.66). The object of his apprehension is presumably the snake that rears up before him, but it emerges from behind a seated woman who reclines quite calmly. The scene is flanked to either side by Athena (left, with Kadmos) and Ares; neither looks at all alarmed, although that may be more the style of the painting than a narrative detail. The other pot, a bell krater, has Kadmos approaching cautiously (this time with spears and hydria); the snake now rises up over the head of the woman (NY 22.139.11). The identity of this woman has occasioned some uncertainty. Harmonia is one possibility, but the figure seems too closely linked to the snake for that to be possible, and probably we should imagine some divinity of the spring (or else a proleptic personification of Thebes herself, as on a late-fifth-century hydria where names are given and Thebe is one of several divinities present: Berlin:Lost F2634). In any case, both these kraters reaffirm the idea that Kadmos went to the spring for water, and the rock that he uses as a weapon on the calyx krater is that which we found in Euripides' *Phoinissai*. But the exact role played by the gods continues to be obscure. Given the range of variation in our evidence, it may be that the nature of their participation, beyond helping Kadmos, was not firmly fixed in the earliest versions.

Later literary sources have little to add on this or any other point; Ovid gives the fullest account (with a blood-curdling description of the dragon) but omits Ares altogether, so that Athena alone counsels the sowing (*Met* 3.1–137). A scholion to the *Phoinissai* does offer an eighteen-line hexameter version of the oracle given by Delphi to Kadmos, in which we learn that the cow was to have a white mark like the circle of the moon on each side of its back (Σ *Pho* 638). In general, all our late sources that narrate the story of the founding give the standard details, including the combat among the Spartoi; Hellanikos remains alone in suggesting that there were only five Spartoi to begin with. Likewise, Hellanikos (or at least ΣA *Il* 2.494) and Apollodoros are the only preserved sources to report a period of servitude by Kadmos as penance for killing Ares' dragon.

We saw above that as early as the end of the *Theogony* Kadmos receives Harmonia, daughter of Ares and Aphrodite, to wife (*Th* 937), but no writer ever explains why he was honored in this way (ΣA *Il* 2.494 does suggest that it was somehow part of the reconciliation with Ares). We should note in this regard that Harmonia, although her parentage should make her a full-fledged divinity, never quite achieves the status of Thetis. On the contrary, writers generally seem to imagine her growing old with Kadmos in normal domestic tranquility, her godhood somehow forgotten in the process. Theognis notes that the Mousai and the Charites attended the wedding (15–18), and Pindar compares the two marriages, that of Thetis and that of Harmonia, as occasions on which the gods honored men with their presence (*Py* 3.86–96). In art the wedding was shown on the Amyklai Throne (Paus 3.18.12: the gods bring gifts), and the happy couple appears in a chariot on a fifth-century Black-Figure neck-amphora (Louvre CA 1961: names provided),[5] but regrettably nothing survives to match the splendor of Thetis' wedding as we see it in the works of Sophilos and Kleitias. The *Iliad* scholia state, however, that all the gods brought gifts, and Diodoros provides a list of these, including the necklace that will play such a large role in the future history of the race (DS 5.49.1). Here Diodoros makes it a gift from Athena (together with a peplos); earlier he had described it as a present from Aphrodite (DS 4.65.5). In Apollodoros, Kadmos himself makes the presentation, the necklace having been fashioned by Hephaistos (ApB 3.4.2). But as we saw in chapter 6, Apollodoros found in Pherekydes the idea that Kadmos acquired the necklace not from Hephaistos but from Europa who got it from Zeus (3F89). Presumably this is the gift referred to as given to Europa by Zeus in the *Ehoiai* after they have arrived on Krete (Hes fr 141 MW). Presumably, too, Pherekydes did not have Europa leave Krete to find her brother, but prevailed upon Zeus or one of the other gods to deliver the present. Whatever the route of transmission, the necklace is clearly always of divine manufacture, and thus a prized heirloom for future generations. Only Statius offers the idea that Hephaistos made the necklace as a source of evils for Harmonia and her descendants, in revenge for Aphrodite's adultery with Ares; in addition to Harmonia herself, he names Semele, Iokaste, Argeia, and of course Eriphyle among those who suffered from it (St: *Theb* 2.265–305, followed by VM I 151 [citing Statius] and VM II 78).

The end of the *Theogony* lists five children of the union of Kadmos and Harmonia, four daughters, Ino, Semele, Agaue, and Autonoe, and a son Polydoros (*Th* 975–78). No later author rejects any of these or makes further additions; we will return to their misfortunes in the following sections. As for Kadmos' final fate, after so much disaster in his family, Pindar places him on the Isles of the Blessed, with Peleus, Achilleus, and others (*Ol* 2.78). Euripides does not contradict this, but does provide via Dionysos (in the *Bakchai*) a startling prediction about his old age: the god ordains that he and Harmonia will be changed into snakes, and that at the head of a vast army (driving an ox-cart) they will sack many cities, until they come to their defeat in assaulting the oracle of Apollo (*Bkch* 1330–39). But Ares will then save them and transport them to the land of the Blessed. This revelation stands in our text immediately after a substantial lacuna (perhaps fifty lines), and thus whatever preceded the metamorphosis (obviously an exile of some sort) has been lost. But both the speech itself and Kadmos' response to it (*Bkch* 1354–60) establish that he and his wife will become snakes *before* they lead barbarian hordes back into Greece, bizarre as this notion may seem. One wonders, too, if they will remain snakes when they go to the land of the Blessed (surely not). The lost *Kadmos* of Euripides might have dealt with these matters, and thus paved the way for the *Bakchai*, although here too such events would probably have to be covered by prediction. Apollonios notes that Kadmos and Harmonia are buried in the country of the Encheleis, in Illyria (AR 4.517–18), and Apollodoros agrees that this was their place of exile (ApB 3.5.4). But Apollodoros is not prepared to accept their snake transformation until after their further deeds are accomplished; thus in human form they are chosen leaders of the Encheleis in their battle against the Illyrioi, and Kadmos even begets another son, Illyrios. Only at the close of their lives do they become serpents before being sent by Zeus to the Elysian Fields.

Ovid, too, makes the metamorphosis the climactic event of their existence, as we might expect; in his account Kadmos, tired after long wandering (no battles or kingship are mentioned) thinks of the snake he slew at Thebes, and prays that if the gods are angry with him for this they might turn him into a snake (*Met* 4.563–603). They do so, and as he curls himself up in Harmonia's lap she also is transformed; they slither off together. Hyginus develops this notion of divine anger further by stating that Ares destroyed Kadmos' children for that reason; the additional point that he and Harmonia become snakes *may* imply the same cause (*Fab* 6). Elsewhere Hyginus offers a story not otherwise known, that Agaue in her wanderings came to Illyria and married the king Lykotherses, then slew him so that she might give the kingdom to her father Kadmos (*Fab* 184, 240, 254). That Kadmos came to Illyria in his old age seems well enough agreed upon by everyone. The snake motif is more puzzling, but may go back to some dimly remembered ancestor worship of our hero himself or his divine wife.[6]

Semele and Ino

Kadmos' most famous daughter Semele, like her sister Ino, is already known to Homer, for Zeus in *Iliad* 14 reminds us that she is the mother of his son Dionysos (*Il* 14.323–25). To be fair, Zeus does not actually call her a daughter of Kadmos, but he does place her with Alkmene in Thebes, and the inference as to her father is very likely. The end of the *Theogony* gives us the first explicit statement of her origins, as we saw above, and also recognizes the unusual circumstances attending the child she conceives: although mortal she gave birth to Dionysos, an immortal, and subsequently obtained divine status herself (*Th* 940–42). In *Homeric Hymn* 1, despite a large gap in the text,[7] we learn first of the different locales where Semele is thought to have delivered the god, and are then informed that these are all erroneous, since Zeus was the one to bring the child to birth (on Mount Nysa). The author of the poem clearly intends to say more on the subject, but unfortunately this is where the lacuna occurs, and when the text resumes Zeus is just finishing a prophecy. In the remains of this Hymn, Dionysos is three times called *eiraphiôtês*, a word debated even in antiquity (see ΣA *Il* 1.39). If it derives from *rhaptô*, "to sew," or could have been thought to do so by our poet, it could refer to the idea that Dionysos was sewn up in Zeus' thigh. On the other hand, we must admit that the whole tale of the sewing might have been invented (at whatever point) to explain an otherwise obscure epithet. What we can say for certain is that as early as this Hymn there is something unusual about Dionysos' birth, and that he does seem to be brought forth from some portion of his father's anatomy. The poem also offers at its close the first occurrence of Semele's other name, Thyone.

Unfortunately little else is said about Semele in the rest of the seventh and sixth centuries. Tyrtaios mentions her, but the fragment is from a papyrus, and there is no usable context (20 W). Sappho in a similar fragment names Thyone, almost certainly as the mother of Dionysos, when the god is being invoked together with Hera and Zeus (17 LP). In art, Semele appears together with Dionysos (both named) on a charming Black-Figure cup by the Kallis Painter in Naples; only the heads are shown, and mother and son look at each other intensely as he holds up a kantharos (Naples Stg 172). The two are also found on a hydria in Berlin, from the Leagros Group, with Dionysos entering a chariot while his mother watches; here she is named both Semele and Thyone (Berlin:Lost F1904). Finally, Dionysos and a woman named only as Thyone stand behind the chariot of Peleus and Thetis on another late sixth-century hydria in Florence (3790). In addition to these three vases, there are quite a number of other Black-Figure examples in which Dionysos is shown with an unnamed woman in a chariot setting or the like, and some of these have even been interpreted as the bringing-up from Hades of Semele. But, of course, any such pairing could as easily represent Dionysos and Ariadne, or perhaps even more likely Dionysos and a goddess, such as Aphrodite: we must remember that the god of wine is a staple feature of generic/metaphoric scenes in art, and his appearance with Aphrodite would well illustrate the pleasures of the grape combined with those of love.[8] In any case, such uncertainty should prevent us from drawing any firm conclusions about stories present or not present in the sixth century.

From the first half of the fifth century we have several useful references in Pindar, and what must have been a very detailed treatment in Aischylos' *Semele*, which was possibly part of a larger connected production. In *Olympian* 2, composed for Theron of Akragas in 476 B.C., we find note of the sufferings of the daughters of Kadmos balanced against the greater blessings that Semele and Ino ultimately obtained (*Ol* 2.22–27). In the case of Semele this means that "dying in the blast of the thunderbolt she lives among the Olympians, and Pallas loves her always, and Zeus the father exceedingly, and her son the ivy-bearer." This is, surprisingly, our first concrete evidence for the manner of Semele's death, although something out of the ordinary has already been guaranteed by the fact that in *Homeric Hymn* 1 Zeus must bear the child. The opening of *Pythian* 11 confirms that Semele is to be found among the gods (*Py* 11.1), while *Pythian* 3, after observing again the misfortunes of Kadmos' daughters, offers the consolation that at least Zeus came to the bed of Thyone, here too clearly Semele (*Py* 3.96–99).

Aischylos' play or plays on the subject are surrounded by intriguing plot possibilities and major controversies.[9] The one certain fragment of any use is a single line: "Zeus, who killed him" (fr 221 R). The context of this sparse quote is a discussion of linguistic forms, so that we derive no help there, and cannot even be sure that the thought is relevant to the action of the play. If it is, then Dionysos himself, mistakenly believed to have perished with his mother, is one candidate for the victim; I believe, however, that there is another likelier figure, to be discussed below. Turning for the moment to a still more crucial problem, we find that Plato in Book 2 of the *Republic* complains of (among other things) playwrights who bring Hera onstage disguised as a temple priestess and collecting alms for the "life-giving children of the Argive river Inachos" (*Rep* 2.381d = fr 168 R). The same line and its predecessor are cited by the scholia to Aristophanes' *Batrachoi* 1344, with the added information that Asklepiades attributed these lines to Aischylos' *Xantriai*. From other sources we know that the *Xantriai* contained at least a reference to the death of Pentheus (fr 172b R), and very likely dramatized that event (see below). That Hera would have a role in such a play is surprising, although there is always the possibility that she stirred up Pentheus or the chorus against the worship of Dionysos. But at this point we encounter a remarkable coincidence: the later sources that recount in full Semele's story—Diodoros, Apollodoros, Ovid, Hyginus—are unanimous in stating that she met her doom because she was deceived by Hera, and Ovid and Hyginus specify that this came about through Hera's transforming of herself into Semele's nurse Beroe (references below). If this last detail is not exactly what we find in Aischylos, it does seem clear that the standard run of the tale made Hera in disguise offer the fatal suggestion to her husband's paramour. Assuming this was the case in Aischylos' *Semele* as well (someone after all must make the suggestion), we can hardly avoid the thought that Asklepiades has miscited the source of his information, and that Aischylos' disguised temple priestess is indeed from the *Semele*.

Furthering this suspicion is an Oxyrhynchus papyrus fragment containing these same lines about Hera and giving us what precedes and follows (POxy 2164; text in Radt's fr 168). We do not learn as much as we would like, but the chorus, in speaking just prior to Hera's entrance, mentions Semele (twice) and Kadmos; thus the play was surely part of a Semele/Thebes trilogy. Hera herself after her opening lines continues to speak of the daughters of Inachos, but in connection with marriage, modest brides, the begetting of children, and the marriage bed, which all sounds like a veiled attack on Semele's adulterous relationship with Zeus rather than a diatribe against Dionysos. On balance I would argue that the motif of a Hera in disguise in order to bring Semele to disaster is probably as early as this play. For the rest of the work we know with certainty only that Aischylos brought Semele on stage pregnant and divinely inspired, and that those women who touched her belly became inspired as well (p. 335 R). The drama's alternate title *Hydrophoroi* ("Watercarriers") might refer to water being brought for the expected delivery, or simply to a general occupation of the chorus.

Sophokles' play *Hydrophoroi* may or may not have dealt with the same topic as that of Aischylos; nothing survives. The latter state of affairs holds as well for a comic *Semele* by Eubolos and a poem, *The Birthpangs of Semele*, by Timotheos, and for several fourth-century tragic efforts. But Euripides does assure us in the prologue to the *Bakchai* (spoken by Dionysos himself) that Semele was consumed by lightning as she gave birth to the god, and that Hera's hybris (an odd word here) against her was the cause (*Bkch* 1–9). A fragment of the same playwright's *Antigone* addresses the god as the child of Dione, apparently in a conflation with Thyone (fr 177 N²). And the scholiast who cites the line also suggests that in Panyasis Thyone was Dionysos' nurse, someone distinct from Semele (Σ *Py* 3.117 = fr 8 *PEG*); the line quoted as evidence does not quite prove that (unless a *trophos* could never be one's mother), but of course our citer had access to the rest of the poem.

Of later (and fuller) accounts the earliest is that of Diodoros, who assigns in two separate places two different motives for the misfortune. In the first of these Hera comes to Semele in the guise of one of her friends, and goads her to seek honor equal to that of Zeus' wife (DS 3.64.3–4). In the second version Hera does not appear at all; instead Semele herself becomes distressed because Zeus does not speak to her when he visits, and thinking herself despised she asks him to come to her bed as he does to that of Hera (DS 4.2.2–3). Zeus therefore arrives for their lovemaking with his lightning and thunder. Semele perishes in the fire, having delivered her child prematurely, and Zeus gives the baby to Hermes to convey to the Nymphai of Nysa. This is our first clear explanation of the accidental nature of Semele's death by the thunderbolt; very early accounts *might* have been different. In Ovid, as we noted, Hera initiates the catastrophe in the guise of Semele's Epidaurian nurse Beroe (*Met* 3.256–315). Thus concealed, she causes Semele to doubt that her lover really is Zeus, and encourages her to seek proof. Semele extorts from Zeus an oath to grant her an unnamed request, much as Phaethon does from Helios, then makes the same wish as in Diodoros. Zeus brings his very lightest, tamest bolts, but the effect is still too much for the expectant mother. Apollodoros gives the same general account, but limits himself to noting that Semele was deceived by Hera into making her request, and died of fright when seeing the lightning and thunderbolts being hurled (ApB 3.4.3).

Hyginus, like Ovid, has Hera visit Semele in the form of the nurse Beroe; here, however, the suggested motive for the request is so that Semele may know the greater pleasure of lying in love with a god (*Fab* 167, 179). Hyginus also records as we saw in chapter 2 the idea that Zeus took the pulverized remains of the heart of the god (Liber, i.e., Dionysos/Zagreus) born to him from Persephone and gave them to Semele in a potion, from which she conceived the second Dionysos (*Fab* 167: see Appendix A). Finally, a variant account of Semele's delivery may be preserved on a late-fifth-century Red-Figure hydria now in Berkeley: Semele herself lies (eyes closed) on a bed in the center, while Hermes to the left carries the child away, apparently forestalling Iris (winged cap, kerykeion) who approaches from the right for the same purpose; behind her stands a taller woman with scepter who will surely be Hera, as from above a thunderbolt descends (Berkeley 8.3316). If Zeus' wife did plot to steal away the child herself, the idea has not survived elsewhere. This seemingly normal birth of a viable child might also seem to preclude the second birth from Zeus' thigh, a detail hinted at in *Homeric Hymn* 1 and made fully explicit on several Red-Figure pots of the fifth century (see chapter 2).

We saw at the beginning of this section that both the end of the *Theogony* and Pindar recognize Semele as a mortal woman who becomes immortal and joins the gods on Olympos. Such a development seems obvious enough, given the status of her son; the Cyzicene Epigrams (*AP* 3.1), Diodoros (4.25.4), Apollodoros (ApB 3.5.3), Plutarch (*Mor* 565f-566a), and Pausanias (2.31.2) all report that Dionysos actually went down into Hades and brought his mother up from the dead, an action paralleled only by that of Orpheus, albeit unsuccessfully. Diodoros adds that Dionysos renamed his mother Thyone on this occasion. The three Black-Figure cups cited earlier as showing Semele (named) and Dionysos together certainly reflect some such tradition for the sixth century. One might have hoped to see the actual fetching of Semele in art, but without further appearances of her name nothing presents itself very securely. The best candidate is probably a lip cup by the Xenokles Painter in London on which we see Dionysos and Hermes and women who could be Semele and Persephone (London B425). The other side of the cup shows Zeus, Poseidon, and probably Hades, which might encourage us to see the reverse as an Underworld scene, yet Ariadne or simply undefined goddesses are always possible. If Aischylos' *Semele* (or the trilogy of which it was part) has any kind of resolution flattering to Zeus we must expect Semele's apotheosis to be predicted or narrated there, as compensation for her unhappy treatment by Hera. To me this seems extremely likely, but the question has much to do with one's general view of Aischylos' gods, and opinions will obviously vary.[10]

In all, Semele remains a unique figure, the only mortal woman to become the mother of a god, and a major one at that. She is also a rare example of a continuing sexual affair between god and mortal (as opposed to goddesses and mortals), although Apollo and Koronis might constitute another instance. Of course a continuing affair is necessary if she is to meet her fate as tradition describes it, and probably her destruction by thunderbolt was always an important part of her image, lending as it does an air of sacrality. The motif of the unwitting request plays its part in this, and has a folktale look about it, but we must still allow that in some early accounts Zeus might have intentionally slain Semele, as indeed Apollo slays Koronis. Diodoros actually cites a Naxian version to this effect, with Zeus wishing his son to be born from himself and not a mortal woman, so that he would be a god (DS 5.52.2). This seems unlikely to be early, given the close bond between Dionysos and Semele in our Archaic sources, but it does give an idea of the possibilities. Another (and darker) cause for Zeus' potential displeasure will emerge in the next section, when we look at Aktaion's fate. That Semele (like Koronis) miscomported herself and paid the penalty in some versions of the story is, of course, not impossible, and in that case Hera's jealousy might have been added as a later element to shift the blame for her fate. But on present evidence we have no reason to suppose that the goddess' role was not always a part of Semele's tale.

On the artistic side in this connection we should note a number of vases on which Zeus threatens a woman with a thunderbolt poised and ready to throw (e.g., London E313, by the Berlin Painter). Such a tableau has been taken by some to denote Zeus and Semele, and while it could scarcely represent the familiar story (where Zeus brings his thunderbolt only reluctantly), it might conceivably anticipate Diodoros' version noted above. But as we saw in chapter 6, on one such vase the female in question is named Aigina (NY 96.19.1), so that probably all of them represent that object of Zeus' affections.[11]

As for Ino, Semele's sister who in some accounts cares for the infant Dionysos, we have already surveyed the various myths about her and her husband
Athamas in chapters 2 and 5. Here it may perhaps be repeated that, although
she does appear in the *Odyssey* as the sea goddess Leukothea, Homer says
nothing of what brought her to that pass. Pherekydes is our first source to
make her a nurse of Dionysos, although Aischylos presumably dramatized a
similar situation in his lost *Athamas*, with the consequent madness sent by
Hera. For the other tales, of Ino as vanished first wife of Athamas come back
to save her children, or second wife bent on destroying her stepchildren, we
must await Euripides' *Ino* and two *Phrixos* plays, or rather our reconstruction
of them based on Hyginus. The leap into the sea with Melikertes was apparently part of the *Ino*, and is mentioned (*sans* Melikertes) in the *Medeia*; it
seems, however, already implied by the *Odyssey*, and Melikertes' death is in
Pindar the origin of the Isthmian games. One emerges from these many different stories with a suspicion that Euripides (or perhaps Sophokles before him)
took Ino from the basic tale in which she is driven mad by Hera and arbitrarily
replaced other names with hers in myths about other wives of the multifaceted
Athamas. In origin she would seem a counterpart to Semele in Hera's wrath
against Dionysos; indeed Aischylos' *Athamas* and *Semele* may have been part
of the same trilogy. Her ultimate fate as a sea goddess is certainly regarded by
Pindar (and probably Homer) as a blessing; whether in all accounts it out-
weighed her suffering is more difficult to say.

Aktaion   The fate of Aktaion, son of Autonoe (sister of Semele and Ino), follows logically
enough here as part of the fortunes of the family, but we will also see that it is
not completely separate from the tale of Semele herself. After Semele's union
with Zeus the *Theogony* notes, for Autonoe alone of the three other daughters
of Kadmos, a marriage, to Aristaios (*Th* 977); no children are given, and we
cannot even be sure who this Aristaios was, although he may be the son of
Apollo and Kyrene by that name. Our first encounter with offspring is in the
Ehoiai, where according to a very fragmentary papyrus summary Aktaion son
of Aristaios and Au[. . .] desires to marry someone whose name ends in -le
(Hes fr 217A MW).[12] He suffers something at the hands of his grandfather
(presumably Kadmos), is turned into a stag by the will of Artemis, and torn
apart by his own dogs. The text is part of a series of capsule summaries of
mythological figures suffering metamorphosis, with this particular summary
attributed specifically to the *Ehoiai*. Unfortunately, given its brevity and the
slight gap between Aktaion's desire for someone and his death, the motive
behind Artemis' deed remains unclear. But other authors almost certainly help.
Although Stesichoros rationalizes the affair slightly by saying that Artemis
threw a deerhide over Aktaion to bring about his fate, he also says that she did
this to prevent him from marrying Semele, thus giving us (surely) the name
missing in the *Ehoiai* (236 PMG). Akousilaos probably completes the picture,
for according to Apollodoros he offered as motive that Zeus was angry because

Aktaion was courting Semele (2F33). Possibly there are two different accounts here, with two different divinities holding center stage, but more likely the conflict is the same in both cases, and Zeus sends Artemis to eliminate Aktaion so that he may reserve Semele's favors to himself. Likely too, with so little room in the *Ehoiai* summary for a separate offense to Artemis (and no special reason to mention desire for Semele otherwise), that work also made Aktaion's relationship to his aunt the cause of his troubles.[13]

In the early fifth century, Phrynichos wrote an *Aktaion* attested only by the *Souda*; more intriguing are the remains of Aischylos' *Toxotides*, which dealt with the same subject. To judge by the title, the chorus of that play consisted of huntress attendants of Artemis, who are probably the ones to note that Aktaion never returns from a day's hunt without some quarry (fr 241 R). But other fragments turn us back to the question of maidens and marriage: Aktaion speaks something about glances and marriage beds (the text is very corrupt), then also says, "The blazing gaze of a young girl does not escape me, if she has tasted of a man; for such I have an experienced eye" (frr 242, 243 R). On the assumption that any chorus of huntresses, whether devotees of Artemis or not, will be virgins, we must suppose Aktaion's remark to be directed elsewhere. Nothing will prove that he is thinking of Semele, but if he desires marriage in this play, then here (as in the *Ehoiai*, Stesichoros, and Akousilaos) she is probably the object of his intentions, and we imagine that the affair with Zeus has already begun. Admittedly that is a great deal to assume; on the other hand, if the play revolves around any of the later-attested causes for Aktaion's demise his concern with young women here will be very hard to explain. To take speculation just one step further, the *Toxotides* and *Semele* may also have been part of a connected dramatic production, in which case issues raised in the first play could carry over into the second. In that regard we might then wonder if the line preserved from the *Semele*—"Zeus, who killed him"—does not refer to Aktaion, for whom Semele may or may not have cared. Whatever the case, the brutal removal of a rival would certainly seem to reflect badly on Zeus, as does the treatment of Semele in her play, for though Zeus may not cause her destruction he is ultimately responsible for it. We must remember, however, that Dionysos' birth is in question, and then too Aktaion's interests may have been directed more toward exposing Semele's shame than seeking her hand. In all, though we can say nothing with certainty, Aischylos' handling of this material seems likely to have agreed with that of his predecessors, and to constitute a version quite different from the one made familiar by Kallimachos and Ovid.

We will see shortly that there is an extensive artistic tradition, reaching back into the middle of the sixth century, on the subject of Aktaion's death, with Artemis virtually always in attendance. Certainly this material is of interest, but since it shows only that one phase of the story it does not help us much in establishing the whole narrative. At the end of the fifth century Euripides in the *Bakchai* offers a brief glimpse of other details: Aktaion is here torn apart by his dogs because he boasted to be better in the hunt than Artemis herself (*Bkch* 337–40). Fragment 241 R of the *Toxotides* has already emphasized Aktaion's hunting prowess in that play, and conceivably it was a dramatic issue for Aischylos. But the context of the *Bakchai* reference is Teiresias' advice to Pentheus after the latter has slighted Dionysos, and Euripides might very naturally have reshaped Aktaion's offense to conform to the point required. That the crime exactly parallels that of Agamemnon at Aulis in the *Kypria* could mean equally that it is old or that Euripides thought of the *Kypria* in inventing it.

Our more familiar tradition, that Aktaion (inadvertently) saw Artemis while the goddess was bathing, surfaces first in Kallimachos' *Hymn* 5, on the Bath of Pallas (5.107–18). In this poem Athena, who has just blinded Teiresias for a similar offense against her, tells his mother, Chariklo, to be grateful that he was not treated as Artemis did Aktaion. The parallelism between the two situations raises (obviously) the suspicion that Kallimachos might have invented the one for the sake of the other, but that cannot be proved, and in any case, since Teiresias' deed is related in far more detail, one might reasonably suppose his tale, not that of Aktaion, to be the innovation. For what it is worth, Apollodoros tells us that the bathing motif (rather than the courting of Semele) is the version of most authors (ApB 3.4.4); very probably, then, it is older than the Hellenistic period. Our most famous description of the bath and Aktaion's subsequent fate is, of course, that of Ovid in the *Metamorphoses* (3.138–252). Somewhat different is Diodoros, who suggests that Aktaion actually desired to marry the goddess, having presented her with the fruits of his hunting,[14] or else (as in the *Bakchai*) that he claimed to be a better hunter than she (DS 4.81.4–5). Hyginus combines two of these ideas (or perhaps expands upon what Diodoros meant) by having Aktaion see Artemis while she is bathing and desire to violate her (*Fab* 180). We seem in all to have three main lines of thought: (1) that Aktaion angered Zeus by desiring a woman the god had appropriated to himself; (2) that he behaved outrageously toward Artemis in some way; and (3) that he innocently viewed the naked goddess. I have argued above that (1) is the most likely motif for Aischylos' *Toxotides*, but (2) might conceivably be possible, if the lines on marriage and maidens could refer to Artemis (does Aktaion mean that he wants the one woman who has assuredly tasted of no man?). Such aggressive hybris strikes me as difficult to make plausible on stage, although it would unquestionably be dramatic.

As for the artistic tradition, we find in all early cases the actual rending of Aktaion by his dogs, rather than any other part of the story, and the surrounding elements are less informative than we might expect. The earliest example, an Attic Black-Figure cup of the mid-sixth century, featured a running Aktaion attacked on all parts of his body by dogs; two women flank the scene (Lost: from Bomarzo). Two lekythoi from the end of the century offer the same composition (Athens 488, 489); others vary only in arming Aktaion with a sword or club. Such a detail may be artistic license, since a metamorphosed Aktaion would not hold any weapon. That he is in fact human in these paintings is only to be expected, given the need to make the scene comprehensible (and pathetic). All the same, if we remember that in Stesichoros Artemis envelops the hero in a deerskin, we may ask if there was not a general tradition in which the goddess simply made the dogs believe their master was a stag. A number of Attic Red-Figure pots of the early fifth century do show Aktaion wearing such a covering as the dogs attack, as does the famous metope from Temple E at Selinous (3921C). But it is hard to say whether these artists are expressing a literal mode of thought or simply trying to convey Aktaion's dual nature. Attempts of the latter sort unquestionably appear, beginning with a terracotta plaque of about 470 B.C. now in Reggio Calabria (4337). Here Aktaion actually has a stag's head; later efforts in the same direction will give him just the antlers and sometimes the ears.

One other detail found on occasion from the late fifth century on is the figure of Lyssa (Madness), so named on a bell krater by the Lykaon Painter of about 440 B.C. (Boston 00.346). She may represent either the madness of Aktaion as a stag, or perhaps that of the misguided dogs. Also on this krater is Zeus standing to the side observing. One is tempted to view such a scene as drawn from a tragic production, with Lyssa an onstage character (as in the *Herakles Mainomenos*) and Zeus relating his role in the slaying. It must be admitted, however, that this is a completely isolated instance of Zeus' presence, and if Semele was involved, one might have expected her to be portrayed. Indeed, the central role of Artemis in every representation of Akataion's story, often in complete isolation with her victim, does seem to suggest that she was originally more important to the story than the Stesichoros-Akousilaos version would imply. The bath is completely absent in art before Kallimachos, but it would be a bold artist who undertook to show her nude (or even disrobing) in Archaic or Classical times; thus this absence may not be very significant.[15] We are left, on the whole, with a good many unanswered questions regarding Aktaion's complicity in the events that caused his doom.[16]

Agaue and Pentheus   Neither Agaue's marriage nor her son is mentioned at all in our literary sources prior to the fifth century, although Pentheus and one Galene (named) do appear on a Red-Figure psykter by Euphronios; the subject is, as we might expect, Pentheus' *sparagmos* (Boston 10.221). The earliest known narration of the tale occurs in one or more lost plays of Aischylos—the *Pentheus, Xantriai,* and *Bakchai.* Of these titles we know almost nothing, save the claim (in Aristophanes of Byzantium's hypothesis to Euripides' *Bakchai*) that the story had already been told in the *Pentheus.* Strictly speaking, that might seem to eliminate the other two titles from consideration here, but with Aischylos the connected trilogy form is always a likelihood, and a scholion to *Eumenides* 26 notes that in the *Xantriai* Pentheus' death occurred on Mount Kithairon. By itself this might be a chance reference in a play on another topic; yet if the entire story of Pentheus was told in Aischylos' *Pentheus,* we might expect our scholiast to think of and cite that work, not an unrelated one. More likely the chorus of the *Xantriai* ("Carders") "carded" Pentheus by tearing him apart, and we are dealing with a group production whose third element was probably the *Bakchai* (although nothing whatever is known of that play, and *Semele* is frequently included instead).[17] If that is right, then Aristophanes in citing one title really meant a whole trilogy, and Aischylos extended the story of Pentheus to some length. Even so, we understand virtually nothing of how the narrative might have been handled. The remark of the Pythia in the *Eumenides* which gave rise to the scholion is simply to the effect that Dionysos led out *(estratêgêsen)* the Bakchai, contriving for Pentheus "death as for a rabbit."

From about 510 B.C. comes the Red-Figure psykter by Euphronios with women pulling at the upper body of Pentheus (named); named too as one of the women is Galene (Boston 10.221). Slightly later is a hydria with women holding various limbs and the head (Berlin:Ch Inv 1966.18), and then (perhaps contemporary with Aischylos) several more such Red-Figure pots, including a stamnos by the Berlin Painter (Oxford 1912.1165). As in the case of Aktaion, these and subsequent efforts concentrate almost entirely on the rending, and thus contribute little to our notions of how the story progressed. For what it is worth, however, we should note that nowhere prior to Euripides do we find Agaue and her sisters specifically named or shown as agents of the deed.

Before Euripides' version came certainly that of Xenokles (winner in 415 B.C. with a *Bakchai*), and probably also that of Sophokles' son Iophon. But the preserved *Bakchai* constitutes our first real narration of the story. Here Dionysos returns to the scene of his birth, intent on vengeance against those who besmirched his mother's name, that is, Semele's sisters, who claimed that Zeus' thunderbolt destroyed her for falsely naming him as her child's father. Accordingly, all the Theban women have been driven mad (or inspired, at least) and sent out to the hills, while Dionysos prepares to confront the skepticism of Pentheus. The latter is presented as the son of Agaue and Echion, who already in Pherekydes was one of the original five Spartoi (3F22). What has happened to Echion, or where he has gone, we do not hear; Pentheus is clearly in charge of the city of Thebes, and determined to eradicate completely the presumed perversion of Dionysiac worship. Some of the Theban women are captured, but their bonds do not hold them, and when Pentheus applies the same treatment to Dionysos (who is disguised as one of the god's devotees) the whole palace collapses. More crucial to the drama, in the exchanges between Pentheus and the god we see the emergence of the former's repressed sexual conflicts, now channeled into voyeurism and intense longing for the very licentiousness he has condemned. Playing on his desire to infiltrate the ecstasies of the Theban women (including his own mother), Dionysos entices him into a Mainad's costume, then takes him out to the hills alone so that he might spy on the supposed orgies. But when he has gained his perch high in a fir tree the god betrays him to the women, who surround the tree and uproot it. Agaue here takes the lead in tearing her son apart; in the play's finale she appears on stage with his head, boasting of her hunting of a great lion. Only gradually with Kadmos' help does she perceive the truth, before Dionysos enters to announce final punishments for all those who doubted his divinity. Agaue must go into exile, and even Kadmos, as we saw before, will have to leave Thebes, ultimately to be metamorphosed into a snake. Pentheus' own ill-assumed arrogance, plus the hypocrisy of his professed morality, seems ample justification for his wretched fate, which is after all the heart of the story. But the harsh treatment of other members of the family reveals a surprisingly grim Dionysos; we can only speculate on whether this was Euripides' conception alone, or that of Aischylos or other playwrights before him, just as we must speculate on whether mother and aunts previously participated in the *sparagmos.*

Other evidence of this time or later rarely departs from the narrative line set down by Euripides. A number of pots show Pentheus arrayed for hunting or actually armed for battle as he sets out to capture the raving women. If any of them could be dated to (or soon after) the time of Aischylos we might suspect that this was the version of his plays; as it is, they are end of the century at best, leaving us uncertain of the origin of such an idea. Possibly artists simply developed the logic of the situation into an appropriate scene, with Pentheus' basic hostility thus portrayed. Apollodoros tells the story very briefly, and with nothing new: Pentheus tries to hinder the worship of Dionysos and goes out to Kithairon to spy on the women; Agaue tears him apart thinking him a quarry (Ap*B* 3.5.2). Ovid offers a lengthy account, but the bulk of it is the tale of Dionysos and the sailors as told by the captured Acoetes (Dionysos?); only at the end of *Metamorphoses* 3 does Pentheus charge out to confront the enemy (how we are not told) and meet his usual fate at Agaue's hands while spying on the women (*Met* 3.511–733). Neither of these writers considers at all the plight of Agaue herself. In Hyginus we have already seen that she abandons Thebes for Illyria, where she marries the king Lykotherses and later kills him (to help her father: *Fab* 184, 240, 254). One other story about her surfaces only in the Second Vatican Mythographer, who says that her scorn for Dionysos was such that climbing a tree she lay in ambush for him with a weapon (VM II 83). The text then shifts to Pentheus, and we are left to supply the outcome. In all, it does seem true that Pentheus' transvestitism and deception by Dionysos appears only in Euripides (and much later Nonnos: 46.81–127). With relatively few later accounts, however, this may be mere coincidence.

On two occasions the *Bakchai* tells us that Kadmos handed over his throne to Pentheus, the son of his daughter Agaue, while at no time does the play ever mention Polydoros, the son of Kadmos attested by the end of the *Theogony.* This Polydoros does, however, reappear toward the end of the fifth century: in Herodotos, Sophokles' *Oidipous Tyrannos,* and Euripides' *Phoinissai* he is son of Kadmos and father of the Labdakos who will father Laios (Hdt 5.59; *OT* 267–68; *Pho* 5–9). Diodoros at one point implies that he accompanied Kadmos into exile, for in that writer he returns to claim the throne after the death of

Thebes

the Niobidai (DS 19.53.5). But this is as much as we ever hear about the details of his life. Pausanias seems to suggest that he was king when Pentheus met his fate (9.5.3); in Apollodoros he marries Nykteis, daughter of Nykteus, the son of Chthonios (another of the original Spartoi), and the child is again Labdakos (ApB 3.5.5). The father-in-law Nykteus is for Apollodoros the same as the Nykteus who with his brother Lykos provides the background for Euripides' lost *Antiope*, and Antiope in turn will lead us to Amphion and Zethos, the second founders of Thebes.

We saw in chapter 6 that this role of the brothers is as old as the *Nekuia* (*Od* 11.260–65), although in that work Antiope is the daughter of Asopos. Apparently there was a tradition that saw no need to link her to a current ruling house in Thebes (as in Pherekydes, where her children founded Thebes *before* Kadmos?), and which perhaps knew nothing of her problems with her father or uncle. In the *Kypria*, however, we read that Nestor's digressions included the tale of Epopeus' ruin (probably the sack of his city) after he had seduced the daughter of Lykourgos (error for Lykos?: p. 40 PEG). We will see shortly that this cryptic summary is probably relevant, the daughter in question being Antiope, although elsewhere her father is always Nykteus. To complicate matters, Apollodoros, having first made Nykteus a son of the sown man Chthonios, later offers a different ancestry in which the father and uncle (Nykteus and Lykos) are *not* descended from the Spartoi, but are the children of Hyrieus, who in turn is the son of Poseidon and the Atlantid Alkyone (ApB 3.10.1). This latter tradition seems also to have invaded the previous one, for even in ApB 3.5.5, where Nykteus is sprung from Chthonios, he and his brother arrive at Thebes (from Euboia [or Boiotia?] by way of Hyria, after killing Phlegyas), and settle there because of the friendship of Pentheus. Apollodoros may mean us to understand that they moved away from Thebes at some earlier point, but more likely he has conflated different traditions. Whatever the case, Lykos is in this first version chosen regent by the Thebans (presumably after the death of Pentheus). As for Labdakos, who might reasonably have been expected to succeed to the throne, Apollodoros tells us that he perished also, thinking the same sort of thoughts as Pentheus. The exact meaning of this sinister phrase is not explained, and no other author clarifies it. Pausanias relates a slightly different story in which Nykteus receives the rule as regent for a very young Labdakos; he then dies in the course of the Antiope story and leaves the office to Lykos, who invests Labdakos with it when the latter comes of age (9.5.4–5). But Labdakos himself dies soon after, and Lykos then becomes regent for the son Laios.

In one manner or other, then, our later sources put the line of Kadmos aside for the moment, and the way is cleared for Antiope and her children to hold center stage. Her tale, or at least its latter phases, was dramatized as we saw by Euripides, and in addition to numerous small fragments we have an *Antiopa* by Pacuvius based on it (Cicero, *De finibus* 1.2) and an avowed summary of the play by Hyginus (*Fab* 8).[18] From these we learn that in Euripides, as in Pausanias, Nykteus is king of Thebes, and that Antiope his daughter, having been embraced by Zeus, flees the anger of her father and comes to Sikyon, where the king Epaphos (probably garbled for Epopeus: see above on the *Kypria* and below *passim*) marries her. One might suppose this would save matters, but Nykteus is not appeased, and on his deathbed asks Lykos the new king to see that she is punished. Lykos does so, killing Epaphos and bringing Antiope back to Thebes in chains; on the way (near Kithairon) she gives birth to twins, who are abandoned. At Thebes Dirke, the wife of Lykos, takes charge of Antiope and keeps her in continual torment until she manages to escape and return to the cave in Eleutherai where she delivered the children. Here the play actually begins, and here she finds the twins, Amphion and Zethos (now grown), without, of course, recognizing them. To her appeals for sanctuary Zethos turns a deaf ear; Amphion was no doubt more amenable, but nothing is decided and after the brothers leave the stage Dirke enters with some Bakchai, sees Antiope, and drags her off to be executed. By this time, however, the herdsman who raised the twins has convinced them that Antiope is their mother, and offstage they rescue her and tie Dirke to a bull.

In the play's denouement, Lykos is also dealt with; summoned by a ruse he is almost slain by Amphion, but Hermes intervenes at the last minute (10 GLP). Naturally the throne is to be handed over to the children, and there is a prediction as well of the role of Amphion's lyre in bringing stones to help the builders; thus we see that his musical powers are as old as this play. Zethos too was given some role, but our papyrus evidence suffers a gap here. The play also contained a theoretical debate between the two brothers, on the active versus the contemplative life—at what point and in what regard we do not know. One other detail, supplied by the sixth-century A.D. Byzantine writer John Malalas, is that in this drama Zeus took the form of a Satyros to rape Antiope (pp. 410–11 N²).[19] In art we see nothing of any of this tale until after the time of Euripides; a Sicilian calyx krater of the early fourth century offers the most complete representation, with the bull trampling Dirke in the background while Amphion and Zethos draw their swords to kill Lykos as Antiope watches and Hermes prepares to intervene (Berlin:Ch F3296).

Pausanias and Apollodoros both know this same basic story, and add some variants for the initial stages of it. In Pausanias, Epopeus of Sikyon carries off Antiope, and her father Nykteus launches a war against Sikyon to get her back (2.6.1–3). The Thebans lose, and Nykteus dies, but not before passing the reign over to his brother Lykos and commanding him to continue the effort, with a view toward chastising Antiope. Why Antiope should be chastised is not here explained. As matters turn out, Epopeus has also received wounds in the battle, and dies; his successor returns Antiope to Lykos, and she delivers her twins on the way back, as in Euripides. That the twins appear even when Zeus has not been mentioned suggests that Pausanias has attempted to minimize the tale of the rape in order to create a more historically plausible motive for Theban-Sikyonian hostilities; obviously, though, Zeus' contribution to the story is going to resurface at points, producing an awkward conflation. Apollodoros follows Euripides more closely, and in fact his one significant new detail, that Nykteus kills himself in shame after a pregnant Antiope has fled to Sikyon, may be taken from the play (ApB 3.5.5). Here too, as against Pausanias, Lykos defeats Epopeus in battle after Nykteus' death, and thus recovers Antiope; the remainder of the story is recounted too briefly to add anything else. The scholia to Apollonios, which offer an account similar to that of Hyginus, also know that Zeus takes the form of a Satyros to rape Antiope (cf. Nonnos 7.123), and that Nykteus, who is grieved/annoyed, then dies (Σ AR 4.1090).

Two other sources supply greater novelties. Book 9 of Pausanias attributes to the oracle Bakis the idea that because Dirke was a devotee of Dionysos the god became angry over her death and sent madness upon Antiope, until Phokos, grandson of Sikyon, cured and married her (9.17.6). On the other hand, Hyginus, who in *Fabula* 8 explicitly follows Euripides, precedes that tale with one in *Fabula* 7 in which Antiope is married to Lykos but raped by Epaphos (again surely a mistake for Epopeus), as a result of which Lykos repudiates her. Zeus then embraces her, while Lykos marries Dirke. The latter, suspicious that her husband still harbors affection for his first wife, imprisons Antiope, but Zeus effects her escape and she delivers the twins on Mount Kithairon; the revenge of her children then follows the normal pattern (although we do not know what happens to Antiope while they are growing up). This is an odd story with a Hellenistic look to it; nevertheless, parts of it may be old, as we shall see below.

Having thus entered the development of Antiope's tale in midstream, via Polydoros, his wife Nykteis, and her father Nykteus, we must turn back to our earliest sources and the tradition that Antiope's ancestors were not originally Thebans, or even lived in Thebes. The *Nekuia*, as we saw, makes her the daughter of Asopos; beyond that it says only that she bore Amphion and Zethos to Zeus, and that they were the first to settle and fortify Thebes (*Od* 11.260–65). Our three-line fragment from the epic poet Asios also makes her the daughter of Asopos and mother of Amphion and Zethos (in language clearly not borrowed from the *Nekuia*: Paus 2.6.4 = fr 1 *PEG*). But the third line adds, surprisingly, that she bore the children after having conceived by both Zeus and Epopeus. Whether such wording could ever be a loose expression for the bearing of children to one's husband in appearance but a god in reality I do not know (cf. Hes fr 17a MW, of the Moliones). If not, then of the two children only one is here Zeus' son. No other author suggests such a split paternity, although our late paraphrases and summaries are not always explicit on the matter. Assuming this is what Asios meant, the three lines as they survive still give no clue as to which son he supposed to be by which father; if one had to guess one would, I suppose, assign Amphion to Zeus, since he possesses wonderful musical skills not matched by anything we can see in Zethos. Indeed, we might hazard that those skills encouraged the notion of separate parentage, although music elsewhere always comes to mortals from Apollo or the Mousai, not Zeus. The *Nekuia* does not mention musical abilities at all; Pausanias notes that the poet of the *Europa* (apparently not Stesichoros' effort, but the epic poem sometimes ascribed to Eumelos) called Amphion the first to play the lyre, with Hermes his teacher, and that Amphion's singing caused animals and stones to follow him (9.5.8 = Eum fr 13 *PEG*). Presumably, this uncertainly dated epic precedes Euripides' play, where we find explicitly stated the fact that the lyre could construct walls (10 GLP, as above).

The *Ehoiai* may also have included such a motif: Palaiphatos, who begins his account of the building of Thebes with the words, "Hesiod and others say that they put up the walls of Thebes with a lyre," then continues, "and some believe that they played the lyre while the stones jumped into place of their own accord" (Pal 41). These last words might seem to cast doubt on the magical properties of the lyre in "Hesiod" as opposed to other writers. Yet it is hard to see what else the words "put up the walls with a lyre" could mean; most likely, the *Ehoiai* was simply not explicit enough to please Palaiphatos, and the tradition of a lyre moving stones does go back to that poem. Pherekydes, incidentally, tells us that the Mousai gave Amphion his lyre (3F41).

We found above that in Pherekydes the Thebes of Amphion and Zethos takes shape long before the time of Kadmos, in defense against the Phlegyes, and is destroyed by that people under the leadership of Eurymachos after Amphion and Zethos have died. In this way Kadmos is free to rebuild the city, and there is no conflict between the two foundations. Since no tradition before Apollodoros is known to have linked Nykteus and Lykos with the Spartoi and thus with Kadmos (and some pointedly do not), Pherekydes' solution may have been the one universally employed in early times, although the *Nekuia's* language does not absolutely exclude that Antiope's children refortified a city once inhabited by Kadmos. Certainly this last is the version of Diodoros and Pausanias: Kadmos builds the upper city, or Kadmeia, and Amphion and Zethos enlarge that with the lower city of Thebes, so that the Kadmeia becomes the citadel (DS 19.53.5; Paus 9.5.6). In Diodoros this happens between the reigns of Kadmos and Polydoros, but Pausanias and Apollodoros probably follow a more canonical line in putting it somewhere between the death of Pentheus and the adulthood of Laios. In Pausanias, we found Lykos as a double regent, first for Labdakos, then for Laios; upon his defeat by Amphion and Zethos, Laios is spirited away by friends until he should be full-grown. In Apollodoros, Lykos apparently usurps the throne from the infant Laios and reigns for twenty years (ApB 3.5.5). When Amphion and Zethos kill or expel him (Apollodoros says both) they also exile Laios, who goes to the Peloponnesos. Hyginus likewise says that they exiled Laios, son of the king Labdakos (by order of Apollo?: *Fab* 9). No very good reason for such high-handed behavior is offered; most likely it arises as a simple narrative necessity when the Antiope-Lykos-Dirke founding of Thebes and the tradition of the Labdakidai come into conflict.

It remains to consider briefly the domestic life of these twins. Amphion is from the time of Aischylos' *Niobe* onward clearly married to the daughter of

Tantalos, and the father of the children whom Apollo and Artemis slay (frr 154a, 160 R). That he is not so named earlier, even in Homer where the death of the children is recounted, is presumably just coincidence; the *Ehoiai* will certainly have specified a father, since we know it gave the number of the children (twenty: Hes fr 183 MW), but from that part of the poem no actual quotes survive. The tale itself, and Amphion's ultimate fate (of which there are several versions), will be discussed in the next chapter, when we deal with the family of Tantalos. As for Zethos, we have already touched upon his marriage in covering the travails of Prokne and Philomela in chapter 7: *Odyssey* 19 tells us that the daughter of Pandareos (Aedon, either the nightingale or a proper name) slew her own child Itylos, the son of Zethos, by mistake (*Od* 19.518–23). Several different scholia agree that she was one of the three daughters of Pandareos, and that in jealousy of the many children of her brother-in-law Amphion and his wife Niobe she plotted to kill one of the latter; unfortunately, she miscalculated the beds and killed her own son, then prayed to be turned into a nightingale. Some or all of this story seems to be ascribed to Pherekydes, who elsewhere is said to have named one Nais as a daughter of Zethos (3F125). The scholia also know a version in which Aedon succeeds in killing one of Amphion's sons, then kills her own to forestall Niobe's vengeance, much as Euripides' Medeia does. Pausanias refers very vaguely to the Homeric story when he says that Zethos' wife killed their son through some sort of error, and that Zethos died of grief (9.5.9). Apollodoros registers nothing of this; he simply notes Zethos' wife as Thebe, eponym of the city, and moves on to the calamity of Niobe without further comment (Ap*B* 3.5.6). There seems no other mention of the misfortune in antiquity.

Laios

At the beginning of the last section we saw Sophokles, Herodotos, and Euripides as guarantors for the direct line of descent from Kadmos (via Polydoros, Labdakos, and Laios) to Oidipous. Labdakos is not, in fact, mentioned as an ancestor of the house (or anything else) before Sophokles' *Antigone* (593), and Laios himself first appears by name in Pindar's *Olympian* 2 of 476 B.C. But presumably this pedigree is of some antiquity, since the epic *Thebais* has Oidipous' sons serve him with the cup of his father and the table of Kadmos, both seemingly family heirlooms; elsewhere, of course, Polyneikes is in possession of the necklace of Harmonia. The previous section showed that in those accounts where Antiope's children intrude into the line, Laios' early manhood is usually the victim, and he must wait for their demise to assume the throne. Fortunately both Amphion and Zethos suffer disaster to themselves and their children, thus paving the way for Laios' return. Meanwhile we may, if we like, follow Apollodoros in assigning his exile to Elis, so that he might meet and carry off Pelops' son Chrysippos.

This story of the first homosexual abduction among mortals is the only tale told of Laios, other than his death at the hands of his own son, and its antiquity is a matter of some question. The earliest sure appearance is the dramatization in Euripides' lost *Chrysippos*, where little survives beyond the title but enough to guarantee the situation. More detail comes down to us from a scholion to the same poet's *Phoinissai*, where we find an extended account of Theban misfortunes, including the idea that Hera sent the Sphinx because the people had failed to punish Laios' unlawful (and contrary to the rites of marriage) passion for Chrysippos (Σ *Pho* 1760 = 16F10). The source cited by the scholiast at the end of his lengthy narrative is one Peisandros; if this could be Peisandros the epic poet of Kameiros, we would have a solid Archaic pedigree for a great many things, but given the long run of the story and some of its details the account surely belongs rather to a Hellenistic mythographer of the same name.[20] What sources he used (including the *Oidipodeia?*) and in what combination we cannot say, nor can we be sure that his Chrysippos material does not depend on Euripides or post-Euripidean sources. One pre-Euripidean work in which attempts have, however, been made to find room for Chrysippos' kidnapping is Aischylos' *Laios*, where the deed would serve to somehow motivate Laios' subsequent problems with Apollo.[21] Personally I find this unlikely in the context of a drama that must have stressed heterosexual passion and/or desire for a son as the cause of Oidipous's birth. We might have expected too that the third play of the group, the *Hepta*, would at least mention such a crime, but the theory of its inclusion here remains possible. Conversely, nothing absolutely forbids us to conjecture that Euripides invented the pederasty for the sake of a play, although it is a lot to invent.[22] Either way, the Peisandros scholion resolves Chrysippos' plight after his abduction by having him kill himself with a sword in shame (a made-for-the-stage ending), and something of the same sort is surely supposed in the oracle to Laios (cited by the hypotheseis for the *Oidipous Tyrannos* and *Phoinissai*) where the king is told that his child will slay him as Zeus' response to the prayers of Pelops, who has cursed Laios for his crime (cf. Σ *Pho* 60).

About this same Chrysippos there is a second tradition, preserved as early as Thoukydides and Hellanikos, that he was slain by his brothers out of jealousy: Thoukydides actually says only that Atreus had to leave Elis because of Chrysippos (1.9.2), but Hellanikos claims that Atreus took the lead in the murder of this offspring of Pelops by a previous marriage because Hippodameia and her children feared that he would inherit his father's throne (4F157). Plato's *Kratylos* offers the same idea, that Atreus foully slew Chrysippos (395b), and thus it would seem to have had considerable currency (for further details see chapter 15). Such a grim fate does not exclude that the boy was earlier carried off by Laios, but it is hard to put the two stories into the same framework. Two authors who do manage to combine Chrysippos' abduction with his death at the hands of his own family are Hyginus and the undated (but late) Dositheos. In Hyginus, Chrysippos is carried off at the Nemean games but recovered by Pelops and then killed by Hippodameia and sons (*Fab* 85). In Dositheos, Laios is caught by Atreus and Thyestes but forgiven by Pelops when he pleads love for the boy (54F1). Apparently this means that Pelops condones the affair, for when Hippodameia steals into her stepson's bedroom to kill him (her sons hav-ing refused) he is sleeping next to Laios, with whose sword she commits the deed. Laios is naturally suspected, but Chrysippos lives long enough to name the real killer.

In art we have only an Attic Red-Figure vase of perhaps the last two decades of the fifth century (showing a Chrysippos with Aphrodite, perhaps not relevant: NY 11.213.2), plus several later Apulian ones with Laios carrying off Chrysippos and figures in Persian dress left behind in astonishment (e.g. Berlin:Ch Inv 1968.12; Getty 77.AE.14; the same scene also on a Praenestine cista in the Villa Giulia).

Turning from such misadventures to the matter of Laios' marriage, we find again considerable uncertainty. The *Nekuia* calls Oidipous' mother Epi-kaste but offers nothing else about her or Laios prior to his death and her fatal remarriage (*Od* 11.271–73). Of the treatment of any of these matters in the *Oidipodeia* (or *Thebais*, if that work had references backward) no trace remains, and likewise for the Peisandros scholion, whatever the date(s) of its informa-tion. In the fifth century we do extract something from Pherekydes—the my-thographer reports that Kreon gave Laios' wife Iokaste, Oidipous' own mother, to him as wife (3F95)—and from the dramatists.

Aischylos' version of the king's ill-fated end—as recounted in the lost *Laios* and *Oidipous*—we must reconstruct from the third play in that trilogy, the *Hepta*. The chorus there tells us that there was an ancient transgression, a *parbasia* committed by Laios and swiftly punished, although something in this connection has survived to the third generation (*Hepta* 742–49). We also learn that Laios ignored Apollo when the god thrice prophesied from Delphi that dying without issue he would save Thebes. The playwright, of course, supposes us to have seen the first play of the group, the *Laios*; thus he does not specify whether the transgression was the refusal to heed Apollo, or something done earlier for which the prophecy was a kind of punishment. Either way, we must be surprised that Laios' begetting of a child would threaten the city; we expect rather that such an event will threaten Laios, and indeed the chorus' next words relate how, overcome by his own foolish counsels, he brought death to himself in the form of the father-slaying Oidipous. But the son must first grow up, and the killing of Laios many years later does not seem much like the swift punish-ment claimed. Nor is the failure to observe a warning (*not* a command) from Apollo what we usually mean by a *parbasia*. On balance we will probably do better to regard the *parbasia* as a previous offense leading Apollo to offer Laios a cruel choice: either no children, or possible danger to the city he rules. As we saw, the abduction of Chrysippos could be the original transgression; the chorus does not allude to it, but we must admit that they do not allude to anything else either. The peril to Thebes constitutes yet another problem: if it springs directly from Oidipous' engendering, then Aischylos must mean the danger (though not disaster) brought upon the city by the quarrel between Eteokles and Polyneikes, figures who but for Laios' folly would not have been born. If, on the other hand, the danger is arbitrarily imposed by the gods to balance Oidipous' birth, we could argue for the Sphinx, although Laios would then be providing both the cause of the danger and the agent of its elimination. Throughout this morass of questions the link between crime and punishment persists in escaping us: there seems nowhere any swift retribution for Laios, and no very clear reason for involving the city when Laios' neglect of Apollo's advice seemingly redounds first and foremost on himself.

As for the action of the *Laios,* if (as I think) it did not involve Chrysippos (or certainly not directly, for enacting his story here would force Oidipous' entire life into the middle play), the drama probably began with Laios setting out from Thebes (for Delphi?) and ended with a messenger speech announcing his demise at a crossroads. The intervening space would then describe and reflect upon past events—the *parbasia* (Chrysippos here?) and Apollo's oracle, the child's begetting, and the subsequent abandonment (in a belated effort to save the city?). Again, one does not quite see how Laios' death many years after relates to these happenings. In Sophokles' *Oidipous Tyrannos* there is not the slightest hint of any such prologue to the child's birth; Laios and Iokaste simply receive a prophecy that whatever child is born to them will be the slayer of his father, and Laios understandably seeks to be rid of him; hence his exposure when he is only three days old (*OT* 711–19).[23] The same holds for the prologue of Euripides' *Phoinissai,* where Iokaste relates past events: Laios consults Delphi because of his childlessness, Apollo predicts his own death if a child is born, and events take their course. The one new detail here is the notion that Laios lay with Iokaste, after receiving the oracle, in a fit of lust and drunkenness (*Pho* 21–22). The Sphinx's arrival, as in Sophokles, is fortuitous, that is, not linked to any previous event.

Our later mythographers all follow this simpler Sophoklean/Euripidean version of affairs and offer nothing that would help to explain Aischylos' more complicated arrangement, although as we saw, the Peisandros scholion and the oracle of the *Oidipous* and *Phoinissai* hypotheseis do link the abduction of Chrysippos to the Sphinx or to Laios' death. One other point to be dealt with is the name of Laios' wife, or wives. Homer speaks of only the one wife, Epikaste, who is clearly the natural mother of Oidipous, while Pherekydes and Sophokles agree in calling the same person Iokaste (Aischylos fails to name her in the *Hepta*). Such a modest variant is hardly cause for concern, but our Epimenidean corpus says that Laios married one Eurykleia, daughter of Ekphas, and that she bore to him Oidipous (3B15). Our source for this information, the scholia to the *Phoinissai,* fails to include, however, the most crucial point: did its author suppose Eurykleia to be the woman Oidipous later married, or did Laios take a second wife Epikaste/Iokaste, making Oidipous' bride merely his stepmother? The scholiast's subsequent remark, that some sources did give Laios two wives, suggests that "Epimenides" did not, but the idea that Oidipous and his mother were not joined in marriage does therefore seem to have been known, unless we are to understand that in the unnamed sources the second wife, not the first, bore the child. Of Euryganeia and Astymedousa, wives of Oidipous whom some modern scholars have taken to be still other identities of his mother, we will see more in the next section.

Oidipous   The tale of Oidipous' abandonment is presumably basic to all accounts of his story, but we find it first attested only in Aischylos' trilogy, assuming the verb *chutrizein*, cited as from the *Laios*, does refer to the child's exposure in a pot (fr 122 R). Subsequently the story finds a full narration in Sophokles' *Tyrannos*, where in response to the oracle Oidipous is given over by Iokaste to a shepherd, that he might be exposed on Kithairon with an iron pin through his ankles (*OT* 717–19, 1171–76). The shepherd instead entrusts him to a Korinthian colleague with whom he shares pasturage, and the latter brings him to Polybos, king of Korinth, who with his wife Merope adopts the child as his own. Here again the *Phoinissai* scholia offer us some anonymous variants (Σ *Pho* 26). In one, Oidipous is placed in a chest that floats to Sikyon, from whence he is taken up by Polybos. A Hellenistic relief cup shows the scene of this finding, with Periboia (as the wife of Polybos is also called by Apollodoros and others) taking the infant Oidipous from a basket and handing him to her husband (Louvre MNC 660).[24] The same story of Periboia's discovery (while she is washing clothes) appears in Hyginus (*Fab* 66), and might reflect a situation (and means of recognition) in Euripides' *Oidipous*, if Periboia there came to Thebes in later times to seek her son (as she does in *Fab* 67). Intermediaries in this version may be indicated by the *Odyssey* scholia, where shepherds from Sikyon actually raise Oidipous (Σ *Od* 11.271).

The other variant takes us further afield, to Olympia, for the same *Phoinissai* scholia suggest a version (something is lost at the beginning) in which Hippodameia, daughter of Oinomaos, presents the child to someone (surely Pelops?) as his. Subsequently, Oidipous having grown, Laios appears and abducts his son's presumed brother Chrysippos, and Oidipous in trying to intervene kills his father. When Iokaste arrives to claim the body, he then meets and marries her, thus completing the disaster. Bizarre though this story seems, it does link together the abduction of Chrysippos and Laios' death in an ingenious fashion, and obviates the need for a curse by Pelops. That it could represent the plot of Aischylos' *Laios* seems discounted, given the range of time and place required. If it is not from some other early source, it is certainly a shrewd late attempt to improve on original elements. In this context we should at least note another remark elsewhere in the *Phoinissai* scholia, that Oidipous killed Laios because both men were enamored of Chrysippos (Σ *Pho* 60). Art offers us, besides the Hellenistic cup noted above, only a Red-Figure amphora by the Achilleus Painter: a man with petasos and spear (thus presumably a traveler) named as Euphorbos carries the infant Oidipous (also named); on the reverse is an unnamed bearded man holding a staff, presumably the recipient of the child (CabMéd 372).

For the story of Oidipous' departure from Korinth and arrival at Thebes (that is, when he grows up in Korinth, not Olympia), there is likewise some diversity of narrative. In Sophokles, as Oidipous himself relates the tale, the day came when a Korinthian, overfilled with wine at a banquet, called him a bastard, and taking the words to heart he questioned his father on the matter (*OT* 774–813). Naturally Polybos avowed himself as parent, but doubts gnawed at Oidipous until he resolved to take his questions to Delphi. There Apollo refused to answer his query about real parents; the god did, however, tell him that he was fated to slay his father and marry his mother (this latter detail withheld from Laios and Iokaste). Accordingly he determined to put as much distance as possible between himself and his supposed homeland, and thus set out eastward. At a place where three roads meet he encountered Laios (we may guess, but are not told, that the latter was headed to Delphi, although Kreon does call him a *theôros*) with a party of five men and a wagon. The herald attempted to push him off the road so that the wagon might pass, and he pushed back. Laios then struck him with his goad as the wagon went by; at this Oidipous lost his temper completely and toppled the old man backward out of the wagon, killing him, whereupon he also killed all the rest, no doubt in self-defense. We know, of course, that this account is not precisely right: one attendant, the same man who took Oidipous away at his birth, has escaped and returned to Thebes with a tale fabricated for his own protection, that robbers in great number set upon the king.

Euripides in his *Phoinissai* gives a slightly different version of these events, that Laios and Oidipous were both on their way to Delphi when they met, Oidipous to seek his parents, Laios to ask if his child had survived (*Pho* 32–45). Oidipous is told that he is dealing with a king, but the same altercation ensues, with Laios' horses trampling on Oidipous' feet. After killing his father, Oidipous takes the horses back to Polybos, so that he seems not to have reached Delphi or to have received any prophecy. The scholia note this point and offer as explanation that he felt he could not consult the god in his polluted condition; no source is named, and the scholiast may be guessing (Σ *Pho* 44). A further note suggesting that Oidipous on his return to Korinth obtained purification and then went on to Delphi, as in Sophokles, likewise seems muddled and is not what Euripides' text implies. Iokaste at this juncture in the prologue proceeds to speak of Kreon's offer of her in marriage (*Pho* 45–50), which might seem to imply that Oidipous came directly from Korinth to solve the riddle and claim the prize, not in flight from Polybos. Such a deviation from the Sophoklean norm, if we have correctly understood it, does offer one distinct advantage: if Oidipous has not been warned by the oracle, there is nothing unreasonable in his slaying a man old enough to be his father or marrying a woman old enough to be his mother. Unfortunately, Euripides' lost *Oidipous* has nothing preserved on this point, and neither does Aischylos' Oidipous trilogy, although there the killing seems to have taken place near Potniai, slightly over a mile south of Thebes (fr 387a R), which might well indicate for both men intended goals quite different from those in Sophokles, and here too no actual visit to

Delphi.[25] Otherwise, about the encounter in Aischylos we know only that Oidipous spat out the murdered man's blood (fr 122a R).

In Antimachos' *Lyde*, Oidipous also takes the horses back to Polybos, offering them to his father as an appreciation for his rearing (70 W), so that Antimachos (whose poem is perhaps older than the *Phoinissai*) like that work has failed to bring Oidipous to Delphi. Diodoros, too, like Euripides, has Oidipous and Laios meet on the same road *to* Delphi, although he says nothing of what follows the killing (DS 4.64.2). As a sheer bit of speculation, the detail of two men meeting on a road to the same place would explain (as Sophokles' version does not) why the encounter takes place at a point where three roads come together. In Nikolaos of Damascus, like Diodoros a late first-century B.C. writer, Oidipous is on his way to Orchomenos for horses, and Laios has Epikaste with him when they meet (90F8). The killing takes place as usual, Epikaste is spared (the servants come up too late to help), and Oidipous hides in the woods for a while before returning to Korinth (oddly enough, the *Phoinissai* scholia state that Oidipous did kill his mother in some versions: Σ *Pho* 26). Here again the animals (this time mules) are taken back to Korinth to be given to Polybos. Seneca's *Oedipus* offers no problems of any sort, and only the briefest mention of the encounter (*Oed* 768–72), while Hyginus follows for the most part what we considered for the *Phoinissai*—a meeting with Laios on the way to Delphi, and a subsequent journey to Thebes to solve the riddle (*Fab* 67).

By contrast, Apollodoros returns us to the Sophoklean account, with Oidipous told at Delphi specifically what will happen if he does not avoid his homeland (ApB 3.5.7). The same author calls Laios' herald Polyphontes and says that he killed one of Oidipous' horses when the latter refused to make way for him (in Pherekydes there is a herald named Polypoites: 3F94). But in all, given the general lack of emphasis on Oidipous at Delphi, we must ask whether Sophokles could have invented the detail of the second prophecy for his play, where it serves to intensify the irony of a man fleeing toward that which he thinks to escape, and tightens the sequence of events working inexorably toward Oidipous' doom. I myself find this attractive, and we should remember that in Aischylos' *Hepta* not even the first prophecy is as we see it in Sophokles, but for the Archaic period there is really no evidence. A visit to Delphi in some early versions might easily have been altered by later writers for the reasons cited above, to eliminate seeming carelessness of behavior in a man forewarned of his fate.

Either way, in flight from Korinth or lured by the promise of reward for defeating the Sphinx, Oidipous comes to Thebes. His encounter with the Sphinx is not actually attested before Aischylos, who mentions in the *Hepta* that Oidipous overcame her and who presumably dramatized that event in the immediately following satyr play *Sphinx;* for the same period we have the famous cup in the Vatican on which Oidipous contemplates the creature as she perches on a column (Vat 16541). Comparison with this virtually certain presentation (see below) permits us to suppose that a Chalkidian (?²⁶) hydria in Stuttgart (65/15), datable to perhaps 530 B.C., also shows the confrontation: here too the Sphinx is on a column, and before her sits a single man on a folding chair, while eight small women heavily swathed in robes look on from various positions. We will see shortly that this type of scene, with numerous men gathered around the column and no single figure identifiable as Oidipous, repeats itself often in the late sixth and early fifth centuries. But the Sphinx's role as a bane of Thebes certainly goes back much farther, to the *Theogony* and the *Oidipodeia*, in fact.²⁷ The first of these says simply that she (called Phix) brought destruction to the Thebans (*Th* 326–27); in the second she apparently causes the death of the "fairest and most desirable of all, the child of Kreon, glorious Haimon" (fr 1 *PEG*). The *Phoinissai* Peisandros scholion claims, as we saw before, that Hera sent the Sphinx to devour whatever Thebans she came across because they had dishonored her by failing to punish Laios' abduction of Chrysippos (Σ *Pho* 1760). The same source includes Haimon among her victims, thus confirming the incomplete quote from the *Oidipodeia*. From other scholia to the *Phoinissai* we learn that Euripides somewhere (probably in the *Antigone*) has Dionysos send the Sphinx, although the reason remains unclear (Σ *Pho* 1031 = fr 178 N²). Among later sources Apollodoros also says that Hera sent the Sphinx (with a riddle learned from the Mousai) to eat Thebans but gives no motive (Ap*B* 3.5.8). No other source offers any reason at all for her appearance at Thebes; perhaps, since she is a monster, we should not expect one.

The *Theogony* and *Oidipodeia* material cited above constitute our entire stock of literary evidence for the Sphinx in the seventh and sixth centuries. The art of the same period fleshes out her portrait, but often in uncertain ways. As we saw in chapter 1, Sphinxes do populate Corinthian and early Attic Black-Figure vase-painting as generic decoration, and likewise crown Attic grave stelai and dedicatory columns of the sixth century. But our first clear piece of narrative unfolds on a Siana cup by the C Painter which depicts some eight youths running away from a Sphinx while their comrade, a ninth youth, clings to the underside of her chest and belly, much like Odysseus and his ram (Syracuse 25418).²⁸ This curious pose is repeated on a *c.* 500 B.C. lekythos (Athens 397), and (though on neither vase is the Sphinx flying) might perhaps anticipate the description of Parthenopaios' shield in the *Hepta*, where an apparently airborne Sphinx carries one of the Kadmeans under her as a protection against missiles (*Hepta* 539–44). A Red-Figure lekythos now in Kiel certainly does show a Sphinx in flight, with her paws wrapped around her young victim (Kiel B555), and another lekythos in Athens depicts the moment of takeoff with her prey (Athens 1607; so too now Getty 85.AE.377, where the youth appears to be dead). Such scenes, while striking, are relatively rare; far more common is the moment of capture, with the Sphinx either leaping against the chest of a young man to knock him down, or crouched over him in triumph as he lies supine. But in almost all such examples the victim is, remarkably, a young, naked, unbearded man (on two occasions there are beards). In all, this material, taken together with the *Hepta* shield and that play's later reference to her as a "man-snatching bane" (*Hepta* 776–77), appears to indicate a tradition in which the Sphinx flies off with her quarry (so probably already the intention of the C Painter). What purpose might be served by abducting rather than simply killing her victims is hard to say.[29] That she shunned other possible quarries seems confirmed by a series of similar Black-Figure lekythoi on which she crouches over a boy while grown men on either side make deprecating gestures (e.g., Louvre CA 111; Syracuse 12085).

The above conclusions, if correct, might also suggest a tradition in which there is no riddle, for youths rather than grown men will scarcely have been sent out to try to solve it. What we may have instead is a monster who snatches up young boys (including Haimon) at will, for whatever purpose. In literature the idea of a riddle first surfaces with Pindar, in the barest of fragments quoted as part of a metrical treatise: "the riddle from the savage jaws of a maiden" (fr 177d SM). Presumably this does refer to the Sphinx, and if the expression "savage jaws" (*agrian gnathôn*) is not just poetic coloring for the source of a deadly puzzle, it might imply that here too she ate people (as in the Peisandros scholion and Apollodoros) while adding riddle-posing to her repertoire. That the Sphinx did ask riddles of the Thebans is not absolutely certain until the *Tyrannos* (OT 130–31, 391–94), and not before Asklepiades do we learn what the riddle (quoted in dactylic hexameters) was. Yet the words *kai tri*[. . .], appearing as they do between Oidipous and the Sphinx on the Vatican cup, would seem with their allusion to something three-footed to guarantee that Oidipous' thoughtful pose there is a response to a riddle. With this much granted we must surely take that riddle back at least to the Stuttgart hydria of *c.* 530 B.C. where we found the same pose. Asklepiades' version of the conundrum runs as follows: "Two-footed and four-footed and three-footed upon the earth, it has a single voice, and alone of all those on land or in the air or sea it changes form. And when it goes supported on three [or its most?] feet, then the speed of its limbs is weakest" (12F7a; manuscript uncertainty between three and most). The hexameter form employed could indicate an origin in an epic source such as the *Oidipodeia*, but Asklepiades generally takes his stories from tragedy, and hexameter is the meter used for riddles on the stage.[30] We have seen that the riddle is not specified in Sophokles, and while it was referred to in Euripides' *Oidipous*, the very scant fragment that survives reveals a different wording from that of Asklepiades (fr 83.22–24 Aus). Presumably, then, the latter's quote derives from some other Oidipous play, and Aischylos' *Sphinx* (where the encounter must fill a whole drama) will be a likely possibility (keeping in mind that whatever play Asklepiades drew on could itself have borrowed from epic sources).

Asklepiades' further account of the story may actually provide a bridge between the motif of the riddle and the youth-snatcher so popular in art: he says that the Thebans gathered daily in their assembly to ponder the riddle, since they could not rid themselves of the Sphinx until they had answered it, and whenever they failed to so do she snatched away whomever she wished of the citizens (12F7b). Something of this sort is perhaps indicated by the many Black- and Red-Figure vases which, beginning about 510 B.C., portray the Sphinx on her column surrounded by seated and/or standing men, mostly bearded, all with cloaks and staffs (e.g., Basel BS 411, Louvre G228). Of this group the most suggestive is probably Vienna 3728, a pelike by Hermonax on which the men certainly appear engaged in a fervent discussion. Conceivably this combination of riddling and snatching is the explanation of the apparent split in our earlier evidence, but it may also be a subsequent invention designed to reconcile that split. Sophokles not only fails to give the actual riddle, but also never specifies under what conditions it was posed, or what exact harm befell the Thebans because of it. Euripides in the *Phoinissai* has Iokaste say that the Sphinx burdened Thebes with her snatchings, prompting Kreon to offer the queen to whoever could solve the riddle (*Pho* 45–49). Later in the same play we find that the Sphinx sang a riddle and alighting on the walls snatched up the Thebans and carried them off (*Pho* 806–11; the scholia say that she tore them apart and dropped them), and later still that she snatched up *young* men (*Pho* 1026–31). From the same poet's *Elektra* we may add (ornamenting Achilleus' helmet) "Sphinxes bearing off song-involving quarry with their talons" (E:*El* 470–72: the adjective is perhaps being stretched to indicate the riddle). All this fits well enough with Asklepiades' version, but is too sketchy to be the sole source for it. We must remember of course that many other fifth- and fourth-century tragedians wrote Oidipous plays, including Achaios, Philokles, and Xenokles. As for Aischylos, we really know nothing at all for certain of his *Sphinx*, not even (though few will doubt it) that Oidipous was a character. Possibly some accounts offered a mixed tradition in which the Sphinx carried off young boys but resorted to a riddle contest when forced to contend with a grown, more powerful man. In any case the cause of her downfall is probably always Oidipous; nothing in any of our ancient sources suggests otherwise.

Regarding that downfall, we have surprisingly no good early information. In both Sophokles and Euripides Oidipous destroys the Sphinx in some manner after answering the riddle, but we are not told how; Aischylos says simply that he "removed" her (*Hepta* 775–77). Force as the method might seem indicated by a squat Red-Figure lekythos of the late fifth century on which Oidipous aims a spear at a cowering or collapsed Sphinx, but there is a column in the background, and she has perhaps already fallen from that, or else gives herself up to death by Oidipous' spear because the riddle has been answered (London E696).[31] In any case the use of real force against a resisting Sphinx should be linked to the presence or absence of the riddle, for in versions (if any) where riddles played no part Oidipous can only have resorted to violence, while in versions where the riddle was posed its solution would accomplish nothing if the monster was to be (and could be) overcome by brute strength. Be that as it may, Palaiphatos in the fourth century is our first source to say that she threw herself from a rock and died after the riddle was answered (Pal 4). His account offers as well what most of us probably think of (based on Sophokles) as the standard Sphinxian *modus operandi*, namely her sitting on the Phikion mount outside the city and posing her riddle to all Theban citizens who passed by, with death the penalty for those who could not answer it. This odd notion of a winged being who can commit suicide in such a fashion we have already noted in chapter 1. In Diodoros, too, she throws herself to her death after Oidipous' correct response; Diodoros suggests that this was in accord with some oracle (DS 4.64.4).

Apollodoros appears to conflate a number of these different traditions, for his Sphinx, like that of Palaiphatos, is a riddler who sits on the Phikion mount, and yet the Thebans gather in assembly and suffer the loss of whomever she snatches up when they cannot discover the answer, just as in Asklepiades (Ap*B* 3.5.8). Cohering with the Peisandros scholion is the fact that she here eats her prey, and with Diodoros the oracle that the Thebans will be rid of her when they have solved the riddle (although why she is forced to suicide is less clear). Finally, as in the *Oidipodeia* and the Peisandros scholion, Haimon is here one of her victims, causing Kreon to offer the rule and Iokaste to whoever can deal with the problem. Hyginus has the Sphinx first ravage the Theban land, then strike a bargain with Kreon that she will leave Thebes when her riddle is solved but will devour anyone who fails to solve it (*Fab* 67). Kreon accordingly advertises throughout the Greek world, and Oidipous succeeds only after many other aspirants have been eaten; once again the Sphinx throws herself from a cliff. One final bit of rationalizing comes from Pausanias, who cites an account in which the Sphinx was actually a bastard daughter of Laios to whom he had confided the oracle given to Kadmos by Delphi; when she ruled after her father's death she used this secret as a test to discourage claimants, until Oidipous came, having learned the prophecy in a dream (9.26.3–4). The presence of an oracle here as in Diodoros is suggestive, but what exact role it might have played in the beginning I do not see.

On his arrival at Thebes itself Oidipous invariably marries the queen and assumes the throne. In Sophokles this appears to be the offering of a grateful people after his victory over the Sphinx; in Euripides' *Phoinissai* and other sources it represents the pre-announced reward to anyone who accomplished that task. After the marriage (and in some sources begetting of children: see below), there are no incidents of any sort to record until the discovery of Oidipous' parentage. This most famous point in Oidipous' life is first and most fully preserved in Sophokles; Aischylos' *Oidipous* may have dealt with the same events, but it may also (as I shall argue later) have treated problems of his old age at Thebes. With or without this tragic model, Sophokles will have had at least one epic precursor, the *Oidipodeia*; we have no idea what use he made of such material, or if other dramatizations for the Athenian stage preceded his.

As the *Tyrannos* opens, Thebes is beset by a plague, and this fact will subtly determine all of the subsequent action. Oidipous sends his brother-in-law Kreon to Delphi for help; the city is told in response that it must find the murderer of Laios if the disease is to abate. Oidipous accepts the challenge of this new riddle with confidence, but there are few leads to such an old killing, although the one surviving witness is sent for. Also summoned, meanwhile, is Teiresias, who concedes knowledge of the solution but refuses to divulge it. When Oidipous in natural frustration threatens force, the seer does finally accuse him, using language that gives the king little chance to guess the truth. Suspicion of Teriesias leads to suspicion of Kreon, for Oidipous from the outset supposes his predecessor's death to have been politically motivated. Kreon's protest that he derives greater advantage as the king's brother-in-law is to no avail, and he is about to be exiled (or worse) when Iokaste enters and separates the quarrelers. On hearing of her husband's problems with Teiresias she cites her own experience with a spokesman for Apollo who told her that her son would kill his father; thus the child was abandoned with a pin through his feet, and the father instead met his death in a meeting with bandits at a place where three roads converged. This chance topographical detail undoes all the intended consolation of the story, for Oidipous now realizes that he may after all have slain Laios. Accordingly he tells Iokaste of his own background, beginning with his trip to Delphi and the oracle's pronouncement to him that he would kill his father and marry his mother. These he supposes, despite some previous doubts, to be Polybos and Merope of Korinth, and thus when a messenger now arrives to announce that Polybos has died of old age he allows himself to feel some measure of relief. But the same messenger then admits that Oidipous was adopted, brought to Korinth in fact by the messenger himself. Iokaste, who knows to whom she gave her child and where he was to be exposed, now grasps the truth, and rushes into the palace to hang herself.

For Oidipous there are several gaps still to be filled in, but the eyewitness to Laios' murder proves to be the same man who took the child to Kithairon, and on his admission that he received that child from Thebes' queen all the pieces fall into place. Oidipous hurries after Iokaste, finds her dead, and puts out his eyes with the brooches from her gown; Kreon reassumes power, only to face immediately the knotty question of whether to exile the polluter. Here the play ends, with Oidipous' fate unresolved. Sophokles has stressed primarily the role of the gods and *moira* in springing the trap so cunningly laid, and the ironic distance between what we must assume and what we can know.

By contrast, our few scrappy fragments of Euripides' *Oidipous* reveal a plot with surprising deviations from the Sophoklean account. Most important, Oidipous is blinded by the servants of Laios, presumably at Kreon's command (fr 541 N^2). At this point in the play he is called son of Polybos, so that the discovery must have been made in two distinct stages, first that he killed the previous king (for which he is punished), then that he is the king's son. This second revelation probably takes place after Polybos' wife has arrived in Thebes (see above), but we have no certain details. Between the two points of emerging truth, Iokaste seems to assert her loyalty to her husband, a position she may or may not have maintained after finding him to be also her son (fr 543 N²). In general Oidipous is contrasted with Kreon, if certain gnomic utterances are rightly interpreted (frr 551, 552 N²); mention of the latter's envy may indicate that he, not Oidipous, took the lead in discovering the murderer, and that the unfortunate king was here a comparatively passive figure.³² Obviously we would give much to have the conclusion, so that we might see exactly what the play intended with such characters. Of later sources, neither Diodoros nor Apollodoros says anything beyond the fact that Oidipous' situation did come to light. The Peisandros scholion offers, however, quite a novel variation on the means by which the truth is revealed: Oidipous buries Laios and the other dead with their cloaks, but takes away the sword and zôstêr of Laios (Σ Pho 1760, as above). Subsequently he finds himself near the same place while traveling back with Iokaste from the completion of certain sacrifices, and being thus reminded of the event relates it to his wife while showing her the zôstêr. At this she recognizes him as the murderer of Laios, but not as her son, and therefore keeps silent. The second part of the secret is revealed only when a stablehand arrives from Sikyon to relate how he found Oidipous as a child and took him to Merope; swaddling clothes and the ankle-pins are produced as evidence, and a reward sought, thus bringing the parentage into the open. The more leisurely pace of this version reminds us how intensely dramatic Sophokles' onstage one-play treatment is, and rouses suspicion that this scholiast's account, or at least parts of it, are far more likely than Sophokles' to derive from early epic. One other variant from the Phoinissai scholia, that Polybos blinded Oidipous when he heard the predictions concerning the slaying of fathers, would seem eccentric in the extreme, jeopardizing as it would much of the subsequent action (Σ Pho 26); possibly this too arose from the need of some dramatist to create a new tragic situation, with Polybos subsequently discovering his mistake, although we may wonder how Oidipous will then manage to fulfill the oracle.

We have seen that in the Nekuia, as in Sophokles, Iokaste (or Epikaste, as Homer calls her) does indeed commit suicide by hanging, "and she left behind to him exceedingly many pains, as many as the Erinyes of a mother accomplish" (Od 11.279–80). In Euripides' Phoinissai, on the other hand, she is alive long after the discovery, and may be also in the recently found Lille fragment of Stesichoros (see below); for Aischylos' Oidipous trilogy we cannot tell. The whole problem of her fate is linked to that of Oidipous' blindness and/or subsequent remarriage, to which we must now turn. The Nekuia also says that after Oidipous killed his father and married his mother "the gods soon made these things known to men" (Od 11.274). The word used for "soon" here, aphar, normally means "quite soon," and already in antiquity we find Pausanias arguing that such language precludes the begetting of any children by Epikaste (9.5.10–11). As further support for such an un-Sophoklean state of affairs he offers the Oidipodeia, where he says that Euryganeia, daughter of Hyperphas, was the mother of the four children, and as well a painting by

Onasias at Plataia (of unknown date) in which Euryganeia is the woman bent down with grief while the two sons fight. Whether this was indeed the understanding of the *Nekuia* we cannot say for certain, but that Book's subsequent observation that Oidipous continued to rule Thebes after Epikaste's death does suggest that he was not blind, and thus might well have remarried (*Od* 11.275– 76). The central part of the Lille Stesichoros fragment features an address by the mother of Oidipous' two sons as they seek some means to avoid a dire prophecy made by Teiresias about their fate (PLille 76a, b, c; PLille 73).[33] Oidipous' possessions appear to be in dispute, so he is presumably dead, but we have no way of knowing whether the unnamed mother is Iokaste, here not a suicide, or a second wife such as Euryganeia (and consequently no way either of knowing whether the children are here any more than in Homer the product of incest).

In Aischylos' *Hepta* we find for the first time a definite statement that Oidipous begat his children by his own mother, and these children are clearly the usual four, Polyneikes, Eteokles, Antigone, and Ismene (*Hepta* 752–57). Pherekydes offers a more complicated situation: in the continuation of his account previously mentioned Iokaste bears to Oidipous Phrastor and Laonytos, who perish at the hands of the Minyes (3F95). Apparently Iokaste disappears as well, for after a year Oidipous marries Euryganeia, daughter of Periphas, who becomes the mother of the four standard offspring. And to this state of affairs Pherekydes adds, after Euryganeia has died, a third wife as well, one Astymedousa, daughter of Sthenelos. The scholiast source for all this then concludes by noting that, according to some, Euryganeia was a sister of Iokaste. The scholion to *Phoinissai* 1760 also knows of a wife Euryganeia whom Oidipous marries after the death of Iokaste and his blinding and who is the mother of the four children; that information is noted under a "some say" heading and may have been found in that form in the mythographer Peisandros, our supposed source for the entire entry. Finally, although no wives of Oidipous are to be found in the *Ehoiai*, a papyrus fragment of that poem does appear to describe his funeral just before turning to Elektryon and his children (Hes fr 193 MW). Some link with the sons of Perseus must therefore be involved, and as Astymedousa is a daughter of Elektryon's brother Sthenelos, it seems more than likely that his branch immediately preceded, with Astymedousa's marriage to Oidipous concluding it. That his funeral is recorded (in some detail) may or may not mean that she married him in his old age.

From Oidipous' wives we turn finally to his ultimate fate. In *Iliad* 23 Homer remarks that Mekisteus, son of Talaos (thus brother of Adrastos), attended the funeral of the "fallen" Oidipous at Thebes (*Il* 23.677–80). The word for "fallen" used here could be meant figuratively, but it would be very remarkable if it did not imply death in battle or by some sort of violence, that is, not old age. Similarly the holding of a funeral at Thebes (with games, no doubt) suggests that Oidipous was a man of some honor and position there when he died, which would agree with the *Nekuia's* apparent concept of him as continuing to rule after the discovery. In Hesiod's *Works & Days* we encounter the idea that the conflict of the great heroes of the fourth age at Thebes was over the flocks of Oidipous, again indicating that he possessed considerable wealth on his death (*W&D* 162–63). And as we saw above, the funeral appeared too in the *Ehoiai*, a social event attended, it seems, by all the women of Thebes and accompanied by wonderment at the corpse of much-grieved Oidipous (Hes fr 193 MW); a scholiast to the *Iliad* passage adds that Argeia, daughter of Adrastos (and at some point the wife of Polyneikes), came "with others" (Hes fr 192 MW). The same scholiast too, after noting that Homer does seem to suppose Oidipous dying in his own land, adds, "not as the *neôteroi*" (ΣT *Il* 23.679). In fact, Euripides in *Phoinissai* (if this part of the play is his) and Sophokles in *Oidipous at Kolonos* are the first known sources to take him away from Thebes after the discovery, and the idea may well have been an Attic tradition of relatively recent vintage.[34] We shall find in the next section that the epic *Thebais* certainly knows of quarrels at Thebes between Oidipous and his sons in his old age, when he is weak and dependent upon them (and here seemingly no longer king).[35] As a last point, the A scholia to *Iliad* 4.376 offer an unattributed story to the effect that after Oidipous has put aside Iokaste, his new wife Astymedousa accuses the two sons of attacking her, thus causing her husband to curse them.

None of this amounts to a consensus, but from many quarters we have hints that Oidipous remains in Thebes after the discovery, often with his kingship and perhaps his sight intact, and that he takes one or even two more wives, with his children at times (perhaps always before Aischylos, though I doubt it) the product of a union different from that with his mother. That the *Iliad* implies him to have died in battle remains a puzzle; later sources follow pretty uniformly the Sophoklean account of his death at Athens, and thus offer no clues.

Polyneikes and Eteokles   The expedition of the Seven against Thebes, and the quarrel between Oidipous' sons which caused it, appear as early as *Iliad* 4, but we learn nothing beyond the fact of Tydeus' pre-attack embassy into the city and its bloody aftermath (*Il* 4.376–98). Eteokles and Polyneikes are mentioned nowhere else in Homer, and not anywhere in Hesiod, while the *Ehoiai* has only a passing reference to Polyneikes (Hes fr 193 MW). The *Thebais* was an epic devoted entirely to this event, since we know its opening line to have been "Sing, goddess, of thirsty Argos, whence the lords . . ." (fr 1 *PEG*). This might seem to begin the poem with Adrastos, but other fragments show that the poet went back to the source of the conflict, as we would expect. Whether any such origins of the dispute were recounted in the *Oidipodeia* we do not know. What the *Thebais* does tell us about the beginnings is that Oidipous on at least two separate occasions cursed his sons for poor tendance of him. In the first of these incidents, Polyneikes serves his father using the silver table of Kadmos and a golden cup (fr 2 *PEG*). The introductory summary by Athenaios (11.465e), before quoting the lines in question, makes clear that Oidipous has forbidden the use of these heirlooms of his father; when he perceives them lying before him, great pain fills his heart, and he prays that his children will share out their patrimony amidst wars and battles. The Greek cited here rather implies that Oidipous can see, since he recognizes the items for what they are, but possibly the poet meant that he knew by feeling them. The same holds for the second occasion, when the sons, through carelessness or some other reason, send Oidipous not his customary portion from the sacrifice, that is the shoulder, but rather the haunch (fr 3 *PEG*). Oidipous is again angry, believing himself insulted, and prays to Zeus that his sons might die by each other's hand. The two events are clearly doublets of the same motif, but such is the stuff of epic, and the second occasion may be justified too by the greater precision that the curse there acquires. Once more, however, we learn nothing of *why* Polyneikes and Eteokles quarreled, only that they were fated to do so.

From epic we turn to Stesichoros' account of these matters as attested by the new fragment in Lille (PLille 76a, b, c).[36] As we saw, Oidipous is here probably dead, but the boys' mother is not, and she speaks all the lines in question. From her words we gather that Teiresias has just uttered a prophecy concerning their mutual slaughter and the danger to the city. That Teiresias should predict, rather than Oidipous pray for, this result, seems puzzling; possibly the poem's time frame is limited, and for that reason the seer is called upon to state more clearly how the gods intend to implement a curse made earlier by the father. If not, then the prophecy must spring from some cause unrelated to Oidipous (in Aischylos' *Hepta* we will find Apollo's anger [against Laios?] given great emphasis, but there the curse is very much in evidence). In any case, the mother (we remember that she is unnamed) despite her despair thinks to see a way of escape that will still accord with Teiresias' words: she proposes that one son retain the gold and other possessions of their father but leave Thebes, while the other remain behind in the city (and presumably occupy the throne, although this is not stated). The choice will be made by lot, and as the fragment breaks off both sons prepare to obey. Something very similar (minus the lot) is preserved for us by Hellanikos, who says that Eteokles offered Polyneikes his choice, either to rule Thebes or take a share of the property and leave; Polyneikes chose the chiton and necklace of Harmonia, abandoned the throne to his brother, and went to Argos, where he gave those items to Argeia, daughter of Adrastos (4F98). Why such an arrangement in either Stesichoros or Hellanikos should lead to conflict we are left to guess; probably Polyneikes like Esau regretted his bargain, and unlike Esau decided to renegotiate. But our scholiast source for Hellanikos points out that not everyone followed this version: in Pherekydes it seems that Eteokles expels Polyneikes by force, and thus that there is no bargain (3F96; cf. ΣA *Il* 4.376, where Eteokles as the older son expels his brother, and Sophokles' *Oidipous at Kolonos* [see below]).

One might think that at this juncture we could consult Aischylos' version of the quarrel in his *Hepta,* where Polyneikes' assault on Thebes forms the action of the play. Yet that drama is surprisingly reticent on the subject. As the play begins, we find Eteokles at the battlements of Thebes preparing for the attack; the play remains with Eteokles for its entire course, and neither he nor the chorus chooses to discuss what led to such a state of affairs. It is, of course, clear that Eteokles has the kingship and that Polyneikes wants it, but we do not learn the basis of the former's tenure or the latter's claim. At one point, Polyneikes does call his brother (via messenger speech) an exiler (*Hepta* 637–38),[37] which might seem to support Pherekydes' version, and both brothers claim to have Dike on their side. But the larger action of the play suggests, I believe, a background closer to that documented by Stesichoros and Hellanikos. Although Eteokles is, from the beginning, aware of his father's curse on himself and his brother, for much of the play's length he seems to trust that that curse has been deflected. Only when he discovers that Polyneikes will face him at the seventh gate does his hope waver; indeed, it collapses altogether as he abandons himself to the Erinys of his father's imprecation and prepares for battle.

This shift from defiance to utter capitulation is truly abrupt, and has caused some critics to locate responsibility in an Erinys-sent madness that deprives Eteokles of his reason.[38] It may be, however, that we here pay the price of not having the second play, where the curse must have taken place. From what remains, its terms are not quite clear, but it appears that the sons were fated to divide the property by the sword (*Hepta* 785–90). If such a prediction offers little basis for optimism, there was also a dream (to whom we do not know: *Hepta* 709–11) which may have spoken of a foreign mediator coming to allot the shares (*Hepta* 727–33). This dream apparently served the same role as the mother in the Stesichorean version, that is, it held out hope that the most extreme implications of the curse—mutual fratricide—could be avoided. Probably, then, in the *Oidipous* the two brothers worked out an arrangement by lot, thus leading Eteokles to hope that the curse had been averted or at least softened. Instead, when he finds that an *allotment* held by the Argive champions has brought Polyneikes opposite him in battle, he realizes finally the grim truth: the foreign mediator is simply iron, and curse and dream both point to the same inexorable outcome.[39] Thus he arms himself, despite the chorus' protests, and sets out for the last gate in the knowledge that he and Polyneikes are destined to die there, sharing out only whatever land their corpses will occupy.

If this interpretation of the *Hepta's* dramatic action is correct, it leads to a further conclusion, namely that the action of the preceding *Oidipous* was set at a time when the two brothers were old enough to be cursed, that is, when their father Oidipous had become an old man. In that case, the trilogy omitted the staging of his great discovery about himself, relegating it no doubt to choral odes or the audience's previous knowledge, a situation that many scholars are reluctant to suppose. But the alternative is to conclude that Oidipous cursed his sons when they had done nothing to him, and indeed were too young to understand his words. The Second Stasimon of the *Hepta* has seemed to some to imply this, for we learn there that Oidipous, when he became apprised of what he had done, "carried away in pain over his wretched marriage, with maddened heart accomplished a twin evil. With the hand that killed his father he took away his eyes, dearer than children [?]. And wrathful at the fostering/tendance he cast bitter-tongued curses upon his children, that they would someday share out the property with an iron-wielding hand" (*Hepta* 778–90).[40]

The last sentence of this passage begins a new antistrophe, and so might be separated from the rest, yet the apparent meaning of the Greek, with its epexegetic asyndeton and subsequent connective, is that Oidipous after the discovery committed two unfortunate deeds: he blinded himself and cursed his sons. If he did both these things immediately, his motive for the curse will have been that his children were the product of an incestuous union. But the form of that curse is then strange indeed. We might expect that a father would wish such children swallowed up by oblivion as quickly as possible, but not made to incur further pollution through fratricide. And why, if the motive is the children's begetting, is the curse made to address only the sons, not the daughters? What Aischylos shows us is a man who is angry, certainly, but angry *at* his sons; hence the precise shape of his curse. The cause must then somehow be found in the word *trophas*, "care, upbringing, tendance," whatever the meaning of its modifier (if it has one): the sons' care of their father in his old age has in some way been at fault, perhaps for one or both of the reasons given in the *Thebais*, perhaps for something else. The transgression may have been shown or related, but the curse will form the first part of the play, and efforts to avert or soften it the second. As one possibility for the latter, Eteokles may have triumphed in a winner-take-all lottery and thus been able to exile Polyneikes. Such conclusions still leave us, however, with the "twin evil" of *Hepta* 782 to be explained. Either the curse was proclaimed many years after the discovery, or the evil in question was the putting out of one's "twin" eyes, as a scholiast supposed. I am not entirely happy with either of these proposals, straining as they both do the Greek, but I find them preferable to a reconstruction that treats the curse too casually. We should remember, too, that Aischylos' audience knew very well what he meant to say, having just seen the *Oidipous;* thus some obscurity of expression would be more tolerable. In all, our evidence suggests that for the Archaic period Oidipous' old age at Thebes and ill-treatment by his sons was an important part of his story, perhaps even as important as the catastrophe of his earlier days.

For the end of the fifth century we have evidence from both Euripides and Sophokles. Euripides' *Oidipous*, since it treated the discovery, probably had nothing to say about later events, although it might have predicted Oidipous' future. Much more information comes from the same poet's counterpart to the *Hepta*, the *Phoinissai*, especially the prologue spoken by Iokaste. Obviously, in this version Oidipous has only one wife, and she remains alive long after the discovery and his self-blinding. Oidipous himself is, as the play opens, also still alive, but his sons on coming to manhood have shut him up in hopes of causing their shame to be forgotten. For this reason he curses them to divide their inheritance by the sword, and they respond by agreeing to remain apart. But here for the first time we encounter the idea of an exchange of roles, that is, that the two brothers have agreed to alternate between ruling Thebes and staying in exile. Polyneikes takes the first shift of a year away from Thebes, then finds himself permanently ousted when Eteokles fails to adhere to the bargain. As their subsequent debate shows, Eteokles stands throughout this debate as the villain; he acknowledges the injustice of his conduct but holds it of no account when set against the chance to retain power. By contrast, in versions where Polyneikes is compensated for his departure (as in Hellanikos) the subsequent conflict seems entirely his doing as the one abjuring the agreement. Either way, however, we find in this play, as in Stesichoros and Hellanikos (and, I believe, in Aischylos), the idea that the brothers are cursed to kill each other, and seek to avoid that fate by physical separation. In Sophokles' *Oidipous at Kolonos,* our only preserved source of this period to send Oidipous away from Thebes before his sons' death, matters take a different turn, owing probably to the fact that Sophokles wished to present the curse onstage rather than earlier. We learn here that after the initial shock of discovery of his deeds Oidipous repented of his wish to leave Thebes and desired to stay; Kreon, however, turned him out nonetheless, and his sons did nothing to help him. Even so, he held his peace for the time, and his sons fell to quarreling over the throne of their own accord. Eteokles got the upper hand with the people and expelled his brother, who in the course of the play comes to his exiled father for his blessing and receives instead his curse.

Thus we have a variety of possibilities for the quarrel, including that of Aischylos' *Hepta* where the mutual fate (hence mutual transgression?) of the two brothers is stressed rather than anything one did to the other. Later authors such as Diodoros and Apollodoros give us the same version of the dispute as the *Phoinissai,* so that the rotating-year motif, whatever its antiquity, has become far and away the most familiar form of the story (DS 4.65.1; ApB 3.6.1; *Fab* 67 makes Oidipous ordain this alternation of rule after his self-blinding). In all accounts, after leaving Thebes Polyneikes makes his way to Argos, where he marries the daughter of Adrastos and mobilizes the Argives for a military expedition against his homeland. We shall return to his checkered fortunes in the next two sections, after we have considered the larger background of this ill-fated expedition.

Adrastos, Eriphyle, and Amphiaraos In chapter 5 we found that for the *Ehoiai* (although not for Pherekydes) Bias and Pero's marriage is blessed with a son Talaos (Hes fr 37 MW). The *Ehoiai* does not develop the family further at this point in the poem, but in Bakchylides a Talaos is the father of Adrastos of Argos (9.19), and Pindar speaks of Adrastos and the other sons of Talaos who confer their sister Eriphyle on Amphiaraos, son of Oikles (*Nem* 9.9–17). Adrastos (no parentage mentioned) has already appeared in the *Iliad* as ruler of Sikyon (*Il* 2.572), father-in-law of Tydeus (*Il* 14.121), and owner of the divinely fast horse Areion (*Il* 23.346–47). He does not appear in the *Odyssey*, but the *Nekuia* tells of Eriphyle as the woman who took gold for her husband (*Od* 11.326–27), and later we hear of Amphiaraos as the man who died at Thebes "because of gifts to a woman" (*Od* 15.246–47). The details of this latter event, namely Amphiaraos' fatal participation in Polyneikes' expedition, are well known to later writers, and must have been recounted in detail by both the *Thebais* and Stesichoros' *Eriphyle*.

The famous Middle Corinthian krater once in Berlin (and considered in chapter 5 for its illustration of the funeral games for Pelias) shows on its other side Amphiaraos' departure for the battle (Berlin:Lost F1655). As he steps into his chariot he turns his head back to view the crowd of well-wishers waving goodbye from the doors of the palace. To the rear stands Eriphyle (so named); one hand holds a necklace. There are also a half-grown son and another child sitting on a woman's shoulder; unfortunately, these are not named, but we will see that they are important. A Black-Figure lekanis lid offers fragments of a very similar composition (Athens Akr 2112), and Pausanias would appear to have seen much the same scene on the Chest of Kypselos (5.17.7–8), so that perhaps all were inspired by a large-scale composition. On the Chest, if Pausanias is actually reading inscriptions, the group in front of the house waving goodbye to Amphiaraos includes an old woman carrying the infant Amphilochos, Eriphyle with the necklace, her daughters Eurydike and Demonassa, and a naked Alkmaion; Baton stands in the chariot and Amphiaraos again turns around as he steps in. Certain from this group, on a Black-Figure amphora of about 520 B.C., are Eriphyle and Alkmaion, both named as the mother holds up the child to the departing warrior (Chiusi 1794).[41] In Attic Red-Figure beginning about 450 B.C. we actually see Polyneikes handing the necklace to Eriphyle (e.g., Lecce 570). Our later sources will specify that the whole story started with a dispute between the families of Adrastos and Amphiaraos, and indeed Pindar does say that Adrastos once fled Amphiaraos, with Eriphyle's bestowal to the latter becoming the token of reconciliation (*Nem* 9.13–17). But neither Bakchylides nor Pindar discuss Eriphyle's subsequent transaction in what survives of their work (although Pindar seems to have mentioned it: fr 182 SM), and our actual account comes from Amphiaraos himself in Euripides' *Hypsipyle*, plus scholia to Pindar and the *Odyssey*.

As the Pindar scholia relate these matters, there was a quarrel over something (land and power, presumably) between the descendants of Melampous (i.e., Amphiaraos) and those of his brother Bias (Talaos and his family: Σ *Nem* 9.30 *passim*). In a version then cited as from the fourth-century historian Menaichmos of Sikyon, Pronax, son of Talaos, is king of Argos but dies, and his brother Adrastos flees to Sikyon where he inherits the kingdom of his mother Lysimache's father Polybos (Σ *Nem* 9.30 = 131F10; on this last point cf. Hdt 5.67). According to others, however, the dispute leads to Amphiaraos' slaying of Talaos, after which Adrastos flees as before but gets the kingdom of

Sikyon by *marrying* Polybos' daughter (Σ *Nem* 9.30b). Either way, Polybos dies without heirs, and the throne of Sikyon passes to Adrastos. Subsequently there is a reconciliation between the two sides, with as in Pindar the marriage of Eriphyle, sister of Adrastos, to Amphiaraos.

The further developments are offered by the *Odyssey* scholia at 11.326, and since these are credited to Asklepiades they probably reflect one or more Attic tragedies, including Aischylos' *Epigonoi* and Sophokles' *Epigonoi* and *Eriphyle* (these last probably, though not certainly, separate plays). None of these dramas will have presented the actual betrayal, but all of them may have referred to it in exposition; the same is true for numerous *Alkmaion* plays by different authors (including two by Euripides) treating either the matricide or its aftermath. Whether the betrayal could ever be said to have a humorous side I do not know, but Sophokles did write a satyric *Amphiaraos* of unknown content (perhaps culminating in the marriage to Eriphyle). In any event, Asklepiades' account begins on a slightly different note from what we found in Pindar, for here Amphiaraos and Eriphyle are already married when the dispute arises (12F29). Somehow she resolves the argument, and the two men declare that in future they will always abide by her decision in disputes between them. When the expedition for Thebes is taking shape, Amphiaraos tries to warn the Argives of their impending doom, but is himself forced to join them by Eriphyle, who has received from Polyneikes the necklace of Harmonia. Her husband has seen her take the gift, however, and while he has no choice but to go, he does exact from his son Alkmaion a promise to avenge him. Later sources all follow this basic narrative without any significant deviation, save that in one note of the Pindaric scholia Adrastos harbors a grudge against Amphiaraos, and himself uses the necklace to bribe his sister, so that her husband might be destroyed (Σ *Nem* 9.35).[42] The scholiast may have a genuine tradition for this, but he may also be guessing in an effort to explain *Nemean* 9's aphoristic line 15.

Backtracking now from this early attested phase of Polyneikes' recruitment of allies, we must start at the beginning of the affair, his actual arrival in Argos and marriage to Adrastos' daughter. The *Iliad* says nothing on this point, although there must be some reason for Argos' support of a Theban exile in that poem, and Homer does mention Tydeus' similar marriage (*Il* 14.121, as above). All later sources, beginning with Pherekydes (probably), call the daughter whom Tydeus marries Deipyle (3F122), and likewise they agree that Polyneikes' bride was Argeia. Previously in this chapter we saw that an Argeia, daughter of Adrastos, came to the funeral of Oidipous at Thebes in the *Ehoiai* (Hes fr 192 MW). Possibly she was at that time already married to Polyneikes, although our text says simply that she came with others. Alternatively, Polyneikes might still have been living at Thebes, and have met his future bride for the first time on this occasion, subsequently going to Argos to seek her hand (and Adrastos' support). The Lille Stesichoros papyrus provides just enough text (after the brothers have drawn for throne and property) to show that Teiresias predicted Polyneikes' migration to Argos, where Adrastos would offer him his daughter; more details must have been given, but they do not survive, nor do we have any idea what the *Thebais* might have contributed. The first preserved accounts of Polyneikes' wooing are in three plays of Euripides, *Hiketides, Hypsipyle,* and *Phoinissai;* Polyneikes himself gives the most complete version in the last of these, but the main details have already been anticipated by Adrastos in the first. In this play Polyneikes comes to Adrastos' door by night, seeking shelter, and apparently finds a bed (or at least porch) available for that purpose (E:*Hik* 131–61). Soon after, another exile, Tydeus, son of Oineus, arrives seeking the same thing, and the two begin to fight over the available space. When Adrastos comes out to investigate the commotion he remembers an oracle given to him by Apollo, that he should marry his daughters to a boar and a lion, and from the manner of their fighting deduces that these two men are what the god intended. Polydeukes and Tydeus thus become his sons-in-law; to each of them he promises restoration to their homeland, beginning with Polyneikes.

With this much as evidence we can understand more clearly a Chalkidian calyx krater of about 530 B.C. on which we see a scene of the arrival: to the right Adrastos (named) reclines on his couch, with a woman standing to one side; both look to the far left where two men are seated on the ground, their mantles wrapped round them, with two more women standing over them talking to each other (Copenhagen VIII 496). One of the two seated men is inscribed as Tydeus, the other (perhaps: the inscription is not immediately beside him) as [Pr]omachos. No other names survive, but it seems a reasonable guess that the female figures are Adrastos' wife (Amphithea?) and two daughters, and that Promachos (or whoever) is meant to be Polyneikes, come like Tydeus in search of shelter. Aischylos' *Hepta* presumably understands the same basic events, since Adrastos, Amphiaraos, and Tydeus are all part of the expedition with Polyneikes (Adrastos in a noncombat role), and no explanation of their presence is considered necessary.

One other question raised by Euripides' detailed account of Adrastos' bestowal of his daughters concerns the role of Apollo in counseling a course of action that leads to disaster. In *Hiketides,* Theseus comes close to exculpating the god by intimating that Adrastos misinterpreted the oracle in marrying his daughters to two total strangers (E:*Hik* 135–45). Polyneikes in relating the same events to Iokaste in *Phoinissai* has no such doubts about its meaning, but we will expect his perspective to be different. The chorus of the lost *Hypsipyle* also recounted the conflict of Tydeus and Polyneikes and their subsequent marriages, perhaps in more detail than either of our preserved Euripidean plays, but only scraps confirming the oracle about animals remain (12 GLP). Our later sources, including Apollodoros (ApB 3.6.1) and the *Iliad* and *Phoinissai* scholia (ΣA *Il* 4.376; Σ *Pho* 409), plus Statius (St:*Theb* 1.390–497) and Hyginus (*Fab* 69), all adhere to the view that Apollo's oracle did command the marriages, and usually add more convincing grounds for Adrastos' reading of it: either the two heroes bear on their shields the insignia of a lion (Polyneikes) and boar (Tydeus: Ap*B*, Σ *Pho*) or they are clad in the skins of those animals (Σ *Pho*, Σ*A Il*, St:*Theb*, Hyg). Sometimes the creatures even become symbols for the lands of those they designate, with the lion indicating the Sphinx and the boar the Kalydonian Boar (Σ *Pho*, Hyg). Conceivably these details are late inventions to make Adrastos' deduction more plausible than it appears in Euripides. Yet the motif of bridegrooms recognized through prophecy does have solid credentials in folklore, and perhaps it is here an early part of the story toned down by Euripides in order to serve the desired characterization of Adrastos as a man who does not use good judgment in dealing with the gods. If that is so, we are left with an Apollo as obscure as ever in his maneuvering of the Argives toward catastrophe. In any event, the result of Polyneikes' marriage is always the same: Adrastos promises his help, Eriphyle is bribed to commit her husband to the endeavor, and an expedition of Argives and their allies sets forth for Thebes to restore the exile to the throne his brother occupies.

The Expedition of the Seven   As we saw above, the *Iliad* knows of the march on Thebes by a generation prior to the one at Troy, and we learn from Sthenelos that his father Kapaneus and Diomedes' father Tydeus joined Polyneikes in his unsuccessful assault (*Il* 4.405–10). Agamemnon adds the tale of Tydeus' embassy to which we will return shortly. The *Works & Days* counts the event together with the siege of Troy as the two great exploits of the age of heroes (*W&D* 161–63), and the epic *Thebais*, as the opening line showed us, began (and no doubt concluded) with it. From this last work we gain the name of another participant, Parthenopaios (fr 6 *PEG*), and perhaps a speech in honor of Amphiaraos (fr 10 *PEG*) but little more (possibly Tydeus' devouring of Melanippos' brains: see below). Pausanias saw Eteokles and Polyneikes actually fighting each other on the Chest of Kypselos (with a Ker: Paus 5.19.6). And Hekataios is named among those who made Parthenopaios a son of Talaos (and thus it would seem a brother of Adrastos: 1F32). But beyond these few scraps we must rely on the fifth century, and in particular Pindar, Bakchylides, and of course Aischylos, to be followed at century's end by Euripides' two plays previously mentioned, the *Hiketides* and *Phoinissai*.

For the preliminaries to the expedition we do, however, have useful information from the *Iliad*: Polyneikes and Tydeus together come to Mykenai to seek assistance, and the citizens there are minded to help them, but Zeus sends contrary omens, and the mission fails (*Il* 4.376–81). Homer then proceeds to the embassy to Thebes (logically enough, since Tydeus is the topic at hand) and omits the stop at Phlious. Our first reference to this second phase of their journey comes from Simonides, who says that they lamented the death of the child [Archemoros] (553 *PMG*). Bakchylides takes matters a step further: at Phlious the Argive heroes set up the Nemean games in honor of Archemoros, whom a snake has slain in his sleep; the event is somehow taken as an omen of Argive failure at Thebes (Bak 9.10–20). Pindar agrees, in *Nemean 9*, that

Adrastos founded the Nemean games on the banks of the Asopos (the river that flows past Phlious and Sikyon) but does not say why (*Nem* 9.9). The hypothesis to the *Nemean Odes* as a whole offers several different versions of the story, including the fact that in Aischylos, among others, this Archemoros is the son of Nemea.[43] Presumably, then, the child's death and the games' founding were the subjects of his lost play *Nemea*. Unfortunately, neither the hypothesis nor any other source tells us anything more about Aischylos' handling of the tale.

The loss of Aischylos' play is the greater because Euripides in his partially preserved *Hypsipyle* offers us quite a different mother for the same child, one Eurydike, wife of Lykourgos, a priest of Nemean Zeus; Hypsipyle, the former paramour of Iason, is involved because she has become the child's nurse, after being exiled from Lemnos and captured by pirates. The child here has as his given name Opheltes, to be changed to Archemoros in the course of the story. As the action of the play opens, Amphiaraos and his companions are on their way north to Thebes, and encounter Hypsipyle while searching for water with which to perform a sacrifice.[44] She takes the seer to a spring guarded by a serpent, and there the serpent somehow manages to kill the child. Eurydike is naturally bent on revenge, but Amphiaraos persuades her that what has happened was destined: the child will be called Archemoros, as signaling the beginning of the expedition's doom, and games will be established. Eurydike yields to this explanation, and the remainder of the play—Hypsipyle's recognition of her sons, who have come to find her—need not concern us here. Apollodoros (Ap*B* 3.6.4), Hyginus (*Fab* 74, with a prophecy that the child is not to be put down until he can walk), and the *Nemean Odes* hypothesis all provide a similar account of Archemoros' parentage and death. The hypothesis' one other significant variation lies in the presenting of a third set of parents, Euphetes and Kreousa. That Aischylos told this same story of Lemnian nurse and snake in his *Nemea* with merely a different name for the mother (and perhaps the father) is possible, but I doubt it: surely neither Aischylos nor anyone else would have named such a play after the child's mother if the plot focused on the misfortunes of the nurse who failed to guard her charge. We must allow, I think, that Aischylos' version may well not have included Hypsipyle at all.

Elsewhere there is some scant evidence that might relate to the Euripidean parents, and which in any case should be noted. Pausanias tells us that on the Amyklai Throne Adrastos and Tydeus halt a fight between Amphiaraos and Lykourgos, son of Pronax (3.18.12). The same scene is apparently represented on the elbow guard of a shield-strap from Olympia where a central figure named as Adrastos stands with raised arm between two warriors closing in battle; other unarmed men to either side forcibly restrain them (B 1654). Other names preserved, though unfortunately incomplete, identify the left-hand combatant as [. . . mph.ar.o . . .]—surely Amphiaraos—and someone on the right side (not necessarily the combatant) as [. . .]orgos—very likely Lykourgos. If this is the Lykourgos of the *Hypsipyle,* and if he was present to witness or hear of his son's death in some accounts (in Euripides, he is out of town), he might well blame Amphiaraos for the tragedy and seek vengeance. But against this possibility is the fact that the shield-relief offers no sign of a woman or child, although there is certainly room for them. We saw, too, that in the *Nemean Odes* scholia Pronax is the son of Talaos and brother of Adrastos, and this arrangement occurs also in Apollodoros (Ap*B* 1.9.13). Thus, if Pausanias' information is right, the Lykourgos of the Throne would be Adrastos' nephew, and more likely a part of the expedition setting out from Argos than someone encountered along the way at Nemea. For what it is worth, Apollodoros himself distinguishes two Lykourgoi in his discussion of these legends, the one a son of Pronax of whom we hear nothing more, the other a son of Pheres (and brother of Admetos) who marries Eurydike and begets Opheltes (Ap*B* 1.9.14). How early this latter figure might be we cannot say; our Archaic sources neither mention nor exclude him. In any case, and with one father or other, the child and his death seem an established part of the tale. Whether Opheltes and Archemoros might ever have been two separate children, with the one usurping the death of the other, remains less certain.

As for the quarrel on the Throne, it is apparently also portrayed on a Lakonian cup by the Hunt Painter of which only a small fragment has been found (Cyrene, no #). The part preserved shows a warrior grasping the wrist of a comrade who has drawn his sword, and the restrainer is clearly named as Parthenopaios; behind him is another figure whose name ends in -os (Adrastos?). This does not help us much, but it does seem to ensure that the quarrel was somehow a part of the story of the Seven (unless Parthenopaios is here in his capacity as a member of Talaos' family). We will see shortly that in Aischylos (and probably earlier) there is bad blood between Amphiaraos and Tydeus, and it has therefore been suggested (since both are present on the Throne) that Pausanias failed to attach the right names to the right figures in making his description. The shield-strap might confirm this view *if* the (restored) name "Lykourgos" there refers to one of the on-lookers, with the name of Tydeus lost over the head of the right-hand warrior.[45] But perhaps there is a dispute alluded to in these works which we have simply lost. Hekataios offers the odd remark that Amphiaraos once fell asleep while standing guard, and suffered the consequences of it (1F33); perhaps this error, whatever its circumstances, was what aroused Lykourgos' (or Tydeus') anger.

The third event preliminary to the actual assault on Thebes is that mentioned several times by the *Iliad*, the sending of Tydeus into the city alone to negotiate with Eteokles. In *Iliad* 4, Agamemnon says that this happened when the forces had come to the Asopos River, and completed a good part of their journey; thus he is thinking, as we would expect, of the Boiotian Asopos that runs south of Thebes, not the Sikyonian Asopos where the Nemean games were founded (*Il* 4.382–400). Tydeus arrives in the city with a message for the Kadmeians, and finds the leaders gathered together in feasting at the home of Eteokles. Undaunted, he challenges them all to contests, and with Athena's help wins everything easily. The losers are sufficiently angered that they send a force of fifty men, led by Maion and Polyphontes, to ambush Tydeus on his way back to the Asopos. He kills forty-nine of these, sparing only Maion, whom he sends back to Thebes on the advice of the gods. Athena and Diomedes both mention this same event more briefly in later parts of the poem (*Il* 5.800–808, 10.285–90); the only new detail is Diomedes' statement that Tydeus was carrying a "gentle message," that is, not just a threat. What we do not learn from any of these passages is how the Kadmeians responded to the message; presumably they rejected any appeal for negotiation, and then too Tydeus' *aristeia*, not his diplomatic skill, is the point of the story. In Diodoros' version, Adrastos sends the hero all the way up to Thebes from Argos to seek Polyneikes' return (DS 4.65.4). Conceivably here the ambush takes place before he reaches Thebes, but in any case he slays all and returns to Argos, and only then is the expedition mobilized. Statius devotes most of Book 2 of his *Thebais* to the episode; Tydeus leaves from Argos as in Diodoros, but here there is a lengthy confrontation with Eteokles, who refuses any claims based on justice, and the ambush occurs as usual on the return. Apollodoros returns to the Homeric version, with Tydeus dispatched just south of Thebes and killing all but Maion (ApB 3.6.5). Likely enough the adventure played a major role in the epic *Thebais* or some other early narrative as a foretale to the actual assault; Statius' lengthy treatment well shows how easily the story lends itself to elaboration.

Given, then, this likelihood of a substantial early telling of Tydeus' advance exploits at Thebes, we may consider here too the odd tale of Tydeus and Ismene, for the encounter between them must occur either during the embassy or as part of the general attack, and the possibilities for such a story in the earlier context will obviously be greater. Our first evidence comes from Mimnermos: a scholiast says that in his poems Tydeus, on the command of Athena, slew Ismene while she was consorting sexually with one Theoklymenos (21 W). The scholiast concedes the strangeness of this, as he does the version of Ion of Chios in which both Antigone and Ismene are burned to death in a temple of Hera by Laodamas, son of Eteokles (740 *PMG*), but offers no motive for either event. A Late Corinthian amphora now in the Louvre adds pictorial support: Tydeus (all figures named) advances with drawn sword toward a bed on which Ismene reclines, her breasts uncovered, and with his free hand seizes her by the arm; behind him a naked Periklymenos runs away (Louvre E640). Even without Mimnermos, we should not have had much trouble divining the situation presented here; what we are still lacking, however, is any reason for Tydeus' interest in the misbehavior of an unrelated Theban woman. Intriguing, too, is the variant "Periklymenos" for Mimnermos' Theoklymenos, since in the epic *Thebais* Periklymenos is the Theban champion who defeats Parthenopaios. We should also note fragments of an Attic Black-Figure skyphos from the Akropolis: only Ismene (again named) actually survives, and appears to be kneeling on a bed while someone to the right of her grasps her by the wrist;

to the left survives an arm holding a spear vertically (Athens Akr 603). A White-Ground cup in the Louvre (G109: male figure leans over a second [female? center missing] with clearly hostile intent) has also been cited in this connection; I am dubious, but in any case with only the two figures the scene has nothing to tell us.[46] The same is true of a Red-Figure skyphos by the Triptolemos Painter now in Berlin on which a man in armor with drawn sword pursues a (clothed) woman as Athena watches, all in an architectural setting (Berlin:Ch Inv 1970.9).[47] To conclude, we have a reference in Pherekydes: among Oidipous' children is Ismene, whom Tydeus kills by a spring that is then named after her (3F95).

Such is the sum total of our information about the slaying; the story does not appear in any later author, and we are left with one of the more baffling situations in Greek myth. Tydeus' presence in any locale appropriate to intimate activities between Ismene and a lover seems impossible unless he has some claim on her as relative or betrothed. The former, of course, is not the case, and the latter automatically excluded by the fact that he only comes to Thebes by virtue of having married Deipyle, unless we postulate that all this took place before his arrival in Argos. Mimnermos' statement that Athena advised the slaying may help us here, since it implies that the goddess, not the mortal, was the one who was angry. But deducing a cause for Athena's anger at a trysting of lovers is not much easier, and her sending of Tydeus into Ismene's boudoir is almost as unconvincing as his entry there on his own initiative. Pherekydes' transfer of the slaying to a site outside the city removes the latter difficulty, but it may also remove the lover insisted upon by both Mimnermos and the Louvre amphora, and thus might represent a change in motive. Clearly the original story is very well hidden; just possibly its earliest forms involved an Ismene (such as the daughter of Asopos?) other than the Theban offspring of Oidipous.[48] Whatever we conclude, one cannot say that the cause of the expedition seems in any way advanced by her demise.

We come finally to the actual attack on the city, and in this connection must consider the identity of the seven champions who mount the assault. For seven or any specific number in the *Thebais* there is no evidence, unless Asklepiades' comment that Pindar borrowed lines from that work for his *Olympian* 6 refers to 6.15 (with its seven pyres; so too *Nem* 9.22–24) as well as the lament for Amphiaraos which follows (Σ *Ol* 6.26). But even if that were so (and it seems unlikely) we would have to debate for the *Thebais*, as we will for Pindar, what those seven pyres might signify. In *Olympian* 6 and all other preserved accounts, Amphiaraos is swallowed up by the earth and does not require cremation; likewise Adrastos, on all occasions on which he is one of the attackers, survives. In theory, then, Pindar should have just five or six pyres, if there were originally seven champions. Possibly though, as the scholia suggest, he means that there was a pyre for the *armies* of each of the seven champions (Σ *Ol* 6.23d), or perhaps a pyre for the fallen at each of Thebes' seven gates. But we cannot totally exclude the idea that an original group of seven did all perish in some early versions, or the possibility that from a larger group some survived. Indeed, Pausanias specifically claims that Aischylos brought the number down to seven from something larger, including heroes from Messenia and Arkadia (2.20.5). To such a notion we might object that seven champions is the logical number to utilize when one is assaulting a city with seven gates, but nothing before Aischylos pairs off the attackers with the gates, and surprisingly few sources after him, leaving us to wonder whether this motif has any early authority. All that we have then for the period before the fifth century is a group of uncertain size, from which we can guarantee Polyneikes, Tydeus, Kapaneus, Amphiaraos, and Parthenopaios, plus perhaps Lykourgos and of course Adrastos, if he is in early versions a combatant.

For the fifth century itself, there is the famous list/description of Aischylos' *Hepta*, where a band of seven champions (excluding Adrastos) is assigned one by one to each of the city's gates, with Eteokles then appointing seven defenders to oppose them. Later in the century Euripides will offer his own lists (slightly different from each other) in his *Hiketides* and *Phoinissai*, and Sophokles too in *Oidipous at Kolonos*. There is also from the first half of the century an Etruscan gem, now in Berlin, which shows five of the heroes (names inscribed) in conversation or brandishing weapons (Berlin:Ch GI 194).[49] The names provided are Parthenopaios, Amphiaraos, Polyneikes (all sitting), plus Tydeus and Adrastos standing in arms; of those we might definitely have expected to find only Kapaneus is lacking. That only five figures appear is probably not significant, given the difficulty of putting even that many on a gem.

In Aischylos we find the Seven saying a last farewell to Adrastos, who is present but not of their number, and giving him tokens for their loved ones before proceeding to the allotment of the gates (*Hepta* 42–56). That allotment is as follows: (1) Tydeus attacks the Proitid gate, with the moon and stars on his shield (Melanippos defends); (2) Kapaneus stands at the Elektran gate, a man with a torch on his shield (Polyphontes defends); (3) Eteoklos is at the Neistan gate, bearing on his shield a man scaling a siege-ladder (Megareus of the house of Kreon defends); (4) Hippomedon assaults the gate of Athena Onka, with a shield showing Typhon (Hyperbios, son of Oinops, defends); (5) Parthenopaios of Arkadia is at the North gate, a Sphinx on his shield (Aktor, brother of Hyperbios, defends); (6) Amphiaraos at the Homoloid gate bears no device at all on his shield (and engages in verbal abuse of Tydeus, whom he blames for the war; Lasthenes defends); (7) Polyneikes advances to the seventh gate, with Dike on his shield leading him back to his city (Eteokles defends). Such an arrangement lies for the most part along anticipated lines, with five of the six previously named heroes involved, and Adrastos escorting them but held out of battle. The resulting two openings fall to Hippomedon and Eteoklos. Both these names will reappear in later (perhaps also contemporary) lists, thus lessening the possibility that they were invented by Aischylos. Otherwise we might have been inclined to suppose novelty at least for Eteoklos, a name that might seem to represent an omen for Eteokles as the gates are assigned.

We should also note that there is here no sign of Periklymenos as the defender who slays Parthenopaios, in contrast to the account of the *Thebais*. Aischylos' *Epigonoi*, which must in some way have dealt with the sons of the Seven, presumably named some or all of the fathers, and its list might well have differed from that of the *Hepta*, but the play is completely lost, leaving behind no information of any sort.

Sophokles' *Antigone* reiterates the idea of seven champions at seven gates, without however offering names or details (*Ant* 141–43). In Euripides' *Hiketides* we find a list identical to the *Hepta*'s; Adrastos is again not an actual attacker, and survives to seek from Theseus and the Athenians the recovery of the bodies of the slain (E:*Hik* 857–931). The only new information advanced here is that Parthenopaios becomes specifically the offspring of Atalanta, and Eteoklos emerges as the son of Iphis, whose daughter Euadne is married to Kapaneus. In the *Phoinissai*, by contrast, although six of the seven champions are the same, the warrior at the seventh and last gate is Adrastos, replacing Eteoklos; he withdraws after witnessing Kapaneus' fate and Zeus' displeasure (*Pho* 1104–38). Sophokles' *Kolonos* dramatizes only the anticipation of the conflict, but a full list is given, matching that of the *Hepta* and *Hiketides*; Eteoklos is here simply Argive-born, but Hippomedon is called a son of Talaos, which ought to make him another brother of Adrastos (*OK* 1311–25). Of later sources, Diodoros agrees with the *Phoinissai* in including Adrastos at the cost of Eteoklos (DS 4.65.4–5), and so too Statius (St:*Theb* 4.32–250), Apollodoros (Ap*B* 3.6.3), and Hyginus (who makes Kapaneus and Hippomedon sons of sisters of Adrastos: *Fab* 70). But Apollodoros in the same place cites a variant according to which Eteoklos and Mekisteus (yet another brother of Adrastos: Ap*B* 1.9.13; so too *Il* 2.566 and 23.678, where we saw him at the funeral of Oidipous) replace Polyneikes and Tydeus in the list of seven. Mekisteus is also a combatant, though not necessarily a leader, in Herodotos, where he is again a brother of Adrastos and a victim (like Tydeus) of Melanippos (Hdt 5.67.3); Pausanias at 9.18.1 says exactly the same. Conceivably, this alternate roster could represent a very old Argive version of the tale before outsiders became involved, but it might also reflect a desire in Argos for an all- (or largely) Argive seven, with less concern for the motivating role played by Polyneikes in the story. Adding Adrastos' two sons-in-law to such a group would give a total of nine, which might in part explain what Pausanias meant in saying that Aischylos *reduced* the number to seven.

One other source of uncertain date to be considered is Pausanias' description of the monument at Delphi showing the Seven, a monument set up by the Argives near the beginning of the Sacred Way to commemorate their victory over the Spartans at Oinoe (10.10.3). The victory, won by the Argives with the help of Athens, does not lend itself to a precise date, but most scholars would now agree on a time somewhere in the 450s b.c.[50] More to the point for our purposes is the source of Pausanias' identification of the various figures, since we do not know if he is working from inscriptions or local tradition, and if the former, whether the inscriptions are as old as the monument. The names given are: Adrastos, son of Talaos; Tydeus, son of Oineus; Kapaneus, son of Hipponoos, and Eteoklos, son of Iphis (these last two both descendants of Proitos); Polyneikes; Hippomedon, son of Adrastos' sister; Amphiaraos (or at least his chariot, in which stands a charioteer Baton); and finally one Alitherses. Thus we would seem to have eight heroes rather than seven. Conspicuously missing is Parthenopaios; the usual explanation, that the sculptors omitted him because he was not Argive (or even married to one) is probably correct. As for the large number, Pausanias' language certainly suggests that he thought all eight figures were participants, but of course he may be wrong; possibly the sculptors conceived of Adrastos, placed as he is at one end, in the escort role he so often plays elsewhere. Or we could drop the totally unknown Alitherses at the other end and consider him like Baton a supernumerary. If we could be sure of a *c.* 450 date for these names we would have a more secure background for Eteoklos, whose antiquity we suspected above as oddly similar in name to Eteokles. Conceivably Aischylos utilized this figure rather than Adrastos as one of his Seven so that all the attackers would perish. But we must admit that in the final analysis we do not know whether Adrastos was ever a combatant in early times. Our one real piece of evidence for that point comes from Pausanias, who says that in the *Thebais* Adrastos flees Thebes on his horse Areion, wearing "mournful clothing" (8.25.8). His flight and torn (?) garments might suggest that he was one of the fighters, but the latter might also signify that he himself tore his clothing when he saw the fate of his friends. For my own part, I do not see why Euripides would have placed Adrastos at the seventh gate (it makes little difference to his play) if he had not found such an idea in earlier works, and then too there is no reason why as one of the instigators of the expedition Adrastos should not fight in the earliest versions of the story. But for all that, he may not have.

We should note in concluding that even among the Argives the list of participants seems not to have been firmly fixed: Pausanias at Argos itself saw an undated Epigonoi group that included sons of Parthenopaios (here the son of Talaos), Hippomedon, Polyneikes, Tydeus, Kapaneus, Amphiaraos, Adrastos, and even Mekisteus, but no son of Eteoklos (2.20.5).[51] I suggested above that Parthenopaios was missing from the Delphi dedication of the Argives because of his Arkadian origin. If so, this Argive claim of parentage from Talaos, first found as we saw in Hekataios, probably represents an attempt to convert him to Argive status and thus justify his participation.

Turning now to details of the combat, we must for the period before 500 B.C. content ourselves with the two small bits of certain information seen above from the *Thebais*, that Periklymenos defeated Parthenopaios and that Adrastos fled the scene on his famous horse. Surprisingly there is nothing preserved from Black-Figure or other Archaic art until the very end of that period (*c.* 460 B.C.), when we find the battle portrayed on the central antepagmentum in the pediment of Temple A at the Etruscan port of Pyrgi.[52] Here two scenes elegantly overlap: from the left Athena approaches, a small jar in her hand, while the center stage shows two warriors sprawled on the ground, the one biting into the skull of the other, and behind them Zeus preparing to hurl his thunderbolt at yet another warrior. Already in the *Hepta* Eteokles has hinted that Zeus will strike down the boaster Kapaneus (*Hepta* 444–46), and this is uniformly the later tradition. As for the remaining figures, both Bakchylides (fr 41 SM) and Pherekydes (3F97) tell us that Athena intended to make Tydeus immortal, and Pherekydes further explains the occasion as the moment of Tydeus' death in battle: he has been wounded by Melanippos, and when Amphiaraos kills the latter and throws Tydeus the head, he begins to gnaw on its brains in his rage. At this critical juncture Athena arrives from *ouranos* bearing immortality, but when she sees Tydeus' savage behavior she throws it away in disgust. Tydeus perceives this before he dies, and exhorts the goddess to bestow the favor on his son instead. The immediate source of this account is the *Iliad* scholia at 5.126 (AbT); all three manuscript traditions credit it to Pherekydes, and we have no reason to doubt them. But much the same account, although in different language, appears in the Geneva scholia to the *Iliad*, with the words "the story is from the Cyclic poets" appended by a later hand.[53] If this is correct, then the tale of Tydeus' lost immortality probably goes back to the *Thebais* (Bernabé includes the scholion as part of his *Thebais* fr 9). The story reappears in Apollodoros (who specifies that Amphiaraos' intention in giving Tydeus the head was precisely to rob him of Athena's gift: Ap*B* 3.6.8), and is clearly what our Etruscan antepagmentum intends. Apollodoros does omit the transfer of the immortality to Diomedes, but Athena's bestowal of that status on the latter is noted by Pindar (*Nem* 10.7) and explained as above by the appended scholia (Σ *Nem* 10.12). In art, we also have a fragmentary Red-Figure bell krater in New York on which a man, presumably Tydeus, is seated on a rock and accompanied by Athena and Athanasia ("Immortality": NY 12.229.14); a now lost bell krater by the Eupolis Painter or his like, showing Athena leading a maiden away from a seated warrior, may intend the same scene (the Rosi Krater).[54] The Pyrgi terracotta contains as well a sixth figure, another warrior, who stands between and behind Zeus and Kapaneus; possibly he represents Kapaneus' original Theban opponent whom Zeus supplants.

For these two of the Seven, then, we have special stories, obviously Archaic in origin, which remain standard in later times. Adrastos is as we saw always saved, combatant or not, and the other attackers are all simply killed by their Theban counterparts, with the exception of Amphiaraos. His fate, to be swallowed up by the ground while still alive, is first preserved in Pindar's *Nemean* 9 and *Nemean* 10. *Nemean* 9 says that Zeus accomplished this, chariot and all, so that he might not be slain by the pursuing Periklymenos (*Nem* 9.25–27); *Nemean* 10 adds that the god split the ground with his thunderbolt (*Nem* 10.8–9). That the seer continues to exist under the earth seems indicated by *Pythian* 8, where he delivers a prophecy as the Epigonoi set out for Thebes (*Py* 8.38–55). Aischylos has, save for the allusion to Kapaneus' fate, none of this; a messenger simply reports back to the chorus that at six of the gates all has gone well, while at the seventh Oidipous' two sons have killed each other. Quite possibly the same poet's *Eleusinioi* or *Argeiai*, although they dealt with the aftermath of the expedition, contained a fuller account of the combats; Kapaneus' fate is mentioned in one fragment of the *Argeiai* (fr 17 R). Sophokles' *Antigone* has nothing relevant about the battle, and Adrastos' funeral speech in Euripides' *Hiketides* merely repeats what we already know of Kapaneus and Amphiaraos while omitting Tydeus' misfortune. But in the *Phoinissai* we get a more unusual sequence of events: after an initial pitched battle in which Kapaneus is struck by a thunderbolt and Parthenopaios is slain by Periklymenos, the Thebans gain the upper hand, and Adrastos pulls his forces back (*Pho* 1141–99, 1219–39). Eteokles then offers to fight Polyneikes in single combat to decide the entire outcome; in the resulting duel, he uses a Thessalian trick to deliver a fatal wound to his brother, but fails to finish him off before taking the spoils (*Pho* 1356–1424). With his dying breath Polyneikes returns the favor, and Iokaste completes the picture by killing herself over the two bodies (*Pho* 1455–59).

One other important detail to be noted in the *Phoinissai* is the prophecy of Teiresias that the city will be saved only if Menoikeus—a hitherto unattested son of Kreon—should throw himself from the walls to the spot where Kadmos slew the dragon, in atonement for that deed (*Pho* 903–1018). Menoikeus tricks his father into leaving the stage, then hurries off to the walls to perform the required sacrifice. Makaria and Iphigeneia are two other examples of Euripides' fondness for voluntary self-immolation, and he may well have invented its appearance here, but we cannot say for certain. Apollodoros includes both the single combat and Menoikeus, and seems by his account to be drawing directly from the tragedian (*ApB* 3.6.7–8). Statius also presents them, but in the context of a much broader tapestry in which the seven attackers fall one by one over several books until only Eteokles and Polyneikes are left to fight; again we miss the strict symmetry of the seven combats at seven gates found in Aischylos. Art has relatively little to offer, other than those pieces with Tydeus noted above: A volute krater of the mid-fifth century does offer a panorama of all the combatants (Ferrara 3031). But amidst these latter, only Amphiaraos is distinguished in any way, as he and his charioteer and horses sink down into the earth at the bottom of the scene; the other figures are merely stock warriors (for a slightly earlier version of Amphiaraos' fate, shown in isolation, see Athens 1125, a Black-Figure lekythos by the Beldam Painter).

*Antigone
and the
Burial of
the Seven*

Next in the sequence of events following the attack of the Seven comes Kreon's refusal to inter their bodies, and the defiance of this proclamation by Antigone when she buries the corpse of her brother Polyneikes. We have seen that Pausanias strongly implies a knowledge in early epic of Oidipous' children, and presumably the ones known to us, but no source prior to the fifth century ever mentions Antigone, in this context or any other. Both she and Ismene emerge at the end of Aischylos' *Hepta* to lament the loss of their brothers, and this is her first appearance in literature or art (*Hepta* 961-1004). The sisters' dirge is, however, interrupted at line 1005 by a herald bearing Kreon's decree, and Antigone in response to this vows at the play's end that she will bury Polyneikes nonetheless. For a variety of reasons, including stylistic ones, most scholars have come to feel that this last section of the drama cannot have been written by Aischylos, and I believe that to be the case.[55] More likely, the final scene with its hanging conclusion was added onto the *Hepta* to update it for a later revival, when the story of the negated burial had become virtually mandatory due to audience familiarity with it. Harder to say is whether the sisters should be excised from the *Hepta* altogether, or allowed to perform their lament. But they are both mentioned as Oidipous' daughters by Pherekydes (3F95), and thus they have some standing prior to Sophokles.

Nevertheless, if the above conclusion about the *Hepta* is correct, then Sophokles is our first source to say anything about Antigone's act of heroism. As his play *Antigone* opens, she is lamenting the decree prohibiting burial of Polyneikes as the latest in a series of catastrophes afflicting their house. Her sister Ismene sympathizes but feels they are too weak to act; Antigone dismisses her scornfully and prepares to bury the body by herself. Her initial step, the covering of the corpse with earth, is found out by the guards after she has left to fetch offerings, and when she returns she is apprehended. In the confrontation with Kreon, she refuses to concede validity to any position but her own; by the terms of the proclamation she is led off to be imprisoned alive in a cave. Haimon, Kreon's son and her betrothed, then pleads with his father for leniency, but Kreon turns a deaf ear when he finds his son siding against him. Finally Teiresias appears, to announce that the gods are rejecting all Theban sacrifices. At this Kreon yields, but too late: Antigone has hanged herself in her prison, and Haimon, discovering the body, draws his sword to meet the same fate. At the end, even Kreon's wife commits suicide, leaving him to mourn a chain of disaster caused partly by his own folly but partly too by Antigone's martyr-like determination to be proved right at all costs. As we saw in chapter 3, the play does not argue that Polyneikes will be in any way benefited by Antigone's devotion to him, and the gods through Teiresias are the ones who accomplish his burial. The intensely confrontational nature of the whole situation might seem to argue that it was created for drama, and we must certainly allow the possibility that Sophokles did invent it. Leaning in this direction too is the fact that in the *Oidipodeia* Haimon is carried off by the Sphinx long before the present action, and we have also found early sources in which Ismene is killed before the assault of the Seven. On the other hand, neither of these figures is essential to Antigone's situation, and they might be simply dramatic additions to a story that Sophokles did, after all, find in epic.

Complicating further the question of dramatic inventions are the remains of Euripides' lost *Antigone*, a play whose plot has sometimes been linked to Hyginus' *Fabula* 72. In Hyginus' account, Antigone and Polyneikes' wife Argeia carry his body in secret to the same funeral pyre on which Eteokles has been placed. When they are discovered Argeia flees, but Antigone is taken before Kreon, who orders her betrothed Haimon to lead her off to execution. Haimon pretends to do so but actually entrusts her to shepherds, and she bears him a child who comes to Thebes years later to compete in games. Like all the Spartoi he has a birthmark that Kreon recognizes, and thus the parents are discovered; when Herakles' pleas on their behalf are to no avail, Haimon kills both Antigone and himself. Admittedly, all or even part of this would be difficult to stage, and it has been thought, too, that Hyginus is drawing from the fourth-century *Antigone* of Astydamas rather than that of Euripides. As an alternative for the latter, following hints from the Sophoklean hypothesis and the fragments, we might set the play at the time of the burial, with Haimon caught helping Antigone and both of them in trouble until Dionysos arrives to save the situation and bring about their marriage. Certain in any case is the fact that at some time in the story (not necessarily the action) of this play Antigone, though caught burying her brother, is married to Haimon and bears him a son Maion (hypothesis to *Ant*; Σ *Ant* 1350). Conceivably, all this could be made to square with Ion of Chios' notion that both Antigone and Ismene are burned to death in a temple of Hera by Laodamas, son of Eteokles (740 *PMG*), but more likely Ion has found (or invented) yet another tradition. We should note too that a Maion, son of Haimon, has already appeared in *Iliad* 4 as the one ambusher spared by Tydeus on the return leg of his embassy to Thebes; if this is the Haimon we know, he will have been married to Antigone (or someone) long before the attack of the Seven. In Statius, Haimon is omitted altogether; Argeia and Antigone meet by chance while searching for Polyneikes, and as in Hyginus cremate him on Eteokles' funeral pyre (St:*Theb* 12.177–463, 677–804). But here, in contrast to Hyginus, both are captured, and saved from execution by Kreon only because of Theseus' attack on the city. Apollodoros simply outlines the story in its Sophoklean form (without Haimon); the one new feature of his account (manuscript reading not certain) is the notion that Kreon caught Antigone himself (ApB 3.7.1). It has also been suggested that behind the uncertain title of Aischylos' *Argeiai* (sometimes transmitted as *Argeioi*) may actually lie *Argeia*, that is, a play about the joint efforts of Polyneikes' wife and sister to secure his burial. Certainly that is possible, but we might have expected the title to be *Antigone*, unless Argeia plays more of a role than we see in Statius and Hyginus. As matters stand, we must concede Sophokles' primacy, without being able to say whether anything in his version or those of later authors draws from earlier periods. As a final point, the speeches in Euripides' *Hiketides* do seem to imply that there Polyneikes' corpse is recovered by Theseus along with the others for burial; one would like to know if and how Aischylos' *Eleusinioi* dealt with this matter.

As for those other burials and the fate of the rest of the Seven, we have already seen in chapter 9 that Aischylos' lost play is our first evidence for such a prohibition of burial or Theseus' intervention; the *Iliad*'s statement that Tydeus is buried at Thebes (Il 14.114) and Pindar's description of the seven corpse-devouring pyres there (Nem 9.24) may or may not imply ignorance of such actions. In Euripides' Hiketides, we see Theseus and the Athenians defeating the Athenians in battle to obtain the corpses, but Plutarch tells us that in Aischylos' version the same result was accomplished by diplomacy (Thes 29.4). The one significant detail of the funeral in Euripides, once the bodies are recovered, is that Euadne, wife of Kapaneus, throws herself on her husband's pyre. Such events could easily find a place in epic (more easily, I think, than Antigone's heroism) although we must ask how early Theseus and/or the Athenians are likely to have played such a central role. Later accounts offer nothing useful, but Pausanias does mention seeing the tombs on the road out from Eleusis (1.39.2). As noted before, the antiquity of this kind of veneration (or rather, the objects of it) is a question that only adds to our uncertainties.

The Epigonoi From Herodotos we learn that there was also an epic *Epigonoi*, at times attributed to Homer (Hdt 4.32). From this title, and the fact that in the poem Manto, daughter of Teiresias, was sent to Delphi from the spoils by the Epigonoi (there to marry one Rhakios, the first person she met: fr 3 PEG), we assume that the work related the sack of Thebes by the children of the Seven, who were known as the Epigonoi, or "After-born." This successful attack is, of course, well known to the *Iliad*: Sthenelos, son of Kapaneus, boasts of how he and the other sons succeeded in assaulting Thebes (with fewer men) where their fathers failed (Il 4.405–10). He cites as cause for this their observance of signs from the gods and Zeus' help, suggesting once again that the Olympians opposed (or at least tried to discourage) the original expedition. The *Odyssey*, for its part, names Alkmaion and Amphilochos as sons of Amphiaraos (Od 15.248: we saw above that the latter's leave-taking in art often shows two sons, an older and a younger) but Homer has no more to tell us than this, and the term "Epigonoi" does not appear in either *Iliad* or *Odyssey*. The second assault may also have been related (or referred back to) in the epic *Alkmaionis*, but our knowledge of the content of that poem is virtually nonexistent. The same is true of Stesichoros' *Eriphyle*, where the one real fragment apparently shows Alkmaion, son of Amphiaraos, leaving some sort of feast at which Adrastos exhorts him to remain (148 SLG).

In the fifth century we have first of all Pindar, whose *Olympian* 2 identifies (in an unrelated context) Thersandros as the son of Polyneikes (Ol 2.43–45), and whose *Pythian* 8 offers a prophecy from the dead Amphiaraos while the Epigonoi (so named) approach Thebes on this "second march" (Py 8.39–55). The seer discerns Alkmaion as first through the gates, and Adrastos, who was beaten in the previous venture but is now enjoying better fortune, save in his son, who shall be the only one of the attackers to die. One should like to think that this ironic arrangement—Adrastos alone suffering loss here after being the only one to escape in the original expedition—was an early part of the story. From tragedy we have numerous titles but little in the way of facts, even regarding plot. For Aischylos' *Epigonoi* we really know nothing beyond the title, our only reason for thinking that the play even concerned these events. An actual assault on Thebes as part of the dramatic action seems unlikely here (in contrast to the *Hepta*, this attack has no curse and no Eteokles), and we should note, too, that Sophokles' similarly titled play deals with the slaying of Eriphyle. Curiously, in the *Hepta* Aischylos seems to overlook this notion of a second expedition, since that play calls Eteokles and Polyneikes *ateknous* (*Hepta* 828), which would eliminate at least Thersandros. Against this view it has been argued that the chorus specifically refers to the Epigonoi by using that term to refer to those to whom the brothers' property remains (*Hepta* 902–5).[56] But the word *epigonoi* there occurs in a line for which there is no strophic responsion (i.e., we must postulate a lacuna in the matching strophe to save it), and even if it is genuine it will more likely refer to future generations in general.[57] Nor should we wonder that Aischylos takes this course: the tragic impact of the brothers' destruction and the relief over Thebes' safety will be considerably lessened if we are in any way reminded of the sequel, although that does not mean the audience was unaware of it. Either the *Epigonoi* of this same poet resurrected those sons or—not impossibly—his version of the sequel did not require them, since desire for vengeance against Thebes (and Kreon) by the offspring of Amphiaraos, Kapaneus, and others of the Seven could provide ample motive without further help from the house of Oidipous.

With Sophokles we do scarcely better on story lines. As noted above, his *Epigonoi* included the matricide, with a hostile exchange between Adrastos (the deceased's brother) and Alkmaion after the deed (if Radt is correct in his attribution of these lines: fr 187 R); what role the second generation of attackers could have played to merit becoming the title is not clear. Asklepiades' statement that Amphiaraos commanded his son to avenge him *before* marching on Thebes with the Epigonoi (12F29) would seem to suggest that in some dramatic accounts the expedition *followed* the matricide, so that perhaps the other sons here formed a group supportive of Alkmaion. The same poet's *Eriphyle* might be another title for the above; if not, it must have offered another version of the same events or else perhaps the original betrayal of Amphiaraos. Euripides' contribution consists of two Alkmaion plays, both relating adventures after the matricide and thus not directly connected with Thebes' fall. Turning to Thoukydides, we find that Amphilochos, son of Amphiaraos, is responsible for the founding of Amphilochian Argos in Akarnania (2.68); the same information without specification of father has earlier surfaced in Hekataios (1F102c), although we will see later that there is some confusion surrounding personages of this name. As to the other participants, we have from Pausanias an account of the monument of the Epigonoi at Delphi, placed by the Argives next to that of the Seven and commemorating the same event, the victory over the Spartans at Oinoe (10.10.4). Here again he gives names, which again are likely but not necessarily from fifth-century inscriptions: Sthenelos, Alkmaion, Promachos,

Thersandros, Aigialeus, Diomedes, with Euryalos between the last two. Pausanias says in passing that Alkmaion was honored before Amphilochos because he was older, which may mean that the younger brother was also present. That would give us a total of eight figures, but nowhere are we ever told that the sons of the Seven were themselves seven in number. Of those named we have already met Sthenelos, Diomedes, Thersandros, and Alkmaion and Amphilochos (as the offspring of Kapaneus, Tydeus, Polyneikes, and Amphiaraos respectively). Aigialeus we will find identified by Hellanikos as the doomed son of Adrastos (4F100), leaving only two names to be accounted for; these, like their fathers, will vary somewhat in the tradition.

Among later sources Apollodoros offers us the same names read by Pausanias at Delphi, with the additional information that Promachos was the son of Parthenopaios and Euryalos the son of Mekisteus (Ap*B* 3.7.2–3). This Euryalos, son of Mekisteus (son of Talaos), is in fact also one of the Achaians at Troy in the *Iliad* (where his appearance is the occasion for the two places where his father is named: *Il* 2.565–66, 23.677–78). That father, Mekisteus, we recall as a brother of Adrastos and a member of Apollodoros' "all-Argive" seven who march with Polyneikes and Tydeus. Presumably, this was the genealogy followed by the Argive commission at Delphi, although it is curious that neither Parthenopaios nor Mekisteus is included on the companion monument showing the Seven. The undated Epigonoi group that Pausanias saw at Argos offers itself a variation on the Delphi version (2.20.5). Here, in addition to Sthenelos, Diomedes, Thersandros, Aigialeus, Alkmaion, and Amphilochos with the usual fathers, we have Promachos, son of Parthenopaios, and Polydoros, son of Hippomedon; added immediately after are Euryalos, son of Mekisteus, and two other sons of Polyneikes, Adrastos and Timeas. The eight of the first group (with the same fathers) recur in the scholia to Sthenelos' *Iliad* 4 speech, save only that Promachos, son of Parthenopaios, becomes Stratolaos, son of Parthenopaios (Σb *Il* 4.404; ΣT *Il* 4.406); added here as a ninth is Medon, son of Eteoklos, perhaps because Eteoklos rather than Adrastos is here accepted as the seventh in the original party. In fact, any source that does not count Adrastos as one of the Seven but does admit his son will probably wind up with nine Epigonoi, assuming that each of the Seven sends at least one son and Amphiaraos sends two. Hyginus' list also matches that of the group at Argos and the *Iliad* scholia (minus Amphilochos and Medon), with the son of Parthenopaios now Tlesimenes or Biantes (*Fab* 71).

As for the assault itself, both the Townley and b scholia agree that Laodamas, son of Eteokles, was killed and Thebes razed. In Apollodoros, too, Laodamas is slain (by Alkmaion) after himself killing Aigialeus; Pausanias by contrast has Laodamas spared and sent off to Illyria with those Thebans who escaped (9.5.13). Elsewhere he locates the initial battle on the plain of Glisas to the northeast of Thebes, but he also places there the tombs of Promachos and others who fought with Aigialeus, implying a tradition in which the son of Adrastos was not the only one of the leaders to fall fighting. One other facet of the tale of the Epigonoi, found first in Diodoros and subsequently in Apollodoros, presents us with a doublet of Polyneikes' original bribing of Eriphyle (DS 4.66.3; ApB 3.6.2). On that first occasion she receives the necklace of Harmonia, but Polyneikes also possesses (as Hellanikos has guaranteed for the fifth century: 4F98) a robe of Harmonia, and his son Thersandros now uses this to bribe Eriphyle to send her son on the second campaign. Apollodoros adds to this that Alkmaion discovered the deed only after the campaign was over. One is hard put to square this, as Apollodoros tries to do, with the idea we found in Asklepiades that Amphiaraos ordered Alkmaion to avenge him as soon as he should be old enough: if Alkmaion already knows of the original bribery he is not likely to yield to his mother's wishes on this second occasion. But then this doublet even on its own terms is a bit lame: Eriphyle does not send her son to his death as she did his father, but rather toward a glorious enterprise, and neither does she have the special hold over him that she did with his father. On the other hand, Asklepiades' version is not so tightly plotted either, for if Alkmaion kills his mother before going on the expedition, as his father commands, we must ask how he could participate in such a joint venture in his polluted condition, and why the Erinyes did not then pursue him. But either of these motifs could be early, although probably not at the same time. Our scant fragment of Stesichoros' *Eriphyle* sounds much as if Alkmaion is departing hastily from a victory banquet to kill his mother, which might suggest that he has just learned (from a drunk and boastful Thersandros?) of her duplicity in the matter of his father. If this is so, there would certainly be room in that poem for the second bribing, which might have originally developed, like the double offense to Oidipous by his sons, in the congenial confines of epic.

Regarding the final destruction of the city, in Diodoros the Thebans are advised by Teiresias to leave their town before the final assault, and most of them do; captured, however, is the seer's daughter, as she was in the epic *Epigonoi*, although here her name becomes Daphne rather than Manto (DS 4.66.4–6). Again she is sent to Delphi as a thank-offering, but now remains in Apollo's shrine as the first Sibyl. Pausanias matches the *Epigonoi* in the matter of Manto's name and union with Rhakios, even if, as he tells the story, Rhakios is from Klaros, not Kolophon, and Manto meets him when she is sent out with other prisoners to found a colony (9.33.2). Teiresias himself dies soon after the evacuation, as we will see below.

Alkmaion and Eriphyle Whether conscious of Eriphyle's treachery before the expedition of the Epigonoi or not, and whenever he carries out the deed, Alkmaion does slay his mother for her treachery in sending his father to Thebes. The confrontation between mother and son, so parallel to that of Klytaimestra and Orestes in the *Choephoroi*, must have been narrated by the *Alkmaionis* and Stesichoros' *Eriphyle*, and dramatized in Sophokles' *Epigonoi* and possibly the play of the same title by Aischylos. The end of the epic *Thebais* may also have included it, although we cannot be sure on this point. Nothing survives from any of these works, but the end of our *Odyssey* scholiast summary from Asklepiades says that Alkmaion suffered madness after the matricide, and was subsequently cured by the gods because he had acted in defense of his father (12F29). Our one preserved piece of Archaic evidence from art is a Tyrrhenian amphora from Orvieto (Berlin:PM VI 4841).[58] Here we see a woman collapsed in death over what is probably a grave mound, with blood spurting from her neck. Just to the right an armed warrior steps into a chariot whose charioteer has already whipped up the horses. As the warrior turns to look back over his shoulder, a huge snake rises up from behind the mound and threatens him, fangs bared. Further to the right, in front of the horses, a woman races toward the center of the scene; most of her head is missing, but one raised hand appears to hold a bow or snake. Behind the horses are traces of another (male) figure, and on the left of the mound four women, perhaps mourners. The inscriptions, as so often on Tyrrhenian amphoras, are meaningless; nevertheless, the tableau does surely illustrate the death of Eriphyle. Whether such a snake could represent an Erinys (we will return to this problem with Orestes at Foce del Sele) and whether an Erinys portrayed as a woman would carry a bow are harder questions. But it does seem evident that Alkmaion's deed has stirred up some sort of malignant nether powers, and that he will need to come to terms with these, if possible.

In the Classical period we find, apart from the effort(s) of Sophokles, two plays of Euripides dealing with problems after the matricide, *Alkmaion in Psophis*, presented with *Alkestis* in 438 B.C., and *Alkmaion in Korinth*, part of the posthumous production that included the *Bakchai* and *Iphigeneia at Aulis*. Both plays are lost, but from Pausanias and Apollodoros we derive what must have been their basic plots, and probably that of Sophokles' *Alkmaion* as well. Psophis is a locality in western Arkadia, just south of Mount Erymanthos. In Apollodoros, Alkmaion arrives here to seek purification from the king Phegeus, since his mother's Erinyes are pursuing him (ApB 3.7.5–6). The purification accomplished, he marries the king's daughter Arsinoe and gives her the necklace and robe of Harmonia, which he has taken from his mother. But the land becomes infertile, and Apollo commands him to seek further purification from Acheloos. In Pausanias, the daughter is named Alphesiboia, and it is Alkmaion's own sickness, whether physical or mental, which causes him to seek Apollo's aid (8.24.8–10). The Pythia advises him that he must seek a land not in existence at the time of his mother's death, and he finally understands this to mean the delta recently formed at the mouth of the Acheloos river. This latter part of the story is also found in Thoukydides (2.102.5–6); Apollodoros acknowledges it as well, but clearly is not always drawing from the same source as Pausanias. As Pausanias and Apollodoros continue the story, Alkmaion arrives at the far western shore of Aitolia and marries the daughter of Acheloos, Kallirhoe, by whom he has two sons, Akarnan and Amphoteros. But alas, Kallirhoe has heard of the fame of Harmonia's robe and necklace, and forces Alkmaion to return to Psophis to get them. Alkmaion does so, concocting a story for Phegeus that he needs to take the items to Delphi to complete his purification. Unfortunately, the father and/or his sons discover the truth from a servant, and the sons set an ambush for Alkmaion in which he is killed. Pausanias stops here; in Apollodoros' continuation, Arsinoe accuses her brothers and is sold as a slave by them, while Kallirhoe prays to Zeus that her sons might immediately become old enough to take vengeance on their father's slayers. After Zeus grants this and the vengeance is accomplished, Alkmaion's sons also kill Phegeus and his wife, then return to the far west to colonize Akarnania.

The other story, that of Alkmaion in Korinth, is specifically assigned by Apollodoros to Euripides, and smacks like the former of dramatic elaboration (ApB 3.7.7). Alkmaion has here begotten two children, Amphilochos and Tisiphone, by Manto, daughter of Teiresias. These he has left for safekeeping with Kreon of Korinth when they are very young, but at some point subsequently Kreon's wife gives the girl away into slavery, fearing her beauty, and by an incredible coincidence she is eventually purchased by Alkmaion himself, without recognizing her, as a personal servant. As the play begins, our hero has come back to Korinth to find his children, not realizing that he already has the one and not recognizing the other when he sees him.[59] From fragments we learn in addition to this that Amphilochos has been brought up as Kreon's son, and that Alkmaion undergoes a fit of madness and is nearly killed by the Korinthians, led by Kreon. Somehow, though, the children's identities are established and Kreon's plot defeated, so that Amphilochos may go off to found Amphilochian Argos. Where the Alkmaion of the earlier play would have found time for all this is a question we are probably not supposed to ask; the plot may owe much to Euripidean invention, but we must remember that the epic *Alkmaionis* covered a broad range of material, and likely put considerable emphasis on foundation legends for northwest Greece. If that is true, conflicting stories explaining different events may have crowded together under its aegis. In any case, since Euripides is credited by Apollodoros with this story, Sophokles' *Alkmaion* (where the protagonist suffers from madness) probably dealt with the story of Euripides' Psophis play, whether before or after his colleague. An unassigned fragment mentioning Alphesiboia may indicate that he, like Pausanias, gave Phegeus' daughter this name (fr 880 R). Both Agathon and Achaios also wrote *Alkmaion* plays, to name only two, but we know little of any of them (although Achaios' was satyric). One other activity credited to Alkmaion by Ephoros (apud Str 10.2.25) and reappearing in Apollodoros (ApB 1.8.6) is a journey to Aitolia with Diomedes to help the latter restore the throne to his father Oineus.

Last, we turn to Alkmaion's brother Amphilochos, founder in Thoukydides of Amphilochian Argos, "after the Trojan expedition, having returned home and not being pleased with the situation in Argos" (2.68.3). That Amphilochos went to Troy is certainly not known to the *Iliad*, where he is never mentioned, but an Amphilochos is named as one of the three warriors holding the victim on the Tyrrhenian amphora portraying the sacrifice of Iphigeneia (London 1897.7–27.2). The name also appears in an unascribed hexameter quote where Amphilochos is exhorted by some older person to adapt (like the *polupous*) to whatever land he might come to, and this is sometimes assigned to the *Thebais* (fr 4 *PEG*). In the Hesiodic Corpus, according to Strabo, an Amphilochos dies at the hands of Apollo at Soloi in Cilicia (Hes fr 279 MW). This last Amphilochos, whom Strabo and other late sources show departing from Troy with Kalchas and becoming embroiled in a dispute with Mopsos (son of Apollo and Manto), is generally understood by them to be a relative of Alkmaion, if not his brother. Strabo himself relates the most important of these tales, that Amphilochos and Mopsos together founded Mallos on a site just east of Soloi (Str 14.5.16). Subsequently in this account, Amphilochos goes back to Argos, but then returns to Cilicia to claim a share of the new settlement; Mopsos refuses, and in the ensuing duel both die. We find a veiled allusion to this mutually fatal combat in Lykophron (439–46), and thus it must be older than the Hellenistic era; Amphilochos' death via Apollo in "Hesiod" could well be a variant of it, with Apollo intervening on behalf of his son (or after Mopsos has been killed). Strabo elsewhere knows a story in which Amphilochos makes his way to the southern coast of Spain, where he dies (Str 3.4.3).

In Apollodoros we find Amphilochos and Kalchas traveling down from Troy to Kolophon, where they meet Mopsos and the famous contest of seers ensues (ApE 6.2; for this contest see chapter 17). A later reference by the same author has Amphilochos blown by storm from Troy to the home of Mopsos, thus triggering their combat (ApE 6.19). In most of these cases, our hero is identified as the brother of Alkmaion rather than the latter's similarly named son, but we must allow that some confusion may have existed between the two separate figures (in origin probably the same person with variant parentages). As a hero Amphilochos has a broad-ranging cult, including Athens and Sparta as well as Mallos, Rhodes, and Aitolia, and the need to account for the various locales may explain some of his peregrinations. Apollodoros adds one other interesting note, that according to some he shared in the slaying of his mother Eriphyle (ApB 3.7.5). We hear nothing else of this, or its consequences; Kallistratos' late-fifth-century tragedy *Amphilochos* might have dealt with such a topic, but of course the events surrounding the conflict with Mopsos and/or Apollo are also a possibility.

Teiresias   Last, as a bit of unfinished business in this chapter, we may consider briefly the career of Thebes' illustrious seer. We first see him in death, in the *Odyssey*, for Kirke tells us that to his shade alone Persephone has granted to retain his wits, and that Odysseus must go to the edge of Hades to consult him (*Od* 10.490–95). No reason at all is given for this special privilege, and we find in fact that any shade can speak intelligently to Odysseus once it has drunk the sheep's blood. Teiresias' own remarks include nothing about himself, and Kirke describes him only as the blind Theban prophet. But the Hesiodic Corpus—

probably the *Melampodia*—seems already to have related the odd story of his gift of prophecy with most of the details known to later times. According to the summary (courtesy of Apollodoros), while near Mount Kyllene Teiresias saw two snakes mating; he struck them and was turned into a woman (Hes fr 275 MW). At some later date, on observing the same two snakes mating again, he was changed back into a man. For this reason, when Zeus and Hera fell into dispute over which sex derived more pleasure from the act of love, they turned to Teiresias for an answer. Here something has gone afoul in the account, for Apollodoros first says that, reckoning such pleasure into nineteen parts, man enjoys nine and woman ten, then cites two hexameter lines in which man enjoys one of ten shares and woman all ten. Both confusion in the first version and interpolation of the second have been suspected. But the second version with its hexameter quote and one-to-ten ratio also appears in the scholia to *Odyssey* 10.494, and something very close to it in the scholia to Lykophron 683. This last, however, also brings in something about nine shares, and knows too a version in which the ratio is one to nine out of a total of ten. This slight difference probably reflects uncertainty over whether men and women could be rated separately on the same scale or had to share out the ten parts of it between them; the resulting ten parts for women in the first instance and nine parts in the second may then have led to the erroneous notion of nineteen parts and Apollodoros' probable error. In any case, and whatever the exact response of the *Melampodia*, women were clearly the greater beneficiaries of the sexual act, and thus Zeus won the argument. Hera in anger blinded Teiresias; Zeus in compensation gave him mantic skills and a long life. These last gifts we find lamented by the seer in a quote assigned specifically to the *Melampodia*, and here he claims to have lived through seven normal life-spans (Hes fr 276 MW). One oddity of Apollodoros' version is that he does not make Teiresias strike the snakes on the second viewing, as the seer does in all other accounts. Possibly he omitted this through carelessness, supposing it to be understood by his audience.

As for variations in other versions, the scholia to *Odyssey* 10 say that on seeing the snakes copulating Teiresias struck just one of them, the female, and after killing her became a woman; then, killing the male (on the same occasion? subsequently?), he regained his original form (Σ *Od* 10.494). Tzetzes at Lykophron 683 says much the same, with the implication that the gender of the snake slain controlled the form Teiresias assumed. The second-century A.D. writer Phlegon, drawing (so he says) from Hesiod, Dikaiarchos, Kallimachos, and other sources, has Apollo advise Teiresias on how he might undo the original transformation (257F36). Ovid has both snakes struck on each occasion, with Teiresias testing out the premise that every such act will cause a change from whatever sex one happens to be at the moment (*Met* 3.322–38). A new (for us) detail from the same account is the length of Teiresias' career as a woman: seven years. Sadly, Ovid's version of the dispute merely says that Teiresias sided with Zeus; Hyginus, who mentions trampling on snakes (perhaps a garbling of a Greek source), is equally laconic on the matter of the argument (*Fab* 75).

Turning back to Apollodoros, we find that Teiresias' bisexual experience and ill-fated pronouncement to Hera are not the only possible cause of his blindness. Before relating the events described above, the mythographer concedes that there are other explanations, including the idea that the seer divulged to men what the gods wished kept secret (as in some accounts did Phineus) and Pherekydes' tale that he saw Athena naked (3F92). This unfortunate accident seems somehow to have taken place because Athena and Teiresias' mother Chariklo were friends; probably Teiresias stumbled upon the two of them while they were bathing. In any case, Athena places her hands over Teiresias' eyes, and he becomes blind. To Chariklo's anguished laments the goddess replies that she cannot undo the blindness, but she does allow Teiresias to understand the speech of birds, and she gives him a staff with which he can walk as if sighted. This same version of events is narrated at greater length by Kallimachos in his *Hymn* 5 ("The Bath of Pallas"). Here Chariklo and Athena are in fact bathing, in a spring on Mount Helikon, when Teiresias, fresh from the hunt and thirsty, comes to the same spring to drink. At Athena's mere words he loses his sight; Chariklo's protest prompts the justification that the laws of Kronos require such punishment. Athena adds too that Teiresias may consider himself lucky compared with Aktaion, who will soon lose his life for a similar transgression. But here too there are compensatory gifts—the profession of *mantis*, with the ability to utter prophecies and distinguish between good- and ill-omened birds, the guiding staff, a long life, and the retention of his senses among the dead (this last as we saw given by Persephone in the *Odyssey*). From Athena's address to her victim we learn that his father is one Eueres, and this is supported by Apollodoros and Hyginus as well. In Apollodoros, he is furthermore descended from Oudaios, one of the five original Spartoi. Presumably, this ancestry derives from the father, but we know nothing else about Eueres; indeed, Kallimachos is the first writer to mention either parent. Because of his long life Teiresias makes a suitable foil for a variety of mythic plots: Oidipous' discovery of his birth, the quarrel of Oidipous' sons, the sacrifice of Menoikeus, Kreon and Antigone, even Herakles in his nursery at Thebes. But the seer has no further adventures of his own, and his life does finally come to an end on the flight out of Thebes at the time of its destruction: he dies after drinking from the spring Tilphoussa, near the mountain of the same name in the region of Haliartos (Ap*B* 3.7.3).

15   The Line of Tantalos

Tantalos himself is never mentioned in the *Iliad*, not even when Achilleus relates the tale of Niobe to Priam. In the *Odyssey* he does appear once, but only in the *Nekuia,* among the transgressors whom Odysseus sees at the very end of his visit (*Od* 11.582–92). Here we encounter already the punishment so familiar in later tradition: Tantalos stands in a pool of water up to his chin, but when he attempts to drink, the water disappears into the ground; likewise when he reaches up for the branches of fruit overhead—pears, pomegranates, apples, figs, olives—a breeze blows them beyond his grasp. The lines also call him an old man, but say nothing about the transgression that brought him to this state of affairs. Elsewhere in the epic tradition, in a work referred to by Athenaios as the *Return of the Atreidai* (likely the more familiar *Nostoi* under another name[1]), we find a rather different account of the situation: here Tantalos has been enjoying the freedom of socializing with the gods, and on one such occasion receives from Zeus a promise to have whatever his heart should desire (*Nostoi* fr 4 *PEG*). Displaying a weakness for divine pleasures, he asks to live always the same life as the gods. Naturally Zeus is aghast at this suggestion, yet has no choice but to fulfill it; at the same time, though, so that Tantalos might be unable to enjoy the things set before him, he suspends a rock over the mortal's head. Athenaios closes his account by saying that Tantalos is unable to obtain any of the proffered items, implying that the unlucky banqueter fears the rock will fall if he so much as reaches for them. The items in question are presumably food and drink, in which case the preventive role of the rock will serve a purpose not so very unlike that of the pool and branches in the *Nekuia.* That the rock also played a major role in the versions of other authors is guaranteed by references in Archilochos (91 W), Alkman (79 *PMG*), Alkaios (365 LP), Pindar (*Is* 8.9–10), and Pherekydes (3F38), but although Alkman does mention sitting among pleasant things, and Archilochos and Pindar use "Rock of Tantalos" as a proverbial expression (like "Sword of Damokles"), we do not learn anything else of interest regarding either crime or punishment.

We will see shortly that the Archaic period also offers evidence of another transgression altogether, one involving Tantalos, Pandareos, and a dog, but that seems to be a separate story with its own resolution; for the situation that in most accounts brings Tantalos to his tormented fate we have only the epic cited by Athenaios, plus a variant account described in Pindar's *Olympian* 1. This ode, probably his most famous, we know to have been composed for Hieron of Syracuse in 476 B.C., on the occasion of a victory in the single horse race. Hieron's mythical counterpart in such victory, as the first to triumph with horses at Olympia, is Pelops, and that thought brings with it a narration of events leading up to the hero's winning of his bride. But the story that emerges is not quite what later sources would lead us to expect, and Pindar himself seems conscious that his audience will be surprised at times by his version. Pelops, he tells us, was he whom "Earth-shaker Poseidon fell in love with, when Klotho pulled him forth from a pure cauldron, and he was resplendent with his ivory shoulder" (*Ol* 1.25–27). From this brief reference we are likely to presume the later-attested familiar tale of Pelops' resurrection by the gods after his father has tried to serve him for dinner, and Bakchylides seems to confirm knowledge of some such story for this time, since the scholia tell us that in his work Rheia cured Pelops in a cauldron (fr 42 SM).[2] Problems arise, however, when we consider subsequent developments in Pindar's poem, for the poet (after a warning about novelties) goes on to relate that Tantalos offered the gods a "most lawful/well-arranged" banquet at Sipylos in return for the feasts to which they had invited him. The term "most lawful" would seem designed to counter any notions of a meal at which Pelops becomes the dinner, and in fact it is on the occasion of the banquet that Poseidon carries the boy off to Olympos in a fit of passion. His disappearance then leads neighbors to speculate that the gods have eaten him, and thus arises the familiar but (in this poem at least) mistaken tale of a cannibalistic feast. The difficulty is that nothing in this revision of the facts will explain Pindar's opening scene, for if Pelops has not been cut up for dinner he has no need to be in a cauldron, or reason to possess an ivory shoulder. Attempts to explain the former as part of a birth ritual seem dubious (would Poseidon fall in love with a newborn child?) and still leave the shoulder to be dealt with.[3] Whatever we make of this conundrum, Tantalos is here exonerated of trying to kill his own son, and thus needs a new transgression for which he can be punished. Pindar makes this the sharing with his friends of the nectar and ambrosia with which the gods made him immortal. For such unauthorized extension of their favors, Zeus suspends over him a rock that he constantly desires to keep away from his head, and thus absenting himself from happiness he has a helpless life, a fourth toil with three others (*Ol* 1.54–64). What these "three others" are remains an insoluble problem; if Tantalos and his rock are in the Underworld we might think of other transgressors, or even other torments (hunger, thirst, and ?), but Pindar can hardly have expected his audience to provide a specific meaning for such a terse allusion. More likely the expression is proverbial, indicating something like "toil upon toil," that is, the hopeless eternity of Tantalos' predicament.[4] Whether Pindar himself supposed the additional torment of unreachable food and drink we cannot then say, but he certainly might expect his audience to supply those details from earlier epic, once the rock was mentioned.

As one further response of the gods in *Olympian* 1 Pelops is sent back to earth, to grow into manhood and assume mortality, and apparently this development is the real point of Pindar's story: the gods' experiment in making men immortal has failed, as Tantalos' sharing of his good fortune with others shows, and thus Pelops must work out a new relationship between man and god, in a world of heroes and darkness occasionally irradiated by divine light. To convey that idea Pindar needs a transgression that will illustrate Tantalos' failure as an immortal, not (as in Athenaios) improper aspirations in that direction or any entertaining of gods with human flesh; thus he settles on the redistribution of nectar and ambrosia as the crime. Whether he invented it is harder to say. Whatever we decide, the cauldron and shoulder remain as tangible vestiges of a different tale with which he clearly supposes his audience to be familiar.

From perhaps only slightly later in the fifth century we have Polygnotos' painting of Hades for the Knidian Lesche at Delphi. Here, as Pausanias tells us, Tantalos is made to endure the same torments as in Homer, and in addition that of the rock suspended over him (10.31.12). Pausanias credits the artist's knowledge of the rock to Archilochos, who he says may well have been the first to tell of it. We saw, however, that our own brief Archilochian reference is essentially a proverb ("May the rock of Tantalos not hang over this island") and the poet must have narrated the story at greater length elsewhere if Pausanias' belief has any merit. In any event, the writer clearly believes that no source before Polygnotos thought to combine the punishments of rock and pool. Euripides' *Orestes* begins with Elektra lamenting the fortunes of the house; we are told that Tantalos "hovers in the air, fearing the rock hanging over his head. And he pays this penalty, as they say, because being a man, and having equal honor at the table of the gods, he could not keep his tongue in check" (*Or* 4–10). Elektra also calls Tantalos a son of Zeus, as will most later authors. But why he should float in air remains unexplained, even if the idea apparently reappears later in the play, when the chorus prays to be taken to the place where the rock (the sun?) swings on golden chains, so that it might lament the fortunes of the house to Tantalos (*Or* 982–85). The scholia to the earlier passage suggest that Tantalos was thus placed between heaven and earth so that he might not hear more of the gods' conversation on Olympos or reveal more of it to mortals (Σ *Or* 7).[5] Scholia to the *Odyssey* refer to Zeus as binding Tantalos' hands and suspending him from a high mountain, with Asklepiades given as source (Σ *Od* 11.582). We cannot say, of course, whether Asklepiades had other sources besides this play, or to what extent the *Orestes* scholia might be guessing. It would seem, however, that such a punishment must certainly preclude the pool and probably also the rock. As for the offense, the scholia obviously suppose that it was similar to that of the Thracian Phineus: disclosing too much of the gods' plans to other men. But Euripides' language could allow for other possibilities: excessively arrogant speech at the table of the gods, or boasting of his good fortune to others, or even the same ill-considered request as in Athenaios. But a crime of the tongue will at least eliminate two possibilities, the cooking of his son and sharing out of the food of the gods. We may add that Sophokles and other playwrights are credited with works entitled *Tantalos* of which we know nothing; the usual assumption is that most if not all of these dealt with Pandareos' theft of the dog.

Later sources have very little to add on any of these points. Both Plato (*Kratylos* 395d) and Hypereides (fr 173 Kenyon) in the fourth century mention the rock (Plato, like Polygnotos, locates it in Hades), and this mode of punishment remains consistently popular in subsequent times. But Horace (*Epodes* 17.65–66; *Satires* 1.1.68–69) and Ovid (*Met* 4.458–59) repeat the Homeric version, and Apollodoros (*ApE* 2.1) and Hyginus (*Fab* 82) combine those torments with the rock, again like Polygnotos. Apollodoros also notes that in some accounts Tantalos is punished for revealing the *mustêria* of the gods, and Hyginus says that he divulged the counsels of the gods which Zeus had confided to him. A poem in the *Greek Anthology* stresses too that Tantalos' tongue was what brought him to grief (*AP* 16.131.9), and Loukianos speaks of his babbling (*Sal* 54.3; *De sacrificiis* 9.10), while Cicero quotes a line from an unknown play in which the miscreant is accused of *suberbiloquentia* (*TD* 4.16.35).

As for the crime that Pindar denies, Euripides' Iphigeneia also finds unbelievable the "banquet of Tantalos for the gods, that they would enjoy the taste of a child's flesh" when she is forced by the Tauroi to sacrifice men to Artemis (*IT* 386–88). And Menelaos in the same poet's *Helen* offers the wish that Pelops had perished "when persuaded you made a feast for the gods" (*Hel* 388–89); the oddity of phrasing (to what was Pelops persuaded?) may indicate some corruption. But we learn nothing further until Lykophron, where for the first time we see Demeter devour Pelops' shoulder (152–55), and then Ovid, who knows of the ivory replacement and specifies that Tantalos was the one to cut up his son (*Met* 6.403–11). Hyginus, too, relates this last fact, and adds that Demeter contrived the new shoulder (*Fab* 83). We saw before that Pindar rather implies (in the version he then rejects) the gods as the perpetrators of the feast (so perhaps also Euripides), but as such a version would not explain Pelops' survival (surely mandatory in all accounts), it is not likely to have ever constituted a tradition. Oddly enough, none of these sources says why Tantalos should have wished to serve the gods in such a fashion; various scholia suggest that he was attempting to be hospitable, or to make a significant contribution to the *eranos* to which the gods had invited him (Σ Lyk 152; Σ *Ol* 1.40a), while Servius seems the first to suppose that he wished to test the divinity of the gods (Σ *G* 3.7; cf. the motives of Lykaon in chapter 18). Some of these later sources also state that Demeter was upset over the loss of Persephone when she ate the shoulder (Σ Lyk 152), and that Zeus ordered Hermes to restore Pelops with the ivory replacement (Σ *Ol* 1.40). The Pindar scholion notes as well that according to some, Themis (or Thetis: manuscripts vary), rather than Demeter, was the inadvertent consumer of the shoulder.

Amid such a range of transgressions and two distinct punishments we might suppose Tantalos free of other misadventures. But there exists yet another tradition, one distinct from everything considered above in that no part of it is ever interchanged with what we have already seen. On a sixth-century Black-Figure cup by the Heidelberg Painter now in the Louvre we find a man in stately dress, followed by a very large dog, a winged figure, another man running up with a leash (?), and two women (Louvre A478). There are alas no names, but the cup presumably illustrates a story found in scholia to the *Odyssey* and *Olympian* 1 and in Antoninus Liberalis. The *Odyssey* scholia are those concerned with the daughters of Pandareos in *Odyssey* 19 and 20: by way of justifying the consignment of these girls to the Erinyes we are told that Zeus' shrine on Krete possessed a live golden dog, and that the Milesian Pandareos, son of Merops, stole it (ΣΣ *Od* 19.518, 20.66). Fearing, however, to take the dog back to Miletos, he left it for safekeeping with Tantalos in Phrygia. When Hermes came to look for the dog, Tantalos swore by all the gods that he did not have it, but Hermes found it anyway; Zeus punished Tantalos by placing Mount Sipylos on top of him. The account of these scholia also relates that Pandareos and his wife Harmothoe first fled to Athens and then to Sicily, where Zeus discovered them and killed them both.

The Pindaric scholia tell the same story, although the dog, which is not here said to be golden, now guards the shrine of Zeus on Krete, and the punishment of Pandareos is omitted (Σ *Ol* 1.91). In Antoninus the dog has been set by Rheia to guard the goat that nourishes Zeus (AntLib 36). Pandareos steals him as before, and deposits him with Tantalos, but here he himself returns to claim the animal, and it is to him that Tantalos swears that he does not have it. Zeus punishes Pandareos for the theft by turning him to stone, and Tantalos for the false oath by (again) burying him under Sipylos. A further variant surfaces at the end of the *Odyssey* 19 scholia: the scholiast says that Tantalos was the stealer of the dog, and that Pandareos, receiving it from him, denied the fact (leading to the punishment of his two younger daughters). Possibly this is a genuine tradition, but the scholiast may well have reversed the roles of the two malefactors.

In all, there seems little likelihood of bringing Tantalos' various offenses and chastisements together into a coherent whole, and in particular making this last misdeed fit with the rest. The one possibility for overlap would seem to lie in the fact that a false oath is a crime of the tongue, which we saw to be one of the transgressions of the rock/pool Tantalos. But our first reference of this sort, Euripides' *Orestes*, pointedly connects the man's "unrestrained" speaking with his access to the gods' table, so that an oath on earth to Hermes or anyone else would seem excluded. Having a mountain fall on one also seems suspiciously close to waiting for a rock to do the same, but the point of the rock is after all that it never falls; in the epic cited by Athenaios, as we saw, its function is much closer to that of the branches and pool. Nor do any of these fates bear much resemblance to a Prometheus-type binding on a mountainside. Surprisingly, there are no preserved artistic representations to help us with any of these matters.[6]

One final entanglement takes us in another direction altogether, though it survives only in late sources. Mnaseas, a third-century B.C. mythographer with Euhemerizing tendencies, apparently had Tantalos rather than Zeus abduct Ganymedes, after which the latter died while hunting (ΣbT *Il* 20.234).[7] Related to this, it might seem, is the report of Diodoros that Tantalos was driven out of Paphlagonia by Ilos, son of Tros (DS 4.74), and indeed the third-century A.D. historian Herodian makes the connection by stating that Ilos and Tantalos went to war over the abduction of Ganymedes, as brother and lover respectively (1.11; so too Σ Lyk 355). Seemingly this tale is incompatible with that in which Zeus takes Ganymedes up to Olympos, and may well have been created as a rationalizing variant on that one, but why in that case Tantalos should play the part of the miscreant is not immediately clear.[8]

Before concluding this section, we should consider also Tantalos' parentage and wife. Our earliest information on the first of these points is Euripides, where Tantalos is a son of Zeus (*Or* 5); later sources all agree on that much, save for the scholion to this same passage, which names Tmolos as the father. The mother seems, however, on all occasions when she is named, to be one Plouto (Paus 2.22.3; Σ *Od* 11.582; Σ *Or* 4; *Fab* 82, 155; Nonnos 7.119 [union with Zeus only]). Hyginus calls her the daughter of Himas (*Fab* 155), but we know nothing else about her. Tantalos' wife and the mother of Pelops is Euryanassa in the scholia to *Orestes* 4 and Dositheos (54F1), but in the scholia to *Orestes* 11 Euryanassa, daughter of Paktolos, or Eurythemiste, daughter of Xanthos, or Klytia daughter of Amphidamas, this last credited to Pherekydes (3F40). For Hyginus she is instead Dione, a daughter of Atlas (*Fab* 9, 83).

Niobe   Tantalos' daughter Niobe (though without parentage) makes her first appearance in *Iliad* 24, when Achilleus uses her as an example to Priam of the need to eat, even amidst great grief (*Il* 24.602–17). The resulting suggestion that Niobe does not immediately succumb to her grief clashes in fact with most later accounts, and has roused suspicions that Homer is here innovating (as perhaps also in the case of Meleagros in *Iliad* 9) to make a point.[9] What Achilleus tells us is that Niobe compared herself to Leto because she had many children and Leto only two; in anger Apollo and Artemis, two though they were, slew her twelve offspring, Apollo the six males and Artemis the six females. The dead lay in their own blood for nine days, since there was no one to bury them, Zeus having turned the people to stone. Finally on the tenth day the gods themselves buried them, and Niobe took thought of food, when she had tired of weeping. But now, he continues, she is among the rocks in the lonely hills of Sipylos, and continues to nourish her grief, although she is stone. The oddities here are of two kinds. On the one hand, Niobe's decision to resume the normal activities of life seems much in conflict with her subsequent metamorphosis, which we presume is in some way caused by her grief, and here Homer may well have added some new material.[10] But the other surprises—for we see no reason why the gods should turn the local populace to stone, or take it upon themselves to bury corpses—are not really necessary to Achilleus' purpose at all, and may form part of an older tradition that has not survived. Based on what we have, the gods would seem to have intensified Niobe's punishment by threatening for a time to keep her children unburied, even though this was not their ultimate intent. Nothing guarantees, however, that Homer has given us all the facts, and the true story may be much more complicated, involving, for example, some transgression on the part of the Thebans (but does Homer mean that they remained stone?).

For the rest of the Archaic period we have virtually no literary evidence beyond what late sources (primarily Aelian, Aulus Gellius, and a *Phoinissai* scholion) tell us about the number of Niobe's children in different early authors. A surprising number of authors are cited, although we do not know for most of them whether they actually narrated the story. More often than not the total figure is divided equally between males and females, as in Homer; after his twelve we have the following: in "Hesiod" nine and ten, or else ten and ten (Hes fr 183 MW); in Alkman ten in all (75 *PMG*), in Mimnermos twenty in all (19 W); in Sappho nine and nine (205 LP); in Lasos seven and seven (706 *PMG*); in Pindar (fr 52n: see *apparatus*) and Bakchylides (fr 20D) ten and ten; in Aischylos, Sophokles, and Euripides seven and seven (Σ *Pho* 159); in Pherekydes six and six (3F126); in Hellanikos four and three (4F21); in Herodoros two and three (31F56). Of these writers we can say that Aischylos and Sophokles wrote *Niobe* plays, and that Euripides apparently did not (the figure attributed to him comes from his *Kresphontes*). We have also a single line from Sappho to the effect that "Leto and Niobe were exceedingly good friends" (142 LP); probably this is meant as a parallel to some current reversal of feeling charted by Sappho, but it may suggest that Niobe's acceptance by the gods as a near-equal brought about her downfall, as it did that of her father. Not before Aischylos do we learn (via a papyrus fragment) that she is the daughter of Tantalos, and married to Amphion (fr 154a R), although no later author ever disputes these points.

Aischylos' dramatization apparently began with Niobe veiled and seated at the tomb of her children, and for some time refusing to speak, so that her boast and the slaying of those children have already taken place. At some point in the play Tantalos will appear (to take his daughter home?) but this is all we know of the action. The fragments do offer some odd statements, most especially the lines quoted by Plato to the effect that "God creates a cause in mortals, whenever he wishes to destroy a house entirely" (*Rep* 2.383b). This would seem to shift the blame from Niobe, but we do not know if the speaker was right; the papyrus fragment mentioned above also includes these lines, and shows that there followed immediately after a caution against mortals speaking too boldly in the midst of their prosperity (fr 154a R). Still, an earlier part of the speech offers an anguished query as to what anger the gods had against Amphion, that they should so strip the leaves from his house; we gather therefore that at least part of the play entertained a questioning of the gods' actions. Tantalos, when he does appear, remarks that his fortune has fallen from *ouranos* to earth, and says, "Learn not to honor too much the things of man" (fr 159 R). That he should already have committed his transgression, as it would seem, and still be free to come to Thebes, is remarkable; perhaps it was necessary for the plot. His own experience with the gods may have put him in a position to help his daughter grasp more clearly the error of her ways, but here we are guessing. The one other fragment of interest says that Amphion's house (i.e., the actual building) will be destroyed by the thunderbolt; we will see possible reasons shortly. In his *Poetics*, Aristotle tells us that Aischylos is to be commended for treating only a part of the story of Niobe; this may mean that her metamorphosis to stone in Lydia was not included, or it may refer simply to the play's commencement after the slaughter (18.1456a.15–19). In Pherekydes' recounting, Niobe goes back to Lydia by herself (thus not as in Aischylos) and sees her city destroyed and the rock suspended over her father; in her grief she prays to Zeus to become stone (3F38; so too in Bak 20D Zeus in pity turns her to stone). Something of this sort could conceivably lie behind Homer's version, with Niobe at first taking courage after her own disaster but then broken by the further misfortunes in her homeland.

In Archaic art we have only one representation, that on a Tyrrhenian amphora of about 560 B.C. showing Apollo and Artemis with between them three fleeing victims (Hamburg 1960.1). The scene does not resurface until the famous calyx krater of the Niobid Painter from about 450 B.C. (Louvre G341). Subsequently it becomes especially popular in sculpture, but the scene represented is always the massacre, and thus we learn nothing further about the story.

In the Classical period we have above all Sophokles' *Niobe*, which seems to have taken quite a different approach in staging from that of Aischylos. Papyrus fragments now make it clear that Artemis and Apollo appeared in person to hunt down the daughters—Apollo even calls his sister's attention to one who is hiding and must not be allowed to escape (fr 441a R). The sons have, it seems, already been killed elsewhere, which is a trifle puzzling because Plutarch tells us that in this play one of the sons when shot calls upon his lover (*Mor* 760d), and Athenaios that the homosexual attachments of the sons were treated in some fashion (13.601a). Presumably this last feature was to increase the pathos of their deaths, and the actual slaughter of them, with whatever appeals were made to loved ones, was reported in a messenger speech. *Iliad* scholia add to all this that Sophokles had the children perish in Thebes, and Niobe then return to Lydia (ΣT *Il* 24.602). Unless we suppose a very unlikely change of scene, a god must have predicted this journey or Niobe announced it herself; we cannot say whether the metamorphosis was foretold. In any case, the overall impact, with the innocent daughters cut down by the gods virtually on stage, must have been considerable.

Later sources do provide some interesting bits of information. We should first note that Telesilla has two of the children, Amyklas and Meliboia, spared (721 *PMG*); of the sources so far considered, only Homer actually states that all were killed (although we should probably assume this in versions where Niobe returns to Lydia, or asks to become a rock). Pausanias adds to the notion of survivors the idea that Meliboia became permanently pale as a result of the ordeal, and was renamed Chloris (2.21.9–10). Apollodoros, our source for Telesilla, has as his own names for the saved pair Amphion and Chloris, which latter he equates with the wife of Neleus (ApB 3.5.6). In fact the *Nekuia* does make Neleus' wife a daughter of Amphion, but that Amphion is said to be the son of Iasos and ruler of Orchomenos, as also in the *Ehoiai* (*Od* 11.281–84; Hes fr 33a MW). Probably then some confusion has taken place between two figures of the same name, and Neleus' wife has in origin nothing to do with Niobe. But how old the tradition of children surviving might be we cannot say (Pausanias, despite his information, rejects it on Homer's authority). One other odd variant to record is that of the Hellenistic (and rationalizing?) Timagoras, who claims that the Thebans themselves slew the children from ambush, being annoyed at treatment received from Amphion and his friends (381F1).

In Ovid, Niobe finds the Theban women worshipping at Leto's altars, and dares (on the basis of lineage, beauty, and fourteen children) to claim Leto's honors as her own (*Met* 6.147–312). The sons are dispatched as they exercise their horses outside the city; Apollo is tempted to spare the last, hearing his appeal, but the arrow has already slipped from his fingers. The father Amphion kills himself at the news. Although Niobe also laments, she cannot help noting that her seven daughters are still more than Leto's brood, and so of course these are killed as well. The metamorphosis then occurs immediately, the result of shock and grief; a whirlwind carries the rock to Lydia to take its accustomed place as a local landmark. Apollodoros, like Homer, has Apollo kill the sons (while hunting on Kithairon) and Artemis the daughters (in their father's house); their mother's crime, as in Ovid, was to boast of her larger family (ApB 3.5.6). We have seen that like Telesilla this author spares two of the children, and like Pherekydes and Sophokles he takes Niobe back to Lydia, where as in Pherekydes her prayer to become stone is granted. Hyginus offers much the same: in his version Apollo slays the sons in a forest while Artemis deals with all the daughters (save Chloris) in the palace; Niobe again turns to rock in Lydia through her weeping (*Fab* 9).

As for Amphion, Telesilla has the two gods slay him also, in contrast to Ovid's notion of suicide. Pausanias says that he pays a penalty in the Underworld (he does not say what, or how the man died) for being among those to mock Leto and her children, and cites the *Minyas* as one source for this idea (9.5.8–9). In Hyginus, who may or may not know the same story as Telesilla, he attempts to attack the temple of Apollo, and dies by the god's arrows. One would like to know whether in this version he was simply angry over the loss of his children (as Hyginus' order of narration implies) or had as in Pausanias already begun to participate in the scorning of divine powers. We remember that in Aischylos' play his palace is destroyed, and perhaps there too he does something personally to merit the gods' wrath.

Pelops and   In discussing Tantalos we have reviewed the evidence for his son's narrow es-
Hippodameia cape from the banquet of the gods at Sipylos. Pelops' one appearance in Homer occurs in *Iliad* 2, when we learn that Agamemnon has a scepter that has passed from Hephaistos to Zeus to Hermes to Pelops, lasher of horses, to Atreus to Thyestes to Agamemnon (*Il* 2.98–108). I suppose we are to understand that Hephaistos made it for Zeus to give to Pelops (via Hermes) as a symbol of authority, although on our later evidence Hermes presenting a gift to Pelops is a bit odd, and Atreus passing on power peacefully to Thyestes, or Thyestes to Agamemnon, distinctly puzzling. Aristarchos supposed Homer therefore ignorant of the family's problems, but the poet may simply have considered them inappropriate to the point he wanted to make about the scepter. We should also keep in mind that the word used for each transfer, "leave," might indicate that power passed to the successor via the previous holder's demise, rather than his approval. In any case, and whatever Homer knows, we have an early link between Pelops and the house of Atreus. That he is in fact Tantalos' son (not said in Homer) is attested by the *Kypria* (fr 15 *PEG*) and Tyrtaios (12 W), while the feast we found first noted by Pindar in a context that showed it to be well known (in some form). The *Ehoiai* seems (based on a very fragmentary papyrus) to have charted the courting of his daughters by the sons of Perseus, as in later accounts; certainly an Astydameia is mentioned (Hes fr 190 MW).

The most famous myth concerning Pelops is, however, his race with Oinomaos for the hand of the latter's daughter. The *Megalai Ehoiai* mentioned some (perhaps all) of the previous entrants who died in this contest; Pausanias cites the work for Alkathoos as one victim and may have drawn from it for others on his own list, which totals seventeen (6.21.10 = Hes fr 259a MW). The Pindaric scholia for their part assign to "Hesiod" and "Epimenides" a total of thirteen (Σ *Ol* 1.127b), and provide three different lists of names, with thirteen, fifteen, and thirteen respectively (Σ *Ol* 1.127b, c, d); only a few suitors like Alkathoos, Lasios, and Eurymachos figure repeatedly in all of these. Pausanias elsewhere reports seeing the race between Oinomaos and Pelops (the latter with Hippodameia) depicted on the Chest of Kypselos; he notes that each driver has two horses, but that Pelops' are winged (5.17.7). For this chariot race in which Pelops wins his bride our first real narration is again *Olympian* 1, whose mythic portion after telling of Tantalos' fall focuses on his son's earthly life. Here, with his beard growing and his thoughts turned toward marriage, Pelops decides to sue for Oinomaos' daughter, and calls on his own former wooer Poseidon for help. The god bestows upon him a golden chariot and tireless winged horses; with these he defeats strong Oinomaos (thirteen previous suitors were unsuccessful) and takes Hippodameia as his bedmate. As this paraphrase shows, Pindar's account passes rather summarily over the race itself, but we presume that the victory is owed to the gift of the god.

Yet another, darker tradition surfaces as early as Pherekydes, to the effect that Myrtilos the charioteer of Oinomaos played a major role in the victory. Our source for the mythographer here, the scholia to Apollonios, strictly speaking mention Pherekydes only (in mid-stream of their account) for a variant detail (Σ AR 1.752 = 3F37a). But since they do not record him as diverging in other matters, we may assume that they found him in agreement on most details of the story. As they relate the tale, Oinomaos establishes the bride contest for his daughter because an oracle has told him that his son-in-law will kill him. Hippodameia, however, becomes enamored of Pelops when he presents himself, and asks Myrtilos, son of Hermes, to assist his victory. In Pherekydes this is accomplished by omitting to insert the linchpin in Oinomaos' chariot, so that it will fall apart; in other versions, rather more plausibly, a waxen linchpin that will disintegrate as the race progresses is utilized. Whether in Pherekydes Myrtilos was promised anything for this service we do not know, but other scholia report that in the mythographer's account Pelops did throw Myrtilos into the sea one day when the two of them were riding around the Peloponnesos with Hippodameia and the charioteer attempted to kiss her (3F37b). The same reference mentions that the horses pulling the chariot were winged, which seems an odd detail to include in an account stressing other means of victory. Indeed, one might be tempted to suppose the wings a Pindaric invention designed to dignify the triumph, and from there conflated into an older tradition, were it not for Pausanias' report of the same motif on the Chest of Kypselos. As it is, both versions must boast some antiquity, different though their approaches to the winning of victory are.

In fifth-century art we have the famous sculptures from the east pediment of the Temple of Zeus at Olympia. Here Zeus occupies the center, presumably indicating his approval of the outcome. To the left are Oinomaos and his wife Sterope (according to Pausanias), to the right Pelops and Hippodameia, and then toward each corner the chariot teams of the two competitors.[11] No fewer than four different of the crouching figures (B, C, L, N) have been identified as Myrtilos, assuming him to have been present; the one kneeling (by Oinomaos' chariot wheel?: C) is perhaps the most likely, though nothing in his pose makes him especially remarkable. To judge from the remains both sets of horses were unwinged. Perhaps the artist has deliberately suppressed both treachery and divine horses in order that Zeus alone might seem to determine the outcome; but perhaps too he presupposes Myrtilos' role, and seeks with this understatement to heighten the tension between the calm demeanor of the figures and the fatal "accident" to follow. From much later in the century a neck-amphora now in Arezzo shows Pelops and Hippodameia together in his chariot (Arezzo 1460).[12] She stands straight up, unaffected by the action, but he leans well back as he strives to control the horses and looks back over his shoulder. Clearly, then, the race is in progress, and if Hippodameia is already at Pelops' side (here as on the Chest of Kypselos), we might guess that this race is actually a kind of mock bridal-rape, with the suitor taking the prospective bride into his chariot as if to abduct her, and the father setting out after in pursuit. This would explain, too, the grouping at Olympia, with Hippodameia next to Pelops, not her father, as they prepare to start the race. We will see shortly that various later authors confirm this notion.

As for literature in the later fifth century, both Sophokles and Euripides wrote plays entitled *Oinomaos*. Of the first we know only that Hippodameia was passionately fired by Pelops' gaze (fr 474 R), that Oinomaos used the suitors' skulls for some architectural project (fr 473a R), and that the race began onstage, with no doubt a messenger report of the subsequent action. But one would like to think that Myrtilos was involved, and he *is* mentioned by the chorus of Sophokles' *Elektra* as thrown headlong from the chariot into the sea (S: *El* 505–15).[13] For Euripides' version we have nothing at all, save perhaps the possibility that Oinomaos was sympathetically treated; in a choral ode of the *Orestes*, however, we find Myrtilos again thrown into the sea, near Geraistos at the southern end of Euboia, and this is now the origin of a subsequent curse on the family (*Or* 988–96). From the contemporary Hellanikos we have already seen Oinomaos' genealogy as son of Ares and Sterope, daughter of Atlas (4F19).

Our later sources support most of these details and flesh out the story. In Apollonios, Iason's robe, made for him by Athena, shows Pelops and Hippodameia together in flight, while Oinomaos and Myrtilos give chase (AR 1.752–58). Oinomaos holds his spear poised, clearly to throw or thrust into Pelops' back, but before he can do so the axle of his chariot breaks and he falls. Diodoros makes Oinomaos (here too son of Ares) learn from an oracle that he will die when his only daughter marries (DS 4.73.1–6); we saw this motif already in the scholia to Apollonios, which probably draw from Pherekydes among others. Faced with such a prospect, he sets up the race for Hippodameia's suitors, giving them a head-start from Pisa in a four-horse chariot while he sacrifices to Zeus; then he overtakes them before they reach the Isthmos and kills them with his spear. Pelops duly appears and persuades Myrtilos to help him, but we are not given details: his chariot simply beats that of Oinomaos to the Isthmos and Oinomaos kills himself, convinced that the oracle has come true.

Apollodoros relates two separate motives for Oinomaos' treatment of his daughter, first that he was in love with her himself and did not wish another to marry her, and second that he received an oracle of his doom as above (ApE 2.4–9). The notion of an erotic attachment to his daughter we find also in the scholia to the *Orestes*, which credit the idea to the "more accurate of the historiographers" (Σ *Or* 990).[14] Apollodoros continues with the usual account, agreeing in many particulars with the Apollonios scholia: here Myrtilos, son of Hermes, is specifically in love with Hippodameia, and thus agrees to help her when she falls in love with Pelops. The race is again to the Isthmos, with the suitor taking Hippodameia in his chariot and trying to prevent Oinomaos from overtaking him. As in Pherekydes, Myrtilos removes the linchpins from the wheel hubs; Oinomaos becomes entangled in the reins and is dragged to his death. But Apollodoros also cites a rival version in which Pelops kills his opponent himself (we are not told how). Whatever the means of death, Oinomaos has somehow perceived Myrtilos' treachery, and he curses his charioteer to perish by Pelops' hand. In Apollodoros' conclusion to the story, Pelops, Hippodameia, and Myrtilos are subsequently out together on an excursion, in the course of which Myrtilos tries to rape Hippodameia after Pelops has gone to seek water; on Pelops' return he casts Myrtilos into the sea (again by Geraistos), and is himself cursed by his rival on the way down.

Hyginus also uses the motif of the oracle to begin his account, but has Pelops approach Myrtilos directly after seeing the skulls of previous suitors fixed on Oinomaos' palisade (*Fab* 84). In return for his help, Myrtilos is promised half of Oinomaos' kingdom, and the pins are withheld, but Pelops then regrets his offer and hurls Myrtilos to his doom instead. Pausanias gives us a similar narrative, save that here Pelops offers not half the kingdom but rather a night with Hippodameia; again he fails to keep his word (8.14.11). In the Vergil scholia, the result is the same but Hippodameia the one who promises herself to Myrtilos in return for his help (Σ G 3.7). The *Orestes* scholia (Σ 990 as above), after establishing Oinomaos as enamored of Hippodameia, follow closely the version of Apollodoros: Myrtilos being also enamored of Hippodameia is persuaded by her to remove the linchpins, and suffers his master's curse as a consequence. But at this point we are offered two possibilities: either Myrtilos tries to rape Hippodameia and is thrown into the sea, or he is falsely accused of rape by her. The latter version also appears in the *Iliad* scholia, where Hippodameia, who has engineered Myrtilos' treachery because of her love for Pelops, now falls in love with Myrtilos as well, and in Pelops' absence (he has again gone to get water) begs the charioteer not to scorn her advances (ΣA *Il* 2.104). He does so, however, and to protect herself she accuses him of rape to Pelops, thus bringing about his doom. We see, therefore, some variation in Myrtilos' role and relationship to Hippodameia, but none at all in his fate; in every account he is thrown to his death.[15] Possibly his status as the son of Hermes means that the race and his part in it was related as early as the *Alkmaionis*, where we know that Hermes for some reason began the quarrel between Atreus and Thyestes (see below), but on present evidence this is a guess.[16] As for Pelops, our summaries never really make clear whether in some versions he might have been ignorant of his intended's machinations to ensure his victory. Both Apollodoros and the *Orestes* scholia send him off to Hephaistos to be purified of the murder, and it seems generally agreed that Myrtilos' curse will fall upon his children rather than himself.

Pindar's *Olympian* 1 assigns to Pelops and Hippodameia six sons but does not name them (*Ol* 1.89). We saw that in the *Iliad* Pelops is said to have left his scepter to Atreus, and Atreus in turn to Thyestes, but there we have no indication of the exact relationship between the three men. In fact, no Archaic source specifies that Atreus and Thyestes were the sons of Pelops; the closest we come is Aischylos' *Choephoroi*, where Orestes calls himself a Pelopid (*Cho* 503); not until Sophokles' *Aias* (1291–94) and the prologue of the *Orestes* is the line of descent made explicit. Given the link established in Homer, however, there seems little reason to doubt that Atreus and Thyestes were always two of the sons. Presumably they were so named in the *Ehoiai*, but the relevant passages have not survived, nor can we say anything about other of Pelops' sons, if any, in that work. Other writers of the Archaic period do offer some suggestions of their own for these sons: a Sikyon is named in Ibykos (308 *PMG*: probably in the *Ehoiai* a son of Erechtheus [Hes fr 224 MW]), Kleonymos and Argeios (husband of Hegesandra, daughter of Amyklas) appear in Pherekydes (3F20, 3F132), and Alkathoos, founder of Megara, in a section of the Theognid Corpus referring to the Persian invasion of 480 B.C. (Theog 773–74). These names are, of course, primarily place eponyms (not surprising, given that Pelops' own name serves as source for the word *Peloponnesos*), and such offspring may be the sort of sons Pindar has in mind. Euripides' *Medeia* and *Herakleidai*, for their part, add a more substantive figure, namely Pittheus of Troizen, the grandfather of Theseus (*Med* 683–84; *Hkld* 207). Whether his link to the house of Pelops stems from Athenian pride in Theseus or goes back to something older we do not know; he does appear frequently in later lists. Apollodoros for example names him (with Atreus, Thyestes, and "others": Ap*E* 2.10) and so too the scholia to *Olympian* 1 (Σ *Ol* 1.144). These last actually offer three slightly different lists, as follows: (1) Atreus, Thyestes, Pittheus, Alkathoos, Pleisthenes, Chrysippos; (2) Atreus, Thyestes, Pittheus, Alkathoos, Hippalkmos, Dias, plus the bastards Chrysippos and Pleisthenes; (3) Atreus, Thyestes, Pittheus, Hippalkmos, Pleisthenes, Pelops the younger. Pindar's six children are all borne by Hippodameia; the scholia's suggestion of sources which included Chrysippos and Pleisthenes in that group might seem then to indicate versions in which they were legitimate. The scholia at *Orestes* 4 name Atreus, Thyestes, and Pittheus, plus ten other legitimate sons (largely eponyms), two daughters, and Chrysippos by one Axioche. Probably Apollodoros, too, had divergent lists from which to draw, and therefore contented himself with the three generally agreed-upon names followed by "others." In Hyginus there are only three legitimate children, Atreus, Thyestes, and Hippalkos (*sic*), plus the bastard Chrysippos whom Atreus and Thyestes kill (*Fab* 85).

As we saw in chapter 14, Atreus' exile because of the death of Chrysippos occurs as early as Thoukydides (1.9.2), and Hellanikos relates the full story as we might expect it, that Pelops favors this son from a previous liaison, and that Hippodameia and her children plot his death, lest he receive preference for accession to his father's throne (41F57). As the two eldest, Atreus and Thyestes take the lead; when Pelops discovers the deed he exiles them, with a curse that they and their race may die at each other's hands. Plato also mentions the murder in passing (Atreus alone cited as agent, since the point is a play on his name: *Kratylos* 395b). The *Orestes* scholia noted above (at *Or* 4) have a tale similar to that of Hellanikos, with Chrysippos' mother here a certain Axioche, and the other sons together with Hippodameia persuading the two eldest (again Atreus and Thyestes) to do the deed in envy of Chrysippos' favored status. Having killed him, the two brothers throw the body in a well, but Pelops suspects the truth and exiles them with an unspecified curse. Dositheos has an unusual variant that we considered earlier in connection with Laios: here the Theban king is sleeping together with the boy when Hippodameia, having failed to persuade her sons to stain their hands, steals into his room and commits the murder herself with a sword taken from Laios; presumably she hopes that Laios will be blamed, but Chrysippos survives long enough to reveal the truth, and Hippodameia is banished (54F1). Some version of the tale as a whole *may* have been the subject of Sophokles' lost *Hippodameia*, if there really was such a play;[17] possibly, too, it formed the basis of Accius' *Chrysippus* or his *Pelopidae*. Neither of Chrysippos' fates—death at the hands of his family and suicide after his abduction by Laios—claim our attention before the fifth century; how much older than that period either might be is difficult to say. For Hippodameia's fate in those versions where she is involved our earliest sources are silent; Hyginus speaks of suicide (*Fab* 85), Pausanias (6.20.7) as well as Dositheos of exile. The other children we shall deal with in the following sections.

Turning from Pelops and Hippodameia's sons to their daughters, we found in chapter 10 that a papyrus fragment of the *Ehoiai* probably listed three of these, although only the names "Astydameia" and "Nikippe" (the latter from scholia) survive, and that they were there courted by the three sons of Perseus, Alkaios, Sthenelos, and Elektryon; the third name, that of Elektryon's bride, we can supply from later sources as "Lysidike," although these names for the daughters and even Elektryon's marriage to a Pelopis are not universally agreed to.[18] Such unions obviously give the family of Pelops a certain foothold in the Argolis, and we will see shortly how this device (sometimes in conjunction with the murder of Chrysippos) enabled storytellers to justify the transfer of the sons Atreus and Thyestes from Pisa to Mykenai (though in some early versions Oinomaos may already have ruled all the land between Pisa and the Isthmos).

Atreus and Thyestes Whether cursed by Myrtilos for their father's slaying of him, or by their father himself for the murder of Chrysippos, these two most famous sons of Pelops seem destined to a tragic feud with each other. The *Iliad* stands alone in suggesting, if that is indeed its intention, a peaceful transition of power (via the scepter) from one brother to the other; in every later account they are at each other's throats, vying for the throne of the land to which they have come. Possibly their struggle was recounted in the *Nostoi* as background to Agamemnon's demise, and the *Orestes* scholia record that in the epic *Alkmaionis* a golden lamb sent by Hermes in anger was the initial cause of the trouble, with one Antiochos the shepherd who brought the creature to Atreus (Σ *Or* 995 = fr 6 *PEG*). An epic concerning Alkmaion is not likely to have dealt with the Atreidai at length, and admittedly we find no other trace of their conflict before Aischylos' *Agamemnon,* but Kassandra's dark hints and barely coherent allusions in that drama show that the story was well known, at least in its general outlines. What we learn from her ravings and visions is that Thyestes entered his brother's bed, and that Atreus in turn fed Thyestes the flesh of his own children (*Ag* 1191–93, 1219–22). Aigisthos' entrance late in the play brings further information: Atreus had exiled Thyestes but allowed him back as a suppliant, and under pretext of sacrificing for a feast day served him the dreadful meal (*Ag* 1583–1611). On discovering the nature of the feast Thyestes vomited forth what he had eaten, kicked over the table, and cursed the whole Pleisthenid race. What Aischylos supposed to have happened after this we do not know; we see only Aigisthos, claiming that Agamemnon's death is vengeance for that deed. Pherekydes in this same period apparently gave an account similar to that of the *Alkmaionis,* but with the anger of Artemis, not Hermes, causing the lamb to be produced and the difficulties begun (3F133).

The latter part of the fifth century offered Athenians quite a range of dramatic treatments: Sophokles' lost *Atreus* and *Thyestes in Sikyon,* plus at least one (possibly two) more *Thyestes* plays, and Euripides' similarly lost *Kressai* and perhaps a *Thyestes;* for the latter poet we have as well substantial references in his *Elektra* and *Orestes.* Of the lost plays, both the *Atreus* and the *Kressai* probably related the power struggle preceding the feast, and Dion of Prusa comes close to saying that in both playwrights the golden lamb was again a factor (66.6). Somewhere, too, Sophokles must have dealt with the feast, for we are told that he made the sun abandon its usual course in horror at Atreus' deed (*AP* 9.98), but this might have been in a *Thyestes* play or even a choral ode of an unrelated drama; the same is true of the throwing of Aerope into the sea, which may come from the *Aias* (see below). Euripides' *Kressai* told the story of Aerope's seduction on Krete, and her father's consequent consigning of her to Nauplios to be drowned, but judging from the fragments this was all prologue, and the actual plot concerned the adultery *and* the feast that followed. If the play followed the pattern of Euripides' other dramas on profligate women, the emphasis may have been upon Aerope's seduction of Thyestes for reasons of passion, rather than his seduction of her to gain power. There is also a *slight* hint in the fragments that the children killed may have been born to Thyestes and Aerope, not to Thyestes and a legitimate wife (fr 460 N²). If that is true, we should have to imagine the affair between Thyestes and Aerope as long-term, and the resulting children raised by Atreus in the belief that they were his; his anger on discovering this truth might also be thought to better motivate the terrible vengeance he takes. We know that Agathon and perhaps the younger Karkinos wrote plays entitled *Aerope,* and that in some such play the performance of the actor Theodoros as Aerope supposedly moved Alexander of Pherai to tears (*VH* 14.40); whatever the truth of that story, the implied focus on Aerope (rather than Atreus or Thyestes) as a pathetic figure might mean that there too the children were hers. Certainly she and Thyestes are the parents in Hyginus (*Fab* 246); our one piece of evidence to the contrary is the scholion at *Orestes* 4, where Thyestes marries a Laodameia who bears to him Orchomenos, Aglaos, and Kalaos.

For other details of the story we must rely on what we find in the *Orestes* (and scholia) and Apollodoros. From the *Orestes* itself we see clearly enough that there was a quarrel over the golden lamb (*Or* 812–13, 997-1000). The scholia offer two slightly divergent accounts, but both link the lamb to the kingship. In the one, that lamb, provided by Hermes as a way of causing trouble for those who slew his son Myrtilos, is proclaimed by Atreus as a sign of his right to the throne (Σ *Or* 998; so too Σ *Or* 995, Byz Σ *Or* 812[19]). Thyestes then seduces Aerope, and she gives her lover the lamb that he uses to become king in place of his brother. In the other version, supplied also by Apollodoros and the *Iliad* scholia, Atreus promises to sacrifice to Artemis whatever is most beautiful among his flocks, but when he discovers the golden lamb hides it away in a chest instead (Σ *Or* 811; ApE 2.10–11; ΣA *Il* 2.105). As before, Thyestes seduces Aerope to get the lamb, then proposes to Atreus in an assembly of the people that whoever possesses the lamb should be king; Atreus agrees, thinking himself the possessor, and discovers the truth too late. Since Pherekydes attributes Atreus' problems to Artemis, it seems likely that he presented this latter account, in which case Apollodoros as elsewhere may have drawn from him.

The events following the transfer of power from Atreus to Thyestes seem likewise to order themselves according to several slightly different patterns. In a choral ode of Euripides' *Elektra*, we find that after Thyestes' deception Zeus causes the stars and the sun to change course, so that the sun now moves from east to west, and there are general shifts in the climate (E: *El* 699–736). Apparently this is a permanent reversal of an earlier order, as we find too in Plato's *Politikos*, where the Stranger maintains that Zeus altered the rising and setting places of the sun and stars to their present arrangement in order to assist Atreus (269a). In *Orestes*, however, the alteration consists of turning the sun back from the west toward the dawn, thus just a temporary aberration from the normal state of affairs (*Or* 1001–6). Either way, the reason for this celestial portent is surely that offered by scholia and Apollodoros: after Thyestes' theft of the lamb Zeus sends Hermes to arrange with Atreus a stratagem in which the latter either announces that he will display a portent greater than the lamb, or gets Thyestes to agree to surrender power when the sun changes course (Σ *Or* 811; ΣA *Il* 2.105; ApE 2.12–13). Zeus then brings about the miracle, and Thyestes is forced to step down (cf. Σ *Or* 998, where the sun and Pleiades fail to set because of Thyestes' impiety). One further complication to consider is a Euripidean fragment in which Atreus says, "Demonstrating the opposite path of the stars I saved the people and made myself ruler" (fr 861 N[2]). The citer,

Achilles Tatius, seems to think that this refers to the sun's retrocession when compared to the stars, as Loukianos (without referring to Euripides) specifically argues was the means by which Atreus recovered his throne, in other words a scientific discovery rather than a miracle (*De astrologia* 12). This is, of course, rationalizing of a myth, but one which Euripides seems to have used somewhere. The same should probably be said of Sophokles, since Achilles cites him in the same context and says that he credited Atreus with the discovery of astronomy (fr 738 R).

By contrast with all this, we saw earlier that somewhere in Sophokles the sun turns backward in the sky of its own accord in revulsion when Atreus serves to Thyestes his own children. That change in motive has some important consequences, for if the portent is a response to Atreus' crimes rather than those of his brother, then it becomes simply a decorative motif and will not explain how Atreus recovered the throne from Thyestes. The Byzantine scholia at *Orestes* 812[20] do seem to suppose such a sequence of events, for in their exegesis, immediately after Thyestes' trick, Atreus "not enduring his misfortune and being angry that he was unjustly deprived of the rule (1) revenged himself on his wife Aerope (both because of her adultery with Thyestes and because she gave away the lamb) by casting her into the sea, as Sophokles says, and (2) killing Aglaos, Orchomenos, and Kaleos the three children of Thyestes served them to their father and later killed him also." Here too the sun in horror travels from west to east for one whole day. Possibly, then, we are to assume that Thyestes abandons the throne after such a horrible experience, but as the king one might expect him rather to seek revenge in his turn. In both Seneca's *Thyestes* and Hyginus (*Fab* 88), where again the sun's motive is a reaction to the feast (as at *Ibis* 429), Thyestes returns from exile for his grim banquet, indicating that Atreus has resecured power long before. Aischylos, we saw, does bring Thyestes back to Mykenai (or Argos) as a suppliant for the feast, but from this alone we cannot tell which version of the story (if either) he intended. On the whole it might seem, given the similarity in the function of the celestial portent, that much of the Byzantine scholia entry is drawn from a play of Sophokles, even allowing that said scholia's specific reference to Sophokles may well derive from an entirely different context (the *Aias:* see below). Atreus as the slayer of Thyestes is in any event surprising; elsewhere Thyestes has the final revenge, and perhaps that is what the scholiast meant.

As for the feast itself, in Seneca's play it forms the centerpiece of the drama, and may have done so in productions by Sophokles and Euripides as well. Seneca gives to Thyestes three sons, Tantalos, Pleisthenes, and a third child unnamed; Atreus slaughters them all for the banquet. At the play's climax Thyestes, having eaten his fill, asks to have his sons brought in, and Atreus presents him with the heads and other remains, advising him that what he does not see he already has. The work closes with laments and protests on the part of Thyestes, but no predictions of any specific vengeance to be taken. Such a treatment of the story seems obvious enough, and could well draw from both

Sophokles and Euripides. In Aischylos' *Agamemnon*, on the other hand, Aigisthos appears to say that he was the thirteenth of Thyestes' children, and the only survivor, being still in swaddling clothes (*Ag* 1605–6). The slaughter (and even partial consumption) of twelve children seems unnecessarily grotesque; more likely there is a corruption here in our single manuscript tradition, with the word for "ten" intruding and converting an original "three" into "thirteen."[21] In that event, two children would constitute the Aischylean meal. Whatever the number, though, Aischylos does attest to an Aigisthos already born at the time of the meal, which we shall see is not always the case.

In Apollodoros three sons are again killed and cooked, and the extremities produced only after Thyestes has finished (*ApE* 2.13); the names—Aglaos, Orchomenos, and Kallileon—are virtually the same as those in the *Orestes* Byzantine scholia at 812 (see above) and scholia vetera at 4 (Aglaos, Orchomenos, Kalaos). Hyginus, on the other hand, reports the same names—Tantalos and Pleisthenes—as did Seneca, although he seems to know of only two children (*Fab* 88, 246, with Aerope the mother); Seneca does not name the third, and may have borrowed the number "three" from the tradition represented by Apollodoros and the *Orestes* scholia. One other story occurs only in Hyginus, namely that after his expulsion Thyestes sends Atreus' son Pleisthenes, whom he has brought up as his own, to Atreus in order to kill the man; Atreus, still believing this to be his brother's son, has him killed instead (*Fab* 86; cf. perhaps the garbled Σ *Or* 16). We will see below that other accounts involving this same son of Atreus do not square well with such a tragedy, even though Pleisthenes does as a rule die young. But Euripides composed a lost work entitled *Pleisthenes* for whose plot there are few candidates other than this one, and thus the story may well be as old as the fifth century, or before. It forms a curious counterweight to the perhaps also Euripidean notion that Atreus for a time believed Thyestes' children by Aerope to be his own.

Regarding Thyestes' children, there is yet one more tale to note, that of Klytaimestra's first husband as alluded to by Klytaimestra herself in Euripides' *Iphigeneia at Aulis* (1149–52), where she says that she was originally married to one Tantalos, and that Agamemnon killed both him and their child. She adds that Agamemnon then married her by force, and the implication is thus that his motive for the murders was to obtain her, although the text does not actually say that. Apollodoros repeats the story, calling the Tantalos in question a son of Thyestes (thus not slain for the feast: *ApE* 2.16), and Pausanias agrees with this genealogy and the marriage, although he omits the child (2.18.2). Subsequently, however, the latter writer calls this same first husband of Klytaimestra Tantalos, son of Thyestes or of Broteas (2.22.3), this last presumably the same Broteas who appears as a son of the original Tantalos at 3.22.4 (and at Σ *Or* 4). Apollodoros does not recognize such a variant, but he does mention a Broteas (between his accounts of Tantalos and Pelops) as scorning Artemis and boasting that not even fire can harm him; he becomes mad and throws himself upon flames (*ApE* 2.2; cf. Ovid *Ibis* 517–18). Clearly then, this Bro-

teas is a member of the family, but certainly the intrigue surrounding Klytaimestra's first marriage will be much greater when her husband is the son of
Thyestes. Aischylos' Klytaimestra has ample opportunity to accuse Agamemnon of that husband's murder and does not do so, nor does she mention him in
any way; in any case, the slaughter of Iphigeneia to win a war probably suited
the playwright's purposes far better than a deed for which Agamemnon could
plead passion as an excuse. That the story was known to the Catalogue Poet,
in whose *Ehoiai* Agamemnon plays an influential role in persuading the Dioskouroi to give Helen to his brother after he himself has married their sister,
may seem unlikely, but hardly impossible.

Thyestes in
Sikyon

We know that Sophokles wrote a play of this title, and part of Hyginus' *Fabula*
88 does indeed take Thyestes to Sikyon, where he begets a child by his own
daughter; given that he has no other reason to be in such a place, even as an
exile, Sophokles' plot surely in some way related that unusual event. Further
evidence may well be offered by an Apulian calyx krater of about 340 B.C., the
work of the Darius Painter (Boston 1987.53). Here, in what certainly looks like
a stage confrontation, we find Thyestes at the center of the scene, looking left
to a servant who holds the infant Aigisthos (all figures named). To the right of
Aigisthos stands Adrastos, and beyond him Pelopia and Adrastos' wife Amphithea. Adrastos is presumably present as ruler of Sikyon, while the child must
belong to the unwed Pelopia. Thyestes, of course, will almost certainly know
that he is the father; less certain is whether Pelopia and Adrastos also know
this. Either way, as fatherless bastard or the product of incest, the child seems
about to be exposed, as Thyestes and his daughter agonize over an action probably mandated by Adrastos.

Whatever we make of this plot, and whatever play it represents, Hyginus'
version of Thyestes' stay in Sikyon (no sources credited) would seem to offer
no room for such dramatics. As he tells the story, Thyestes after the banquet
flees to a certain king Thesprotos, and thence to Sikyon, where he chances upon
rites to Athena being conducted by his own daughter Pelopia. Fearing to defile
the ceremonies he hides in a grove, and thus happens to see the priestess disrobed when she comes to the same place to wash her bloodstained garment.
Face veiled, he leaps out from his hiding place and rapes the girl, who in the
process pulls his sword from its scabbard and subsequently hides it in the
temple. On the next day, Thyestes departs for Lydia. Meanwhile, barrenness
of the land has forced Atreus to seek his brother, and he pays a visit to Thesprotos; although he arrives too late to find Thyestes, he does meet Pelopia,
whom he obtains from Thesprotos, thinking her to be the latter's daughter. She
then bears Aigisthos from the embrace of her nocturnal assailant; the child is
abandoned but shepherds have him nursed by a goat and ultimately Atreus
finds and raises him. At some later point, Agamemnon and Menelaos capture
Thyestes as he is consulting the Delphic oracle and bring him back to Atreus,
who commissions the son he thinks to be his own, Aigisthos, to kill his bitter

enemy. Aigisthos is prepared to carry out this order in Thyestes' prison when his victim recognizes the sword he lost on the night of the rape. Pelopia as the person who provided the sword is sent for; realizing now the identity of her child's father she seizes the sword and stabs herself. Aigisthos then returns to Atreus with the bloody weapon as proof of Thyestes' death. Atreus goes down to the beach to sacrifice in thanksgiving and Aigisthos there kills him, thus restoring the throne to his father.

Obviously such a long and contorted story cannot have been dramatized in its entirety, and there are some logical inconsistencies, such as why Atreus finds Pelopia with Thesprotos rather than at Sikyon, and why Thesprotos allows Atreus to suppose the girl his daughter. But the last series of events— arrival of a captive Thyestes in Mykenai, Atreus' order to Aigisthos, Aigisthos' confrontation of Thyestes, Pelopia's entrance and death, and a messenger report of the death of Atreus—would work well enough on stage, with the preceding action related in the prologue (either by Pelopia or a god). Such a play would not, however, be likely to bear the title *Thyestes in Sikyon*, when all the stage action takes place in Mykenai. Since we do have one or even two other Sophoklean *Thyestes* dramas to account for, we should probably apportion the story out between two productions, with *Thyestes in Sikyon* relating the events of the rape itself (or perhaps the conflict shown by the Darius Painter), and another *Thyestes* (or even *Atreus*) presenting the outcome years later when Thyestes is captured. Possibly the two plays were even part of a connected trilogy, although a *Thyestes in Sikyon* presenting the Darius Painter's plot will not have been compatible with any subsequent story in which Atreus believes the child to be his.

One other aspect of the union between father and daughter which may shed light on Sophokles' dramas is the question of Thyestes' motivation. In Hyginus' *Fabula* 88 we see Thyestes stumbling upon the sacrifice by chance and being tempted to his deed by the priestess' state of undress, which rather suggests that he does not recognize his daughter and is simply overcome by the passion of the moment. But the same writer's *Fabula* 87 tells us that Thyestes had been advised by an oracle to beget a son by Pelopia to avenge him, and we find a compressed version of that story also in Apollodoros and the Euripides scholia (ApE 2.14; Σ *Or* 15).[22] The emotional pressures on a man advised to violate his own daughter might seem to offer much to a tragedian, especially if the father is then threatened with the exposure of the child he has so terribly desired. On the other hand, Sophokles may well have preferred a version in which Thyestes is ignorant of his deed, and condemns his daughter as severely as Adrastos (or more so) until the truth and his own complicity are revealed. Either way, it does seem that in the situation presented by the Darius Painter Thyestes must know the truth about Aigisthos' birth, or come to learn it soon after the child is born.

Apollodoros goes on to say that Agamemnon and Menelaos eventually seized power from Thyestes and exiled him again, this time to Kythera; we have no evidence as to his ultimate fate. Aischylos' *Agamemnon*, as we noted above, has Aigisthos alive at the time of the banquet, which would seem to exclude the more scandalous account of the child's conception. That Aischylos knew that tale is not impossible; clearly, though, he would have no use for it here if he did, since an Aigisthos who has already avenged his brothers' death on Atreus will have no plausible claim to the life of Agamemnon on the same grounds (quite the opposite). Presumably, those accounts that did acknowledge the tale of Pelopia presented Aigisthos' later act of bloodshed as an attempt to regain his father's power or (as Homer implies) to appropriate Klytaimestra for himself. That Pelopia's travails could on the other hand be simply an invention of Sophokles or his time must also be allowed, although it seems unlikely. Of Euripides' *Thyestes* mentioned before, we know virtually nothing, save that Atreus was a character. The capture of Thyestes and death of Atreus *could* conceivably have been the subject, and such a play might even have preceded that (or those) of Sophokles.

Pleisthenes   We come last of all in this chapter to the most perplexing member of the house of Tantalos. Homer never mentions him, either in *Iliad* 2's succession account or elsewhere, and while the standard epithet *Atreidês* can mean simply "descendant of Atreus," both the *Iliad* and *Odyssey* on occasion call Agamemnon or Menelaos specifically a *son* of Atreus. But the Hesiodic Corpus saw matters differently: *Iliad* scholia tell us that while Homer makes Agamemnon the son of Atreus and Aerope (she is not mentioned in the *Iliad* or *Odyssey*; presumably the scholiast gets this from the Epic Cycle), in Hesiod he and his brother are the sons of Pleisthenes (ΣA *Il* 1.7 = Hes fr 194 MW). Another *Iliad* scholion repeats this idea, although *without* mentioning Hesiod; it does cite Porphyrios and "many others" for it, and adds that Pleisthenes died young, having done nothing of note, whereupon his sons were raised by Atreus (ΣA *Il* 2.249). Tzetzes (in his *Exegesis in Iliadem*) explains further what we will have already guessed, that in this version Pleisthenes is the son of Atreus. He goes on to say that for Hesiod, Aischylos, and others, Pleisthenes is born of Aerope, and that this Pleisthenes, wed to Kleola, daughter of Atreus' brother Dias (she is thus his own first cousin), begets Agamemnon, Menelaos, and Anaxibia (pp. 68–69 Hermann, reproduced in part as Hes fr 194 MW).[23] Here too we find the father dying young, so that the grandfather Atreus raises the sons who come to be thought of as his. Whether the "Hesiodic" source for all this could be the *Ehoiai* is unclear, for fragmentary lines of that poem just preceding the tale of Alkmene appear to attest that Aerope (not Kleola) is the mother of Agamemnon and Menelaos (and a third son: Anaxibios?), although whether by Atreus or Pleisthenes we cannot tell (Hes fr 195 MW). If that is correct, then either Tzetzes has drawn some of his information from his other named sources alone, or his reference to "Hesiod" intends another part of the Hesiodic Corpus.

We should note here (as likely happens in Euripides) that a father adopting his deceased sons' children might plausibly marry the mother as well; thus it would be no surprise to find Aerope (or even Kleola) in some accounts married to first Pleisthenes and then Atreus. But in the scholia to the *Orestes* (where Dias is again a brother of Atreus), we find just the opposite: here Atreus marries Kleola, daughter of Dias, she who was the wife of Pleisthenes in Tzetzes, and the two of them become the parents of the (infirm of body) Pleisthenes (Σ *Or* 4). We might suppose that the roles of Aerope and Kleola have simply been reversed, were it not that Pleisthenes marries someone quite new, one Eriphyle by whom he becomes the father of Agamemnon, Menelaos, and Anaxibia. But it remains possible that Atreus was wed to Kleola and Pleisthenes to Aerope in the *Ehoiai*, and that Tzetzes' account of "Hesiod" inadvertently reversed those two women. As noted above, Euripides seems likely to have passed Pleisthenes' wife Aerope on to Atreus (in the *Kressai:* see below).

Tzetzes offers one other curious bit of information, not in his *Exegesis* but in his scholia to that work: while in Homer Agamemnon and Menelaos are the sons of Atreus, son of Pelops, in Hesiod they are the sons of Pleisthenes, the hermaphrodite or lame one, who wore a woman's mantle (addendum to Hes fr 194 MW).[24] What the first of these terms might imply about Pleisthenes' actual physical condition is hard to say, nor is it clear whether one item of feminine dress is sufficient to categorize him as desirous of a gender change. But the lameness concurs with the elsewhere reiterated idea that he was weak or sickly, and we find it supported in particular by Loukianos in his play *Podagra*, where the title character (Gout) is humorously credited with afflicting various mythical figures (*Podagra* 250–57). Among these are Achilleus, Philoktetes, and Oidipous, people with foot afflictions, to be sure, but not gout, so that when Pleisthenes is also included his lameness is probably meant.

The remainder of the Archaic period provides some further references, if not help. Stesichoros uses the name "Pleisthenides" of someone, probably Menelaos, in a fragment showing Helen conversing with Telemachos (209 *PMG*). From the same poet's *Oresteia*, we have two lines relating a dream of Klytaimestra in which she sees a snake with bloody head which becomes or from which springs or after which appears "a king Pleisthenides" (219 *PMG*). We will be obliged to consider the exact identity of this king more fully in chapter 17; for present purposes it will suffice to note that the Pleisthenid ought to be some member of Agamemnon's rather than Aigisthos' line, most likely Agamemnon himself or his son Orestes, as a Pleisthenes son of Atreus would certainly guarantee. With Ibykos, however, matters take a more confusing turn, for in his poem to Polykrates on the heroes at Troy he speaks of Agamemnon as "the king Pleisthenides, leader of men, son of a noble father Atreus" (282 *PMG*). Either the poet here heedlessly combines two conflicting descriptions (from different epic traditions?), or he knows of a genealogy other than those we have found so far.

For the fifth century we have first of all Bakchylides, who calls Menelaos "Atreides" and "Pleisthenides" in the same poem (15.6, 48), and then Aischylos. The *Agamemnon* shows us Klytaimestra after the murder of her husband offering to bargain with the *daimôn* of the Pleisthenidai for acceptance of the present situation if he will leave to afflict some other house (*Ag* 1568–73). One would suppose she means to include all the misfortunes of the family, in which case Pleisthenes ought to be at least an ancestor of Atreus and Thyestes. But perhaps that is to press a generic epithet too closely in a situation where the audience cannot mistake the meaning. Further on in the drama Aigisthos appears, and in relating the grim feast of Atreus describes how Thyestes on learning the truth kicked over the table and prayed that all the race of Pleisthenes might thus perish (*Ag* 1598–1602). Whom Thyestes means by that designation is again unclear, especially as just previously at line 1600 he has called down destruction upon the Pelopidai. This last wish would, of course, include himself and his line, and perhaps at this moment he indeed wishes to see the entire race blotted out. But Aigisthos cites the curse primarily as proof of the justice of Agamemnon's death, so he seems to understand it as an appeal for vengeance against Atreus, not total obliteration of everyone in the family. If that is the case, then Pleisthenes must in some way indicate Atreus' branch of the family but not Thyestes', and this condition will again be satisfied if Pleisthenes intervenes between Atreus and Agamemnon. Against such a conclusion, however, we must admit that the play elsewhere and Aigisthos himself in this very speech call Agamemnon the son of Atreus (*Ag* 60, 1583). We saw above that Tzetzes credited the Pleisthenes son of Atreus who died young to Aischylos as well as to "Hesiod," but we do not know whether Tzetzes drew that conclusion from *Agamemnon* 1598–1602 alone, or whether he found more detailed, certain information in a lost play (the *Iphigeneia?*). On balance, all we can really say is that Aischylos has here conflated Homeric and non-Homeric tradition, with Homer holding sway most of the time but Pleisthenes thrown in at one point for good measure. What he did elsewhere may or may not have been quite different.

Scholars also equate at times the Pleisthenes under discussion with the Pleisthenes named by the *Olympian* 1 scholia as a son (not always legitimate) of Pelops. But making this brother of Atreus the important Pleisthenes (rather than a separate figure of the same name) will not resolve any of our previous difficulties, for he would still have to be the father of Agamemnon and Menelaos if the patronymics we have encountered are to make sense, and his children still adopted by Atreus, who would remain only their stepfather. If Agamemnon (or Menelaos) was ever truly both "son of Atreus" and "Pleisthenides," then Pleisthenes must at some time have been a direct ancestor of Atreus, and for this our tradition would *seem* to leave no room.

Turning to Sophokles' *Aias*, we find on the part of Teukros in that play total adherence to Homer: Pelops begets Atreus who begets Agamemnon (*Ai* 1291–97). He adds too (by way of insult to Agamemnon) Thyestes' feast, and then Agamemnon's Kretan mother, "in whose bed finding an alien man the father enjoined that she be quarry for the fishes." As those words stand the reference would seem to be to Katreus, Aerope's father, who found her with a slave and gave her to Nauplios to kill. But the word here translated as "alien" *(epaktos)* would more naturally refer to an adulterer, since in the bed of an unmarried woman any man would be inappropriate, and only a small adjustment to the text (involving the word *father*) would produce rather a reference to Aerope and Thyestes. Either way, Aerope must be the Kretan mother, married to Atreus, but if the manuscript correction is accepted we would have here our first reference to Aerope being thrown from a cliff as punishment for her adultery. The account of the Byzantine *Orestes* scholia at line 812, where Sophokles is said to attest that fate for Aerope, seems to guarantee that it appeared somewhere in his work, but of course the scholiast might be referring to this same passage of the *Aias,* where the meaning is as we have seen controversial.

No later source says anything at all about Aerope's death, although Atreus would be expected to put aside such an adulteress, and those versions involving a new marriage to Pelopia must suppose some such action. The scholia for the *Aias* passage tell us that in Euripides' *Kressai Nauplios* (as usual disobeying Katreus' order to drown Aerope) gave her to Pleisthenes in marriage (Σ *Ai* 1297). Beyond this information we are left to speculate about Euripides' drama, but if, as Apollonios of Alexandria suggests, Aerope's further wantonness was the topic (Σ *Batr* 849), we might reasonably conjecture that by the time of the play's opening Pleisthenes has died, leaving his father Atreus to both adopt the children and marry his son's wife. Indeed, in all versions where Pleisthenes intervenes between Atreus and Agamemnon, this would seem the logical means of bringing Atreus and Aerope together, unless Tzetzes' notion that Atreus was originally married to Aerope and Pleisthenes to Kleola has some basis after all.

We saw before that a play entitled *Pleisthenes* is also attributed to Euripides, and that the only conceivable plot for it, unless a story has been completely lost, is Hyginus' *Fabula* 86, where Atreus unwittingly kills his own son Pleisthenes sent to him by the foster-father Thyestes. Such a tale could certainly be dramatized, and it would explain Pleisthenes' early death. But nowhere else is it suggested that Pleisthenes is not known to be Atreus' son from birth, and by the time he dies, the traditional Pleisthenes is a grown man with a wife and several children. When we add these difficulties to the inherent improbability of such parental confusion, we may well feel that Euripides has here given us a new story, perhaps a twist on the confusion over Aigisthos. Whatever the exact genealogy in these lost plays, Euripides is in our preserved dramas quite ready to follow Homer: both the *Helen* and the *Orestes* present a direct Pelops-Atreus-Agamemnon line of descent, with no possibility of intervening members and in both cases Aerope as Agamemnon's mother (*Hel* 390–92; *Or* 11–18).

Later sources have virtually nothing to record on these matters. Apollodoros does confirm Aerope's rescue by Nauplios and betrothal to Pleisthenes, to whom she bears Agamemnon and Menelaos (Ap*B* 3.2.2), but we hear nothing more of him, nor does the mythographer say how Aerope later comes to be married to Atreus when he relates the tale of her infidelity with Thyestes (Ap*E* 2.10). Hyginus' only reference to Pleisthenes is the story just discussed; at no point does he name him as father of Agamemnon and Menelaos. In concluding our look at this odd figure, we may be tempted to ask why storytellers bothered to create or preserve him, since with or without him the Atreidai remain effectively the sons of Atreus. There are, of course, his mysteriously bisexual tendencies in the Hesiodic Corpus (if Tzetzes' allusions are accurate), but the one real instance in which he appears to serve a purpose is the story we postulated for Euripides' *Kressai*, with a young Aerope married to a (perhaps) much older Atreus after her first husband has died, and for that reason attracted to the (perhaps) much younger Thyestes. Admittedly, such a reconstruction sounds archetypally Euripidean, especially when we note that the play was written in his "fallen women" period of the 430s B.C.. But given the need to explain Pleisthenes' presence much earlier, in the *Ehoiai* and other early sources, it may be that this plot of unhappy younger wife is quite old, and forms an important starting point for the conflict between Atreus and Thyestes.

16   The Trojan War

In *Iliad* 20 the Trojan Aineias comes face to face with Achilleus, and in response to the latter's taunts provides a capsule history of the race of Troy (*Il* 20.215–41). First among the rulers is Dardanos, son of Zeus, who founds a settlement on the slopes of Mount Ida, Troy itself not having yet been built. Dardanos' son is Erichthonios, whose wealth includes three thousand mares, and with some of these Boreas consorts in the form of a horse, producing twelve colts who run across blades of asphodel and sport above the breakers of the sea. To Erichthonios is born Tros, and to Tros three sons, Ilos, Assarakos, and Ganymedes. The last of these, because of his beauty, is snatched up by the gods to become wine-pourer for Zeus, but Ilos begets Laomedon and Assarakos Kapys. Laomedon in turn has five sons—Tithonos, Priam, Lampos, Klytios, and Hiketaon—while Kapys produces just one, Anchises who will father Aineias, the point of this whole recitation.

Lampos, Klytios, and Hiketaon all appear briefly with Priam in *Iliad* 3, as elders sitting on the wall of Troy (together with Panthoos, Thymoites, Oukalegon, and Antenor: *Il* 3.146–48); Tithonos we will naturally not expect to find, since he has been abducted by Eos. Homer never elsewhere alters any part of the above genealogy, but he does at *Iliad* 6.23–24 add a sixth son for Laomedon, one Boukolion who is the eldest and apparently illegitimate. And Diomedes in *Iliad* 5 varies the tale of the acquisition of the horses a bit by having Zeus give them to Tros as compensation for the loss of his son Ganymedes (*Il* 5.260–72: nothing else is here said about the abduction). The same speech adds that after the horses had passed to Laomedon Anchises bred foals from them by his own mares without the owner's knowledge. That Herakles bargained with Laomedon for some or all of the horses is established by *Iliad* 6, as we saw in chapter 13. From a number of references throughout the poem we also discover that Aineias is Anchises' son by Aphrodite, although the circumstances of such a mating are never explained. Against this overall picture, the use of "Dardanides" as a patronymic elsewhere in the *Iliad* has been thought to betray an earlier, less developed family line, with the patriarch Dardanos originally much closer to the generation involved in the Trojan War.[1] In particular there is the application of that adjective (ten times) to denote Priam (*Il* 3.303, etc.), but also the presence at several points of a tomb of Ilos Dardanides in the middle of the Trojan plain (*Il* 11.166, 371–72; tomb without the patronymic also at 10.415, 24.349). Possibly in both these cases the patronymic's range has simply been (remarkably) extended. But possibly too Ilos, son of Tros, was in earlier times viewed as a brother of Erichthonios and son of Dardanos, and came to occupy a different niche only as the family expanded.

The *Ehoiai* for its part offers one small bit of evidence to support this last conclusion in the form of a papyrus fragment with only the left edge preserved (Hes fr 177 MW). From what survives we see that Dardanos' mother was apparently Elektra, and we should probably make this figure as in Hellanikos (where she bears Dardanos to Zeus: 4F19a) a daughter of Atlas. The fragment further gives Dardanos a brother Eetion (Hellanikos [4F23] calls him both Eetion and Iasion), and like the *Iliad* a son Erichthonios. But here there is also a second son Ilos, after whom the papyrus breaks off, so that we cannot tell through which of the two sons the royal line continued. If through Ilos, there might have been a tradition rival to Homer, perhaps reflected by Ilos' tomb even within the *Iliad*. But the *Ehoiai* probably supposes (as perhaps the *Iliad* in its use of Ilos Dardanides) a cadet brother of Erichthonios. One other brief reference assigned to the *Ehoiai* calls Tros the son of Teukros (Hes fr 179 MW); nothing, however, indicates how these two figures would relate to any of the others. The *Little Iliad* (or a similar poem) also mentioned Ganymedes' abduction in some unknown context (probably the arrival of Eurypylos at Troy), and here we do find a significant change in the line, for the abductee is now the son of Laomedon, not of Tros, while Zeus' gift to the bereaved father becomes the vine, in some way ornamented by Hephaistos (*IlMik* fr 29 *PEG*).

In the *Homeric Hymn to Aphrodite*, the goddess' allusion to Ganymedes follows the same general outline presented by Diomedes in the *Iliad*: the youth is again the son of Tros, who finds considerable consolation in the news of his son's fate (as revealed by Hermes) and the present (from Zeus) of the horses (*HAph* 202–17). Here though, in contrast to *Iliad* 20, it is Zeus alone, not the gods as a whole, who does the abducting, "on account of his [Ganymedes'] beauty, so that he might be among the immortals and pour for the gods in the house of Zeus, a wonder to see, honored by all the immortals, drawing off red nectar from a golden krater." Admittedly, Aphrodite's point in telling this story (and that of Tithonos which follows) is to excuse her own descent into Anchises' bed by stressing the undoubted good looks of the race of Troy. But while the attraction in Eos' case and her own is sexual, we are not entitled on that account to assume the same for Zeus and Ganymedes. On the contrary, emphasis here as in the *Iliad* remains on Ganymedes' beauty as something admired and shared by all the gods as they watch him serve them; quite possibly, then, the sexual element in this relationship has not yet taken shape. Whatever Zeus' motive, the boy does seem in the Hymn to have been carried off to Olympos by a whirlwind, much as Penelope envisions happening to her in the *Odyssey*.

The main body of the *Hymn to Aphrodite* tells, of course, how the goddess, by the contrivance of Zeus himself lest she boast of sending other gods to bed with mortals, conceived a desperate passion for Anchises, and how she came to him claiming to be the daughter of the Phrygian king Otreus. Her tale—of being snatched up by Hermes and brought to Mount Ida to become Anchises' wife—is not perhaps overly plausible, but it allays his fears that she is a goddess, and on that assumption he is only too willing to take her to bed. Only afterward does she reveal her true identity and announce the child who is to be born to them, a child who will be cared for by the Nymphai until he is old enough to come to his father. Anchises' subsequent fate—perhaps alluded to here by the goddess but not confirmed until Sophokles' *Laokoon* and then, of course, the *Aeneid*—has already been considered in chapter 2, under the heading of Aphrodite's amours. The end of the *Theogony* also notes briefly this mortal-immortal union (*Th* 1008–10), while the *Iliad* makes mention of daughters of Anchises by an unnamed mother (seemingly his wife) of whom the eldest and most-admired—Hippodameia—is wed to the ill-fated Alkathoos (*Il* 13.427–35). We should keep in mind, of course, that the *Kypria* and other poems of the Epic Cycle may have offered their own background on the royal house of Troy, even if nothing survives.

What little there is from the later Archaic period all relates to Ganymedes, save for the previously discussed tale of Herakles and Laomedon. In literature we find a brief mention by Theognis, who is our first source to specify that Zeus' interest in Ganymedes was erotic (*Theog* 1345–48) and then Pindar, who concedes the same point as a precedent for Poseidon's abduction of Pelops (*Ol* 1.43–45). Ibykos, too, seems to have related the tale, but we have no details beyond the fact of the abduction (289 *PMG*). In chapter 15 we considered the evidence (from *Iliad* scholia and the historian Herodian) for Tantalos rather than Zeus as the abductor; the same scholia also know of a version in which Minos played that role (ΣbT *Il* 20.234, credited to Dosiadas [458F5]). In art, the earliest sure rendering of the gods' intervention is the Red-Figure cup by Oltos in Tarquinia (RC 6848) on which Ganymedes (named and portrayed as a naked young male) pours nectar for Zeus and the other gods. Soon after, however, Zeus begins to appear as perpetrator of the kidnapping, as on a (lost) White-Ground alabastron by the Diosphos Painter with Zeus (prodded by Eros) pursuing Ganymedes while Tros looks on (Berlin:Lost F2032: names again furnished), and then a whole series of Red-Figure pots.[2] The final sequence of this action, the actual abduction, appears on a cup by Douris (Louvre G123) and a terracotta group at Olympia (T 2), both dating to about 475–70 B.C. In the case of the cup, the scene could possibly be one of human activity (despite the presence of a scepter), but a statue dedication of this type at a sanctuary of Zeus must surely represent the god. Both the statue and many of the pots include a cock as love gift, either clutched or pursued by Ganymedes. In a number of cases the child seems indifferent or unwilling, and Zeus must resort to a certain amount of tugging (e.g., Ferrara 9351). On no occasion, however, do we see any sign of an eagle, either as agent of the abduction or in any other capacity.

From the literature of the time we might have expected at least a satyr play, but there is no record of any drama bearing the title *Ganymedes*, and only the briefest mention of him in one of our preserved tragedies (*Tro* 820–24). The middle of the fourth century brings us our first traces of the eagle as abductor, most notably in a lost work of Leochares described by Pliny (*NH* 34.79). The later literary tradition offers two explanations of this form of the tale: Ps-Eratosthenes (*Katast* 30), Vergil (*Aen* 5.254–55), Apollodoros (*ApB* 3.12.2), and Pliny himself suppose the eagle to be a servant of Zeus bringing Ganymedes to his master, while the (Hellenistic?) *Peri Apiston* of one Herakleitos (28) as well as Ovid (*Met* 10.155–61) and Loukianos (*DD* 10) make the eagle Zeus in disguise. Under such circumstances, we cannot tell what most artists intended in representing the eagle in this role, although one Hellenistic sculptural group in Naples portrays an unmistakable exchange of looks between eagle and boy (Naples 6351). For the more important issue here, namely how early the eagle became a part of the story, we are likewise at a loss. We have seen that in the *Hymn to Aphrodite* a whirlwind is the instrument of abduction, but of course this may not have been the only early form of the story. Admittedly, though, a whirlwind as the standard device in the Archaic period would explain why we never see for that period an artistic portrayal of the abduction, in contrast to the ever-popular Europa and her bull.

As for other members of the Trojan line in our late sources, Lykophron has a cryptic reference to a Trojan ancestor who swims (with the help of some sort of craft) from Samothrace to the Troad during the great flood (Lyk 72–80). Konon and other writers establish that this was Dardanos himself, although in Konon's version the motif for the migration is grief over the death of his brother Iasion, killed for desiring Demeter (26F1.21). In this account, as in Hellanikos (and probably the *Ehoiai*), the brothers are sons of Zeus and Elektra, daughter of Atlas; Konon adds that, having left Samothrace on a raft, Dardanos comes to the mainland, and there, after a covenant with Teukros, son of Skamandros (the local king), founds a city Dardania at the place where he first arrived safely. Upon Teukros' death, he then comes into possession of the entire kingdom. Hellanikos may well have related all of this, since we know that in his *Troika* Dardanos marries Bateia, daughter of Teukros (4F24). The same writer also appears to have said that Dardanos was advised by Apollo against settling on the site of Troy, and for this reason made his way to Mount Ida where he founded Dardania (4F25). Possibly this last detail is meant to explain why Dardanos settles so very far away from what would be the most natural landfall for one arriving from Samothrace. Diodoros too, though he says nothing about a journey from Samothrace, has Dardanos marry Bateia, daughter of Teukros Skamandrides, ruler of the land, and found a city named after himself (DS 4.75). In Lykophron this daughter is Arisbe, and her father Teukros comes

originally from Krete, having journeyed to the Troad with his father Skamandros on a raid (Lyk 1301–8).[3] As for Troy, Lykophron calls its site "the hill
founded by the wandering cow" (Lyk 29), and both Apollodoros and the Lykophron scholia explain that Ilos followed this cow to find the site for his city.
Apollodoros makes the cow a gift from the king of Phrygia (Ap*B* 3.12.3); in
the scholia Ilos has a herd of cows, and he is told to watch for the one who will
lie down. But in each account he clearly acts on instructions from an oracle, so
that this tale is a virtual doublet of the founding of Thebes. Diodoros likewise
says that Ilos founded the new city of Ilion out on the plain, and both he and
Konon agree on one other point, that Assarakos ruled Dardania (26F1.12). This
is what we might expect, at least after Assarakos' brother Ilos has moved north
to found his new city, and such a division probably means that Assarakos' line
was believed to remain near Mount Ida. Certainly in the *Iliad* we see the great-
grandson Aineias bitter toward Priam over his lack of status at Troy (*Il*
13.459–61), and Achilleus in his speech to Aineias boasts that he once chased
his opponent from Ida to Lyrnessos (*Il* 20.188–94). The remainder of Apollodoros' account repeats much of what is found in Konon and Diodoros, saving
only the rulership of Dardania, and adds (as in the *Ehoiai*) an Ilos, son of
Dardanos, who here dies without issue (Ap*B* 3.12.1–3). Subsequently he includes also Ilos, son of Tros, as a second figure of that name; possibly the *Iliad*
had already supposed such a doublet. To Laomedon's family (sons alone named
in Homer) Apollodoros assigns as well three daughters, Hesione, Killa, and
Astyoche, and of the sons as given by Homer makes Boukolion offspring of
the Nymph Kalybe, thus clearly illegitimate. Purely Latin is presumably the
tradition in which Dardanos and Iasion have their original home in Italy (*Aen*
3.163–68), and Dardanos at least makes his way from there to both Samothrace
and the Troad (*Aen* 7.205–8).[4]

The Birth and Childhood of Paris

Priam's parentage, his alternate name Podarkes, and his accession to his father's
throne after the affair with Herakles and the horses we have already considered
in chapter 13. In all accounts he is the son of Laomedon, with his mother
Zeuxippe according to Alkman (71 *PMG*) and Strymo according to Hellanikos
(4F139). Of his wife Hekabe, the *Iliad* says that her father was Dymas (and her
brother Asios: *Il* 16.717–18), and Pherekydes agrees on this point (3F136);
Euripides on the other hand makes the father Kisseus (*Hek* 3), and later tradition offers still other names. The *Iliad* also makes clear that Priam has fifty
sons (twenty-two are named, among them Hektor, Paris, Helenos, Deiphobos,
and Troilos) and twelve married daughters living with him (most notably Laodike); the unwed Kassandra and Polyxena (the latter never mentioned by
Homer) must be added to these last, plus perhaps other unmarried daughters or
married ones living elsewhere. Some of these offspring are specifically Hekabe's
and some are not; Priam at *Iliad* 24.496 finally discloses the actual number of
sons (not daughters) which she has borne to him—nineteen—but Homer offers no other details of their marriage or life together, and we must wait till

Apollodoros to hear of Priam's previous union with one Arisbe, daughter of Merops, who bears him a son Aisakos, or of Kreousa as his daughter by Hekabe (Ap*B* 3.12.5; cf. Σ Lyk 1232 on the latter). Already in Stesichoros, however, we find the idea that Hektor was Apollo's son, not Priam's (224 *PMG*), and so too Ibykos (295 *PMG*), Lykophron (Lyk 265), and Euphorion (fr 56 Pow); Homer clearly knows nothing of this. That Troilos was also a son of Apollo has no preserved authority earlier than Lykophron, as we will see later in this chapter.

In any case, there is no hint in the *Iliad* of any problem or decision at the time of Paris' birth, despite the numerous insults and imprecations leveled at him in the course of the poem. Our first trace of such a story comes from Pindar, whose *Paian* 8a (from a papyrus) tells of a dream or vision vouchsafed to Hekabe while she was pregnant with Paris: she seemed to give birth to a fire-breathing Hundred-Hander, and he with harsh strength destroyed the whole of the city of Ilion. Another figure (a *mantis?*) then replies, mentioning something about forethought, and here the papyrus breaks off. The obvious implication, that Priam and Hekabe were warned of Paris' future before he was born, is confirmed by the A scholia at *Iliad* 3.325, where Hekabe dreams that she gives birth to a flaming torch that burns down both Troy and the forests of Mount Ida; seers then advise that the child be abandoned on Ida as food for wild beasts, and this is done, only to be thwarted by a shepherd who finds Paris and raises him. A similar story formed the prologue of Sophokles' and Euripides' *Alexandros* plays, both of which dealt with Paris' return to Troy as a young man. For the reconstruction of those plays we have a few fragments, plus a papyrus hypothesis of Euripides' version (POxy 3650),[5] but our primary knowledge of plot comes from Hyginus, so that we cannot say which details belong to which playwright, much less whether any might have been added from other sources. As Hyginus tells the story, Hekabe in her dream gives birth to a blazing torch from which numerous serpents issue (*Fab* 91). Diviners therefore advise that whatever offspring she is carrying should be destroyed when she delivers it, and the infant Alexandros is handed over to servants to be killed. The servants, however, in pity expose the child, and of course shepherds discover him and bring him up as their own, calling him Paris. Grown to young manhood, he finds one day that men sent by the king are leading off his prize bull to be used as an award for games to be celebrated in honor of Alexandros. With no other way to recover his property he follows them to Troy and enters the contests, where he defeats all comers including his own brothers. Such a defeat prompts Deiphobos to draw his sword against the unknown upstart; Paris flees to an altar of Zeus for sanctuary, and Kassandra then reveals his true identity as son of Priam. Priam himself acknowledges this lost child, and apparently no more is said about the omen of his future.

Of this eminently dramatic plot we can assign for certain to Sophokles only the context in which a herdsman defeats men of the city (fr 93 R), but this seems enough to guarantee the playwright's use of the whole Hyginian tale in some form. For Euripides we have more substantial fragments showing that Kassandra appeared, that Deiphobos took his defeat extremely hard, in contrast to Hektor, and that Hekabe, finding the victory of a supposed slave over free men intolerable, proposed that her sons should kill the newcomer (9 GLP).[6] Briefer fragments from Stobaios seem to indicate that wealth and poverty, slave and free man, and the illusory difference between them, were key issues, as we see reflected in the same poet's *Elektra*. From the preserved *Troades*, produced together with the *Alexandros*, we have an allusion to the dream and Paris as a torch (*Tro* 920–22); presumably, the *Alexandros* itself did not contradict this. In a separate play altogether, the later *Andromache*, the chorus relates how Kassandra called upon everyone in the city to destroy the infant Paris, to no avail (*And* 293–300). Varro tells us that Ennius used Euripides' etymologizing of the name "Alexandros" for his own play of that title (*LL* 7.82), which has led some scholars to suppose the whole of Ennius' play drawn from Euripides, but obviously he could have conflated different plays, and in any case we do not have much of his effort either. What does survive from it includes a prologue spoken by Kassandra (in which Hekabe again dreams that she is delivered of a burning torch, and Apollo interprets the omen: *Ex incertis* fr V Rib), the fact that the shepherds gave Paris the name "Alexandros" (*Alexander* fr V Rib), and a call by Kassandra to the populace to come quench the brand, that is, Paris (*Alexander* fr VI Rib). This last detail suggests a different means of recognition than in Hyginus, for Kassandra is not likely to stop her brothers from killing Paris by revealing his name and then incite them to kill him anyway. Servius knows a version in which the identification is made by means of a rattle or amulet *(crepundia)* given to him as an infant (Σ *Aen* 5.370); it has also been proposed that Hekabe might observe the resemblance between her sons and the stranger, or Paris make some chance remark about his origins which could lead to the discovery. In either case the servant who failed to kill the child may be called upon as well, much as in Sophokles' *Oidipous*.

The story was also quite popular on late Etruscan urns, where Paris in his Phrygian cap crouches on an altar and a Trojan (presumably Deiphobos) tries to kill him; Aphrodite generally intervenes. Other figures include Priam and Hekabe and also Kassandra, who holds an axe and wishes for reasons of her own prescience to dispatch her brother. That Aphrodite appeared in tragedy as well to identify Paris and/or resolve the crisis is certainly possible, but we would then expect her (or any *deus ex machina*) to repeat the initial warning about Paris, which would leave Priam in a difficult position. More likely, Kassandra is disbelieved, as usual, and the omen is forgotten in the joy of the moment. Surprisingly, there is no record of the story in vase-painting. Although he omits any details of the recognition, Apollodoros tells much the same tale as Hyginus, with the dream of the torch (as in Ennius no snakes) and an interpretation by Priam's son Aisakos, after which the child is exposed on Mount Ida and nursed by a bear for five days (ApB 3.12.5). Here too, as in

Ennius, shepherds name the child Alexandros, in contrast to the *Troades* and Hyginus, where his parents give him that name. Already in Homer we find both appellations used, though with no explanation of their source; conceivably, Sophokles used one version of the dual naming and Euripides the other. We should note in that connection that while Varro has Ennius borrow Euripides' etymology for Alexandros he does not quite attest that the circumstances—shepherds bestowing the title—were also the same, even if that seems likely. On the whole we must admit, as so often, that though the motif of prophecy and abandonment is certainly old, we cannot say how old it is in the particular case of Paris. Proklos' summary of the *Kypria*, where we might have expected to find it, has nothing on Paris' early life at all, and one does not immediately see where else it might have been told. The problems involved in fitting it together with the judgment of the goddesses we will return to below.

One additional tale of Paris' birth, alluded to quite obscurely in Lykophron and explained in the relevant scholia, suggests that Hekabe had a sister Killa, married to Thymoites, with whom Priam secretly lay; she bore a child Mounippos, and when an oracle advised Priam to kill both the woman who had just given birth and her child he slew Killa and Mounippos rather than Hekabe and Paris (Σ Lyk 319). Earlier, however, the same scholia make the father of the child Thymoites himself; here too the child is killed with his mother after Aisakos has advised slaying the offspring born on that day (Σ Lyk 224). We have seen above that in Apollodoros Killa is the sister of Priam, not Hekabe (Ap*B* 3.12.3), and that Homer mentions Thymoites once, as one of the elders sitting with Priam and his brothers (*Il* 3.146). Diodoros calls Thymoites a son of Laomedon, although he does not relate any part of the above story (DS 3.67.5). In Vergil, meanwhile, we find the remark that Thymoites "is the first to encourage our bringing the horse within the walls and placing it on the *arx*, whether through treachery or because the fates so now ordained" (*Aen* 2.32–34). The mention here of treachery seems really too casual to have more sinister overtones, but Servius after relating the same tale of Priam's killing of the wife and son of Thymoites in response to an oracle (again the utterance of his son by Arisbe) argues that Vergil may be alluding to a grudge on the part of the angered father (Σ *Aen* 2.32); it does seem clear, though, that he has no independent source for such an idea.

Tyndareos and the Wooing of Helen

We have seen that in Homer Helen is consistently a stepdaughter of Tyndareos, and a half-sister of the Dioskouroi (since they share a common mother). About her wooing and bestowal upon Menelaos, neither the *Iliad* nor the *Odyssey* has anything to say, despite Menelaos' seeming lack of stature for such a role. Likewise, neither poem makes mention of any oath taken by suitors to defend the eventual bridegroom's rights; we are presented rather with heroes who have come to Troy for glory and spoils.[7] Possibly such obligations on the part of the suitors have been omitted from the *Iliad* because they would inevitably affect our response to Achilleus' withdrawal from battle, but other sources solve that problem by dropping Achilleus from the list of suitors, and Homer could have done the same. If he has heard of the oath, perhaps his motive for its exclusion is the hope of imparting greater effectiveness to those scenes in which the Achaians, Agamemnon included, contemplate abandoning the war. But, of course, Homer may not have known the story at all. The *Kypria,* or rather our summary of it, also ignores all aspects of the wooing, beginning rather with the wedding of Peleus and Thetis and the Judgment of Paris, after which Paris sails to Sparta, where Menelaos and Helen are already married. The same summary does, however, relate subsequently the incident of Odysseus' feigned madness to avoid participating in the expedition, behavior that might lead one to suppose that he is under some commitment to Menelaos.

In the *Ehoiai,* at any rate, there was an extremely detailed report of the wooing, in part preserved, with a catalogue of all the suitors who sent gifts to Sparta (Hes frr 196–204 MW). That they sent gifts rather than coming in person seems to have been the standard procedure, at least at first, for the Berlin papyrus that is our main source of information notes that one suitor (name lost) knew of Helen only by hearsay, and that in contrast to the others Idomeneus did come himself to plead his case. Yet ten lines later in the same fragment, after a most inconvenient gap in the papyrus, we find someone extracting a clear oath from the suitors to pursue anyone carrying off Helen by force. From this event it might seem that all the suitors are now present in Sparta, but given the brevity of the missing space in which they would have to assemble it may be that the oath is administered severally via messenger, and that there never is an actual gathering of wooers. As to the names of the aspirants, the fragments offer the following: Odysseus; Thoas, son of Andraimon; Podarkes, son of Iphiklos; Protesilaos, son of Aktor; someone from Athens who is very likely Menestheus; Aias; Elephenor, son of Chalkodon; Idomeneus; and the two sons of Amphiaraos. Of these all but the last are familiar figures in the *Iliad.* Unfortunately, we have no idea of the original length of the list or of how many names were included. We do, however, find Kastor and Polydeukes mentioned repeatedly as recipients of the various envoys, and at one point the poem says that the two brothers would have given Helen to (name lost, alas), had their brother-in-law Agamemnon not interceded on behalf of Menelaos (Hes fr 197 MW). From this passage we see that (1) the Dioskouroi, rather than Tyndareos, seem to have the decisionmaking role, and (2) Agamemnon is not among the suitors, being already married to Klytaimestra. Why Klytaimestra should have been married before Helen is something of a puzzle; perhaps we are to understand that she was older, or perhaps storytellers wished to avoid explaining Agamemnon's defeat in the wooing by his own brother. Other fragments tell us that Odysseus sued but sent no gifts (knowing that Menelaos would win as the wealthiest of the Achaians: Hes fr 198 MW), that the Athenian contestant believed himself the wealthiest (Hes fr 200 MW), and that Aias of Salamis offered sheep and cattle from Troizen, Epidauros, Aigina, Megara, etc. (Hes fr 204 MW). Finally the oath is sworn by all, after which we are told very simply that Menelaos is chosen because he has furnished the most goods. All the same, the poet adds, he would not have won had Achilleus been among the suitors; the latter's absence is here ascribed to the fact that he is still with Cheiron on Mount Pelion, and perhaps that he is still very young. Beyond this we have only a reference from scholia which adds the Kretan Lykomedes to the list of suitors (Hes fr 202 MW).

In the mid-sixth century, Stesichoros seems also to have recounted the wooing, almost certainly in his lost *Helene*. Our one reference to his treatment of the occasion (a scholiast's summary) regards the oath: Tyndareos fears to make enemies of the other Greek leaders by preferring one of them, and so extracts a common oath that they will all defend the rights of whoever should win her; this done, he gives her to Menelaos (190 *PMG*). The same general rationale appears in the fifth century in Euripides' *Iphigeneia in Aulis*, where Agamemnon describes the oath as conceived by Tyndareos to preserve order after the suitors (here clearly assembled) begin to threaten each other (*IA* 49–71). But when they have all agreed to protect Helen from any sort of abduction, he allows her to choose her own husband according to the whims of her heart. Of later sources our best accounts are from Apollodoros and Hyginus, both of whom give lists of the suitors. That of Apollodoros contains thirty-one names, familiar as Achaian leaders in the Catalogue of Ships and elsewhere in the *Iliad* with the exception of Amphilochos, son of Amphiaraos (Ap*B* 3.10.8). Among those mentioned, there are thus few surprises, save perhaps for the inclusion of Patroklos and the absence of Idomeneus and Meriones. The omission of Idomeneus in particular, combined with those of Podarkes and Lykomedes, would seem to show that Apollodoros is not here basing himself directly on the *Ehoiai*, unless he is reciting (fallibly) from memory. The one other notable detail in this account (in which the suitors are again clearly together at Sparta) is the claim that the idea for the oath comes from Odysseus, after Tyndareos has expressed fears about anger among the losers. Odysseus makes this offer of help in exchange for Tyndareos' assistance in securing the hand of Penelope from Ikarios. Tyndareos then chooses Menelaos; we are not told why. Hyginus' list of thirty-six suitors is a bit more chaotic, as we might expect, and also omits Podarkes and Lykomedes (as well as any son of Amphiaraos), so that the same conclusion applies as for Apollodoros (*Fab* 81). Regarding the selection of the winner he says that Tyndareos "fearing lest Agamemnon repudiate Klytaimestra and lest discord arise out of the matter, on the advice of Odysseus bound himself by oath and made Helen the selector of her own husband" (*Fab* 78). Thus Odysseus is again the instigator, but there is (unless something has been misunderstood) no suitors' oath, and Helen here as in Euripides makes her own choice, although Hyginus does not say why she should prefer Menelaos. Our one other bit of evidence comes from Pausanias, who points out the Tomb of the Horse on the road out of Sparta toward Arkadia and says that Tyndareos here sacrificed a horse and took the suitors' oaths over it (3.20.9). One emerges from this survey with the impression that storytellers found Helen and Menelaos irrevocably linked, despite the presence of seemingly more attractive suitors, and made the best of the situation.

The *Iliad* has just one solitary reference to the event that formed the cause of the Trojan War, and even that is couched in terms vague enough to be controversial. Hera and Athena several times in the course of the poem state their bitter enmity toward Troy and their determination that it be destroyed, but only in Book 24 is any cause stated for this anger. When the poet tells us that all the other gods urged Hermes to steal back the body of Hektor from Achilleus he excepts three—Hera, Poseidon, and Athena—and adds that Troy and Priam and the people were hateful to these "because of the folly of Alexandros, who created contention with the two goddesses, when they came to his courtyard, but approved the one who furnished to him an object of grievous lust" (or "made him desirable in a way which caused grief": *Il* 24.28–30). If we cannot get the exact sense of these last words, we have still enough to say that this is the Judgment as we know it: two goddesses are disappointed, while the entire *Iliad* proclaims that the third, here chosen by Paris, has provided him with Helen.[8] That Homer does not mention the story elsewhere may seem surprising, but the anger of such goddesses must have some origin, and we will understand that Homer does not wish to stress too strongly divine responsibility for the war. Nor should Poseidon's inadvertent involvement in this passage be an issue: the poet knows that his audience will not confuse the god with the real contestants, and they have already heard Poseidon's own reason for wrath, namely his ill-treatment by Laomedon at the time of the building of Troy's walls (*Il* 21.441–57). Thus, nothing really supports Aristarchos' athetizing of these lines; their allusive quality indicates rather the familiar nature of the tale, as so often in Pindar.

What details we miss in Homer are certainly atoned for by the *Kypria*, where Paris' famous decision seems to have been fully narrated, to judge by Proklos' summary. There Eris, being present at the wedding of Thetis, starts the quarrel among Hera, Athena, and Aphrodite as to beauty, and Zeus orders Hermes to take them to Paris on Mount Ida to resolve the matter. Paris, swayed by the promise of a marriage with Helen, chooses Aphrodite; we are not told what if anything Hera and Athena offered. Prior to all this the *Kypria* has begun with Zeus and Themis plotting together to bring about the Trojan War; our summary says no more than that, but the *Iliad* scholia offer a quote from the poem showing that Zeus' motive was to relieve the earth of the weight of so many mortals, in an act of pity (ΣA *Il* 1.5–6 = fr 1 *PEG*). The quote is preceded by a more general narrative of the situation which is probably also drawn, at least in large part, from the *Kypria*. This tells us that Gaia is burdened not only by the number of men, but also by their impiety, and that she makes an appeal to Zeus to lighten the weight. His first response to her request is the war at Thebes. Subsequently he plans to employ thunderbolts and great floods as well, but Momos prevents him, and advises Thetis' marriage to a mortal and his own engendering of a beautiful daughter, from which two events will arise a great war. That either Helen's birth or Thetis' union with Peleus was a preplanned device to trigger the Trojan conflict is not an idea found elsewhere, and then too another source reports that in the *Kypria* Zeus gave Thetis to a mortal out of anger, because she rejected him (Philodemos: fr 2 *PEG*). But however we take these details, the central theme of overpopulation and large-scale war as a solution is obviously early, although Paris' ultimate responsibility as a cog in this plan remains uncertain. The Berlin fragments of the *Ehoiai* appear to know something of the same story, for immediately after Helen's marriage and the birth of Hermione (unexpected, for some reason) they tell us that the gods were divided in strife, as Zeus continued to set the earth in turmoil and to blot out much (or all?) of the race of men (Hes fr 204 MW). The problems of this passage, with its mention of *hêmitheoi* and a life of the blessed ones apart, we have already discussed in part in chapter 3. An event involving heroes falling in strife, as the text says at one point, and following so closely upon Helen's appearance, must surely be the Trojan War. Yet the motive, whatever it is exactly, obviously differs from that of the *Kypria,* and what we see next in the fragments of the *Ehoiai* is some sort of natural disaster with high winds (after which the papyrus breaks off), rather than any of the usual preludes to the war. Possibly we are to understand, as in the *Kypria,* Momos' intervention and a change of plan, but certain words do suggest that war and natural devastation are both part of Zeus' plan from the very beginning. In any case, we cannot say whether the Judgment of Paris appeared in the *Ehoiai* at all, or just how the war there began. Our one other literary source of the Archaic period on this point is Akousilaos: apparently in his version Aphrodite somehow arranged the war, so that Aineias' house might become the ruling one (2F39).

In art we have a substantial number of early representations, the Judgment of Paris being a favorite subject of the Archaic period.[9] The very earliest are an ivory comb from Sparta, of uncertain date but usually regarded as seventh-century, and the Protocorinthian Chigi Olpe of about 640 b.c. The comb shows Paris seated to the left on an elaborate chair or throne, and the three goddesses approaching him, Hera with a cuckoo, Aphrodite with a goose (presumably these are attributes, not bribes: Athens 16368).[10] On the Chigi Olpe in the Villa Giulia much of the lower part of the scene is broken away, but here there are in recompense names to guarantee the artist's intention (VG 22679). Alexandros now stands to the left, greeting a missing figure who by the tip of his kerykeion must be Hermes; behind the latter are the three goddesses, of whom, since the second and third are Athena and Aphrodite, the first must be Hera. Neither of these depictions adds much to our knowledge of the story, but they do attest it for the seventh century, and much as we see it in the *Kypria.* For the sixth century we have first of all the Chest of Kypselos, where an inscription quoted by Pausanias assures us that here again Hermes is leading the three goddesses to Alexandros, who is to resolve the issue of their beauty

(5.19.5); our guide saw the same scene also on the Amyklai Throne (3.18.12). Unfortunately, in neither case does he note any indication of the prospective judge's attitude toward this contest. It is a question of some interest because from about 570 B.C. onward Attic Black-Figure representations often show Zeus' designated arbiter displaying a certain reluctance to assume his assigned role. On a tripod kothon by the C Painter in the Louvre Paris steps away gingerly to the right as Hermes (looking back) and his charges approach (Louvre CA 616). Between the two men a female figure faces Paris with a garland in each hand; she may be one of the contestants sneaking ahead for a private interview, although (since there *are* three females behind Hermes) she may also be Paris' lover, Oinone. A neck-amphora and column krater by Lydos develop this reluctance still further: Paris now vigorously strides away, virtually running, while Hermes increases his own pace and raises his arm as if to halt his quarry (Florence 70995; London 1948.10–15.1). Such attempted discretion might seem to accord ill with the subsequent acceptance of Aphrodite's bribe, but this last feature of the story was no doubt locked in, leaving us with a Judgment in which Paris is prudent enough to foresee the dangers of his task, but not prudent enough to avoid them. Whether this attractively dubious characterization derives from a literary source or represents an artistic innovation of the sixth century remains open.

In non-Attic art of the period we have a Pontic amphora from Vulci now in Munich (837), and the British Museum's Boccanera slabs from the cemeteries of Caere (no #). Both works display a Paris waiting calmly for the divine procession to reach him, as on the Chigi vase; the Munich amphora has as well cows behind the Trojan, our first concrete reference to his herding activity. The Attic pieces so far considered (and others of the same time) show him rather in long chiton (and himation on occasion) and sometimes carrying a scepter (or at least an elegant staff) which gives him quite the look of a royal personage. Not until around 520 B.C. do the trappings of a shepherd begin to appear: a dog, animals from the herd, and Paris himself seated on a rock, often with a lyre for entertainment. At the same time, or a little later, the fleeing Paris motif begins to become less common, in part perhaps because Hermes and the goddesses alone, without Paris, emerge as the most popular type. In Red-Figure, Paris on his rock resurfaces as the standard mode of representation, and as the century progresses emphasis shifts from the procession to the goddesses crowded around the handsome, youthful Trojan. In two such cases from the early part of the century one goddess offers to Paris what certainly looks like an apple (a piece of fruit, in any case), so that we see here for the first time the prize to be awarded (London E178, E257).[11] Oddly enough, Hermes in the earlier representations is never given custody of this item; as we saw in chapter 1, its first literary appearance is quite late (ApE 3.2; *Fab* 92; *Sal* 45).

The artistic evidence thus suggests that the Archaic period for most of its length chose to portray Paris as a prince of the house of Troy, rather than a shepherd tending his livestock. Indeed, we might suppose his role as herdsman to begin as late as the latter sixth century, were it not that the *Kypria* does place him on Mount Ida for the goddesses' visit. But since *Iliad* 20 speaks of Aineias as herding cattle on Mount Ida when he is unlucky enough to encounter Achilleus, it seems clear that livestock-tending is not inappropriate for royalty. More problematic is the relationship of Paris' abandonment to the Judgment: one would like to know whether in the *Kypria* and other early accounts the goddesses agreed to be judged by a shepherd of no supposed birth or distinction, or whether they came to him after his restoration to royal status at Troy, when he had become a royal shepherd rather than a common one. Both solutions seem slightly anomalous (although I suppose Zeus could have revealed Paris' identity to his wife and daughters), and not impossibly the visit to Paris on his hillside was originally conceived in a world where he was always a royal shepherd, never an abandoned waif. If that were true we might suppose the tale of prophecy and abandonment a later elaboration, one inspired by his shepherding duties but never quite accounting for the honor of his role in the Judgment.[12]

For the fifth century our evidence comes from a variety of dramatic sources, and serves on the whole to reinforce what we have already seen. Aischylos does not mention the Judgment in the *Oresteia* (scarcely surprising since human responsibility is such a primary issue) and there is no trace of it elsewhere in his work, or any hint among the lost titles. Sophokles did write a satyric *Krisis* which dramatized the conflict; our source, Athenaios, suggests that Athena's intellectual nature and athletic prowess may have been contrasted to Aphrodite's hedonism in a kind of philosophical allegory (fr 361 R). Presumably the Satyric chorus had in mind rather a physical display of the goddesses' charms. In the *Dionysalexandros* of Kratinos (430 or 429 B.C.), the Judgment was caricatured, with Dionysos (i.e., Perikles) disguised as Paris rendering the verdict and causing the war. Here for the first time, if our summary of the play is accurate, do we hear of three bribes: Hera promises an unshaken *tyrannis*, Athena success in battle, and Aphrodite that Paris will be most handsome and desirable (POxy 663 = vol. 4, p. 140 *PCG*). The particular form of Aphrodite's offer *may* reflect what *Iliad* 24 meant, or was thought to mean, if it does not arise from something in the Periklean comparison intended; in any case, it leads to the usual result, Paris' seduction of Helen. Only shortly after this comedy comes Euripides' version of the same events, as related by Helen in the *Troades*: Pallas begins the contest by promising that as general of the Phrygians Paris will destroy Hellas, and Hera in her turn offers a tyranny over all Asia and Europe (*Tro* 924–37). Finally Aphrodite extols the marvels of Helen, and Paris makes his choice. Helen then adds that as a consequence of that choice the Greeks have been saved from Eastern domination, as would have happened had Paris taken either of the other offers; probably the poet has exaggerated those offers for the sake of just this argument (which Hekabe not surprisingly ridicules as absurd, since Hera and Athena would never abandon their favorite Greek cities). Likely Kratinos has not invented the three bribes, given that they become a standard part of the later tradition. But we have seen that only Aphrodite's appears in our brief evidence from the *Iliad* and the *Kypria,* and whether the others were always present must remain uncertain; conceivably in the earliest accounts Hera and Athena merely flaunted their charms, while Aphrodite alone presented an additional inducement for Paris' consideration, her rivals' attempts to do likewise representing a post-*Kypria* development.

Elsewhere, Euripides' references to the Judgment come from choral odes and other allusions in a variety of plays. From the *Andromache* we have an ode lamenting that Paris ever survived, or judged the contest (*And* 274–92). Here as before Hermes brings the goddesses—a triple-yoked team—to Mount Ida, where the emphasis is very much on the solitary nature of Paris' existence among his livestock. The goddesses pause to wash in a nearby spring before actually arriving, and then "pushing themselves forward past each other with the going beyond of their hostile words they came to Paris"; the awkwardness of the translation reflects the ambiguity of these words, which may mean simply that the goddesses tried to outdo each other in disparaging the allurements of their rivals. Briefer mentions in the *Helen* (23–30) and *Iphigeneia at Aulis* (1283–1309) also establish Paris as a shepherd on Ida at the time of the Judgment, and seem to imply that he has set up permanent housekeeping there, as we saw before.

In the fourth century the story finds a place in Isokrates, whose encomium to Helen likewise includes mention of the three offers made to Paris (10.*Helen* 41–44). Here Athena promises victory in battles, Hera rule over all of Asia, and Aphrodite Helen. The author also adds a surprising defense of Paris' choice, namely that he preferred Helen not for the sake of pleasure but in order to become a son-in-law of Zeus, with the consequent advantages to his future children. The very earnestness of this last argument suggests it is new, nor does it ever reappear. For the bribes in essentially this form we have also Apollodoros (Ap*E* 3.2), Loukianos (the *Dearum Iudicium*), and Hyginus (*Fab* 92), the latter adding from Hera unsurpassed riches and from Athena knowledge of all skills. Later artistic representations continue the trend of the latter fifth century, with the goddesses grouped around Paris and Eros sometimes in attendance. Obviously, they are seeking to cajole or influence him, but a painting cannot tell us by what means. Regarding one other aspect of Paris' early career, his lover Oinone whom he abandons for Helen, we find nothing until Hellanikos, who knows of their child who came to Troy to find his father; we will return to that story and her fate later in this chapter, when we come to the death of Paris.

The Abduction of Helen

The *Iliad* twice mentions Paris' journey from Sparta back to Troy with Helen, once when he himself reminds Helen how they made love on the island of Kranae (presumably for the first time: *Il* 3.443–45), and again when the poem mentions the elegantly woven robes brought back by Paris from Sidon on his return (*Il* 6.289–92). The location of Kranae is a mystery, and even the name itself, which means "rocky," may be nothing more than an epithet. Pausanias identifies the island as one just off Gythion south of Sparta on the coast, which is perhaps the most logical guess (3.22.1); Strabo says rather the island of Helene off Sounion (9.1.22), and so too Lykophron (110–11). The terms of the single combat in *Iliad* 3 also establish that Helen brought with her substantial property belonging to Menelaos (*Il* 3.67–72, etc.), and Paris confirms this in *Iliad* 7 when he announces to the assembled Trojans that he is willing to give back those possessions but not Helen (*Il* 7.362–64).

For anything beyond these sparse details we must turn to the *Kypria*, where Aphrodite tells Paris to build ships for his voyage to Greece and to take Aineias with him, while Helenos and Kassandra (in apparently two separate scenes) foretell the future. On his arrival in Lakedaimonia he is greeted first by the Dioskouroi, and then at Sparta by Menelaos, who entertains him in his home; Paris for his part reciprocates by giving gifts to Helen. For reasons unstated, Menelaos then sails off to Krete, after instructing Helen to make sure that the visitors have everything they need. Aphrodite now takes a hand in bringing Paris and Helen to bed together, after which they take a good deal of property and sail away during the night. Hera sends a storm that drives them to Sidon, where Paris captures the city. On reaching Troy they are then formally married. So runs Proklos' summary, with the same theft of possessions and stopover at Sidon found in the *Iliad*; scholia add for the *Kypria* that Helen also takes her child Pleisthenes with her to Cyprus, and bears to Paris one Aganos (fr 12 *PEG*). Puzzling in comparison with all this is Herodotos' remark that in the *Kypria* Paris with a fair wind and a calm sea reaches Troy on the third day (counting the one on which he set out), as opposed to Homer where he visits Sidon and generally wanders around (Hdt 2.117). Various explanations have found support, among them that Herodotos was mistaken, that Proklos' summary is contaminated by material from the *Iliad*, that *Kypria* poems by two different authors existed, and that the version of Herodotos' time was subsequently expanded (to better conform to Homer?) into the one known to Proklos.[13] It should be added here that we also do not know why the *Kypria* bears the title it does; reference to a stopover on Cyprus and an acknowledgment of Aphrodite as the Kyprian goddess are two possibilities (neither very convincing).

Of other authors relating the flight from Sparta, Diktys of Krete has Paris welcomed by the king of Sidon, whom he murders once inside the palace (Dik 1.5). Such a sequence of events—certainly more plausible than an assault on the city with the few men Paris should have with him coming from Sparta—is perhaps what Proklos found in his *Kypria* as well, if not an attempt to rationalize that account. In Apollodoros as in the *Kypria* Menelaos departs for Krete while Paris is his guest, here in order to bury his grandfather Katreus, whereupon Helen abandons her nine-year-old daughter Hermione and sets sail with Paris by night (ApE 3.3–4). Again she takes much of her husband's property with her, and again Hera's storm forces them to Sidon. But of a capture of the city Apollodoros has no word; Paris simply delays in Phoinicia and Cyprus to throw off pursuit. Homer, as we saw, does not actually attest more than a visit to that area. Regarding offspring of the adulterous pair, *Odyssey* 4 begins by noting that the gods granted to Helen only one child, Hermione (*Od* 4.12–14); given the context this might mean only one child from Menelaos, but the wording suggests otherwise. As we saw in chapter 11 Kinaithon and the *Ehoiai* mention a son Nikostratos (fr 3 *PEG*; Hes fr 175 MW), and the Lakedaimonians are cited for two sons, Nikostratos and Aithiolas (ΣA *Il* 3.175); the *Kypria's* Pleisthenes seems nowhere else mentioned. Helen in later sources will bear a number of sons to Paris (32F11; Σ Lyk 851), none of them very important unless Korythos is in fact hers (see below). As a variant to Paris' usual motive for visiting Sparta we should also note the Antheus whom Lykophron says was loved (in a sexual sense) by Paris (Lyk 134). The scholia thereto relate that this Antheus was a son of Antenor whom both Paris and Deiphobos desired; after accidently killing him Paris fled Troy in fear, sailing with Menelaos to Sparta where he met Helen. Of this story, too, there is no other trace, and seemingly when it was told it replaced the Judgment of Paris.

In art, though the abduction is frequently represented, especially in Attic Red-Figure, the nature of the scene is not such as to provide narrative detail.[14] Possibly it surfaces as early as the Geometric period, if the famous departure/abduction on the Late Geometric krater from Thebes now in London does show this couple, rather than Theseus and Ariadne or Iason and Medeia (London 1899.2–19.1), but for our purposes nothing will really be gained by a positive identification when the *Iliad* already guarantees the event. The same is true of a number of shield-bands from Olympia on which a warrior seizes the wrist of a woman. But a Middle Corinthian krater does offer names, as Paris and Helen (cloak held out modestly to shield her face) arrive at Troy in a chariot; Hektor is named among the couples flanking them (NY 27.116). In Attic Red-Figure we have Makron's cup in Boston on which Paris, now armed with helmet and spear, leads away by the wrist a downward-gazing Helen; Aineias, Aphrodite, and Peitho are also present while overhead hovers a small Eros (Boston 13.186). Another cup by the same painter in Berlin offers much the same general scene, but without the divine figures. Here instead Aineias seems to be fending off Timandra, Helen's sister, who hastens toward him imploringly while one Euopis informs Ikarios and Tyndareos of the event (Berlin:Ch F2291). Both cups do suggest a certain reluctance on the part of Helen, who must be led along by her would-be lover. We have already seen Helen in *Iliad* 3 as a woman who has under Aphrodite's persuasion made her choice, for better or worse, and blames no one else for her decision, however much she may regret it (cf. too *Od* 4.259–64). Yet we have also seen that both the *Ehoiai* and Stesichoros cite Aphrodite's anger as the cause of the Tyndareides' adulterous comportment, because (in Stesichoros at least) Tyndareos once neglected to sacrifice to her (Hes fr 176 MW; Stes 223 *PMG*). Thus there may well have been a tradition that attempted to mitigate Helen's behavior in leaving Menelaos. No source, however, goes so far as to argue that she is actually kidnapped against her will, although this may be implied in some of the versions in which she never arrives at Troy (see below). From Homer's picture of her as lured away from a better husband by the cajoling of Paris we turn to the similar portrait in the choral odes of Aischylos' *Agamemnon*, where she trips lightly through the gates of Troy, bringing death as a dowry to her new in-laws (*Ag* 403–8); the poor figure she cuts in Euripides' *Troades* as she seeks to excuse her actions we have already noted. That tragedy should judge her in these harsh terms is perhaps to be expected; with the war itself frequently weighed and found wanting, as it was not in epic, she becomes a natural scapegoat. Vase-painting of the later fifth century generally concentrates on her first meeting with Paris and his attempts to seduce her; Eros is again frequently present to assist in overcoming her reservations.

There was, however, also an early tradition that exonerated Helen altogether by the simple expedient of denying that she ever ran off with Paris. Our first evidence for this version is the so-called Palinode of Stesichoros, written, according to Plato and others, because the poet had lost his eyesight after telling the generally known tale of Helen's flight to Troy in a previous poem (probably the one implicating Tyndareos). His solution was to compose a new poem in which he recanted that account, saying instead (as Plato quotes the lines): "That was not a true tale; you did not sail in the well-benched ships, nor did you come to the towers of Troy" (192 *PMG*). Thus it seems that in the Palinode Helen never leaves Sparta, or at least not in the normal fashion. But Stesichoros can hardly have recanted the whole Trojan War, and Plato elsewhere discloses the device used by the poet to generate the conflict without her: Paris has taken an *eidôlon* of Menelaos' wife to Troy, and over this the two sides fight in ignorance of the truth (*Rep* 9.586c). Plato does not actually say that Stesichoros invented such an idea, but he does seem to suppose that, and so too later authors who discuss this radical variant. The one exception is a paraphrase of Lykophron which gives "Hesiod" priority in the matter of the *eidôlon* (Hes fr 358 MW [*dubium*]); probably it is mistaken, or else means by Hesiod a very late part of the Hesiodic Corpus. Admittedly, though, we cannot say how the Trojan War began in the *Ehoiai*, or what role Helen played.

Another issue regarding the Palinode on which we should like to be better informed involves where Helen resided while her *eidôlon* was at Troy. From our one quote we have seen that she did not sail away with Paris, and (if she in fact did not enter "well-benched ships") not with anyone else either, although of course a god (as below in Euripides) could presumably take her wherever he liked. More specific on the matter is Dion of Prusa's Egyptian informant in his Trojan discourse, who states that in Stesichoros Helen does not sail anywhere, while other writers have Paris carry her off to Egypt, where she remains (DP 11.41). The implication of the Greek here is, I think, that Helen neither sails nor goes anywhere, in which case Stesichoros would seem to have made her spend the war at home. But other sources claim just the opposite, that is, that

Stesichoros did somehow bring her to Egypt: in particular, a papyrus commentary on the melic poets says quite directly that when in Stesichoros the *eidôlon* went to Troy, Helen was lodged with Proteus (193 *PMG*). The scholia to Aristeides (at 13.131) go still further with the statement that Stesichoros had Paris take her to Egypt where Proteus rescued her (cf. Σ Lyk 113). This last is not impossible, for even in a version which exonerated Helen she might have been taken as far as Egypt by force, but given the lines quoted by Plato it seems best to suppose the attribution of this account to Stesichoros as in error. If we agree on the other hand that Helen can hardly remain in plain sight in Sparta for the whole length of the war we may feel inclined to side with the commentary, and to suppose that a god in fact brought her to Proteus so that the war might take place. Our earliest sources, the *Odyssey* and the *Nostoi*, both show Menelaos driven down to Egypt after the sack of Troy by a divine storm, with the real Helen already at his side; perhaps this well-established stopover gave Stesichoros (or whoever) the idea of hiding Helen with Proteus until Menelaos, who was scheduled to put in there anyway, could come to pick her up. Our fragments of Hekataios also show Helen in Egypt, but no more than that, and here as in Homer she may have come with Menelaos (1F308, 309).

For the Archaic period Stesichoros' probable translation of Helen to Egypt during the Trojan War is in fact the only appearance we have of that story. The later fifth century brings us to Euripides' *Helen* of 412 B.C., which fully dramatizes the reunion of Menelaos and his wife after he has unwittingly traveled down to Egypt with the *eidôlon*. Much of this drama is likely to be Euripidean invention, but the basic situation—Helen's stay in the house of Proteus—is also referred to in Euripides' *Elektra* (1280–83: Zeus creates the *eidôlon* to start the war), the metrics of which appear to guarantee an earlier date than that of the *Helen;*[15] thus Helen in Egypt, even if not Stesichorean, would precede this telling of the tale. As Helen herself explains matters at the beginning of the latter play, the *eidôlon* was the work of Hera, who angry over her loss in the Judgment begrudged Paris his prize. The Trojan received the *eidôlon* when he came to Sparta, while Zeus sent Hermes to transport Helen though the air to Egypt where Proteus might guard her until the war was over. The play's dramatic conflict arises from the fact that Proteus has since died, and his son Theoklymenos wishes to keep Helen for himself. We shall come back to this delicate situation in chapter 17 when we consider the returns from Troy. Existence of this version prior to Euripides is also indicated by its appearance (in a far more rationalizing form) in Herodotos, who says that according to the priests of Egypt Paris brought Helen there when he stopped with Proteus, the current king, for a rest on his way back to Troy (Hdt 2.113–19). On discovering his guest's treatment of his previous host Proteus was suitably shocked, and announced that he would keep Helen and the stolen property in his palace until the rightful owner should come to claim them. In this account, Helen is not completely exonerated, but she is presented as a woman temporarily seduced and deceived by Paris' charms, while Paris as the seducer must shoulder most of the blame. As for the *eidôlon*, it never materializes here, for Paris returns to Troy without Helen, and the Greeks attack, refusing to believe that she is not in the city. Only when Troy is sacked do they at last realize the truth, and Menelaos sails down to Egypt to find his wife safe and sound.

Apollodoros has the same version of these events as Euripides, citing unnamed writers for whom Hermes brings Helen from Sparta to Egypt while Paris and the *eidôlon* go to Troy (ApE 3.5). Philostratos, on the other hand, repeats Herodotos' version faithfully in his life of Apollonios of Tyana, where Achilleus, granting a rare interview, adds that the Greeks did learn the truth before Troy's fall but would have been ashamed to leave without accomplishing some deed of note (ApTy 4.16). Accounts of Menelaos' wandering after the sack may in some cases have had him aware of the *eidôlon*'s true nature, and thus searching for his wife when he reaches Egypt; in Euripides, as we saw, this is not the case, and the *eidôlon* reveals itself (by disappearing) only after Menelaos has encountered the real Helen. In any case, those versions in which Paris (rather than Hermes) brings Helen to Egypt and leaves her there leave room for the possibility that she was abducted against her will, so that this form of the story, like that in which she never goes away with him, may have served to exculpate her.

The First Mobilization at Aulis   At this point in the account of preparations for the expedition against Troy, the *Kypria* digresses to record the fate of Kastor and Polydeukes, so that listeners will understand why they do not mobilize with the other Achaians to seek out their sister's abductor. Iris then informs Menelaos of his loss, and he begins plans for the expedition with Agamemnon. They go first to Nestor, who accompanies them on their recruiting efforts elsewhere, including Ithaka where Odysseus feigns madness until the leaders threaten recriminations against his son on the advice of Palamedes. Subsequently the heroes all gather at Aulis and observe the omen of the snake and the sparrows (interpreted by Kalchas) before setting sail. But when they come to the shore of Asia Minor they mistake Teuthrania in the land of Mysia for Troy and attack. The local king Telephos slays Thersandros, son of Polyneikes, but is himself wounded by Achilleus. As they depart, the Achaians encounter a storm that disperses them and takes Achilleus to Skyros, where he marries Lykomedes' daughter Deidameia. From here, without further explanation, the action shifts to Argos and Telephos' arrival to seek from Achilleus a cure for his wound in exchange for guiding the army to Troy. So the summary of Proklos; there are no fragments or quotes touching on this part of the story, and we can only guess at what the original poem contained by way of detail.

Homer relates nothing of such a prologue, save for the omen of snake and sparrows recalled by Odysseus in *Iliad* 2, after the troops have been summoned back from the ships (*Il* 2.299–330); aside from this passage and a listing in the Catalogue of Ships (*Il* 2.496), Aulis is not mentioned in either *Iliad* or *Odyssey*. What Homer does tell us about the omen is that while the Achaians were sacrificing at Aulis a snake came out from under the altar and devoured eight baby sparrows plus their mother, after which Zeus turned him to stone. Kalchas then predicted that the Greeks would fight at Troy for so many years before capturing the city. The reference in the *Kypria*, where the Greeks are also sacrificing, is too brief for us to say whether the full version would have agreed with the *Iliad's*, and whether it was simply derived from that poem. More crucial is the question of the two mobilizations found in the *Kypria*; nothing in Odysseus' words in *Iliad* 2 suggests such a situation, or a mistaken landing in Mysia, but his purpose in speaking is to stress the foretold victory, not past hardships. We therefore cannot really say how much Homer did or did not know of the *Kypria's* complicated chain of events prior to the arrival at Troy. One of those events in particular might seem necessary to any account of the war, for if Achilleus does not come to Skyros he will not beget a son Neoptolemos, who will be vital to the final taking of Troy. But we will see that there is an alternative to the *Kypria's* means of bringing him there: in quite a number of later sources Achilleus arrives on Skyros in flight from the original mobilization, sent by his mother to hide. In fact, very little in the *Kypria's* prelude is essential to the war as conceived by the *Iliad*, and may or may not be post-Homeric elaboration. One point perhaps in conflict between the two poems is the fact that Kalchas (rather than Telephos) is credited at *Iliad* 1.71–72 with leading the Greeks to Troy by means of his prophetic skills, but this may just be characterization of the moment.

One other event not mentioned at all by Proklos but apparently part of the *Kypria* concerns the daughters of Anios. Diodoros makes Anios a son of Apollo and Rhoio, daughter of Staphylos, and locates him on Delos (DS 5.62.1–2). Lykophron alludes to the fact that he invited the Achaians to stay with him, and that his daughters somehow provisioned the army at Troy (see below), but for details we must turn to the scholia. These attest that one Dorippe bears to Anios (same parentage as in Diodoros) the Oinotrophoi,[16] that is, Oino, Spermo, and Elais (Σ Lyk 570). Dionysos gives these daughters the power to take (? *lambanein*) grain whenever they wish, and Pherekydes is then cited for the idea that Anios persuaded (tried to persuade?[17]) the Achaians to remain with him for nine years until the time of Troy's fated fall should arrive, with his daughters supplying all their needs for that period (3F140). The note concludes with the claim that this material is also to be found in the *Kypria*. Some lines later, the same scholia assert that Oino made wine, Spermo seed, and Elais oil, and that these girls saved the Greeks from starvation by going to Troy (Σ Lyk 580); Palamedes, in fact, goes to fetch them when the troops find themselves short of food (Σ Lyk 581).

The *Odyssey* has what may be a reference to such a story, for Odysseus tells Nausikaa that he once visited Delos in connection with the war, and the scholia to the passage claim that he had gone there with Menelaos to fetch the Oinotrophoi, citing Simonides' *Kateuchai* as a source for the tale (Σ *Od* 6.164); the scene is illustrated, with Menelaos alone appealing to Anios at an altar and the three girls holding respectively a grapevine, stalks of grain, and an olive branch, on an Apulian calyx krater by the Darius Painter [PrColl, Miami]).[18] One wonders if Odysseus and Palamedes were here rivals trying to accomplish the same task in competition with each other (in Servius' comment at *Aen* 2.81, Palamedes does succeed in obtaining grain for the army after Odysseus has failed to do so, though Servius says that they [or at least Odysseus] went to Thrace). What we find in Lykophron's version itself is the same invitation by Anios to the Achaians to remain on Delos for nine years, and the daughters again somehow capable of creating provisions—grain, wine, and oil (Lyk 569–83). But though the offer is refused by the Achaians, here too, as in the scholia, those daughters journey to Troy to provide for the needs of the Greeks, suggesting that Agamemnon in time thought better of his refusal. In Ovid, Dionysos' gift is the power of the daughters to turn whatever they touch into wine, grain, and oil (*Met* 13.632–74). On learning of this capability, Agamemnon sends armed forces to claim them for his expedition. Two of the (here four) daughters flee to Euboia while the other two seek their brother Andros on the island of the same name (seemingly they were at or on their way to Aulis). Andros yields to pressure and surrenders them, but Dionysos saves them by turning them into white doves. Lest we suppose that this metamorphosis is Ovid's own invention, we should note that Lykophron at one point also calls the sisters *phabes* ("doves" or "pigeons"); admittedly, though, the scholia offer no explanation of this word, and it can hardly allude to precisely the same story told by Ovid if in Lykophron the girls do go to Troy (willingly or unwillingly). For Apollodoros, the special power of the Oinotrophoi consists of the ability to produce the wine, grain, and oil from the earth (ApE 3.10). He mentions them amid the preparations for the first mobilization but without connecting them in any way to the narrative; apparently their role was lost in the course of epitomizing. Finally, from Diktys we have the statement that Anios and his daughters provided the Greeks with supplies before they left Aulis; how they generated the supplies he does not say (Dik 1.23).

From this digression we return to Telephos. In the fifth century, Pindar refers briefly to Achilleus' heroism in wounding him and to Mysia with its many vines (*Is* 8.49–50). His travails were also the subject of plays by all three of the major tragedians, although none have survived. In the case of Aischylos certainly and Sophokles probably, the works in question were connected trilogies covering (one assumes) both the attack on Mysia and the healing in Argos, with in Sophokles, perhaps, Telephos' birth and/or the fate of his son Eurypylos as well. Euripides' effort, entitled *Telephos* and part of his production of 438 B.C., showed Telephos' appeal to the Achaians at Argos to cure his wound; we know that the hero appeared as a beggar in rags (mercilessly parodied by Aristophanes) and that he seized the infant Orestes as a hostage after his disguise was penetrated. Subsequently, the Achaians were mollified by the discovery that he really was a Greek by birth, and he agreed to guide them to Troy in exchange for Achilleus' aid to heal the wound. Aischylos' *Telephos* must have dealt with the same situation, but we know only that he *may* have anticipated Euripides in the use of Orestes as a hostage (Σ *Acharnes* 332 says so, but has been questioned[19]). Red-Figure, however, certainly begins to illustrate that detail in the second quarter of the fifth century (e.g., London E382). If Sophokles, too, dramatized this part of the story, he must have done so in the *Syllogos Achaiôn*, which obviously dealt with some phase of the mobilization. Both Aischylos and Sophokles also wrote plays entitled *Mysoi*, which may or may not have treated the attack and wounding. For the third Aischylean title nothing presents itself; that completing Sophokles' group may have been the *Aleadai* or the *Eurypylos*. In neither case can we say what the overall pattern of the story was.

Later sources of information include Apollodoros (ApB 3.17–20) and the A scholia to *Iliad* 1.59, which agree that Telephos after killing many Greeks came face to face with Achilleus and fled; becoming entangled in vines (the scholia say that Dionysos was angry with him because he had deprived the god of honors) he was wounded in the thigh by his opponent. On being advised by an oracle that the wound could be cured only by he who caused it, he journeyed to Argos, and after promising to show the Achaians the way to Troy and not to help the Trojans himself (so the scholia) he was healed by Achilleus. Apollodoros adds that Achilleus used the rust from his spear to effect the cure, a motif we find first in Propertius (2.1.63–64), Ovid (*Ex ponto* 2.2.26), and an undated painting seen by Pliny (*NH* 25.42; 34.152); in all likelihood, this folktale-laden motif goes back to the *Kypria*. Indeed, the general similarity (including the absence of Orestes) between the *Iliad* scholia (citing the *neôteroi*) and Apollodoros on the one side and the *Kypria* on the other has prompted the belief that these later sources are drawing directly from the Epic Cycle,[20] although Apollodoros' rags should come from Euripides if Aristophanes' jabs are to have any point. In Hyginus' version there is the wound and the oracle, but no rags; Telephos seizes Orestes on the advice of Klytaimestra and the Achaians capitulate when they receive a prophecy that they will not take Troy without his help (*Fab* 101). Achilleus arrives and denies any knowledge of healing, but Odysseus points out that Apollo means the spear, not the man wielding it. Again Telephos points the way to Troy, although he declines to fight himself, being married to Priam's daughter Laodike. All this sounds like a play, but without the rags it may be that of Aischylos or Sophokles, or a melding of different sources.

From Diktys, finally, comes the seemingly innocuous detail that Diomedes carried the body of the slain Thersandros out of the battle in Mysia (Dik 2.2). Such elaboration is typical of Diktys, but in this case it leads us back to the early fifth century and a Red-Figure calyx krater by Phintias of which only fragments survive (Leningrad St 1275).[21] What remains are Patroklos (named), Diomedes (also named, and bent forward under the weight of something, surely a fallen comrade), plus the inscription "Dionysos" (figure not preserved). Seemingly, then, the main part of the krater represented Achilleus and

Telephos, with the god's role in the latter's wounding thus guaranteed as at least this early.

For further information on the other events of this first mobilization we must generally look again to the later mythographers. Odysseus' attempt to avoid service by feigning madness may be hinted at in the *Odyssey*, for Agamemnon in the Underworld states that he and Menelaos persuaded their comrade with some difficulty (*Od* 24.115–19). More likely, though, mention of persuasion means that they had no real claim on his services, and had to talk him into fighting at Troy. On the other hand, one might reasonably expect to find his ruse described in the *Palamedes* plays of all three major tragedians, and Sophokles put the tale on stage in his *Odysseus Mainomenos*, but in no case are useful fragments or references preserved. As we saw above, Proklos' report of the *Kypria* simply mentions the assumed madness and Palamedes' threat to kill Telemachos without specifying what form the stratagem took. In Lykophron, Kassandra wishes that Odysseus had stayed home, "hitching up a lustful ass to the yoke in the counterfeit contrivances of madness" (Lyk 815–19), which gives us some suggestion of the familiar story of plowing. In describing a painting of unknown date Loukianos mentions a wagon, a team of two different animals, and Palamedes threatening to kill Telemachos with his sword unless Odysseus ceases his pretense (*Oik* 30).

But the full story does not survive before Hyginus, who says that when the envoy came to Ithaka Odysseus, knowing from a prophecy that his absence would be for twenty years, donned a rough cap and yoked a horse and an ox together to his plow (*Fab* 95). Here Palamedes, rather than personally menacing the child, puts him directly in front of the plow, and Odysseus is forced to turn aside, thus conceding his sanity. The *Kypria*'s version, although Proklos' language is vague, seems rather to agree with Loukianos on this last point, and so too Apollodoros, who has Palamedes take Telemachos from his mother's arms and brandish his sword until Odysseus relents (ApE 3.7). Beyond this, Apollodoros like Proklos simply says that Odysseus behaves as one mad, which may mean that he is drawing from a summary of the *Kypria* no more detailed than ours. He does seem to put all the actors in Odysseus' house, not out in a field, and this could mean that in the *Kypria* no plow was involved, but he could also be guessing. Both Servius and the Lykophron scholia follow the account of Hyginus, with the plow, different animals, and Palamedes placing the child in harm's way; Servius adds that Odysseus sowed salt (Σ *Aen* 2.81), the scholia that he yoked a horse and an ox or an ox and an ass (ΣΣ Lyk 384, 815). The one constant feature of the story in all forms is Palamedes' role as the unmasker of Odysseus' deception, thus setting the stage for Odysseus' subsequent plot against him at Troy.

Last, there is the matter of Achilleus' recruitment. The *Kypria*'s notion that he came to Skyros as part of the return from the first expedition is unique to that poem, the *Little Iliad* (fr 24 *PEG*, probably as background to the fetching of Neoptolemos to Troy), and possibly the *Iliad*, where Patroklos' bedmate

Iphis is said to have been provided by Achilleus on conquering Skyros (*Il* 9.666–68).[22] In all later sources the situation is quite different: Thetis determines to hide the youthful Achilleus when the mobilization first begins, and takes him to Skyros to conceal him among the women of King Lykomedes' court. It has been argued (Proklos notwithstanding) that this was actually the version of the *Kypria*, since the *Iliad* scholia (see below) credit it to the Cycle.[23] Otherwise, our earliest evidence is a painting by Polygnotos, showing Achilleus among the women, which Pausanias refers to in describing works in the Propylaia in Athens (1.22.6).[24] Sophokles' play *Skyrioi*, once thought to have dramatized the hero's discovery by Odysseus and Diomedes, is now believed to have presented (probably) the summoning of Neoptolemos. But a papyrus hypothesis tells us that Euripides' *Skyrioi* was definitely about these events, with Lykomedes at first unaware that his young charge is not a girl (PSI 1286).[25]

As the play opens, it seems that Deidameia is already pregnant, having been raped or at least surprised by Achilleus, and Lykomedes is soon to be informed of the situation. Thus, when Odysseus and Diomedes arrive, Achilleus will find himself torn between his new family and the military needs of the Greeks. Nothing, however, shows us exactly how Odysseus made the identification, and we must look to later sources for that part of the story. Bion's (or an imitator's) poem on the subject breaks off in midstream, while Achilleus is still persuading Deidameia to share his bed (Bion 2), but in Ovid Odysseus himself explains the trick: he placed weapons among the feminine goods he had set forth, and waited to see who would pick them up to admire (*Met* 13.162–70). When Achilleus alone of all the women of the household did so, he had his man (so too Σ Lyk 277). The version of Apollodoros has a slightly different notion, that Achilleus was discovered by means of a trumpet (ApB 3.13.8). This same trumpet appears in Statius' account of the event, but only as an afterthought following Achilleus' betrayal of himself with the arms (*Ach* 1.750–920). Not until Hyginus do we see what must have been its original purpose: here Achilleus is not so foolish as to commit himself on first seeing the weapons, but Odysseus orders a trumpet to be sounded, whereupon the disguised hero supposes the city under attack, and rushes to the arms (*Fab* 96). Possibly this device is taken from Euripides, although we must note that Hyginus in contrast to the Euripidean hypothesis has Lykomedes aware of the deception from the beginning, and then, too, what we know of Euripides' play suggests perhaps that Achilleus will have to make his own decision whether or not to fight. One other detail of interest in Hyginus is Achilleus' name: the maidens of the palace call him Pyrrha from his reddish hair. Presumably this explains the son's name; the *Kypria* says that Lykomedes called that son Pyrrhos, and Phoinix Neoptolemos (fr 21 *PEG*).

As a final problem, the story of Achilleus' concealment is told in the scholia to *Iliad* 19, after Achilleus has mentioned his son Neoptolemos on Skyros. In these scholia (crediting the Cycle), Peleus rather than Thetis becomes the one to hide his son with Lykomedes, who as in Hyginus is party to the deception and provides the women's clothes (Σb *Il* 19.326). On receiving an oracle that Troy will not fall without Achilleus, the Achaians send Odysseus, Phoinix, and Nestor to visit the old man, and subsequently they make their way to Skyros where Achilleus is entrapped exactly as in Ovid. The scholiast then notes the birth of Neoptolemos to Deidameia and his participation at Troy, and concludes with the ascription to the Cyclic poets, in contrast with our evidence for both the *Kypria* (Proklos) and the *Little Iliad* (direct quote). That the scholiast could mean just the material immediately preceding his comment, that is, the birth of Neoptolemos and his deeds, seems unlikely, and hence the uncertainty about the epic tradition(s) must remain.

Iphigeneia and the Second Mobilization at Aulis

In *Iliad* 9 Agamemnon speaks of three daughters who are available for Achilleus to wed, Chrysothemis, Laodike, and Iphianassa (*Il* 9.144–45). Neither here nor elsewhere does Homer ever mention Iphigeneia or any difficulty in departing from Aulis. That Iphianassa should have a name so similar to that of Iphigeneia has been taken by some as a signal that Homer means to reject the tale of the sacrifice,[26] but this is dangerous ground, and the use of a slightly different name is surely too subtle a touch to make the intended point. Rather, I think, the poet is concerned to avoid imbuing Agamemnon with the sort of tragic depth which might well accrue to him if he has sacrificed his own daughter for the expedition, on the grounds that such depth would be ill-suited to his general character in the *Iliad*. The poet of the *Kypria* seems to have agreed at least with the notion of distinct persons for the names in question, for in his work there are four daughters, including both Iphigeneia and Iphianassa (fr 24 PEG). The scholiast who tells us this does not give the other two names, although his wording implies that the *Kypria* has simply added Iphigeneia to the three names supplied by Homer.

Our first actual sources for the sacrifice at Aulis are the *Kypria* and the *Ehoiai*. In Proklos' summary of the former, Artemis becomes angry because Agamemnon upon shooting a deer boasts that not even the goddess is his equal in the hunt, and in her rage sends winds that keep the fleet at Aulis from sailing. Kalchas then informs the leaders that they must offer up Iphigeneia if they are to appease Artemis, and they undertake to do so, after bringing her to Aulis with the promise of marriage to Achilleus. The sacrifice, however, is not carried out, for the goddess substitutes a deer on the altar in place of Iphigeneia, who is taken off to the Tauroi and becomes immortal. For the *Ehoiai*, our evidence consists of the same passage in which we have previously seen Leda's children and grandchildren described (Hes fr 23a MW). The text, which has some major gaps, runs as follows: "Agamemnon <lord of men> married the dark-eyed daughter <of Tyndareos, Klytaimestra, for the sake of her beauty (?)>. And she in his halls <bore slim-ankled Iphimede> and Elektra who rivaled the goddesses in beauty. Iphimede the well-greaved Achaians slaughtered on the altar of famed <Artemis of the golden arrows> on that day <when they sailed in their ships> to Ilion <to exact> a penalty for the <slim-

ankled> Argive woman, an *eidôlon*, that is. For <Iphimede herself the hunt-ress> showerer of arrows easily saved, and poured down upon her head <lovely ambrosia, so that her flesh might be unchanging>, and she made her immortal and ageless all her days. And now the races of men upon the earth call her Artemis of the wayside, <the attendant of the famous> showerer of arrows." As if this narrative were not remarkable enough, Pausanias asserts that in the *Ehoiai* Iphigeneia does not die, but becomes Hekate by the will of Arte-mis (1.43.1 = Hes fr 23b MW), and that same notion (with the same attribu-tion to "Hesiod") also appears in Philodemos (*Peri Eusebeias* p. 24 Gomperz).

That "Iphimede" is here simply a variant name for "Iphigeneia" seems an inevitable conclusion, even if we did not allow the same for the Homeric Iphianassa. More troubling is the equation with Hekate, an equation for which there seems no room in our present text (the lines immediately following deal with the birth of Klytaimestra's third child Orestes). Possibly she is hidden in the supplemented gaps, or perhaps the equation was made elsewhere in the poem. But perhaps, too, these authors (or their sources) took it upon them-selves to interpret the preserved words "Artemis *einodia*" ("Artemis of the wayside") as indicating Hekate, whether correctly or not. We saw in chapter 1 that *einodia* is used of Hekate as early as Sophokles (fr 535 R), but it is also used of Demeter and Persephone. We saw as well that Hekate (Iphigeneia or not) is not elsewhere attested in early Greek thinking as closely linked to Ar-temis, certainly not so closely linked that she should become simply an aspect of Artemis bearing the goddess' name. On the other hand, Philodemos says that Stesichoros in his *Oresteia* followed "Hesiod" in making Iphigeneia He-kate (= fr 215 *PMG*); unless Stesichoros used exactly the same (ambiguous) phrasing as the Catalogue Poet, we must suppose that he at least made explicit an idea that may or may not have been in the *Ehoiai*.

Whatever we make of this problem of Artemis and Hekate, it does seem at first glance that all three of our earliest sources—the *Kypria*, the *Ehoiai*, and Stesichoros—agree on the essential outcome of the sacrifice, namely that Iphi-geneia/Iphimede is saved by Artemis and becomes an immortal of some sort. But it has been argued that our text of the *Ehoiai* contains an interpolation of much the same sort as that generally supposed for Herakles' "appearance" in the *Nekuia*, for here too a narrative seemingly headed in a different direction is corrected by a line beginning with an *eidôlon*.[27] In line 17 of the fragment we are told that the Achaians "butchered" Agamemnon's daughter, not just that they intended to (aorist tense), and the Greek verb *sphazô* surely conjures up images of bloodshed and iron cutting into flesh. But four lines later we are assured that the maiden only appears to die, for what is sacrificed is an *eidôlon* (which dies convincingly in her place?) while the girl herself is rescued. That this version requires such an improbable replica of Iphigeneia when the *Kyp-ria's* deer was available can only mean that its author knew a tradition in which Iphigeneia did die, and wished to modify that; almost certainly this was the *Ehoiai* in its original form. Dating the six lines of the addition is another matter; for all we know, they may have been supplied well before the end of the Archaic period, and been part of the text read by Aischylos and others. In any event, if the lines are an interpolation, then both rescue and slaughter versions will have been known in early times, and there seems no criterion by which we could even begin to guess at the priority of one over the other. One further consequence of conceding an interpolation here would be the reordering of our time sequence in the matter of Iphigeneia-Hekate: while the *Ehoiai* is probably earlier than Stesichoros, the interpolation could well be later, and thus inspired by a Stesichorean innovation rather than vice versa.

In art the tragic story, which might seem to lend itself to illustration, is barely known. For the seventh and sixth centuries our one possibility is a Protoattic krater by the New York Nessos Painter preserved only in fragments (Boston 6.67). On one of these we see two men carrying a woman horizontally; only her feet and the skirt of her garment are visible. On the other piece, a bearded man turns his head to look back over his shoulder. Possibly this is Agamemnon averting his gaze as he prepares for the sacrifice, but there are no names to guarantee the interpretation, and no way to tell whether Artemis' intervention was anticipated or not. Certain on the other hand is a white-ground lekythos of the fifth century by Douris now in Palermo (Palermo NI 1886). A warrior identified by inscription as Teukros and wielding a drawn sword gently leads Iphigeneia (also inscribed) toward an altar. To the rear another sword-bearing warrior (name lost, if there was one) follows. Iphigeneia here seems resigned, but scarcely enthusiastic, while the presence of Teukros in a commanding role suggests that the sacrifice was supported by the entire army. One other pot to be mentioned is a Red-Figure pyxis in the British Museum on which Iphigeneia stands in the doorway of her house, seemingly preparing for her wedding (London E773). Danae approaches to offer her something from a chest, and other figures in various domestic scenes labeled as Helen, Klytaimestra, and Kassandra confirm that the artist has conflated heroines from different stories to produce a series of unrelated vignettes. Once again there is no sign of Artemis, and thus no clue to Iphigeneia's actual fate.

Turning to the fifth century in literature, we find Pindar and Aischylos in agreement that the girl did die at Aulis, both authors using this fact as part of the motivation for Klytaimestra's subsequent wrath against her husband. Pindar alludes to the event in the course of his *Pythian* 11 (written probably in 474 B.C.),[28] asking whether Iphigeneia slaughtered far from her homeland or the pleasures of a stranger's bed did more to turn her mother to murder (*Py* 11.17–25). The verb employed for the slaying of Iphigeneia is again *sphazô*, as it was in the *Ehoiai*, and of course Klytaimestra's response shows her to believe her daughter dead, as she would not if Artemis had been seen to intervene at Aulis. The same holds true for Aischylos' *Agamemnon*, where a description of the sacrifice occupies much of the parodos, and the elders, who were present at Aulis ten years before, certainly suppose the victim dead (*Ag* 228–49). Probably we should expect no less, for the chain of transgression and revenge with which the *Oresteia* is concerned will lose a very important element if Iphigeneia is saved. But Aischylos' presentation of the sacrifice via the elders remains problematic all the same, and both Artemis' motive and Agamemnon's freedom of choice have triggered controversy. In contrast to the account of the *Kypria*, there is here no initial offense against the goddess, no boast or anything else to which the chorus can point as cause of the disaster. Instead we find at Aulis a new omen, two eagles that appear to the assembled army and proceed to devour a pregnant hare (*Ag* 109–20). Kalchas pronounces that Artemis is angry at this feast of the "hounds of the father," who are clearly Agamemnon and Menelaos, and prays that she will not block the expedition. Despite his appeal, the constraining winds do arise, and finally the seer is forced to reveal the one solution that will allow the fleet to sail. Agamemnon, after some hesitation and a speech that the chorus reports verbatim, consents; Iphigeneia is then slain (we are not told how she was brought to Aulis) in a most pitiable description, and the expedition's success is assured.

This lack of clear motivation on the part of Artemis has been quite variously explained: for some scholars the crux of the matter is a conflict between Artemis and her father, with Agamemnon a helpless victim caught in the middle, while for others the eagles' consumption of burgeoning new life symbolizes the indiscriminate destruction that Agamemnon will visit on Troy, and the goddess, anticipating his intent, commands him to begin the slaughter with his own child, if he can.[29] Artemis' purpose would thus be dissuasive, rather than vengeful, but not prohibitive; Agamemnon has the choice left open to him. Aischylos also composed a lost play entitled *Iphigeneia* about which we know absolutely nothing. Unless some other story concerning her has been lost, we must choose for the plot between a full-length treatment of the sacrifice and the Euripidean tale of Iphigeneia among the Tauroi, with her recovery by her brother Orestes. In the former case, we cannot even say whether Iphigeneia would have been killed or rescued by Artemis, since Aischylos' treatment of the myth in one play need not preclude a totally different version in another. Neither do we know whether the *Iphigeneia* was an independent play or part of a connected trilogy; similarly "orphaned" Aischylean titles such as the *Hiereiai* ("Priestesses") and *Thalamopoioi* ("Marriage-chamber Builders") might be brought together with it to form a continuous narrative of sacrifice and transfer to the Crimea,[30] but this is speculation of an extreme sort.

From later in the century we have a similarly lost *Iphigeneia* of Sophokles (where fragments do seem to guarantee that the subject was the sacrifice), plus references to the event in the same poet's *Elektra*, and then a description of both sacrifice and rescue in the parodos of Euripides' *Iphigeneia among the Tauroi* followed by a full dramatization of these events in the *Iphigeneia at Aulis* (produced posthumously). Of Sophokles' lost play we know for certain only that the stratagem of a marriage with Achilleus was employed to lure Iphigeneia to Aulis, since we have a line (almost certainly addressed to Klytaimestra, who must therefore have been a major character) mentioning the acquisition of a great son-in-law (fr 305 R). In his *Elektra*, the title figure attempts to justify her father's actions in a debate with Klytaimestra by recalling the crisis at Aulis (S: *El* 563–76). We are told here that Agamemnon was amusing himself in a precinct of Artemis and surprised a deer, which he succeeded in shooting, whereupon he uttered some sort of boast. The goddess, becoming extremely angry, determined that he should not leave until he had sacrificed his daughter, and so made it impossible for himself or the army to go anywhere, either to Troy or homeward, before the deed was carried out. Obviously, both these details are designed to exculpate Agamemnon by making the goddess seem unnecessarily vindictive and by giving the mortal no choice whatever, in contrast to Aischylos' *Agamemnon*. That Agamemnon was in a sanctuary of Artemis when he shot the deer may or may not have been a detail of the *Kypria* skipped over by Proklos' summary. The same holds for the notion that the army was totally trapped at Aulis, although I very much suspect that this is a Sophoklean invention of the moment to aid Elektra's argument. That Iphigeneia here actually dies, or is believed to die, is of course (as in Aischylos) necessary if Klytaimestra is to have any defense at all for her own actions.

In Euripides' *Iphigeneia among the Tauroi*, to take his earlier play first, yet another device is found to trigger the crisis as the army prepares to sail. The winds arise without explanation, and Kalchas then reveals that by failing to sacrifice Iphigeneia long before, Agamemnon has neglected to fulfill a vow once made to Artemis, that he would give her the most beautiful thing the year should bring forth, which for the year in question happens to have been his daughter, now long overdue (*IT* 15–25). Odysseus is dispatched to Argos with the ruse of a marriage to Achilleus, and Iphigeneia arrives at Aulis where the sacrifice is prepared. But Artemis takes her away and substitutes a deer without the knowledge of her father or any of those watching; thus Orestes, when he arrives in the land of the Tauroi to fetch the image of Artemis, has no notion that he will find his sister there, and the surprise is the greater. The effect of the new motivation is again to exonerate Agamemnon, since a vow once made to a god must be fulfilled, whether or not one wishes to sail to Troy. But it is of course a folktale motif, seen as well in the homecoming of Idomeneus, and may have been part of the story in some earlier version. Odysseus' role will become standard, as we might expect, since the bringing of Iphigeneia involves deception, and might be early, although here again Proklos' summary of the *Kypria* is not specific. We should note, too, that while Iphigeneia's stay among the Tauroi certainly goes back to the *Kypria*, she is in that work a goddess; Euripides' conception of her as a priestess sacrificing strangers to Artemis is surely a different matter, and not attested before this play (although it *may* have appeared in Aischylos).

In *Iphigeneia at Aulis* the situation is somewhat different, for now as in Aischylos the winds arise without any provocation, and Agamemnon may clearly (if he chooses) disband the expedition (*IA* 87–107, 352–53). But vanity and the promptings of his brother cause him to heed Kalchas' call for the offering of Iphigeneia to the goddess to whom that place is sacred, and thus he has informed Klytaimestra by letter of the supposed betrothal to Achilleus. Subsequently he repents of this deception and sends a second letter repudiating the first, but it is intercepted by Menelaos, who strongly rebukes Agamemnon for his weakness and lack of patriotism. Iphigeneia does then arrive, accompanied by Klytaimestra, and Menelaos weakens in his resolve; Agamemnon perceives, however, that with his daughter actually in camp Odysseus will surely reveal the prophecy to the troops, and they will then demand her death so that they might sail. He hopes to keep his wife ignorant of this until after the deed is done, but Achilleus, impatient for action and ignorant of the promise made in his name, comes to the tent when only Klytaimestra is there, and at her mention of the marriage the whole deception comes out. In his indignation, Achilleus at first declares that he will protect the girl single-handedly; his attempts to persuade the army, however, are unsuccessful, and he even risks being stoned as they clamor for war and Troy. Finally Iphigeneia herself resolves the situation by deciding that she will voluntarily surrender her life for the good of all concerned. She exits, and a messenger returns with a final speech describing to Klytaimestra the deer substituted for her daughter (some of this last material may have been rewritten from fragments in later times).[31] There is also a line of a speech by Artemis, concerning the deer, which has been attributed by Aelian to this play (*NA* 7.39); if that is correct, then (in a section now lost) the goddess appeared to Klytaimestra before the messenger came back and revealed to her the whole truth about her daughter's fate. Naturally there have also been suspicions that the whole ending is a post-Euripidean addition, and that the play as he wrote it did send Iphigeneia to her death. But with such a playwright we are never likely to be very sure of anything.

Our sources subsequent to the fifth century are, as usual, Apollodoros and Hyginus. The former offers the same reason for Artemis' anger as the *Kypria*, that on shooting a deer Agamemnon had boasted to be her equal, but also a curious variant on the *Iphigeneia among the Tauroi*, namely that Atreus had failed to give the goddess the golden lamb after promising her the finest thing in his flocks (*ApE* 3.21–22). Agamemnon here sends Odysseus and Talthybios to Argos with the fabricated betrothal, and they bring back Iphigeneia. Sacrifice and rescue also follow the lines of the *Kypria*, but while that work had Artemis take the girl to the Tauroi and make her immortal, Apollodoros has Iphigeneia either among the Tauroi (as a priestess) *or* immortal. Probably this reflects influence from Euripides, who as we saw has a different idea of Iphigeneia's life among the Tauroi from that of the *Kypria*. Hyginus, too, gives the motive of the slain deer and consequent boast as the cause of the trouble (*Fab* 98). At Kalchas' subsequent prophecy Agamemnon himself wavers, but Odysseus comes up with the scheme of the marriage deception, and he and Diomedes here make the journey to Argos for the girl. She is again rescued with a deer as substitute and taken to the Taurian land to become a priestess. Given the presence of deer and Odysseus as executor of the ruse, Hyginus cannot here be drawing from either of Euripides' plays exclusively, or even both together. Odysseus as creator of the marriage deception *might* go back to Sophokles' *Iphigeneia*, where Odysseus is a character, but in that work Klytaimestra seems to have come to Aulis, as she does not in Hyginus; perhaps we should think instead of Aischylos or even the *Kypria*. A quite different outcome of the sacrifice appears in Diktys, who bypasses the miraculous by having Achilleus save Iphigeneia and entrust her to the conveniently present king of the Scythians (Dik 1.22). What more might have passed between rescuer and rescuee in such an account we cannot say, but for the third-century (?) b.c. historian Douris (76F88 apud ΣbT *Il* 19.326) and Lykophron (324), Neoptolemos is the son of Iphigeneia; Douris appears to add that she was taken (by Achilleus) to Skyros and left there. Her career as a priestess in the Crimea, and her return to Greece with Orestes, we will return to in chapter 17.

As one final curiosity to mention in connection with the Achaians' departure for Troy, Odysseus' impersonation of Aithon (a younger brother of Idomeneus) during his interview with Penelope in *Odyssey* 19 brings with it the tale that the real Odysseus was on his way to Troy when he was blown off course at Cape Maleia and driven to Krete (*Od* 19.172–202). There, "Aithon" says, Odysseus found Idomeneus already departed for Troy some ten days before, and left himself after he had enjoyed the local hospitality and the north winds had diminished. Conceivably, the *Odyssey* means that both men were on their way to Aulis in order to mobilize for Troy, but that is not really what the text (twice) says. More likely, Aulis has been forgotten for the moment in order to make this tale of an encounter with Odysseus plausible, but we must admit the possibility of a version in which the Achaians first assembled at Troy, or somewhere nearby.

The Journey to Troy: Philoktetes and Tennes With the expedition finally launched (for a second time), the Achaians now make their way over to Troy with relatively little trouble or incident. The *Kypria* (or rather, as always, our epitome) notes only two stopovers, Tenedos, where Philoktetes is bitten by the snake while the troops are feasting, and Lemnos, where he is left behind because of the smell of the wound; there is also a quarrel between Agamemnon and Achilleus, the latter "having been invited late," but the summary does not make absolutely clear at which of the two stops this took place. If "invited late" means (as one would assume) to a feast, we might logically suppose it to be the one on Tenedos during which Philoktetes is bitten. On the other hand, Agamemnon's speech of reproach to the troops in *Iliad* 8, when he reminds them of their boasts of military valor while they ate and drank on Lemnos (*Il* 8.228–34), would seem to indicate a feast here too. But Aristotle in the *Rhetoric* makes reference to Achilleus' anger at not being invited to dinner on Tenedos (*Rhet* 2.24), and he of course will be drawing from some complete work, not an ambiguous summary. Of any further details of the quarrel Proklos says nothing, and even the *Iliad* has no allusion to it. Possibly relevant, however, is a passage in *Odyssey* 8, when the Phaiacians' singer Demodokos offers the tale of a quarrel between Achilleus and Odysseus (at a banquet) at which Agamemnon rejoices, having been told something by Apollo at Delphi which leads him to believe that this signals the beginning of disaster for the Trojans (*Od* 8.75–82).

On the surface these would seem to be two separate quarrels, and the scholia agree, making this latter tale one of an Achaian discussion at Troy, after Hektor's death, on how best to take the city. But in Plutarch's *Moralia*, we read that in Sophokles Odysseus once incited Achilleus by claiming that the latter's professed anger over a dinner was really a ruse to conceal his fear of battle and Hektor, now that he had seen the walls of Troy (*Mor* 74a). Possibly this is still another dinner, but it sounds very much as if the Achaians have just arrived at (or near) Troy, and Hektor is clearly still alive. Perhaps then, at the feast on Tenedos, Achilleus is originally angry with Agamemnon because of the late invitation and threatens to leave, but then becomes embroiled in an argument with Odysseus when the latter tries (successfully, as matters prove) to taunt him into staying with accusations of cowardice. Unfortunately, Plutarch does not name the play of Sophokles from which he quotes; it may have been the *Syndeipnoi* (probably satyric) or the *Syllogos Achaiôn,* if these are not two titles for the same play. To this whole reconstruction one might, I suppose, object that Agamemnon has little reason to rejoice in the first year of the war. But it is technically the beginning of troubles for the Trojans, and then too Agamemnon may have misinterpreted an oracle referring in fact to his own dispute with Achilleus nine years later.

From quarrels we turn to the unfortunate Philoktetes. In the *Iliad's* Catalogue of Ships we find much the same story given by the *Kypria,* that the hero, son of Poias and here leader of a contingent of seven ships from the territories around Mount Pelion, was bitten by a snake and consequently abandoned by the Achaians on the island of Lemnos in great pain (*Il* 2.716–25). But Homer does not say anything about where he was bitten, or why, only that the Achaians will eventually come back to get him. This same passage plus a reference by Odysseus in the *Odyssey* (8.219–20) also establishes Philoktetes' skills as an archer, and we have seen in chapter 13 the tradition that he or his father Poias received the bow of Herakles upon the latter's death. But we have no other information at all about him until the fifth century, when Pindar gives him a brief mention (as one whom great heroes will bring back from Lemnos to sack Troy: *Py* 1.50–55), and Aischylos, Sophokles, and Euripides all write plays about the Achaians' return to Lemnos to fetch him. Of these only Sophokles' effort survives, and since it was produced in 409 B.C. it was probably the latest of the three. All three gave some background regarding the cause of the abandonment, to judge from Dion of Prusa's discussion of their plots (DP 52), but of Aischylos' version of these events he offers nothing. For Euripides, thanks to his paraphrase of the prologue, we know that Philoktetes was bitten when he showed the other Greeks the altar of Chryse, where it was necessary that they sacrifice if they were to win the war (DP 59). In Sophokles we find that Philoktetes has been bitten on/at Chryse (*Ph* 263–70), and Neoptolemos later adds that the snake in question was a sacred one guarding the unroofed shrine of the divinity Chryse (*Ph* 1326–28).

Already in about 460 B.C., Hermonax shows this moment on a stamnos, with Philoktetes lying on the ground, Achilleus, Agamemnon, and Diomedes looking on in alarm, and the statue of Chryse (named) off to one side (Louvre G413). The location of the Homeric Chryse has always been a problem, but Pausanias speaks of the wounding taking place on a small island named Chryse near Lemnos which had sunk into the sea before his own time (8.33.4). As to the cause of such a change in geography from that of the *Kypria* we can only speculate, but if Euripides and Sophokles do mean the same place as Pausanias, they (or an earlier tradition) might have been motivated by the seeming illogicality of taking a man wounded on Tenedos all the way back to Lemnos in order to abandon him. The A scholia at *Iliad* 2.722 solve this problem more simply by locating the incident on Lemnos itself; here Philoktetes is cleansing the sacred precinct (again of Chryse) when the snake strikes. For Hyginus, who also places the wounding on Lemnos, the cause is rather Hera's anger because Philoktetes aided in the cremation of Herakles; thus she sends the snake expressly to bite him (*Fab* 102). Apollodoros seems considerably closer to the *Kypria* (as often) in his account, for there the attack is again on Tenedos, with the snake crawling out from the altar while the heroes are sacrificing to Apollo (Ap*E* 3.27). Both the stench of the wound and Philoktetes' cries are cited as the reason for the abandonment, as in Sophokles; Odysseus takes him to Lemnos on orders of Agamemnon.

For another quite different version of the wound we have Servius and the Vatican Mythographers (Σ *Aen* 3.402; VM I 59, II 165). These all relate the same story, that Herakles wished no one to know where his mortal remains lay, and extracted a promise from Philoktetes to that effect. When the other Achaians pressed Philoktetes for that information later, not believing Herakles dead, he stamped on the ground with his foot to indicate the place, hoping thus to maintain his oath. But on the way to Troy an arrow (poisoned with the Hydra's blood) accidentally fell from his quiver and struck the offending foot as payment for the transgression. The Lykophron scholia repeat the tale of the *Iliad* scholia that Philoktetes was cleaning an altar (of Athena), but they also know one in which Chryse is a Nymph who falls in love with Philoktetes and has him bitten by the snake when he rebuffs her advances (Σ Lyk 911). Whether any of these stories are early we cannot say, although they perhaps show a developing pattern of attempts to find clearer reasons for Philoktetes' misfortune. His subsequent rescue and deeds at Troy we shall return to toward the end of this chapter.

One other tale that must be placed in this time frame of the voyage to Troy survives only in Lykophron (allusive as usual) and later authors—Konon, Diodoros, Apollodoros, Plutarch, Pausanias, and scholia. Lykophron tells us that two children died together with their father, who was killed by a millstone; he then adds that these children had narrowly escaped death before when they were cast adrift in a chest by a gull-reared father who believed the lies of a flute-player (Lyk 232–42). There follows mention of someone who forgot to declare the commands of a goddess mother, and died by the sword. As Konon tells this story, one Kyknos ruler in the Troad (as we will see, probably not the ally of the Trojans slain by Achilleus) has two children, Tennes and Hemithea, but upon the death of their mother he remarries, and the new wife, becoming enamored of Tennes and being rejected, falsely accuses him (26F1.28). As in all such stories the father is convinced, and locks both Tennes and Hemithea (when she sides with her brother) in a chest that is thrown into the sea. It drifts to an island known as Leukophrys where the inhabitants rescue it and make Tennes their king, renaming the place Tenedos in his honor. Subsequently Kyknos arrives to ask forgiveness, but as he speaks from his ship Tennes takes an axe and cuts the hawser cables to prevent him from landing.

Diodoros confirms most of this except the last, adding that a flute-player had supported the slanders of Tennes' stepmother and that Tennes himself was killed by Achilleus when the Achaians sacked Tenedos on their way to Troy (DS 5.83.4–5). Apollodoros gives the name of the first wife as Prokleia (daughter of Laomedon) and the second as Philonome; the flute-player is identified as Eumolpos (ApE 3.25–26). The story then proceeds as in Konon, save that instead of coming to Tenedos after he learns the truth Kyknos puts both wife and flute-player to death. More to the point for present purposes, we hear that Thetis has warned Achilleus not to slay Tennes (actually the son of Apollo according to some) lest he himself die by Apollo's hand. But as the Achaians approach the island Tennes tries to ward them off with stones, and Achilleus kills him with his sword. Plutarch offers an elaboration of this same motif: Thetis not only warns Achilleus, but charges a servant to remind him of the warning should the occasion arise (*Mor* 297d-f). As the Achaians are ravaging Tenedos, Achilleus comes upon Tennes' sister, who is extremely beautiful, but Tennes interposes himself to save her and is slain. When Achilleus realizes what he has done, and the fact that the servant though present failed to stop him, he kills the man, and buries his fallen opponent. The first part of the story is here only briefly told, but the flute-player is called Molpos. Pausanias gives us almost exactly the same tale as Konon, with the addition of the names of the two wives as given by Apollodoros, and Poseidon claimed as Kyknos' father (10.14.1–4).

In the Lykophron scholia, Kyknos is the son of Poseidon and one Skamandrodike, who abandons her child near the shore, to be found by a swan and then kindly fisherman (Σ Lyk 232). Here too when grown he marries Prokleia, daughter of Laomedon, and then a second wife Phylonome, leading to the story of the chest and the arrival of the children on Leukophrys. But as we have seen, none of the versions recounted so far will allow Achilleus to slay father and both children in the same place, as Lykophron implies. Whether from other sources or just guessing, the scholia on this point maintain that upon discovering the truth about his children Kyknos came to Tenedos and lived with them, and that Hemithea died when the earth swallowed her up as Achilleus was pursuing her. One other novelty is that the servant who fails to advise Achilleus is called Mnemon, and his crime is the greater because it is fated that Achilleus die soon after he has killed a son of Apollo, as Tennes here is. One wonders if Apollo's sometime paternity of Hektor and Troilos was used to activate the same motif. As for Kyknos himself, we will see below that the Kyknos whom Achilleus slays at Troy is sometimes killed with a stone, but that hero has intimations of invulnerability about him, and Lykophron has probably conflated aspects of the two (although they may well go back to a single original).

How early this story of children cast adrift and arriving on Tenedos might be is, as usual, uncertain. The absence of any reference to the killing of Tennes in Proklos' summary could indicate that it was not a part of the *Kypria*, but we really have very little means of controlling how complete that summary is. Several uncertain references suggest that Euripides or Kritias (fr 21 Aus = 43 fr 20 Sn), and perhaps as well Aischylos,[32] may have written plays entitled *Tennes*. The first of these works, for which a fragmentary hypothesis does exist, apparently recounted the Potiphar's wife adventure in the home of Kyknos, with the stepmother finally put to death and Apollo ordering the island to be called Tenedos; the second, far less certain, is conjectured to have related rather the hero's defense of his island.

To the tale of Tennes we should add briefly that of Trambelos, whom we saw in chapter 13 to have been a son of Telamon and a Trojan captive Theaneira. Istros, who with Lykophron (467) is the earliest to mention him, says that he was slain by Achilleus during a raid on Miletos, and that Achilleus on discovering his identity built a tumulus for him (334F57). Parthenios relates in addition to this a story from Euphorion that Trambelos fell in love with one Apriate on Lesbos; she resisted and died either at his hands or while trying to flee him; his own subsequent death is here seen as punishment for that deed (Par 26 = fr 27 Pow).

The Landing: Protesilaos, Kyknos, and the Embassy to Troy

At this point in our epitome of the *Kypria* we are told simply that the Greeks attempted to land on the shores of Troy, that the Trojans opposed them, with Hektor killing Protesilaos, and that Achilleus then took charge of the situation, slaying Kyknos, son of Poseidon, and routing the Trojans. As in the case of Philoktetes, the Catalogue of Ships has an entry for Protesilaos, son of Iphiklos and thus first cousin to Philoktetes, even though he is no longer alive to lead his contingent: the poet tells us that he died at the hands of a "Dardanian man," being the first to leap down from the ships, and that he left behind a wife tearing both cheeks and a home only half-completed (*Il* 2.698–702). There is no trace here of either a prophecy or a wife whose husband visits her one last time after his death. Pausanias does tell us that in the *Kypria* the wife's name is Polydore, daughter of Meleagros (4.2.7), so that poem may have told something of her story, but on the other hand in all those later accounts where we do find the tale of Protesilaos' last visit she is called Laodameia. Sophokles wrote a (lost) *Poimenes* that recounted in some way the events of the landing and the death of Protesilaos at the hands of Hektor, but this seems to have been told from the viewpoint of the Trojans, and to have included as well the exploits of Kyknos (frr 497, 500, 501 R). The earliest preserved trace of the tale of what followed his death is Euripides' lost *Protesilaos,* in which, as a scholiast tells us, the protagonist after just one day of marriage is summoned to join the expedition for Troy (p. 563 N²). He is the first to touch shore, as in the *Kypria,* and dies, but appeals to the gods of the Underworld and is allowed one more day to spend with his wife. Fragments of the play seem to indicate that this is prologue, and that the drama showed the actual day of his return, with probably (as we shall see below) Laodameia's suicide when he finally departs. Laodameia's father Akastos would also seem to have been a character, perhaps trying to exhort his daughter to remarry.

After the fifth century we have Ovid's *Heroides* with a letter from Laodameia to her husband after he has departed for Aulis (*Her* 13), and Loukianos' version of Protesilaos' overtures to Hades in the Underworld (*DMor* 28), but no further information until Apollodoros. Here we learn for the first time that Thetis has warned Achilleus not to be the first to disembark at Troy, since the first to land will be the first to die (*ApE* 3.29–30). Instead, Protesilaos (who, it would seem, does not know the oracle) is the first, and after killing a number of Trojans is slain by Hektor. His wife Laodameia in grief then has a statue made in his likeness with which she "associates" (*prosomileô,* often used in a sexual sense). The gods observing this behavior take pity on her, and Hermes brings Protesilaos back from Hades. Laodameia believes him restored to her alive from Troy; when Hermes comes for him and she realizes the truth she kills herself. Obviously the last part of this is a bit unclear, perhaps because the epitomator of Apollodoros has omitted something. Hyginus also relates the prophecy that whoever landed first at Troy would die, but in his account this fact is clearly general knowledge, for when all the others hesitate Protesilaos takes the initiative, paying with his life at Hektor's hands (*Fab* 103). The strange notion here that Protesilaos was actually Iolaos, son of Iphiklos, and renamed only after his valorous sacrifice, presumably means that the mythographer has confused two figures of similar parentage (Iphiklos, Iphikles) who both receive favors from the gods regarding their mortality (resurrection, rejuvenation). He goes on to relate that Laodameia requested the return of her husband for a period of three hours. When Hermes finally led him away, she despaired and caused a bronze (or waxen?) statue in his image to be made, which she embraced and took with her to bed (*Fab* 104). After this fact was discovered by a servant, who mistakenly believed he had caught her with a lover, her father learned the truth and ordered the statue burned to spare her further pain, but she threw herself on the pyre constructed for it and died.

Following close upon the death of Protesilaos in the *Kypria*, as we saw above, comes the death of Kyknos on the Trojan side, slain by Achilleus; our epitome notes nothing unusual about this seemingly normal battlefield event. Homer does not mention Kyknos, while Pindar, who does, simply reiterates that Achilleus killed him (*Ol* 2.82; *Is* 5.39). To judge from a remark by the character of Euripides in Aristophanes' *Batrachoi* (962–63), Aischylos may have brought him on stage, but we do not know in what play, or if his whole story was dramatized. Sophokles included him in his *Poimenes* (as a rather brash character: fr 501 R), and that play may actually have focused on his arrogance and death. One curious fragment says that "neither bronze nor iron takes hold of (someone's) flesh" (fr 500 R), so that probably we have already here the idea of Kyknos' invulnerability. In any case, such an idea, whether Sophoklean or not, is confirmed by a chance remark of Aristotle, who tells us in the *Rhetoric* that Kyknos prevented the whole army of the Achaians from landing, and was unwoundable (*Rhet* 2.22.12). How he was nevertheless slain is perhaps explained by Ovid, who has him strangled by Achilleus with the straps from his own helmet after attempts to pierce him with spear or sword have failed (*Met* 12.72–144). But in Apollodoros (where nothing is said of invulnerability) Achilleus slays Kyknos with the cast of a stone (ApE 3.31), so that perhaps in early versions the latter's protection against harm covered only bronze and iron (keeping in mind fr 500 R above), or else objects that cut. Either way, the magical element would be quite appropriate for the Epic Cycle, but with no help at all from Proklos we cannot say more than that. Another rather unusual detail seems to have been provided by Hellanikos, who according to a scholiast related that Kyknos was white with respect to his skin from birth (i.e., an albino?: 4F148); the same scholiast notes that somewhere in the Hesiodic Corpus it is simply his head (*kephalê*: hair?) which is white (Hes fr 237 MW). All sources seem to agree that Kyknos was a son of Poseidon, although there is nothing to link him with the similarly named son of Poseidon whom we have met as father of Tennes.

With the Achaians now successfully in command of the beach at Troy, the *Kypria* proceeds to the sending of an embassy into the city to demand the return of Helen. Some later accounts (including Apollodoros: see below) place this request earlier, when the Greeks are still at Tenedos, but the event remains essentially the same. Antenor mentions it in *Iliad* 3, when he supports Helen's assessment of Odysseus by recalling how that hero and Menelaos had come and stayed in his house when they addressed all the Trojans on the question of Helen's return (*Il* 3.205–24). The mission apparently involved some danger, for we learn in *Iliad* 11 that Antimachos, having been bribed by Paris' gold to oppose their request, urged the assembled Trojans to slay Menelaos on the spot rather than allowing him to return to the Greek camp (*Il* 11.122–42). Neither the *Iliad* nor our *Kypria* epitome assigns to Antenor any special role in preventing this action, but we will see below that the Epic Cycle was probably familiar with that detail. A Late Corinthian krater of the early sixth century now in the Vatican offers us a tableau of the embassy: Menelaos, Odysseus, and Talthybios sit to the left on a gradated tier of seats while Theano (Antenor's wife) and attendants come to meet them (Vat K40099). Horsemen follow, some named, but there is surprisingly no sign of Antenor himself. In any case, these are obviously formalities of welcome preliminary to the actual request for Helen.

Turning to the fifth century, we find in the corpus of Bakchylides a fragmentary dithyramb entitled "The Antenoridai, or the Demand for Helen" (Bak 15). Here too Theano is prominently positioned, for the poem begins (somewhat abruptly) by speaking of her as a priestess of Athena who does something (edges of text missing) for Odysseus and Menelaos. There are then apparently speeches by one or more of these parties in a lacuna, after which the sons of Antenor must have led the embassy to the Trojans' agora; Antenor himself proceeds to alert Priam to the proposal about to be offered, while heralds summon the people to the assembly. These as they gather pray to the gods, and it seems that they desire respite from their sufferings, but the final section of the poem (if it is complete) is devoted entirely to Menelaos' speech, in which he contrasts Dike with Hybris, the ruin of the Gigantes, and suggests that it is open to the Trojans to save themselves from their sufferings. Obviously they fail to do so, and the poem was probably meant to draw impact from the contrast between what we see and what we know will follow, as often in Bakchylides.

Sophokles' lost drama *Helenes Apaitesis* ("The Request for Helen") seems likely to have brought on stage the whole story, including perhaps the proposal to murder Menelaos, but we have no real evidence for any part of its plot, and just possibly it dramatized instead the attempt to recover Helen from Egypt. On the other hand, in the same poet's *Aias Lokros*, there is certainly a reference to a leopardskin placed on the door of Antenor's house (fr 11 R; cf. Str 13.1.53). The bT scholia to *Iliad* 3.205–6, where the embassy comes from Tenedos, say that Antenor not only offered hospitality but actually saved the ambassadors when they were about to be treacherously slain, and that in gratitude Agamemnon placed a leopardskin on his door during the sack of Troy in token that this house should be spared; we find this same idea of leopardskin and safety for the family in Polygnotos' painting of the Trojan Sack for the Knidian Lesche at Delphi (Paus 10.27.3), so that it is very likely older than the fifth century. This last conclusion is perhaps reinforced by the fact that in the *Little Iliad* Odysseus carries a wounded Helikaon, son of Antenor, out of danger during the night assault (Paus 10.26.8), although such an action might conceivably have been motivated simply by bonds of guest-friendship. The safeguarding of Antenor's family is a theme that appears again, although in the altered form that the Greeks spared these people because they supported the return of Helen, at the very beginning of Livy's history of Rome. Apollodoros, like the *Iliad* scholia, deviates from the *Kypria* in having the embassy set out from Tenedos, before the Greeks have landed on the shores of Troy; like the *Iliad* scholia, too, he has Antenor save Menelaos and Odysseus when they are threatened with death

(ApE 3.28–29). He does not in the epitomator's account of the sack report any formal amnesty for Antenor, but we are told that Odysseus and Menelaos saved Antenor's son Glaukos (ApE 5.21), so that some such theme may have appeared in the full version.

Achilleus and the Early Years of the War

Next in the *Kypria* comes Achilleus' desire to actually see Helen (suggesting here again that epic tradition did not think of him as one of the original suitors). We are told simply that Aphrodite and Thetis brought them into the same place, with no further detail. Presumably, Aphrodite led Helen secretly out of Troy to a place where Thetis was waiting (in equal secrecy) with her son, but this is a guess. No other source so much as mentions this story, but we do have a curious remark in Lykophron, where Kassandra prophesies that Helen shall have five husbands—Theseus, Menelaos, Paris, Deiphobos, and Achilleus, whom she causes to toss and turn upon his bed at Troy as he sees her in his dreams (Lyk 139–74). Since the same lines also describe Achilleus as the future husband of Medeia, Lykophron cannot be thinking here of a union with Helen in Elysion (such as we find in Pausanias). Whether in that case he supposed a rendezvous as in the *Kypria*, with erotic consequences, I do not know; both the scholia to this passage (Σ Lyk 143) and those to the *Iliad* at 3.140 (b only) claim that Achilleus was Helen's fifth husband "in a dream," surely a strange notion. At *Iliad* 19.325, for what it is worth, Achilleus calls Helen *rhigedanê*, "chilling," but of course the whole situation of the *Iliad* requires from him a certain lack of enthusiasm for the goals of the war.

After this encounter, the *Kypria* presents an otherwise totally unrecorded event, namely that the army revolted and wished to return home, but was held back by Achilleus. That this particular hero, who had himself earlier threatened to leave, should play such a role may seem odd; perhaps we are to think that his viewing of Helen has inspired him to remain and win her back. No reason is given for the army's action; possibly supplies were short, and this was the point at which Agamemnon decided to send for the daughters of Anios, if in fact the *Kypria* contained that story. On the other hand, the arrival of those daughters now would eliminate all difficulties in finding provisions, and the next event in the poem is Achilleus' seizure of the cattle of Aineias, followed by the sack of Lyrnessos (both incidents alluded to in *Il* 21), plus Pedasos and other of the nearby cities. From *Iliad* 2 we learn that Briseis was acquired at Lyrnessos, where Mynes and Epistrophos, the sons of Euenos Selepiades, were slain (*Il* 2.688–93). Briseis' own speech in *Iliad* 19 adds that Mynes was the king of Lyrnessos, and that her husband (perhaps this same Mynes) was also one of Achilleus' victims (*Il* 19.295–96).

The other city that we know from the *Iliad* to have been sacked is Thebe, the home of Andromache's father Eetion, who perished on that day with his seven sons, although Achilleus allowed Andromache's mother to be ransomed back (*Il* 1.366–67; 6.414–28). From somewhere in this general raid Chryseis too emerges as part of the booty; the scholia suggest that the people of Chryse had all fled to the better-defended Thebe because of the war (ΣA *Il* 3.366), or else that Chryseis was visiting Iphinoe, sister of Eetion, on the occasion of a sacrifice to Artemis and thus was captured (bT scholia ad loc.). Whatever the *Iliad* in fact supposed, Eustathios tells us that the visit-and-sacrifice version appeared in the *Kypria* (although he also notes that in other accounts she was a native of Thebe: *Kyp* fr 28 *PEG*). Achilleus himself in *Iliad* 9 refers to a total of eleven cities that he has captured on land, in addition to twelve by sea (*Il* 9.328–29); he gives no names, although earlier in the same book Agamemnon mentions Lesbos in this latter category (*Il* 9.128–30), and further on we find Skyros as well (if this is, in fact, the island: *Il* 9.666–68); we have already seen possibilities for Tenedos and perhaps Lemnos. Pedasos is a site occupied by Trojan allies at *Iliad* 6.33–35; the scholia assign to the Hesiodic Corpus the tale that Achilleus besieged this town, aided by a maiden of the community who became enamored of him and sent a message advising that water supplies were low (Hes fr 214 MW). The taking of Lesbos presumably preceded Odysseus' wrestling contest with someone there at *Odyssey* 4.324, if the two poems know the same story. In later times the list and range of territory covered was predictably expanded; thus in Apollodoros we find such places as Smyrna, Klazomenai, and Kolophon.

Troilos and Lykaon

Our *Kypria* summary closes its one sentence noting all the places that Achilleus sacked with the laconic remark that Achilleus also "slew Troilos," as if it were of little consequence in itself and, moreover, somehow related to the raids of surrounding territory. From our other sources this seems not the case, but the fact remains that our epitomator was not very interested in this episode, or else wished to pass over it quickly. The *Iliad* does speak of Troilos, but just barely: Priam in Book 24 lists him among those of his sons who have perished, and calls him "delighting in horses," but this is all we learn. For the entire remainder of the Archaic period our only certain literary evidence is a casual reference in Ibykos' Polykrates poem, where Troilos' beauty is stressed (282a.40–45 *PMG*), and a line from an unnamed play of Phrynichos speaking of the "light of love glowing on his reddening cheeks" (3 fr 13 Sn). But Ibykos probably told elsewhere of Troilos' slaying outside the city walls, to judge from the commentary in an Oxyrhunchus papyrus scrap (224 *SLG*). To the citation with the above information the commentator adds that [Achilleus] lay in wait for Troilos and slew him outside the walls of Troy, in the Thymbraion precinct; it is not clear, however, whether this detail might be drawn from Ibykos' poem, or simply appended to it as a clarification from other sources. In any case, the Thymbraion we know from other authors to have been an area sacred to Apollo,[33] since Thymbra in the Troad formed the basis for one of his cult titles, and we will see later that this detail may be significant.

Early vase-painting and other artwork presents quite a wealth of material covering several different phases of the exploit, although of course this evidence cannot speak to the most important question of all, Achilleus' motive in slaying an essentially helpless and unoffending opponent. The earliest of these illustrations is conceivably a Protocorinthian aryballos of the seventh century on which a warrior in armor walks behind an unarmed man on horseback, but there is no certainty that pursuit is involved here (London 1969.12–15.1). The contrary is, however, the case on a subsequent Protocorinthian aryballos of about 650 B.C. where the name "Troilos" and part of the name "Achilleus" are painted in (Kanellopoulos Coll 1319). Here Troilos (spear or sword in hand) rides off rapidly to the left as Achilleus behind him pursues on foot. In metalworking, we have a bronze tripod-leg relief from the end of the seventh century and two shield-band reliefs from the first quarter of the sixth century at Olympia. On the tripod leg, although the upper right corner is missing, a large, fully armed warrior seizes the hair of a much smaller figure, as the latter seeks to climb a set of stairs, and menaces him with a sword (Olympia B 3600). On the first of the shield-bands we see a young boy, naked, crouching on a raised platform with his left arm around a slender tree (B 988). His right arm is caught by the wrist and raised high in the air by the figure to his left, an armed warrior with helmet and breastplate who seems (once again) intent on dispatching the boy with his sword. Conceivably, both these scenes could represent the death of Astyanax, or indeed any young Trojan victim on the night of Troy's fall, but the child is rather old for our usual understanding of Hektor's son, and the platform would seem likely meant as an altar, an element that will emerge as central to Troilos' story. The second shield-relief offers much the same picture, but the tree is gone, the boy now faces his assailant, and the platform has clearly become a formal altar; moreover, there is a cock sitting upon it (B 1912). This last element inevitably causes one to think of the tradition (preserved only very much later) of Achilleus' sexual passion for Troilos, with the cock here as love gift; to dismiss it as nothing more than a coincidence here is difficult, to accept such a theme this early perhaps equally so.[34]

Of Attic vase-paintings there are quite a number beginning about this same time, c. 575 B.C., with the earliest also the most famous, the band directly below the Wedding of Peleus and Thetis on the François Krater. To the left in this band is a fountain house behind which stand Apollo and a young Trojan who is collecting water in a hydria. Before the same fountain, to the right, are one Rhodia and Thetis, then Hermes with his head turned back toward Thetis, then Athena. This last figure has her left hand held out at her side as if in encouragement, and indeed in the center of the band a running figure (upper body and name lost) is pursuing a mounted Troilos, who is beardless, clad in tunic, and riding one of two horses galloping in tandem. Below these horses is a hydria on its side; to the right, in front of them, a running woman, for whom the upper body and name are again lost, save for two letters of the latter which are probably enough to guarantee her as Polyxena. The object of their haste, as pictured on the far right, is Troy; before the walls we see Antenor turning back and gesturing to a seated Priam, while emerging from a gate in the walls are Hektor and Polites in hoplite armor. A simpler form of the same scene appears on a Siana cup by the C Painter dating to about 570 B.C.: to the left the fountain house, then the armed Achilleus in pursuit of Troilos and the two horses, the fallen hydria (here between Achilleus' legs), and to the far right Polyxena (NY 01.8.6; no names given). A second Siana cup by the same artist shows a slightly earlier moment: although Troilos has already wheeled his horse around to flee and Polyxena starts away in fright, Achilleus is crouched behind the fountain house, demonstrating that he has hidden there to ambush his prey (Louvre CA 6113).

As the century progresses, we see these same basic elements over and over again on numerous Attic Black-Figure pots and a few non-Attic examples, including a Middle Corinthian bottle with ambush and fountain house (signed by Timonidas: Athens 277) and a Late Corinthian amphora on which Troilos turns to aim a bow at Achilleus while the latter prepares to hurl his spear (Zurich ETH 4).[35] Since the fountain house is not the same as an altar (and Troilos runs *away* from it in any case), these scenes would appear to indicate that Achilleus here catches Troilos and pulls him off his horse, in contrast to the version of the Olympia bronze reliefs (and other depictions noted below) where the slaying and altar are joined. Illustrations of the actual moment of overtaking are rare, but this phase of the action does appear on one of the Etruscan Loeb Tripods now in Munich (SL 66: tripod B), as well as on a Pontic amphora in the Louvre (E703). In both cases, Achilleus seizes the hapless Troilos by the hair to drag him down to his doom. On another Pontic amphora, however, he has Troilos slung over his shoulder, and appears to be carrying him toward an altar while mounted warriors pursue (Reading 47 VI 1). Possibly, therefore, the full form of the story had Troilos taken from his horse to the Thymbraion to be killed there (as a deliberate insult to Apollo?); perhaps he was even riding toward that precinct in hope of sanctuary, and Achilleus, catching him just before he got there, took him into the precinct to demonstrate his contempt for Troy's gods. But we cannot exclude the possibility that altar and fountain house represent two quite different versions of the story that have (on the Reading amphora) become confused.

As for the more precise details of these scenes, some of the above-mentioned examples show Troilos holding several spears, and wearing a cloak or tunic or both, but on only one occasion does he have any kind of defensive armor (a helmet and shield, plus a sword, on a cup by Oltos: Louvre G18). In the great majority of cases we see two horses, as on the François Krater, rather than just one; we will return to this point shortly. Achilleus waiting in ambush behind the fountain house (rather than in pursuit) is shown on quite a number of the pots, on a metope from Heraion I at Foce del Sele (no #) (Troilos lacking, but see below), and possibly on one of the poros pediments from the sixth-century Athenian Akropolis (Akropolis 52). The vase-paintings present quite a consistent picture: Achilleus in armor crouching behind the vertical façade of the fountain (which is usually fitted out with a lion waterspout) while on the other side Polyxena prepares to fill her jug as a mounted and undefended Troilos waits with the two horses. A bird often perches on top of the fountain, but whether he was a traditional decorative element or a part of the narrative we cannot say. One additional detail on two Lakonian representations is the presence of a snake at Achilleus' feet (VG 106349, Troilos and Polyxena in exergue; the second, from Samos, lost);[36] in neither instance does it seem to concern him, and it is probably a guardian of the spring. We have already considered yet a third such cup on which the warrior actually aims his spear at the snake as more likely part of the story of Kadmos (Louvre E669; see chapter 14).

Of the manner of Troilos' death there is also some sixth-century information via Attic Black-Figure. Two Tyrrhenian amphoras of about 570 B.C. agree on the grimmest detail, that Achilleus has decapitated his victim, and done so at what is again unmistakably an altar. On the tamer of these, Achilleus holds the severed head by the hair, as if to hurl it at the Trojans (Hektor, Aineias, Agenor) who approach from the other side of the altar; the headless corpse slumps on the ground (Florence 70993). The second amphora offers essentially the same scene: Troilos' head now appears to be impaled on the point of Achilleus' spear as he aims it at the advancing Trojans, but perhaps we are to understand that it is in midair, having already been thrown by Achilleus (Munich 1426). Here Hermes and Athena stand behind Achilleus; Hektor is now joined by Aineias and Deithynos. Nor is this a notion confined to the Tyrrhenian series of Attic pots: a band cup of about 560 B.C. shows Achilleus holding Troilos by the leg with one hand while he raises the head in the other as if to throw it at his opponents (PrColl, Basel), and a memorable hydria of the Leagros group offers Troilos' corpse beginning to fall to the ground as Achilleus strides upward on the altar to brandish the head at the attacking Trojans (London B326). A Middle Corinthian column krater may illustrate the stage just prior to this, for Achilleus here holds up the intact body by the foot (over an altar) as Hektor, Aineias, and other Trojans close in (Louvre E638). Attic Red-Figure has none of this; the emphasis falls entirely on the pursuit of the horse, with a cup by the Brygos Painter showing once again Achilleus seizing Troilos' hair in order to pull him from his mount (Louvre G154); on numerous other examples the Achaian's outstretched hand has Troilos almost within reach. The sequel is illustrated on a cup by Makron where the horse is lying on the ground, and Troilos, still clinging to his neck, finds himself in the grasp of his pursuer, who plunges a sword into his shoulder (Palermo V659). In a great many (though not all) of these scenes, we continue to find Troilos with two horses, although the second plays no useful part in the story once its master has turned to flee; that artists persisted in including such a detail may suggest a literary (or artistic?) predecessor of remarkable impact. The original motive for these horses we will return to below. Before leaving the artistic evidence altogether we should also note a second metope from Foce del Sele (no #) showing a figure clinging to a column with one arm while another figure with drawn sword tries to pull him away. If this is a further stage of the Troilos story (after the metope with Achilleus hiding behind the fountain), we would have additional evidence for the version first seen in the Olympia shield-reliefs, but the scene is perhaps better interpreted as Orestes and Aigisthos.[37]

Turning back to literature in the fifth century, we find rather less than we might have expected. Neither Aischylos, Pindar, nor Bakchylides mention Troilos at all in what is preserved of their work; in the case of Pindar this is perhaps significant, since Achilleus' other exploits are noted with approval on several occasions in his *epinikia*. In fact the only fifth-century writer (other than Phrynichos) known to have dealt with Troilos at all is Sophokles, who wrote a play of that title. Scholia to the *Iliad* tell us that in this drama Troilos was ambushed[38] while exercising his horses near the Thymbraion (ΣT *Il* 24.257); otherwise we know only that the city itself was the setting, a eunuch spoke some lines, and that Polyxena and Troilos' mutilation may have been involved. We have already encountered the Thymbraion as the site of the slaughter in the Ibykos commentary (perhaps drawing from just this play), but the more specific detail that the *ambush* took place there, plus the presence of horses being exercised, brings us back to a previous uncertainty, whether the fountain house, Polyxena, and the flight are always part of the same story as the slaying at an altar. For although Sophokles (and even Ibykos before him?) might quite reasonably put the fountain house near the Thymbraion, and bring Troilos there after exercising to water his horses, such a sequence leaves no plausible reason for Polyxena's presence; one expects, I think, that in the beginning Troilos came with her directly from Troy, perhaps as an escort. Then too, in the fountain house version, Troilos is clearly run down by Achilleus, a feat that loses much of its point if the Thymbraion where he is killed is essentially adjacent to the point of ambush; on the François Krater, we may remember, he seems to be fleeing back toward the city. Nevertheless, Troilos' watering of his horses (somewhere) does seem to have been a part of the play, since one of the few fragments preserved mentions an approach to spring drinking water (fr 621 R). Whatever we conclude, the mention here of the Thymbraion, together with the numerous altars in the artistic tradition, certainly suggests an early account in which that precinct was the site of the slaying.

From this intriguing state of affairs we move to Lykophron, where in just seven lines we find two entirely new details, first that Achilleus had fallen in love with Troilos, who remained "unwounded" by the one he conquered, and second that the Trojan was in fact a son of Apollo, at whose altar he was decapitated (Lyk 307–13). Lykophron's language is highly obscure, as usual, and one would be surprised if this motif of Achilleus' passion was something that he had invented. Presumably we are to understand from the word "unwounded" that Troilos did not return Achilleus' affections and was slain for that reason. This last, at any rate, is the version of the scholia, in which Troilos takes refuge in the precinct of Apollo to avoid Achilleus' advances; when the latter is unable to persuade him to come out, he goes in and kills him at the altar (Σ Lyk 307). The erotic motif occurs too in Servius, where Achilleus in his desire lures Troilos to him by offering doves; on trying to take them the boy is seized, and dies in Achilleus' embrace (how or why not said: Σ *Aen* 1.474).

A quite different (and more honorable) motive for his demise first survives in Plautus, who tells us that Troilos' death was one of the events necessary to the fall of Troy, like the stealing of the Palladion (*Bacchides* 953–55). If this notion could go back to the *Kypria* it would explain much; as matters stand, however, our epitome of Apollodoros, where we might hope to find it in that case, says only that Achilleus ambushed Troilos in the sanctuary of Thymbraion Apollo (ApE 3.32), much as he appears to do in Sophokles. Apollodoros' one other contribution is to reiterate the idea that Troilos might have been a son of Apollo (by Hekabe: ApB 3.12.5). Hyginus is even less help; although he mentions Troilos' death in several lists he never narrates it in any form. By contrast the First Vatican Mythographer elaborates on what we found in Plautus by claiming that Troy was destined never to fall if Troilos reached the age of twenty, and thus that Achilleus killed him from ambush as he was exercising outside the walls of the city (VM I 210). His very brief narrative adds that Troilos' lifeless body was dragged back to Troy still tied to his horses. In Dares we find for the first time Troilos as warrior (of the first rank), leading the Trojans after the death of Hektor and even wounding Diomedes and Agamemnon, until his horse is brought down and Achilleus seizes his opportunity (Dar 33).[39] That he or any warrior should fight (even briefly) from horseback seems very much a post-epic invention, one no doubt designed to accommodate to a military context the long-established tradition of a mounted Troilos meeting his fate.

On the whole, the only respectable motive for Achilleus' deed emerging from this survey is that of the prophecy that guarantees Troy's safety if the boy should live, late though that is in our sources. The brutal death of Rhesos (to keep his horses from watering at the Skamandros) considered below would be then an obvious parallel, and one missing even in Homer. But we cannot in either instance be sure that the device of a prophecy has not been imported into the story to palliate unseemly actions. The versions in which Troilos' killing is at an altar must surely involve desecration of a precinct, especially if the altar is the Thymbraion of Apollo, and no prophecy will explain the brutality (to say nothing of insensitivity) with which Achilleus decapitates the body and throws the head at the boy's brothers in sixth-century art. We will see below that in some accounts Achilleus is slain in this same precinct, indicating perhaps Apollo's revenge.

Before leaving Troilos altogether, we should perhaps note briefly the later, post-Classical developments that bring (heterosexual) romance into his life. No such motif appears in Dares, but his elevation of Troilos to a fully grown adult appearing on one occasion in combat with Diomedes, plus the telling of the familiar tale of Briseis, perhaps opened the door to a more innovative approach by the twelfth-century Benoit de Sainte-Maure in his *Le Roman de Troie*, a poem of some thirty thousand lines which includes an account of the love of

Troilos for the Trojan Briseida, here daughter of Kalchas. Benoit claims to have drawn much of his poem from Dares, and possibly he had a fuller version of that author than we do. In any case, Troilos and Briseida are lovers, but her father Kalchas, having gone over to the Greek side, asks Priam to send her to him, and the latter does so. She then falls prey to Diomedes' entreaties and forgets Troilos, and although she reproaches herself later, she feels she cannot return to Troy; the tale ends somewhat abruptly with Achilleus as usual dispatching the unhappy Troilos. Subsequently the same tale appears in the *Florita* of the early fourteenth-century Armannino and the *Filostrato* of Boccaccio slightly later in the same century, both (perhaps independently) substituting the name "Criseida" for that of Briseida. The change may or may not have arisen from a confusion between Kalchas and Chryses, the fathers, possibly aided by a misreading of Ovid's *Remedia Amoris* 467–74. Whatever the truth of the matter, Boccaccio's lengthy poem served as the source for Chaucer's even longer work some fifty years later, and from thence to Shakespeare's play, so that for better or worse Cressida has become in Western literature the object of Troilos' affections.

One other exploit of Achilleus to be discussed in this same general context is the capture of Lykaon, whom we meet in a memorable scene in *Iliad* 21. There Achilleus accosts this son of Priam as the latter is escaping from the river, and discovers him to be the same youth whom he had once before ambushed by night while the latter was cutting fig branches in an orchard in order to make chariot rails (*Il* 21.34–48). On that occasion Achilleus sold him to Euneos of Lemnos, but Euneos in turn allowed him to be ransomed by one Eetion of Imbros, apparently a family friend, and this last sent him to Arisbe, north of Troy on the Hellespont. The intention seems to have been that he remain there, but he escapes, and has been enjoying his return to Troy for eleven days when he falls into Achilleus' hands again, only to meet his death this time. *Iliad* 23 adds that Euneos gave Patroklos a splendid silver krater as the price for the captive (*Il* 23.740–47); otherwise we learn from the *Iliad* only that he was Priam's child by Laothoe, daughter of Altes, with no explanation of why he should risk so much by going out at night, or why Achilleus should have been waiting for him. But the Townley scholia remind us here that Achilleus does earlier claim to have spent "many sleepless nights" in prosecuting the war (*Il* 9.325), and this present incident taken together with the death of Troilos may suggest that there was a period at Troy during which open hostilities were less in evidence, and warriors gained fame and booty by more devious means. The *Kypria* also knows of this story, although our summary mentions it only in a roundabout fashion in noting that Patroklos takes Lykaon off to Lemnos and sells him; nothing is said of his capture. Possibly, of course, the *Kypria* included this event based simply on what was recorded about it in the *Iliad*.

Palamedes   Homer never mentions this figure, not even in the Catalogue of Ships, although we have seen that the abandoned Philoktetes and the deceased Protesilaos found room there. Earlier in this chapter we encountered him in the *Kypria*'s account of the recruitment of Odysseus, when at his suggestion the Achaians somehow threatened the infant Telemachos and thus discovered the father's ruse. Proklos (near the close of his summary) says only that Palamedes died, but Pausanias cites the poem to the effect that he drowned while fishing, and that Diomedes and Odysseus were responsible. Why they should want to do this is not stated. Otherwise, our only references to this hero before the fifth century occur in the *Nostoi*, Stesichoros, and (probably) the *Aigimios* of the Hesiodic Corpus, for Apollodoros says that according to Kerkops (one reputed author of the latter work) Nauplios and Hesione begat Palamedes, Oiax, and Nausimedon, while in the *Nostoi* his mother was instead Philyra, and for the tragedians Klymene, daughter of Katreus (ApB 2.1.5). We have met this Nauplios already before, in chapter 6, as the offspring of Poseidon and the Danaid Amymone; we will see shortly that as father of Palamedes he plays a crucial role in the aftermath of his son's demise, and probably did so from an early date, given that he is mentioned in the *Nostoi*. Stesichoros is our first source for the idea that Palamedes discovered or invented something (*stoicheia* [letters?]: 213 *PMG*); for more exact details we must turn to the fifth century.

From that time period we have Pindar's remark that Palamedes surpassed Odysseus in some fashion regarding *sophia* (fr 260 SM) plus *Palamedes* plays (all lost) by each of the three major tragedians; to these last should perhaps be added as well Sophokles' *Nauplios Katapleon*, if in that play Palamedes' father defended his departed son (see below). For Aischylos we know (from a scholion to the *Desmotes*) that the playwright elsewhere assigned many of Prometheus' cultural improvements to Palamedes (Σ *PD* 457–59a), while an actual Aischylean quote says that Palamedes organized the army into units, and determined the proper times for meals (fr 182 R). Stobaios adds to this another citation, unattributed, which shows Palamedes describing his invention of arithmetic for a confused and muddled Greek world (fr 181a R). Sophokles somewhere had Nauplios credit his son with a similar range of discoveries, weights, numbers, measures, military tactics, and how to read the movement of the stars (fr 432 R), and another fragment adds dice and draughts (fr 429 R).[40] That Euripides followed suit is guaranteed by a quote expressly from his play in which we hear again of writing as a new skill, the "drug of forgetfulness, voiceless yet speaking" (fr 578 N²). Seemingly, then, all three poets shared this characterization of Palamedes as benefactor of the Greeks through gifts in some respects similar to those proffered by the Aischylean Prometheus. Other traces of this tradition appear in Gorgias' rhetorical defense speech for Palamedes, where military tactics, writing, written laws, weights and measures, counting, beacon fires, and draughts are listed (82B11a), and in Plato's *Republic*, where Sokrates remarks on how foolish Agamemnon looks time and again in tragedy, given that prior to Palamedes' discoveries the Achaian general was seemingly unable to count the number of his ships or even his feet (*Rep* 7.522d).

As for the plot of these plays, the *Orestes'* title character attests Oiax's desire for revenge against Agamemnon for Palamedes' death (*Or* 432–33), while (according to Dion of Prusa) Euripides' *Philoktetes* made Odysseus claim to have destroyed Palamedes by a false charge of trafficking with Priam's sons (DP 59). But for any continuous narration of the story of his downfall we must look to later sources, beginning with the *Orestes* scholia.[41] These tell us that while the Achaians were becalmed at Aulis, Palamedes solved difficulties with the rationing of food by showing them the use of Phoinician letters, that is, writing, and that to distract them he invented as well games using dice, adding in the bargain measures and arithmetic (Σ *Or* 432). For these innovations he acquired a great reputation, and in jealousy of his fame Agamemnon, Odysseus, and Diomedes plotted his downfall, suborning a servant to hide gold that they had intercepted from a Trojan messenger under his bed. To complete the trap the same messenger was forced to write a letter linking Palamedes in a scheme with Priam to betray the Greeks, and thus when the plotters demanded a search of his tent the incriminating evidence resulted in his being stoned to death by the army. In Hyginus, by contrast, Odysseus alone plots against Palamedes, because he has been "deceived by the ruse of the latter," a reference surely to the feigned madness on Ithaka (*Fab* 105; cf. *Fab* 95 and *Met* 13.56–60). Toward this end the Ithakan convinces Agamemnon that a dream has advised the moving of the Greek camp for a single day. Agamemnon does so, and in the interim Odysseus buries the gold in the spot where Palamedes' tent has been pitched. After the camp is moved back and Palamedes repitches his tent in the same place, Agamemnon receives a letter purportedly from Priam to Palamedes noting this hidden gold; its discovery seems to confirm all charges, and Palamedes is again stoned.

Apollodoros' version is too brief to add much to this, although here too, as in Hyginus, Odysseus acts alone, and we find the letter of the Phrygian captive, planted gold, and the death by stoning at the hands of the army (Ap*E* 3.8). Servius' account likewise follows much the lines of Hyginus, save that the camp is not moved (Odysseus somehow buries the gold in the dead of night with the help of a bribed slave) and that Odysseus pretends to support Palamedes after the letter is found, calling on the Greeks to exonerate Palamedes by searching his tent. And the second-century A.D. Polyainos in his *Stratege-mata* notes that in the tragedians Odysseus' stratagem of hiding the gold in the tent results in Palamedes, the wisest of all the Greeks, being convicted of treason; there is a hint here too that the trial may have been viewed as a battle of wits between the two rivals (1 *prooem* 12).

Taken as a whole, this body of post-*Kypria* material is remarkably consistent. The variations that do exist would seem to reflect perhaps two basic versions, one in which jealousy of Palamedes' accomplishments (by Odysseus, Agamemnon, and Diomedes) is the motive for his death, with letter and gold found together in his tent and perhaps summary execution, and a second in which Odysseus carries out solitary vengeance, with the letter produced first and a trial or at least debate held, followed by the discovery of the gold which convinces Agamemnon and the troops. For our purposes it will not matter a great deal which version was used by which tragedians, but a fragment of Aischylos' play (asking for what cause the speaker's son was killed: fr 181 R) does seem to indicate that Nauplios appeared in that play, and thus that the action was either *all* set after Palamedes' death or else very briefly dramatized in its opening phases.[42] By contrast, a fragment defending Palamedes in Sophokles' play of that name (fr 479 R) will surely not have been spoken by the father if, as seems likely, his trip to Troy to protest his son's death was dramatized by that same poet's *Nauplios Katapleon*. In that case, Odysseus may well be the defender, pretending as in Servius to side with Palamedes in order to more effectively (and maliciously) spring his trap.[43] Finally, in Euripides' play someone addresses Agamemnon with the remark that all men, those who are friends of music and those who are not, strive for money (fr 580 N²). Presumably this is Odysseus speaking, there is a debate, and Agamemnon is as in Servius and Hyginus an uninvolved arbiter whom Odysseus must convince. These points being so, it has not unreasonably been proposed that Servius has followed Sophokles, Hyginus Euripides, and the *Orestes* scholia (which, in fact, conclude with Nauplios' visit) Aischylos, although of course we cannot say how much contamination of different authors these later sources may contain.[44]

Notable in any case is the agreement of said sources that Palamedes was judged guilty of treason and executed by the army, in marked contrast to the *Kypria* where his death is a private matter at the hands of Odysseus and Diomedes and there is presumably no question of treason. The reason for their deed in that early work remains a mystery. Certainly the *Kypria* contained Palamedes' uncloaking of Odysseus' madness on Ithaka, but if revenge is the sole motive here it is difficult to see why Diomedes should help, so that we should perhaps suppose rather jealousy the cause as in the *Orestes* scholia. Conceivably, in fact, something like the *Kypria's* account survives in Diktys, the only other retelling we have in which Palamedes suffers a similar death: here he becomes envied because an oracle of Apollo has selected him to perform a great sacrifice, and because he is generally popular with the troops (Dik 2.14–15). Accordingly, Diomedes and Odysseus persuade him to go with them to a well where they claim to have found gold, and lower him down to retrieve it. When he reaches the bottom they throw stones down on top of him and thus kill him. Relevant, too, may be Servius, where as we saw in discussing the daughters of Anios Palamedes succeeds in securing grain for the army at Troy after Odysseus has failed, thus increasing the latter's enmity (Σ *Aen* 2.81, followed by VM I 35, II 200).

There is finally the above-noted coda to the tale of Palamedes, the wrath of his father Nauplios and journey to Troy to accuse those responsible for his son's death. The *Orestes* scholia constitute our clearest source for this event, stating as they do that Nauplios came to Troy after his son's death to protest, but received little attention because the army wished to please the leaders (Σ *Or* 432: we remember that a number of heroes including Agamemnon conspire toward Palamedes' death in this account). We saw above that this voyage was almost certainly part of Aischylos' *Palamedes*, and probably too Sophokles' *Nauplios Katapleon*, assuming that play is not the same as his *Nauplios Pyrkaeus*. In any case, the one fragment of protest specifically assigned to a Sophoklean Nauplios (fr 432 R) indicates that the poet dramatized the story in some work. In Euripides, matters were handled a bit differently: here after the trial and execution of Palamedes his brother Oiax ponders how to inform their father of what has happened. With commendable ingenuity, if not plausibility, he decides to inscribe the story on oars that will then float back to Greece; the device is brutally parodied by Aristophanes in the *Thesmophoriazousai* (768–84; see scholia at 771). Given this emphasis on a painfully slow method of transmitting events, it seems impossible that Nauplios could have arrived at Troy in the play; if we hear anything more of him, it will be of his final vengeance, via a *deus ex machina*.

That vengeance involved, to judge by our later sources, two different actions. Lykophron hints pointedly at the first of these, making Kassandra prophesy that the Greeks shall not be happy in their return from Troy, for the "hedgehog ruining homes by such devices shall deceive the roosters' hens who keep the roosts, so that they become hostile" (Lyk 1093–5). What he means is surely explained by Apollodoros, who says that after Nauplios returned from his unsuccessful voyage to Troy he visited the homes of a number of the Greek leaders and managed to turn their wives to adultery (we are not told how; perhaps by tales, true or not, of their husbands' paramours at Troy: ApE 6.9). Included in the list are Klytaimestra's affair with Aigisthos, that of Aigialeia, wife of Diomedes, with Sthenelos' son Kometes, and that of Meda, wife of Idomeneus, with Leukos. But this last liaison turns sour, for Leukos kills Meda and her daughter Kleisithyra (after they have taken refuge in a temple) and seizes possession of part of Krete, repelling even Idomeneus when the latter returns. That tale is in fact also alluded to by Lykophron, and with Apollodoros' help we now see that there too Nauplios is implicated:

> Not calmly does the fisherman with his net row his two-oared craft, meaning to cause confusion for Leukos guardian of the throne and weaving his hatred into deceitful devices. And that one, savage in his mind, will spare neither the children nor the wife Meda, nor the daughter Kleisithera, whose hand her father will promise with bitter consequences to the nursling snake. And with unholy hands he will kill them all in the temple [Lyk 1216–24].

It would seem, then, that Leukos is a foster child brought up in the home of Idomeneus, and that he was betrothed to the latter's daughter before his regrettable loss of restraint, although there is no clear mention here of adultery with the mother; we will return to these problems in chapter 17, when we consider the returns of the Achaians. One other detail is reported by the *Odyssey* scholia, that Nauplios persuaded Antikleia of Odysseus' death, whereupon the grieving mother hanged herself (Σ *Od* 11.197, 202, credited to the *neôteroi*). On this phase of Nauplios' vengeance we have no other information; just possibly it (rather than the debate at Troy) was the subject of Sophokles' *Nauplios Katapleon*, if that play was distinct from the *Pyrkaeus*. The matter of this latter drama was certainly the second phase of the retribution, a phase surely in the *Nostoi* and indicated by both Apollodoros and the *Orestes* scholia: as the Achaians prepared for their return from Troy, Nauplios proceeded to the promontory of Kaphereus at the southern end of Euboia and lit deceptive fires that lured the ships to destruction. Again, this is an event to which we shall return in chapter 17.

The Actors of the Iliad

Before turning to the *Iliad* itself, whose plot forms the next sequence of action in the war, we might pause here to consider the main figures encountered in that work, as found primarily in Book 2's Catalogue of Ships. Homer's list of Achaians in this catalogue is arranged geographically, rather than by importance, but the various councils held, plus valorous deeds in battle, show us clearly whom to regard as the major figures. From Mykenai and Sparta, respectively, come Agamemnon and Menelaos, the sons of Atreus and chief prosecutors of the war, Agamemnon with a hundred ships, Menelaos with sixty (*Il* 2.569–90). Pylos sends the aged Nestor, son of Neleus, whose reminiscences on problems with Herakles and Augeias have been mentioned already in chapter 13; ninety ships follow him (*Il* 2.591–602), plus his sons Antilochos and Thrasymedes. From Krete arrives Idomeneus, son of Deukalion, the son of Minos (*Il* 13.448–53), accompanied by Meriones, son of one Molos (*Il* 10.269–70), and eighty ships. From Argos and Tiryns are the two sons of the Seven against Thebes already encountered in chapter 14, Diomedes, son of Tydeus, and Sthenelos, son of Kapaneus; with them is Euryalos, son of Mekisteus, the son of Talaos, and eighty ships again follow (*Il* 2.559–68). Aias, son of Telamon, comes from Salamis with just twelve ships (*Il* 2.557–58); his half-brother Teukros (for whom see Herakles' sack of Troy in chapter 13) is not mentioned in the Catalogue but appears frequently elsewhere. The other Aias, this one the son of Oileus (*Il* 2.527–35), comes from Lokris with forty ships.

From Athens arrives Menestheus, son of Peteos, a marshaller of men and horses second only to Nestor, with fifty ships (*Il* 2.546–56); we have seen in chapter 9 that Theseus' sons Demophon and Akamas are not named in the *Iliad* but are present in the closing stages of the Cycle to recover their grandmother Aithra. Ithaka and the surrounding islands (Kephallenia, Samos, Zakinthos, etc.) are led by Odysseus, of course, but with only twelve ships (*Il* 2.631–37); the nearby islands of Doulichion and the Echinades are led by Meges, son of Phyleus, with forty (*Il* 2.625–30). Finally, there is from Phthia and Pelasgikon Argos Achilleus with his Myrmidones (*Il* 2.681–84) and close friend Patroklos, son of Menoitios. This last is also not mentioned in the Catalogue; we learn about him from various other parts of the poem, including the fact that, angered over some game, he killed a companion when very young and was compelled to go into exile (*Il* 23.84–90). Fifty ships follow Achilleus and Patroklos. Of Phoinix, former tutor of Achilleus, we hear first in Book 9, where he tells his story, and then briefly in Books 16, 17, 19, and 23. In 16 he leads a group of the Myrmidones into battle, and he himself admits in 9 that Peleus sent him with Achilleus from Phthia, but earlier in that same Book he has been with the rest of the Achaians in their debate, rather than with his own contingent, perhaps one more sign of reworking in this part of the poem. His father is Amyntor, son of Ormenos, with whom he once quarreled over the affront shown to his mother by the latter's preference for a certain concubine (*Il* 9.447–84). His mother called upon him to usurp the girl's affections, and when he did so Amyntor pronounced a curse that he should never have children. For nine days his friends guarded him lest he do violence to his father, but on the tenth he escaped and came finally to Phthia, where Peleus put him in charge of the infant Achilleus (for the non-Homeric tradition that his father blinded him, see below).

This concludes the list of the major figures present before the walls of Troy, but Homer includes the minor leaders of a number of other contingents whom we should note here: from Boiotia, fifty ships and five leaders, Penelaos, Leitos, Arkesilaos, Prothoenor, and Klonios (*Il* 2.494–510): from Orchomenos, Askalaphos and Ialmenos, sons of Ares, and thirty ships (*Il* 2.511–16); from Phokis, Schedios and Epistrophos, sons of Iphitos Naubolides, and forty ships (*Il* 2.517–26); from Euboia, Elephenor, leader of the Abantes, and forty ships (*Il* 2.536–45); from Arkadia, Agapenor, son of Ankaios, and sixty ships (borrowed from Agamemnon: *Il* 2.603–14); from Elis, four groups of ten ships each, manned by Epeians and led by Amphimachos, son of Kteatos (this father one of the Moliones), Thalpios, son of Eurytos (the other Molion), Diores, son of Amarynkeus, and Polyxenos, son of Agasthenes, the son of Augeias (*Il* 2.615–24); from Aitolia, Thoas, son of Andraimon, with forty ships (*Il* 2.638–44); from Rhodes, Tlepolemos, son of Herakles (*Il* 2.653–70: see chapter 13); from Syme, Nireus, son of Charopos, the most handsome of the Achaians after Achilleus but not very warlike (*Il* 2.671–75); from Kos and nearby islands Pheidippos and Antiphos, sons of the Heraklid Thessalos (*Il* 2.676–80: see chapter 13); from Phylake and Pteleos, as we saw above, Podarkes, younger brother of the slain Protesilaos, with forty ships (*Il* 2.695–710); from Pherai, Eumelos, the son of Admetos and Alkestis, with eleven ships (*Il* 2.711–15); from the land around Mount Pelion the contingent (just seven ships) of Philoktetes led by Medon, a bastard son of Oileus by one Rhene (*Il* 2.716–28); from Oichalia, city of Eurytos, the two sons of Asklepios, Podaleirios and Machaon, with thirty ships (*Il* 2.729–33); from Ormenios Eurypylos, son of Euaimon, with forty ships (*Il* 2.734–37); from Argissa and environs, Polypoites, son of Peirithoos and Hippodameia, with forty ships (*Il* 2.738–47); from around Dodona, Gouneus with twenty-two ships (*Il* 2.748–55); and from the land of the Magnetes, Prothoos, son of Tenthredon, with forty ships (*Il* 2.756–59).

On the Trojan side there are (perhaps fortunately) fewer main figures, with a limited number of Trojans themselves playing any substantial role other than to be killed, and of the allies only Sarpedon and Glaukos, leaders of the Skamandrian Lykians, distinguishing themselves at all. We have already met Priam and Hekabe earlier in this chapter, and a number of Priam's children in various other places. *Iliad* 24.496–97 reveals that nineteen of his fifty sons were borne to him by Hekabe, but the only ones so identified are Hektor and one Antiphos. At least two sons (Troilos and Mestor) have died before the start of the *Iliad*, and eleven others (Hektor, Antiphos, six illegitimate, three uncertain) will die in the course of the poem. *Iliad* 24 lists nine surviving ones— Helenos, Paris, Deiphobos, Polites, Agathon, Antiphonos, Pammon, Hippothoos, and Agauos (or Dios: *Il* 24.249–51)—but of these only the first four are ever mentioned elsewhere. In the first section of this chapter we also saw the cadet line that produced Aineias. His wife is a more difficult question: Homer says nothing of such a person, while both the *Kypria* (fr 31 *PEG*) and the *Little Iliad* (fr 22 *PEG*) appear to have called her Eurydike, and so too Ennius in his *Annales* (Cicero *Div* 1.20.40). Pausanias, our source for that name in the two Greek epics, saw a woman labeled Kreousa among the Trojan captives in Polygnotos' painting of the Sack for the Knidian Lesche at Delphi (10.26.1); from his vantage point he assumes Polygnotos meant this figure to be the wife of Aineias, but we cannot say whether the artist would have agreed. We did find earlier that Apollodoros knows of a Kreousa, daughter of Priam and Hekabe, yet here too there is nothing about Aineias' wife. Only in the *Aeneid* is she firmly assigned that status, and neither Vergil nor Servius say anything else about her. For the rest, the only Trojans of real note are Antenor and his sons, a number of whom are also killed as the poem progresses, although as we saw the remainder of the family will be spared in the final sack of the city. Antenor's wife Theano makes several minor appearances; Homer calls her the daughter of Kisseus (in Euripides, though not Homer, the father of Hekabe) and priestess of Athena (*Il* 6.298–300, 11.223–24).

The Events of the Iliad   Proklos closes his summary of the *Kypria* with the statement that after the death of Palamedes came the "plan of Zeus, so that he might lighten the burden of the Trojans by causing Achilleus to abandon the Greek alliance, and a catalogue of those helping the Trojans." What this might mean is unclear, if it does not anticipate the opening books of the *Iliad*; perhaps the poet in shaping the work thusly meant to stress the continuity between *Kypria* and *Iliad*, and to advertise a bit for the next tale in the series that had come to be formed. Admittedly, the *Iliad* itself does not begin with a plan of Zeus to help the Trojans, but rather with a quarrel between Achilleus and Agamemnon which leads Zeus to agree, somewhat reluctantly, to Thetis' request for such a result. Probably this divergence stems from a debatable interpretation of *Iliad* 1.5, where Homer says that when Greeks perished in large numbers the *boulê* of Zeus was accomplished. While such phrasing could mean that Zeus foresaw the quarrel from the very beginning and planned its consequences, what follows in

Iliad 1 suggests rather that Zeus' plan mentioned here is nothing more than the plan to accommodate Thetis' request, and springs from no personal motive at all, however much he might favor the Trojans. But seemingly the poet of the *Kypria* differed with this view, or else Proklos has introduced a motive of his own for the action in concluding his summary.

In any case, the next event in our preserved picture of the Trojan War is certainly the quarrel between Achilleus and Agamemnon, brought about by the fact that Chryses, father of Agamemnon's war prize Chryseis and priest of Apollo, is (unusually) still alive. His request for the return of his daughter, accompanied as it is by an offer of ransom, might seem nothing more than an exchange of goods, but Agamemnon chooses to regard the loss of the girl (low though slave women generally are in the Iliadic scale of values) as a serious loss of status, and thus rejects the offer. Chryses in his anger appeals to Apollo as the god's loyal priest, and Apollo acknowledges that responsibility by sending plague to ravage the army. When the troops finally assemble at Achilleus' summons, Kalchas reveals the cause of the problem, but Agamemnon is still unwilling to acquiesce without an immediate replacement for Chryseis. Achilleus not unreasonably points out that this is impossible at the moment, and adds some remarks about Agamemnon's general greed; the upshot is that Agamemnon finds himself compelled to forcibly appropriate Achilleus' own war prize, Briseis, in order to save face. At this threat Achilleus nearly dispatches Agamemnon on the spot, but with Athena's encouragement settles for a few more insults and the pronouncement that he himself will no longer fight for such a leader, nor will his men. The loss is clearly more than the Achaian side will be able to support (Nestor hints at as much), but to make sure of Agamemnon's humiliation without him, Achilleus asks his mother Thetis to intercede with Zeus, requesting victory for the Trojans until Agamemnon should apologize. Zeus foresees problems with Hera over this course of action, even though it will not affect the eventual outcome of the war, but finally succumbs to Thetis' pressure. Meanwhile, Odysseus has been delegated to return Chryseis to her father, and Briseis is removed from Achilleus' tent by heralds sent by Agamemnon.

Thus the action of *Iliad* 1. From this point on, the course of events proceeds forward in a more desultory fashion, and for the purposes of this book we need only mention the more critical moments. In Book 2, Zeus sends a false dream to encourage Agamemnon; the latter's failure to recount this to the troops combined with an odd sense of the appropriate time to test their loyalty leads to a rush for the ships, halted only by Odysseus and Athena. We meet also in this book Thersites, the ugliest and most unpleasant man in the army, who reviles Agamemnon for his lack of leadership, until chastised by Odysseus. After the leaders on both sides have been itemized with their contingents (the Catalogue of Ships) we proceed to Book 3 and a single combat between Paris and Menelaos designed to resolve the war for good (the Achaians to leave if Paris wins, the Trojans to hand back Helen and all stolen goods and pay a penalty in the opposite event). But though Menelaos has no problems with the unwarlike Paris, Aphrodite intervenes as her favorite is being dragged back to the Achaian side by his helmet, breaking the strap and carrying him back to Troy where she induces Helen to indulge in lovemaking with him. As Book 3 closes, Menelaos and the Achaians are claiming victory over the vanished Paris, but in Book 4 Hera protests this too-peaceful result and, after offering to abandon Argos or Sparta or Mykenai when their time comes, obtains Zeus' permission to send Athena down to earth to restart hostilities. This Athena does, in the guise of Laodokos, son of Antenor, by tempting one Pandaros to fire a shot at Menelaos during the current truce so that the Trojans will not have to admit defeat; she also assures, however, that the arrow so fired only wounds Menelaos. Both sides rush back to arms, the truce is forgotten, and battle joined. As Agamemnon exhorts his men, at times with criticism, we find the memorable exchange with Diomedes and Sthenelos concerning their fathers and the expedition of the Seven against Thebes.

In Book 5 Diomedes occupies center stage, creating havoc in the Trojan ranks and wounding two of the gods supporting their cause. First he scratches Aphrodite on the wrist as she seeks to protect her son Aineias, felled by a stone; she drops him and flees in Ares' chariot up to Olympos where her mother Dione comforts her (Apollo accomplishes the actual rescue of Aineias). At the close of the same book, with Athena's special permission, he wounds Ares, who has been literally fighting for the Trojans, in the belly; this departure from approved methods of support for one's chosen side is apparently the reason for Zeus' approval of such harsh treatment, as Ares goes bellowing and complaining back to his father's palace. Book 5 also brings the death of the treacherous Pandaros at Diomedes' hands, having failed to obtain any of the gifts that Athena/Laodokos promised.

In Book 6 Hektor returns to Troy to advise Hekabe to appeal to Athena for relief from the devastations of Diomedes; Hekabe offers a robe, which Athena refuses. Hektor also visits the house of Paris to bring his brother back to battle, and engages in a poignant meeting with Andromache and his son Astyanax on the walls of the city, where they have been watching the war. The manner in which the child here shrinks back from the image of his father in full armor as the latter stoops to pick him up surely encourages us to suppose an allusion to Astyanax's ultimate fate, and thus strengthens the notion that Homer was generally familiar with events outside the compass of his poems. In Book 7, for no very clear reason, we are treated to a single combat between Telemonian Aias and Hektor; night intervenes before any serious damage can be done, although Aias more than holds his own. At a subsequent assembly of the Trojans, Paris agrees to give back Menelaos' stolen property but not Helen, and a burial truce is arranged during which the Achaians construct a wall and trench to protect their ships. In Book 8 Zeus sets about fulfilling his promise to Thetis, and thus forbids the other gods to descend to the battlefield. The Achaians are accordingly pushed back, and by the end of the book have conceded the entire plain to the Trojans, who are (for the first time?) camped upon it, their many fires like to the stars above.

Accordingly, in Book 9 Nestor and the other Achaian leaders pressure Agamemnon to offer Achilleus the necessary apology, that is, the return of Briseis (untouched) together with numerous other handsome gifts. Odysseus, Aias, and Achilleus' old tutor Phoinix bring this offer to Achilleus, but he is adamant in his refusal, stressing the extent of his pain and the hurt of the insult. Phoinix here tells the story of Meleagros discussed in Chapter 11, seemingly to no avail though Achilleus does recant his announced intention to leave immediately. In Book 10 the Achaians, depressed over this failure, feel the need to scout out Trojan intentions, and Odysseus and Diomedes volunteer for the mission. At the same time Hektor has sent out one Dolon, son of Eumedes, to scout the Greek side, promising him the horses of Achilleus if he should succeed. He is, however, captured by his Greek counterparts and killed after revealing the location of a new contingent of Trojan allies, that of the Thracian Rhesos, who has splendid white horses. Odysseus and Diomedes then raid this camp while its occupants are sleeping; Odysseus takes the horses while Diomedes butchers thirteen men, including Rhesos himself, and they make their escape back to their own side. In Book 11 various Achaians are wounded— Agamemnon by Koon Antenorides, Diomedes by Paris, Odysseus by Sokos Hippasides, Machaon by Paris, Eurypylos by Paris. Nestor brings Machaon back to the ships, and Achilleus seeing them pass by sends Patroklos to confirm the wounded man's identity—a fatal act of concern. Nestor offers Patroklos the story of his family's conflict with Herakles and with the Epeians of Augeias, and then suggests that Patroklos might enter the battle in Achilleus' place. At the book's close, on his way back to the tents of the Myrmidones, Patroklos is intercepted by Eurypylos, who asks for help in tending his wound. Book 12 opens with the tale of how Poseidon and Apollo later destroyed the wall of the Achaians, after the war was over, and then proceeds to the Trojans' successes before the wall. These last are somewhat negated by an omen sent by Zeus—an eagle whose prey of a snake twists around in his captor's clutches to bite him and escape. The seer Poulydamas quite properly interprets this portent to mean that the Greeks will similarly escape the Trojans' grasp, though Hektor is unable to accept that fact. As this book closes Hektor smashes the gates of the Achaians' wall with a stone, and calls upon his allies to follow him through to the ships.

Book 13 brings Poseidon onto the battlefield to encourage the Achaians as they struggle to hold back Hektor, and we see the death of Alkathoos, husband of Hippodameia, Aineias' half-sister. Also dying in this book is Euchenor, son of Polyidos, who upon being told by his father that he will die either in battle or of a painful sickness chooses the former. In Book 14 Agamemnon once again proposes returning to Greece, but Odysseus, Nestor, and Diomedes rebuke him, and suggest lending their presence, albeit wounded, to the battle without actually fighting. Hera also assists by concocting a story (of a planned visit to the quarreling Okeanos and Tethys) which allows her to request from Aphrodite the latter's embroidered *himas*, or strap, source of all desire, and with this she has no trouble luring Zeus away from the battle and to bed, hidden away in the clouds on Mount Ida. For good measure she bribes Hypnos—with the gift of Pasithea, one of the Charites, to wife—to put Zeus to sleep after their lovemaking, and Poseidon is left free to further aid the Achaian side.

Book 15 features Zeus' awakening and command to Poseidon to abandon the battlefield, accompanied by the first prediction of Patroklos' fate and Hektor's doom following close upon it. Apollo on his father's command then shakes the aigis, and the Achaians are panicked into running for the ships, where Aias virtually alone is forced to hold off Hektor and the Trojans. At this most critical point of danger, Book 16 brings Patroklos back from his tendance of Eurypylos to Achilleus with the suggestion that he lead the Myrmidones out in the latter's place to save their comrades from total destruction. Achilleus agrees, but only to the extent that Patroklos push the Trojans away from the ships, lest he win too much glory for himself or come to grief at Apollo's hands. Patroklos thus takes all of his friend's armor except the spear that only Achilleus can wield and, with Automedon as charioteer and the horses Xanthos and Balios, sets out for battle. After notable successes he comes face to face with Sarpedon, and here Zeus makes his famous suggestion to Hera that he might avert fate and save his son. Hera expresses appropriate alarm that *aisa* and the laws of mortality should be thus flouted, and Zeus relents, agreeing instead to her proposal that Hypnos and Thanatos carry the body back to Lykia, after he has sent Apollo to rescue it from the battlefield. Hektor in fear now turns back to Troy, where Patroklos in pursuit assaults the walls three times, to be turned back each time by Apollo with his bare hands. On the fourth attempt, Apollo calls out that Troy is not fated to fall to Patroklos or even Achilleus, and Patroklos desists. But his own death is now near, for as he continues fighting Apollo comes up behind him in a mist and strikes him on the back, causing his helmet and breastplate to fall away and his spear to shatter in his hand. Euphorbos takes advantage of his defenseless condition to wound him with a throw of his spear, but does not dare confront him, and it remains for Hektor to dispatch the hero with a sword-thrust. Patroklos' dying words predict death in turn for Hektor at Achilleus' hands, but the Trojan boldly suggests that Achilleus, not he, might die in such an encounter.

Book 17 deals with the battle over Patroklos' body, after Hektor has returned from his vain pursuit of Achilleus' horses to strip off the armor. Menelaos sends Antilochos to announce the death to Achilleus, and as the book closes he and Meriones shoulder the corpse while the two Aiantes hold off Hektor and Aineias. In Book 18 Achilleus does finally hear of Patroklos' fate, and in response to his lament Thetis once again rises up out of the sea. To his insistence that he will now return to battle to fight Hektor she accedes, but proposes that she first obtain new armor from Hephaistos to replace that which Hektor has taken. After her departure Iris arrives, sent by Hera, and suggests that Achilleus go out to the ditch and shout, so that the Trojans might be frightened and the Achaians given a chance to bring back the body. This is done, and as night falls Poulydamas (whom we now learn was born on the same night as Hektor, and is better in counsel) advises retreat to safety within the walls, a plan rashly rejected by Hektor and the other Trojans. Meanwhile, Hephaistos produces the armor requested by Thetis, and as Book 19 begins she brings these items, including the wondrous shield, back to her son. Agamemnon then tells the story of Zeus and Ate as part of a reiteration of his apology, and the same gifts offered the day before are taken to Achilleus' tent, together with Briseis. But Achilleus himself has little thought for anything except Hektor, and refuses even the food that Odysseus suggests the army needs. In this book we also see Briseis' lament over Patroklos (with the remarkable claim that he would have persuaded Achilleus to marry her had he lived), and Achilleus' only reference in the *Iliad* to his son Neoptolemos on Skyros. Finally, there is the most fanciful moment of the poem: Achilleus' call to his horses not to leave him to die as they did Patroklos, and Xanthos' reply (inspired by Hera) that *moira* and Apollo slew his friend, while he himself will soon fall to a mortal and a god.

Book 20 brings us to Achilleus' entrance into battle, while the gods themselves are given leave by Zeus to go down and help their favorites (Hera, Athena, Poseidon, Hermes, and Hephaistos to the Achaians, Ares, Apollo, Artemis, Aphrodite, Leto, and Xanthos the river to the Trojans). Aineias now confronts Achilleus, but after each have missed with their spears Poseidon proposes to the other gods that they should save Aineias from a certain death, since he is fated to carry on the line of Dardanos, dearest of Zeus' sons, and rule over future generations of Trojans. Hera remains indifferent, but Aineias is duly carried out of battle to safety. Achilleus then loses Hektor as well, for Apollo wraps the Trojan in a mist and carries him away as they prepare to fight. By the beginning of Book 21 the Trojans are in full flight to the Xanthos, where Achilleus proceeds to slaughter them, filling up the river with carnage and slaying, among others, his former captive Lykaon. At this glutting of its waters the river itself protests, and rises up in pursuit of the hero to drown him, in the process calling to the Simoeis for aid. Poseidon and Athena come to Achilleus in his flight to promise support, but it is Hera who appeals to Hephaistos to take action; he responds by setting fire to the banks of the Xanthos, and the river quickly yields. From this first encounter between rival gods the narrative proceeds to other confrontations. Athena has no difficulty knocking Ares down with a stone after he has tried to stab her; Aphrodite helps the defeated war god away, but is herself struck to the ground by a blow of Athena's hand at Hera's urging. Poseidon challenges Apollo, chiding him for supporting the Trojans after their own ill-treatment by Laomedon, but Apollo will not fight with a god his senior and yields the victory, much to the disgust of Artemis. She, however, fares little better against Hera, who strips her of her bow and boxes her ears. Finally, Hermes and Leto find themselves face to face.

Hermes, like Apollo, declines such a match, and offers Leto the chance to boast of her superiority; she prefers to pick up her daughter's fallen arrows and head back to Olympos. At this book's close Apollo buys the Trojans time to retreat by snatching Agenor, son of Antenor, out of battle as he prepares to face Achilleus and, in the guise of Agenor, leads Achilleus away from the battle by feigned flight.

Book 22 brings finally the death of Hektor, whose time has run out. Apollo reveals his true form to Achilleus, and the latter turns back to the walls where Hektor is waiting for him, determined to atone for his folly in keeping the Trojans out on the plain by a showdown with his rival. Yet this long-awaited duel is hardly climactic: Hektor's courage fails before they have even begun to fight, and Achilleus must chase him back and forth before the walls as he looks for help from his comrades above. As the two come back around by the hot and cold springs of Skamandros for the fourth time, Zeus sets up his golden scales, placing in one the *kêr* of death for Achilleus, in the other that of Hektor. Hektor's sinks down, and Apollo abandons him. To further his destruction Athena in the guise of Deiphobos gives him encouragement to make a stand; after both Achaian and Trojan have thrown their spears and missed, she brings back Achilleus' spear but not Hektor's. Seeing himself deceived and with no second spear, Hektor launches a desperate rush with his sword and is easily slain by Achilleus' spear cast, the latter aiming at an opening in the neck of the armor he knows so well. Hektor, like the horse Xanthos, has a prophecy to deliver, naming Paris and Apollo as the mortal and god who will contrive Achilleus' own death. Unimpressed, Achilleus drags the body behind his horses before the walls and then takes it back to the ships in the same fashion, as Hektor's parents and wife look on.

Book 23 offers the funeral of Patroklos and the games, after twelve Trojan prisoners have been slaughtered in his honor. The chariot race brings Diomedes home first, since his prayer to Athena results in an accident to the chariot of Eumelos, whose horses were fastest. Antilochos is second, followed by Menelaos, Meriones, and Eumelos, but Menelaos questions Antilochos' dangerous tactics at a narrow part of the course and their order of finish is reversed. Even so, when Antilochos yields, Menelaos is appeased and passes back to his opponent the mare that is second prize. For Eumelos there is a special prize, in recognition of his misfortune, and the phiale originally intended for the fifth-place finisher is given to Nestor. In boxing Epeios drops Euryalos with one punch, while in wrestling Odysseus and Aias after a long struggle are called upon by Achilleus to accept a draw. The footrace features Odysseus, Antilochos, and Aias, son of Oileus; Odysseus is just behind this last in the final stage of the course when, like Diomedes in the chariot race, he prays to Athena. As a result, Aias slips in the blood and dung near the finish line and must settle for second. The general amusement greeting his fate, combined with his contentious attitude during the viewing of the chariot race, reminds us of his generally unpopular character and perhaps his ultimate folly. For the duel in armor, Diomedes and Aias are the opponents, and while the combat is soon halted for fear of harm, Achilleus judges Diomedes to have had the better of it. In the throwing of a huge iron weight (which is the prize), Polypoites far outstrips Aias, Leonteus, and Epeios. In archery, Teukros and Meriones compete; the latter wins when Teukros fails to pray to Apollo for success. Finally, there is the spear throw; Agamemnon and Meriones present themselves, but Achilleus declares Agamemnon the winner by common consent, without an actual competition.

Book 24 then concludes the *Iliad* with the real climax of the poem, the confrontation between Achilleus and Priam when the latter comes to the Achaian camp to ransom the body of Hektor, which is still being maltreated by Achilleus. After some discussion among the gods, Zeus sends Thetis to tell Achilleus that he must release the corpse to Priam, asserting that the rights of the dead cannot be ignored. At the same time Iris is sent to Priam with instructions for the ransom, including the assurance that Hermes will meet him on the way for protection. Priam accordingly sets out, although when Hermes does appear it is in the guise of a young Myrmidon who offers to take Priam secretly into Achilleus' compound. This done, Priam slips into the latter's quarters and takes his hands in supplication, reminding him of his own father Peleus soon to be bereaved of his son. The two share a mutual lamentation and food, Achilleus arranges the body for the journey, and contracts with Priam for an eleven-day period of mourning during which he shall hold back the Achaians from battle. When Priam returns to Troy with the body there are formal eulogies from Andromache, Hekabe, and Helen, and then the building of the pyre and the final rites, and here the *Iliad* ends (although the Townley scholia tell us that in some versions the last line was altered so as to create a link with the first line of the *Aithiopis*).

Of other or later versions of all these events there is not much to say; the monumental form of the *Iliad* as we have it seems to have become highly canonical, and while lyric poets might refer to the events of the war in general as a model of heroic times, no literary source deals with the story again in any detail until Aischylos, whose lost Achilleus trilogy (*Myrmidones, Nereides,* and *Phryges*) clearly dramatized the entire central action from original abandonment of the war to reconciliation with Priam. Unfortunately, we know very little of the particulars, much less how Aischylos viewed the overall situation. In the first play, a chorus of Myrmidones seems to have visited Achilleus in his tent, exhorting him to return to battle. From these, or Phoinix, or someone, there may also be a threat of stoning by the army, and finally the report of the ships' peril which induces Achilleus to send out Patroklos. Before the play ends news will come back of the latter's death, and fragments preserved at this point do indicate a sexual element in the two friends' relationship, in contrast to the *Iliad* (frr 134a-136 R). The second play brings on the Nereides (probably with Achilleus' new armor), and he then appears to have gone out to face Hektor, returning subsequently with the corpse. In the third play, Achilleus once again sits brooding in his tent, until Hermes comes to tell him that the body must be returned, and Priam follows with the ransom, apparently weighed out pound for pound against Hektor's body (ΣAT *Il* 22.351). Aside from the sexual attachment and the threat of stoning, this all might be nothing more than Homer's tale put on stage just as he wrote it, with an *Oresteia*-like reconciliation at the end, but we may underestimate the poet's originality.

Sophokles too *may* have dramatized the last part of the *Iliad* in his *Priamos* (or *Phryges?*),[45] but otherwise neither he nor Euripides appears to have dealt with any part of the poem's *narrative*, and the same is by and large true of other tragedians as well, save of course for Rhesos' death in the play of that name (see below).[46] But we should note the comment of Tekmessa in the *Aias* to the effect that Hektor was dragged to his death by means of the belt he received from Aias, while Aias died by the sword he got from Hektor (*Ai* 1026–33); presumably this is Sophoklean invention.

There were also *Phoinix* plays by Sophokles, Euripides, and Ion, among others; of these, Sophokles' perhaps and Euripides' certainly told of Phoinix's conflict with his father. In Euripides' version we have reason to suspect that the mother is dead, that the concubine attempts to seduce Phoinix, rather than vice versa, and that Amyntor, believing her subsequent slander, orders his son blinded.[47] Apollodoros gives a similar account, adding that Peleus brought Phoinix to Cheiron, who restored his sight (Ap*B* 3.13.8; this may all have been drawn from Euripides). The Cyzicene Epigrams, on the other hand, seem to assume the same story of mother and concubine as in the *Iliad*, with the mother (here Alkimede) still alive and in the relief described trying to prevent Amyntor from blinding his son with a torch (*AP* 3.3). The same is true of Lykophron, where Phoinix is blinded for entering the concubine's bed (Lyk 421–23); the scholia call the mother who requested this favor from her son Kleoboule and the concubine Klytie or Phthia (she is Phthia also for Apollodoros). In the A scholia at *Iliad* 9.448, the mother is Hippodameia and the concubine again Klytie; the rest of the comment simply repeats Homer's version, in which, as we have seen, Amyntor's punishment of his son is rather a curse of childlessness.

As for the preserved Greek tragedy entitled *Rhesos* handed down to us under Euripides' name, scholars remain dubious of the attribution and therefore completely uncertain as to date (early fourth century?).[48] Nevertheless, the play offers some interesting variations (one might even say improvements) on the account in *Iliad* 10. As the drama opens, the Trojans are in some alarm at seeing the many fires lit in the Achaian camp, and the army gathered around Agamemnon's hut. Hektor, fearing that they mean to leave by night, calls for a volunteer to spy out the situation, and here as in the *Iliad* Dolon comes forward, naming on his own initiative the horses of Achilleus as the desired reward. Dolon then departs, clad in a wolfskin and promising to bring back the head of some Achaian—Odysseus, say, or Diomedes—as proof of his venture. Next a shepherd announces the arrival of Rhesos, son of the river Strymon

and a Muse, from Thrace together with a huge force, and Rhesos himself follows, pleading war with the Scythians at home as excuse for his late appearance. The chorus is much impressed, and Rhesos is confident that his forces
can defeat the Greeks in a single day. All exit the stage, and Diomedes and
Odysseus now enter, carrying the spoils they have taken from Dolon, who is
already dead. Their original intent seems to have been to kill Hektor in his
sleep, but Athena appears and steers them to Rhesos, whom she says no
Achaian will be able to withstand if he survives that night. As in the *Iliad*,
Diomedes does the killing while Odysseus takes the beautiful white horses;
Athena assists with an imitation of Aphrodite when Paris arrives suspecting
trouble. The play then closes with the Trojans' discovery of the deed, bitter
accusations by the surviving Thracians against Hektor, and the coming of the
Muse (unnamed) to take her son away. All this does not perhaps have a great
deal of bite, but treachery is countered by treachery, and the Achaian sortie
now has some real purpose and consequence.

If we may trust the *Iliad* scholia, Pindar too gave the story better motivation: in his version, Rhesos actually fought at Troy for a day, and wreaked such
havoc among the Achaians that Hera and Athena advised Diomedes and others
to undertake the night raid (ΣbT *Il* 10.435 = fr 262 SM; ΣA *Il* 10.435). The
remarks in the latter of these two scholia go further still, and cite an account
of "others" (Eustathios says the *neôteroi*) in which Rhesos arrived at Troy
during the night, and died before he could taste the water there. For it was
fated, the scholia continue, that if he should taste the water, or his horses drink
from the Skamandros and feed on its banks, that he would become invincible.
Vergil seems to know something of the same story, since the *Aeneid*, too, has
Diomedes take the horses of Rhesos before they have grazed at Troy or drunk
the water of the Skamandros (*Aen* 1.469–73); Servius at 469 reports this to
mean that there was a prophecy of Troy's invincibility should the horses thus
feed or drink. Thus we find in this version (whether it is the warrior or the
city at risk) much the same notion attached to Troilos by the *Bacchides* of
Plautus (although the latter's list of three such prophecies does not include
Rhesos).

In art there is a rich collection of representations from the *Iliad*, beginning
with scenes of the embassy and final ransom on shield-bands from Olympia
and continuing on to Corinthian and Attic Black-Figure pots, but the events of
the poem have nothing like the popularity accorded to Herakles or even Perseus, and the illustrations that survive do not offer much that differs from
Homer's account.[49] On a fragment of a dinos by Sophilos, for example, we see
the funeral games for Patroklos (so labeled): there are the stands with cheering
crowds and the first horses coming into view, but we cannot tell to whom they
belonged, save that his name ended in -*os* (Athens 15499). An inscription also
tells us that Achilleus was portrayed on the other side of the stands, but he is
entirely lost. The François Krater offers as part of its second band precisely the
same event: Achilleus stands to the far right next to a tripod, waiting for the

arrival of the competitors, who are (in order) Olyteus (i.e., Odysseus), Auto-medon, Diomedes, Damasippos, Hypothoon (*sic*) (Florence 4209). Diomedes is, as we saw, the winner of the race in the Homeric version, and Automedon, although he does not compete there, is at least a charioteer of Achilleus and Patroklos. But Odysseus, here the winner, is likewise not a competitor in the *Iliad*, where nothing is ever said of his horses, Damasippos does not appear in the poem at all, and Hippothoon (as close as we can get to the last contestant) fights only on the Trojan side. That this scene could represent an alternate version of the race remains a possibility of course, but when both of the otherwise unfamiliar names contain the root *hippos*, or "horse" (Damasippos, "horse-tamer"; Hippothoon, "swift-horsed"), we may be forgiven for suspecting that the painter has done some inventing to augment a less-than-perfect memory of the Homeric version.

From about the same time is a metope of the Heraion I temple at Foce del Sele (no #): here, a figure who is surely Patroklos reaches up for what is apparently his breast-plate while another warrior (Hektor? Euphorbos?) stabs him in the back with a spear.[50] In *Iliad* 16 we saw that Patroklos' armor falls off from the force of Apollo's slap to the back; here the armor seems almost to be flying away, and conceivably the artist envisioned (or knew from variant epic accounts) something more magical than simply a god's intervention in battle. Other metopes from the same structure *may* show Helen and Andromache with infant Astyanax (on one section) and Hekabe with the corpse of Hektor (on another) in a general mourning scene.[51] From Korinth about 570 B.C. comes an olpe with Thetis' visit to a prostrate Achilleus, apparently engrossed in his grief for Patroklos and unwilling to eat (Brussels A4). For the rest of this century, and extending on through the fifth century, we have quite a number of Attic Black- and Red-Figure vases with scenes from the epic, including the leading away of Briseis, the duel between Aias and Hektor, the embassy to Achilleus, the carrying away of the corpses of Sarpedon and Patroklos, the making of the new armor and its consignment to Achilleus, the combat between Achilleus and Hektor, the slaughter of Trojan prisoners, and the ransoming of Hektor's body. Especially noteworthy from an artistic point of view are the New York Euphronios krater with Hypnos and Thanatos carrying off the body of Sarpedon as Hermes supervises (NY 1972.11.10), the Sosias Painter's intimate portrait of Achilleus bandaging Patroklos' arm in the tondo of a kylix (Berlin:Ch 2278), and the ransoming scenes on cups by Oltos (Munich 2618) and the Brygos Painter (Vienna 3710). But all these show simply expected elements of Homer's story, or details (such as Patroklos' wound) which can easily be extrapolated from it.[52]

The same is true of the relief panels from the east frieze of the Siphnian Treasury at Delphi (no #): to the left sit the gods, Trojan allies (Ares, Aphrodite, probably Artemis, and Apollo) on one side of Zeus, Achaian allies (possibly a kneeling Thetis and Poseidon, certainly Athena, Hera, and Demeter) on the other. On the right a battle rages over a fallen corpse, either that of Sarpedon or Patroklos, with Glaukos, Aineias, and Hektor on one side, Menelaos, ?, and Automedon on the other. From all this we learn that someone put Demeter (not named as a participant in the *Iliad*) on the Greek side, but otherwise the frieze's (considerable) values are entirely artistic.

Penthesileia and Memnon

The additional last line of the *Iliad* quoted from the Townley scholia above shows that the following poem in the Cycle, the *Aithiopis*, began with the arrival of the Amazon Penthesileia to help the Trojans, and so too Proklos in his summary of that work. What Proklos tells us beyond that is simply that Penthesileia was a daughter of Ares, Thracian in origin, and that after displaying great valor on the battlefield she was slain by Achilleus and buried by the Trojans. Thersites then reviled Achilleus for supposedly being in love with the Amazon, and Achilleus in anger slew him as well, creating dissension among the Greeks and necessitating a trip to Lesbos where he was purified by Odysseus. Subsequent to this account there are no literary references at all until Hellanikos, for whom we learn, courtesy of Tzetzes, that the Amazon was thought to have come to Troy to win glory in battle against men so that she might marry, since it was forbidden to Amazones to consort with men before they had done so (4F149). I have no explanation for such an idea. Lykophron alludes to the death of Thersites as due to Achilleus' wrath after Thersites had struck a blow to the eye of Penthesileia as she was dying (Lyk 999-1001; on this blow to the eye see also Σ *Ph* 445). The scholia relate that in fact the Aitolian gouged out her eye, but they know as well the versions in which Thersites' tongue is his undoing, and in which his accusation against Achilleus seems in fact one of necrophilia. Diodoros remarks briefly that Penthesileia came to Troy because she had killed a relative, and although she was queen of the Amazones she had to go into exile (DS 2.46.5). In Apollodoros, too, she has killed someone, namely Hippolyte, bride of Theseus, but inadvertently, while they were fighting together at the wedding of Theseus and Phaidra; here she is the daughter of Ares and one Otrere, and is purified at Troy by Priam, after which she slays Machaon and falls to Achilleus (ApE 5.1–2). Apollodoros also includes the death of Thersites as in the *Aithiopis* (he seems to regard Thersites' revilements as true, as does Propertius: 3.11.15–16) but says nothing about Achilleus' purification. In Eustathios, Achilleus accomplishes the slaying with a blow to the face, and as the *neôteroi* are cited, this may go back to the Cycle (Eu-*Il* 2.219, p. 208; cf. Σ *Ph* 445, Σ Lyk 999).

Of other authors, Quintus makes Penthesileia's accidental victim her own sister Hippolyte, slain by her while casting at a deer (QS 1.18–25). Here she brings with her twelve other Amazones, and after her death Achilleus falls in love with her when he has removed her helmet; Thersites dies as in the *Aithiopis* (his criticism is of Achilleus' weakness in loving a woman) and the corpse of Penthesileia is given back to the Trojans for burial. As for the aftermath in Quintus, as sole kinsman of Thersites (son of Agrios, Oineus' brother) Diomedes is alone among the Achaians in protesting his cousin's murder, and nearly comes to blows with Achilleus until the other Greeks reconcile them. In chapter 11 we saw that long before this Pherekydes (or someone) makes Thersites the son of Agrios and Dia, daughter of Porthaon (3F123: slight manuscript uncertainty), and thus such a conflict between Diomedes and Achilleus may be what Proklos refers to in saying that at this point in the *Aithiopis* there is stasis over the killing. Only in Diktys of Krete does Achilleus fail to completely dispatch Penthesileia (who here comes solely for glory and spoils); after some discussion Diomedes drags her nearly lifeless body to the Skamandros and throws it in (Dik 4.3). The Lykophron scholia (at 999) report the same deed, but there she is already quite dead and Diomedes' motive is specifically the fact that she brought about the death of his cousin.

Art offers a number of representations of Achilleus slaying the Amazon, beginning with shield-band reliefs from Olympia and elsewhere dating as early as perhaps 625 B.C. (Olympia B 112; name included on the later B 1555). In painting there is the famous neck-amphora by Exekias in the British Museum (London B210) and of course the name-piece of the Penthesileia Painter from about 455 B.C. (Munich 2688); one Black-Figure hydria of the Leagros Group even shows Achilleus carrying the body of his opponent out of battle (London B323). But otherwise our examples are straightforward combat scenes; nothing survives of any other part of the story (save Thersites' death: Boston 03.804, an Apulian volute krater), so that here as largely for the *Iliad* we learn nothing new from the artistic tradition, not even whether Achilleus' love for his fallen foe was generally credited.

After the death of Penthesileia and Achilleus' purification, the *Aithiopis* turns to yet another new ally of the Trojans, this time Memnon, son of Eos, who also wears armor forged by Hephaistos; the *Theogony* names Tithonos as his father, as we might expect (*Th* 984–85). Thetis tells Achilleus something about this next opponent, and in the ensuing battle Achilleus defeats him after Antilochos has fallen to him. Eos then obtains immortality for her son from Zeus. The *Odyssey* twice refers to the death of Antilochos, on the second occasion specifying that he was slain by the son of Eos, so that the author of that poem clearly knew much the same story (*Od* 3.108–12, 4.186–88). The only other Homeric reference is that of the *Nekuia*, where in speaking to Achilleus Odysseus asserts that Neoptolemos was the most beautiful of all those at Troy after Memnon (*Od* 11.522). For the seventh and sixth centuries there are just two brief allusions, a line of Alkman in which "Aias rages with his polished spear, and Memnon lusts for blood" (exact meaning of this last verb uncertain: 68 *PMG*), and Strabo's assertion that Simonides wrote a dithyramb *Memnon* in which the hero was buried in Syria (on the coast, near Paltos: 539 *PMG*).

In art there is the well-known amphora from (probably) Melos with Apollo in chariot greeted by Artemis which dates to about 640 B.C.; on the neck are two warriors confronting each other with armor stacked up between them, and in panels to either side a concerned woman looking on (Athens 3961). In the absence of names the armor (rather than a corpse) between the combatants has been taken to signify the duel between Aias and Diomedes at the funeral games for Patroklos (where the armor of Sarpedon was in fact the prize), or perhaps the conflict between Aias and Odysseus for the armor of Achilleus. But such scenes will not in any way explain the women, and more likely we do have here our first look at Achilleus and Memnon, accompanied by their mothers.[53]

Subsequently, a Middle Corinthian column krater of about 580 offers the two warriors (names inscribed; there is nothing between them) flanked by horses (Berlin:PM F1147) and a second krater of perhaps twenty years later has sons, mothers, and corpse of Antilochos, all named (Korinth C 72–149; so too a Chalkidian amphora in Florence [4210], among others). From Athens a Black-Figure amphora shows all five figures of the group, but while the warriors and their mothers are named as we would expect, the corpse in the center is Phokos, not Antilochos (PrColl, Athens). The presence of Hektor behind Eos (when he should be long since dead) suggests that the artist did not take his identifications as seriously as we might like. The combat also appeared on the Amyklai Throne (Paus 3.18.12: only the two fighters are mentioned) and the Chest of Kypselos (Paus 5.19.1, here definitely with the mothers), and even perhaps on a small terracotta altar from Agrigento on which one mother (Eos?) holds a second spear for her son.

In the fifth century we have several Pindaric allusions to Achilleus' victory over Memnon, but no details of interest beyond the fact itself (*Ol* 2.83; *Nem* 3.61–63, 6.51–55). In *Pythian* 6, however, we learn that Antilochos' father Nestor risked falling to Memnon after one of his horses (struck by Paris' arrows) hindered his chariot from flight; he called for his son, and Antilochos "purchased with death the safe return of his father" (*Py* 6.39). Admittedly this is remarkably like the moment early in *Iliad* 9 when Nestor's horse is similarly wounded by Paris, and the old man, busy trying to cut the traces, is saved by Diomedes as Hektor threatens (*Il* 8.80–91). Pindar's version is not a story found elsewhere, but as his point is the rather strained one of a comparison with Thrasyboulos, son of Xenokrates, who drove his father's chariot to victory, he is probably drawing on something already known to his audience. Even more enlightening, if only we had it, would certainly have been Aischylos' lost Memnon trilogy, consisting of *Memnon*, *Psychostasia*, and perhaps *Phrygioi*. The first of these, though there is little hard evidence, brought Memnon onstage from Aithiopia and probably included the death of Antilochos. In the second, as Plutarch tells us, Aischylos reshapes the weighing of the *kêres* (of Achilleus and Hektor) in *Iliad* 22 into a weighing of the *psychai* of Achilleus and Memnon, with beside the scales of Zeus Thetis and Eos, one to each side pleading for the life of her son (*Mor* 17a). What difference there might be between *kêres* and *psychai* remains a matter for dispute. Other evidence for the play comes from Pollux, who says that the *theologeion* was a platform above the *skênê* used for example for Zeus and those with him in the *Psychostasia* (4.130 = pp. 375–76 R). From such information it would seem that Zeus himself appeared onstage, and that there was an elaborate weighing scene, with perhaps actors playing Achilleus and Memnon actually standing in a pair of giant scales. It has, however, been objected that the technical requirements of that kind of tableau were probably quite beyond the capabilities of the Aischylean stage, and that Pollux's information may refer to some much later performance (or rewrite) of the play (nor does Plutarch actually say that in Aischylos Zeus held the scales).[54]

Vase-painting of the sixth and fifth centuries offers us a number of representations of this weighing, and while one of the earliest of these, an Ionian hydria in the Villa Giulia (the Ricci Hydria, no #), does show Zeus seated on his throne holding scales (Eos and Thetis kneel/stand before him, Achilleus and Memnon square off to the right), the others agree in portraying rather Hermes with the scales. The earliest of all (c. 540 B.C.) is an Attic Black-Figure dinos on which a seated Zeus and Hermes with scales are flanked by Thetis and Eos, thus establishing that Hermes performs the weighing as an agent of Zeus (Vienna 3619). Here too we see on each tray of the scales an *eidôlon* or miniature image of one of the contestants. Subsequently we have a Black-Figure lekythos of about 500 B.C. which omits Zeus and the mothers but again shows the two small images of the real warriors on the scales, while Achilleus and Memnon themselves are shown lifesize (London B639: no names). Other representations are all Red-Figure, including a very fine cup by Epiktetos on which Thetis and Eos both appeal to Zeus while looking back at Hermes, who stands between their sons holding the scales (VG 57912). But in all, the evidence is clearly sufficient to tell us that the motif of a weighing of the *psychai* (or *kêres* or whatever) of Achilleus and Memnon is older than Aischylos' trilogy, in contrast to what Plutarch seems to believe. The question has, of course, special importance because his remarks about Aischylos reshaping the *Iliad* would otherwise have led us to the conclusion that such a weighing did not appear in the *Aithiopis*. Sixth-century representations will not by themselves establish that the weighing was a part of that epic, but it seems likely, in which case Plutarch was not as familiar with the poems of the Cycle as he ought to have been.

As for Aischylos, we should probably conclude that Eos and Thetis appealed to a Zeus not physically present, and that Hermes as his representative (silent, if the play was two-actor) performed the onstage weighing in the *Psychostasia*. A further comment by Pollux (not mentioning this play by name) says that Eos came by means of the *geranos* to fetch the body of her son, again probably part of a later staging or version. We have no evidence as to how Aischylos' drama ended; possibly Eos' loss here was thematically related to the action of the third play of the trilogy, where Thetis probably lost her son Achilleus (see below). In any case, art represented also this sad mourning by the dawn goddess of her mortal son, perhaps on the Black-Figure name vase of the Vatican Mourner Painter (Vat 350), certainly on the fine Red-Figure cup by Douris, where the poses of Eos and Memnon resemble a pre-Christian pietà (Louvre G115). Of later literature there is little to say; Sophokles' *Aithiopes* may have treated this story or it may not, and subsequent authors have nothing new to add to the basic events.

As we saw in our brief look at the *Iliad*, not only does Thetis several times prophesy Achilleus' imminent death if he should slay Hektor, but Hektor himself as he lies dying in *Iliad* 22 predicts that Paris and Apollo shall bring death to the hero beside the Skaian gates. Earlier, Achilleus' horse Xanthos has said much the same thing in Book 19 by speaking of a mortal and a god as the agents, although Achilleus in Book 21 uses the phrase "arrows of *Apollo*" in recalling his mother's words (*Il* 21.276–78). The *Aithiopis* adds to this that Achilleus put the Trojans to flight and was actually pursuing them into the city when he was killed by Paris and Apollo. We have no other literary references until the fifth century, when Pindar's *Paian* 6 appears to tell us (the relevant section of papyrus has many gaps) that Apollo in the mortal form of Paris kept back the day of Troy's destruction and restrained Achilleus with death, casting/ shooting (something) at him (*Pa* 6.75–86). The implication of the adjective *opsiteros*, used to define "taking (of Troy)," would seem that Apollo here acts to protect *moira*, much as he does in *Iliad* 16 when Patroklos tries to assault the walls, or as Poseidon does in *Iliad* 20 when he rescues Aineias. From somewhere in Aischylos' work comes the quote given to us by Plato in which Thetis takes the god of prophecy to task for telling her that her children would live long lives, then slaying her only child (fr 350 R). I suspect this occurs in the third play of the Memnon trilogy, in a play specifically about the death of Achilleus and perhaps titled *Phrygioi*,[55] but even if that is true it does not help us much; the statement that Apollo killed her son should not in the circumstances be taken to mean that Paris played no part. The same holds for Neoptolemos' description of his father's death in Sophokles' *Philoktetes* (334–35: "no mortal destroyed him, but the god Apollo"), since the point here is the hero's invincibility under normal circumstances and the god's maliciousness. On the other side of the coin, Euripides twice has characters suggest that Paris was responsible (*Hek* 387–88; *And* 655); again, where the point is the culpability of the Trojans, the failure to mention Apollo is probably not significant. Vergil's *Aeneid* is, remarkably, the first work to state what the *Iliad* implies, that Paris shot the arrow and Apollo guided it to its mark (the "body" of Achilleus: *Aen* 6.56–58; cf. *Met* 12.598–606).

Nevertheless, despite such a wealth of sources, nothing in them (or in what is preserved, at least) ever speaks of a uniquely vulnerable foot, or of Achilleus' being struck there. Our first known author to even touch on such an idea is Statius, in whose *Achilleis* Thetis recalls a dream in which she seems a second time to be dipping her son in the Styx (*Ach* 1.133–34). The brevity of the reference shows that Statius alludes to some story already familiar to his audience; further clues appear at *Achilleis* 1.268–70, where Thetis laments that she did not arm her child completely in the waters of the Styx, and *Achilleis* 1.480–81, where she says that carrying him in secret through the Styx she made his fair limbs impervious to iron. Lactantius' commentary adds to this picture that Thetis, fearing death for her son, dipped him in the Styx, and that he became invulnerable in his whole body save for that part by which he was held (ΣΣ *Ach* 1.134, 296, 480; so too Servius at *Aen* 6.57, in virtually the same words). But none of these writers ever say that the part held was the foot, much less what particular part of the foot might be involved. Apollodoros, who with Hyginus is in fact the first to mention feet, says that Achilleus was struck in the *ankle (sphuron)* by an arrow shot by Paris and Apollo (ApE 5.3); the epitomator does not specify if he was vulnerable only there or not. We are, however, surely meant to understand that Achilleus dies (on the battlefield) from this wound (were it only incapacitating, the actual slayer would surely be credited). Hyginus, like Pindar, has Apollo operate in the guise of Paris, angered because Achilleus has boasted that he will sack Troy all by himself (*Fab* 107). He adds to this that Apollo struck and killed Achilleus with an arrow to the ankle *(talum)* "which alone mortal he is said to have had," thus giving us our first specific reference to the foot (and ankle) as the vulnerable part alluded to by Statius.

On the artistic side, we have some important early evidence which may anticipate details of the literary tradition. First is a Protocorinthian lekythos of about 670 B.C. with no names but a number of warriors in a battle scene (Athens, no #). To the left of the four main combatants an archer kneels, and an arrow he has just fired is about to strike the shin of the first of the opposing figures. Next comes a Pontic amphora from Copenhagen dating to perhaps 540 B.C.; again there are no names, but as two warriors square off against each other a third in Phrygian dress moves in from the right, aiming an arrow down toward the buttock or thigh of the man in front of him (Copenhagen 14066).[56] The third piece is a lost Chalkidian amphora, formerly in the Pembroke-Hope collection, of about the same date. Here we have quite a vigorous battle scene, with names for most of the figures. At the center lies Achilleus' corpse, with an arrow through one ankle (or more accurately the part of the foot just above the ankle) and seemingly another in his back. Over him Aias plunges his spear into Glykos (i.e., Glaukos: cf. ApE 5.4, where Aias slays this Lykian over the corpse), who had tied a rope around that same foot of Achilleus and was in process of dragging away the body. To the left Athena supervises (and Sthenelos binds up a wound of Diomedes); to the right Paris moving away in flight turns back to fire an arrow, while Aineias and other Trojans come up to help. Fourth is an Attic Red-Figure pelike by the Niobid Painter on which Paris to the left takes aim at a casually standing Achilleus to the right (Bochum S1060). Neither figure is named, but the clear presence of Apollo in the center of the composition with one hand held palm open toward Achilleus surely guarantees the moment in question (rather than for example that of *Iliad* 11 where Paris wounds Diomedes in the foot), and Paris here even wears a laurel crown like his divine patron. Though he draws back an arrow to fire again, one has already been released, and drops downward ominously toward Achilleus' foot (perhaps guided by the god?).

Taken together, these four pots would seem to leave little doubt that Achilleus was wounded in the foot (and that Glaukos was slain by Aias in the fight over the corpse) at an early point in the tradition. That being the case, we might well hypothesize that Apollodoros' account with its references to Glaukos and Achilleus' ankle is taken more or less directly from the *Aithiopis*. But it should then follow (given that in the *Aithiopis* as in the *Iliad* Apollo helps) that the wound to the foot is deliberate, rather than (as when Paris wounds Diomedes) an off-center shot to a peripheral part of the body.[57] In other words, if Paris did in the *Aithiopis* strike Achilleus' ankle with divine aid, he did so surely because only there could Achilleus be slain, and only with Apollo's assistance could he hope to hit such a difficult target. Seemingly then, at least one early version did know of Thetis' attempt to make her son physically invulnerable. As an alternative, certain points in the *Iliad* have been thought to support the theory that in some accounts it was Achilleus' armor, the work of the gods, which was invulnerable (thus explaining Patroklos' necessary loss of it before his defeat).[58] In that case we might suppose that Apollo simply guided Paris' arrow to one small part of Achilleus' (very vulnerable) body not covered by his invulnerable armor, and that this arrangement was somehow transformed into or replaced by the concept of the (almost) invulnerable body.

Complicating both these views, however, and all other accounts of Achilleus' death, there stands the puzzling fact that a vulnerable ankle ought not to be the cause of a *fatal* wound, as opposed to a disabling one; we need only to compare Diomedes, who simply limps off the field of battle after Paris puts an arrow through his foot in *Iliad* 11. True, Quintus of Smyrna does have Achilleus expire from such an ankle wound (after fighting on bravely for a considerable time: QS 3.60–185), but such overblown rhetorical elaboration is probably the result of accepting a long-standing tradition without the magic behind it. What we really need, if this fatal blow to the ankle is to make sense, is a story in which the hero's vital organs are displaced to a part of his body where his opponents will not expect to find them, or against which they will have difficulty mounting an assault. Perhaps in such a story the obtaining of personal invulnerability required as a tradeoff that one vulnerable spot be left in which all the recipient's vitality could be concentrated, with of course fatal results if anyone learned the location of that spot. But this kind of motif, if it did exist for Achilleus, has clearly been lost, and could never have been accounted for by the bath in the Styx, which will at best explain only the child's quasi-invulnerability. I suspect then that already at an early point the full magical ramifications of Achilleus' peculiar situation have dropped out of the tradition, leaving behind a vulnerable ankle that somewhat implausibly remains the cause of his death. If that is so, then the bath may have been invented quite a bit later, perhaps even (as has been suggested) under the influence of Christian baptism.[59] One final point concerns the hero's better-known invulnerable *heel*. We have seen that all our evidence, both Greek and Latin, specifies the ankle, and this holds even for the Second and Third Vatican Mythographers, where the part not impregnated is the *talus* (VM II 205; VM III 11.24; VM I 178 says the *planta*, or sole of the foot). But seemingly the referent of *talus* shifted downward in the later Latin form *talone*, as the modern French *(talon)* and Italian *(tallone)* words for "heel" would indicate.

Added to this uncertain picture is the fact that late authors also offer quite a different version of Achilleus' death, one based on his desire for Priam's daughter Polyxena. Our best sources for this story are the scholia to the *Hekabe*, Hyginus, Servius, and Lactantius, plus the uncertainly dated Diktys and Dares. The *Hekabe* scholia suggest that, according to some, Achilleus died in the precinct of Thymbraian Apollo while he was negotiating with Priam for the hand of Polyxena in marriage (Σ *Hek* 41). Servius adds that Achilleus first saw her when she came with her father to ransom Hektor's body, was falsely promised her hand if he would stop the war, and on coming to the precinct of Apollo for the treaty was slain by Paris from ambush (with an arrow: Σ *Aen* 3.322); Lactantius has Paris hiding behind a statue in the precinct when he commits the deed (aiming, as we saw, at the vulnerable ankle: Σ *Ach* 1.134). Hyginus' very brief note (given only as an explanation of Polyxena's sacrifice) is vaguer, but Achilleus is here again slain by Paris (and Deiphobos) when he comes (somewhere) to discuss a union with their sister (*Fab* 110). In Diktys' pro-Greek version, Achilleus first sees Polyxena by chance at a religious festival and offers to bring the war to an end if he might marry her (Dik 3.2). Nothing comes of this, but Priam later brings Polyxena with him when he arrives to fetch his son's body, and asks Achilleus to keep her with him (Dik 3.27). Achilleus defers that decision for the moment, and Priam subsequently sends some sort of message to him on the subject in the Thymbraion via the herald Idaios. Paris and Deiphobos take advantage of the situation to approach Achilleus in the same precinct as if bringing a further communication; Deiphobos seizes and immobilizes him in an embrace so that Paris coming forward may stab him in the side (Dik 4.10–11). Dares' pro-Trojan version begins in much the same way, with Achilleus first seeing Polyxena when she and her parents come to pay honor at the tomb of Hektor. He proposes that he will personally abandon the war in return for her hand; Priam counters that only a complete cessation of hostilities will suffice. The issue is then dropped, but later Hekabe, angered at the death of Lykaon and Troilos, sends a message in Priam's name asking Achilleus to come to the same precinct of Apollo to discuss the marriage (Dar 34). When he and Anticholos arrive, they are overwhelmed by superior forces and cut down by Paris in person. Conceivably this variant mode of death was created to explain the otherwise rather unusual sacrifice of Priam's daughter at the tomb of Achilleus, an event found already in the *Iliou Persis;* certainly such a demise was not part of the *Aithiopis*, where Proklos' summary guarantees that Achilleus died on the battlefield.[60]

The Fate of Aias	With Achilleus now dead, however that event was brought about, the *Aithiopis* proceeds to the struggle over his body and the wondrous armor. We are told by Proklos that after a considerable battle Aias, shouldering the corpse, brought it back to the ships, with Odysseus holding off the Trojans to the rear (this last also at *Od* 5.308–10). Antilochos was then buried and Achilleus laid in state for the mourning of Thetis, the other Nereides, and the Mousai, after which Thetis snatched her son from the funeral pyre and took him away to the White Island (or perhaps in the original an island named Leuke). The Achaians piled up a mound nonetheless and held funeral games, and then Odysseus and Aias disputed the disposition of his armor. Proklos' summary of the *Aithiopis* ends here, but a Pindaric scholion, if trustworthy, would have the poem include the suicide of Aias (toward dawn: *Aith* fr 5 *PEG*). We know in any case that the following poem, the *Little Iliad* of Lesches, began with the contest for the arms and that same suicide. Here Odysseus wins by the contriving of Athena, and being maddened Aias outrages the herds of the Achaians and then kills himself. Scholia add that in the poem Nestor recommended the sending of spies to listen under the walls of Troy to Trojan opinions of the disputing heroes; these heard one maiden comment on Aias' valor in carrying back Achilleus when Odysseus was unwilling to do so, but heard another (inspired by Athena) respond that even women can carry burdens, but not everyone can fight (*IlMik* fr 2 *PEG*, with *appuratus*). We learn elsewhere that because of the anger of the king, Aias' body was buried in a coffin rather than being cremated (*IlMik* fr 3 *PEG*). Interestingly enough, a papyrus fragment from what is apparently early epic suggests that in at least one account Odysseus actually was the one to carry back the body (*IlMik* fr 32 [*dubium*] *PEG*; cf. Σ *Od* 5.310).

The *Odyssey* has its own version of a few of these events, for Odysseus on seeing Aias in the Underworld notes the latter's continued anger over the contest for Achilleus' arms, which Thetis proposed and *paides Trôôn* plus Athena judged (*Od* 11.543–60).[61] His further words make it clear that Aias perished on account of those arms, but he does not say how, nor is there any mention of madness. Scholia to this passage expand Odysseus' account a bit by suggesting that Agamemnon specifically asked Trojan prisoners which hero had harmed them most; with no source given we might perhaps suspect this to be the version of the *Aithiopis* (Σ *Od* 11.547). *Odyssey* 24 also contains a description of Achilleus' burial by Agamemnon, who tells us that after a whole day of contending over the body Zeus sent a storm, and the Achaians brought the corpse back to the ships (*Od* 24.36–92). There they washed it, and (as in the *Aithiopis*) Thetis, the Nereides, and the nine Mousai arrived, here lamenting for seventeen days. On the eighteenth, the Achaians cremated the body and placed the bones together with those of Patroklos in a golden jar contributed by Thetis, and after the mound had been piled up Thetis obtained prizes from the gods for funeral games. That Thetis does not then snatch the body off the pyre, as she does in the *Aithiopis*, is only to be expected, given that for both *Odyssey* 11 and 24, Achilleus' shade is in the Underworld like that of any other mortal. Apollodoros' epitomator says, rather oddly, that the *Achaians* buried Achilleus and Patroklos together on the White Island (possibly compression is responsible for this) and that in the games in his honor Eumelos won the chariot race, Diomedes the stadion, Aias the diskos throw, and Teukros the archery contest (Ap*E* 5.5). We have already noted the evidence from other Archaic authors (Ibykos 291 *PMG;* Simonides 558 *PMG*) concerning Achilleus' life with Medeia after death, and likewise in Pindar he has a blessed existence (*Ol* 2.79–80; *Nem* 4.49–50; cf. *IlMik* fr 32 [*dubium*] *PEG*).

Aias' downfall continues as an important theme in the fifth century, when both Aischylos and Sophokles compose plays on his fate and Pindar offers some strong comments in his defense. Once again Aischylos seems to have composed a trilogy, consisting of *Hoplôn Krisis* ("Judgment of Arms"), *Threissai,* and *Salaminiai.* The first play certainly presented the dispute, with Aias casting aspersions on Odysseus' ancestry (fr 175 R) and the Nereides *perhaps* serving as judges (someone does call upon them to do so: fr 174 R). In the second occurred the suicide, with Athena or some other female divinity showing Aias the one place where he was vulnerable (the armpit: fr 83 R). For the third drama we do not even know the location, much less the plot; it may have been at Troy, on the island of Salamis when Teukros returned home, or even on Cyprus, and (depending in part on location) Aias' burial, or Teukros' concern for him, may or may not have been issues. Pindar speaks of the vote in two odes written for Aiginetans: *Nemean* 7.23–30 asserts that the Achaians were blind to the truth when they valued Odysseus above Aias, causing the latter to commit suicide, while *Nemean* 8.21–32 suggests that lies were told, to make the Danaans favor Odysseus with their secret vote when Aias clearly did more to win back Achilleus' body. Both in these poems and in *Isthmian* 4, where Aias' suicide in the night (by throwing himself on his sword) is said to have brought reproach to the Greeks at Troy, Pindar seems to suppose that the Achaians themselves made the decision (although since he criticizes that decision, we can hardly expect him to stress Athena's role).

Sophokles' preserved *Aias* (produced in the 440s B.C.?) gives us our first full account of the story. The play begins with Odysseus gingerly approaching the tent of Aias, after the army has become alarmed over the slaughter of some of their flocks. It is thus the night after the judgment, and Athena comes to inform her favorite hero of the situation. We learn from this and other parts of the play that here too, as in Pindar, the Achaian leaders themselves voted (as they may have done in the *Aithiopis,* the *Hoplôn Krisis,* and even perhaps in the *Odyssey* and *Little Iliad,* if the Trojan opinions there were simply advisory), and that Aias believes Odysseus and the Atreidai to have unfairly influenced the result against him. Accordingly, he has plotted to strike at the leaders that night in their sleep, and only here has Athena intervened, sending madness to turn him instead against the flocks, which he mistakenly believes are the Achaians. At the height of this folly he has dragged a particularly large ram back to his tent in the belief that it is Odysseus, and proceeds to lash it with a whip. Athena invites Odysseus to exult at his enemy's ruin, but he is more horrified at the downfall of a comrade and fellow mortal. Aias' delusion now ends, and realizing what he has done he determines on suicide, despite the appeals of his concubine Tekmessa, by whom he has a son Eurysakes. The deed is carried out at the beach, where he throws himself on his sword, and the second half of the play revolves around a conflict between the Atreidai, who have forbidden burial, and Teukros. The dispute is only resolved when Odysseus reappears and asks burial for his fallen opponent as a personal favor, arguing that it is not right to carry hatred past the limit of death.

The play thus emerges as something of a contrast between Aias' steadfast intransigence and Odysseus' flexibility, with the latter's viewpoint seemingly more effective. For Athena's treatment of Aias, moreover, the one defense offered is that Aias once dismissed her offer of help on the battlefield, claiming that he by himself would be sufficient (*Ai* 770–77). We saw above that madness and the issue of burial were also elements of the *Little Iliad*, but we do not know if the madness there was of the same type (Proklos does not say what Aias supposed himself to be doing when he attacked the herds), nor whether there was any protest at the proposal for inhumation. Apollodoros is here again too brief to be of much help, and what he does offer is as in Sophokles, but we do find repeated as well the detail of the *Little Iliad* that on Agamemnon's order Aias (alone of all the Achaians) was buried in a coffin (ApE 5.7).

As for Aias' near invulnerability, no writer before the fifth century preserves any trace of it (although it may be hinted at in art: see below), and Homer certainly excludes it (*Il* 23.820–23). Aischylos thus is our first certain source for the idea. But in Pindar's *Isthmian* 6, Herakles comes to the house of Telamon and prays that his friend might have a child as unbreakable in form as the hide of the Nemean Lion (*Is* 6.42–49). Possibly such words are simply a request for strength, and the scholia do not elaborate, but under the circumstances they should probably be taken as an allusion to the impenetrability of the Lion's hide and that of the child. That Herakles' visit was the occasion on which Aias became invulnerable is at any rate the view of Lykophron, who says that Herakles' prayer was made after Aias was already born, that he held the child in his arms, that the lionskin conferred the invulnerability, and that the one place where Aias could be killed was the part covered by Herakles' quiver (Lyk 455–61). The scholia clarify this somewhat by adding that Herakles wrapped the child in the skin, and that the part not covered was either by the ribs or the collarbone (cf. ΣAb *Il* 23.821). Scholia to the *Isthmian* 6 passage add that the story of Herakles' prayer as Pindar tells it is taken from the *Megalai Ehoiai* (Σ *Is* 6.53 = Hes fr 250 MW), so that the whole tale probably goes back that far; whether it was found in the *Aithiopis* or the *Little Iliad* we cannot say.[62] Aischylean in any event might still be the curious appearance of a goddess to Aias to tell him where he is vulnerable, since that information is something he might well know by himself in earlier accounts.

For these events in art we have a fine Late Corinthian hydria with Thetis and the Nereides gathered around the body of Achilleus (Louvre E643), while a problematic Athenian Black-Figure amphora of the Leagros Group with a large warrior running across the sea (there is a ship below) *may* mean to suggest Achilleus' journey to the White Island (London B240). Beyond these two pots there are a good number of representations of three other scenes, the rescue of Achilleus' body, the dispute over the arms, and Aias' suicide. For the first of these, illustrations may begin as early as the end of the eighth century, if we accept scenes of a man being carried on an ivory seal from Perachora (Athens, no #) and the repeated seal impressions on a clay vessel from Samos (T 416). Toward the middle of the seventh century we start to find more detailed, and hence more convincing, recreations of this motif: a terracotta relief from Tarentum offers us on the top band of a woman's skirt a male figure carrying on his shoulder another man (in helmet and almost twice the bearer's size) (Naples, no #). The same disproportion appears even more vividly on several slightly varying shield-band reliefs from Olympia, where the bearer wears corselet and greaves, the corpse a chain-link corselet and helmet (B 1921, B 1911), and on a terracotta mold from Lemnos (1205), both of the second half of the century. In no case are there names, but nothing at any point in our tradition assigns this role to anyone but Aias, while the large size of the deceased (in the absence of any known story involving the porting of oversized opponents; Alkyoneus would not be armed) seems an early attempt to convey Achilleus' stature as a fighter.

By the sixth century Thetis' son assumes more normal dimensions in this scene, as we see on both handles of the François Krater, where the names of the two men are included (Florence 4209). Here Aias is in the *knielauf* position (looking quite elegant) and Achilleus without arms; probably Kleitias wished by this latter device to increase the pathos of his death. Subsequently, Exekias produced a powerful version of his own, with a fully armed Aias bent under the weight of a fully armed and very heavy-looking Achilleus (Munich 1470: both sides). The face of Aias is all but hidden by his shield in each version, and the effort involved, in contrast to the opinion of Lesches' Trojan maidens, is very pointed. The same artist assayed yet another version of this tableau for a lost amphora once in Berlin (Berlin:Lost F1718); his general compositional scheme seems to have set the fashion for virtually all future illustrations of the story. In later Black-Figure portrayals, there are supporting figures, including at times one who might be Odysseus, but it cannot be said that his role is at all emphasized. The only other figural scheme illustrating this story is that of Aias beginning to lift the body of Achilleus from the ground, or supporting him on one arm, as on an odd late sixth-century amphora in Munich on which the dead Achilleus is shown full face, looking more like a Satyros than a human (Munich 1415).

The dispute over Achilleus' arms, while obviously known to epic tradition and possibly illustrated as early as the Melos amphora discussed above (Athens 3961), cannot be identified with absolute certainty in art until the Red-Figure period, when several Attic cups offer the spectacle of partially armed warriors drawing swords against each other while their comrades (including a bearded man in the center) try to restrain them (Douris: Vienna 3695; Brygos Painter: Getty 86.AE.286; London E69). By themselves these representations could intend as well combats in funeral games for Patroklos or Achilleus, but in each case we see on the other side of the cup the voting for the arms, thus virtually guaranteeing that at some point the dispute between Aias and Odysseus threatened to resolve itself by force. Conceivably this notion was suggested by the dramatic trilogy of Aischylos, but against such a theory are a small number of Black-Figure pots where we find the same sort of scheme, albeit without an accompanying vote. In this category are a lekythos from the third quarter of the sixth century (two naked men oppose each other with swords, a third stands between with a spear or staff; armor on the ground: Berlin:Lost F2000), an amphora of the last quarter (two old men restraining in the center, while younger men to each side pull on the sword arms of the disputants, who are fully armed: Munich 1411), and an oinochoe of the same period (combatants again naked except for swords, and numerous restrainers: Louvre F340). In neither of the last two cases are any arms shown as prizes or spoils, but it seems a reasonable conjecture that all three pots represent the conflict, an event that perhaps led the Achaian leaders to agree to decide the disposition of the arms.

A first stage of that disposition appears on a late (*c.* 500 B.C.) Black-Figure pelike with Odysseus (named) standing on a platform and arguing his case while Aias (also named) listens (arms between them: Naples 81083). The vote itself then follows on several Red-Figure cups, including the above-mentioned pieces by Douris and the Brygos Painter: on all of these a platform or low block stands in the center, and at one end or the other the Greeks place their pebbles as ballots, approaching from both sides. At least three examples feature Athena in the center, supervising the process; Aias stands off to the side and puts his head in his hand as he sees the vote going against him. I suggested above that the threat of decision by combat probably preceded the resort to a vote, but of course it could also have come afterward, with Aias attacking Odysseus in his frustration at losing.

Finally, we turn to artistic versions of the suicide. Aias is the only figure in mythology known to have thrown himself on his sword, so that the surprisingly large corpus of such representations all presumably illustrate this story (on a steatite intaglio from the latter seventh century he is in fact named: NY 42.11.13). Oldest in time is certainly a Protocorinthian aryballos of about 700 B.C. which shows Aias slanting across a vertical sword amid a general parade of unrelated figures (Berlin:PM VI 3319). Subsequently, there are quite a number of Corinthian offerings, including the "Eurytios" krater of about 600 B.C. on which warriors in poses of astonishment stand to either side of the transfixed Aias (Louvre E635); the sword point here seems split in two, perhaps suggesting early knowledge of the (almost) invulnerable hero found in Aischylos. A Middle Corinthian cup of the early sixth century also shows a number of Greeks (named) flanking the prostrate corpse: Phoinix and Nestor are closest, seeming almost to remonstrate with each other, then Odysseus and Diomedes to the left and Agamemnon, Teukros, and Aias (obviously the son of Oileus) to the right (Basel, Loan). Meanwhile, the scheme of the krater resurfaces on shield-band reliefs from Olympia, with again warriors facing each other over the corpse, hands held out (Aias himself has his face touchingly buried in his hands: B 1636, B 1654). The death even appears on an unfinished metope from Foce del Sele (no #), where Aias, here all alone, leans awkwardly over the upright sword. From Athens there is above all the amphora by Exekias showing not the fact of death but rather Aias carefully planting the sword in the ground, his whole attention wrapped up in that one deliberate act (Boulogne 558). Less poignant but still affecting is a Red-Figure lekythos of about 460 B.C. on which, the sword now planted, the intended suicide kneels and holds both hands up to the sky (Basel, Loan). In a masterful tondo by the Brygos Painter, on the other hand, we see Aias lying on his back, with the sword protruding upwards from his chest, while a woman (surely Tekmessa) prepares to spread a cloak over him (Getty 86.AE.286). The entry of the sword from the back is here clearly more appropriate to a murder than a suicide, thus prompting some scholars to think rather of Klytaimestra and Agamemnon.[63] But the woman's gesture seems one of tenderness, an empty scabbard to upper right suggests that the sword was the man's own, and (as we have already seen) the outside of this cup presented the quarrel over the arms and the vote. Finally, an Etruscan mirror of the early fourth century depicts the moment of suicide (and Aias' invulnerability): the sword clearly bends back against his chest as Athena appears, her hand outstretched to indicate (one presumes) the correct spot (Boston 99.494).

One other story (if it is that), to be mentioned here for want of a better place, is the game of dice or draughts between Aias and Achilleus. The confrontation appears only in art, beginning about 550 B.C. with a Black-Figure cup now in the Vatican (343). The scene of fully armed warriors seated or crouching with a small gaming table between them appears on both sides; on one of these, other warriors and older men look on, while on the reverse the warriors turn away, as if heading out to battle. Only nonsense inscriptions appear here, but the famous Vatican amphora by Exekias, which shows the two men alone, leaning intently over the table on which their tokens lie, provides the names of Aias and Achilleus (Vat 344). By the 520s B.C. a central Athena has been added to the composition (overseeing the game or calling the warriors to battle?) and knucklebones are sometimes in use. In all, there are over 125 vase-paintings of the scene, plus Olympia shield-band reliefs (B 4810) and probably a statue group (including Athena) on the Akropolis in the last decade of the sixth century.[64] Most likely, the moment intended is that before Achilleus' last battle, but it is difficult to think of a literary plot line in which such an event could hold much importance, unless Achilleus and Aias played for some stakes (such as Achilleus' armor after he died?). The sudden spate of illustrations in the latter part of the sixth century may argue rather for a fanciful invention by a sculptor or monumental painter.

Next in the sequence of events charted for us by the *Little Iliad* comes the capture by Odysseus of the Trojan Helenos, son of Priam, "from ambush." Already in the *Kypria* Helenos possessed prophetic skills (mentioned only once by Homer: *Il* 6.76), and so too here, for he predicts something that leads Diomedes to sail back to Lemnos for Philoktetes. Returning to Troy, Philoktetes is healed of his wound by Machaon and slays Paris in a single combat; Paris' corpse is then maltreated in some way by Menelaos but recovered by the Trojans for burial. We saw above that the *Iliad* too knows of this return, although without offering any details (*Il* 2.721–25). No other treatments of the story surface until the fifth century, when Pindar uses it as an exhortation to Hieron in his *Pythian* 1, and all three of the major tragedians dramatize the envoy to Lemnos. Pindar's allusion, in an ode composed for a chariot victory in 470 B.C., presents us with the surprising idea that Philoktetes is not healed when he fights at Troy: "But now he [Hieron] has gone to war in the fashion of Philoktetes. For even the proud courted that man under necessity, and they say that godlike heroes went to bring him from Lemnos, worn out though he was from his wound. And he sacked Troy and brought an end to the Achaians' labors, plying a strengthless frame, for so it was fated" (*Py* 1.50–55). The scholia note here that Hieron was at the time suffering from some form of stones, and probably Pindar has himself changed the myth on this one occasion for the sake of the analogy, since his purpose is to encourage Hieron to endure his malady. The same scholia also tell us that a dithyramb by Bakchylides contained this story, and that there Philoktetes was brought back because Helenos had prophesied that Troy would not fall without the bow of Herakles (fr 7 SM).

Of the three dramatic versions of the tale only that of Sophokles survives, but we do have the two discourses by Dion of Prusa noted above, one comparing the three plays, the other reproducing in dialogue form material almost certainly from the prologue of Euripides' effort (DP 52, 59). From the comparison we learn less about the plays than we might have hoped, but we can say that in Aischylos the chorus consisted of men of Lemnos, and that Odysseus himself played the primary role in separating Philoktetes from his weapons and so persuading him to come back. This he was able to accomplish because Philoktetes failed to recognize him after so much time, and he took advantage of the fact to fabricate a story in which Agamemnon was dead, Odysseus charged with some sort of base deed, and the army in general in a wretched condition. Such deception apparently served the purpose of cheering up Philoktetes and making him more trusting of his visitor, but we do not know anything else of Aischylos' plot, in particular how reluctant Philoktetes was or was not to return and how Odysseus managed to persuade him. Dion's failure to mention any other characters does suggest that the play had only two actors, and perhaps only two main roles. Euripides' drama was probably written before that of Sophokles, given the late (409 B.C.) date of the latter, and took advantage of the third actor to have Odysseus and Diomedes come together. Odysseus has here been disguised by Athena so that Philoktetes will not recognize him, and the chorus again consists of Lemnians, who apologize at some point for having ignored Philoktetes for so many years. Discourse 59 adds to this picture a dialogue between Odysseus and Philoktetes which reproduces closely four of the fragments actually attributed to Euripides' play, and is thus surely modeled on the prologue of that work, which we know to have been spoken by Odysseus.

In this discourse, Odysseus muses on the difficulties that a reputation for wisdom brings, since such men are always embroiled in difficult situations as the most likely to succeed. As in Bakchylides, Helenos has named Herakles' bow (and apparently Philoktetes as well) as necessary to the taking of Troy, and while Odysseus at first refuses the mission because he himself abandoned the wounded hero, Athena persuades him to change his mind. The situation is complicated, however, by the fact that the Trojans are themselves in process of sending a delegation to Lemnos, hoping to persuade Philoktetes to come back with them so that Troy will never fall (Dion attests this to be a Euripidean innovation). Odysseus' story to Philoktetes is that he is an Achaian driven from the Greek camp by Odysseus because he was a friend of Palamedes, whom Odysseus has destroyed. Somehow he has managed to arrive alone on Lemnos in his flight, and Philoktetes calls upon him to share his own lot for the moment. Philoktetes adds that the pain from his foot is not as great as it once was, but here the dialogue ends, and once again we know nothing about the resolution of the play, save that a Lemnian named Aktor who was known to Philoktetes made an appearance.

In Sophokles' drama, Odysseus is again the leader of the expedition, but here he has brought with him Neoptolemos rather than Diomedes. As we will see in the next section, the summoning of Neoptolemos from Skyros to Troy happens in the *Little Iliad* only *after* Philoktetes' return, so that Sophokles has altered the epic chronology. A second innovation concerns the island of Lemnos, now completely deserted save for Philoktetes; the chorus consists of the Achaian sailors who came with Odysseus and Neoptolemos. But as before, Philoktetes hates the Greeks who abandoned him, and Odysseus' plan is that Neoptolemos carry out the necessary deception by acknowledging his identity but claiming to have left Troy in anger after the Atreidai and Odysseus refused to give him his father's armor. Although Odysseus does not say what precisely he thinks this tale will accomplish, Philoktetes' response is to ask to be taken back to Greece on Neoptolemos' ship, a wish intensified by the arrival of a sailor from Odysseus with the news that the Greeks are coming for Philoktetes. So far this is as we might expect, but Philoktetes then gives Neoptolemos his bow to hold while he rests after an attack of pain, and Odysseus, finding the bow in Neoptolemos' hands, declares that the weapon alone will suffice, if Philoktetes refuses to come to Troy with it. Whether he believes this or is simply bluffing to frighten Philoktetes we never learn, for Neoptolemos balks at depriving a crippled man of his only means of support and gives the bow back, over Odysseus' protests. He does also, however, try to persuade Philoktetes that it will be in his own interest to come back to Troy, citing Helenos' prophecy and the glory he will win there and revealing now for the first time, toward the close of the play, that Philoktetes can be cured of his terrible wound if he will consent to come. Yet Philoktetes still refuses, and only the appearance of the divine Herakles at the play's close convinces him that what is fated must after all be carried out. As such, the drama is as much a study of Neoptolemos' character under pressure and temptation as it is of Philoktetes, and Sophokles is likely to have invented a good many of the details of his plot to serve that purpose. We should note, though, that other playwrights of the fifth century (e.g., Achaios, Philokles) also wrote dramas entitled *Philoktetes*, and we cannot say what they may have added to the tradition. Later writers offer us nothing of any interest on the matter of the actual fetching, adhering as they do to one or other of the above authors; for what it is worth, Apollodoros sends Odysseus and Diomedes to fetch the bow and wounded hero.

As for the events following Philoktetes' return, namely his physical recovery and the death of Paris, we know that Sophokles wrote a *Philoktetes at Troy* that must have covered some of this material. The scanty fragments show that the hero still suffered from the excruciating pain of his wound for at least part of the play, and it seems to have been a matter of some concern to him. Given the difficulties in finding much tragedy in this situation if he knows he is to be cured, we might conjecture that he does not know (in contrast to the later Sophoklean play set on Lemnos), and that he spends much of the drama lamenting his condition. If so, the work will have had a difficult time finding room for the combat with Paris, save as a prophecy, and perhaps that was how matters were handled. But equally, the combat may have held center stage as the primary event. Either way, the confrontation between Philoktetes and Paris offers one puzzle. The language of our summary of the *Little Iliad* certainly implies that these two noted archers fought a duel, which one would expect to be a traditional combat with sword and spear (*monomachia* as found here is the term used in the Alexandrian book headings of the *Iliad* for the single combats between Menelaos and Paris and Aias and Hektor, i.e., combats fought while the rest of the army watched). In that case, it seems certainly odd that both men should change weapons (especially when Philoktetes' bow is the presumed key to his success) and that these two in particular should be chosen to meet. Diktys, however, does present a single combat with bows (Dik 4.19), and conceivably this was after all the epic version as well; Paris is here wounded in the left hand, then the right eye, and finally both feet (cf. Σ Lyk 911). On the *Tabula Iliaca Capitolina*, a pictorial relief from Augustan times with scenes supposedly drawn from the *Little Iliad* (as well as from Homer, Arktinos, and Stesichoros), we do see a figure who must be Paris falling backward in death with a bow in his hand,[65] but we cannot say how precisely the artist (or his pictorial sources) would have followed the original text. Lykophron and Apollodoros report simply that Philoktetes did shoot Paris with an arrow (Lyk 914–15; ApE 5.8).

Other differences between Apollodoros' version and epic are the curing of Philoktetes by Podaleirios, not his brother Machaon (necessary because in Apollodoros Machaon is by this point already dead, having been killed by Penthesileia) and the delivery of the prophecy about Philoktetes and the taking of Troy by Kalchas, not Helenos. This last change probably stems from the incorporation of an event (related first by Konon and then Apollodoros) which requires Helenos' presence in Troy at this moment (and for some time after): following Paris' death he and Deiphobos contend for Helen's hand, and when Deiphobos is chosen (Konon says by force and intriguing, although he was younger), Helenos leaves Troy for Ida in anger (26F1.34; ApE 5.9). He is, however, captured by Odysseus on Kalchas' recommendation, and delivers various prophecies about Troy's fall to which we shall return in the next section. Servius at *Aeneid* 2.166 gives much the same account, adding that Priam assigned Helen to Deiphobos, and that once captured Helenos revealed the secret of the Palladion out of hatred. Obviously, the *Little Iliad* cannot have told this story of a dispute over Helen, for there Helenos is captured by the Greeks before Paris dies; where Konon and Apollodoros might have found such a tale we do not know.

One other sequence of events connected with Paris' death can likewise not have come from the *Little Iliad*, where he clearly dies on the battlefield and his corpse is disfigured by Menelaos before its recovery for burial. The key figure in this sequence is Oinone, daughter of Kebren, about whom Parthenios tells two tales. In the first, which he credits to Hellanikos and Kephalon (i.e., the Hellenistic Hegesianax[66]), Korythos, Paris' son by Oinone, comes to Troy to fight and is much taken by Helen, who receives him quite kindly, since he is very attractive (Par 34 = 4F29, 45F6). On discovering this fact, Paris kills him. The author then adds that according to Nikandros Korythos was instead the son of Paris and Helen, and offers a quote to prove it. In the second tale, credited to Kephalon and Nikandros, Paris is actually married to Oinone before he abducts Helen (Par 4 = 45F2). This former love possesses for whatever reason the gift of prophecy, and foretells to Paris that he will leave her to find a bride in Europe, thus bringing war to his people and to himself a wound in battle which only she can heal. Matters proceed as she predicts, he is wounded by Philoktetes' arrows and, remembering her words, sends a messenger to ask for her help. She replies that he would do better to seek help from Helen, whom he preferred to her, and hearing this refusal from the messenger he dies. When she sees that he is indeed dead she laments bitterly and kills herself.

Konon has a fuller version (or combination) of these two tales, as perhaps Hegesianax before him, with Paris and Oinone parents of a child Korythos who surpasses his father in beauty (26F1.23). His mother deliberately sends him to

Helen at Troy, hoping to make Paris jealous and create trouble with his new wife. This in fact happens, for Paris, entering their bedroom one day, sees Korythos sitting next to Helen and, inflamed by suspicion, kills him. On hearing of her son's death, Oinone proclaims that Paris will one day need her when he is wounded by the Greeks. The rest of the story proceeds as in Parthenios, with Paris carried toward Mount Ida in a wagon and the messenger going on ahead. Here, however, Oinone has a change of heart after sending the messenger away and arrives with the necessary herbs too late, hanging herself when she learns of Paris' death. The latter part of this story is certainly as early as Lykophron, who speaks of the jealous bride, skilled in healing, who threw herself from a high tower to share the death of her bedmate Paris, although Lykophron deviates from Parthenios in making Oinone send her son "to inform about the land," apparently telling the Greeks how they may find Troy (Lyk 57–68). The scholia to this passage offer nothing not found in Konon and Parthenios, save that Oinone was hindered by her father when she wished to heal Paris.

Apollodoros gives much the same version as Konon, but without mention of any son; Oinone, daughter of Kebren (the river), having learned the art of prophecy from Rheia, warns Paris against abducting Helen; he fails to heed her, is wounded by Philoktetes, and appeal, death, and repentant suicide follow (ApB 3.12.6). In Ovid's *Heroides*, too, the son is absent; Oinone speaks of a marriage with Paris while he was still an unknown shepherd, and laments his abandonment of her for Helen (*Her* 5). The tale as a whole has an obvious overlay of Hellenistic romanticism, but although it cannot have been told in the *Little Iliad*, we cannot say for certain that it is not in some form as old as the Archaic period.[67] If Hellanikos on the evidence guarantees for us only a son of Paris by Oinone whom his father rashly kills, at least this means that the union of Paris and Oinone was known in his time.

By all accounts, whether there was a dispute or not, Helen does marry Deiphobos after the death of Paris; probably this was known even to the author of the *Odyssey*, for the story of Helen's attempt to reveal the secret of the Wooden Horse includes the fact that Deiphobos accompanied her there, although Menelaos does not call him her husband, and when the Achaians emerge from the Horse Odysseus and Menelaos proceed to Deiphobos' house (*Od* 4.274–76, 8.517–20).[68] Next in the *Little Iliad* comes the bringing of Neoptolemos from Skyros to Troy by Odysseus, a maneuver that may or may not have been required by Helenos for the taking of Troy. In the *Nekuia*, Odysseus tells Achilleus exactly the same story, that he himself went to Skyros to bring back the latter's son to the war (*Od* 11.508–9). The event does not surface again until Pindar's *Paian* 6 (which simply confirms the summoning: *Pa* 6.98–104) and Sophokles' *Skyrioi*, for which our few fragments indicate only that someone (Lykomedes and/or Deidameia?) tries to discourage Neoptolemos from the possible dangers of following in the footsteps of his father (fr 555 R, possibly also 554 R).[69] In the same poet's *Philoktetes*, Neoptolemos himself mentions that Odysseus and Phoinix came to fetch him, offering the argument that with his father dead it would not be *themis* for Troy to fall to anyone but him (*Ph* 343–47). The timing of his arrival here, right after his father's death, is probably due to the need to make plausible the false quarrel with Odysseus over the arms. Apollodoros also has Odysseus and Phoinix undertake the mission, adding that they had to persuade Lykomedes to let his grandson go (Ap*E* 5.11), and the same two Achaians are named on a Red-Figure volute krater of about 470 B.C. where they appear together with Lykomedes and his (unnamed) daughter and grandson (Ferrara 44701). In Quintus, on the other hand, the envoys are Odysseus and Diomedes, the same two who induced Achilleus to leave Skyros for the war, and the reminder of the loss of her husband does much to influence Deidameia's feelings toward this new request (QS 6.56–113, 7.169–393. Among other details in Quintus' lengthy account, there is a warning by Lykomedes of the dangers of the sea which matches closely the content of Sophokles' fragment 555 Radt, and scholars have suggested that his version may draw heavily from the *Skyrioi*.

To the same sentence of Proklos' summary of the *Little Iliad* relating Neoptolemos' arrival and receiving of the arms of his father from Odysseus are added the words "and Achilleus appeared as a *phantasma* to him." Presumably this means that Achilleus' ghost somehow manifested itself to Neoptolemos (rather than to Odysseus), but for what purpose we do not learn. PRylands 22 may have placed the event at Achilleus' tomb, if a substantial supplement is correct;[70] perhaps Neoptolemos went there in hopes of receiving encouragement from his dead father. In any case, Neoptolemos requires some sort of formidable opponent if he is to display his military skills; thus Eurypylos, son of Telephos, arrives to assist the Trojans, performs various heroic deeds (including in this poem, according to Pausanias, the killing of Machaon: 3.26.9 = fr 30 *PEG*[71]), and is then slain by the son of Achilleus. His defeat is recounted by Odysseus to the shade of Achilleus in the *Nekuia*, speaking of Eurypylos' magnificence and beauty (second only to Memnon), and of how many Keteians perished with him because of "womanly gifts" (*Od* 11.519–21). Homer does not explain that last phrase; the scholia credit Akousilaos with the story that Eurypylos was the son of Telephos and Astyoche, and that when Priam sought his help as the inheritor of the kingdom of Mysia his mother at first refused, until Priam sent her a golden vine (Σ *Od* 11.520 = 2F40). One line later, other *Odyssey* scholia repeat this tale, adding that the vine was a gift from Zeus to Tros in recompense for Ganymedes, that Priam had inherited it, and that Astyoche was his sister (Σ *Od* 11.521). They also, however, cite an alternative explanation for Homer's words, namely that Priam had promised Eurypylos one of his daughters in marriage, much as Kassandra was betrothed to the foreigner Othryoneus.[72] Neither of these persuasive devices is mentioned by Proklos in his summary of the *Little Iliad*, but we saw earlier in this chapter that a fragment of that poem (or similar epic: *IlMik* fr 29 *PEG*) does speak of a golden vine (the work of Hephaistos) given by Zeus to Laomedon in compensation for Ganymedes, so that Priam's gift to Eurypylos' mother was very likely the version used by Lesches.

Sophokles seems also to have treated the story of the combat, probably in a play entitled *Eurypylos* that would have brought the hero to Troy and included his death and the lamentation of his mother.[73] Elements of this drama apparently included frequent references to Telephos and his healing by the spear of Achilleus, pointed emphasis on the irony of that same spear being used by Achilleus' son to slay Telephos' son, and reproaches by Astyoche against Priam, who persuaded her (fr 211 R). Unfortunately, this last section is quite mutilated in the papyrus source, and does not quite allow us to say for certain whether her acceptance of gold in return for her son was included here.

In art we have only one early illustration, a Black-Figure hydria of about 510 B.C. on which Eurypylos already lies dead, the spear protruding from his chest, while Neoptolemos pursues his chariot (slaying the charioteer) and Apollo with drawn bow closes in from the right (Basel BS 498). Before Apollo lies the dead body of Helikaon (in the *Iliad* son of Antenor and husband of Priam's daughter Laodike [*Il* 3.121–24]); we have seen and will see again that in the *Little Iliad* Helikaon is rescued by Odysseus on the night of Troy's fall. If Apollo and the son of Achilleus did engage in a confrontation after Eurypylos' death, no literary source preserves it; Apollodoros via our epitomator says no more than we learned from Proklos (although, as we saw, he reassigns Machaon's death to Penthesileia).

Next in the *Little Iliad* we find the Trojans in desperate straits, being now truly besieged, and at this point Athena suggests to Epeios the building of the Wooden Horse. Such at least seems to be the sense of the Greek word *proairesis*, that the stratagem was at Athena's choosing. In the *Odyssey* we hear on two occasions of how Epeios built the horse, once with Athena's help, and we are told as well that Odysseus took the lead in the matter, opening and closing the hidden door and generally showing courage when other Achaians were frightened, but nowhere does Homer go so far as to say that the idea was his (*Od* 8.492–95, 11.523–27). No doubt Arktinos' *Iliou Persis* and that of Stesichoros had something to say on the subject, but we do not know what, though Arktinos does seem to have given the Horse a movable tail, knees, and eyes (fr 2 PEG). In Konon, the instigator is Helenos, who after his capture says that it is fated that Troy be captured by a wooden horse (26F1.34); Apollodoros on the other hand makes the conception entirely that of Odysseus, who persuades Epeios to do the building (ApE 5.14). Likely his growing reputation for deceit, not just strategy, led to this shift of responsibility, but we cannot say when.

From the building of the Horse one might expect Lesches to proceed to the abandonment of the camp by the bulk of the Achaians so that the Trojans might come out to claim their trophy, but instead the *Little Iliad* offers two final adventures, both involving the infiltration of the city. In the first, Odysseus enters the city alone, disguised as a beggar, in order to spy (he has been in some way wounded or mutilated by Thoas as part of the deception); when Helen recognizes him they plot together for the destruction of the city and he returns to his own camp, after killing a number of Trojans. The second concerns the return of Odysseus with Diomedes in order to steal the Palladion, an image of Athena housed in the city. Why Odysseus should need to spy, or what he hopes to learn, is not clear. But two such similar adventures side by side might well seem tedious if they were not connected; possibly, therefore, Odysseus learned from Helen only after he had entered the city that the Palladion must be stolen, and being unable to accomplish that alone went back to camp to fetch Diomedes, with whom he returned in the dead of night. Alternatively, Odysseus may have known already from Helenos of the need to secure the Palladion and ventured into the city in disguise to scout out its location or otherwise plan the theft, with Helen offering assistance after she recognized him.[74] Apollodoros follows at least the logic of this latter proposal, for he compresses matters into one foray in which Odysseus leaves Diomedes outside the walls while he goes in with his disguise, steals the Palladion with the aid of Helen, and uses Diomedes' aid to get it back to the ships (ApE 5.13).[75]

In *Odyssey* 4, Helen relates the story of the visit (not the theft), but tells us little more than Lesches, namely that Odysseus entered the city disguised, was recognized by her alone, admitted his identity after she had washed and anointed him and sworn not to betray him, and then revealed to her the *nous* of the Achaians (*Od* 4.242–64). Here too as in Lesches he kills Trojans before departing, and when he has left, Helen is pleased at the thought of rejoining her husband. This claim by her, combined with the word *nous*, which should properly mean here a plan, strongly suggests that Odysseus has told her about the Horse, as Lesches' account also leads us to suppose. Such a conclusion may seem contradicted for the *Odyssey* by Menelaos' subsequent story of how Helen and Deiphobos tried to trick the Greeks inside the Horse into giving themselves away. But this contradiction is already inherent in *Odyssey* 4, to whatever end, given that Helen herself claims she was longing at that point to return to her first husband. That she says nothing of the Palladion may indicate that even as early as the *Odyssey* Odysseus' role in that venture was not entirely glorious (see below).

Euripides' *Hekabe* provides the next bit of evidence about the first mission: Hekabe there asserts that when Odysseus came to spy, Helen did reveal his identity to her, and that he was thus forced to supplicate her for his life, which she granted (*Hek* 239–50). Why the Trojan queen should be so charitable is not explained, and since she here mentions the incident in order to reproach Odysseus pointedly for failing to save Polyxena in return, we may well suspect that Euripides invented the whole idea. The (interpolated) list of plays drawn from the *Little Iliad* in Aristotle's *Poetics* includes *Ptocheia (Begging)* that must have been based on the spy mission, but we know nothing about it (*Poet* 23.1459b6). The list also cites a *Lakainai*, and this we do know to have been composed by Sophokles, and to have dealt with the theft of the

Palladion. Our one really informative fragment reveals that two people entered Troy together through a sewer (fr 367 R), while the title of the play can only mean that they contacted or were found by Helen after they got in, since her attendants must have been the chorus. A second fragment justifying the Greek position in the war might, however, more logically be addressed to a Trojan (fr 368 R), and later sources (e.g., Σb *Il* 6.311) do make Theano the one to hand the image over, after Diomedes and Odysseus have purportedly come on an embassy to Priam (cf. Σ Lyk 658, where Antenor serves as middle-man). Finally, an unplaced fragment in which Odysseus reviles the ancestry of Diomedes (fr 799 R) has caused some scholars to suppose the subsequent quarrel over the Palladion took place here as well, but of course such a speech might appear in a number of contexts.

Servius at *Aeneid* 2.166 confirms the fact that in some accounts Diomedes and Odysseus were thought to have entered the city through a sewer, while Aristophanes in the *Sphekes* probably refers to the same idea (so the scholia) in describing one of Philokleon's attempts to break out of his house, dressed like Odysseus in rags (*Sph* 350–51). That rags and sewer should be part of the same venture here might seem to agree with Apollodoros' account of just one raid, but given the oddity (clearer than in Apollodoros) of someone donning rags and then stealing surreptiously into Troy we should probably suppose conflation of two separate expeditions for the sake of the parody. Yet the version of Aristophanes' contemporary Antisthenes, in whose *Aias* Odysseus allows slaves to beat him in the face and back and then, clad in rags, infiltrates Troy at night to steal the statue (*Aias* 6), poses the same problem in a more serious context, so that perhaps we might after all think of an earlier (if not very logical) literary source. The *Rhesos* envisions a more plausible sequence in which Odysseus' foray to get the Palladion is followed later by a completely separate mission in rags, one presumably carried out in broad daylight (*Rh* 499–507). As we noted above, though, the two separate devices for infiltrating the city can be made to work together if only Odysseus is allowed to enter first in the daytime in his rags and then again at night for the actual theft. Lykophron follows Lesches in having Thoas disfigure Odysseus for his disguise but says nothing about the Palladion; he does state that Odysseus fooled even Troy's leader, presumably Priam, with his tears (Lyk 779–85). The scholia argue that he blamed these on Agamemnon, so that he was presumably recognized as a Greek, but what sort of Greek he claimed to be we do not know.

As for the quarrel between Odysseus and Diomedes which forms the aftermath of the theft of the Palladion, the *Little Iliad* must have recounted this part of the story in some form, since Hesychios makes the poem the source of the proverbial phrase "Diomedean compulsion" which he says arose from the theft (fr 25 *PEG*).[76] But for any explanation of that expression we must turn to later sources, most explicitly the account of Konon in which we find (in complete contrast to what we have seen so far) that Diomedes stood on the shoulders of Odysseus in order to climb over the city wall, and then failed to pull his comrade up after him although Odysseus stretched up his hands (26F1.34). Thus he was able to secure the Palladion all by himself; to Odysseus' queries as they went back across the plain to the ships, knowing the trickery of the man, he replied that he had not taken the Palladion specified by Helenos, but another one instead. The statue itself, however, moved or stirred in some way (by the will of a god) so that Odysseus knew it to be the proper one, and being behind Diomedes he drew his sword to kill the man and bring the image back himself. But Diomedes saw his sword glitter in the moonlight and forestalled him; for the rest of the journey he made Odysseus walk ahead of him, striking him with the flat of his sword to keep him moving, and hence the origin of the proverb. Presumably we are to understand this summary account to mean that from the outset of the venture Diomedes feared treachery on Odysseus' part, and concocted the story of a second, false Palladion in hopes of discouraging any attempt to kill him for it. But we must admit that the invention is not very plausible (why has Diomedes taken the statue at all if it is not the right one?) and curious too is the statue's identification of itself, for if Athena is responsible she only exposes Odysseus to humiliation thereby.[77] Numerous later writers gloss the saying with a more or less similar story, and Servius specifies, as we assumed, that Odysseus tries to kill Diomedes because he wants all the credit for himself (Σ *Aen* 2.166).

We must note, however, that while in this tradition the second Palladion seems simply an invention of one of the characters, we *may* have literary evidence for a false Palladion already in epic: Dionysios reports that in Arktinos the real Palladion was a statue given by Zeus to Dardanos, and hidden away in an *abaton* for safekeeping while an exact duplicate was put on display; this latter image was what the Achaians stole (DH 1.69.3). Obviously such a story cuts against the run of Lesches' tale and is not entirely logical, either, for if Troy falls despite the Achaians' failure to obtain the right statue, then Helenos' prophecy is wrong. Indeed, the concept of a genuine Palladion not stolen by the Greeks serves only one real need, namely the Roman claim that the statue had been brought to Italy by Aineias, and one would normally suppose that the Romans themselves invented the story to support that claim. We must therefore consider the possibility that Dionysios is somehow mistaken in ascribing this tale to Archaic epic; perhaps he was working from an interpolated text.[78] In any case, we see that such a version requires the Achaians to be fooled by the stratagem, in contrast to Konon's account in which Diomedes claims to have taken a false Palladion but actually has the genuine article.[79]

Art has, however, a concept of this tale surprisingly different from what we have found so far.[80] On a Red-Figure cup by Makron in Leningrad Diomedes and Odysseus, at the far left and right of the scene respectively, are engaged in a vigorous dispute with drawn swords; between them, acting as peacemakers, stand Demophon, Agamemnon, Phoinix, and Akamas (Leningrad 649: all figures named). What is here remarkable is that both Diomedes and Odysseus hold a Palladion in their free arms. That Makron has not simply indulged in a bit of whimsy seems guaranteed by a similar scene on a belly amphora by the Tyszkiewicz Painter: Athena now substitutes for the restraining Achaians, and the Palladion held by the right-hand figure is just barely visible (the top of her helmet appears just above his shoulder), but there are again two such statues (Stockholm:Med 1963.1). The idea resurfaces on an Apulian oinochoe of about a hundred years later, with Athena now pointing at something, either the Palladion carried by Diomedes or (beyond him) an unidentified woman with (probably) a torch (Louvre K36). One might guess that she in some way resolves the dispute between the two warriors, for a dispute there must have been (as the Leningrad cup shows) if both Diomedes and Odysseus returned to camp with a Palladion that they claimed was the one necessary to the taking of the city. Literary support for a double theft is not entirely lacking: Ptolemaios Chennos (whom we should certainly otherwise have thought to be fabricating) says that Odysseus and Diomedes stole two of them (3.8 [p. 24 Chatzis]). Unfortunately we know nothing more about what story he recounted.

Although Theseus' sons might plausibly be added to any Attic scene of the Achaians at Troy, their special presence on the Leningrad cup (as arbiters?) has led some scholars to suppose the tale of two Palladia an Athenian invention, with Akamas and Demophon given the real image (in gratitude for their intervention?) and bringing it back to Athens to become enshrined at the court/precinct of the Palladion southeast of the Athenian Akropolis. Were that true, however, we should expect these sons to be present also on the Stockholm amphora; Athena in the role of arbiter there suggests that it was the quarrel itself, not who resolved it, that mattered. Likewise the idea of inventing a second Palladion in order to justify the awarding of the first to the Theseidai seems unnecessarily complex; Dionysios of Samos says simply that the statue was entrusted to Demophon (15F3, apud Cl:*Pro* 4.47.6), while Pausanias reports (specifically in connection with the Palladion court) that Demophon made off with it after an inadvertent clash between his people and Diomedes' Argives as the latter returned from Troy (1.28.9).[81] Perhaps, though, the two statues represented an Athenian response to claims by other cites (such as Argos) that they possessed the true Palladion.[82] But all this is definitely speculation. Makron's tableau (and for that matter the story itself) does not seem the sort of thing easily handled by the two-actor tragedy mandatory in his time, so that his source will probably have been another medium.

We should add finally the account in the b scholia to *Iliad* 6.311, where after Odysseus and Diomedes have brought the Palladion (handed over to them by Theano) back to camp a dispute arises between Aias and Odysseus over who shall take the image home. As the hour becomes late, the statue is left with Diomedes for safekeeping until morning, but during the night Aias dies mysteriously and Odysseus is suspected. In Diktys we find many of the same details: Antenor brings the Palladion to the Achaians and after the sack Aias Telamonides (still alive), Diomedes, and Odysseus dispute ownership; Diomedes eventually withdraws, but Aias persists, and when the leaders have voted,

Odysseus is the winner. Enraged, Aias makes threats; the next morning he is found dead, with suspicion falling primarily on Odysseus. For his part, Quintus ignores the incident of the Palladion altogether.

One other requirement before Troy may fall surfaces in Lykophron and Apollodoros. Lykophron's cryptic remark says only that the city's destruction was aided by the remnants of the son of Tantalos (Lyk 52–55), but Apollodoros explains (what we would have guessed) that the Achaians were required to fetch the bones of Pelops (ApE 5.10; so too the Lykophron scholia). In this latter author, the prophecy of this need is made by Helenos, who adds to it the further tasks of the fetching of Neoptolemos and the theft of the Palladion. Conceivably, Pelops' Lydian origins have something to do with the notion of his presence if the Achaians are to capture an Asian town, but neither of these authors (nor the scholia) offers any further explanation.

The Fall   In *Odyssey* 8 the blind singer Demodokos tells how the Greeks set fire to their
of Troy   camp and sailed away, while Odysseus and others remained hidden in the Horse (*Od* 8.499–510). The Trojans pulled this object as far as their acropolis and then debated what to do next, some arguing that it should be cut open, some that it should be thrown down from a high place, and others that it should be left intact as an offering to the gods; this last opinion of course prevailed. Nothing is here said of Sinon or Laokoon, but in such a brief summary we should not expect to find them, and then, too, Demodokos' song is about Odysseus. Lesches for his part relates that the Greeks caused the leaders to enter into the Horse and then set fire to their camp, taking the fleet out to Tenedos. The Trojans, thinking to be released from their difficulties, received the Horse into the city (destroying a part of their wall to do so) and celebrated in the belief that they had won the war. A reference to the *Little Iliad* in the Lykophron scholia adds to this epitome that Sinon did appear in Lesches' version, lighting a beacon as a signal to the other Greeks in the dead of night, when the moon was just rising (fr 9 *PEG*, with *apparatus*); we are told too by Aristotle that a *Sinon* play (probably by Sophokles: see below) was drawn from the epic (*Poet* 23.1459b). There is, however, no word in Proklos of Laokoon, and we cannot tell if he formed part of the *Little Iliad* or not.[83] Our first certain appearance of this latter figure is in the *Iliou Persis* of Arktinos, which begins (in our epitome) at the point where the Trojans are uncertain what to do about the Horse. As in the *Odyssey* there is a debate, with some wishing to push it from a cliff or burn it and others to dedicate it to Athena. When this last opinion gains the upper hand the Trojans turn back to their celebration, supposing that they are rid of the war. But at this point two serpents appear and destroy Laokoon and one of his two children. "Bearing badly" *(dusphorêsantes)* such a portent, Aineias and his followers abandon the city for Ida; Sinon then lights the signal fires, having before gotten into Troy by claiming for himself (or pretending) something. As we should expect, Proklos' summary of the narrative does not entirely square with the best-known ancient account of these

events, that of Vergil's *Aeneid* 2. But Arktinos' Sinon (and that of Lesches?) may well have played much the same role as he does in Vergil, for the Greek word *prospoiêtos* can certainly mean a fabrication (or "taking a new identity to oneself") such as the *Aeneid* offers when Sinon claims to have been destined for human sacrifice by Odysseus and to have barely escaped with his life (*Aen* 2.77–144).

Vergil's epic makes Sinon go on to state that the Horse is a present to Athena, made large so that the Trojans might not bring it into the city; that idea is contested by Laokoon, who casts his spear at the wooden creature, nearly exposing it before the serpents put an end to him (and his two sons). All this seems entirely logical: Laokoon is removed by the gods because he endangers the success of the Greeks. In Arktinos, by contrast, Laokoon's fate plays no direct role in the decision of the Trojans to accept the Horse because it happens only after the fact. Possibly he was nonetheless an advocate of the Horse's destruction, and perished (albeit late) so that the Trojans might believe they had done the right thing, but as Proklos presents the situation the primary result of his demise is to stir Aineias to flight. We cannot, however, be certain that Proklos reproduces accurately the cause and effect sequences of his original, and then, too, the word used of Aineias' response properly suggests that he is angry or vexed about something; perhaps the other Trojans were not sufficiently grieved at the death of his sometime (*Fab* 135) uncle. It has even been suggested that Arktinos' portent signifies the fall of Troy and the elder line of the ruling house (as Laokoon and one son perish) but the survival of the cadet branch as represented by Aineias.[84] In any case, the latter is here not available to help with the final defense of the city as he is in Vergil, and his escape is more plausibly (though less heroically) explained (for other versions of his fate see below). To all this we can add that Bakchylides somewhere made the serpents come from the Kalydnai Islands (Kalymnos and Leros?) and had them changed into humans; he also involved Laokoon's wife in some way (fr 9 SM).

Such represents the sum total of our evidence for either Sinon or Laokoon in the Archaic period. Sophokles composed both a *Sinon* and a *Laokoon;* from the former (where the emphasis was surely on the duplicity of the title figure) nothing whatever remains, but of the latter we know that here, too, Aineias leaves before the fall of the city, carrying his father, and that he does so on his father's advice, for the latter recalls warnings from Aphrodite and also recent signs concerning the sons of Laokoon (fr 373 R). If used precisely (our source is Dionysios), this last phrase should mean that two (or more) children are killed, but that Laokoon himself survives. Sophokles also gave the names of the snakes (fr 372 R), which might suggest that they became human as in Bakchylides. In Apollodoros' version both Kassandra and Laokoon object to the Horse on the grounds that there are armed men inside; what follows—diverse support for hurling it from a cliff, burning it, and making it a dedication, with the latter prevailing, then feasting and the snakes sent by Apollo as a "sign" *(sêmeion)*—is remarkably close to the version of Arktinos (ApE 5.16–19). Here, though, it is the two sons alone who die (devoured, in fact), as perhaps in Sophokles, and Sinon (who may or may not have gained access to the city) lights the beacon fire outside Troy, at the tomb of Achilleus. What exactly the death of Laokoon's sons is a sign of is not clear, at least not in the epitome. The Lykophron scholia follow Sophokles in giving names to the snakes (Porkis and Chariboia—one male and one female) and Bakchylides in bringing them from the Kalydnai Islands (although with the odd expression that they sailed); they add that Laokoon was a son of Antenor, and that his child or children were killed in the precinct of Thymbraian Apollo (ΣΣ Lyk 344, 347).

First in Hyginus do we find the notion that a previous transgression was the motive for the snakes' assault. Laokoon is here the brother of Anchises and a priest of Apollo; although the god does not wish him to marry and beget children this is done, and as a consequence Apollo sends the snakes (from Tenedos) to kill the sons Antiphas and Thymbraios (*Fab* 135). Laokoon is at the moment sacrificing to Poseidon, having been drawn by lot to do so (exactly as in Vergil); when he tries to help his sons he perishes as well. Servius, on the other hand, cites as the transgression Laokoon's intercourse with his wife Antiope in the precinct of Thymbraian Apollo, before the images of the gods (Σ *Aen* 2.201). Earlier in the same note he has mentioned Euphorion (as the source for the Trojans' killing their priest of Poseidon when he failed to prevent the arrival of the Greeks), but what follows is probably drawn from elsewhere. We should remember that Bakchylides made Laokoon's wife a significant character in his version, so that one of these two accounts *might* go back to him (although see below). Just possibly in some versions where Laokoon has committed a previous offense the attack of the snakes takes place at a time quite removed from that of Troy's fall. For Vergil, on the other hand, his demise is the key factor in persuading the Trojans to bring the Horse within the walls, and we assume that the snakes are sent by the gods for just such a purpose. A previous offense might also have played a part in Sophokles, given tragedy's fondness for guilt themes, although there the reference to Aineias' flight makes clear the time frame.

Against this literary tradition, art has surprisingly little to offer. But almost certainly depicting the story in some form is a Lucanian bell krater of the late fifth century now in Basel: a woman raises an axe and rushes at two snakes that coil themselves around a cult statue of a beardless male crowned with and holding laurel; on the ground before the statue is a child in pieces, behind the woman a distraught bearded male cloaked in a mantle and behind him Apollo himself (Basel, Slg Ludwig, no #). A very similar scene appears on an Apulian vase fragment found at the end of the last century: here Apollo is to the left, turned away toward Artemis, while the snakes coil around the cult statue as before and the woman rushes in (something raised over her head) from the right (Ruvo, no #). As before, pieces (legs) of a child lie on the ground, but in contrast to the Basel krater one of the snakes here has an arm in his mouth (the head of the second snake is lacking); new also is the tripod next to the statue, while Laokoon (if he was present further right) has been broken away. Seemingly then, we have a version in which the attack takes place in the precinct of Thymbraian Apollo, only the children (or one child?) are killed, and Laokoon's wife makes a (vain?) attempt to avenge them, perhaps perishing in the process. Conceivably this act of daring on her part is what our sources refer to when they place her in Bakchylides' version, and constitutes the limit of her involvement. On the other hand, such a role in the climax of the story may indicate a greater complicity in its causes, that is, a forbidden procreation version such as Hyginus and Servius attest. By comparison with such tantalizing hints, the famous Hellenistic (or Roman) sculpture unearthed in the Golden House of Nero in the early sixteenth century tells us only that its sculptors preferred to show all three males of the family as victims.[85]

From the preliminaries we pass to the actual night of the Sack. The Greeks hiding in the Horse (three thousand according to Lesches, if Apollodoros is correct, but something smaller has surely been garbled in transmission[86]) are referred to three times in the *Odyssey*, first in Book 4 when Menelaos tells the tale of Helen's attempt to disclose their presence (4.271–89), second in Book 8 when Demodokos sings of the Sack (8.499–520), and third in Book 11 when Odysseus describes Neoptolemos' bravery to the shade of Achilleus (11.523–32). The first of these brief notices remains a puzzle even in its own context, since the notion that Helen imitated the voices of the leaders' wives in hopes of surprising them into speech contradicts her own just finished claim that she longed to return home.[87] The event is not mentioned elsewhere until Apollodoros (who surely takes it from the *Odyssey*), and the name of the Achaian whom Odysseus must restrain from calling out, Antiklos, is one not found in the *Iliad*; if the *Odyssey* poet has not here indulged in a bit of invention to praise Odysseus, he at least draws on an epic tradition not entirely in line with the *Iliad's* cast. Whatever the truth of the matter, Helen's gambit fails, and the Achaians within the Horse are left to emerge at their leisure, presumably after the Trojans have gone to sleep. In Proklos' summary of Lesches we saw that a part of the city wall was destroyed to bring in the Horse, leaving one to wonder whether the risk of hiding men inside it was really necessary. The summary of Arktinos says nothing on this point; Apollodoros, who *may* be following him, since he quotes Lesches' number of men as a variant, reports that the (fifty) stowaways open the gates, as we might expect. Eustathios adds that in Stesichoros the number of men was one hundred, but elsewhere twelve, whom he names as Menelaos, Diomedes, Philoktetes, Meriones, Neoptolemos, Eurypylos, Eurydamas, Pheidippos, Leonteus, Meges, Odysseus, and Eumelos (Eu-Od 11.522, p. 1698). Conspicuously absent are Agamemnon and Idomeneus, but of course someone must command the fleet. Sinon's role in these events is less clear. In the *Little Iliad* we know only that he lit a fire; in the *Iliou Persis*, where he pretends to something, we presume that he is taken into the city, and lights the fire from there, but conceivably he left the city to do so. We saw that he is certainly outside the walls (at the tomb of Achilleus, in fact) in Apollodoros' version, perhaps because the fire was meant not only as a signal but also as a guide to ships attempting a landing in the dark. In Vergil, Sinon's primary function is to persuade the Trojans to admit the Horse; here he lights no fire at all, but rather opens the panel that lets the Greeks out of the Horse. At any rate the beacon brings back the army from Tenedos, and they join forces with those already inside the city to carry out the massacre of the inhabitants. To all this the second *Odyssey* reference adds that Odysseus and Menelaos went together to the house of Deiphobos, where there seems to have been an actual combat won by Odysseus (*Od* 8.517–20).

From other evidence we know that the *Little Iliad* contained a description of the massacre, despite Proklos' (or an epitomator's) failure to record the fact. For the battle itself in this poem our best source is Pausanias, who recounts in detail the points at which Polygnotos' painting of the Sack for the Knidians at Delphi recalls the version of Lesches (10.25–27). Among the parallels are the wounding of Meges in the arm by Admetos, son of Augeias, and a similar wounding of Lykomedes, son of Kreon, in the wrist by Agenor. A Trojan Astynoos was also mentioned, as was the Helikaon (son of Antenor) rescued from the fighting as we saw before by Odysseus, presumably because of his family's support of the Greek cause (see above). Of other Trojans or their allies, Axion, son of Priam, is here slain by Eurypylos, Agenor and Eioneus are dispatched by Neoptolemos, and Admetos falls to Philoktetes. Priam himself also dies at Neoptolemos' hands, but only after having been dragged away from the altar of Zeus Herkeios to the doorway of his house. One figure slain here by Diomedes but elsewhere by Neoptolemos is Koroibos; his appearance (as a corpse) in Polygnotos' painting prompts Pausanias to note that he was a son of Mygdon of Phrygia, and that he came to Troy to wed Kassandra, but we are not given any source for this tale.[88] Mygdon is mentioned by Priam in *Iliad* 3 as a leader of the Phrygians (*Il* 3.186); Homer never speaks of any son at Troy. In *Iliad* 13 we find Kassandra betrothed to Othryoneus, but as he dies in that book, I suppose she might have been promised to yet another foreigner. As for Astyanax, both Pausanias and specific lines from the *Little Iliad* quoted by Tzetzes make Neoptolemos responsible for throwing him from a tower, but this (the quote says) is done on Neoptolemos' own authority, not because the Greeks as a whole voted on or approved such an action (fr 21 *PEG*). The quote, which describes the deed in just three lines, may imply that Neoptolemos performed it in his capacity as the winner of Andromache. Finally, in both the *Little Iliad* and Ibykos, according to Aristophanes scholia, Menelaos dropped the sword with which he proposed to kill Helen when he saw her disrobed (Σ Ar:*Lys* 155 = fr 19 *PEG*). We will see below that such a tableau is also attested in seventh-century Greek art; certainly, though, it does not accord very well with the earlier suggestion (from Proklos' summary) that in this poem Helen and Odysseus somehow came to an agreement or plan for the fall of the city.

Compared with these bits and pieces of the carnage in the *Little Iliad* we have Proklos' full summary of the assault as found in Arktinos' *Iliou Persis*. Presumably, though, this has been compressed a good bit, for the only events recorded are Neoptolemos' slaying of Priam after the latter had fled to the altar of Zeus Herkeios, Menelaos' slaying of Deiphobos and leading away of Helen to the ships, and Aias Oileiades' accidental dragging away of a statue of Athena while trying to separate Kassandra from it. This last bit of tactlessness so enrages the other Greeks that they attempt to stone him, and are only thwarted by his seeking of refuge at an altar of Athena. There follows after the burning of the city the death of Astyanax, here at Odysseus' hands, and as well the sacrifice of Polyxena and recovery of Aithra, to be discussed below. The summary closes with the statement that Athena contrived destruction for the Greeks after they had put to sea, an unexplained action given that they have done their best to punish Aias. The few fragments we can add to this picture note only that Astyanax was thrown from the walls (fr 5 *PEG*), as Andromache at *Iliad* 24.734–38 predicts with the reasoning that some Greek will be angry over the many deaths brought about by Hektor. Here too, as before, we know nothing of the versions presented by the *Little Iliad* poems of Kinaithon and Diodoros of Erythrai, if these are different from the one ascribed to Lesches.

As for Stesichoros' *Iliou Persis*, the scholion telling us of Astyanax's fate in Arktinos may or may not say that he met a different fate in this lyric work (202 *PMG*); we know for certain about the poem only that those wishing to stone Helen dropped their stones at the sight of her (201 *PMG*). Some further information might appear on the *Tabula Iliaca Capitolina*, which claims for its representation of the Sack to illustrate Stesichoros' poem.[89] But whatever the exact truth of this statement, Vergil has also clearly been used,[90] and the scenes offered (aside from that of Aineias' departure, for which see chapter 17) are essentially standard repertoire (Aias and Kassandra, Neoptolemos and Priam, Menelaos and Helen, Demophon and Aithra, sacrifice of Polyxena, etc.) which tell us nothing new. From recent papyrus finds, we know that Alkaios also dealt with Aias' impiety, probably as part of an attack on Pittakos; nothing survives but the fact that an insane Aias tore Kassandra away from Athena's protection, and thus caused hardships at sea for the other Greeks because they failed to punish him (262 *SLG*).

From the fifth century and later in literature, there is not a great deal of interest. Neither Pindar nor Bakchylides has anything to offer, and in tragedy only Sophokles' lost *Aias Lokros*, with presumably a description of the dragging forth of Kassandra (presented as background to a trial?), seems to have dealt with any of these events. Euripides' *Troades*, which one might think would review the horrors of the city's taking, concerns itself entirely with the happenings of the morning after (including the decision of the Greeks as a whole to hurl Astyanax from the walls at Odysseus' insistence). Lykophron assigns part of Sinon's task to Antenor, calling him a traitor who opened up the Horse to let out the Greeks (Lyk 340–43); the scholia claim that he had made a pact with the Greeks in exchange for the rule of the city afterwards. In the epitome of Apollodoros, we hear of one Echion, son of Portheus, who dies attempting to leap down from the Horse; the others more prudently lower themselves by means of a rope (ApE 5.20). They then open the gates to those coming back from Tenedos. Neoptolemos slays Priam at the altar of Zeus Herkeios as before, Menelaos slays Deiphobos and takes Helen away, Odysseus and Menelaos intervene to save Glaukos, son of Antenor, and Aias offers some sort of violence to Kassandra when she has wrapped herself around an image of Athena; the Greek verb used, *biazomai*, is a standard term for sexual assault but can also denote the simple application of force. In the A scholia to the *Iliad*, however, all doubt is removed: Aias rapes Kassandra in the very precinct of Athena, so that the statue of the goddess turns its eyes upward toward the roof; here too, as in Alkaios, the deed serves as the root cause of the Greeks' subsequent difficulties at sea (ΣA *Il* 13.66). The portent of the statue turning its eyes upward at Kassandra's plight also appears in Lykophron (361–64) and, as we shall find below, in Quintus.

Aineias, we have seen, always survives the Sack, as Poseidon predicts at *Iliad* 20.300–305, but the means by which he does so vary considerably. In both the *Iliou Persis* of Arktinos and the *Laokoon* of Sophokles he leaves Troy well before the city's destruction, warned, it seems, by the fate of Laokoon and carrying (in Sophokles at least) his father on his back. Xenophon, however, speaks of him as among those defeated by the Greeks, for he says that by saving the ancestral gods of his parents, and as well his father, he gained a reputation for piety *(eusebeia)* that caused the Greeks to leave him undespoiled (*Kyn* 1.15); Apollodoros seems to understand something similar, for he places Aineias' departure (carrying his father) squarely in the middle of the Sack, and says that the Greeks allowed him to depart, again because of his piety (ApE 5.21). That the Greeks should leave any male Trojans alive, other than their benefactor Antenor, may sound surprising, but perhaps Aineias' mother Aphrodite contributed to his safety in some versions. Nevertheless, the notion of his piety recurs again and again. In Lykophron he is said to have abandoned wife, children, and property, selecting rather the household gods and his father when the Greeks permitted to him alone to choose out something from his house (Lyk 1261–69); no reason is given for this favor. Diodoros suggests that the Greeks made a truce with Aineias and others who still held a part of the city and allowed each to take away as much as he could carry; while others chose their valuables Aineias lifted up his father, and on being given for that reason a second choice took the household gods (DS 7.4). In Aelian, the option is one item alone; here Aineias' first choice is the gods, the second his father, whereupon the Greeks vote to abstain from his property altogether (*VH* 3.22). Neither account, however, says anything about a wife or children. In contrast to this notion of choice, Dionysios, who claims that his entire narrative here derives from Hellanikos, has Aineias mobilize a mass withdrawal from the city during the Sack, sending out first women, children, and the aged to Mount Ida, then defending the citadel, and finally retreating in good order with his father, gods, wife, children, and others as the situation becomes hopeless (DH 1.46.2–4 = 4F31). There is no suggestion in any of this that Aineias sacrificed family or property, or that he gave any preference to gods or father. Finally, although the Lykophron scholia simply paraphrase what the *Alexandra* contains, they do give Kreousa as the name of the wife and Askanios and Euryleon as the two children to whom Aineias prefer gods and father (Σ Lyk 1263). The subsequent quote from Lesches in these same scholia to the effect that Aineias is taken away from Troy in Neoptolemos' ships as a captive is quite doubtful (especially as the same lines are elsewhere ascribed to one Simias); we will consider the problem more fully in chapter 17. Likewise the extensive artistic tradition on Aineias' departure is here postponed to chapter 17, since it inevitably involves the question of where he goes after Troy.

Turning from these Greek sources to Vergil we find a continuous and detailed narrative of events, although of course the capture of Troy is seen entirely through Aineias' eyes, and he departs before the night is entirely over. Prior to that point, however, he provides a vivid account, with Kassandra (here first, followed by Apollodoros[91]) joining Laokoon in predicting Troy's demise, and Sinon opening the Horse for the Greeks inside. The ghost of Hektor appears to Aineias in a dream, warning him to flee; Panthoos, the priest of Apollo, running away with conquered gods and a grandchild, offers the same message. We meet again Koroibos, son of Mygdon, betrothed to Kassandra as he is in Pausanias (from Lesches?); when he sees his intended dragged away from Athena's precinct by her hair, he dashes to her aid and is cut down by Peneleos (a leader of the Boiotians in Homer). Even Panthoos dies, and Aineias finds himself by a secret door in the palace, where he witnesses first the slaughter of Polites by Neoptolemos before Priam's eyes, then the death of the old man himself, impiously butchered at the courtyard altar where his family has taken refuge. Such atrocities put Aineias in mind of the danger to his own family, but before he gains his house he sees Helen lurking in the shadows of the shrine of Vesta, and must be dissuaded by his mother from killing her. When he does arrive home, he faces objections to flight on the part of his father Anchises; these having been surmounted by an omen, the party sets forth, Aineias carrying Anchises and the household gods and leading Askanios, with Kreousa following behind. On finding her subsequently missing Aineias turns back, but her ghost advises him that Aphrodite has protected her from the Greeks. To all this *Aeneid* 6 adds a brief report from the shade of Deiphobos in the Underworld, who stresses Helen's treachery in leading the women of Troy in Bacchic revelry while she planned the city's destruction, and her removal of his sword while he slept so that Menelaos might enter the house and mutilate him. Some of these details obviously serve Vergil's own special purposes and may have been invented by him; about others, such as Helen's assistance to the Greeks, we cannot say. The Polites who appears at *Iliad* 2.791–94, for example, seems to be a grown warrior, although we will see shortly that the question of a child slain by Greeks during the Sack is a controversial matter in early Greek art.

As for Diktys and Dares, both writers bring about quite different resolutions of the siege: in the former, Antenor and Aineias negotiate a peace that the Greeks break (the walls having been breached to bring in the Horse), while in the latter Antenor, Aineias, and the rest of the Trojan peace faction betray the city after Priam insists on further fighting. We should note too that Diktys, like Vergil, has Menelaos cut off portions of Deiphobos' anatomy. In Quintus' version, Sinon is tortured by the Trojans but maintains his story (the same as in Vergil); Laokoon's protests against the Horse lead Athena to blind him, and when he continues to object she sends the serpents (swimming again from Kalydne) to destroy his children. Kassandra's predictions are simply ignored, and Odysseus leads the Greeks out of the Horse at Sinon's summons. For the rest (although Diomedes, here as in Pausanias, is the one to slay Kassandra's fiancé Koroibos, who seems to have offered his aid to Troy in return for her hand), matters proceed much as in the *Aeneid*. Of interest, however, are Priam's prayer that Neoptolemos kill him, and the clear rape of Kassandra by Aias, who cannot restrain himself despite the warning given by the statue, which turns away its eyes as in Lykophron and the *Iliad* scholia at 13.66.

In art we have an assortment of scenes, beginning with the Horse itself on a bow fibula (from Thebes?) dating to perhaps 700 B.C.: only the Horse itself is shown, but the presence of wheels instead of hooves (and what are perhaps windows) makes its identity certain (London 3205). A pithos from Mykonos dating to the second quarter of the seventh century elaborates on this theme, with again wheels for the Horse and windows (seven in all) from which the heads of the Greeks inside can be seen as they peer out, handing down their weapons; other warriors (Trojans? Greeks?) parade around outside (Mykonos 69).[92] On the body of the same vessel in three rows is a series of nineteen panels, at least six of which show bleeding children or warriors actually stabbing children with swords while their mothers watch (one warrior has no weapon and dashes his child down to the ground head-first); seven other panels have women supplicating warriors who threaten them or (in one case) a woman brutally stabbed by her assailant. In no case do any Trojan warriors seem to be present. One specific scene is very likely identifiable, that in which the woman's conspicuously exposed breast identifies her as Helen, mounting her own defense against Menelaos and his drawn sword (panel 7); a second, the warrior throwing his child to the ground, may be Neoptolemos (panel 17), but the atrocity of Astyanax's death would be rather lost in the general carnage shown here (indeed the two stabbings of children [panels 14, 19] are far more horrific). Such emphasis on the slaughter of innocents seems strange to be sure when set against a literary tradition in which the women and children were largely spared, in accordance with the usual practice of war. But it cannot be denied that even in the subsequent vase-painting tradition of Athens the accent is heavily on the less attractive aspects of the Sack—the slaughter of Astyanax (or Polites?), the death of Priam, and the dragging away of Kassandra from the statue of Athena.

This last was illustrated on the Chest of Kypselos (Paus 5.19.5 gives no useful details) but our first preserved evidence is a series of shield-bands from Olympia starting at about the same time, in the first quarter of the sixth century. On all of these the general composition remains the same: Aias moves in from the left, seizing Kassandra's arm with his left hand while the right holds a threatening sword (B 1801, B 1654, B 975, etc.). She herself seems to clutch at the dress of the Athena to the right, a figure with raised spear and shield which has been interpreted as both the goddess and a statue (would a live goddess permit the impending impiety?). The girl's apparent nudity on the oldest example might be taken as no more than an indication of youthfulness, but when later pieces clearly delineate her breasts we must assume that the artist wished to emphasize her nakedness. The same situation holds for a good many of the illustrations in vase-painting, where the other Trojan women are fully clothed; seemingly then, Aias' lust for and rape of Kassandra was a part of the early tradition, although the ever-present sword (surely unnecessary to force such a victim) remains curious, as does her subsequent presentation to Agamemnon as a prize.[93] In Attic Black-Figure the earliest known example is a Siana cup in the manner of the C Painter: Kassandra is half-hidden as she crouches behind Athena (the latter again in something approaching a Promachos pose: London B379). Numerous later Black-Figure paintings repeat this exact same composition: heavily armed Aias with sword, crouching Kassandra (sometimes half-draped or dressed), and Athena with shield held out and spear horizontal. On some examples the tip of the sword is dangerously close to Kassandra's neck, and did we not know better we would surely assume that she was executed on the spot. In Red-Figure versions the Athena becomes more clearly a statue on a pedestal, sometimes in the Promachos position, sometimes not; the most elegant account forms part of the Kleophrades Painter's general representation of the Sack on a hydria from Nola wherein Aias seizes by the hair a quite alluring Kassandra who is fully naked, save for a cloak knotted around her neck (Naples H2422). As Red-Figure progresses, Kassandra is more often running toward the statue than crouching beside it, and Aias holds a spear rather than a sword; sometimes, too, the statue is turned away from Aias, as in Lykophron, but the basic narrative shows no signs of having changed. Noteworthy are several caricatures, including one of the fourth century on which Aias clings to the statue while Kassandra grasps him by the helmet (VG 50279); perhaps the reference is in part to his seeking of shelter (as we saw in Arktinos) when the other Greeks wished to stone him.

Next in the artistic repertoire of the sack comes the death of Priam, which we find again and again linked with the death of a child whom we usually take to be Astyanax. This latter event is perhaps first seen on a Late Geometric pot fragment, where a man holds an upright child by the lower leg (Agora P10201),[94] and perhaps also as we saw above on the Mykonos pithos, where one of the panels shows a warrior holding a child by his ankles and striking him against the ground (Mykonos 69). Possible, too, is an Olympia shield-band relief where a warrior with raised sword holds a child off the ground by the wrist (B 847). Both these latter poses will return in vase-painting in scenes that appear connected with the death of Astyanax; that with the sword may or may not reflect a version of the death by means other than falling from the battlements. Priam's own death first appears on an Olympia shield-band (where the prostrate figure lying upon an altar can be no one else: B 160) and perhaps the left corner of the Artemis temple pediment on Kerkyra (although here the victim is on a throne).[95] In each case the method of execution is a spear, in contrast to what we will see below. On a Black-Figure lekane cover of about 565 B.C. by the C Painter, a warrior swings a child by the ankle back over his head and dashes toward an altar behind which stand an old man and woman, their hands raised in alarm; behind the warrior a mounted figure gallops toward the altar, and behind him are warriors on foot (Naples, no #). If this is Neoptolemos, we will have the deaths of a Trojan child (whatever we call him) and Priam brought together for the first time. Such a link is in any case certain on a slightly later Black-Figure lekythos where the warrior holds the child (dangling by a leg) over a corpse stretched out upon an altar and threatens him with drawn sword (Syracuse 21894). Subsequently, however, this sword gives way to a much more popular composition, beginning with Lydos in the 550s and perhaps prefigured by the C Painter lekane: the pose found there (child brandished above head like a club) is now combined with the old man on the altar, so that Neoptolemos appears to be dashing the child down upon the body of Priam (Louvre F29; so too Berlin:Ch F3988, a tripod kothon). The same arrangement appears too on an Olympia shield-band of the last quarter of the century (B 4810). In these instances Priam seems to be dead, but in several Black-Figure examples of the latter half of the century he is clearly alive, and raises his hands to protect himself as the child is swung toward him (e.g., Louvre F222; Bonn 39). On none of these vases is the child identified as Astyanax (although he will be in Red-Figure: see below). More uncertain is a hydria of the Leagros Group on which the child is about to be dashed against an altar while an old man crouches behind the warrior rather than in the line of fire (Munich 1700; battlements on the shoulder). In this instance (and perhaps also that of the C Painter lekane), we *may* want to think of Troilos, or at least of confusion between the details of his story and that of Astyanax.

In Red-Figure there are fewer occurrences of the scene, but on at least one of those the child is identified as Astyanax (Athens Akr 212). On the Brygos Painter cup in Paris, meanwhile, a young boy named as Astyanax flees the slaughter, while on the other side Priam on his altar is as usual threatened by a warrior with a similar but unnamed youth, leading us to wonder if the child could appear twice on the same pot (Louvre G152). This cup provides in any case a vivid picture of the Trojan women's desperate struggle against the Greeks, for while their men lie dying on the ground Andromache has picked up a pestle or the like and rushes into battle; Astyanax stands behind her, starting away in fear. One other curious detail of this cup is the pair to the left of Priam and Neoptolemos: Akamas leads away Polyxena, who looks back gently at the death of her father. A mistake in the names has been suggested, but after all someone must take the girl captive, even if this is not recorded in what little survives of the literary versions. Finally, we have the hydria of the Kleophrades Painter in Naples, where Priam sits on the altar with his already dead child (numerous stab wounds) in his lap as a Greek prepares to deliver the final blow (Naples H2422). To the left is the previously mentioned scene of Kassandra's seizing, with beyond that Aineias carrying off Anchises; to the right is another Greek menaced by a woman with a pestle, and then the rescue of Aithra by her grandsons (see below). On none of these pots is Neoptolemos named, but with the manner of executing the child so impiously conceived he is the obvious candidate; certainly we will not think of Odysseus here. Whether the killing of child and grandfather together is an artistic compression by painters disinclined to show battlements, or whether it really does derive from a literary tradition, is a more difficult question. Likewise, we cannot say whether an early story of Polites slaughtered in his father's arms might be illustrated here (or drawn upon to furnish iconography for a death of Astyanax), as opposed to being a late invention of someone like Vergil, perhaps inspired by that very death of Astyanax in Greek art.

One other quite popular scene, Menelaos' recovery of Helen, we have seen illustrated as early as the Mykonos relief amphora of the seventh century. Subsequently, the same theme, or at least a man in armor leading off a woman or threatening her with a sword (or both) appears on a sixth-century grave relief from Sparta (Sparta 1), on the Chest of Kypselos (Paus 5.18.3: Menelaos advances on Helen with sword drawn), and then in Attic Black-Figure from the time of Lydos (Berlin:PM F1685, where the juxtaposition with the death of Priam guarantees the scene).[96] But only in Red-Figure does the encounter take on any emotion: in the late work of the Berlin Painter we see Menelaos for the first time fling away his sword and run toward Helen with (presumably) something other than murder on his mind (Vienna 741; Naples 126053). Subsequently, this form of representation becomes quite popular, with an Eros sometimes added overhead. In no instance does Deiphobos ever appear. As a final point, Helen is again in a state of undress (naked to the waist, in fact) on the *Tabula Iliaca Capitolina,* in the part supposedly drawn from Stesichoros' *Iliou Persis.* In that poem we saw that the Achaians as a group threaten Helen with stones (fr 201 *PMG*); here Menelaos stands alone with his sword.

The first of these two events certainly appeared in both the *Little Iliad* and the *Iliou Persis.* In Lesches, Aithra made her way out of Troy at its fall to the Greek camp, where Demophon sought formal possession of her from Agamemnon; the latter consulted Helen, as the proper owner of the woman, and when she consented, grandmother and grandchildren were reunited. Of Arktinos' version we are told only that Demophon and Akamas found Aithra and took her away with them. We have seen the recovery illustrated above as part of the general sack of Troy by the Kleophrades Painter (Naples H2422; so too London E458, a calyx krater by Myson), and it appears as well on the *Tabula Iliaca Capitolina*. From Euripidean scholia (at *Hek* 123) we learn that in some writers the sons of Theseus came to Troy for this purpose alone, presumably providing a convenient excuse for their failure to appear in the *Iliad*, where Menestheus leads the Athenians. The same scholia add that in Hellanikos they come hoping to get Aithra as spoils if Troy falls, and to ransom her with gifts otherwise; they have been in exile in Euboia, not wishing to be ruled by Menestheus (4F142). That they first tried diplomacy in recovering their grandmother might be indicated too by Lykophron's claim that Laodike, daughter of Priam, stole into the bed of one of them and bore to him Mounitos, who was later killed by the bite of a snake to his heel (Lyk 494–500). Parthenios attests that the son of Theseus in question was Akamas; he adds, however, that Diomedes and Akamas had come to Troy to seek the return of Helen, and that this was the occasion on which the unmarried Laodike conceived a passion for him (Par 16; we have seen that in the *Iliad* Laodike is married to Helikaon, son of Antenor). With the help of friends, both visit the town of Dardanos (further north, on the coast of the Hellespont) at the same time, and there the mating is accomplished; the child Mounitos is brought up by Aithra until Troy falls, and then given over to Akamas, only to be slain by the snake while hunting in Thrace. Parthenios credits all this to one Hegesippos of Mekyberna (east of Olynthos), of perhaps the fourth or third century B.C. The scholia at Lykophron 447 and 495 relate much the same details of the affair, with Euphorion cited for at least Mounitos' death.

The fate of Polyxena, however, like the fall of Troy itself, is missing from our summary of the *Little Iliad*, and we do not know whether Lesches related it. Surprisingly, it does appear in a place we would not expect to find it, namely the *Kypria*, and in a totally unique form: Polyxena is wounded by Odysseus and Diomedes in the course of the Sack, and dies of her wounds (*Kyp* fr 34 PEG). The problem of fitting such an event into a poem whose narrative ends long before the Sack has generated suspicion that something is misattributed here, although the device of a prophecy might provide a solution.[97] In Arktinos we first encounter the familiar form of her death, that she was slaughtered at the tomb of Achilleus; Proklos' summary gives no further details. The scene is clearly illustrated on a Tyrrhenian amphora of about 570 B.C., where three Greeks—Amphilochos, Antiphates, and Aias (Oileiades, we presume)—hold Polyxena horizontal while Neoptolemos cuts her throat so that the blood runs down upon a tomb or mound (London 1897.7–27.2). Behind Neoptolemos to the left stand Diomedes and Nestor in attendance; behind Aias to the right is Phoinix, but with his back turned as if disapproving or unable to watch. Dramatic though this scene is, we are once more left without explanation of the reason for such brutality, and the tale reappears on only one other occasion in Archaic literature, when Ibykos confirms that Neoptolemos was the slayer.

In the later fifth century, however, Polyxena finds a place in plays by

Sophokles and Euripides, and as well in one of the paintings of Polygnotos displayed in the Athenian Propylaia. The painting, according to Pausanias, simply showed her about to be killed beside the tomb of Achilleus, and is thus not much help (1.22.6). Sophokles' play about her was the *Polyxena*, which featured someone's ghost or shade, a second sacrifice to placate Athena, and grim predictions about the Achaians' future; the tomb appears to have been onstage, and both ghost and sacrifice may have been vividly presented (although probably not actually shown). But here again we do not see why a human sacrifice was necessary. Only with Euripides' preserved *Hekabe* is a purpose for the deed revealed: Achilleus' ghost has appeared above his tomb as the Greeks prepared to sail, and demanded the life of Polyxena as the price of their departure (*Hek* 35–44). The language used (by Polydoros' ghost) in recounting this fact, as well as the words of Hekabe, the chorus, and Odysseus later in the play, suggest that the matter is one of honor to the departed hero, a distribution to him of his share of the spoils (*Hek* 93–95, 113–15, 309–10). Neoptolemos' remarks at the sacrifice itself (reported) convey in addition the notion of a blood offering to the dead (*Hek* 534–38). There is to be sure debate in the Greek camp: Agamemnon opposes the idea (out of sympathy for Kassandra, his own prize), but the sons of Theseus support it and Odysseus finally carries the day. At no point in the play, however, do we ever hear of any amorous passion for Polyxena on the part of Achilleus; she is simply valued because she is among the most beautiful of the captives, and is therefore an appropriate gift for Achilleus to choose. The same playwright's later *Troades* also touches on the event, with Talthybios there telling Hekabe that Polyxena will "tend" the tomb of Achilleus (*Tro* 264). That Achilleus actually desires her as an object of love is first hinted in Lykophron, if the words "savage bridal rites and marriage sacrifices" can be taken with that sense (Lyk 323–24). Subsequently, as we have seen in Diktys and Dares, Achilleus falls in love with the girl while he is still alive, and dies in the precinct of Thymbraian Apollo while trying to negotiate for her (so too *Fab* 110). Ovid follows Euripides in stressing Achilleus' honor as the cause of his demand (*Met* 13.445–48), but in Seneca's *Troades* Achilleus requests Polyxena's death so that he might become her "husband" in Elysion; she seems not displeased by the prospect (Sen:*Tro* 938–48). Philostratos takes matters even further, for in his account Polyxena reciprocates Achilleus' love, and commits suicide at his tomb in order to be with him (*ApTy* 4.16). The evidence thus seems to suggest that Achilleus' feelings of passion for Polyxena arise at some point after the fifth century, but we must admit that the Archaic period is largely a blank here.

Hekabe and Polydoros The tale of Polydoros' murder by the treacherous Polymestor of Thrace, and Hekabe's subsequent revenge against him, is not mentioned anywhere in our remains of the Epic Cycle. If, as in Euripides' *Hekabe*, the whole series of events took place in the Thracian Chersonese, where the Greeks were encamped prior to departure, we might expect it to have been related at the beginning of the *Nostoi*, as part of the difficulties with that departure. But Proklos says nothing of it in his summary, and neither does the *Odyssey*, which ought to have told of it if it was part of an Odyssean stopover further on in Thrace. In point of fact, Euripides' play is our very first trace of the story, and that circumstance, combined with the presence in the *Iliad* of a Polydoros, son of Priam, slain by Achilleus on the field of battle (*Il* 20.407–18), must make us suspect Euripidean innovation on a substantial scale. Admittedly, this Iliadic Polydoros is not the child of Hekabe, but rather of Laothoe (and thus brother of the twice-captured Lykaon of *Iliad* 21); nevertheless, Homer calls him the youngest of Priam's children, as does the *Hekabe*, and Euripides' character probably has no other counterpart in epic. In the *Hekabe*, Polydoros himself speaks the prologue as a ghost, relating how toward the end of the war Priam sent him out of Troy with a certain sum of gold to his friend Polymestor, king of Thrace, so that the line might be preserved in case of disaster to the city. With the city's fall, however, Polymestor has slain his guest and cast the body into the sea, to be found washed up on shore by Hekabe's servant in the opening part of the play. Hekabe appeals to Agamemnon for justice, and he allows her to summon Polymestor and his sons. Lured by a promise of hidden Trojan gold, he enters Hekabe's tent, where his sons are killed by the women and he himself blinded. With his appeals to Agamemnon denied, the play closes on his strange prediction that Hekabe will climb the mast of the ship taking her to Greece and be changed into a dog, with her final resting place commemorated by the name "Kynossema." An unascribed lyric fragment that may well be earlier than this play also shows her becoming a dog, although we learn nothing of the circumstances (965 *PMG*).

The story of treachery by this king of Thrace is further improved upon in Pacuvius and Hyginus by the presence of one Iliona, eldest daughter of Priam and Hekabe, who has married Polymestor and borne him a son Deipylos at about the same time that Hekabe bears Polydoros (Pac *Iliona* frr I–XVIII, plus [probably] *Ex incertis* fr XLII Rib; *Fab* 109). Priam thus sends Polydoros to his daughter to be raised together with her son, for the same reasons as in Euripides. She, however, from suspicions not explained, raises her own son Deipylos as Polydoros and her brother Polydoros as Deipylos. In time, Polydoros (the real one) finds his own reasons to suspect the situation and goes off to an oracle of Apollo to seek his true identity. Meanwhile, Troy falls, and the Greeks, not wishing to leave any of Priam's sons alive (save Helenos), inform Polymestor that they will give him Elektra, Agamemnon's daughter, to wife if he kills Polydoros for them. He of course then kills his own son Deipylos by mistake, thinking him to be Polydoros. At the oracle, the real Polydoros receives an ambiguous answer to the effect that his mother is a slave and his homeland is in ashes. Hastening home in alarm, he learns the whole truth from his mother, and persuades her to bring about the blinding and subsequently the death of Polymestor. She then kills herself. Much of this is worthy of Euripides; since it seems not to derive from him, however, it may stem from the Alexandrian

---

era (like the tale of Atreus and Aigisthos?). Surprisingly, Apollodoros has no mention of any version of Polydoros' fate, but Vergil creates an unforgettable picture of his betrayal with the thicket of cornel wood which speaks to Aineias from above his grave in *Aeneid* 3 (22–68). The nature of the scene requires (as against Euripides' version) a burial, but otherwise Vergil's few details are in accord with the *Hekabe;* he clearly expected his Roman audience to know the story.

As to Hekabe's ultimate fate, dog or not, there are some other points to note. Most often we think of her as assigned to Odysseus, but in truth our preserved bits of the Epic Cycle say nothing about her allotting, and she never appears as a companion or shipmate of Odysseus at any point in the *Odyssey*. Her despair at such a future is most memorably portrayed in the *Troades* of Euripides, who seems once again the first to mention it. Earlier, in the *Hekabe*, nothing at all is said of whose slave she will be; the plot rather implies that Agamemnon controls her destiny. In any case, there is an early variant of all this in the *Iliou Persis* of Stesichoros, where she is taken to Lykia by Apollo (198 *PMG:* we should remember that in some traditions she is the mother of Troilos [or Hektor] by the god). Dares, on the other hand, takes her across to the Chersonese with Helenos, Kassandra, and Andromache (Dar 43). Nikandros retains her canine conversion, although apparently at Troy, after she sees the city in ruins and dashes into the sea (Σ *Hek* 3). In Lykophron the setting is also Troy: Hekabe curses the Achaians and is stoned by them, becoming a dog at some point in the process (Odysseus casts the first stone: Lyk 330–34, 1174–88). The scholia at 1176 seem to suppose that she turns into a dog first and is stoned in that form. Either way, she goes down to Hades, where Lykophron says that she serves as the hound of Hekate. In Diktys she is again stoned by the Achaians for her curses, but this author omits any transformation (Dik 4.16); Quintus, by contrast, omits the stoning, but has her turned into a dog by the gods (no stated reason) and then turned to stone (QS 14.347–51). In Ovid, she is stoned by the Thracians immediately after she has blinded their king (*Met* 13.565–71).

Last, we find first in Lykophron the idea that Laodike is swallowed up by the earth and goes down to Hades alive (Lyk 316–18, 496–98). Although Apollodoros too mentions a chasm that opens up and swallows her (ApE 5.23), only Quintus offers the explanation that she requests this fate, lest she become a slave, and some unspecified god fulfills it (QS 13.544–53). One might suppose that as the wife of Helikaon, son of Antenor (*Il* 3.121–24), who is saved in the *Little Iliad* by Odysseus, or at any rate as the mother of Akamas' child Mounitos (see above), she would have reason to expect a better fate than slavery, but her role as one of Priam's more beautiful daughters may have dictated the situation here.

17   The Return from Troy

Menelaos and Nestor Proklos' summary of Arktinos' *Iliou Persis* concludes with the laconic remark that following the division of booty the Greeks sailed away, and Athena contrived their destruction at sea. Both the epic *Nostoi* and Nestor in the *Odyssey* speak more specifically of a quarrel between Agamemnon and Menelaos after the taking of Troy, when the ships were preparing to leave. If our epitome is correct, in the *Nostoi* Athena created the quarrel (concerning something about the leave-taking), and Agamemnon remained behind, offering sacrifices to appease her anger, while Diomedes, Nestor, and after them Menelaos, among others, departed immediately. Hermes in *Odyssey* 5 (speaking to Kalypso) claims that the Achaians on the return "transgressed" against Athena, causing her to send a storm from which Odysseus survived to reach Kalypso's island (*Od* 5.108–11). This last detail—that Odysseus was involved in the general catastrophe—is not supported by the rest of the *Odyssey* or any other source, and is probably an oversimplification of the moment. Likewise the phrase "on the return" is presumably short for "during preparations for the return," if as we would guess the transgression involved some lack of proper behavior to the gods before departing.

Nestor in *Odyssey* 3 is more loquacious, but he too will not say exactly what caused Athena's anger; we are told only that some of the Achaians were not prudent or just, and thus Athena's wrath was visited upon them via Zeus (*Od* 3.130–36). Possibly this means simply Aias' violation of Kassandra's sanctuary during the Sack (which it seems the Achaians failed to punish), but Nestor may also be alluding to the more general lack of gratitude to Athena advanced by later authors, or to something else that has not survived. In any case, the dispute between the Atreidai caused by Athena results in a general assembly called near sundown, at which Menelaos (following, it seems, the view of Nestor and Odysseus) advises all to leave as quickly as possible, while Agamemnon wishes to stay and carry out sacrifices in the hope of appeasing the goddess. As Nestor sees the situation, and as events prove, this last is a vain effort. Nevertheless, about half the army determines to stay. At dawn the other half departs, Nestor, Diomedes, and Odysseus among them, but when they reach Tenedos, doubt reassails Odysseus' crews, and they and Odysseus turn back (thus explaining why Nestor knows nothing more of their fate). At

Lesbos, where Nestor and Diomedes have stopped to consider their best route across the Aegean, Menelaos catches up with them; they sacrifice to the gods, who advise them to sail above rather than below Chios. At Euboia they put in at Geraistos and sacrifice to Poseidon in thanks for their safety. The fourth day from their departure sees Diomedes safe at Argos, and Nestor continues on to Pylos without incident.

So runs Nestor's first account of the return in *Odyssey* 3. But when Telemachos quite properly wonders what has happened to Menelaos, if Agamemnon's death on his return went so long unpunished, his host concedes that at Sounion Apollo shot the pilot of Menelaos' ship, one Phrontis, son of Onetor, and that Menelaos remained behind there to bury him (*Od* 3.276–302). The rest we must assume he learned from Menelaos after the latter's return: the storm sent by Zeus at Cape Maleia which drove his fleet to Gortyn on Krete, where many ships foundered; the passage of five of them down to Egypt; and Menelaos' sojourn there (collecting provisions and gold), with a successful voyage back to Sparta only in the eighth year, after Orestes had avenged Agamemnon. Further details of the stay in Egypt are then provided by Menelaos himself in *Odyssey* 4, when it is his turn to entertain Telemachos. He speaks of time spent in Cyprus and Phoinicia (Sidon), in Aithiopia and Libya and among the Eremboi, as well as in Egypt (*Od* 4.81–85). Seemingly he was in no great hurry to return to Sparta, for his actual becalming on the island of Pharos at the mouth of the Nile occupies only twenty days out of the eight-year period. At the end of those twenty days Eidothea, daughter of Proteus, approaches him with a solution to his dilemma (*Od* 4.351–569): she tells him that he and three of his crew must hide among the seals in the cave where her father comes to rest each day at noon. She herself provides the sealskins to cover them, and ambrosia for their nostrils so that they may withstand the smell. When Proteus arrives and settles down, having failed to notice them, they spring forth and seize him, holding on despite his transformations (lion, serpent, panther, boar, water, tree) until he agrees to reveal the source of their becalming: they have failed to sacrifice to Zeus and the other gods before setting out and must return to the Nile to do so properly. At the same time, the old man also discloses information about other events (Aias Oileiades' fate, Agamemnon's death, and the whereabouts of Odysseus) to which we will come in due course. The pronounced cure for the lack of wind is, of course, successful; Menelaos sets up a barrow for his dead brother after completing the sacrifices at the Nile and sets sail for home, arriving just in time for the funeral of Aigisthos, whom Orestes has slain. The *Nostoi* epitome's account of all this is much more limited, but there too Menelaos reaches Egypt with five ships after the rest are lost at sea, and his return to Sparta is effected only after Orestes and Pylades have taken vengeance for Agamemnon.

In the *Odyssey* certainly and the *Nostoi* presumably, Helen really was at Troy, so that there was no need to retrieve her in Egypt. In Stesichoros, where the *eidôlon* first takes her place, matters proceed rather differently, but we still do not know for certain that Helen stayed with Proteus in his Palinode,[1] and we cannot say much about Menelaos' return voyage in that work; it may not even have been included. Moving down to the fifth century, we have a full dramatization of the encounter with Proteus in Aischylos' lost satyr play *Proteus*, the fourth drama in his *Oresteia* production of 458 B.C. Presumably there were thematic connections between Menelaos' problems here (adverse winds) and those of his brother at Aulis in the opening play of the production, the *Agamemnon*.[2] Presumably too, after the chorus' attack against Helen in that play, the *Proteus* continued to represent her as a genuine runaway rather than an innocent victim. But we do not know at all what else this satyr play might have contained. Only with the *Helen* of Euripides (preceded as we saw in chapter 16 by a brief allusion in his *Elektra*) do we find clearly told the story of Menelaos' finding of Helen in Egypt after he has departed from Troy. In both plays she has spent the war in the house of Proteus (here more king than sea god), but in the *Helen* Proteus has since died, and his son Theoklymenos wishes to keep Helen in Egypt permanently as his wife. At this point Menelaos arrives, thinking the *eidôlon* that accompanies him to be Helen, and is thus understandably confused at seeing the genuine article. Matters are eventually straightened out, aided by a report of the miraculous disappearance of the *eidôlon*, but Theoklymenos (who kills all Greek visitors on the chance that they might be Menelaos) remains to be dealt with. Helen solves this problem by announcing that messengers have come with news of her husband's death, and that to mourn him properly she must be sent out on a ship into the harbor for a special Greek ritual. Too eager to claim his bride, Theoklymenos falls for the ruse, and Helen and a disguised Menelaos make their escape, aided by the *deus ex machina* appearance of the Dioskouroi to halt pursuit. Their subsequent life together, as we see it in *Odyssey* 4, seems unmarred by any conflict or controversy; even the marriage of Menelaos' bastard son Megapenthes (on the same day that Hermione is being sent to Neoptolemos) causes no difficulties.

Agamemnon Not surprisingly, the *Iliad* tells us nothing of Agamemnon's forthcoming death when he reaches the plain of Argos. But the *Odyssey* has a good deal to say about that event, much of it in the context of an unfavorable comparison between Klytaimestra and Penelope as model wives and a likening of Aigisthos to the suitors.[3] Indeed, in the opening passage of the epic, Zeus observes that Hermes was sent down to earth by the gods to tell Aigisthos not to kill Agamemnon and take his wife, lest he suffer the consequences, as he subsequently did (*Od* 1.35–43). Nestor in Book 3 adds details of Klytaimestra's seduction by Aigisthos: at first it seems she was unwilling to accede to his blandishments, and then too she was attended by a singer left behind by Agamemnon to guard/ protect her (*Od* 3.263–75). But presently, "when the *moira* of the gods constrained her to succumb" (whatever that means), the singer was taken to a deserted island to become prey for birds, and she went willingly to Aigisthos' house. This last phrase may simply be a carryover of the normal Greek idiom for marriage, and Nestor later states that Aigisthos for seven years ruled golden Mykenai, having subdued the people (*Od* 3.304–5). All the same, we will see shortly that there is some reason to believe that the *Odyssey*'s Klytaimestra took up residence with Aigisthos, rather than vice versa. Aigisthos' residence, by the way, is here located by Nestor "in a nook/recess of horse-pasturing Argos," that is, somewhere in the Argolid. Nestor's further statement that after the successful seduction Aigisthos made many costly sacrifices and dedications to the gods (*Od* 3.273–75) might seem to indicate that his motive was primarily one of passion, rather than a desire for power or revenge against Agamemnon's side of the family. The same conclusion is probably what we should understand from Zeus' words in *Odyssey* 1, although in both cases such a coloring of the event may be influenced by a desire for contrast with the faithful Penelope and the lustful suitors. Zeus also emphasizes Aigisthos' part in initiating both seduction and murder, but Athena (as Mentor) attributes the latter to the deceit of lover *and* wife (*Od* 3.232–35); we will see Klytaimestra's role given more prominence as the poem progresses.

In *Odyssey* 4 Telemachos acquires further information on the killing via details given by Proteus to Menelaos in Egypt (*Od* 4.496–537). A storm, it seems, caught the ships of Aias and Agamemnon at the Gyrian rocks (Tenos? Mykonos?); Aias was drowned, but Hera saw Agamemnon safely through and he found himself almost about to put in at Cape Maleia when a wind carried him back out onto the open sea. At this point the text becomes somewhat puzzling, and must be quoted: "to that far edge of land, where Thyestes had his home before, and then Aigisthos son of Thyestes lived. But when also from that place a safe return was in view, the gods turned back the wind, and they came to their homeland." Here Agamemnon kisses the ground in his joy, but he has been spotted by a lookout, paid by Aigisthos, who has been watching for a whole year and now reports the return to his master. Aigisthos takes twenty men and sets up an ambush; "on the other side" (of the megaron?) he orders a feast prepared and sallies forth in his chariot to invite Agamemnon to dinner. Unwitting, the latter comes, and after the meal, is cut down "like an ox in his stall." There is, moreover, a general struggle of forces, for none of Agamemnon's companions survive, and none of Aigisthos' either.

Some obvious questions arise here. Specific mention of Aigisthos residing where his father Thyestes used to live strongly implies that he is in fact there at the moment, not in Agamemnon's palace. Certain in any case, I think, is the fact that he invites Agamemnon to his own house, where the murder takes place, for how on any logic can he invite his cousin to dinner in the cousin's house without making it obvious that he has moved in? Textual emendation has been proposed at various points,[4] but it seems simpler to try to interpret the narrative on its own terms, and to assume that Aigisthos remains in his own house, to which he invites and in which he slays Agamemnon. Homer's text will then have intended something like the following: because of the winds Agamemnon nearly lands near Aigisthos' home (somewhere further east in the Argolid?) where he is not expected and no lookout is posted; from there he would have been able to make his way, either to Aigisthos' house where he would have found his wife and cousin together, or homeward to Mykenai where rumors of the truth (and Klytaimestra's absence) would have alerted him to his danger. Instead with a change of wind he comes to Nauplia, where he is seen, and thus Aigisthos' invitation intercepts him before he can reach his (wifeless) home; he detours instead to Aigisthos' house where the ambush has been prepared. This is admittedly a cumbersome chain of events, but logical; presumably the audience was familiar with it from more detailed versions. Alternatively, given Nestor's earlier reference to ruling at Mykenai (*Od* 3.304), we might suppose Aigisthos and Klytaimestra there, from which point, when the warning arrives, Aigisthos sends men to arrange the banquet and ambush back at his house (could this be the meaning of *heterôthi*?) and rides out as if from that house to intercept Agamemnon. Either way, the locale of the murder gives greater point to the need for advance warning: Agamemnon must not simply be prepared for, but diverted from his natural goal, namely his own palace. Such an arrangement also allows for a more realistic treatment of Agamemnon's political power: as a king he returns from Troy with subjects and retainers, men who will contest his murder and with whom Aigisthos can deal far better on his own territory. Klytaimestra for her part will be hidden until the trap is sprung (Proteus in fact never mentions her, either as motive or agent). Admittedly, such a role does not give her quite the duplicity we might have imagined from the words of Athena/Mentor in Book 3, or those of Menelaos at 4.91–92 (when he laments his brother's demise at Aigisthos' hands through the treachery of an accursed wife), but perhaps this notion of treachery refers simply to her adultery, or else to the planning of her husband's death in advance of the actual event. That she did participate in the killing may or may not be supposed in these first accounts; certainly it is the case in two later ones to which we must now turn.

The first of these later narrations is in the *Nekuia,* where Agamemnon's shade describes the scene of the murder to Odysseus (*Od* 11.405–34). We hear nothing about where the victim puts into harbor, but here as in Book 4 he has been invited to dinner by Aigisthos (the term *oikonde* surely refers to the latter's house), and there having feasted he and his men are slaughtered. His contrasting the scene with a battlefield suggests that there is no real combat with Aigisthos' forces, but only a massacre, with much blood running over the floor. As he raises his hands and (apparently) beats the ground in an appeal for vengeance he hears the cries of Kassandra, killed near him by Klytaimestra, who turns away and does not even close his eyes or mouth. The text here offers some slight ambiguity: either Agamemnon dies pierced by someone else's sword (presumably that of Aigisthos), or he throws his hands about Klytaimestra's in a vain attempt to prevent her from killing Kassandra. Kassandra's presence with Agamemnon in Aigisthos' house should mean (as we would expect) that he is still en route from Troy to his own home; presumably, Klytaimestra has been in hiding until the trap is sprung. Odysseus' response to this account does specifically link the notion of her deception with planning the deed in Agamemnon's absence at Troy. The second passage, the *nekuia* of *Odyssey* 24, brings back the shade of Agamemnon to lament again his ill-fortune. At one point here he says that Aigisthos and Klytaimestra performed the deed together (*Od* 24.96–97); at another he seems to credit his wife alone, perhaps because of the contrast with Penelope (*Od* 24.199–202). Either way, the beginning of this Book states once again that the murder occurred in the house of Aigisthos, with Aigisthos thus surely the host (*Od* 24.21–22). Such is precisely the opposite of the situation in Aischylos' *Agamemnon*, but Homer's arrangement allows him to emphasize the role (and transgression) of either lover or wife as uppermost, depending upon the current situation. On the other hand, we should note that the poet never mentions Orestes' killing of his mother, and probably has no desire to do so, or even suggest it, given the favorable parallel he wishes to establish between Orestes and Telemachos; for this reason it is in his interests to minimize Klytaimestra's direct complicity as party to a homicide, however much he may stress her infidelity.

In the *Nostoi* epitome, too, Agamemnon is said to have been slain by Aigisthos and Klytaimestra (see below for a possible illustration on a "Homeric" bowl); no other details are given. One additional event of interest in this poem is the appearance of the ghost of Achilleus (as in the *Little Iliad*) to the ships of Agamemnon as they are leaving Troy, in an attempt to dissuade their departure by predicting what will happen. What follows in the summary is the storm at the Kapherides rocks and the death of Aias, a disaster that may or may not have coinvolved Agamemnon; we will return to that problem too below, in discussing Aias and Nauplios. Stesichoros' lyric *Nostoi* may also have included an accounting of Agamemnon's travails, but we have no idea at exactly what point his *Oresteia* begins, and thus cannot say what part of the return and slaughter was covered in either of those poems, although we assume that the story was told in one or the other (if not both). Philodemos, as we saw in chapter 16, attests that the *Oresteia* spoke of Iphigeneia's transformation into Hekate, so that this poem may well have treated in detail the background to Orestes' vengeance. One detail that did appear somewhere was the placement of Agamemnon's kingdom in Sparta rather than Mykenai; our source, a Euripidean scholiast, notes that Simonides also located it there (216 *PMG*). Scholars have naturally seen such a variant as politically motivated: Agamemnon as a Spartan ruler would give the kings of that city an Achaian as well as a Dorian ancestry, thus allowing them to claim whichever was more advantageous for a given moment.[5] Whether this is true or not, the change of venue means that Stesichoros may well have contrived a completely different logistical situation for Agamemnon's death than that seen in Homer. But in the absence of any notion of where Aigisthos would have lived when Agamemnon ruled Sparta we cannot say more, and we have no other information for this poet or for Simonides. The same is true of Xanthos, the obscure older poet on whom

Stesichoros is supposed to have drawn. One other detail from Stesichoros seen earlier regards the cause of the Tyndareides' problems: a wrathful Aphrodite causes their infidelity after their father forgets her sacrifices (223 *PMG*). In the *Ehoiai*, too, the goddess' anger (at Tyndareos?) is the root of the difficulty; a direct quote offers the picture of Klytaimestra leaving glorious Agamemnon to bed with Aigisthos, thus choosing an inferior husband (Hes fr 176 MW). Elsewhere in the latter poem the Catalogue Poet tells us that after two daughters (Iphimede and Elektra) Klytaimestra bore Orestes, who "coming to full youth avenged himself on the *patrophoneus* and killed his own mother" (Hes fr 23a MW). *Patrophoneus* is properly a male agent noun, and is used of Aigisthos with this exact same wording at *Odyssey* 3.197. All the same, the Catalogue Poet must have envisioned Klytaimestra as closely involved in the murder, if Orestes is to be at all justified in killing her.

From the early literary tradition we now turn to art of the same period, before considering the abundant evidence of the fifth century.[6] The theme of Agamemnon's death is probably illustrated as early as a terracotta relief plaque from Gortyn of the late seventh century on which we see a woman and a man flanking a seated figure and seemingly engaged in a struggle with him (Iraklion 11512). Given a less-than-perfect pressing, the details of the scene are fuzzy and arguable, but the woman (on the left) does appear to be bending over the seated man and grasping his right wrist (as he raises his arm) with her right hand, while her left arm passes behind his body and is obscured. The man to the right catches the seated figure's spear just below the blade with his left hand and presses down on the top of the man's head with his right. The victim (if he is that) has something over his head which may be either his hair or part of a garment. On the whole, this seems likely to be the event in question, with both Klytaimestra and Aigisthos participating, but given the murkiness of the representation in its present condition it is hazardous to go further; we cannot really say with any certainty that the enveloping cloak is here shown, or even that Klytaimestra rather than Aigisthos is meant to be striking the fatal blow.[7]

Much clearer is the next item, a shield-band relief from Olympia, dating to the second quarter of the sixth century, with a woman and two men in a deadly struggle (B 1654).[8] Here the men grapple with each other as if wrestling; the one in the center of the composition aims a blow of his hand at the one on the right, who has him caught in a headlock. Behind him, to the left, the woman seizes his drawn-back elbow to impede him and plunges a sword/knife into his back or side. Behind the right-hand figure a spear stands upright: Agamemnon's weapon, perhaps, put aside incautiously, or a symbol of his rule. A very similar composition on a fragmentary shield-band from Aigina (no #) probably illustrates the same scene, although the left-hand figure here is not definitely a woman.[9] In any case, we finally have an early version in which Klytaimestra plainly does the killing herself, treacherously striking from behind while Agamemnon is engaged with Aigisthos. Earlier than any of these pieces, however, is a fragment of bronze sheathing from the Argive Heraion,

of the mid-seventh century, which probably shows Klytaimestra slaying Kassandra: one woman seizes a second by a lock of her hair and stabs her in the
side with a short sword or dagger (Athens, no #).[10] Obviously we cannot guarantee this interpretation, but one is hard pressed to think of any other story or
situation involving two women in such a pose.

Having surveyed this much, we must now consider several less certain
examples which, if they do represent the death of Agamemnon, would, like the
Olympia shield-band, give Klytaimestra quite a central role. The first, a steatite
gem from Krete known already in the last century and dating to perhaps 700 B.C.
(NY 42.11.1), shows just two figures, a seated man and a woman bending over
him.[11] The woman's right hand (gem, not impression) holds or rests over a
water jug; her left is extended out toward the man's midsection. He in turn has
his right arm extended out toward the woman's waist, while his right leg is
raised almost to the same point and his left arm placed back behind him for
support. If this is Klytaimestra and Agamemnon, it is not only the earliest
illustration of their story, but assigns Klytaimestra a primacy in the killing we
might not have expected. But given the limitations of space on such a gem, it
may be that the scene as we see it has been cut down from a fuller representation like that on the Olympia relief: Klytaimestra strikes from ambush in Aigisthos' house while Aigisthos himself (not shown) distracts the victim. On the
other hand, the interpretation of the scene in question as the death of Agamemnon (when we cannot even be sure a murder is in question) is very far from
certain. The alternative suggestion of Eurykleia washing the feet of Odysseus
seems equally plausible, if not more so, leaving us (as so often for the earliest
stages of Greek art) without the sort of evidence on which we can base any
really sound conclusions.

A second category of tantalizing representations involves the device of
Agamemnon's bath, a detail not firmly attested until Aischylos' *Oresteia*. On a
relief amphora from Thebes of the seventh century a damaged (and quite uncertain) scene offers a totally different composition from what we have seen so
far (Boston 99.505).[12] Aigisthos (if it is he) now stands to the left, his left hand
clutching the wrist of the man in the center, his right outstretched and perhaps
holding a weapon. Of the central figure all except the head and one hand are
lost, but toward the bottom are what appear to be the legs of a stool, or perhaps
a tripod. The woman in the scene stands to the right, not directly involved, but
her right hand may hold the hilt of a lost sword. Such a tableau has generated
other interpretations, including Apollo and Herakles struggling for the Delphic
tripod, or even Orestes and Aigisthos,[13] but the fact that the central figure is
behind (or *in*) the tripod might suggest that the missing section showed the
lebes used to heat water for a bath. That there was a lebes, as opposed to just a
tripod (in which, for example, Herakles might be sitting, to establish his own
oracle), has been argued on the parallel of the previously discussed metope
from Foce del Sele where a man is definitely so sitting in such a vessel.[14] Unfortunately, the left side of this metope, where another figure must have been

positioned, has been broken away, as has the final surface of what remains. But the man in the lebes does have his left hand raised (the right is missing) in a gesture that looks like alarm. We saw in chapters 8 and 12, however, that there are several other possibilities for this metope, including Minos slain by the daughters of Kokalos, Pelias slain by Medeia (although there the daughters do the actual deed before putting the pieces in water), Aison or Iason rejuvenated, or even the resurrection of Pelops. Relevant to this scene also is the small terracotta relief band (reputedly from Sicily), now in Basel, on which a quite similar figure sits in a lebes, with the left side of the scene now completed by a woman who holds a water jug in her right hand and a weapon (or the man's upraised right arm?) in her left (Basel BS 318).[15] To the far right stands a figure with a long cloak who is probably male and who seems relatively uninvolved in the action. Certainly bathing appears to be involved in this last example (even if no one ever actually bathed in a lebes—probably tub and cauldron for heating water have been combined for reasons of space), but even so, Minos is perhaps as likely as Agamemnon here, with a daughter of Kokalos on one side (pouring in the fatal hot water) and Kokalos himself on the other. In that case the parallels offer no sure early evidence for Agamemnon's bath, and we must reserve judgment on the Boston amphora as well. If the Foce del Sele metope *could* represent the death of Agamemnon, it might provide further evidence for versions in which Klytaimestra takes the leading role (assuming Aigisthos was not in a lost metope to the right), but we are in dangerous waters here.

Two last, still more uncertain pieces remain to be mentioned. One is a Protoattic vase, the so-called Oresteia Krater formerly in Berlin (Berlin:Lost A32) and known at present primarily from drawings.[16] A male with drawn sword follows another male and, reaching around his body, grasps a long strand of something that seems to attach to the latter's forehead. The latter in turn reaches back in a supplicating gesture, so that he seems about to be killed. Beyond him to the far right a woman stands turned away, her hand to her cheek. The strand in question has recently been interpreted as a schematic representation of the net or garment pulled over Agamemnon's head,[17] but it cannot be said to be very convincing, nor does one quite see why the woman would look distressed at (or at least uninterested in) the proceedings. We shall return to this vase below in the context of its more familiar interpretation, Orestes slaying Aigisthos.

The other piece is a "Homeric" bowl of the second century B.C. now preserved in Berlin (Berlin:PM 4996).[18] Here we have without question the death of Agamemnon and Kassandra (as proved by inscriptions) and some indication of the artist's source. To the left Klytaimestra reaches out with drawn sword and grasps the hair of the helpless Kassandra. To the right a male figure in long cloak over one shoulder charges (with similarly drawn sword) at a reclining Agamemnon, the latter with a garland on his head and drinking cup in hand; a robe or blanket covers his lower body. Similarly dressed are three men behind him in various stages of starting up to flee. Their way, however, is blocked by

two armed warriors who poise their spears for the kill. Of these three companions of Agamemnon, two have names that can be read: Alkmeon, and Mestor,
son of Aias; the henchmen of Aigisthos are Antiochos and Argeios. To this
primary mold design, the potter casting the actual bowl has made two clear
additions: using the segments of the mold to overstamp, he has added the upper
torso of Agamemnon at the feet of Klytaimestra in her scene, and represented
Kassandra as falling onto the legs of Agamemnon in his. Most important, in
the area between the arms of the original Kassandra and Aigisthos, there is an
inscription that identifies the scene as the death of Agamemnon and probably
specifies before that the source of the story. Not all the letters are preserved,
but what remains seems to indicate the *Nostoi of the Achaians* as responsible,
in which case we would have a valuable illustration from that lost epic. What
is here shown, even without the overstamping to bring Agamemnon and Kassandra into closer proximity, is essentially what the *Nekuia* tells us. Agamemnon and his men are having dinner when they are surprised by the ambush
launched by Aigisthos and his band; the latter deals with Agamemnon while
Klytaimestra dispatches Kassandra, and there is no sign of any bath. Either
then the *Nekuia* and the *Nostoi* were very similar in their account of this event,
or the artist drew his inspiration from the more familiar *Odyssey* but credited
the work to which the story narratively belongs.

In all, the only certain thing we can conclude from all of our artistic evidence prior to the fifth century is that Klytaimestra (based primarily on the
Olympia shield-band) did at times assume an active role in killing her husband.
Seemingly, Homer brings her out from ambush in Aigisthos' house, where
Agamemnon has been invited to dinner; the conflicting notion of a bath during
which he was killed may or may not have developed prior to the fifth century,
and may or may not indicate at the same time a shift of the scene of action to
the palace at Mykenai (since Agamemnon might as well expect to be bathed in
Aigisthos' house after a long journey as he would in his own). More definite
conclusions seem to me undesirable, although the possibilities for different
early versions are unquestionably intriguing.

For the first half of the fifth century we have in literature Aischylos' *Agamemnon* plus allusions in Pindar's *Pythian* 11, and in art the detailed representation of the Dokimasia Painter on an Attic Red-Figure krater in Boston (Boston 63.1246).[19] Complicating the deductive process here is the uncertainty of
relative dating, for while the *Agamemnon* is firmly fixed by its hypothesis to
the spring of 458 B.C., *Pythian* 11 could (from its scholia) celebrate a victory
in either 474 or 454, and the krater is dated between 470 and 460, too close to
assure that it precedes Aischylos. Nevertheless, with the reader warned, we
will take Pindar first, then the krater, and finally the *Oresteia*.[20] *Pythian* 11,
written for Thrasydaios of Thebes, moves from the land of Pylades to the tale
of his Lakonian comrade Orestes, who, his father slain, was saved from the
strong hands and grim treachery of Klytaimestra by his nurse Arsinoe, when
his mother dispatched Kassandra and Agamemnon to the shores of Acheron

with the flashing bronze (Py 11.15–22). The poet then asks, pointedly, whether Iphigeneia's slaughter at the Euripos stirred her hand, or rather was it nights spent in another's bed. Subsequently he locates the murder at Amyklai, where Agamemnon perished himself and brought about the death of Kassandra as well. These few lines offer a number of important points. As noted in chapter 16, Pindar stands as the first extant author (depending on date) to specifically link Iphigeneia's death with Klytaimestra's betrayal (as well as the first, for that matter, to attest unambiguously that Iphigeneia did die). He suggests, again for the first time, that Orestes was in some danger from his mother, who might have killed him had he not been rescued. He follows Stesichoros in moving Agamemnon's home to Sparta, or rather nearby Amyklai, instead of the Argolid. And he is our first literary source to move Klytaimestra fully to center stage, making the initiative and control of the situation hers (as well as the deed?), with Aigisthos reduced to a supporting role.

The first and fourth of these points are crucial to Aischylos' treatment of the story, and thus our interest in knowing whether he or Pindar has prior claim to them. But one might well be skeptical that either poet has introduced wholly new themes here; Klytaimestra's motivation and role in the murder are obvious areas for exploration, and we cannot be sure that the Nostoi and Stesichoros (among others) did not explore them.[21] We should note too that in treating this whole story Pindar is, like Aischylos, concerned with its proper completion, the matricide; thus, like Aischylos (and unlike Homer), we should expect him to underline what justified that extreme measure by a greater emphasis on Klytaimestra's role.

Moving from Pindar to the Dokimasia Painter, we find a scene not entirely in line with these observations. His krater shows without any question both events, the death of Agamemnon on one side and the death of Aigisthos on the other, and the second probably dictated his treatment of the first. What we see on this first side is Aigisthos striding forward from the left, drawn sword in right hand, to seize Agamemnon by the hair as his victim shrinks backward in alarm. Aigisthos is here fully dressed; Agamemnon's body is entirely covered (head and hands included) by a diaphanous bordered garment under which he is completely naked, and there is already a stab wound in his chest. The garment clings in a peculiarly web-like fashion around his right hand, as if failing to provide an expected exit. To each side of this central group a woman runs forward, hand outstretched; that on the left holds an axe in her other hand. Beyond these, two other women run away from the scene in terror, virtually colliding with the columns that form the frame of the whole composition. Obviously we have here at last indisputable evidence for an entangling cloth of some sort, and probably for the bath as well, since Agamemnon is naked (although see below on Seneca and Apollodoros). The woman behind Aigisthos must by virtue of the axe be Klytaimestra running up to help (or to slay Kassandra); that behind Agamemnon might be Kassandra or a daughter of the house, with Kassandra the simply clad slave figure running away right. On the principle of better compositional symmetry, I would favor Klytaimestra and Kassandra balancing each other as the two major figures flanking the men, but it does not much matter for our purposes. Since we have here again, as for Pindar, elements new and vital to Aischylos' presentation of the story, it might seem crucial in this case also to establish priority, and to that end it is frequently argued that Aigisthos would not take the leading role if the painter had drawn from Aischylos. That argument assumes, however, that a painter cannot conflate ideas from different sources, and it also ignores the problem of the other side: if a painter has doubts about showing the death of Klytaimestra in the sequel, he will naturally focus on Aigisthos in the original act, so that slayer and object of vengeance will be the same person. Aischylos could afford to focus on the matricide because he had two full plays in which to explore and justify the deed; the Dokimasia Painter had no such luxury. Nevertheless, I do believe that he illustrates a tradition older than the *Oresteia*, regardless of the date of his work, for reasons explained below.

With Aischylos' great trilogy of 458 B.C. we find ourselves in the presence of the most famous and influential version of the fortunes of the house of Atreus. The *Agamemnon* opens at Mykenai, or rather Argos (a shift usually thought to be prompted by the political realities of the time), but certainly in any case Agamemnon's home. There is here as in Homer a lookout, but on the roof of the palace, posted there by Klytaimestra to watch not for Agamemnon himself but rather for a beacon relay that will announce Troy's taking. The watchman confides that all is not well within, which we take to mean the presence of Aigisthos in the proper owner's place; nevertheless he seems confident that with his master's return the problem will resolve itself. The beacon does now appear, Klytaimestra explains its significance to the elders as they ponder the long-ago death of Iphigeneia, and a herald enters to confirm the expedition's success. We learn from him that Troy was razed to the ground, temples and all; Klytaimestra has already suggested the dangers in such an act, and it develops that the fleet did encounter a catastrophic storm on the way home. But Agamemnon is safe enough, and soon arrives, bringing with him Kassandra, whom he flaunts in front of his wife. She has for her part strewn the path to the palace with purple garments, and persuades Agamemnon to walk on these, hoping to make him even more guilty in the eyes of the gods. His entry into the palace to perform sacrifices of thanksgiving is followed by that of Kassandra, but only after she has delayed some time to predict Agamemnon's imminent demise, and her own, to the chorus. The impact of this scene arises in part from the chorus' inability to grasp darkly worded hints which the audience, based on prior knowledge, understands only too well. In particular, we must suppose that the truncated references to the fatal bath and net, not fully explained on stage until much later, will have little point if they do not refer to a tradition older than the play. In the same way, the net imagery used of Troy's capture earlier by the chorus in the First Stasimon will have no larger implications if the motif of the net is not already known.

In any event, Kassandra like Agamemnon goes to her doom. We hear two cries from Agamemnon himself within the palace, then see Klytaimestra coming out, with the bodies of husband and war prize on some sort of platform, to recount her deed. Kassandra has already implied that he was in the bath (standing up to get out of it, I suppose) and amid garments (*peploi*) when he was struck (*Ag* 1126–29). Klytaimestra speaks now of how she threw a robe (or robes) about him so that he might not escape, and struck him three times, the third as he was going down (*Ag* 1382–92). The implement used is not here in any way specified; at *Choephoroi* 1011 it seems to have been the sword of Aigisthos (borrowed by Klytaimestra?), while in the *Nekuia* we saw a sword to be either the murder weapon of Aigisthos (slaying Agamemnon) or Klytaimestra (slaying Kassandra), depending on how we read a difficult text (*Od* 11.421–24). The Dokimasia Painter is the first known source to give Klytaimestra an axe in this particular situation. We shall see below, however, that for the confrontation with Orestes she is so equipped as early as the Foce del Sele metopes, and in several Red-Figure vases before the time of the *Oresteia*. Thus, her call for an axe in the *Choephoroi* with which to defend herself is not an Aischylean invention, but rather an element of earlier tradition which might have influenced storytellers' choice of her weapon for the slaying of Agamemnon (at whatever point, although we have seen her twice with a sword/dagger in the seventh and sixth centuries). Likewise, of course, the influence might have gone the other way, with an axe first used against Agamemnon subsequently adopted for the confrontation with Orestes (although an artistic corpus of some quantity does not show it before now). In the latter part of the fifth century this axe will become a standard feature (see below).

Two other points need to be made before leaving Aischylos. The one concerns Orestes, whom Klytaimestra has herself sent away to Strophios of Phokis, unlike her counterpart in Pindar (and in Euripides and Sophokles); thus there can be no question of her planning to kill him (*Ag* 877–85). The second point involves Aigisthos, who emerges from the palace long after the killing is over and makes no protest when the chorus suggests that he took no part at all in the deed, but only in the planning. His task, he insists, was to remain hidden, lest he arouse the suspicion of a man who was his enemy. It is clear that he remained hidden longer than was necessary, but his premise is sound: he has been living in Agamemnon's house, and his appearance too soon would have given away Klytaimestra's deception. This whole balance of responsibility, with Klytaimestra playing very much the man's part and Aigisthos the woman's, probably owes a good deal to the trilogy's overall theme of perversion in male-female relationships, a theme adumbrated in the watchman's opening characterization of his queen and worked out only in the *Eumenides*. To what extent Aischylos might have found such a feminine-slanted imbalance in earlier versions of the story remains uncertain. But we can say that Aischylos' setting of the murder in Agamemnon's own home, where the work of deception will fall to Klytaimestra, has effaced general awareness of earlier accounts in which Aigisthos probably played that role.

Subsequently in the fifth century there are several dramatic allusions, although they do not add a great deal. At no point does Klytaimestra yield the status found in Pindar and Aischylos; either the deed is all hers, or she shares it with her lover. Euripides' *Orestes* says that "casting a piece of weaving without exit over her husband she slew him" (*Or* 25–26), and later, that he "lies dead, having fallen in the very last bath offered by his wife" (*Or* 366–67). In the same poet's *Elektra*, Agamemnon dies "in his own home, by the deceit of his wife Klytaimestra and the hand of Aigisthos, son of Thyestes" (E:*El* 8–10); his old tutor here rescues Orestes, as he does in Sophokles' *Elektra*. Three different plays of Euripides, plus this same drama of Sophokles, mention an axe as the murder weapon (*Hek* 1279; *Tro* 361–62; E:*El* 279; S:*El* 96–99), and we see it as well on a cup of the same general period by the Marlay Painter on which Klytaimestra uses it to dispatch Kassandra (Ferrara 2482). There are, surprisingly, no more representations of the death of Agamemnon after the Dokimasia Painter's krater. In Pherekydes we hear that Aigisthos slew the child of Orestes' nurse Laodameia, thinking it to be Orestes himself (3F134); one suspects, even if our scholiast source does not say, that the nurse deliberately sacrificed her own son to facilitate her charge's escape.

Of later sources, Pausanias offers the famous information used to such good effect by Schliemann, that within the ruins of Mykenai were the graves of Agamemnon and all those coming back with him from Troy, whom Aigisthos slaughtered after having given them a feast (2.16.6). Probably this reflects a fusion of the Homeric feast in Aigisthos' house with the rival view that Agamemnon died in his own house at Mykenai. Pausanias' further information, that Agamemnon had one grave, his charioteer Eurymedon another, and his twins Teledemos and Pelops by Kassandra another, may come from local tradition. The notion that Kassandra had time to conceive and bear twins after the fall of Troy is puzzling to say the least; its only other occurrence is in the *Odyssey* scholia, where we are told (in the context of the slaughter, although for no discernible reason) that Teledemos was the son of Agamemnon and Kassandra (Σ *Od* 11.420).

In Lykophron, as in Aischylos and Euripides, there is a bath, and here too as in Euripides a piece of material from which Agamemnon seemingly expects to find some exit for his head, and does not (Lyk 1099–1102). Seneca's *Agamemnon*, which follows the general narrative line of Aischylos' version, also has this feature: Agamemnon is feasting in his palace upon his return when his wife calls upon him to take off his Trojan spoils and put on instead a cloak (*amictus*) that she herself has made for him (Sen:*Ag* 875–905). The cloak does not offer easy exit for his head and hands, and while he is struggling with it, Aigisthos stabs him and Klytaimestra then finishes him off with her axe. Apollodoros, too, puts the murder at Mykenai, and in his version we see more clearly what Seneca, and Euripides and Lykophron before him, must have meant, for here Klytaimestra gives her husband a chiton without places for his hands and without a neck; he is, as in Seneca, killed while trying to put it on (ApE 6.23; so too Σ *Il* 1.7, VM I 147, ΣΣ Lyk 1099, 1375).[22] Such a trick garment sounds remarkably like what Agamemnon is wearing in the Dokimasia Painter's version of the tale, where we saw the entangling material clinging oddly to head and hand. Presumably this device will have been part of the story only in versions where Agamemnon is in his own home and greeted by his wife (i.e., not feasting with Aigisthos). It does not, however, seem what Aischylos intended, for although Klytaimestra does mention robes that she threw over her quarry like a net, she says nothing about any special deviousness in this ploy, as she surely would have had she made a special garment. We might indeed wonder if the bath was not originally an alternative to the garment (only Euripides and Lykophron combine the two), but of course a bath is certainly logical before changing clothes after a journey, and the failure of Apollodoros to mention it means little in an epitome. One other detail of note in Apollodoros is the crediting of the infant Orestes' rescue to Elektra.

We conclude this section with several more curious variants. Diktys, followed by Hyginus, offers a novel but not illogical version in which Oiax, the brother of Palamedes, falsely informs Klytaimestra that her husband is bringing home a concubine whom he prefers to her, hoping to get revenge for his family's wrongs (Dik 6.2). In Hyginus, Oiax's slander consists simply of stating that Kassandra is being brought back as a concubine (which in all other accounts is true); Klytaimestra consults with Aigisthos, and the two kill Agamemnon (and Kassandra) with an axe while he is sacrificing (*Fab* 117). The story, which rather exonerates Klytaimestra, may be based in part on Agamemnon's claim in *Iliad* 1 that he prefers Chryseis to his own wife. Finally, we should note Pausanias' remark that in Kinaithon Orestes has a bastard son by Erigone, daughter of Aigisthos (fr 4 *PEG*). Presumably (although Pausanias does not say), this Erigone is a child of Aigisthos and Klytaimestra; we shall learn more of her later.

Orestes'
Revenge

As discussed above, neither *Iliad* nor *Odyssey* ever says exactly that Orestes killed his own mother Klytaimestra, but the *Odyssey*, after stressing on several occasions that he slew the killer of his father Aigisthos (with the gods' express approval: *Od* 1.40–47), strongly implies a matricide by telling us that Menelaos returned from Egypt on the very day when Orestes was giving a funeral feast for both Aigisthos (whom he had killed) and his own "hateful mother" (*Od* 3.306–12). The lines with this last information (309–10) do not appear in all manuscripts, and have been thought by some an interpolation (even if a funeral for Aigisthos at least is confirmed by *Od* 4.546–47). But Homer never suggests any other form of punishment or future for Klytaimestra, and since she is clearly guilty in his scheme of things, we can only suppose him aware of her death, whatever we do with the questioned lines. On the other hand, there is nothing in *Iliad* or *Odyssey* to help us decide whether that era was aware of Orestes' problems after killing his mother; again, this is the sort of coda that the *Odyssey* (given Orestes' role there) might be expected to suppress, if it did know of it. One other puzzling detail is the notion at *Odyssey* 3.307 that Orestes returned to his homeland for his revenge from Athens, rather than the Phokis of his friend Pylades (admittedly never mentioned by Homer). Zenodotos actually proposed to read "Phokis" for "Athens" here, in keeping with later tradition, and Aristarchos suggested "Athena," Orestes being thus under her protection (at Tegea?) during his exile (Σ *Od* 3.307).

Following Homer we have the *Nostoi*, where Proklos remarks simply that the murder by Aigisthos and Klytaimestra is followed by the vengeance of Orestes and Pylades. What this vengeance consists of is not said, although mention of Klytaimestra's role in the crime might be thought to imply her sharing the punishment. In the *Ehoiai*, as noted earlier, when Orestes comes of age he avenges his father's death on the slayer and also kills his "overbearing [?] mother with the pitiless [bronze]" (Hes fr 23a.30 MW). The matricide is thus simply mentioned in passing, as part of a two-line characterization of Orestes whom Klytaimestra bore as one of a number of children; we cannot say if the poem returned to it elsewhere. Stesichoros' *Oresteia* must have grappled with it, although our only real evidence for that fact is the information that in his poem Apollo gave to Orestes a bow with which he might defend himself from the Erinyes (who would hardly pursue him for the death of Aigisthos: 217 *PMG*). The work's most famous quote, that concerning the dream of Klytaimestra, shows that Aischylos in the *Choephoroi* borrowed this device (although not, it seems, the exact same dream). As our source Plutarch recites the lines, "a serpent seemed to come to her, the top of its head covered with blood, and from it [or after this?] a king Pleisthenides appeared" (*Mor* 555a = 219 *PMG*). We have already considered in chapter 15 the difficulties involved in ascertaining who this Pleisthenes is and hence who his descendant might be. But the snake with its bloodied head must certainly be Agamemnon, and the king either the same person in human form or (more likely) his son Orestes, whose appearance as king indicates that Aigisthos' line will not retain the throne. Either way, we learn little more than we would naturally have guessed about Stesichoros' version.[23] The presence of Erinyes from whom Orestes must defend himself presumably indicates that the matricide was an issue, but how treated, or even how resolved, we cannot say.

In art the earliest presumed representation of the revenge is the abovementioned Protoattic krater from Berlin sometimes taken to show rather the death of Agamemnon (Berlin:Lost A32). Since that is unlikely, given the pose of the woman with one hand to her face, we might well imagine the scene to present Orestes (backed by Elektra: hand visible) leading the two culprits to their deaths, although it would require a very subdued and resigned Klytaimestra.[24] From the same period, or perhaps a bit later in the century, comes a Kretan bronze mitra found at Olympia on which a young man approaches a woman on an elaborate throne (B 4900).[25] Above the woman arches a piece of cloth, which she grasps; the youth may or may not be drawing a sword (the crucial left edge of the mitra is broken away). If the woman is pulling the cloth away to reveal herself (rather than using it in an attempt to hide) we might look rather to Menelaos' recovery of Helen.[26]

Of the early sixth century are several bronze reliefs from Olympia. The shield-band pattern usually taken to present this story shows an elegantly dressed man seated in an equally elegant chair, struggling to unsheathe his sword, while another man, unbearded and perhaps naked except for a sword-strap over his shoulder, seizes his antagonist by the forelock and prepares to stab him with a spear (Olympia B 988 and others).[27] Orestes is an obvious guess here, but there are other possibilities, such as Neoptolemos and Priam or even Zeus and Kronos. The same holds for the sculptures previously considered under those headings in the left corner of the pediment of the Temple of Artemis on Kerkyra (Museum, no #: only the seated figure fully preserved).[28] Much more dramatic is the other Olympia relief, on a bronze strip probably from a tripod: a man seizes the woman facing him by the throat with his left hand while his right drives his sword completely through her body (M 77).[29] To the left, behind the attacker, stands another female, one hand raised with her cloak as if in encouragement; to the right, behind the dying woman, a man moves away hurriedly, reaching out toward a stepped structure (an altar?) while looking back at the scene behind him. Such a scene is almost certainly a rare view of the death of Klytaimestra, one picture making up for all of Homer's reticence (although objections have been raised[30]), and the man moving away to the right becomes then Aigisthos seeking refuge from Orestes.

Of the mid-sixth century also are several problematic metopes from Foce del Sele. On one of these we have a clear illustration of a woman with an axe being restrained by another woman;[31] from the intensity with which the restrainee advances to the right we should probably imagine at least one additional metope linked to this one with her intended victim on it. Conceivably these women are Klytaimestra and Kassandra in an otherwise unattested pose, but the two available candidates for the second metope both suggest rather the death of Aigisthos. On the first of these possibilities a man facing right (Orestes?) draws a sword while a woman behind (Elektra? Laodameia?) appears to encourage him; if that is correct, Aigisthos must have occupied yet a third (lost) metope.[32] On the second example one man stabs another in a pose similar to what we saw on the tripod leg, with the victim grasping a column at the top of a stepped platform while he turns back to supplicate for his life.[33] This last piece comes dangerously close in its composition to shield-bands discussed in chapter 16 where the small size of the victim seemed to justify his identification as Troilos, cut down at the altar to which he had fled.[34] Here, by contrast, with two figures of equal size and insufficient detail to be sure of beards, we have a more difficult problem. But the gesture of supplication appears nowhere else in Troilos iconography, and another part of that story (Achilleus behind the foun-

tain house) is present at Foce del Sele. Quite possibly, therefore, the man clinging to the column is Aigisthos, about to be slain by Orestes while either Elektra
or Laodameia restrains Klytaimestra from intervening with her axe. We must
admit, however, that the other reconstruction, with Orestes and sister threatening a lost Aigisthos (or Klytaimestra herself?), is also possible.

One other metope from Foce del Sele believed by many to portray Orestes
focuses on an entirely different part of the story. We see a man with drawn
sword preparing to strike at a snake that has coiled itself around him and rears
up menacingly: supposedly this is an Erinys threatening Orestes after he has
killed his mother.[35] I would not exclude the possibility, but I confess to some
skepticism in the absence of better parallels than we have. The whole question
of the portrayal of Erinyes re-embroils us in the problems of the Tyrrhenian
amphora with the possible matricide of Alkmaion discussed in chapter 14 (Ber-
lin:PM VI 4841). On that vase a snake certainly rears up over the corpse of the
dead woman (and the tomb on which she lies); at the same time the murderer
prepares for a rapid exit right, suggesting that the snake threatens him and is
thus some sort of avenger of the deceased, regardless of how we interpret the
woman running in from the right with bow/snake. But lacking certainty that
the woman is not an Erinys, and with no literary support of any kind for an
Erinys in purely snake form, I am dubious about the painter's intentions. One
should note in this connection two efforts by the Cactus Painter toward the end
of the sixth century, on each of which two large snakes threaten an unarmed
man (Athens 12821; PrColl, Athens [lost?]).[36] In the second of these a tomb is
indicated, and thus both sets of snakes *may* be tomb guardians, but scarcely
the Erinyes; the context is much too general, and Erinyes are never thought to
protect (or avenge) *all* the dead. Of course they have snaky hair in the *Oresteia*
and other literary works, and they frequently hold snakes with which to
threaten Orestes in fifth-century Red-Figure. But from Homer and Hesiod
onward we understand these divinities (I think) as anthropomorphic. If this
view is correct the Foce del Sele metope will better represent some other hero,
Iason with the serpent guarding the Golden Fleece, perhaps, or Herakles chal-
lenging the snake who guards the Hesperides' apples.[37] The context (that is, the
other metopes flanking this one) may well have helped viewers to a correct
understanding of the artist's intentions.

For the fifth century we have the versions of Pindar (Orestes comes back
from his stay with Strophios and Pylades near Parnassos to kill both mother
and Aigisthos: *Py* 11.15–16, 34–37) and Aischylos; the latter's *Choephoroi* is
in fact the first continuous preserved account of the matricide, to be followed
by the *Elektra* plays of Sophokles and Euripides. In Aischylos, Orestes returns
from the exile in Phokis to which Klytaimestra sent him accompanied by Pylades and determined to recover his patrimony. He has also visited Delphi,
where Apollo instructed him to kill both Aigisthos and his mother, or else
experience dire torments. Accordingly he proceeds to his father's tomb to seek
support. There he meets Elektra, his sister who remained with her mother, and

hears of Klytaimestra's dream wherein she gave birth to a snake; nursing this, she was bitten by its fangs, which drew out blood as well as milk. Orestes naturally recognizes himself as the snake and is further encouraged. The plot devised by the two friends is to present themselves at the palace door, claiming knowledge of Orestes' death (as told to them by Strophios). Klytaimestra is the first to hear this news, and seems (despite her protestations of grief) quite eager for Aigisthos, the master of the house, to hear it as well. In the meantime, she retreats to her own quarters, but is summoned out again by a servant announcing that those supposedly dead have come to life and killed Aigisthos. At this point she calls for the famous axe, but then bares her breast (when she sees Orestes with Aigisthos' corpse) and summons up a child's feelings for his mother. She also attempts some justification of her deed; Orestes wavers, but on appeal to Pylades is reminded of the god's command, and leads her offstage to her death. As he returns to the stage with the fatal garment used to trap his father (it is here called a *pharos*), he sees for the first time the Erinyes, dark-robed women entwined with snakes, eyes dripping blood; their pursuit will send him back to Delphi, where Apollo instructed him to return for protection.

This narrative line of the *Choephoroi*, whatever the source of individual details, likely follows in its general shape the run of the story familiar to most Athenians by the time of Aischylos. When we turn to the third play of the trilogy, however, there is much less to be sure about. In fact, we have seen that well before Aischylos Stesichoros preserves for us the notion of a mother's Erinyes tormenting Orestes (217 *PMG*), but we know nothing about the outcome of the problem in his account, nor what early artists (whether or not the snakes discussed above are Erinyes) thought of the matter. As Aischylos presents the story, Orestes' fate is closely tied to civic developments in Athens, and one might be forgiven for guessing that this and even the flight to Athens itself were the inventions of an Athenian (not necessarily Aischylos). In any event, as the *Eumenides* opens Orestes is back in Delphi, but although Apollo delays his pursuers for a while the god cannot deter them altogether. His advice is that Orestes should go to Athens and seek Athena's help; Hermes escorts him off as Klytaimestra's ghost rouses the Erinyes and they and Apollo exchange reproaches. In Athens both parties, Orestes and the Erinyes, appeal to Athena for justice, agreeing to abide by her decision. She, however, declines to take sole responsibility, and instead turns the case over to a panel of twelve impartial Athenians, the first jury. Apollo arrives to speak for Orestes; the Erinyes present their own case. Their concern is with the fact of matricide and the precedent it creates for disrespect by children to parents. Orestes' claims of the necessity of his revenge are for the most part lost on them, for the deed creating that necessity, a wife's killing of her husband, does not involve any link by blood, and is thus outside their jurisdiction.

As we saw in chapter 1, there is not much effort to secure a consistent theology here; the Erinyes maintain that they protect all blood relationships from harm (*Eum* 605), but they have nothing to say (indeed they are never asked) about Agamemnon's sacrifice of his daughter Iphigeneia. Against their view that a simple admission of the deed by Orestes is sufficient for conviction, Apollo counters with the claim that the father supplies all the genetic input for offspring, the mother being merely an incubator and therefore not related by blood. The Erinyes in turn argue that the whole order of civilization, and the status of the older gods within it, will collapse if such things are permitted. What the audience (or the jury) made of all this we do not know; the entire debate seems inconclusive, with the jury in fact dividing their twelve votes evenly between the two parties. Scholars are not agreed on whether Athena now votes for Orestes to break the tie (because she herself has no mother) or acquits him on the general principle of innocent until proven guilty.[38] Either way the narrative problem of Orestes' future after matricide is resolved, and the jury system has been created. True, the Erinyes remain behind to threaten Athens with crop failure and the like, but once Athena assures them of their place in the new order (as guarantors of punishment decreed by the state) they yield to her persuasion and take up residence under the Areopagos. In such a dramatic treatment Orestes and the merits of his case have not, one may feel, held center stage; he is acquitted and summarily dismissed while the playwright assures us that a method of dispensing justice useful for all situations has been devised.

Following Aischylos in the preserved literary record of the fifth century are the *Elektra* plays of Sophokles and Euripides (both probably from its last twenty years, although we have no way of determining which effort came first). Sophokles adds to the cast Chrysothemis, a child of Agamemnon and Klytaimestra whom we have not seen since her father's casual reference to her in *Iliad* 9 and her (probable) inclusion as one of four daughters in the *Kypria*. In that connection we may remember that she is clearly excluded from the *Ehoiai*, where Agamemnon and Klytaimestra have only two daughters (Iphimede and Elektra: Hes fr 23a MW). Her role in Sophokles is to serve as a foil for Elektra's greater aggressiveness, urging prudence when action might seem required; considering Sophokles' use of Ismene for much the same purpose in *Antigone* (and the existence of tales about Ismene's death at a much earlier point) we might suspect that this daughter too has been resurrected from obscurity by the playwright, were it not for her appearance on a Red-Figure pelike that must be earlier than this play (see below). The play itself focuses primarily on the conflict between Klytaimestra and Elektra, the mother attempting to justify her actions, the daughter (aided by Agamemnon's genuine lack of choice at Aulis) refusing to listen. Orestes, who has returned with both Pylades and his childhood tutor, sends the tutor on ahead to announce to the household his death in a chariot mishap. Elektra then resolves to kill Aigisthos herself, however much Chrysothemis might denounce the plan as folly. At just this moment Orestes appears, with an urn supposed to contain his ashes, and reveals himself to Elektra as soon as he perceives it safe to do so. Aigisthos is for the time being away; with the tutor's help they enter the palace and kill

Klytaimestra as she prepares the urn for burial. When Aigisthos finally appears, having been summoned by the news of Orestes' death, he is shown his lover's corpse and then led in to his own death.

Throughout this play there is a total avoidance of any overt reservations about the justness of matricide. Orestes has here again been to Delphi, but he seems to have asked only about the manner of his revenge, not whom he should kill, and is told only that it must be done by stealth, not direct force. Elektra's plot involves Aigisthos alone; Orestes never discusses his, but simply walks into the palace and slays his mother as Elektra approves. Matters are thus very much in the offspring's hands, with no indications of the sort of future that they or Pylades (a completely silent character) might expect. At one point in the play Elektra does accuse her mother of "engendering children" with Aigisthos, which may be meant to acknowledge existence of a daughter Erigone (S:*El* 587–89); quite possibly she was the subject of the *Erigone* plays by Sophokles, Philokles, and others of which we know nothing (see below for later tales).

Euripides' interpretation brings us to a more surprising (and surely novel) rethinking of some situations. Elektra is here married to a peasant, Aigisthos reasoning that neither husband nor the children thus produced will be a danger to him. Although this husband has not touched her, she feels bitterly her exclusion from the palace and even laments the lack of decent clothes which prevents her from participating in Hera's festival. Orestes on his return comes to her husband's house to find her, and they plot the murders together. Once again Orestes has been to Delphi, or at least in contact with the god. But he says nothing at first about the nature of the response, and it appears for a while that the advisability of matricide is not to be an overt issue in the play. In their opening exchanges Orestes simply asks his sister if she is prepared to kill their mother as well as Aigisthos, and she affirms that she is. Because the intended victims are too well guarded in the palace, however, a stratagem different from those we have seen before must be devised. Orestes will approach Aigisthos down in the meadows, where he is at the moment readying a sacrifice for the Nymphai, while Elektra will send for her mother on the pretext that she has given birth to a child. All goes as planned: Orestes is invited to the sacrifice by the unwitting Aigisthos, and strikes as the latter turns his back to inspect the entrails. Klytaimestra for her part hastens to the hut, where Orestes, seeing her, begins to waver in his resolve. Here for the first time we learn that Apollo did after all command the matricide; when Orestes still hesitates, Elektra takes the lead. At this crucial moment, Euripides offers us an *agôn* in which Klytaimestra's wrongs are more sympathetically treated than they were in Aischylos or Sophokles; she has come too, it seems, to regret the treatment of her children and to be little in control of her own life. Nevertheless Elektra perseveres, luring her mother into the hut where Orestes strikes the blow, his sister urging him on. Both are quite shaken when they re-emerge, as the full horror of the deed sinks in. But before they can reflect further, the Dioskouroi appear, to lament their sister's death, denounce (tactfully) Apollo's oracle as false, and predict Orestes' future as it is played out in the *Eumenides,* complete with Erinyes and a judgment at Athens. The only new details here are Orestes' ultimate settlement near the Alpheios River in southern Arkàdia, and the command that Elektra marry Pylades; this union is also predicted in the *Iphigeneia among the Tauroi,* where Pylades is a grandson of Atreus and cousin to Elektra (*IT* 912–19). In Pausanias and several scholia, that relationship is explained as due to a marriage between Pylades' father Strophios and Agamemnon's sister Anaxibia (Paus 2.29.4, perhaps drawn from Asios; ΣΣ *Or* 765, 1233). Anaxibia is certainly the name of Agamemnon's one sister in the *Ehoiai,* although her marriage in that poem is not preserved; elsewhere in the *Orestes* scholia this same sister and wife of Strophios is Kydragora (Σ *Or* 33; cf. Σ *Or* 1233), while Hyginus calls her Astyoche (*Fab* 117).

The same poet's *Orestes,* securely dated to 408 B.C., treats the aftermath of the matricide in different fashion: Elektra and an Orestes driven mad by his mother's Erinyes face stoning by the Argives, unless Menelaos can arrive to save them. He does arrive, but is dissuaded by an angry Tyndareos from taking any action in his nephew's defense. Orestes' subsequent attempt to address the Argive people directly gains nothing more than a concession of suicide, and at Pylades' prompting he determines to gain some measure of vengeance against Menelaos by killing Helen before he dies. Elektra for her part adds the thought that they might escape their own doom by taking Hermione hostage. In the course of their takeover of the palace Helen mysteriously disappears, but they are about to slay Hermione and fire the whole structure when Apollo appears to resolve matters. Helen, he announces, has been taken up to Olympos to sit with her brothers and the gods; Menelaos should remarry. Orestes shall spend a year in exile in the Parrhasian plain (the same part of Arkadia indicated in the *Elektra*) and then journey to Athens for his trial (here with the gods seemingly as jurors on the Areopagos). Ultimately he (not Neoptolemos, who is fated to die at Delphi before he can do so) shall wed Hermione, and Pylades shall have Elektra (the latter already so promised by Orestes).

The art of the period meanwhile offers us a number of Red-Figure representations of the death of Aigisthos, many of them prior to the production of the *Oresteia* and nearly all of them featuring as a common element Klytaimestra and her axe. Admittedly, it is absent from the earliest pieces, two fragmentary cups of the late sixth century in Florence (4B19 etc.) and Oxford (1973.1032), on which Aigisthos is sprawled helplessly on the ground as Orestes seizes his hair.[39] But on these Klytaimestra herself is missing, probably not preserved. When she does finally appear, in a memorable role on an early pelike by the Berlin Painter (*c.* 500 B.C.), we find a tableau with Aigisthos now on a throne, but again hopelessly unbalanced and ineffective as Orestes grasps his hair (Vienna 3725). Both Orestes and Chrysothemis behind him (named) look back to the left, as if at something approaching, and this we see on the other side of the vase: Klytaimestra charges forward with an axe while an older figure (labeled "Talthybios") seizes the blade in order to restrain her. We have already encountered the axe (plus restraining female figure) on the Foce del Sele metopes, but only now can we be certain that Klytaimestra means to use it to defend Aigisthos rather than (as in the *Choephoroi*) herself. The presence of Chrysothemis, not Elektra, is a surprise so clearly in advance of Sophokles, and we must wonder if (despite her role as a mere foil in his drama) she played some more important part in an Archaic version of the revenge. Subsequently we have a Red-Figure lekythos with similar scene (although there is no sister, and the restraining figure is one Telamedes: Boston 1977.713) and then among others a column krater probably by the Harrow Painter with just Klytaimestra, Talthybios, and the axe (Vienna 1103). On a stamnos by the Copenhagen Painter (*c.* 475 B.C.) Orestes seems in considerable peril as he stabs Aigisthos, for his attention is wholly on his victim and there is no restraining figure as Klytaimestra closes in from the left, axe raised (Berlin:PM F2184). To the other side of Aigisthos' chair Elektra (named) stands, hand outstretched in alarm. The same composition (including both female figures) reappears on a column krater by the Aegisthus Painter, although now a semi-naked young male (Pylades?) grasps the axe blade and Orestes looks back (Bologna 230). A newly published calyx krater by the same painter brings back the older bearded man as restrainer, while between Klytaimestra and Orestes comes a woman holding a small child; to the right the "Elektra" figure now holds one hand up to her forehead (Getty 88.AE.66).[40] The woman with child is a surprise here; most likely she represents a nurse holding Erigone or another of Aigisthos' children by Klytaimestra (see below). Finally, a stamnos by the Berlin Painter (Boston 91.227a, 91.226b) and the other side of our Boston calyx krater by the Dokimasia Painter (Boston 63.1246) introduce yet another new element, a lyre clutched in the left hand of Aigisthos as he is killed. On both of these, as in the Copenhagen Painter's version, Orestes is unaware of his mother's threat, and on both, the "Elektra" figure again runs up in alarm from the other side (the stamnos has a restrainer, the calyx krater none).

Even allowing for the possibility that many of these illustrations derive from a single monumental painting, we seem to have evidence of a highly dramatic version of the story in which Klytaimestra did almost dispatch her son while he was occupied with Aigisthos, and was prevented from doing so only by some third party. Such a version, with Orestes perhaps acting in self-defense to save his life, might also have been designed to mitigate the stigma of a deliberate matricide. Aischylos' more theatrically pointed confrontation of words between mother and son finds no such counterpart in art; indeed, the shield-band from Olympia discussed above is the only direct illustration of her death; other scenes showing a woman fleeing a man *might* be taken for this story (rather than that of Menelaos and Helen), but nowhere do we ever see the telltale axe. Thus the account in which Klytaimestra battles to protect her lover may have been the predominant (or only) version prior to Aischylos. Common to all these representations is the haplessness of Aigisthos; his costume (banqueting dress) suggests that he was taken by surprise, and at no time does he put up a convincing fight. Compared with this generally uniform artistic tradition we may be surprised to find that according to Pausanias a Polygnotos painting of the revenge in the Athenian Pinakotheke showed Pylades dispatching the sons of Nauplios who had come to aid Aigisthos (1.22.6). No other literary or artistic version that we know of includes such allies, although their presence (as enemies of Agamemnon, one of the slayers of their brother Palamedes) is not without some logic.

Later literary sources bring us nothing new on the subject of the deaths of Aigisthos and Klytaimestra, but they do offer new details about offspring of their union. According to the Parian Marble it was [Erig]on[e], daughter of Aigisthos, who brought Orestes to trial on the Areopagos, where the latter was victorious (239F25). Apollodoros knows of this trial (prosecuted by Erigone or perhaps Tyndareos), and adds that Klytaimestra was the girl's mother (ApE 6.25). In Diktys this Erigone hangs herself in disappointment after Orestes is acquitted at Athens (Dik 6.4); the same result appears in the account of the *Etymologicum Magnum* (s. *Aiôra*) after Erigone and Tyndareos have come together to Athens to prosecute the unsuccessful trial. Given that much, we might well suppose the story to have been told by Hellanikos, where the Athenians agree to judge the dispute between Orestes and "those coming from Lakedaimon" (4F169a). Yet the denouement at least is suspiciously close to the tale (claimed for Eratosthenes, whose poem about her is attested) of Erigone, daughter of Ikarios, who hanged herself after she found that her father had been killed by the cowherds to whom he gave wine (ΣAb *Il* 22.29). This latter figure has been thought a Hellenistic conception, but the fact remains that we cannot say for certain whether Sophokles' attested *Erigone* (or similar plays by Philokles, Kleophon, Phrynichos II) concerned the daughter of Aigisthos.[41] Apollodoros also states that Orestes married either Hermione or Erigone (ApE 6.28), drawing perhaps for this latter idea on the same tradition we found ascribed (by Pausanias) to Kinaithon (fr 4 *PEG*): Erigone, daughter of Aigisthos, bears to Orestes a bastard child Penthilos. That the same woman is in one tale Orestes' bitter enemy and in another his lover is to say the least puzzling.

Finally, in Hyginus alone we find the story of a *son* of Aigisthos, Aletes (*Fab* 122). Hyginus does not say that his mother was Klytaimestra, and some of the wording might be taken to mean that she was not, although with Hyginus any such conclusions are perilous. The tale itself is quite simple and smacks of tragedy: Aletes has seized the throne of Mykenai amid false reports that Orestes has been killed by the Tauroi. Elektra, however, goes off to Delphi for confirmation of his death, and there finds her brother and Iphigeneia (nearly killing the latter through ignorance). Reunited, the three return to Mykenai where Orestes kills Aletes and would have killed Erigone as well, had not Artemis snatched her away and made her a priestess in Athens. The last detail seems again to betray confusion with Erigone, daughter of Ikarios, and even a doublet of Iphigeneia's original fate. Sophokles (or a namesake) may have written a play *Aletes*; we know nothing about it.[42] The rescue of Iphigeneia is discussed below, as are Orestes' further deeds, including the slaying of Neoptolemos.

Iphigeneia among the Tauroi
We saw in chapter 16 that as early as the *Kypria* Iphigeneia is rescued at Aulis by Artemis and taken to the Tauroi, where she is made immortal. The implication of this is, I suppose, that she is to be worshipped by the Tauroi, but something may have been lost in the summation. In the *Ehoiai* (or rather, what we took to be an interpolation in that work) there is the same notion of apotheosis but no mention of the Tauroi; rather, Iphigeneia becomes an attendant of the goddess under the name "Artemis *einodia*" or (possibly) "Hekate" (Hes fr 23a MW). This last version seems to have been found also in Stesichoros' *Oresteia* (215 *PMG*), and strengthens our impression of a tradition in which, whatever the differences in detail, Iphigeneia is taken away to a blessed existence of immortality from which she most certainly does not need to be rescued. That she is nonetheless brought back by Orestes and Pylades in Euripides' *Iphigeneia among the Tauroi* probably stems from a variety of factors relating more to the needs of cultic aetiology than narrative considerations. For one thing, she herself had become linked (or fused) with Artemis at both Brauron and Halai Araphenides (north of Brauron), where the Athenians had a cult of Artemis Tauropolos (Str 9.1.22) and kept one version of the statue of her claimed to have been brought back from the Crimea (*IT* 1448–57).[43] For another, the historical Tauroi of that peninsula were described already by Herodotos as sacrificing all foreign sailors to a maiden goddess whom they identified with Iphigeneia, daughter of Agamemnon (Hdt 4.103). How this idea was concocted we cannot say, but certainly it must go back to the time of the *Kypria*; in Euripides, Athena proclaims the cult title "Tauropolos" as derived from the Taurian land, and that derivation (taken in reverse, of course) might well be the truth of the matter.[44] From the land of the Tauroi, at any rate, a desire to bring Iphigeneia narratively into contact with Brauron and Halai, so as to better explain the cults there, might have generated the impetus for Euripides' play. His drama is our first source to say that she was rescued from the Crimea; whoever invented this story invented as well perhaps her shift back to mortal status, making her a priestess rather than the divinity herself.[45]

As the play opens, Iphigeneia describes her situation, brought to these people and their king Thoas after the sacrifice at Aulis and made to consecrate foreigners to the goddess. Orestes and Pylades then appear, seeking just this shrine of Artemis in order that they might carry off the statue within, for Apollo has told them that only thus, when they have conveyed it back to Athens, will Orestes' madness end. They are, however, spotted by herdsmen and captured, so that they come before Iphigeneia as prospective victims, in ignorance of her real identity and she of theirs. But they are Greeks, of course, and she conceives the plan of saving one of them so that he might take back to Orestes a letter from her; when its contents are revealed as a safeguard against loss the whole truth comes out. Iphigeneia then proposes that Orestes' pollution as a matricide may be turned to their advantage; much as in the *Helen*, she tells the king that such a victim must be purified at sea before the sacrifice, and the statue as well, thus acquiring an avenue of escape. The king's forces pursue when they discover statue and victims making for open water, but Athena appears to Thoas and instructs him to desist: Orestes will take the statue to Halai Araphenides in Attika, where he will establish a cult in Artemis' honor, while Iphigeneia shall become keeper of a second shrine at Brauron, where she shall be buried when she dies. These last details patently justify Athenian cult practice, and are much strained to fit the circumstances of a royal family of Argos, but no doubt Athenian audiences enjoyed them.

Later accounts of the rescue follow Euripides without serious deviation, save in the fact that the statue often winds up elsewhere; Pausanias, for example, found the Spartans convinced that Iphigeneia had brought it there, to be the image of Artemis Orthia (3.16.7). But Hyginus adds to the successful return an interlude that we must here consider. In this tale, as Orestes and Iphigeneia make their way back from the Crimea, they have stopped in at the island of Sminthe where they find the priest of Apollo—Chryses—and his daughter Chryseis, who years before on her return from Troy bore a child conceived by Agamemnon whom she named Chryses after her father. Fearing to admit the truth, however, she has claimed that the child is Apollo's. At this point the text shows some obscurity (or rather, reference back to *Fab* 120), with Chryses (the younger) apparently planning to return Orestes and Iphigeneia to Thoas, who is perhaps an ally. The elder Chryses then learns (from his daughter, presumably) the truth, which he reveals to his grandson, namely that these refugees are the latter's half-siblings. The refugees are therefore assisted as they kill Thoas (newly arrived to claim his victims?) and reach Mykenai safely with the statue. Obviously this sounds like a standard recognition play of the later fifth century, and in fact Sophokles is credited with a *Chryses* (of uncertain content) which might then anticipate the rescue in the *Iphigeneia among the Tauroi*. But such a play (if it concerns this Chryses) might also deal with his problems at Troy or elsewhere.

Neoptolemos   Of Neoptolemos, Nestor in *Odyssey* 3 says that he brought the Myrmidones back safely, one presumes by sea and to their homeland of Phthia (*Od* 3.188–89). Admittedly, Homer is concerned here to contrast the blissful condition of the many who did return home gloriously with the special pain of those few (Agamemnon, Odysseus) who did not; when concerned with other stories of the war's aftermath he may have seen matters differently. Whatever the case, Neoptolemos' subsequent misfortunes give special relevance to the issue of his Trojan prisoners. We saw in chapter 16 that the *Little Iliad* made the son of Achilleus responsible (on his own initiative) for the death of Astyanax, while the *Iliou Persis* gave that role to Odysseus. Either way, both works agree that Neoptolemos received as a special prize Andromache, wife of Hektor.

But there is a complication, for Tzetzes, our source for the *Little Iliad* on this point, insists that the hero took on board his ship not only Andromache but also Aineias, and offers an eleven-line quote from Lesches to that effect (Σ Lyk 1268 = fr 21 *PEG*). Of these eleven lines, however, the last six, where Aineias is actually mentioned, are also quoted by the scholia to the *Andromache*, which ascribe them to Simias of Rhodes, a shadowy figure known from the *Souda* and certainly of Hellenistic times (Σ *And* 14). Elsewhere, Tzetzes adds that Aineias was freed after Neoptolemos' death at Delphi, which may also come from Simias (Σ Lyk 1232). Certainly the idea of such a captivity is strange, and would serve little purpose before Aineias has become linked to Rome, for by himself he is (unlike Helenos, who is a seer) of no use to Neoptolemos. In all other versions he either escapes during Troy's fall or is freed by the Greeks.

The *Nostoi* has nothing on this matter; what it does say is that Thetis warned Neoptolemos of the dangers awaiting the Greeks at sea, and that in consequence he journeyed overland, meeting Odysseus at Maroneia in the land of the Kikones. Subsequently he buried Phoinix, who had died, and in the land of the Molossoi was recognized by Peleus (who of course had never seen his grandson). The genuine part of Tzetzes' quote of the *Little Iliad*, with its talk of boarding ships, might seem to contradict this, but perhaps the warning came after he had departed Troy, and he put back in to shore when convenient. Something similar is recorded by Eustathios, who says that Neoptolemos burned his ships at Thessaly by the advice of Thetis after traveling there by sea, and then journeyed to Epeiros, recognizing his destination from a portent given by Helenos (Eu-*Od* p. 1463; cf. Σ *Od* 3.188).[46] Nothing in our summaries of the three epics suggests that Helenos accompanied him; such a detail might not have struck epitomators as especially important.

No other Archaic source mentions the return until Pindar, who notes in *Nemean* 7 that on leaving Troy Neoptolemos missed Skyros and ultimately found himself at Ephyra in Molossia, where he ruled a short time (*Nem* 7.36–39). The earlier *Paian* 6 of the same poet identifies the site as near Mount Tomaros, apparently thinking of the same location. This latter poem also implies that Apollo may have been responsible for the hero's failure to arrive at Phthia, for we are told that the god in his anger vowed that the slayer of Priam would never arrive at his home (*Pa* 6.112–17). But other versions may have chosen to regard the Molossian land as somehow Neoptolemos' proper home, for we have seen that in the *Nostoi* he finds his grandfather Peleus there (though this might be an improperly stated compression of the epitomator). The *Odyssey* hints at one point of a Peleus under some pressure from neighbors in Achilleus' absence (*Od* 12.494–504), and the notion of a recognition in the *Nostoi* might suggest that he was, like Odysseus' family, in difficulty when his grandson arrived, wherever that was. Such a story *might* also have formed the basis of the lost *Peleus* by Sophokles. As often, we have no details of the work, although it must be earlier than Aristophanes' *Hippes* (424 B.C.) and the account in Diktys (see below) may be drawn from it. Euripides offers a likely reference to it at the close of his *Troades*, where Talthybios tells Hekabe that Neoptolemos has already departed for Phthia, having heard news that Peleus has been cast out of the land by Akastos, son of Pelias (*Tro* 1123–28). The scholia add that in some accounts the expellers are rather the *sons* of Akastos, Archandros and Architeles, and that Peleus' setting forth in search of his grandson came after a storm to Kos (or Ikos?) where he was entertained by Molon and died. Kos seems rather too far away to be likely here, but poem 7.2 of the *Palatine Anthology* agrees with the idea that he is buried on Ikos (modern Alonissos), one of the Northern Sporades.

In the version of Diktys noted, Neoptolemos comes first to the Molossian land, but then, while repairing his ships, the hero receives a report that Peleus has been expelled from his kingdom in Thessaly by Akastos (Dik 6.7–9). After sending subordinates to assess the situation, he finally resolves to go himself, but has further troubles at sea, and barely puts to shore on the Sepiades Islands. Presumably by these Diktys means the islands next to the Cape of Sepias in Magnesia, that is, the same Northern Sporades off the entrance to the Gulf of Iolkos. There Neoptolemos finds Peleus hidden in a cave. By chance the sons of Akastos (here Menalippos and Pleisthenes) are coming to hunt on the island, and Neoptolemos takes advantage of the situation to ambush and kill them. Next, disguising himself as a Trojan prisoner, he encounters Akastos and lures him to the cave with a tale of an unguarded Neoptolemos sleeping there. Caught in the trap, Akastos comes close to losing his life, but Thetis appears to appeal for him after berating him severely. He concedes the kingdom to Peleus, and the Aiakidai return to their rightful land. Certainly this sounds like a play, and the *Troades* shows that the premise for it was known in the fifth century; its Sophoklean pedigree remains a guess, if an attractive one.

As for other versions of the return, Apollodoros says that Neoptolemos remained behind on Tenedos for two days (again on Thetis' advice), then set out with Helenos by land, and came to the Molossoi (burying Phoinix on the way), where after a battle he ruled the country (*ApE* 6.12–13). Andromache bears him a son, Molossos, and Helenos founds his own city, having been given to wife Neoptolemos' mother, Deidameia. Only after Peleus has been driven out of Phthia by the sons of Akastos and dies does Neoptolemos obtain his rightful kingdom of Phthia; we are not told how. Much of the first part of this agrees with our epitome of the *Nostoi*, but there is here no recognition by Peleus, unless we assume that he comes to the Molossian land after his expulsion (which is not impossible) and tells his grandson what has happened. Pausanias, like Eustathios, speaks of prophecies of Helenos which guide Neoptolemos to Epeiros, where he has three sons by Andromache—Molossos, Pielos, and Pergamos; after his death at Delphi, Helenos receives Andromache and they have a son, Kestrinos (1.11.1). That Helenos and Andromache should thus wed is an idea first preserved in Euripides, as we shall see below. It reappears, of course, in Book 3 of the *Aeneid*, although with no very convincing explanation; according to Servius it was Helenos (not as elsewhere Thetis) who gave Neoptolemos the initial warning not to sail to Greece by sea, and for this reason he was favored with Hektor's bride after her new master's death (Σ *Aen* 3.297). Hyginus records as the one child of Neoptolemos and Andromache the name "Amphialos" (*Fab* 123).

Regarding Neoptolemos' death itself, Pindar's *Paian* 6 and *Nemean* 7 are in fact our earliest references; both poems place the event at Delphi, but neither involves Orestes in any way, nor says anything about a quarrel over Hermione, daughter of Helen and Menelaos. That Neoptolemos married Hermione is told as early as the *Odyssey*, where Telemachos' arrival at Sparta coincides with the day on which she is to be sent off to Achilleus' son as a bride, having been promised while both father and prospective groom were still at Troy. Homer mentions this event as part of a definite context, a portrait of the domestic felicity not yet vouchsafed to Odysseus and Penelope; he can scarcely here mean us to think of any subsequent assault on the marriage bond by Orestes (who in the *Odyssey* is very much the defender of the home) and perhaps does not know that story.

Pindar's account in *Paian* 6 makes Apollo the cause of death; he is angry with the slayer of Priam, and thus ordains that Neoptolemos shall never return home nor reach old age (*Pa* 6.117–20). Death here comes by the god's hand while the hero is arguing with attendants over fees (presumably for consultation). This apparently too negative characterization is ameliorated in *Nemean* 7 by eliminating all mention of Apollo's wrath and having Neoptolemos journey to Delphi precisely to offer trophies to the god. At the temple he enters into a quarrel over sacrificial victims, not fees, and is slain by "a man," to the great distress of the local populace (*Nem* 7.40–43). Pindar stresses, however, that higher purposes are served by this death, for Neoptolemos thus remains within the sanctuary, to be a watcher for all time over the ceremonies, as *moira* intended.

In Pherekydes there is likewise no mention of Orestes; instead we are told that having married Hermione Neoptolemos goes to Delphi to inquire about their prospects for children (3F64a). There he sees men of Delphi carrying off meat from the sanctuary, and takes it away from them. At this point our text, from a Euripidean scholion (Σ *Or* 1655), adds that he kills himself with a knife *(machaira)* and is buried by the priest under the threshold of the temple. Such an ill-motivated suicide has obviously been questioned; we will see in a moment that textual corruption is probably involved here. The *Odyssey* scholia (and Eustathios) give us the plot of Sophokles' lost *Hermione*, a play offering some version of these same events. The drama centered on a conflict in the girl's betrothing: Menelaos had promised her to Neoptolemos while the two were at Troy, but at the same time Tyndareos back in Sparta gave her to Orestes (Σ *Od* 4.4). Upon his return Menelaos took her away from Orestes in order to maintain his promise; Neoptolemos, however, met his death at Delphi, slain there by a man named Machaireus when he tried to seek satisfaction from the god for the death of his father (this motive only in Eustathios), and thus Hermione was able to return to Orestes, to whom she bore Tisamenos.

Given the basic similarity between the name of the killer here and the *machaira* employed as the murder weapon in our text of Pherekydes, scholars have not unreasonably supposed that such a name (as murderer) stood originally in the latter text, but was mistakenly taken by someone to be a weapon, leading to the change of "him" *(auton)* to "himself" *(heauton)* and the erroneous notion of a suicide.[47] Such a conclusion, with Machaireus in Pherekydes as in Sophokles the killer, seems on the whole likely, the more so as something must be done about that suicide. Curiously though, in Pindar's *Nemean 7*, where we found a murder and a dispute over meat, the name of the killer is omitted but not the murder weapon, which is a *machaira* (*Nem* 7.42). Possibly this is a play on the killer's name, but since a *machaira* was commonly a butcher knife (and "Delphic *machaira*" a proverbial expression for the priests' share of the victims), the idea may in origin have been that Neoptolemos was killed with such a weapon because it was ready at hand when the dispute broke out, said weapon subsequently evolving into a person named after it. Machaireus as killer is also the version of Asklepiades, who says that nearly all the poets agree that Neoptolemos was slain by him, and that although first buried under the threshold he was later removed by Menelaos and buried in the temenos (12F15). As to who Machaireus was (a priest?), or exactly why he committed the deed, we have no other information, nor can we say to what extent Orestes is involved as a character in the *Hermione* (he and Neoptolemos do confront each other at Delphi in Pacuvius' *Hermiona*). But at least there seems some common adherence to a tradition in which someone other than Orestes is the murderer. Further testimony on this point is probably to be found in the *Andromache* scholia: we are told there that in (name has fallen out) Neoptolemos is slain by Machaireus, but that in other writers such as Euripides he is slain by Orestes (Σ *And* 53). If such a remark will not quite prove that Euripides invented the idea, it does link him rather than earlier poets with it.

Regarding Neoptolemos' motive for being at Delphi, Pherekydes' notion of childlessness stands (rather more respectably) against the idea that Neoptolemos wished to lay a claim against Apollo for the death of his father. We saw that this latter motif may have appeared in Sophokles' *Hermione* (if Eustathios is drawing from that source); certainly it is part of both Euripides' *Andromache*, where Neoptolemos makes a second trip to Delphi to apologize for his previous behavior (*And* 49–53), and his *Orestes* (*Or* 1653–57). Quite a number of later writers do report children of Neoptolemos and Hermione, and the tragedians Philokles and Theognis even claim that Hermione was pregnant by Orestes when she was taken by her new husband (Σ *And* 32; the child is Amphiktyon). This last detail may indicate that in some versions Neoptolemos was the villain, taking Hermione away by force from a man she loved and whose child she was carrying.

In any case, we find from this brief survey that Sophokles is the first preserved source to have Orestes marry Hermione, and that prior to the end of the fifth century there is a substantial tradition making Apollo (or Machaireus or some other Delphian) the cause of Neoptolemos' death. That Orestes himself did the deed (or rather, caused it to be done) first survives in Euripides' *Andromache*. That work also introduces another complicating factor, the presence of the concubine Andromache, who emerges as a reluctant rival for Neoptolemos' affections. The play opens with Andromache seeking refuge at the shrine of Thetis, fearing the anger of Neoptolemos' wife Hermione in his absence, for she herself has unwillingly borne to him a child (never named in the play, "Molottos" in some cast lists) while Hermione remains barren. The reason for Neoptolemos' absence is, as we saw above, a second trip to Delphi, undertaken in an attempt to atone for an earlier visit there when he demanded justice from Apollo for the death of his father. Hermione for her part has been joined by her father Menelaos, and accuses Andromache of causing her childlessness through spells or potions. The play's action turns around attempts to extricate Andromache from her refuge. When she refuses to leave the altar her child (seized by Menelaos) is threatened, and although she surrenders on the promise of his safety, her captors announce their intention to execute both. Fortunately, Peleus arrives to save the situation, with Menelaos wilting totally before the latter's anger and deciding he will be safer back in Sparta.

Thus abandoned, Hermione begins to fear the reproach of her husband when he returns and learns of her failed plot, and at just this moment Orestes enters, in passage to Dodona. Seeing Hermione's plight, he recalls the fact that she was promised to him by Menelaos but repromised to Neoptolemos at Troy, his subsequent pleas to Neoptolemos being rebuffed because of his matricide and maddened condition. When Hermione explains her now precarious position, he announces that Neoptolemos is doomed, fated to die by the god and his own slanders already planted at Delphi. The two then make their escape to Sparta, while a messenger enters to report to Peleus the death of Neoptolemos. He had, it seems, on his previous visit despoiled the shrine, and Orestes (somehow present) has spread the rumor that he has returned for the same purpose. Accordingly he is ambushed and killed by the Delphians, despite a noble and heroic resistance. The play concludes with a theophany by Thetis, who consoles the distraught Peleus and orders him to bury the body at Delphi as a reproach to Orestes. She further decrees that Andromache shall marry Helenos (not previously mentioned in the play) in Molossia, and that from her child by Neoptolemos will spring future rulers of that land. Peleus himself will henceforth live with her as a god in Nereus' home beneath the sea; thus the work closes.

The somewhat later *Orestes* of the same writer adheres instead to what might seem a more canonical version of Neoptolemos' death at Delphi: only one visit is made (as in the *Andromache* and perhaps Sophokles' *Hermione* to reproach Apollo for slaying his father) and he dies by a "Delphic sword" (*Or*

1653–57). Since Apollo predicts this outcome to Orestes it seems clear that the latter will not be involved, and that Neoptolemos pays rather the price of his own hybris. By contrast, the *Andromache's* unique notion of a double visit allows Euripides to include Neoptolemos' claim against Apollo while at the same time (since Neoptolemos repents) creating room for Orestes, not Apollo, to be the cause of his death. Again, I think, we see grounds for supposing that Euripides himself concocted Orestes' role in the killing.[48] One other novel element in the *Orestes*, the idea that Hermione has not actually been wed to Neoptolemos, may have arisen from the need to explain why she is with her mother in Mykenai and thus available for Orestes and Pylades to threaten.

Subsequent evidence includes an Apulian krater of about 370 B.C. on which we see a wounded Neoptolemos, sword drawn, in a desperate struggle for his life ("H.A." Coll 239). Above him are the temple, Apollo, and the Pythia, to the left an unnamed attacker with poised spear, to the right the omphalos and behind it Orestes (named). This last crouches cautiously, as if fearing to confront his rival directly, but he too has a drawn sword. Although his role here is more aggressive than that described in the *Andromache*, one has the impression that the artist has taken his scene directly from that play. Much more circumspect is the part Orestes plays in Diktys, who hedges on the critical details. Here Neoptolemos goes to Delphi to give thanks to Apollo (because he has been vindicated against Paris for the death of his father), leaving behind Hermione, Andromache, and the latter's one surviving son by Hektor (Laodamas: Dik 6.12). The action then proceeds as in Euripides' *Andromache*, with the exception that Orestes plans to kill his rival after the latter's return and is apparently forestalled by the death at Delphi, attributed by rumor to Orestes but actually of unknown cause. The first writer to claim that Orestes himself actually slew Neoptolemos seems then Vergil, who in *Aeneid* 3 makes good use of the parallel between Neoptolemos' butchering of Priam at an altar in Troy and being himself killed (from ambush) at an altar by another Greek (*Aen* 3.325–32: the phrase *patrias aras* at 332 [Servius attempts various explanations] remains obscure). Orestes' reason is, as usual, desire for Hermione, the "wife snatched away" from him, with a contributing nod to his mother's Erinyes; Neoptolemos has meanwhile abandoned Andromache to Helenos in order to pursue this marriage. The appropriateness of fate here might tempt us to think that Vergil himself improved upon the account of Euripides by making Orestes the slayer, but a lost intermediary between them has probably already taken that step (see below). The alternative version with Machaireus was not forgotten, however: it appears in Strabo, for example, with again the motif of a demand for redress from the god (Str 9.3.9), and so too in Apollodoros (ApE 6.14). Strabo, like those before him, does not quite say that Machaireus slew Neoptolemos *because* the latter demanded redress, but that is the natural conclusion, as it is for Pausanias, who has a priest of Apollo do the killing at one point (10.24.4), and Delphians on orders from the Pythia at another (1.13.9). Apollodoros makes the connection more explicit by stating that Neoptolemos' hostile actions (taking of meat, looting the shrine) are the result of his failure to obtain satisfaction, with Machaireus acting to protect the sanctuary. The same writer, however, also reports the story that Orestes struck the blow out of jealousy, thus lessening the chances that Vergil innovated here. Hyginus adds his support to this latter version with the detail that Orestes killed Neoptolemos while the latter was sacrificing at Delphi (*Fab* 123). In all, we seem to have two separate strands of thought, the one blaming Neoptolemos for his rash challenge to Apollo and desecration of the latter's shrine, the other shifting much of the guilt to a jealous Orestes. Yet in the first case the greed of the shrine's priests is also sometimes a factor, and in the second Neoptolemos' usurpation of an already betrothed woman often the source of the trouble.

Teukros Of the son of Telamon our *Nostoi* summary says nothing, and likewise the *Odyssey*. Both Pindar (*Nem* 4.46–47) and Aischylos (*Persai* 894–95) speak of his eventual settlement of Cyprus from Salamis, but the problems in his homeland which motivated this event are first recorded by Euripides' *Helen*, and then by Lykophron. Conceivably they formed part of Aischylos' lost *Salaminioi* (or *Salaminiai*) as the final play of his Aias trilogy, although nothing of the plot survives, and for such a title there are many other possibilities, including events at Troy (since a chorus of Salaminians need not be on Salamis). More certain evidence comes from Sophokles, for as early as the *Aias* Teukros anticipates his father's anger, and even possible exile, should he return home without his half-brother (1006–21). Sophokles also wrote a (lost) *Teukros*, which from the remains would definitely seem to have dramatized this homecoming of Telamon's bastard son. One or both of these lost plays were probably a source for Pacuvius' *Teucer*, whose fragments in turn add some details.

Of Sophokles' play we know (virtually for certain) that it was set on Salamis, where Telamon and his visitor Oileus waited for news of their children. Oileus apparently consoled his friend when Teukros arrived with the news of Telamonian Aias' death, but subsequently found himself in the same position when news came of the death of his own son in the storm (fr 576 R and *TD* 3.71). The bearer of this news may have been Odysseus; certainly he is present at some point and accuses the half-Trojan Teukros of likely treachery against the Greeks (frr 579a, b R). We have nothing of the outcome of the debate, although we will naturally suppose Teukros banished for failure to assure his brother's return. Pacuvius' version seems to have included Teukros' mother Hesione, who grieved (for her child's exile?), and an accusation that Teukros has somehow lost (perhaps only for the moment) his brother's son. There was certainly here a detailed description of the return voyage and storm, but whether this means that Lokrian Aias' death was again an issue, or represents Teukros' defense for losing the child, we do not know.

At the beginning of the *Helen* Teukros makes a very brief appearance, stopping off in Egypt on his way to Cyprus, so that Helen may be apprised of the outcome of the Trojan War before Menelaos arrives (*Hel* 68–163). Of himself he tells Helen simply that after he was expelled by his father in anger over Aias' death Apollo ordered him to Cyprus so that he might found a new Salamis. Lykophron says, more precisely, that Telamon banished Teukros because he blamed him for Aias' death, not believing the story of the suicide at Troy (Lyk 450–69). Apollodoros has, surprisingly, no word of this event (although the *Epitome* does say that some Greeks settled on Cyprus), and neither does Hyginus. But in *Aeneid* 1 Dido comments that Teukros came to Sidon, and that her father Belus helped him find a home on Cyprus, having recently conquered it (*Aen* 1.619–26). Servius adds that according to some Telamon was angry because Teukros appeared without Tekmessa and Eurysakes, who had been placed on a ship not yet arrived in port (Σ *Aen* 1.619). Likely enough this is the explanation of the allusion seen above in Pacuvius; it may or may not go back to Sophokles. The Lykophron scholia offer nothing new, save that Teukros on Cyprus married Eue, daughter of Kypros, and had a daughter Asterie (Σ Lyk 450).

One other story of Teukros is preserved only in Justin's epitome of Pompeius Trogus, but could perhaps incorporate early elements: we are told that on learning of his father's death Teukros attempted to return to Salamis from Cyprus, but that his nephew Eurysakes prevented him, and that he then went on to the site of New Carthage in Spain (44.3). New Carthage itself goes back no further than the late third century B.C., but the rest of the tale (with a less ambitious final destination) might be earlier: we know in fact that Sophokles wrote a *Eurysakes*, and this seems the likeliest plot for it. The same story was probably dramatized in Accius' *Eurysaces*, for which fragments show that a homeless, wretched-looking exile was a major character. The Athenians for their part were ready to maintain that Eurysakes and his brother Philaios had given over the island of Salamis to Athens and taken out Athenian citizenship, the one at Melite, the other at Brauron (*Sol* 10).

*Aias
Oileiades
and
Nauplios'
Revenge*

We saw that Homer mentions neither Palamedes nor the vengeance of his father Nauplios against the Achaians returning from Troy. The *Odyssey* does note the disaster at Gyrai and the death of Aias (described briefly by Proteus to Menelaos): here Aias and Agamemnon are seemingly together when the storm strikes, thus both part of the second departure from Troy, after Menelaos and Nestor have led away the first group (*Od* 4.499–513). But what caused the storm is not said, only that Poseidon drove Aias' ship against the rocks. The location of Gyrai is likewise uncertain: Mykonos, Tenos, and Cape Kaphereus (on the southeast tip of Euboia) are variously claimed by later sources; only the last-named site would immediately suggest Nauplios as part of the story. In many later accounts the reason for the storm is the gods' anger after the sacrilege of Aias (or other Achaian misdeeds), with the ships then driven to Kaphereus. Possibly this was always the sequence of events, but perhaps too Nauplios' role in causing the disaster was originally independent, and fused together with Olympian intervention in a later syncretism. What Proteus does tell us in the *Odyssey* is that Aias was saved by Poseidon when his ship went down, and that he would have avoided death, even though he was hateful to Athena, had he not boasted that he had escaped the sea despite the gods. Upon hearing him, Poseidon broke off the section of rock on which he was sitting with his trident, and Aias drowned. Agamemnon himself was somehow saved by Hera and made his way to the Argolid, where he met his usual fate.

Proklos' summary of the *Nostoi* says for this part of the story simply that there was a storm at the Kapherides rocks and that Lokrian Aias perished. The choice of this site for the storm probably means that Nauplios' part was related also, although Proklos does not speak of him and there is no proof that he was always linked to Euboia. In his favor, however, is the fact that he *was* mentioned in some context in the poem, for Apollodoros tells us that his wife in that work was Philyra (Ap*B* 2.1.5). To be perfectly strict, Proklos' wording also does not guarantee that the Kapherean storm and Aias' death were part of the same sequence of events, although this would seem a reasonable assumption.

From epic we turn briefly to lyric and then tragedy. Judging from papyrus fragments, Alkaios dealt with the desecration of Athena's statue by Aias and seems also to have described the storm (the fragments end at just this point: 262 *SLG*). Aischylos' memorable account of this storm in *Agamemnon* gives no particulars of place or victims (*Ag* 646–73); Sophokles' *Aias Lokros*, set almost certainly at Troy after the desecration (since Athena addresses the Argives: fr 10c R), probably concluded with a prediction of divine punishment, now totally lost. The same poet's *Teukros* we have seen to combine Telamon's wait for his son's return with that of Oileus, so that there will have been here at least a messenger speech describing the storm and Aias' death (perhaps without Nauplios). But Sophokles' *Nauplios Pyrkaeus* must have dramatized the actual vengeance as we know it from later sources, with the old man lighting beacons near the rocks of Cape Kaphereus to lure the Achaian ships to destruction, in our first sure appearance of that story; no details of the plot survive. Not impossibly *Nauplios Katapleon, Aias Lokros*, and *Nauplios Pyrkaeus* were linked together as a connected trilogy, with the first two plays bringing Nauplios and Athena to Troy to protest unjust deeds, and the third dramatizing the combined vengeance of the two plaintiffs when their appeals are not heard.

Euripides' *Troades* begins with a prologue shared between Poseidon and Athena in which the goddess asks Poseidon to assist her in vengeance upon the Greeks for the desecration of her shrine (*Tro* 48–97). With the emphasis entirely on her own anger nothing is said here of Nauplios, but Euboia and the Kaphereian promontory are mentioned as site of the disaster (along with other points scattered across the Aegean); here too we encounter the unusual idea that Zeus has promised his daughter that *she* may throw the thunderbolt (*Tro* 80–81). More specific is the same poet's *Helen*, where two brief references confirm the general run of Nauplios' deed (the false fires and ships crashing on the rocks: *Hel* 766–67, 1126–31, with Menelaos' presence at the time perhaps poetic license). In the latter of these passages Nauplios is called *monokôpos,* "rowing alone," suggesting that he rowed out in a small boat to the point where he lit the fires; clearly at any rate Euripides refers to a well-known (and detailed) version of the story. Oddly enough, in describing Nauplios' efforts to corrupt the wives of the Achaians Lykophron calls him a fisherman with a *dikôpon selma,* "two-oared craft," as if he spent a great deal of time in that boat (Lyk 1217). The same work features Kassandra predicting the storm, with cryptic references to Nauplios' fires and Aias' drowning, after which Thetis buries his washed-up corpse on Delos (Lyk 373–407). This last detail is also found in the *Iliad* scholia (ΣA *Il* 13.66) and may, like other parts of that account, be drawn from Kallimachos' *Aitia.*

Of later writers, Vergil follows Euripides' *Troades* in the idea that Athena herself wielded the thunderbolt, for he has her personally hurl one at Aias' ship (*Aen* 1.39–45). The same image reappears (vividly) in Seneca's *Agamemnon* (470–578) and later in Apollodoros, Hyginus, and Quintus (Ap*E* 6.6; *Fab* 116; QS 14.449–589). These last four all present a similar sequence of events: Zeus and/or Athena sends the storm, with Aias' consequent death (Poseidon's doing in Seneca, Apollodoros, and Quintus), and the surviving ships make their way through the night to Euboia, where Nauplios is waiting with his beacons. Apollodoros adds as the place of Aias' burial by Thetis Mykonos (not, as above, Delos), and Hyginus has the further grim detail that Nauplios killed any Greeks who were able to swim to shore. The other part of Nauplios' vengeance, the leading of Achaian wives to betray their husbands, we have already considered in chapter 16. Apollodoros also has one odd variant on all this, that Nauplios made a general practice of luring ships to destruction with beacon fires (presumably for their cargoes), and that he somehow died in the same fashion (Ap*B* 2.1.5).

Idomeneus, The just-mentioned second part of Nauplios' revenge on the Greek leaders, the
Diomedes, corrupting of their wives with false tales, involved in particular Idomeneus and
Philoktetes, Diomedes. Like Neoptolemos, both men are said by Nestor in the *Odyssey* to
and Others have gotten home without incident, the implication being that their homecomings were thus happy ones (*Od* 3.180–82, 191–92). Our *Nostoi* summary says only that Diomedes left Troy with Nestor and came safely home; there is no mention of what he found there, and no mention of Idomeneus at all. If Sophokles' *Nauplios Katapleon* did concern one or more of these corrupted wives there may have been some sort of prediction of their fate at the play's end. Otherwise our first source to treat the consequences of the infidelities (other than that of Klytaimestra) is Lykophron, who presents as we saw in chapter 16 a surprising sequence of events: Leukos, the guardian of Idomeneus' kingdom, is stirred by Nauplios' lies and deceptions to kill in a temple precinct both Idomeneus' wife Meda and her children, including a daughter, Kleisithera, to whom he himself is married (Lyk 1214–25). The apparent deduction to be

made here is that Leukos, far from seducing Meda, is falsely led to believe her infidelity with someone else, in contrast to Nauplios' machinations with Klytaimestra and Aigialeia.

Apollodoros, however, tells us that as a result of Nauplios' schemes Leukos does become the lover of Meda, whom he kills together with her daughter Kleisithyra (sic) in a temple; nothing is said of any marriage to the latter (ApE 6.10). When Idomeneus returns Leukos drives him out, having taken control of ten cities on Krete. This mention of ten cities apparently springs from attempts to explain why *Iliad* 2.649 calls Krete a land of a hundred cities when *Odyssey* 19.174 speaks of it as having only ninety. The scholia to these two passages both suggest a conflict between Idomeneus and Leukos which somehow resulted in the sacking or seizure of ten cities; both also make Leukos a son of Talos who has been adopted by Idomeneus and left in charge of things. But neither scholion says anything about wives, daughters, or adultery, real or imagined. The Lykophron scholia at 386 simply repeat Apollodoros, although his version conflicts with their text. At 1218 they recount instead that Nauplios persuades Leukos to aim at the throne, and the latter then kills Meda and Kleisythera (to whom he was engaged), as well as several male children; Idomeneus on his return blinds him.

Most later sources do agreee with Apollodoros that Idomeneus vacates Krete, for whatever reason. In *Aeneid* 3, for example, his abandonment of the island permits Aineias to attempt a settlement there (3.121–23: no mention of Leukos). Later in the same Book we hear of him settled at Sallentinum (the very tip of the heel of Italy: 3.400–401), while in *Aeneid* 11 we find a cryptic reference to the "overturned household gods" of Idomeneus (11.264–65). Commenting on the first and third of these passages, Servius produces an entirely new (or at least unsuspected) tale, that on his return from Troy, after surviving a storm, Idomeneus promised that he would sacrifice to Poseidon whatever first met him on Krete. This proved to be his son, whom he either did sacrifice or tried to; the people in alarm at his cruelty (or because of the consequent plague) banished their king. The First Vatican Mythographer makes this a daughter rather than a son, but otherwise the details are the same (VM I 195; VM II 210 retains the son). The story seems not to survive elsewhere; one might have thought it or Meda's adultery or both to be the stuff of tragedy, yet suitable titles by any playwright *(Idomeneus, Leukos, Meda)* are entirely lacking. Surprisingly, Diktys, although his narrator is nominally a companion of Idomeneus, has no special story to tell of his leader's return: Idomeneus here dies peacefully and passes on the rule to Meriones. Lykophron has him buried instead at Colophon in Asia Minor (Lyk 424–32), perhaps without returning to Krete (so the scholia, with strong objections to such a version), while Servius claims that he went to somewhere in Asia after having journeyed to Italy (Σ *Aen* 3.401). Like so many others of the Greeks, his travels seemed designed above all to allow various Greek settlements to claim him as founder.

With Diomedes we encounter a similar situation, the more so as he is much more involved in the process of settling the Greek West. After his wounding of Aphrodite in *Iliad* 5, Dione is heard to reflect that his wife Aigialeia (daughter of Adrastos and thus also his aunt) may yet lament his loss; she envisions, it seems, no more than his possible death in battle (*Il* 5.406–15). But later sources, beginning with Lykophron and the scholia thereto, offer us quite a different outcome, namely that Aphrodite in revenge for her wound will cause Aigialeia to become unfaithful. Lykophron's long account of the hero's travails is filled with the usual obscurities, but shows that a detailed version of the story was familiar to his audience (Lyk 592–632). In the first part of this tale we can discern that his wife did indeed madly desire another, and that he narrowly escaped death thanks to an altar of Hera. Subsequently he comes to the Daunian lands in Italy, where he founds Argyrippa (Arpi, near the Garganus promontory). His men are for some reason transformed into birds who roost on the island (off said promontory) which comes to be called after him. There is also in Lykophron a dispute over land, settled in a way that disappoints him by his brother Alainos; he therefore pronounces a curse that only one of his own race shall successfully till it. The scholia explain this dispute as arising from a division of the spoils won in battle when Diomedes helped the local king Daunos: his half-brother Alainos, in love with the king's daughter Euippe and serving as judge, gave Daunos the land taken and Diomedes only the booty, thus the latter's curse (Σ Lyk 592). The scholia further add that Daunos later killed Diomedes, but the motive is not clear; lamenting him, his men are changed into birds. Predating this account is a work loosely ascribed to Aristotle, the *Peri Thaumasiôn Akousmatôn*, in which birds who guard the shrine of Diomedes on Diomedeia are descended from the companions of Diomedes, who were shipwrecked off the island at the time when Diomedes himself was slain by the local king, one Aineas (*Mir* 836a).

The scholia to *Iliad* 5 describe more fully Aigialeia's adultery, saying that at first she missed her husband greatly, but that subsequently because of Aphrodite's anger she carried on with all the young men, and especially with Kometes, son of Sthenelos, to whom Diomedes had entrusted the affairs of the house (ΣbT *Il* 5.412). Upon returning, he himself was almost killed and escaped only because he sought refuge at an altar of Athena. In this account he proceeds to Italy, where he is treacherously killed by the king Daunos, or else by a son of Daunos while they are hunting; Athena then makes him immortal and turns his companions into herons. Apollodoros also knows of Aigialeia's affair with this same Kometes, but attributes it rather to the work of Nauplios, who leads her into temptation as he did Meda and Klytaimestra (ApE 6.9). Unfortunately the epitome says nothing whatever about the events following Diomedes' return to Argos; this is the *Bibliotheke's* last mention of him. Earlier Apollodoros does speak of the help rendered to his grandfather Oineus in Kalydon (see above, chapter 11), but without making its time-frame clear.

For his part, Diktys offers a version of Diomedes' domestic problems which seems to acquit Aigialeia, for in his account Oiax, son of Nauplios, is the one who falsely reports her husband's amours at Troy, and rather than taking a lover of her own she enlists the help of the citizens to shut him out of Argos (Dik 6.2). He then proceeds to Kalydon to assist Oineus as above. Hyginus, like Diktys, makes this conflict with Agrios, brother of Oineus, an adventure after Troy, but says nothing of wives or exile (Fab 175). Vergil in Aeneid 11 has messengers report back to Turnus and Latinus from Diomedes at Arpi: he refuses to aid their cause, and in so doing declares that the gods, hating him since the day he wounded Aphrodite, have kept him from seeing his beloved wife and fair Kalydon (Aen 11.269–77). The mention of a "beloved" wife would seem at odds with her usual adultery; probably this is just exaggeration for effect (but see below on Antoninus Liberalis). Diomedes also refers cryptically to his companions' metamorphosis into birds, which must have been a story generally familiar to Romans; Servius objects that they ought not to have been transformed while their master was still alive, since the cause is grief for his death, but poetic license and a bit of compression is likely at work here. In the Aeneid Daunos is, of course, the aged father of Turnus; Vergil does not, however, say more of him than that, and clearly does not regard Turnus and Diomedes as linked by marriage.

Adultery as the starting point for Diomedes' troubles reappears in Antoninus Liberalis in a story that may come from Nikandros (AntLib 37). Here, too, after leaving Argos Diomedes journeys to Kalydon to help his grandfather, but then intends to return to Argos and is foiled only by a storm that brings him to the Daunioi in Italy, where the king Daunios (sic) promises him land and his daughter in return for aid against the Messapioi. This is done, and Diomedes lives out his life there, being buried on the island Diomedeia. In all, there were clearly some variants regarding the nature of Diomedes' relationship with Daunos and the Italians, although all sources who consider the matter agree that he made his way to Italy after leaving Argos.

Philoktetes we saw was also attested by Nestor at Odyssey 3.190 as safely reaching home (Meliboia and environs, south of Mount Ossa, according to Il 2.716–18), but he too, like Diomedes, seems subsequently destined for Italian shores. Our first hint is again in the Aristotelian Thaumasiôn, where we find him settled at a place called Mykalla (or Makalla) in the territory of Kroton, and honored by the Sybarites (Mir 840a). He has dedicated his bow to Apollo, and he lies buried near the river Sybaris where he aided the Rhodians who came with Tlepolemos (the death of Tlepolemos in Iliad 5 is apparently no impediment to this tale). Lykophron knows something of the same story, for he speaks of Philoktetes received by Krimissa, and buried near Sybaris after his death at the hands of the Pellenioi (from the town near Sikyon) whom he was fighting to aid people from Rhodes (Lyk 911–29). Strabo adds to this that he was driven out of Meliboia following some sort of political stasis, and thus came to southern Italy, where he founded several cities between Kroton and Thourioi, including Krimissa and Petelia (Str 6.1.3). Some of this account he says he has found in Apollodoros (the second-century B.C. Athenian), whom he elsewhere credits with drawing heavily on Demetrios of Skepsis from earlier in the same century (Str 8.3.6), but we cannot trace the development of these wanderings with any precision. From the *Epitome* of our mythographer Apollodoros we learn only that Phikoktetes went to Campania (ApE 6.15), but Tzetzes (presumably working from a more complete version of the *Bibliotheke*) quotes him to the effect that the hero was driven to Campania, and from there, after warring against the Lucanians, he settled in Krimissa and dedicated his bow (Σ Lyk 911 = ApE 6.15b). In Vergil, Helenos' warnings to Aineias likewise include the information that Philoktetes has settled Petelia (*Aen* 3.401–2).

From Lykophron too first comes a story that a Trojan captive named Setaia burned ships of the Greeks near Sybaris, and as punishment was chained to a rock to die of exposure (Lyk 1075–82). Strabo sets his version of the tale at the river Neaithos (modern Neto) in this same area, between the promontory of Krimissa and Kroton: here certain Trojan women fired the ships of their Greek captors because they were weary of traveling; the men accordingly created a settlement, and the river was named after the incident (Str 6.1.12). Apollodoros (apud Tzetzes), although he calls the river "Nauaithos," knows the same story, with the captives here led by the sisters of Priam, Aithylla, Astyoche, and Medesikaste, and acting from a desire not to be taken to slavery in Greece (Σ Lyk 921 = ApE 6.15c). In Vergil the event is transferred to Sicily, where some of the Trojan women in Aineias' party burn ships in order not to continue their journey (*Aen* 5.604–718: they are settled at Segesta). Presumably Vergil borrowed this device from its older setting in Italy, although we cannot be certain.

Other returnees of whom Apollodoros (or Tzetzes citing him) speaks include Gouneus (who went to Libya; so too Lyk 897–98), Antiphos (to Thessaly), Pheidippos (to Andros and then to Cyprus), Agapenor (to Cyprus), Menestheus (to Melos), Podaleirios (to Caria by way of Delphi), and Demophon (to Thrace and then Cyprus). This last, however, is said by Apollodoros to have first married Phyllis, the daughter of the king of Thrace (ApE 6.16–17). When he then wished to leave she gave him a chest with instructions not to open it unless he decided not to return to her. He went to Cyprus and did open it, seeing something that caused him to fall from his horse in fear and die; Phyllis herself had already committed suicide. The orator Aischines knows at least some part of this, for he tells his audience that a son of Theseus (here Akamas, not Demophon) received the place called Ennea Hodoi in Thrace as a dowry (2.31). Loukianos likewise mentions Akamas and Phyllis (perhaps not as part of the same story: *Sal* 40) while the Lykophron scholia relate the tale as in Apollodoros, with Akamas (here too in place of Demophon) frightened by a *phasma* when he opens the chest and impaled on his own sword as his horse falls (Σ Lyk 495). In Hyginus the faithless lover is, as in Apollodoros, Demophon, but there is no word of his death; Phyllis hangs herself, and her grave is shaded by trees that mourn her (*Fab* 59, 243). In Servius, after her suicide she turns into an almond tree that puts out leaves when Demophon embraces it (Σ *Ecl* 5.10). One searches Ovid's *Metamorphoses* in vain for this tale; Phyllis' lament over her abandonment by Demophon does form part of the *Heroides* (2). Two other heroes—Meges and Prothoos—Apollodoros tells us were drowned at Kaphereus (Σ Lyk 902 = Ap*E* 6.15a), and the Aristotelian *Peplos* concurs with this (although it assigns to Gouneus the same fate: fr 640 [pp. 400–401 Rose). Prothoos is mentioned only in the *Iliad*'s Catalogue, but Meges is a figure of some weight in that poem whom we might have expected to survive.

Last we come to Kalchas, the seer of the Achaian expedition. In Apollodoros he, together with Amphilochos, Leonteus, Podaleirios, and Polypoites, does not take ship at all from Troy, but travels by land down to Kolophon where he dies, defeated in a contest of prophecy by Mopsos, son of Apollo and Manto (Ap*E* 6.2–4). Strabo like Apollodoros relates the two riddles involved, and cites lines from the Hesiodic Corpus for the first of them: Mopsos being asked by Kalchas how many figs a certain tree holds replies ten thousand, with one of those left over after the rest have filled the measure of a *medimnos* (Str 14.1.27 = Hes fr 278 MW). When this count proves to be correct, Kalchas dies, so that there was here presumably no second riddle. The same seems true of the version Strabo reports from Pherekydes: here Kalchas asks how many piglets a pregnant sow will bear, and Mopsos replies three, of which one a female, whereupon Kalchas dies of grief (3F142). His death was not always simply a matter of chagrin, however, for Strabo notes that in Sophokles' *Apaitesis Helenes* it was fated for the seer to die when he should encounter a better seer (the contest takes place in Kilikia). At some point both riddles were incorporated into a single story; thus in Lykophron, Kalchas asks Mopsos about the fig tree, and Mopsos having successfully responded counters with the question about the sow (Lyk 426–30). Apollodoros follows the same arrangement, with Kalchas replying that eight piglets will be born and Mopsos declaring that the true number is nine, all male. In the Lykophron scholia, Mopsos asks both riddles, and Kalchas has no answers to offer; the number of piglets is here ten, one male, and recognizing the truth of the oracle Kalchas kills himself (Σ Lyk 427; cf. Σ Lyk 980). Strabo also knows of versions in which Kalchas asks about the sow and Mopsos the fig tree, but in all cases Mopsos prevails. The contest takes on a rather different look in Konon, where the two seers are unable to resolve their dispute until Amphimachos, king of the Lykians, intervenes; Kalchas prophesies to him victory in battle, but Mopsos defeat; when the king is in fact defeated, Mopsos is honored and Kalchas again commits suicide (26F1.6). His fate has one other variant, found at a later point in Lykophron and explained by the scholia: here he is in southern Italy, near the river Siris, and dies when struck by Herakles after announcing the number of figs on a tree (Lyk 979–83). If we can trust the scholia, Herakles tried in vain to fit the leftover fig into the *medimnos*; when Kalchas laughed at his efforts he was killed.

Odysseus

At the beginning of this chapter we found that in Nestor's account of the return Odysseus and his crews for some reason turned back at Tenedos and rejoined Agamemnon, leaving Nestor and Diomedes to go on alone (*Od* 3.159–64). Odysseus in his own accounting to the Phaiakians omits this, saying only that the winds brought him to Ismaros, a town of the Kikones in Thrace. A raid is launched and spoils divided, but Odysseus' men overindulge in wine and do not heed his command to retreat. As a result they are overmatched by a Kikonian counterattack and must flee; nothing is here said of Maron, priest of Apollo, whom Odysseus spares and who gives him in consequence the powerful wine used on Polyphemos. After Thrace there is a storm, and the crews are forced to row to land. Possibly this is the disaster at Kaphereus, but we may wonder that Odysseus does not say so. At Cape Maleia there is more bad weather, winds that blow the ships past Kythera and on for nine days, until they reach the land of the Lotus-Eaters. Three men alone of the crew are sent out to reconnoiter; the locals give them the lotus, causing them to lose all desire for home, and Odysseus must drag them back weeping to the ships.

Next is the island of the Kyklopes, giants lacking most of the trappings of communal life or the civilization brought by fixed agriculture. Odysseus' ship alone goes to explore, and he and twelve others approach Polyphemos' cave (seemingly with half a mind to steal his sheep). There they are trapped when their host proves inclined to eat them (two at a time); because of the huge stone blocking the doorway they cannot even kill him as he sleeps. With the Ismarian wine of Maron—mixed with twenty parts water for most men, but Polyphemos takes it straight—the Kyklops is therefore drugged, leaving Odysseus free to put out his eye with a stake hardened in the fire. At his cry of pain the other Kyklopes come to inquire, but when Polyphemos repeats the name Odysseus has told him ("Outis" ["No one"]), they assume his misfortune to be the work of the gods, and leave. The actual escape is effected by means of Polyphemos' sheep: each member of the crew clings to the underside of three of them tied together as they exit the cave (Odysseus takes one large one), and their master, feeling only their backs, fails to detect the men. From the seeming safety of the ships Odysseus shouts back news of the escape to Polyphemos, and narrowly misses being sunk by a huge rock the Kyklops hurls. His second announcement is his true identity, which gives his victim a name to use in calling on his father Poseidon for vengeance (the failure of Polyphemos to observe the laws of guest-friendship, though often remarked, seems not to be a consideration here).

Book 10, the second of Odysseus' narrative, begins with the arrival on Aiolia, the floating home of Aiolos Hippotades, whose six sons are married to his six daughters (see chapter 5). After a month of hospitality the crews are sent off with a bag in which all the winds except Zephyros are tied up, so that that one will bring them the more speedily to Ithaka. The desired land is actually in sight when Odysseus drifts off to sleep; thinking the bag to contain riches his men open it and a storm ensues. Driven back to Aiolia, they find that Aiolos will not help them a second time, as he supposes them hateful to the gods. In their wanderings they then come to the land of the Laistrygones (named "Telepylos," if this is not an epithet). Here, through no fault of their own, the reconnoiterers are attacked (and one eaten) by Antiphates, whose wife is as large as a mountain. Other Laistrygones then assault the harbor, throwing huge stones and spearing the crews for dinner. Odysseus' ship alone escapes, and makes its way to Aiaia, the island of Kirke, who is like her brother Aietes a child of Helios and the Okeanid Perse.

Unaccountably determined to investigate the inhabitants of this land as well, Odysseus divides his men up into two groups, led by Eurylochos and himself, and they draw lots. Eurylochos, clearly the loser, goes off with twenty-two others to find Kirke in her halls, surrounded by tame wolves and lions and spinning at her loom. A drink of cheese, barley, honey, and wine is offered; all but Eurylochos (who has stayed outside) drink and at the touch of her wand are changed into swine. He reports this back to Odysseus, who sets forth alone on a rescue mission and is intercepted by Hermes in the guise of a young man. The god gives him a root called *moly* that will protect him from Kirke's enchantments. He is warned, however, that while he must accede to her request to share her bed, he must also extract an oath of safety first, lest she unman him when he is naked. All things then proceed as predicted (although we are never told how the *moly* functions): on failing in her enchantment Kirke grasps the identity of her would-be victim, for Hermes had once foretold his coming. She then tries her second ploy, but Odysseus extracts the oath as instructed. There are no more deceptions; at his insistence she returns his men to human form (by rubbing a salve on them) and, returning to the ship, he summons the remainder of his crew (including a most reluctant Eurylochos). They are sufficiently well entertained that they spend a year with the enchantress, until the men, becoming restless, ask Odysseus to think of their departure. He consults Kirke, who makes no protest but tells him that they must first journey to the realm of Persephone to consult the seer Teiresias on how best to reach Ithaka. Nor do all of them leave her house unscathed: Elpenor has apparently gone up to the roof for some cool air after drinking heavily, and on waking and forgetting where he is falls off, breaking his neck.

Book 11 of the *Odyssey* deals entirely with the visit to the Underworld; the details of his journey there we have mostly considered in chapter 3. Odysseus encounters not only Teiresias, but also Elpenor, his mother Antikleia, companions from Troy (Agamemnon, Patroklos, Antilochos, Achilleus, Aias Telamonides), a host of famous women (Tyro, Antiope, Alkmene, Megara, Epikaste, Chloris, Leda, Iphimedeia, Phaidra, Prokris, Ariadne, Maira, Klymene, Eriphyle), Minos, Orion, three transgressors (Tityos, Tantalos, Sisyphos), and finally Herakles, or rather the *eidôlon* of his shade in the poem as we have it. From Teiresias he learns very little of his return, but something of his old age, when he will carry an oar inland until he finds a people who think it a winnowing shovel. There he will sacrifice to placate Poseidon and then go back to Ithaka, where a gentle death will come to him from the sea (or perhaps "far from the sea," that is, when he is long retired from sailing) in his old age (*Od* 11.134–36 for this last).

In Book 12 the wanderers return to Aiaia to bury Elpenor, and are given by Kirke the specific sailing advice we expected them to get from Teiresias. From her island they proceed past that of the Seirenes, Odysseus stopping the ears of his men with wax and ordering them to tie him to the mast. When he hears the song he does indeed wish to be released (signaling so with his eyebrows), but Eurylochos and Perimedes further secure his bonds. On Kirke's recommendation they have avoided the Planktai in favor of the strait between Skylla and Charybdis. The former dwells in a cave turned toward Erebos, barking like a puppy; she has twelve feet, six necks, and three rows of teeth in each head. Only the upper part of her body extends out from the cave, as she snatches up sea creatures and whatever sailors pass by. Kirke's advice is to bear toward her side and probably lose some of the crew rather than come too close to the whirlpool of Charybdis and risk the entire ship; she in fact gets six, and eats them immediately.

Next comes Thrinakia, the island of the Sun, which Odysseus wishes to avoid on the warning of both Teiresias and Kirke. Eurylochos and the others overrule him, however, and they land to spend the night. At first they have the provisions given them by Kirke, but a storm arises and the winds Notos and Euros becalm them for an entire month. At last even hunting fails, and when Odysseus goes off by himself to pray to the gods for help, Eurylochos persuades the others to solve their problem by slaughtering the cattle of the Sun. They feast for a week on the spoils, even as Helios extracts a promise from Zeus that they will be punished. At last the winds shift and they leave, only to be drowned when Zeus strikes the ship with a thunderbolt. Odysseus alone survives, clinging to mast and keel; he is borne back to Charybdis where he must cling to a fig tree while his makeshift craft is sucked under, waiting for it to reemerge. When it finally does so, he is carried to the island of Ogygia, where Kalypso, daughter of Atlas, keeps him as her lover for seven years, until Hermes comes from Zeus to order his release. We see his departure at the beginning of Book 5, the narrative to the Phaiakians having now ended: although Kalypso offers him a permanent life with her, and immortality as well, he is determined to leave, building a raft to do so. At this juncture, however, Poseidon vents his wrath for the blinding of his son Polyphemos (he had been among the Aithiopes when the other gods approved Hermes' mission) by sending a storm. Ino Leukothea intervenes to bid Odysseus abandon the raft and his garments and trust in her veil; he is reluctant to do so, but the raft finally shatters and he has no choice.

The veil aids him to arrive in Scheria, the land of the Phaiakians, where naked and exhausted he meets Nausikaa, daughter of the king, who has come down to the river (as Book 6 opens) to do laundry. With her advice and some new clothes he makes his way into the city, seeks shelter with Alkinoos and Arete, weeps at the tales of the bard Demodokos, reveals his identity, tells of his wanderings, and is promised safe passage to Ithaka by the king. Meanwhile, as the poem has already recounted in Books 1–4, Athena disguised as the Taphian Mentes encourages Telemachos to set off on a journey to Pylos, that he may question Nestor about his lost father. Penelope's suitors, who have encamped in the palace, refuse him aid, but he manages nonetheless, aided by Athena in a new disguise as Odysseus' old companion Mentor. From Pylos, having heard Nestor's account, he proceeds with Nestor's son Peisistratos overland to Sparta to see Menelaos. Nothing essential to the plot results from either of these visits, but the various reminiscences characterize Odysseus and set the stage for his return. The suitors for their part plot to ambush Telemachos on his return voyage; they are of course foiled by Athena, who sends the ship a different way. Telemachos on leaving Pylos has also picked up a new passenger, Theoklymenos of the race of Melampous, who is fleeing a homicide. They arrive back in Ithaka just after Odysseus, who has been set on shore (with many gifts) by a Phaiakian ship. Poseidon cannot prevent this, but he turns the ship to stone on its return. He intends also to surround the Phaiakians with a great mountain; as we leave them for the last time they are sacrificing to him in the hope of averting such a fate.

The second half of the *Odyssey* treats Odysseus' successful reclaiming of his role as ruler of Ithaka, helped as always by Athena. Having hidden his gifts from the Phaiakians he goes first to the hut of the swineherd Eumaios, whose loyalty he tests before revealing his identity. There he is also reunited with Telemachos, who brings him up to the palace disguised as a beggar, so that he might assess the situation and formulate a plan of attack against the suitors. In the course of Books 17–18 he is predictably ill-treated by them, especially Antinoos and Eurymachos; at one point he must fight and defeat a rival beggar, Iros, to maintain his place. In Book 19 he is interviewed by Penelope, to whom he speaks of Odysseus' return, and recognized by his old nurse Eurykleia, who finds a scar on his leg when she washes his feet; in a digression we are told that he received the wound as a boy when hunting with the sons of his maternal grandfather Autolykos on Parnassos. As the book closes Penelope announces to him her intention of holding a competition the following day to settle the matter of her disposition; whichever suitor can string Odysseus' bow and shoot an arrow through twelve axe blades (or handles?)[49] will become her husband. Thus the stage is set for Odysseus' triumph. Telemachos begins the contest in Book 21, and we are told would have finally strung the bow had Odysseus not signaled him to desist; the others all fail miserably. On Telemachos' insistence the beggar is also given a try: he both strings the bow and shoots the arrow through all twelve targets without difficulty, then with his next arrow slays

Antinoos. At this a general combat breaks out, Odysseus and Telemachos aided by their thoughtful previous removal of weapons from the hall, the suitors by the treacherous goatherd Melanthios who recovers some of those arms for them. In the end all are killed except the herald Medon and the singer Phemios, who are absolved by Telemachos of guilt. Twelve serving women of the house who slept with the suitors are then hanged, and Melanthios executed. The final two books of the poem relate Odysseus' recognition by Penelope (only after he reveals the secret of their bed, carved out of a live olive tree) and his father Laertes. Last in the series of reintegrations with his former world is that with the people of his island: the parents of the suitors threaten an armed attack to recover the bodies of their sons, but the ever-watchful Athena intervenes to make peace between the two sides, and the *Odyssey* comes to a close.

As with the *Iliad*, there is little if anything in this account which art or subsequent literary versions present much differently. The *Nostoi* seems, as we would expect, to have ignored his wanderings (although it did note the meeting with Neoptolemos in Thracian Maroneia). Stesichoros' *Nostoi* may or may not have included something of his adventures; certainly the same poet's *Skylla* must have dealt with a part of them. The very end of the *Theogony* mentions the hero's dalliances with Kirke and Kalypso, resulting in (by the first) Agrios, Latinos, and Telegonos, and (by the second) Nausithoos and Nausinoos (*Th* 1011–18). Of these we will return to Telegonos below. In the fifth century we know that Aischylos recounted some phases of the wanderings and return, probably in a connected trilogy with as titles *Psychagogoi, Penelope, Ostologoi*, and *Kirke* as the satyr play. The *Psychagogoi* seems to have dramatized the *Nekuia*, with a chorus of spellweavers summoning up the shades of the dead; our only useful fragment concerns Teiresias' prediction of Odysseus' death (fr 275 R). In the *Penelope* Odysseus confronted his wife, repeating from the *Odyssey* his disguise as a Kretan (fr 187 R). The *Ostologoi* ("Bone-Gatherers") has been taken to refer to both a chorus of beggars in the palace and the relatives coming to collect the remains of the dead suitors. The latter is, I think, the more probable, in which case the end of the *Penelope* probably featured a messenger speech with the account of the suitors' defeat (and the recognition by Penelope?).[50] But in all, we know virtually nothing of the interpretive direction these plays took. *Kirke* (guaranteed as satyric) is a total blank.

Sophokles contributes two titles of his own, *Nausikaa*, or *Plyntriai*, and *Niptra*. Had it not been for the alternate title of the first of these (referring to a chorus of young girls doing the washing) we should probably have assumed the play satyric; as it is, it would seem a tragedy, although one is hard pressed to divine the conflicts at work. There may have been a fair amount of retelling of previous adventures, as seems also the case in the *Niptra*, where Eurykleia washes Odysseus' feet. For this last play we have a version by Pacuvius which includes Odysseus' death; probably he has conflated the *Niptra* with Sophokles' *Odysseus Akanthoplex*, which did deal with that subject. A play *Skylla* involving Odysseus is mentioned by Aristotle, who does not name the author

(*Poet* 15.1454a). We will return to Skylla and the misfortune which in some cases made her a monster in chapter 18.

The earliest artistic representations of the *Odyssey* date from the mid-seventh century, and show Odysseus and his men blinding Polyphemos.[51] On a fragment of a krater from Argos we see the Kyklops stretched out in repose while two much smaller men (the others are missing to the right) from a considerable distance direct the stake toward his eye; he reaches up with one hand to push it away (Argos, no #). On the more famous Protoattic amphora from Eleusis, Polyphemos is seated to the right holding a wine cup; from the left Odysseus (here distinguished from his men by being in reserve) drives the stake into his eye from close range (Eleusis, no #). Once again the victim reaches up with his hand as he awakes from his stupor. The same scene reappears in Italy on the Aristonothos krater, made apparently by a Greek living in Caere; Polyphemos is smaller here, and the men hold the stake at waist level as they move forward (Rome:Conservatori, no #). The last of them pushes off with his foot from the wall behind him for extra power, while behind the Kyklops to the right is a platform on a pole holding six cross-hatched objects, perhaps a drying rack for cheeses. Of about the same time is a Black-and-White-style pitcher from Aigina, the so-called Ram Jug on which we see three of the men clinging to the underside of their sheep (Aigina 566). To these we may wish to add the Melian amphora of the end of the century with a neck panel showing Hermes (clear from his kerykeion and winged sandals) and a woman who may or may not be Kalypso (Athens 354).

In the sixth century Polyphemos continues to be popular. A Lakonian cup of about 550 B.C. portrays him sitting up, a human leg (from the knee down) in each hand (CabMéd 190). Four men approach with the stake on their shoulders; the leader holds out a kantharos to the Kyklops and he starts to drink from it as the stake pierces his eye. On an Attic cup of the same time we see Polyphemos (head missing) surrounded by Odysseus' men with a huge wineskin; those further away have their swords drawn, and Athena has been added to the scene (Boston 99.518). From the end of the century, still in Black-Figure, comes an oinochoe showing two phases of the action: the stake being hardened in the fire and then mobilized against the slumbering Kyklops (his eye now closed in sleep: Louvre F342). Likewise the escape from the cave surfaces frequently, with an Attic krater fragment of *c.* 560 offering us a quite hairy Polyphemos feeling over the back of the very ram under which Odysseus (named) is concealed (Cahn Coll, no #). In all, Attic Black-Figure preserves some forty examples, with among others a krater by the Sappho Painter featuring Odysseus still under his ram but with drawn sword, as if prepared for discovery (Karlsruhe 167).

The sixth century also saw the emergence of two other Odyssean tales in art, those of the Seirenes and Kirke. Portrayals of the first of these might possibly begin about 600 B.C. with a Corinthian aryballos in Basel (Basel BS 425), but on this example the captain of the ship seems busy with the sail, rather than being tied to the mast, and the one Seiren shown is well off to the side (beyond a totally irrelevant chariot, in fact) while a real bird hovers over the vessel.[52] Of the same time period is a small Black-Figure fragment from Naukratis which shows five men sitting in a boat and part of a wing overhead (London B103.19); although this seems a more likely illustration of the story in question, it tells us little in the absence of Odysseus. The first preserved representation with useful detail is that on the Boston aryballos of the mid-sixth century, where the Seirenes are fully in evidence and Odysseus clearly under restraints (Boston 01.8100; curiously enough, two birds also appear here, seemingly about to attack the crew). All further scenes of this type, from the late-sixth-century Attic Black-Figure oinochoe (Stockholm:Med, no #) and White-Ground lekythos (Athens 1130) with flute/lyre-playing Seirenes to the famous Red-Figure stamnos with a (dying?) Seiren plunging down to the ship (London E440), show Seirenes alone (no birds), and a bound Odysseus seemingly lured by their music, as we would expect from the *Odyssey*.[53]

For Kirke, the earliest representation is perhaps that on a pot fragment from the end of the Geometric period found on Ithaka: a man stands before a woman with what may be a branch in his hand while the woman has one hand raised as if in astonishment. Odysseus revealing the *moly* to Kirke is obviously only one possible interpretation, but does have the fragment's find-spot in its favor.[54] Certain illustrations begin about 560 B.C., when we see Kirke with Odysseus' transformed men. On a Black-Figure kylix now in Boston the sorceress stands in the center pouring a drink for one of the men while three others to either side of her are shown with their heads alone changed (into lions, dogs, roosters, etc.: Boston 99.519). From the far left Odysseus approaches, sword in hand. A second cup in Boston (that with Polyphemos on the other side) offers much the same scene, although now Kirke is nude, and three of the men have animal forelegs as well as heads (of sheep, dogs, and boars: Boston 99.518). Again Odysseus appears with drawn sword on the left, but now he raises his arms and draws back a bit, as if in astonishment; behind a lion-man runs off terrified. This method of portraying the transformed men becomes standard in later vases, none of which add anything of note to our literary narrative; most dramatic is perhaps the Red-Figure krater of the mid-fifth century on which Odysseus leaps up from his chair, sword in hand, as Kirke starts back in alarm and the cup falls to the floor (NY 41.83). The crewmen here have tails as well, possibly because the scene was inspired by a satyr play in which Satyroi played their roles (i.e., Aischylos' *Kirke*).

Among less certain scenes to be noted is that of the metope from Foce del Sele on which we see a man astride a large turtle and peering ahead (no #).[55] The idea is unknown to any literary tradition, and the guess that the rider might be Odysseus is based largely on the fact that he spends far more time in (as opposed to on) the sea than any other hero. But it is helped perhaps by a second such rider on a Black-Figure skyphos from the end of the sixth century: this time the man lies flat on his stomach on the back of the turtle in order to see ahead, and behind him is clearly a fig tree such as Odysseus in the *Odyssey* mentions near Charybdis (Palermo P335). There Odysseus uses the fig tree to hang from until the whirlpool sends back up the flotsam on which he has been riding; here we are perhaps to think that he finds instead a turtle that serves to bring him to Ogygia and Kalypso. Admittedly the evidence for such a con-clusion is slim, and would require some non- (or variant) Homeric version otherwise completely unsuspected. I am not myself convinced, but the artists of these pieces surely had some myth in mind.[56] Nausikaa may perhaps be shown on a mid-sixth-century Black-Figure exaleiptron now in Baltimore (WAG 48.198). Around the shoulder a series of women move away in alarm, with the last of them turning back to gesture at a couple who seem lost in animated conversation. Peleus and Thetis have been suggested, but there is no hint of wrestling or transformation, so that Odysseus and Nausikaa seem at least possible. Pausanias claims the scene of the journey to the shore for the Chest of Kypselos, where two women (one veiled) were shown in a mule-cart (5.19.9); he seems however clearly without the aid of inscriptions here, and may or may not be correct.[57]

Fifth-century Red-Figure adds to this modest corpus a number of addi-tional scenes, though most of them not before the middle of the century. Odys-seus naked before Nausikaa (Athena stands between) is now definitely por-trayed on an amphora in Munich (Munich 2322) and again on a lid of a pyxis in Boston (Boston 04.18: Athena here seems to insist that Odysseus accost the girl). Also in Boston (Boston 34.79) is a pelike by the Lykaon Painter with Odysseus, head on hand and sword drawn, sitting before the slaughtered sheep as the shade of a young man, surely Elpenor, rises up from the Underworld to converse; Hermes stands to the right. Other illustrations of this period are all taken from that part of the epic dealing with Odysseus on Ithaka: we see the reunion with Eumaios (probably: Tübingen S/10 1605), Penelope grieving and Eurykleia washing her master's feet (both on the same skyphos, Chiusi 1831), the suitors bringing gifts to their intended bride (Syracuse 2408), and Odysseus dealing out death to his adversaries who seem in the midst of banqueting (Ber-lin:PM F2588). Surprisingly there is no sign of other stories, such as Skylla, or the Laistrygones, or the death of the dog Argos; for these we must await later centuries.

Last there remains to be considered Odysseus' old age, and his son by Kirke. We saw that the end of the *Theogony* speaks simply of the birth of this son, Telegonos, together with two others, Agrios and Latinos (*Th* 1011–16). All three are said to rule over the Tyrsenoi (presumably Etruscans), but prob-ably only the latter two are meant; their names (Agrios = Silvius? Faunus?) would seem to reflect a hazy fusion of Latins and Etruscans in the early Greek West.[58] Telegonos, on the other hand, is the protagonist of a clearly Greek epic, the *Telegoneia* credited to Eugammon of Cyrene as the closing part of the Epic Cycle. Proklos' summary of this work begins with the burial of the suitors, then sacrifices to the Nymphai and a business trip to Elis, where Odysseus is entertained by Polyxenos and tales of Trophonios, Agamedes, and Augeias are recounted. After a return to Ithaka he journeys north to the land of the Thesprotoi, where he marries the queen Kallidike. When war arises between the Thesprotoi and the Brygoi (Odysseus leading the former), Ares gives victory to the Brygoi until Athena intervenes; the two gods apparently come to blows, and are halted only by Apollo. On Kallidike's death Odysseus' son Polypoites (presumably by Kallidike) succeeds her and Odysseus returns to Ithaka. Now Telegonos appears, searching for his father, and not knowing that he has found him ravages the island; Odysseus in attempting to defend his homeland is fatally wounded by this son. On discovering his error, Telegonos takes the corpse, Penelope, and Telemachos back to his mother. There Kirke makes all three of them immortal; Telegonos marries Penelope, and Telemachos Kirke.

Homer, or at least the *Nekuia*, knows too of some later adventures of Odysseus, and his death, for at *Odyssey* 11.134–36 we saw Teiresias prophesy of a journey inland with an oar, and of a gentle death from (or away from) the sea in old age. The events of Eugammon's poem may also have been described in some fashion in an epic called *Thesprotis*, since Pausanias tells us that there Odysseus has a second son Ptoliporthes by Penelope after returning from Troy (8.12.6). For that matter, Clement seems to think that Eugammon borrowed heavily from a work about the Thesprotians which might be this poem (see *Tel test* 3 *PEG*), but of course he will not have had reliable information on which was earlier. Apollodoros' version of Odysseus' later life is close enough to that of Proklos that it might have been drawn directly from Eugammon: sacrifices (to Hades, Persephone, and Teiresias) are followed by the trip to Thesprotia and placating of Poseidon (Ap*E* 7.34). Then comes the union with the queen Kallidike (who offers him her kingdom) and the birth of their son Polypoites, the defeat of neighboring peoples, and the giving up of the kingdom to his son when he leaves. On returning to Ithaka he finds a son Poliporthes borne to him by Penelope. Finally Telegonos comes to the island, searching as before for his father, and in the course of a cattle raid kills Odysseus with a spear having as its point a *kentron*; something has fallen out here which is surely (as in Lykophron [795–96] and many other sources) the *trugôn*, "sting ray," whose tail forms the spear point (cf. Σ *Od* 11.134 and Oppianos, *Halieutika* 2.497–505).[59] Afterwards Telegonos takes the corpse and Penelope back to Kirke; when he has married his stepmother, Kirke sends them both to the Isles of the Blessed. No mention is made here of Telemachos and Kirke, but quite possibly we should combine this summary with that of Proklos (which it nowhere contradicts) to get the gist of the *Telegoneia*.

From the *Odyssey* scholia we have also other kinds of information, including a curious quote from Aischylos' *Psychagogoi*. In that play, as in the *Odyssey*, Teiresias seems to have prophesied Odysseus' death, but with the statement that a heron flying overhead would deposit a load of excrement upon him, including an *akantha* (anything thornlike or spiny) which would cause his aged skin to rot (fr 275 R). Such an unusual notion might prompt us to suspect the text, but Sextus Empiricus confirms that he at least understood the words as we have them (*AdvMath* 1.276).[60] Whether Aischylos invented this bizarre fate we cannot say; whoever did so would seem to have desired a different demise for Odysseus than that brought by Telegonos, and hence concocted a new version that, like that of the *Telegoneia,* conformed with Teiresias' words in the *Odyssey.* Conceivably the encounter with the heron might even be what the *Nekuia* alludes to, assuming it does envision a death *from* the sea, although in that case most of us (with the scholia ad loc.) will probably prefer Telegonos. Sophokles treated the death in his lost *Odysseus Akanthoplex,* but such a title (with the same word *akantha* as in Aischylos) leaves us unable to say for certain even if Telegonos was involved. Yet very likely he was, for Aristotle speaks of the patricide as occurring somewhere in Greek tragedy (*Poet* 14.1453), Pacuvius includes him in his *Niptra* modeled in part (we think) on this play, and the few surviving lines speak of a prophecy from Zeus at Dodona which Odysseus seems to believe false. The content of that prophecy we probably find in Diktys, Hyginus, and a hypothesis to the *Odyssey,* all of which refer to a prediction that Odysseus will die by his son's hand. In Diktys and the hypothesis this not unnaturally causes him to fear Telemachos, against whom he takes precautions (in Diktys Telemachos is actually sent away to Kephallenia: 6.14–15). When Telegonos arrives, Odysseus thus faces him confidently and only after his fatal wounding learns the truth. Likely much of this goes back to Sophokles' play; whether it might also go back to Eugammon (there is nothing about a prophecy in either Proklos or Apollodoros) is another matter. Hyginus does deviate from this proposed plot a bit by having Telemachos accompany his father to face Telegonos; he also has Athena advise the survivors to take the corpse to Kirke, and arrange the two marriages (*Fab* 127). Kirke and Telemachos here beget Latinus, while Penelope and Telegonos beget Italus.

That the two couples thus formed following Odysseus' death live happily ever after (perhaps forever) seems certainly the notion of all the writers so far surveyed. But in Lykophron we encounter veiled allusions to Telemachos' slaying of his wife, and his being slain in turn by her daughter, his own sister the cousin of Glaukon and Apsyrtos (Lyk 807–11). Such a cousin can only be a daughter of Kirke, so that the wife of Telemachos referred to must be Kirke herself, and the avenger who is his own sister a daughter of Odysseus and Kirke. The scholia name this daughter as Kassiphone, but their explanations have Telemachos married to Kassiphone and killing his mother-in-law Kirke (being unwilling to take orders from her), after which his wife exacts revenge (Σ Lyk 808). Another entry in the scholia then recounts a version in which Kirke brings Odysseus back to life with a potion and marries off Telegonos to Penelope and Telemachos to Kassiphone in the Isles of the Blessed (Σ Lyk 805); the purpose of these arrangements is presumably so that, having satisfied everyone else, she might keep Odysseus for herself. Much of this sounds late, but Lykophron's story of Telemachos, wife, sister, and two killings was clearly known to his audience.

One other story of this period is preserved only in Parthenios, who ascribes to Sophokles an otherwise virtually unknown play entitled *Euryalos* (Par 3). He tells us that after the death of the suitors Odysseus went to Epeiros because of certain oracles, and that there he seduced Euippe, the daughter of his host Tyrimmas. The offspring Euryalos, when he grew to manhood, was sent off by his mother with certain sealed tokens to find his father, but when the boy arrived on Ithaka Odysseus was away, and Penelope guessing the truth persuaded her husband on his return to kill the new arrival as a conspirator of some sort. Only afterwards, having shown a lack of self-control and appropriate behavior in this action, did he learn the truth. Parthenios adds to this account his death from the sting of a ray wielded by one of his own race; possibly the play contained a prophecy of such. Our one other reference to this drama is from Eustathios, who says that in Sophokles' *Euryalos* Telemachos kills the boy (Eu-*Od* p. 1796). If this is not a mistake, we must suppose that Odysseus causes his son to be the agent of the deed.

Last there are some other variants cited by Apollodoros (Ap*E* 7.38–40). According to some, he says, Penelope was seduced by Antinoos and thus sent back by Odysseus to her father Ikarios, where she bore Pan as a result of a union with Hermes. We saw in chapter 2 that Penelope as mother of Pan is at least as old as Herodotos, perhaps even Hekataios; only in Douris of Samos, however, does she lustfully consort with all the suitors to produce the child (76F21). Pausanias too reports (as a Mantinean tradition) the notion that Penelope was expelled from Ithaka for inchastity (8.12.6). Apollodoros' second variant is an account in which Odysseus personally kills his wife for adultery with Amphinomos, another of her suitors in the *Odyssey*. He then concludes his *Bibliotheke* (at least in our epitome) with a version in which Odysseus is judged by Neoptolemos for the deaths of the suitors. Convicted by the latter (who hopes to get Kephallenia) he goes to Thoas, son of Andraimon, in Aitolia and, marrying his daughter, begets a son Leontophonos, after which he dies. Plutarch also tells of Neoptolemos' judgment against Odysseus; he does not, however, mention any selfish motives for the exclusion from Ithaka, Kephallenia, and Zakynthos, and Odysseus here retires to Italy (*Mor* 294c-d). Of the union in Aitolia and a final son there is no other word. That he has also in the *Telegoneia* a son by Kalypso, one Teledamos, is perhaps indicated by a somewhat confused comment of Eustathios (fr 3 *PEG*). As for Telemachos, we saw earlier that in the *Ehoiai* he weds Polykaste, daughter of Nestor (Hes fr 221 MW), thus presumably excluding his marriage to Kirke in that poem; in Hellanikos, by contrast, he is married to Nausikaa (4F156).

Aineias Strictly speaking, Aineias is not one of those who returns from Troy, and much of his story is Roman invention. But this seems the most appropriate place, now that we have dealt with the Achaians, to document what early Greeks supposed about his wanderings after Troy fell. In *Iliad* 20 we found him saved from death at Achilleus' hands by Poseidon, otherwise an Achaian supporter, because it was fated that he should survive, lest the line of Dardanos, the favorite son of Zeus, be snuffed out; in so doing Poseidon noted Zeus' anger with the house of Priam as the reason why Aineias' branch of the family and his children's children were henceforth to rule the Trojans (*Il* 20.300–308). Just what Trojans Poseidon imagines will be left to rule is not clear, nor is the logic entirely sound if Aineias already has children (but perhaps he does not: none are ever mentioned in Homer, and Askanios is the name of a Phrygian ally of Troy). In any case the god's words are most naturally taken to mean that Aineias' line will flourish in a new settlement at Troy, or else somewhere close by. Aphrodite too in her *Homeric Hymn* predicts to Anchises that Aineias and his children after him shall rule the Trojans, but gives no details (*HAph* 196–97). We saw in chapter 16 that Arktinos' *Iliou Persis* solved the problem of Aineias' survival by having him abandon Troy for Mount Ida with many of his people after the death of Laokoon, being for some reason displeased at that event. Our summary does not, however, say that these people remained or settled there. From Lesches, assuming the lines of Tzetzes' quote putting Aineias on board ship with Neoptolemos are by Simias of Rhodes (see above), we have nothing; Proklos' epitome of this poem does not even mention him.

Moving down into the sixth century, we must consider again the controversy surrounding Stesichoros and the Augustan limestone relief known as the *Tabula Iliaca Capitolina*.[61] In the panoramic central section of this version of Troy's fall Aineias appears three times: (1) inside the walls, receiving a large round box or other object from a kneeling figure; (2) issuing forth from a gate, with Anchises (and the box) on his shoulder, Askanios led by the hand, and an unnamed woman behind (Hermes precedes); (3) with Anchises, child, and Misenos boarding a ship. In this last scene we find the inscriptions *Anchisês kai ta hiera* ("Anchises and the sacred things"; he is in fact handing a box to a crewman) and *Aineias sun tois idiois apairôn eis tên hesperian* ("Aineias with his people setting out for Hesperia"), while just above to the left, in part of the space between (2) and (3), largest of all, are the words *Iliou Persis kata Stêsichoron* ("The Fall of Troy according to Stesichoros"). If the artist of the relief (one Theodoros) did in fact derive all this from the source named we would have important evidence that Aineias' migration toward western lands was known as early as Stesichoros' treatment of the Sack. But even if everything else in these scenes should be from Stesichoros, the artist might easily have intruded the one word *Hesperia* and the figure of Misenos from later Roman tradition to make the departure more significant. There is, moreover, no reason to think that the other elements are all Stesichorean: the kneeling figure in (1) seems suspiciously like Vergil's priest Panthoos, the woman of (2) has disappeared by the time we get to (3), and not only the *hiera* but the whole tale of Aineias' escape is here given uncommon attention in a poem about a Greek victory. Misenos himself, we should note, is not known as a Trojan before Vergil, and here as he prepares to board he holds something very much like a trumpet (cf. *Aen* 6.164–67). Probably then, as we might have suspected, Theodoros has claimed Stesichoros (along with several epic poems) as sources for his work, but not scrupled to give his Roman audience touches of the *Aeneid* (or its predecessors) at points where that version would be more familiar (and palatable) to them. In that case we have no real evidence at all for what Stesichoros did with Aineias; if the ship can be trusted, the Trojans did at least put out to sea, but perhaps even that is too much to say for certain.

From actual sixth-century art, as opposed to illustrations of later times, comes a substantial series of Attic Black-Figure vases showing Aineias carrying his father away.[62] All date to the second half of the century, and most cluster in the last decade. On the earliest complete scene, from an eye cup in Paris, Aineias strides right while Anchises perches on his shoulder (or upper back) and faces back to the left (Louvre F122). The latter's left hand holds a staff; the right is empty. Below are just visible the legs of a child striding along beside his father. Subsequent examples alter the pose so that Anchises faces forward and clings to the neck and back of Aineias. The child is sometimes but not always present, most memorably on a neck-amphora in Würzburg where Aineias seems to coax him to abandon a dog on which his attention is fixed (Würzburg 218). A woman also frequently accompanies the group, leading the way (e.g., Berlin:Ch F1862), and another sometimes follows (Würzburg 212). The son when present on these occasions usually runs between the leading woman and Aineias; in three instances there are two sons, one to either side (e.g., Munich 1546). In contrast to this figural scheme one vase presents the preceding woman with a small child on her shoulder (Tarquinia RC 976); thus we can say that here at least Aineias' wife is intended (whether Eurydike or Kreousa), but neither she nor any of the children are ever named on these pots.

As the series progresses toward the end of the century the women become more and more just stock filler elements. In many cases, Anchises grasps a pair of spears, reasonable enough since Aineias must use at least one hand to reach back and support his father's legs. But these spears are his total baggage; nowhere can he be said to hold anything like sacred objects or a container for them. We first see such objects for certain on an Etruscan gem of the early fifth century, where Anchises with his free hand pointedly exhibits a flattish pixis or cista (CabMéd 276). An Etruscan Red-Figure amphora of the same period shows the woman in front of Aineias with a long oval container on her head which has also been taken to be a receptacle for such objects, but the straps suggest perhaps rather a piece of luggage (Munich 3185);[63] in any case this woman, like the one on the Tarquinia neck-amphora, must be Aineias' wife. The same is true of the figure seen accompanying Aineias on a silver tetradrachm of about 500 B.C. from the Greek town of Aineia (in the northwest corner of the Chalkidike): Aineias carries a male figure of adult size while the woman walking before him and looking back carries a smaller figure, seemingly female from her long chiton.[64] Since this scene represents not just the departure from Troy but the founding of a new city, we may assume that the artist of the coin (and the people of the city) supposed both husband and wife to have made that departure successfully. On the other hand, there is no sign of any wife in the Kleophrades Painter's version of the Sack in Naples; we see only Aineias with his father on his back and his young son following along. The Parthenon's north metope 28, if correctly interpreted, placed the emphasis rather on the escape of father and son, with Anchises and a woman standing alongside.[65]

It would appear, then, that Athenians of the sixth and fifth centuries were quite familiar with Aineias' rescue of his father from Troy, and with the son who usually accompanied the two of them. As in the later literary sources surveyed in chapter 16, his wife was a less essential element who might be omitted, but she too made her escape at times. What the pots do not tell us is where Aineias is going (in no case is there any sign of a ship). To be sure, the coin type from Aineia offers one answer already in circulation in the sixth century, but we cannot say how widespread an idea this might have been. Virtually all the Black-Figure examples were found in Italy, and while that is not a highly unusual situation, it may indicate already at this time a special interest in Aineias on the part of the Etruscans, possibly as a founder hero who came to their land.

Turning back to literature, we have quite a number of casual references from Dionysios, who surveys as part of his history various traditions on Aineias' departure from Troy and subsequent exploits (1.46–59). In such a context he is our source for the previously noted fragment of Sophokles' lost *Laokoon* in which, as in Arktinos, Aineias takes his father to Mount Ida after the Laokoon affair (fr 373 R). In the fragment itself we see the two of them (Anchises on Aineias' shoulders) preparing to exit the city and surrounded not only by their slaves but also by a "crowd such as you would not believe, who are eager for this colony of Phrygioi." The use of the word *apoikia* ("colony"), plus Dionysios' failure to discuss (here or later) their destination, might suggest that in Sophokles' play the departees intended to take up residence on Ida. But the quote will have been from the end of a play not primarily about Aineias, and the playwright may not have committed himself.

From the end of the fifth century we have (via Dionysios' summary) Hellanikos' *Troika*, offering as we saw in chapter 16 a more militarily oriented account with Aineias in charge of Troy's defense (4F31). As the Achaians begin their successful assault on the city and are engrossed in plunder, he directs an exodus of the Trojans, women, children, and aged first, to Mount Ida, following himself with the troops and his father and native gods in chariots. From Ida, having gathered a large force from the surrounding areas, they hope to return to Troy after the Greeks have left, but the latter instead plan to assault the mountain as well. Finally a settlement is negotiated in which the Trojans agree to vacate the Troad, taking with them their valuables, and the Greeks promise safe conduct. Askanios is sent off to rule the land around Daskylion (southeast of Kyzikos), but the rest sail to Pallene (in the Chalkidike, and not so very far from Aineia). Here Hellanikos' contribution to Dionysios' inquiry presumably ends, as the latter turns to later writers who make Aineias die in Thrace or move from there to Arkadia. As evidence for the journey to the far west and Italy he then cites various aspects of Roman culture, as well as monuments still extant in Greek territories. From these he proceeds to a brief sketch of wanderings after Thrace, from Pallene to Aineia to Delos, Kythera, Zakynthos, Leukas, Actium, Dodona, Bouthroton, and so over to Italy. No sources are given for this part of the story, and while some scholars have supposed that Hellanikos is responsible for all of it, Dionysios' occasional vague references to writers in general suggests just the opposite. At 1.72.2, however, he certainly does say that the compiler of the accounts of the priestesses at Argos, who should be Hellanikos, has Aineias arrive in Italy from the land of the Molossians with Odysseus (!) and found Rome, naming it after a Trojan woman Rhome, who burned the ships to halt their wandering (4F84). The motif is one we have seen earlier in this chapter, when Trojan women in the hands of unnamed Greeks took similar measures in southern Italy; it seems to be a recurring theme of the migration west. To what extent this whole narrative might be in conflict with the *Troika*, and whether Hellanikos really is the author of it, remains uncertain.[66] If it is rightly ascribed to him (Dionysios also names his pupil Damastes of Sigeion as relating something of the same sort) he would become the first known writer to link Aineias with Italy or Rome. In that case, one might guess that there was influence from Italian legends back to Greece.

At any rate, in the following centuries there grew up among the Greeks a vast corpus of tales about Rome's origins, with Aineias becoming the father of sons Romulus and Remus, or Rhome marrying Latinus and bearing these children, or Askanios begetting Romus, or even Odysseus and Kirke doing so (DH 1.72.5, supposedly from Xenagoras). This last suggestion, together with Odysseus' children by Kirke (Latinos and Agrios) at the end of the *Theogony*, shows that there was an effort on the part of some Greeks to derive native peoples in the west from a Greek ancestor rather than a Trojan one. But none of this material, Greek or Italian, can have been formulated much before the fourth century, and as such, like the rest of Aineias' later adventures, it lies beyond the scope of the present book. We should note however that, on the whole, Askanios plays a surprisingly limited role in the Italian adventure; indeed, Dionysios leaves him behind in Asia to settle at Daskylion in Mysia and subsequently return to Troy (DH 1.47.5; cf. the Alexandrian historian Lysimachos at 382F9, where Askanios is given over into Akamas' care for this purpose). In the west Aineias' ancestor role depends almost always on his fathering of other children, if not Romulus and Remus themselves, then perhaps their mother Ilia, as in Naevius and Ennius, so that the twins become his grandchildren. In this respect, as often, what looks traditional in Vergil, Askanios' engendering of the line of Alba Longa, may in fact have been relatively novel.

18 Other Myths

Important and well-known though Ixion's tale is, we have not dealt with it before now because his parentage does not link him into any of the major mythological families discussed in earlier chapters. Homer says of him only that Zeus lay with his wife (unnamed) and begat Peirithoos (*Il* 14.317–18); from this point on our literary sources are completely silent until the fifth century, when Pindar incorporates his exploits into *Pythian* 2, and Aischylos uses them for a production that included the plays *Ixion* and *Perrhaibides*. *Pythian* 2 has long posed problems of dating, and probably does not even commemorate a victory at Delphi.[1] But it is dedicated to Hieron of Syracuse, and thus falls somewhere between 480 and 468 B.C. The mythic section begins with Ixion's punishment, bound as he is to a winged wheel that rolls everywhere while he proclaims the need to honor benefactors. As the cause of this fate unravels, we learn that he was welcomed by the gods (apparently on Olympos) but then in the madness of his mind conceived a passion for Hera, adding this transgression to that of being the first mortal to slay a kinsman. What he lay with when he tested Hera's honor, however, was a cloud in her form fashioned by Zeus (as we saw in chapter 3), and that cloud produced from the union a child Kentauros, "bearing honor neither among men nor in the laws of the gods" (*Py* 2.42–43). Kentauros in his turn mingled with Magnesian mares on the slopes of Mount Pelion, and thus the Kentauroi were born, a dreadful progeny for Ixion to boast of.

Pindar obviously speaks to an audience already familiar with this story, or at least with the first part of it. The scholia explain the murder as that of his father-in-law Deioneus, who expected gifts when he gave away his daughter Dia and was invited by Ixion to come to collect them (Σ *Py* 2.40b). When he arrived he fell into a pit of fire prepared by Ixion and died, and of this murder no one wished to purify Ixion, not even the gods. Finally Zeus took pity on him and not only performed the purification but brought him up to *ouranos* to share the gods' hearth; there he became enamored of Hera. Diodoros tells almost exactly the same story (the father-in-law is Eioneus, the bride Dia: 4.69.3–4), and it is surely what Pindar had in mind, for we see brief glimpses of it also in Aischylos' *Perrhaibides* (a work that might or might not be earlier than *Pythian* 2). Here some character demands gifts belonging to him (including gold and silver cups: fr 184 R), and there is talk of a man who has perished pitiably, cheated of his property (fr 186 R), while someone else spits out the blood of a murder victim (fr 186a R). There are no other details, but Deioneus/ Eioneus' death seems clearly the subject matter. Of the *Ixion*, from presumably the same trilogy, nothing survives, leaving us to speculate that it concerned Ixion's purification on Olympos and his passion for Hera, if that was not reserved for a third play. From the preserved *Eumenides* comes the (curious) insistence of Apollo that Zeus did not err in receiving the supplications of the primal murderer Ixion (*Eum* 717–18).

The Pindar scholia comment as well on the name of Ixion's father, which was a matter of some controversy: Aischylos, they say, made him one Antion, Pherekydes made him Peision, others Ares, and still others Phlegyas (so too ΣA *Il* 1.268; almost certainly this is Phlegyas, father of Koronis). In scholia to Apollonios we find Phlegyas as the father credited to Euripides (with a quote) but Pherekydes' choice now becomes Antion (unless something has fallen out: Σ *AR* 3.62). Diodoros also gives as the name "Antion," who in his account is the son of Periphas (son of Lapithes) and marries Perimele, daughter of Amythaon, to produce Ixion. The scholia to *Odyssey* 21.303 claim that Ixion is a son of Zeus; nothing daunted, Hyginus adds yet another possibility, Leonteus (*Fab* 62). Apollodoros (in the *Epitome* section: see below) does not specify a father. Euripides' preference for Phlegyas probably occurs in his lost *Ixion*, a play of which we know only that it included the punishment of the wheel. The *Ixion* play of Sophokles, if it existed, is a total blank; [2] the chorus of the *Philoktetes* remarks at one point that Ixion dared approach Zeus' bed and was bound to a wheel (*Ph* 676–79).

Later sources concentrate mostly on the attempted seduction of Hera, often ignoring the homicide altogether. Apollodoros' epitomator simply repeats the essentials of that part of Pindar's story, including cloud, wheel (borne through the air), and offspring Kentauros (Ap*E* 1.20). Of interest, though (and making more sense of the cloud than Pindar does), is the detail that Zeus fashioned that cloud in order to see whether Ixion was actually guilty. The same idea appears in the *Odyssey* scholia, where as we saw Ixion is a son of Zeus, and the father suspects that Hera is slandering his children (Σ *Od* 21.303). In addition, this scholion has Ixion partake of nectar and ambrosia on Olympos: hence the punishment of the winged wheel, because he cannot be killed. The scholia to *Phoinissai* 1185 include both homicide and passion for Hera, briefly told, with request for bride gifts, a pit of fire (the father-in-law is again Eioneus), purification by Zeus, the cloud, child, and wheel. Here again Ixion is made immortal, and the cloud is designed to test Hera's accusation against him. New in these scholia, however, are the reports that Zeus sends Ixion down to Tartaros, and that the wheel is fiery. In the Apollonios scholia we find our most precise details about the murder: when Eioneus came to collect his gifts Ixion prepared his pit and then covered it over with thin pieces of wood and fine dust, so that his father-in-law fell in (Σ *AR* 3.62, as above). Subsequently Ixion went mad because of this (a detail seemingly from Pherekydes), until Zeus cured him. Madness is also an ingredient of the A scholia at *Iliad* 1.268, where Ixion suffers this fate after treacherously burning Deioneus, father of his bride Dia, when the latter comes for the gifts. Purification and dalliance with the cloud follow as usual, but here punishment is said to take place only after death, and the wheel to which Ixion is bound rolls around in the Underworld. Our first datable source for this last idea is Apollonios, who has Hera say that she will protect Iason even if he should descend into Hades to free Ixion from his bronze chains (AR 3.61–63). Hades is his place of torment in Vergil as well, both in the *Georgics* (3.37–39 [where the wheel has snakes]; 4.484) and the *Aeneid* (6.601). The latter passage goes on to describe for both Ixion and Peirithoos the fate normally associated with Tantalos—a rock teetering over their heads and food they cannot eat; either a line with Tantalos' name has fallen out, or Vergil here takes some liberties with the normal tradition. Lactantius Placidus and the Second Vatican Mythographer seem the only sources to say that Zeus struck Ixion with his thunderbolt before the binding to the wheel (Σ St:*Theb* 4.539; VM II 106). His reason, they add, was not simply that Ixion desired Hera, but that after returning to earth he boasted of lying with her (so too, perhaps, ApE 1.20).

Finally, as we saw at the beginning of this section, Zeus in *Iliad* 14 claims that Peirithoos is his son by the wife of Ixion (317–18). Both the A and bT scholia hasten to assure us that this was before her marriage to Ixion, when she was still a maiden. Such a sequence of events is not likely to have been supported by the storytellers who made her father claim bride gifts for his daughter, and the scholiasts may be improvising, but at least they appear ignorant of any story in which Zeus' affair with Dia might have been linked (as motive or revenge) to Ixion's attempt upon Hera. Nonnos has a brief reference to Zeus, Dia, and an equine mating (7.125), and Eustathios cites a tale in which Zeus does in fact mate with Dia in the form of a stallion (as a way of explaining the offspring's name: Eu-*Il* p. 101); perhaps the story of Kentauros has influenced matters here.

In art we have a few illustrations, but nothing earlier than the fifth century and little that does more than confirm details already known. Earliest are two Red-Figure cup fragments from the beginning of that century showing the central portion of Ixion's body tied to the wheel (Agora P26228; Rome:Forum, no #). From the middle of the same century comes a kantharos by the Amphitrite Painter with a naked Ixion led before Hera by Ares and Hermes while Athena rolls in a wheel with wings attached to it (London E155); the presence of these wings probably guarantees that Ixion and the wheel were here thought to remain in the upper world. The other side of the same kantharos, with a similar figure seeking refuge at an altar as his victim slumps to the ground and is received by Thanatos, has been thought to show the death of Eioneus, the more so as the killer is in the coils of a snake who threatens to bite him.[3] No literary source ever suggests that Ixion was pursued by the Erinyes (although the notion of his madness could, I suppose, imply this), and as we have seen elsewhere an Erinys as snake is a questionable concept. But still more difficult are other details: the supposed father-in-law is young and beardless, while the supposed son-in-law does have a beard and holds a drawn sword with which he has clearly wounded his victim (no sign of a fiery pit). This is the same scene that we have previously found interpreted as Laokoon and his sons (or Orestes and Neoptolemos), and its meaning remains a problem.

The end of the century brings us a skyphos on which Hephaistos is finishing construction of the wheel (again winged) while Hera converses with a seated Zeus (Cahn Coll 541). Unfortunately, the rest of the scene is broken away. Still later, a Campanian amphora of the late fourth century shows Ixion (as on the two cup fragments) already bound to the wheel, while Hermes and Hephaistos look on from below (Berlin:PM F3023). Tongues of fire seem to be indicated on the wheel, while coiling around Ixion are several snakes, clearly older in the tradition than their appearance in Vergil; whether their pedigree is originally literary or artistic is hard to say. Likewise unclear is the point at which Ixion and his wheel are brought down into the Underworld. On present evidence this would seem to take place in Hellenistic times and probably represents a simple assimilation to the fate of other transgressors. In any case the shift must involve the loss of his function as an admonisher to others of the dangers of ingratitude.

Last, and in utter contrast to any of the above material, is a tale preserved only in the Cyzicene Epigrams, namely that Ixion slew Phorbas and Polymelos in retribution for the penalty enacted against his mother (*AP* 3.12). The introduction explains that her name was Megara, and that she had chosen to marry neither of them, whereupon they killed her. We can only presume that this is the Ixion familiar to us; despite the many authorities for his father's name, Diodoros alone identifies his mother, calling her Perimele (DS 4.69.3, as above).

Orpheus   The name "Orpheus" is not found anywhere in Homer, or the *Hymns*, or Hesiod or the Hesiodic Corpus. The earliest appearance of this figure seems to be, in fact, on the metopes of the Sikyonian *monopteros* at Delphi, where his name painted in guarantees him to have been one of the Argonautai (see chapter 12). One would guess that at some point his musical skills were of special use to the expedition, and indeed in Apollonios he saves the crew by drowning out the song of the Seirenes which would have lured them to their deaths (AR 4.891–911); scholia take this tale back to Herodoros, and add that Cheiron advised Orpheus' inclusion on the voyage for just this purpose (Σ AR 1.23 = 31F43b). The obvious idea that his song could charm savage beasts is first preserved in Simonides, where birds fly overhead and fish leap from the sea in time to the music (567 *PMG*). It resurfaces probably in Bakchylides 28 (trees and the sea may be involved) and certainly in Aischylos' *Agamemnon* (1629–32). With Euripides at the end of the century we find both trees (*Bkch* 560–64) and rocks (*IA* 1211–14) following the singer as well, and one suspects that by this time such magical powers were commonplace for Orpheus.

For the most famous part of his story, however—the descent into Hades to recover his wife and his subsequent tearing apart by Thracian women—the evidence is less plentiful. Nothing whatever survives of either of these tales prior to the fifth century, and even then there is surprisingly little. Difficult in particular is the matter of his appearance in Aischylos' Lykourgos production, a set of plays attested as consisting of *Edonoi, Bassarides, Neaniskoi,* and *Lykourgos.* For the most part these dramas must have related Lykourgos' refusal to accept the worship of the newly arrived Dionysos, as *Iliad* 6 recounts (see chapter 2). But Ps-Eratosthenes' discussion of the Lyre constellation opens up other possibilities: after recounting the passage of the lyre from Hermes to Apollo to Orpheus, who won great renown with it, he says,

> But having gone down into Hades because of his wife and seeing what sort of things were there, he did not continue to worship Dionysos, because of whom he was famous, but he thought Helios to be the greatest of the gods, Helios whom he also addressed as Apollo. Rousing himself up each night toward dawn and climbing the mountain called Pangaion he would await the sun's rising, so that he might see it first. Therefore Dionysos, being angry with him, sent the Bassarides, as Aischylos the tragedian says; they tore him apart and scattered the limbs [*Katast* 24].

If nothing else we can at least say that Orpheus' death was mentioned in the *Bassarides* of Aischylos, and that Dionysos was there responsible. But most likely this was in a choral ode, something recalled by the Bassarides briefly as an exemplum or warning to Lykourgos not to make the same mistake, rather than in a full dramatization of Orpheus' fate in what was otherwise a tetralogy about Lykourgos. If that is the case, we are left to decide how much of Ps-Eratosthenes' account might have been found in such a choral ode. The placement of Aischylos' name, where it is, after specific mention of the Bassarides, makes it perhaps more likely that only their role in the story comes from his work, with the rest—descent into Hades, worship of Helios, equation of Helios and Apollo—deriving from elsewhere. But this is just one possibility, and even if correct will not alter the fact that Aischylos and his audience must have known a myth about Orpheus and Dionysos (and Helios?), whether or not he tells all of it. The narrative logic of Ps-Eratosthenes' tale poses another problem, for it is not immediately clear why that which Orpheus sees in the Underworld should turn him away from Dionysos and toward the sun; does the darkness of Hades cause him to appreciate better the sun's light? Hyginus, who in his *De Astrologia* cites Eratosthenes at this juncture, suggests that Orpheus simply forgot Dionysos in his praise of the gods (rather, it would seem, than consciously determining to ignore him: *Astr* 2.7.1).

If the initial part of Ps-Eratosthenes' narrative does come from Aischylos it would mark our first trace of the tale of Eurydike. Otherwise, that honor goes to Euripides' *Alkestis,* where Admetos boasts that if he had the tongue

and voice of Orpheus he would descend to Hades so that having charmed Demeter's daughter and her husband with songs he might take his wife back (*Alk*
357–62). Strictly speaking he does not here say that Orpheus ever did such a
thing, only that he could do it if anyone could, but to suppose the audience
ignorant of Eurydike would involve a remarkable coincidence. More troubling
to some has seemed the fact that Orpheus did not ultimately rescue his wife,
so that the parallel is a bit ill-omened. Perhaps Euripides knows a version in
which that wife was successfully reclaimed, but Admetos may well mean simply
that he would not repeat Orpheus' crucial mistake. Orpheus also formed part
of Polygnotos' Nekyia painting at Delphi, as described by Pausanias (10.30.6);
here, however, he sits next to a willow tree holding his harp, seemingly one of
the shades rather than a visitor, and there is no mention of Eurydike at all.
In Plato's *Symposion* the speech of Phaidros includes the claim that the gods,
while admiring Alkestis who died for her husband, were not so impressed with
Orpheus, who did not die for his wife but contrived to enter Hades while still
alive; thus they showed him a *phasma* of his wife but did not allow her to
leave (*Sym* 179b-d). The gods' logic here fits the situation too well not to
arouse suspicions of Platonic revision, but at least we see a familiarity with the
story we know. The first actual mention of the wife's name occurs in the *Lament for Bion* ascribed to Moschos, where the singer hopes that Persephone
will restore to him the dead Bion as she once granted to Orpheus Eurydike
because of his music (3.123–24). Hermesianax of Kolophon (in a poem to his
mistress Leontion) is, by contrast, alone in calling this same wife Agriope (or
perhaps Argiope), and has been thought by some to imply that Orpheus succeeds in bringing her back (fr 7 Pow).

Of other Hellenistic and later works, Phanokles' poem *Kaloi* speaks of
Orpheus' love for Kalais, son of Boreas, and his death (with his head torn off)
at the hands of women who objected to his introduction of homosexuality into
Thrace (fr 1 Pow); the poem seems generally devoted to homosexual relationships of Greek heroes, but for Orpheus as so inclined there is supporting evidence elsewhere. In Konon we find first the familiar explanation of Orpheus'
failure, that after winning Eurydike back from Plouton and Persephone by his
songs he forgot their instructions concerning her and so lost her (26F1.45).
The account continues with his death at the hands of Thracian women, either
because he now hated all women or because he refused to admit them to certain
rites. Diodoros will perhaps have been among those believing that the wife is
successfully restored, for he suggests that Orpheus is to be compared with
Dionysos, who had brought his mother Semele up from the Underworld (DS
4.25.4). In the *Culex* of the *Appendix Vergiliana,* Eurydike keeps her part of
the bargain with Hades and Persephone on the journey upward by looking
ahead and maintaining silence, but Orpheus breaks his by turning to seek kisses
from her (*Cu* 268--95). Vergil's famous treatment of the star-crossed lovers
in the *Georgics* puts much of the blame on Aristaios, son of Apollo and
Kyrene, who by pursuing Eurydike with lustful intent caused her to step on a

snake (G 4.453–503). Orpheus' descent into Hades to rescue her proceeds as we would expect, but Persephone (no reason given) requires Eurydike to follow her husband up into the light; when he turns at the very edge of the upper world and looks back in his desire she is lost to him. From this point on he does nothing but lament, with no thought of remarriage, and the Thracian women, thinking themselves despised, tear him apart, casting his head in particular into the Hebros River, where it continues to lament.

Ovid's *Metamorphoses* omits any assault on Eurydike, but in his account also she is bitten by a snake (while taking a walk after her marriage: *Met* 10.1–85). The rest evolves as before, with the novelty of a vow by Orpheus that he will remain in the Underworld himself if his prayer is not granted. As in Vergil he is not allowed to look back until he has reached the upper air, but in concern and desire to assure himself that she is there he falters, an error rather more sympathetically treated by Ovid. Subsequently he returns to Thrace, where although avoiding women he does not shun the love of young boys. After several digressions the women of Thrace again dispatch him for his scorn of them, and here too his head thrown into the Hebros retains the power of song (*Met* 11.1–66).

In Apollodoros, who also makes a snake the cause of Eurydike's death (so too Σ *Alk* 357), there is the novel idea that Orpheus was instructed not to look back at his wife until he had reached his own house (Ap*B* 1.3.2). He founds the mysteries of Dionysos, and is again torn apart by women (no reason given). Pausanias says simply that the women of Thrace in a drunken state killed him because he had persuaded their husbands to follow him in his rovings; he also adds a version in which the death is by thunderbolt, because Orpheus has revealed the mysteries to the uninitiated (9.30.5). In Hyginus the cause of his death is no fault or act of his own, but rather Aphrodite's anger over his mother Kalliope's decision in the matter of Adonis (*Astr* 2.7.3: see below).

Thus literature offers virtually no early evidence for the story of Eurydike, and the same is true for art. Attic Black-Figure ignores her and the descent to Hades altogether, while Red-Figure does not discover her until the fourth century (in southern Italy); we have already seen that Polygnotos omits her. But the question of the antiquity of Orpheus' journey to the Underworld is a complex one, the more so as later "Orphic" tradition claimed the existence of a *Katabasis* poem describing the event.[4] For Orpheus, far more than for most of the figures in this book, mythic hero becomes subsumed to claimed ancestor of a wide variety of mysteries and cults, while the descent into Hades serves as a crucial proof of his shamanistic powers. Under such circumstances we must be even more cautious than usual in assessing what stories were current (and how widespread) in the Archaic period.

What Red-Figure art of the fifth century does show us vividly, beginning with a cup in Cincinnati (1979.1) and a stamnos (by Hermonax) now in the Louvre (G416), is the death of Orpheus. In all cases women attack the helpless musician, sometimes simply with their bare hands or boulders, other times with swords and axes. Even the severed head is shown on occasion, clearly with prophetic powers from the intensity with which the bystanders gaze at it (e.g., Basel BS 481). With this much of the later tradition represented in fifth-century art we might suppose the event that led to it—the loss of Eurydike—guaranteed as well. But we have seen that in some sources there is no direct connection between Eurydike and the Thracian women, the cause of Orpheus' death being rather his refusal to share with them mysteries that he had introduced, his scorn of them, or other such reasons.

One final point of concern is Orpheus' parentage. Pindar in *Pythian* 4 appears to say that he is the son of Apollo, but the scholia claim that the poet elsewhere calls Orpheus the son of Oiagros; they then cite Ammonios' suggestion that the preposition *ek* used in *Pythian* 4 means only "drawing inspiration from," for which there are parallels (Σ *Py* 4.313a). Whatever Pindar did mean in this case, Oiagros is clearly one early father, and Asklepiades gives us additional fifth-century authority for Apollo (and Kalliope) as the parents (12F6). Subsequent accounts keep almost entirely to these two options, with Oiagros seemingly representing the majority opinion (Bakchylides, Plato, Apollonios, Diodoros, etc.); the Apollonios scholia specify Oiagros and Polymnia (so "others," in contrast to Asklepiades' view: Σ *AR* 1.23). The late Pergamean historian Charax and the *Certamen Homeri et Hesiodi* do offer a genealogy for this Oiagros: from Aithousa and Apollo was born Linos, from Linos Pieros, from Pieros and Methone Oiagros, from Oiagros and Kalliope Orpheus (103F62; *Cert* 46–48 [Allen 1912]). The name of Pieros reappears in Pausanias, who maintains that a daughter (unnamed) of his was Orpheus' mother (9.30.4). Apollodoros acknowledges the tradition of both fathers, but adds the odd idea that Oiagros was the real father and Apollo the reputed one, when from a mythographer we might expect just the reverse (ApB 1.3.2).

Lykaon and Kallisto

The tales of Lykaon and his daughter Kallisto and their respective encounters with Zeus are best known to us from Ovid's *Metamorphoses*, where the narratives appear as completely separate stories, linked only by the family relationship of the two protagonists. Both tales can be traced back to Eratosthenes, however, and from there, at least in part, to the Hesiodic Corpus in what is a very tangled development. What we know for certain of the Archaic period is that the relationship of the two as father and daughter did appear in Eumelos (fr 14 *PEG*) but was not uniformly agreed upon: according to Apollodoros, "Hesiod" made her one of the Nymphai (Hes fr 163 MW), Asios a daughter of Nykteus (fr 9 *PEG*), and Pherekydes a daughter of Keteus (3F157). What Ps-Eratosthenes claims to draw from the Hesiodic Corpus (not necessarily from the same poem referred to by Apollodoros) is a story in which the daughter of Lykaon (presumably Kallisto) follows Artemis in the hunt, and having been made pregnant by Zeus hides the fact from the goddess as long as she can (*Katast* 1: *Arktos Megalê*). Finally, though, her pregnancy is discovered while she is bathing, and Artemis in anger changes her into a bear, in which form she gives birth to a son Arkas. Both bear and child are then captured by shepherds and turned over to Lykaon, after which the bear unknowingly wanders into a forbidden sanctuary of Zeus, pursued by her son and the Arkadians. At this point she is about to be put to death, but in consideration of their union Zeus rescues her and makes her a constellation. The text here seems to indicate that Arkas (and others) pursued her only after she had entered the sanctuary, and only because she had done so; we will see a slightly different version shortly. Presumably, the mating with Zeus and birth of Arkas appeared in the *Ehoiai*, and probably some version of Kallisto's final fate, but we will see that this last was subject to some variation.[5] If the catasterism was as early as the Archaic period it could perhaps have formed part of the Hesiodic *Astronomia*. The union of Zeus and Kallisto was also mentioned in the corpus attributed to "Epimenides," where they beget twins, Arkas and Pan (3B16).

In the fifth century Aischylos composed a *Kallisto* from which we probably would have learned a great deal more, but absolutely nothing of it survives. Euripides' *Helen* mentions the girl by name as bride of Zeus and a bear, a metamorphosis that Helen oddly considers as bringing relief from woes, and a happy lot compared to that of her own mother Leda (*Hel* 375–80); this whole passage is difficult, but on the surface it might seem that Euripides is ignorant of or ignores any danger to Kallisto in her bear form. The fourth-century comic poet Amphis offers more detail on the seduction: Zeus here takes the form of Artemis herself to deceive Kallisto, and when Artemis later demands the identity of the guilty party the seducee can only name the goddess (fr 47 Kock); the latter's consequent rage and Kallisto's transformation are thus only too understandable. In Kallimachos, however the seduction was accomplished, it seems that Hera discovered it and herself transformed Kallisto, following which she instructed Artemis to shoot the bear; Zeus saved Kallisto by catasterism, but nothing in the brief account that survives says anything about a child (fr 632 Pf).

Ovid too relates Zeus' disguise as Artemis, although with a bit more verisimilitude: Kallisto realizes the identity (or at least the gender) of her seducer, if to no avail, and thus does not implicate Artemis (*Met* 2.409–530). When her pregnancy is discovered at the bath she is simply banished from the company of the maidens and in human form delivers a human child; only subsequently does she suffer Hera's anger, as in Kallimachos. Arkas grows to manhood, goes out hunting, and nearly kills his own mother; Zeus intervenes to take them up to the heavens. Hera, however, has the final word, for she secures from Tethys the promise that Kallisto and her child shall be debarred from the sea (a detail not found in any of the sources drawn from Eratosthenes). Hyginus in *Fabula* 177 has a very abbreviated version of this, saying simply that Kallisto, daughter of Lykaon, was changed into a bear by Hera in anger at Zeus' affair with her, and that after the catasterism Hera obtained from Tethys the same request as above.

Turning to Apollodoros, we find a somewhat different account; after his discussion of the varied genealogies for Kallisto he proceeds (without naming a source) to relate that Zeus approached her in the guise of Artemis or perhaps Apollo, and then, wishing to conceal the matter from Hera, himself turned her into a bear (Ap*B* 3.8.2). Hera, not fooled, persuades Artemis to shoot the bear (as a wild beast: thus unwittingly) or else Artemis commits the deed of her own volition in anger over Kallisto's lost virginity. Quite probably this last version implies a variant in which Kallisto does not become a bear at all, for Artemis is not likely to transform her *and* shoot her, or to slay her for her own reasons after Hera has accomplished the transformation (cf. *Cert* 117–18, where Artemis again slays Kallisto because she succumbed to marriage, and no bear is mentioned).[6] After her death in Apollodoros Kallisto is changed into a constellation, while Arkas is rescued from her womb, much as Dionysos and Asklepios were taken from their mothers. Apollodoros' last reference before beginning this tale is a favorite source, Pherekydes, and that mythographer may have been responsible for the version he offers. Pausanias returns to Hera as the cause of the transformation, but here too Artemis shoots the bear "as a favor" to her, and the child is taken (by Hermes rather than Zeus himself) from the dying mother soon to be placed among the stars (8.3.6–7).

Hyginus in the *De Astronomia* gives slightly varying versions of most of the above. In the first part of his discussion of the "Arktos Megalê" he follows the same account as *Katasterismoi* 1, save that after Arkas has followed Kallisto into the precinct the Arkadians wish to kill both of them (*Astr* 2.1.2). In the chapter on the "Arktophylax," however, after Arkas is served by Lykaon to Zeus for dinner (see below) he is restored and given to foster parents (*Astr* 2.4.1). When he grows up and goes out to the hunt he sees a bear (his mother, of course, here *not* a pet of Lykaon) and gives chase for the purpose of killing her. The pursuit leads into the forbidden shrine of Zeus, so that here too both mother and child incur the death penalty and must be saved by Zeus (cf. the Germanicus scholia at 27). Later sections under the "Arktos Megalê" heading report that according to others Hera changed Kallisto into a bear and caused her to encounter Artemis, who killed her before realizing who she was (*Astr* 2.1.3: catasterism follows), or that Zeus changed her into the bear to avoid Hera's anger, but that Hera perceived the trick and had Artemis kill her (*Astr* 2.1.4, as in Apollodoros).

We would seem to have then two distinct strands of narrative. In the first, Artemis' anger includes (when she does not shoot the girl on the spot) the metamorphosis of Kallisto into a bear after her pregnancy is discovered; subsequently the bear is threatened by an unwitting son, or both are threatened by the Arkadians (or some combination of the two), and Zeus must intervene to take her/them up to the heavens (possibly Eratosthenes recounted both versions). In the second, Artemis merely expels Kallisto from her company, and Hera enters as jealous wife to accomplish the metamorphosis and then deceive (or perhaps order) Artemis to kill the animal, which she does. In this latter account no catasterism is strictly necessary (although always possible) and the child Arkas is seemingly not involved. For the first of these two narratives our earliest source is Eratosthenes, for the second Kallimachos followed by Apollodoros (perhaps drawing on Pherekydes).

Art offers for certain in the fifth century only the lost painting of the Underworld by Polygnotos in the Knidian Lesche at Delphi: Kallisto is with Nomia and Pero, and sits or reclines on a bearskin (Paus 10.31.10). The skin surely alludes to her transformation; whether her very presence here could be said to exclude a catasterism is a more difficult question. A Red-Figure amphora of about the same time has been taken to show Artemis in the act of shooting a (human) Kallisto as she clutches her child (Seill Coll, no #). There is no sign of any metamorphosis here, and the child's garment does seem to indicate a girl, but the more usual interpretation, that of Artemis and Niobe, would make Artemis' victim grotesquely small. In the fourth century we do find coins from Arkadia showing the shooting of a girl (clearly Kallisto, with Arkas beside her) by Artemis, and on several Apulian pots we see the unfortunate woman beginning to turn into a bear (so Boston 13.206, Getty 72.AE.128). On this latter example Hermes picks up the child; likewise on an Apulian calyx krater in Cremona where Hermes, Arkas, Kallisto, Apollo, Artemis, and Lyssa are all named, and Hermes moves off, surely to take Arkas to new parents (Cremona, no #). Whether Artemis' presence is sufficient to guarantee that she rather than Hera has caused the transformation I do not know, so that we are left quite uncertain of Aischylos' (or earlier) treatments of the story.

Lykaon's story as we find it in Ps-Eratosthenes and most other authors remains on the whole isolated from these events. The Vatican fragments of the Eratosthenes epitome do come close to suggesting that Lykaon invited Zeus to dinner and served him a child because he knew of his daughter's seduction; the account is attributed to "Hesiod" (*Katast* 8R = Hes fr 163 MW). Our other version of this epitome, while ignoring such a motive (and making no mention of "Hesiod"), calls the slaughtered child Arkas himself, who is thus served (unwittingly or not) to his own father (*Katast* 8D). In both accounts destruction of the house and restoration of Arkas follow, plus Lykaon's transformation into a wolf in 8R. That Lykaon should have such access to his grandson may seem surprising, given the boy's birth in the wilds, but we must remember that one version of Kallisto's story (that found elsewhere in Ps-Eratosthenes) has both her and Arkas captured by goatherds and given to Lykaon (who may or may not recognize them: *Katast* 1). Possibly, then, these two stories were part of a single narrative, whether or not part of the Hesiodic Corpus. Arkas as the victim served to Zeus also appears in the scholia to Germanicus' translation of Aratus and in Hyginus' *Astronomia*, the latter stressing that Lykaon wished to test his guest (*Astr* 2.4.1; we are again uncertain whether Lykaon realizes the paternity of the child).

Of other authors, Ovid has Zeus in his own form carry out the visit to Arkadia, wishing, we are told, to investigate rumors of human wickedness (*Met* 1.199–243). His host, who entertains some doubts about his guest's identity, serves him the flesh of a hostage whom he has slaughtered for the occasion. As in Ps-Eratosthenes, Zeus strikes the house with a thunderbolt and turns Lykaon into a wolf as punishment. Apollodoros offers much the same account, with the difference that here Zeus visits the house incognito to test the reputed impiety of the fifty sons of Lykaon, who serve him the intestines of a child (ApB 3.8.1: no motive other than said impiety is cited). Zeus upsets the table and destroys Lykaon and his sons with the thunderbolt, all but Nyktimos the youngest, whom Gaia saves (cf. *Mor* 300b, where two children [the only innocent ones] escape). In the *Fabulae*, Hyginus too makes the sons the primary culprits, serving human flesh to see if their guest is a god, but keeps the changing of Lykaon into a wolf (*Fab* 176). He also begins his brief account with the rape of Kallisto, conveying the impression that that deed took place at the start of this same visit. Lykophron calls the victim served Nyktimos, presumably here as elsewhere Lykaon's own child (Lyk 480–81); in the scholia the other sons are again responsible (and again as a test of divinity), with all those not killed by the thunderbolt turned into wolves. Pausanias reports what may be the core of the myth, or else its rationalization: Lykaon brings a child to the altar of Lykaian Zeus and sacrifices it, thus leading to his metamorphosis into a wolf (8.2.3); subsequently Pausanias speaks of Nyktimos as the eldest of Lykaon's children, and the one who inherits his father's rule (8.3.1).

It only remains to note briefly the line of descent from Arkas, who is the ancestor of a number of figures already treated elsewhere in this book. Apollodoros gives the most complete account: Arkas is the father of Elatos and Apheidas (ApB 3.9.1–2). Of these, Apheidas begets Stheneboia, who will marry Proitos, and Aleos, who fathers Kepheus, Lykourgos, and Auge. Auge we have seen as the mother of Telephos by Herakles, and Kepheus as the ruler of Tegea who perishes with his sons while aiding Herakles against Hippokoon. Lykourgos becomes the father of the Ankaios slain by the Kalydonian Boar, and as well of Iasos and Amphidamas; Iasos will become the father of the Arkadian Atalanta and Amphidamas the father of her consort Melanion. Pausanias has most of this same information (with more geographical details: 8.4.1–5.2) and adds that from Elatos sprang Ischys, the same figure who as early as Pindar's *Pythian* 3 consorts with Koronis as she carries Apollo's child (*Py* 3.31–32).

Smyrna/   In chapter 2 we looked briefly at the parentage of Adonis in the context of his
Myrrha   affair with Aphrodite. The earliest known reference to such a person proved to
and Adonis   be in the Hesiodic Corpus, where we learned that he was the offspring of Phoinix, son of Agenor, and Alphesiboia (Hes fr 139 MW). Nothing guarantees that this Adonis is the same one loved by Aphrodite, but Apollodoros, who gives us

the information, thought so, and he presumably had the whole "Hesiodic" original or something based on it to look at. In any case no later writer supports this parentage; we next find Adonis in the fifth century, where for Panyasis he is the child of Theias, king of the Assyrians, and his own daughter Smyrna (fr 27 *PEG*). In this version it seems that Smyrna is punished for not honoring Aphrodite by being made to fall in love with her father, whose bed she enters for twelve consecutive nights (with the help of her nurse) before he discovers the truth. When he draws his sword to make an end of her she prays she might disappear, and the gods pitying her turn her into a myrrh tree; in the tenth month after, the child Adonis is born from the tree.

Antoninus Liberalis has essentially the same story, although Adonis is born before the transformation and Theias kills himself (AntLib 34). Nor does Ovid's account deviate much from Panyasis, save that father and daughter are now Kinyras and Myrrha; the nurse as in Antoninus persuades the father that a young girl wishes to share his bed, and thus Myrrha accomplishes her desire (*Met* 10.298–514). Kinyras is also the name of Adonis' father at ΣbT *Il* 5.385 and other late sources; the daughter is sometimes Smyrna (so Hyginus and Cinna's lost *Zmyrna*), sometimes Myrrha. In Hyginus the mother of Smyrna is Kenchreis, who causes all the trouble by boasting that her daughter is more beautiful than Aphrodite (*Fab* 58). The goddess responds by instigating the unspeakable desire, but here there is apparently no discovery; Smyrna instead hides in the woods to conceal her pregnancy, and Aphrodite in pity turns her into the myrrh tree. Servius reverts to the more usual pattern, but with the detail that the anger of Helios was responsible for Myrrha's love (Σ *Ecl* 10.18); no further explanation is given.

As for the tale of Aphrodite's dispute with Persephone for custody of the child, Apollodoros and Hyginus are our only real sources. In Apollodoros, Aphrodite takes Adonis while he is still very young and hides him in a chest, apparently to conceal him from the other gods (ApB 3.14.4). The chest is then given to Persephone for safekeeping, but on seeing the child she does not wish to give him back, and thus a conflict arises which Zeus must resolve. His solution is to give Adonis to each of the two goddesses for a third of the year, the remaining third to be at Adonis' own disposition. Adonis gives that third in fact to Aphrodite, so that he is with her for eight months and Persephone for four. Soon after, however, he is slain by the boar (seemingly this would mean that Persephone gained total custody of him, but Apollodoros does not say so). In Hyginus matters are much the same, save that there is no mention of how the dispute arose, and Zeus assigns Kalliope to make the decision (*Astr* 2.7.3). Her award is for six months to each goddess, but Aphrodite, enraged at having to share Adonis, causes in the women of Thrace such passion for Kalliope's son Orpheus that they tear him apart in their eagerness to possess him; nothing more is said of Adonis.

In art we see what is probably the first part of the story on a series of terracotta reliefs from Lokroi in southern Italy dating to about 450 B.C.: a seated woman lifts the lid of a chest or basket in which a small child is sitting, hands on knee (Reggio Calabria, no #). The sanctuary in which these plaques were found has been assigned to both Aphrodite and Persephone; doves on some examples make the goddess shown more probably Aphrodite, but either way we would seem to have a fifth-century attestation of the clash over the child. About a hundred years later come several representations of the decision itself in Apulian vase-painting. Most notable is a pelike in Naples with on the shoulder Zeus seated between a standing Persephone to the left and an Aphrodite kneeling in supplication to the right (Naples Stg 702). Aphrodite clutches in her free hand a small winged Eros, while to the left with Persephone (as we should expect since she has custody at the time of the judgment) a small Adonis grasps the lower part of Zeus' scepter. That he should be awarded, even in part, to Persephone is surely a doublet of his death on the tusks of a boar, whatever the immediate cause, and although there are no specific accounts of Aphrodite bringing him back to life, the essence of his story and the religious practices surrounding it remains his participation in two worlds, and his return from the dead.

Skylla and Glaukos

We saw in chapter 7 that both Vergil and Ovid identified the Skylla, daughter of Nisos and betrayer of her father, with the monster Skylla who threatened sailors attempting the strait between herself and Charybdis. But in fact there is no basis for such an identification, and Ovid himself later reveals knowledge of a completely different story about the monster Skylla's origins. The *Odyssey* tells us that her mother was Krataiis, who "bore her as an evil for men" (*Od* 12.124–25) and assigns to her twelve feet, six heads, and three rows of teeth in each head; we also learn that she barks like a dog and extends the upper part of her body out of her cave to grab sailors, whom she eats (*Od* 12.80–100). Such scant information would seem to suggest that she has had this form from birth. The same conclusion might be drawn for the *Megalai Ehoiai*, where she is the child of Phorbas and Hekate (Hes fr 262 MW), and even more so for Akousilaos, who makes her the daughter of Phorkys (famous progenitor of monsters) and Hekate (2F42; so too Σ *Od* 12.85). Stesichoros apparently wrote an entire poem entitled *Skylla* from which we have only one piece of information, that the mother was Lamia (220 *PMG*); this may or may not be the Lamia, daughter of Poseidon, who became by Zeus the mother of the first Sibyl (*Mor* 398c; Paus 10.12.1). Of the dithyramb (by Timotheos?) *Skylla* referred to by Aristotle, nothing has survived (although it involved a lament by Odysseus: 793, 794 *PMG*), and the rest of the fifth and fourth centuries offer nothing. But the monster returns to play a role in Apollonios' *Argonautika*, where she threatens the homeward journey of the Argo until Thetis lends a hand. Here again she is the daughter of Phorkys (or Phorkos) and Hekate, with "Krataiis" another name for the latter (perhaps correctly: AR 4.825–31). Apollodoros also gives Krataiis as the mother, and Phorkos or Trienos (Triton?) as the father (ApE 7.20). To this picture the *Odyssey* scholia add some further details, namely that she had dogs (or dogs' heads) attached to her flanks, and that the lower part of her body remained in her cave because it was rooted to the rock (Σ Od 12.85).

So far, then, we have a female monster who has from all appearances always been such. But in the Roman authors the situation is quite different, and to judge from the comments of the Vergilian corpus' *Ciris* the concept of Skylla as a beautiful young girl probably goes back at least to Alexandrian times. The *Ciris* says in fact that many poets have turned Skylla, daughter of Nisos, into the Odyssean sea monster, but while it rejects this conflation it reports several origins for said monster, including the idea that Skylla was embraced by Poseidon, and hence changed into a monster by Amphitrite out of jealousy (with poison spread about) or, as a second choice, changed by Aphrodite after flaunting her beauty too outrageously (*Ciris* 54–88). Ovid also attests the transformation of Skylla, daughter of Krataiis (*Met* 13.749), but for other reasons: Glaukos, the half-fish god of the sea, has fallen in love with her, and when she rejects his advances he turns to Kirke for help (*Met* 13.900–14.74). Kirke, however, becomes enamored of Glaukos, and when he spurns her for Skylla she takes revenge against her rival by pouring poisons into the water at the place where Skylla regularly bathes; on entering the pool the girl's lower body turns into the foreparts of dogs. Probably all or most of this can be traced back at least to the third century B.C., for Athenaios tells us that the Samian (?) poetess Hedyle composed a *Skylla* in which Glaukos was in love with the title figure (Athen 7.297b).

Of still other authors, Hyginus follows the Ovidian account precisely (*Fab* 199); likewise Servius, but with alongside it the *Ciris* version (Σ Ecl 6.74: Amphitrite uses the poisons of Kirke). Amphitrite is as well the villain in the Lykophron scholia, where she like Kirke in Ovid pours the poison directly into the place where Skylla bathes (Σ Lyk 46). One other story, that the monster Skylla was slain by Herakles when she tried to take some of the cattle of Geryoneus and was brought back to life by her father by means of fire, survives only in Lykophron (44–49 and scholia [where the father is Phorkys]) and the previously mentioned *Odyssey* scholia at 12.85, the latter crediting a Dionysios of uncertain identity.

Before leaving this section we must consider also the transformation of Skylla's would-be lover Glaukos. Pausanias tells us that both Pindar and Aischylos spoke of the fisherman who ate grass and became a god of the sea with prophetic powers, Pindar briefly, Aischylos in an entire play (9.22.7). From Pindar nothing else survives, but we have a number of fragments from Aischylos' *Glaukos Pontios* confirming the miracle and the eating of the "undying" grass, with the location of the event at the northern end of Euboia (frr 25c-29 R). His prophetic skills are affirmed by Euripides in the *Orestes* (where he announces to Menelaos the death of Agamemnon: *Or* 362–67), and Palaiphatos like most later sources gives as his homeland the town of Anthedon across from Euboia on the Boiotian coast (Pal 27). Various scholia recount that having caught a fish he cast it upon some grass, which it proceeded to eat, thus reviving itself; when he ate the same grass he became immortal and leapt into the sea (Σ *Or* 364; Σ *G* 1.437; Σ *Lyk* 754). This is also the version that Ovid's Glaukos recites to Skylla when he attempts to win her; on eating the grass he here has an irresistible urge to cast himself into the sea, where his fellow divinities pour the waters of rivers and seas upon him to give him his new form (*Met* 13.917–65). With such consistency in all these accounts and no other details it is a bit surprising to find in Athenaios allusions to numerous additional stories by little-known Hellenistic writers, such as that of Theolytos in which Glaukos falls in love with Ariadne on Dia but is defeated and bound by Dionysos (Athen 7.296–97c). Other tales include his identification with Melikertes, or his love for Melikertes, or even being loved by Nereus (this from Nikandros); there are also quite a variety of parentages to choose from. Neither Apollodoros nor Hyginus tells his story.

Maira   In chapter 5 we considered the evidence from Pausanias for one Thersandros, son of Sisyphos, who in turn has a son Proitos (9.30.5). Pausanias, who is looking at the figure of Maira in Polygnotos' *Nekuia* for the Knidians, makes this Proitos Maira's father, and tells us that in the *Nostoi* (with this descent) she dies while still a maiden (*parthenos: fr 6 PEG*). Since Proitos of Tiryns, brother of Akrisios, is elsewhere always of the line of Io (his father being Abas, son of Lynkeus and Hypermestra), one would normally expect the present Proitos to be a separate individual. But the *Odyssey* scholia insist that Maira is the daughter of Proitos and Anteia, the latter as early as *Iliad* 6 the wife of the Tirynthian (Σ *Od* 11.326), so that somewhere a conflation has probably occurred. The *Odyssey* itself at 11.326 simply names Maira as one of the women seen by Odysseus in Hades, expecting, it seems, that we will know her story. The scholia cite Pherekydes as source for their account: although Maira is a devotee of Artemis and the hunt and guards her virginity, Zeus approaches and somehow deceives *(lanthanôn)* her, with the child Lokros the result (3F170). When she no longer comes to the hunt she is shot by Artemis. Proitos and Anteia as her parents appear at the very beginning of this note, and may also derive from Pherekydes. No other writer mentions her save for Eustathios, who adds nothing new; he does, however, regard this story as separate from that in which she dies a maiden (Eu-*Od* p. 1688). Unfortunately, he does not tell us whether he really knows of a second, distinct story, or whether he is simply guessing on the principle that a *parthenos* will not have a child. Strictly speaking, the term *parthenos* does not always indicate a virgin; at *Pythian* 3.34, for example, it denotes Koronis at a time long after she has lain with Apollo, and elsewhere too sometimes means no more than "young" or "unmarried." But whether Pausanias (and other parts of the *Od* 11.326 scholia) would so emphasize the word as characterizing Maira when she had borne a child to Zeus is difficult to say. One wonders too if Pherekydes had Zeus simply abandon the girl to Artemis' anger when elsewhere he usually provides some sort of (quite late) assistance. On the whole we seem unlikely to have the complete story; sadly, the preserved parts of the *Ehoiai* fail to mention Maira at all.

Melanippe   Prior to Euripides the only trace of this figure is in a line of Asios, where she bears Boiotos in the halls of Dios (fr 2 *PEG*); Strabo, who quotes the line, seems convinced that Dios is the father. Euripides himself makes her in the first of his two plays about her *(Melanippe Sophe)* a daughter of Aiolos, son of Hellen, and Hippo, daughter of Cheiron. Melanippe speaks the prologue in person, claiming that her mother, because her charms and cures released men from pain, was turned into a horse by Zeus (14 *GLP*). Several sources attest that this speech (or at least its beginning) is indeed from the *Sophe*; by contrast, Ps-Eratosthenes offers a somewhat different version of the mother's fortunes which he cites as from a Euripidean *Melanippe*. Here the daughter of Cheiron (now Hippe) is seduced by Aiolos and as the time of her delivery nears flees into the forest (*Katast* 18). Her father comes in search of her while she is in labor, but as he is about to discover her secret she prays that the gods might hide her from him by turning her into a horse. Out of respect for the piety of father and daughter, Artemis then places her among the stars, in a part of the sky not visible to the Kentauros (her father), as the constellation called Hippos. Hyginus (*Astr* 2.18.2) and the Germanicus scholia support this summary, so that it seems a genuine account of Eratosthenes' original; possibly Euripides used such material at some point in his *Melanippe Desmotis*. Hyginus goes on to relate as well a story similar to that of the *Sophe*, that Hippe had prophetic powers and was changed into a horse lest she reveal the intentions of the gods (*Astr* 2.18.3), then says that in Kallimachos she ceased to follow Artemis in the hunt, and was transformed by the goddess for that reason (= fr 569 Pf). Hippe's motive for leaving Artemis is not here stated, but surely the cause, as with Kallisto and Maira, was her seduction and consequent pregnancy. Ovid calls his daughter of Cheiron (and Chariklo) Okyrhoe; she too learns the art of prophecy, and after predicting the fate of the child Asklepios and her own father finds herself becoming a horse, apparently at Zeus' command (*Met* 2.635–79).

Returning from this preface to the actual plot of Euripides' *Sophe*, it seems that Hippo/Hippe's daughter Melanippe is herself pregnant, having been forced by the god Poseidon, and that she has borne twins, by name Aiolos and Boiotos.[7] If we can trust Ennius' Latin version of the play, the children are placed in a cowshed, leading to the mistaken notion that they are the unnatural offspring of one of the cows. Hellen (Melanippe's grandfather) persuades her father Aiolos to have them burned; Melanippe tries to defend them without revealing her own complicity, but in the end her secret comes out, putting her no doubt in worse difficulties than before. According to Pollux, there was a special mask for Hippo (as a horse?) in Euripides (4.141); presumably, then, she appeared at the end to declare the gods' will and rescue her daughter. The only illustration of this play (or for that matter any part of Melanippe's travails) is an Apulian volute krater of the later fourth century: a cowherd presents the two infants to a grim Hellen (all characters named), while to one side Aiolos stands observing and to the other Melanippe and her nurse do the same (Sciclounoff Coll, no #). To the far left a young Kretheus (Aiolos' son) crowns a horse with a wreath; whether this detail could be meant to indicate Hippo is uncertain.

The plot of the second play, the *Melanippe Desmotis*, is considerably more complicated, and not entirely compatible with the *Sophe*. The scene is set in Metapontion in southern Italy, where Metapontos is apparently king, and to which place Melanippe has been brought (Str 6.1.15). Athenaios adds that there was a woman in the play named Siris (12.523d), and this was presumably Metapontos' wife. The rest of the story is harder to reconstruct, for Hyginus gives a rather jumbled version of it (*Fab* 186), and Diodoros a historical narrative that includes Melanippe but makes her granddaughter Arne the woman who bears Aiolos and Boiotos to Poseidon and is exiled with them to Metapontion by her outraged father (DS 4.67.3–6). The one useful fragment of the play is a messenger speech in which the queen hears of an abortive attempt by her brothers to slay Aiolos and Boiotos, whose birth and (probably) right to the throne they contest (fr 495 N^2 = 13b GLP). Adding this to what we find in Hyginus, it would seem that Melanippe's children were brought up by the queen as her own, while Melanippe herself, unaware of their identity, served in the palace in some menial capacity. The queen's brothers at this point obviously know the children's true origins, but whether Siris also wishes them dead is not clear; in Hyginus (where she is Theano) she finally produces children of her own, and thus her feelings for Melanippe's sons change. In any case, in the *Desmotis* the queen's brothers are slain, Melanippe threatened (perhaps by the children themselves, if they still do not recognize her), and everything finally revealed, as we would expect; the queen probably commits suicide, leaving Metapontos free to marry Melanippe. Hyginus deviates from this reconstruction slightly by having the children he has assigned the queen (now grown) attempt the ambush in order to eliminate their rivals. He also has Melanippe's father (Desmontes, from a misunderstanding of the subtitle *Desmotis*) blind her; eventually Poseidon restores her sight and the father is killed by his grandchildren. The Cyzicene Epigrams tell us that Aiolos and Boiotos saved their mother from death; the introduction adds that they rescued Melanippe from the bonds in which her father had placed her because of her seduction (*AP* 3.16). Obviously, much of the above is similar in kind to the stories of Tyro, Hypsipyle, and Antiope, and whether it had an early existence of its own may be questioned. In Pausanias, Melanippe is the mother of Boiotos by one Itonos son of Amphiktyon; nothing else is said of her story (9.1.1).

Kresphontes   Kresphontes the elder is a quasi-historical figure, known primarily as the Herakleides who obtained Messenia by using a token of damp earth (or fired clay) when the allotment was made (ApB 2.8.4; Paus 4.3.4–5). Of his subsequent career the usual account is that Messenians or rivals to the throne slew him and perhaps some of his sons (so first Isokrates 6. *Arch* 22–23). But Euripides produced a play *Kresphontes* whose plot can probably be recovered from Hyginus' *Fabula* 137 with help from an Oxyrhynchus papyrus (POxy 2458); some fragments survive also of Ennius' version of the same story. As Euripides' drama begins, the elder Kresphontes has long since been murdered by one Polyphontes, who has taken his wife Merope and seized the throne, killing two of his children in the bargain. Merope, however, has managed to conceal a third infant child, also named Kresphontes, and send him away to Aitolia. In the course of the play he naturally returns, but Merope (aided by Polyphontes) has somehow arrived at the idea that he has killed her son, and his own death at her hands (onstage, with an axe) is barely averted (this from Plutarch: *Mor* 998e = fr 456 N²). She then returns to Polyphontes, pretending to be reconciled to the death of her son, and suggests a sacrifice to which the young stranger will be invited. This stratagem puts a weapon in the son's hands, he kills the usurper, and justice triumphs. Hyginus adds to this bare outline the idea that Polyphontes had advertised a reward for the death of Kresphontes, with as usual the intended victim then presenting himself at the palace claiming to have done the deed; such a standard plot device may well come from Euripides. The Cyzicene Epigrams also celebrate the tale (Kresphontes fixes a spear in Polyphontes' back while Merope strikes the miscreant on the head with a staff: *AP* 3.5), and Apollodoros very briefly recounts Polyphontes' crime and the son's revenge, although he calls that son Aipytos (ApB 2.8.5; cf. Paus 4.3.6–8).

The Daughters of Minyas   Of these ill-fated daughters our first preserved account is in Ovid, but Antoninus Liberalis credits his own version to Nikandros and Korinna, and so we will begin with it (AntLib 10). Minyas, son of Orchomenos, has in fact three daughters, Leukippe, Arsippe, and Alkathoe, who are extremely industrious. For this reason they find fault with all those women who leave the city for the mountains to engage in Bakchic revels, even when Dionysos himself in the form of a young girl advises them not to neglect the rites of the god. Upon their continued refusal he turns himself into a bull, a lion, and a leopard, while milk and nectar flow from their looms. At this they become frightened and draw lots; when that of Leukippe emerges first, she takes her own son Hippasos and with her sisters tears him apart as a sacrifice to Dionysos. They then go out to the hills and join the revels, until Hermes with his *rhabdos* turns them into a bat and two different kinds of owls. Ovid's version follows much the same lines, with Alkithoe *(sic)* and her sisters determined to remain at their weaving while the others run off to the festival (*Met* 4.1–42, 389–415). Here, however, there is no appearance by the god and no sacrifice; their looms are simply overrun by vine tendrils and all three turn into bats. In Aelianus, their motive for refusing the god is a desire not to leave their husbands (*VH* 3.42). Vines, ivy, snakes, and the like appear as they tend their looms, but even this does not impress them, and so they become maddened and slay the young child of Leukippe. When they then try to join the other Mainades they are rejected, and become a crow, a bat, and an owl. For his part Plutarch (where Arsippe becomes Arsinoe) simply comments that they conceived a mad desire for human flesh (apparently to eat) and thus drew lots, killing as before Leukippe's child Hippasos (*Mor* 229e). Among the plays of Aischylos about which little or nothing is known there are two, *Bakchai* and *Xantriai*, which have been thought by some to relate this myth.[8] *Xantriai* (the title means "Carders") might seem especially appropriate, given the girls' attachment to their weaving, but we have seen in chapter 14 that a reference to Pentheus in that play is probably reason enough to assign it to his story. For the *Bakchai*, on the other hand, there is really no evidence one way or another, and thus a fifth-century account of this story is certainly a possibility.

Appendix A

Some "Deviant" Cosmogonies

The choice of what material to include in this section is of necessity arbitrary and subjective. But most scholars would agree, I think, that in our corpus of Greek myths there exist versions of the creation and first beginnings which of their own volition remain outside the mainstream of Greek thought, versions that address a small clique of believers and represent decidedly personal views about the nature of humans and the destiny of the soul. We have touched on some of these in chapters 1 and 2, since it seemed inappropriate to omit them from the main discussion altogether, but I should like at this point to review what we know of their beliefs in a more systematic fashion. The material in question falls into two main categories, that ascribed to the undoubtedly historical Pherekydes of Syros and that ascribed to Orpheus. Had we more of "Mousaios" and the "Epimenides Theogony" they might have been included here as well, since the ideas attributed to them seem cut from much the same cloth. But what survives of their cosmogonies is too scant to make a summary feasible, or even to be sure that their intentions were as "deviant" as they sometimes appear, and their remnants have therefore been incorporated into the main text as variants on our more "canonical" traditions.

Pherekydes of Syros

Pherekydes of the island of Syros west of Mykonos we know to have lived in the sixth century, probably writing in the middle of it, and there are no grounds to suppose him not the source of the ideas attributed to him.[1] He was sometimes regarded as the first writer of narrative prose (or else prose about the gods), and Diogenes Laertios preserves the opening lines of his work, which announce that Zas and Chronos always existed, and Chthonie, she whose name became Ge when Zas gave her the earth as a prize (*geras:* 7B1). Subsequently we learn that Chronos produces from his own seed fire, water, and *pneuma;* these are in some way deposited in five recesses *(muchoi)* where (perhaps in different combinations) they become a second (and numerous) generation of gods (7A8). Meanwhile, Zas is preparing a marriage with Chthonie, and on the third day of the ceremonies gives her a robe or cloth *(pharos)* on which are embroidered Ge and Ogenos and the dwellings of Ogenos; he perhaps indicates as well that marriages will be under her care (text damaged: 7B2). Apparently we are to understand this cloth as the prize mentioned by Diogenes: Zas creates the earth and sea, as symbolized by the cloth with those entities embroidered upon it, and Chthonie receiving the cloth becomes Ge, the earth. The cloth is also associated in Pherekydes with a winged oak tree on which it hangs, according to Isidoros (7B2 again), and we find mention as well of "the oak and the robe" (*peplos:* 7A11), the tree being in some way a support or foundation for earth and sea. This last source mentions too as from Pherekydes the birth of Ophioneus and the battle of the gods. Such a battle proves to have been between Kronos (not Chronos) and Ophioneus, each with their forces (the latter's including his children) drawn up for combat; an agreement is struck whereby whichever should be driven out and fall into Ogenos shall be the loser, the winner to hold *ouranos* (7B4). At another point we learn that Zeus (so spelled) casts down into Tartaros whomever of the gods shows hybris, and that the daughters of Boreas and the Harpuiai and Thyella guard the place (7B5).

Not attested as from Pherekydes, but showing obvious affinities, is a part (not all) of the song sung by Orpheus in Book 1 of Apollonios' *Argonautika:* "how Ophion and Eurynome daughter of Okeanos held the rule on snowy Olympos, and how Ophion yielded his power to the might and force of Kronos, and Eurynome to Rheia, and they fell into the waves of Okeanos" (AR 1.503–6; there follow lines in which Kronos and Rheia rule the Titans until such time as Zeus is born, probably not relevant here).

This is all, leaving us with mostly questions. Scholars have generally assumed that at some point Chronos becomes Kronos, and Zas Zeus, and perhaps Ge Rheia. Such an assumption seems likely to be right, but poses some problems for our understanding of the relationship between Zeus and Kronos: do they clash as in Hesiod after the fall of Ophioneus, or are they allies in that battle and subsequently, with Zeus simply assuming a more prominent role toward the end of the poem? Those holding the first view must confront the difficulty that for Ophioneus to fall into Ogenos the latter must first have been created by Zas, in which case his wedding to Chthonie/Ge will precede Kronos' defeat of Ophioneus. No doubt this obstacle can be circumvented, but there still remains the fact that Zeus (as Zas) and Kronos (as Chronos) have both existed forever, in contrast to Ophioneus, and there seems no good reason why either of them should suddenly engage in conflict with the other. Significant too, as recently pointed out, is the passage of Aristotle placing Pherekydes with those mythographers for whom the initial principles of the world reflect the Good (*Metaphysics* 1091a29–b12). Conceivably this could mean only Zas, but when we consider Chronos' role in the creation of things it seems impossible to regard him as an opposing force of evil. On the whole, then, I think it best to assume that Zas and Chronos work together in harmony from beginning (of which there is none) to end, and that the battle with Ophioneus (from his name clearly a Typhoeus counterpart) and his brood is the only conflict which Pherekydes envisioned.

The Orphic Theogonies

In the case of Pherekydes we have some reason to hope that we are dealing with the ideas of a single individual, conceived, expressed, and preserved in a coherent and consistent fashion. The situation with "Orpheus" is quite different. It has long been argued, rightly I think, that so-called Orphic texts, as collected in Otto Kern's *Orphicorum Fragmenta* (Berlin 1922), are simply works that their authors chose to attribute to Orpheus rather than themselves; by so doing they hoped to achieve for their ideas greater prestige and a more willing reception. Since this option was open to anyone, regardless of the nature of his ideas, we will be hard-pressed to speak of any consistent "Orphic" beliefs; every such text may well be an individual entity with little or no allegiance to others sharing the same claim of authorship. Nevertheless, certain kinds of ideas coming from Thrace and the Near East do seem to have been found more suitable for ascription to the shamanistic Orpheus who had been to the Underworld and returned, and some scholars do still believe in a single unified Orphic religious movement, with corresponding texts, as early as the fifth century B.C. Whatever the truth of the matter, we will certainly see some common threads at work in the different stories designated as "Orphic."

These texts have recently been restudied by Martin West in his book *The Orphic Poems* (Oxford 1983), which is essential reading on the subject, even for those who do not accept his basic premises. Beginning with the end-point of our knowledge, the so-called Rhapsodic Theogony assembled in the first (?) century B.C., West constructs a stemma of the relationships between various texts that were eventually combined to form the Rhapsodic version. His results depend to a considerable extent on material from a newly published papyrus, discovered at Derveni near Thessalonica in 1962. This papyrus, which dates to the later part of the fourth century B.C. or perhaps even earlier, includes a commentary on certain passages of an Orphic text concerned with the beginnings of things. Comparison of this version with that of the Rhapsodic Theogony and several others known to have been in circulation in antiquity leads West to the conclusion that originally two separate lines of tradition existed, both of which go back to the fifth century B.C.; the one is represented in his view by the so-called Protogonos Theogony of which the Derveni version is an abridgement, the other by the Eudemian Theogony (named for its mention in the work of the Peripatetic Eudemos). Both works were then drawn upon for the composition of the Cyclic Theogony, a poem that West believes stood at the head of the Epic Cycle when that entity was organized in the third century B.C. From there the trail leads to Apollodoros, whom West thinks used a prose summary of this material as he did the rest of the Cycle, and to the Rhapsodic Theogony, which combined material from the Eudemian, the Cyclic, and the Hieronyman (Stoic) redaction of the Protogonos Theogony to form its own version.

West's arguments are obviously strongest at the beginning (the Protogonos Theogony, *c.* 500 B.C.) and the end (the Rhapsodic Theogony) of this process because at those two points he has some solid evidence; in between there is a certain amount of guesswork, along with deductions based on very slim testimony. Nevertheless, he manages to suggest some order in what is an immensely complicated body of material, and the overall picture has much to recommend it. Since a reasonably clear presentation of that material is all that is needed here, what follows will adhere to his basic arrangement of the tales, with sources noted from Kern's edition of the fragments and hypotheses distinguished from firm evidence.

In the Protogonos Theogony (as represented by the Derveni papyrus), it is certain that Zeus was preceded by Ouranos and Kronos, as in Hesiod, and that Kronos committed a "great deed" against Ouranos (surely the castration). But in contrast to Hesiod we find that Ouranos is the son of Nyx, and that Zeus becoming ruler swallows (on her advice) the *daimôn* "who first sprang forth into the aither" (West here rearranges lines on what I believe are valid textual grounds to produce this sense, but see below). Said *daimôn* is subsequently named Protogonos (elsewhere known as Phanes), and after Zeus has swallowed him all the immortals and rivers and springs and all other things "attach themselves" *(prosephun)* to Zeus. Apparently he then brings them forth again from his mouth, save for Aphrodite who is a product of his seed. As the Derveni citations end he has created Okeanos and Acheloos (and probably everything else) and desires to lie in love with his mother.

To all this West adds from the Hieronyman and Rhapsodic Theogonies the following material, which he believes goes back to the Protogonos. Chronos creates an egg from Aither (fr 70 Kern), and from that egg springs forth Protogonos (fr 60), four-eyed (fr 76), four-horned (fr 77), with golden wings (fr 78), many animal heads (frr 79, 81), and both male and female sexual organs (fr 81), which he uses to mate with himself (fr 80). At his emergence Chaos and Aither are split (fr 72). His offspring include Nyx (fr 98), who is the mother by him of Ouranos and Gaia (fr 109). Gaia gives the Titans to Nyx to hide and nurse (frr 129, 131), after her first two sets of offspring have been imprisoned by Ouranos. Events (castration of Ouranos, etc.) follow as above and in Hesiod, with Okeanos perhaps reluctant (fr 135). Somehow Zeus replaces Kronos in power and recreates the world through the swallowing of Protogonos (frr 129, 167, 168). Zeus then mates with his mother Rheia who is also Demeter (frr 153, 145); their union in the form of snakes produces Persephone, who may have two faces and horns (fr 58). Zeus in the same snake form mates with Persephone, and the child Dionysos is born (fr 58). Apollo and Persephone produce the Eumenides (fr 194), and probably there is a battle between the Olympians and the Titans. Protogonos creates a golden race and Kronos a silver one (fr 140); Zeus adds a third race, hapless men who know nothing of the avoiding of evils or seizing upon the good (fr 233). The poem as a whole would date to about 500 B.C., composed perhaps for a "Bacchic" society in Ionia.

By contrast, for the second branch of tradition, that called the Eudemian, we know for certain only that Nyx had absolute primacy, appearing first of all (fr 28 Kern). West proceeds on the assumption that Plato's *Timaios* order of succession, in which Okeanos occupies an intermediate genealogy between Ouranos and Kronos (*Tim* 40e), comes from this poem, and that we need only put Nyx at the head of it. Phorkys' mention as a brother of Kronos there may mean that he and Dione (a thirteenth Titan in Apollodoros) assume the places of Okeanos and Tethys to make up the canonical twelve Titans, in which case Dione is probably Aphrodite's mother as in the *Iliad*; the castration of Ouranos is omitted. Zeus is nursed by Adrastea and Ida and guarded by the Kouretes on Krete (ApB 1.1.6; frr 105, 151 Kern). Metis gives Kronos an emetic to swallow (ApB 1.2.1); he is perhaps also intoxicated with honey and castrated by Zeus (frr 148–9, 154, 137 Kern). Zeus and Persephone produce Dionysos on Krete. Spurred on by Hera (or their own jealousy) the Titans tempt the child with toys, tear him apart, and roast and eat the remains (frr 34, 35, 214). Athena, however, rescues the heart (fr 35), and Zeus uses it in some fashion to create a new Dionysos (probably by placing the heart in a body of gypsum: fr 214). As for the Titans, they are destroyed by Zeus' thunderbolt, and a new race of men is fashioned from the ashes (fr 220). Persephone is guarded by the Kouretes but nonetheless abducted by Plouton, to whom she bears the Eumenides (frr 151, 197); at the time of her abduction she is weaving a robe with a skorpion (frr 192, 196). West assigns this poem to the last third of the fifth century at Athens.

I would add here only that in other hands the chronological assessment of these myths can look quite different, and even too the sense. The second edition of Kirk, Raven, and Schofield's *The Presocratic Philosophers*, for example, holds to the originally presented order of lines in the Derveni papyrus, with the result that Zeus swallows not the revered Phanes (as he certainly does in the Rhapsodic tradition), but instead a phallus, apparently that severed from his grandfather Ouranos (Phanes is thus not mentioned at all). The myth in consequence offers a much closer parallel to the Hurrian-Hittite tale of Kumarbi, who cuts off the weather god's phallus and swallows it. Indeed, the authors suggest that Hesiod deliberately eschewed this form of the castration and swallowing motifs in favor of something tamer. They also argue for a single line of Orphic tradition in the fifth century, one that included Chronos but not Nyx as a first principle, and an egg but perhaps Eros (in his Hesiodic role) rather than Phanes as its contents. On the other hand, the tale of Zeus and his daughter Persephone as parents of an original Dionysos torn apart by Titans and reborn does seem to be accepted by most scholars as early Orphic belief, and this is perhaps that body of tradition's most distinctive contribution to the Greek myths as we know them.

Appendix B

Editions of Ancient Texts Cited

Accius
Tragicorum Romanorum Fragmenta, ed. O. Ribbeck. *Scaenicae Romanorum Poesis Fragmenta* 1. Leipzig 1897.

Aelianus
De Natura Animalium: Claudii Aeliani De Natura Animalium libri xvii, ed. R. Hercher. Leipzig 1864.
Varia Historia: Claudii Aeliani Varia Historia, ed. M. R. Dilts. Leipzig 1974.

Aischylos
Fragments: *Tragicorum Graecorum Fragmenta* 3, ed. S. L. Radt. Göttingen 1985.
Plays: *Aeschyli Tragoediae*, ed. D. L. Page. Oxford 1972.

Aithiopis
Poetae Epici Graeci 1, ed. A. Bernabé. Leipzig 1987.

Akousilaos
Die Fragmente der griechischen Historiker 1, ed. F. Jacoby. 2d ed. Leiden 1957.

Alkaios
Poetarum Lesbiorum Fragmenta, ed. E. Lobel and D. L. Page. Oxford 1955.

Alkmaionis
Poetae Epici Graeci 1, ed. A. Bernabé. Leipzig 1987.

Alkman
Poetae Melici Graeci, ed. D. L. Page. Oxford 1962.

Anakreon
Poetae Melici Graeci, ed. D. L. Page. Oxford 1962.

Antimachos
Antimachi Colophonii reliquiae, ed. B. Wyss. Berlin 1936.

Antisthenes
Antisthenis Fragmenta, ed. F. Caizzi. Milan 1966.

Antoninus Liberalis
Mythographi Graeci 2.1, ed. E. Martini. Leipzig 1896.

Apollodoros
Apollodorus, ed. J. G. Frazier. 2 vols. Cambridge, Mass., 1921.
Mythographi Graeci 1, ed. R. Wagner. Leipzig 1894.

745

Apollonios of Rhodes
Apollonii Rhodii Argonautica, ed. H. Fränkel. Oxford 1961.

Apuleius
Apuleius I: Metamorphoseon libri xi, ed. R. Helm. Leipzig 1931.

Aratos
Arati Phaenomena, ed. E. Maass. Berlin 1893.

Archilochos
Iambi et Elegi Graeci 1, ed. M. L. West. Oxford 1971.

Aristophanes
Fragments: *Poetae Comici Graeci* 3.2, ed. R. Kassel and C. Austin. Berlin 1984.
Plays: *Aristophanis Comoediae*, F. W. Hall and W. M. Geldart. 2 vols. Oxford
    1906–7.

Aristotle
Constitution of Athens: Aristotelis Atheniensium Respublica, ed. F. G. Kenyon. Ox-
    ford 1920.
Peplos: Aristotelis qui ferebantur librorum fragmenta, ed. V. Rose. Stuttgart 1886.
Peri Thaumasiôn Akousmatôn: Aristotle: Minor Works, ed. W. S. Hett. Cambridge,
    Mass., 1936.
Poetics: Aristotelis de Arte Poetica Liber, ed. R. Kassel. Oxford 1965.
Rhetoric: Aristotelis Ars Rhetorica, ed. W. D. Ross. Oxford 1959.

Asklepiades
Die Fragmente der griechischen Historiker 1, ed. F. Jacoby. 2d ed. Leiden 1957.

Aspis
Hesiodi Theogonia, Opera et Dies, Scutum, ed. F. Solmsen. 3d ed. Oxford 1990.

Athenaios
Athenaei Naucratitae Dipnosophistarum libri xv, ed. G. Kaibel. 3 vols. Leipzig
    1887–90.

Bakchylides
Bacchylidis Carmina cum fragmentis, ed. B. Snell and H. Maehler. Leipzig 1970.

Bion
Bucolici Graeci, ed. A. S. F. Gow. Oxford 1952.

Certamen Homeri et Hesiodi
Homeri Opera 5, ed. T. W. Allen. Oxford 1912.

Cicero
De Divinatione: M. Tulli Ciceronis scripta quae manserunt omnia, fasc. 46,
    ed. R. Giomini. Leipzig 1975.
De Natura Deorum: M. Tulli Ciceronis scripta quae manserunt omnia, fasc. 45.,
    ed. W. Ax. 2d ed. Stuttgart 1933.
Tusculan Disputations: M. Tulli Ciceronis scripta quae manserunt omnia, fasc. 44,
    ed. M. Pohlenz. Stuttgart 1918.

Claudian
Claudii Claudiani Carmina, ed. J. B. Hall. Leipzig 1985.

Clement of Alexandria
Clément d'Alexandre: Le Protreptique, ed. C. Mondésert. 2d ed. Paris 1949.

Editions of Ancient
Texts Cited

Dares
A. J. Valpy, ed. *Dictys Cretensis et Dares Phrygius: De Bello Trojano*. London 1825.

Demosthenes
Demosthenis Orationes, ed. S. H. Butcher and W. Rennie. 3 vols. Oxford 1903–31.

Diktys
Dictys Cretensis, ed. W. Eisenhut. Leipzig 1973.

Diodoros Siculus
Diodorus Siculus: Library of History, ed. C. H. Oldfather et al. 12 vols. Cambridge,
    Mass., 1933–67.

Diogenes Laertius
Diogenes Laertius: Lives of Eminent Philosophers, ed. R. D. Hicks. 2 vols. Cambridge,
    Mass., 1925.

Dion of Prusa
Dionis Prusaensis quem vocant Chrysostomum quae exstant omnia, ed. J. de Arnim.
    2 vols. Berlin 1893–96.

Dionysios of Halikarnassos
Dionysius of Halicarnassus: Roman Antiquities, ed. E. Cary. 7 vols. Cambridge,
    Mass., 1937–50.

Dionysios Skytobrachion
Die Fragmente der griechischen Historiker 1, ed. F. Jacoby. 2d ed. Leiden 1957.

Ennius
Annales: The Annals of Q. Ennius, ed. O. Skutsch. Oxford 1985.

Epigonoi: Poetae Epici Graeci 1, ed. A. Bernabé. Leipzig 1987.

Epimenides
Die Fragmente der Vorsokratiker 1, ed. H. Diels and W. Kranz. 6th ed. Berlin 1951.

Etymologicum Magnum
Etymologicum Magnum seu verius Lexicon, ed. T. Gaisford. Oxford 1848.

Euphorion
Collectanea Alexandrina, ed. J. U. Powell. Oxford 1925.

Euripides
Fragments: A. Nauck, *Tragicorum Graecorum Fragmenta*. 2d ed. Leipzig 1889.
Plays: *Euripidis Fabulae*, ed. J. Diggle and G. Murray: vol. 1 (Diggle): *Kyklops, Alke-
    stis, Medeia, Herakleidai, Hippolytos, Andromache, Hekabe*. Oxford 1984; vol. 2
    (Diggle): *Hiketides, Elektra, Herakles Mainomenos, Troades, Iphigeneia among
    the Taurians, Ion*. Oxford 1981; vol. 3 (Murray): *Helen, Phoinissai, Orestes,
    Bakchai, Iphigeneia at Aulis, Rhesos*, 2d ed. Oxford 1913.

Eustathios
Eustathii Commentarii ad Homeri Iliadem. 4 vols. Leipzig 1827–30.
Eustathii Commentarii ad Homeri Odysseam. 2 vols. Leipzig 1825–26.

Hekataios
Die Fragmente der griechischen Historiker 1, ed. F. Jacoby. 2d ed. Leiden 1957.

Hellanikos
Die Fragmente der griechischen Historiker 1, ed. F. Jacoby. 2d ed. Leiden 1957.

Herakleitos
Peri Apistôn: Mythographi Graeci 3.2, ed. N. Festa. Leipzig 1902.

Herodoros
Die Fragmente der griechischen Historiker 1, ed. F. Jacoby. 2d ed. Leiden 1957.

Herodotos
Herodoti Historiae, ed. C. Hude. Oxford 1927.

Hesiod
Fragments: R. Merkelbach and M. L. West, *Fragmenta Hesiodea*. Oxford 1967.
Poems: *Hesiodi Theogonia, Opera et Dies, Scutum*, ed. F. Solmsen. 3d ed. Oxford 1990.

Homer
Iliad: Homeri Opera 1–2, ed. D. B. Munro and T. W. Allen. 3d ed. Oxford 1920.
Odyssey: Homeri Opera 3–4, ed. T. W. Allen. 2d ed. Oxford 1917–19.
Homeric Hymns: Homeri Opera 5, ed. T. W. Allen. Oxford 1912.

Hyginus
De Astronomia: Hygin: L'Astronomie, ed. A. Le Boeuffle. Paris 1983.
Fabulae: Hygini Fabulae, ed. H. J. Rose. Leiden 1933.

Hypereides
Hyperidis Orationes sex, ed. C. Jensen. Stuttgart 1917.

Ibykos
Poetae Melici Graeci, ed. D. L. Page. Oxford 1962.

Isokrates
Isocrate: Discours, ed. G. Mathieu and É. Brémond. 4 vols. Paris 1962–67.

Istros
Die Fragmente der griechischen Historiker 3B, ed. F. Jacoby. Leiden 1950.

Kallimachos
Callimachus, ed. R. Pfeiffer. 2 vols. Oxford 1949–53.

Konon
Die Fragmente der griechischen Historiker 1, ed. F. Jacoby. 2d ed. Leiden 1957.

Kypria
Poetae Epici Graeci 1, ed. A. Bernabé. Leipzig 1987.

Little Iliad
Poetae Epici Graeci 1, ed. A. Bernabé. Leipzig 1987.

Loukianos
Luciani Opera, ed. M. D. Macleod. 4 vols. Oxford 1972–87.

Lykophron
Lycophronis Alexandra, ed. L. Mascialino. Leipzig 1964.

Lykourgos
Lycurgi Oratio in Leocratem, ed. N. C. Conomis. Leipzig 1970.

Macrobius
Saturnalia: Macrobius 1, ed. J. Willis. Leipzig 1970.

Menandros
Menandri Reliquiae Selectae, ed. F. H. Sandbach. Oxford 1972.

Mimnermos
Iambi et Elegi Greci 2, ed. M. L. West. Oxford 1972.

Moschos
Bucolici Graeci, ed. A. S. F. Gow. Oxford 1952.

Mousaios
Die Fragmente der Vorsokratiker 1, ed. H. Diels and W. Kranz. 6th ed. Berlin 1951.

Naupaktia
Poetae Epici Graeci 1, ed. A. Bernabé. Leipzig 1987.

Nikandros
Nikander: The Poems and Poetical Fragments, ed. A. S. F. Gow and A. F. Scholfield.
    Cambridge 1953.

Nonnos
Nonni Panopolitani Dionysiaca, ed. A. Ludwich. 2 vols. Leipzig 1909–11.

Oidipodeia
Poetae Epici Graeci 1, ed. A. Bernabé. Leipzig 1987.

Orphic Argonautika
Les argonautiques d'Orphée, ed. G. Dottin. Paris 1930.

Ovid
Ars Amatoria: P. Ovidi Nasonis Amores, Medicamina Faciei Femineae, Ars Amatoria,
    Remedia Amoris, ed. E. J. Kenney. Oxford 1961.
Fasti: P. Ovidi Nasonis Fastorum libri sex, ed. E. H. Alton, D. E. W. Wormell, and
    E. Courtney. Leipzig 1978.
Heroides: P. Ovidii Nasonis Epistulae Heroidum, ed. H. Dörrie. Berlin 1971.
Metamorphoses: Ovidius: Metamorphoses, ed. W. S. Anderson. Leipzig 1977.
Remedia Amoris: P. Ovidi Nasonis Amores, Medicamina Faciei Femineae, Ars Amato-
    ria, Remedia Amoris, ed. E. J. Kenney. Oxford 1961.

Pacuvius
Tragicorum Romanorum Fragmenta, ed. O. Ribbeck. *Scaenicae Romanorum Poesis*
    Fragmenta 1. Leipzig 1897.

Palaiphatos
Mythographi Graeci 3.2, ed. N. Festa. Leipzig 1902.

Palatine Anthology
The Greek Anthology, ed. W. R. Paton. 5 vols. Cambridge, Mass., 1916–18.

Parian Marble
Die Fragmente der griechischen Historiker 2B, pt. 3, ed. F. Jacoby. Berlin 1929.

Parthenios
Mythographi Graeci 2.1, ed. P. Sakolowski. Leipzig 1896.

Pausanias
Pausaniae Graeciae Descriptio, ed. F. Spiro. 3 vols. Stuttgart 1903.

Pherekydes of Athens
Die Fragmente der griechischen Historiker 1, ed. F. Jacoby. 2d ed. Leiden 1957.

Pherekydes of Syros
Die Fragmente der Vorsokratiker 1, ed. H. Diels and W. Kranz. 6th ed. Berlin 1951.

Philochoros
Die Fragmente der griechischen Historiker 3B, ed. F. Jacoby. Leiden 1950.

Philodemos
Philodem: Über Frömmigkeit, ed. T. Gomperz. Leipzig 1866.

Philostratos (Flavius)
Flavii Philostrati Opera 1, ed. C. L. Kayser. Leipzig 1870.

Philostratos the Younger
Flavii Philostrati Opera 2, ed. C. L. Kayser. Leipzig 1871.

Phrynichos
Tragicorum Graecorum Fragmenta 1, ed. B. Snell. Göttingen 1971.

Pindar
Fragments: *Pindarus* 2, ed. B. Snell and H. Maehler. Leipzig 1975.
Odes: *Pindarus* 1, ed. B. Snell and H. Maehler. Leipzig 1971.

Plato
Platonis Opera, ed. J. Burnet. 5 vols. Oxford 1905–10.

Plautus
T. Macci Plauti Comoediae, ed. W. M. Lindsay. 2 vols. Oxford 1904–5.

Pliny the Elder
Pliny: Natural History, ed. H. Rackham et al. 10 vols. Cambridge, Mass., 1938–63.

Plutarch
Lives: Plutarchi Vitae Parallelae 1 and 3, ed. K. Ziegler. Leipzig 1960–73.
Moralia: Plutarch: Moralia, ed. F. C. Babbitt et al. 15 vols. Cambridge, Mass.,
    1927–69.

Polyainos
Polyaeni Strategematôn libri viii, ed. E. Woelfflin and J. Melber. Stuttgart 1887–1901.

Pratinas
Tragicorum Graecorum Fragmenta 1, ed. B. Snell. Göttingen 1971.

Propertius
Sexti Properti Carmina, ed. E. A. Barber. Oxford 1960.

Pseudo-Eratosthenes
Mythographi Graeci 3.1, ed. A. Olivieri. Leipzig 1897.

Ptolemaios Chennos
Der Philosoph und Grammatiker Ptolemaios Chennos, ed. A. Chatzis. Paderborn
    1914.

Quintus of Smyrna
Quintus de Smyrne: La suite d'Homère, ed. F. Vian. 3 vols. Paris 1963–69.

Sappho
Poetarum Lesbiorum Fragmenta, ed. E. Lobel and D. L. Page. Oxford 1955.

Σ Apollonios of Rhodes
Scholia in Apollonium Rhodium vetera, ed. C. Wendel. Berlin 1935.

Σ Aratos
Scholia in Aratum vetera, ed. J. Martin. Stuttgart 1974.

Σ Aristophanes
Scholia Graeca in Aristophanem, ed. F. Dübner. Paris 1877.

Σ Euripides
Scholia in Euripidem, ed. E. Schwartz. 2 vols. Berlin 1887–91.

Σ Germanicus
Eratosthenis Catasterismorum Reliquiae, ed. C. Robert. Berlin 1878.

Σ Hesiod
Theogony: Scholia vetera in Hesiodi Theogoniam, ed. L. Di Gregorio. Milan 1975.
Works & Days: Scholia vetera in Hesiodi Opera et Dies, ed. A. Pertusi. Milan 1955.

Σ Homer
Iliad: Scholia Graeca in Homeri Iliadem, ed. W. Dindorf and E. Maass. 6 vols. Oxford 1875–88.
Odyssey: Scholia Graeca in Homeri Odysseam, ed. W. Dindorf. 2 vols. Oxford 1855.

Σ Lykophron
Lycophronis Alexandra 2, ed. E. Scheer. Berlin 1908.

Σ Pindar
Scholia vetera in Pindari carmina, ed. A. B. Drachmann. 3 vols. Leipzig 1903–27.

Σ Sophokles
Scholia in Sophoclis Tragoedias vetera, ed. P. N. Papageorgius. Leipzig 1888.

Σ Statius
Lactantii Placidi qui dicitur commentarios in Statii Thebaida et commentarium in Achilleida, ed. R. Jahnke. *P. Papinius Statius* 3. Leipzig 1898.

Σ Theokritos
Scholia in Theocritum vetera, ed. C. Wendel. Stuttgart 1914.

Σ Vergil
Aeneid: Servii Grammatici qui feruntur in Vergilii carmina commentarii: Aeneis, ed. G. Thilo and H. Hagen. 2 vols. Leipzig 1881–84.
Eclogues: Servii Grammatici qui feruntur in Vergilii Bucolica et Georgica commentarii, ed. G. Thilo. Leipzig 1887.
Georgics: Servii Grammatici qui feruntur in Vergilii Bucolica et Georgica commentarii, ed. G. Thilo. Leipzig 1887.

Seneca the Younger
L. Annaei Senecae Tragoediae, ed. O. Zwierlein. Oxford 1986.

Sextus Empiricus
Sextus Empiricus, ed. R. G. Bury. 4 vols. Cambridge, Mass., 1933–49.

Simonides
Poetae Melici Graeci, ed. D. L. Page. Oxford 1962.

Sophokles
Fragments: Tragicorum Graecorum Fragmenta 4, ed. S. Radt. Göttingen 1977.

Plays: *Sophoclis Fabulae*, ed. A. C. Pearson. Oxford 1924.

Statius
Achilleis: P. Papini Stati Achilleis, ed. A. Marastoni. Leipzig 1974.
Thebais: P. Papini Stati Thebais, ed. A. Klotz. 2d ed. Leipzig 1973.

Stesichoros
Poetae Melici Graeci, ed. D. L. Page. Oxford 1962.

Strabo
Strabo: Geography, ed. H. L. Jones. 8 vols. Cambridge, Mass., 1917–32.

Suetonius
C. Suetoni Tranquilli Opera 1, ed. M. Ihm. Stuttgart 1908.

Thebais
Poetae Epici Graeci 1, ed. A. Bernabé. Leipzig 1987.

Theognis
Iambi et Elegi Graeci 1, ed. M. L. West. Oxford 1971.

Theokritos
Bucolici Graeci, ed. A. S. F. Gow. Oxford 1952.

Thoukydides
Thucydidis Historiae, ed. H. S. Jones and J. E. Powell. 2 vols. Oxford 1942.

Titanomachia
Poetae Epici Graeci 1, ed. A. Bernabé. Leipzig 1987.

Tzetzes, John
Exegesis in Homeri Iliadem: Draconis Stratonicensis Liber de Metricis Poeticis; Ioannis Tzetzae Exegesis in Homeri Iliadem, ed. G. Hermann. Leipzig 1812.

Valerius Flaccus
C. Valeri Flacci Argonauticon, ed. E. Courtney. Leipzig 1970.

Vatican Mythographers
Scriptores rerum mythicarum Latini tres Romae nuper reperti, ed. G. H. Bode. 2 vols. Celle 1834.

Varro
M. Terenti Varronis De Lingua Latina quae supersunt, ed. G. Goetz and F. Schoell. Leipzig 1910.

Vergil
Aeneid: P. Vergili Maronis Opera, ed. F. A. Hirtzel. Oxford 1900.
Eclogues: P. Vergili Maronis Opera, ed. F. A. Hirtzel. Oxford 1900.
Georgics: P. Vergili Maronis Opera, ed. F. A. Hirtzel. Oxford 1900.
Minor works (*Ciris, Culex*, etc.): *Appendix Vergiliana*, ed. W. V. Clausen, F. R. D. Goodyear, E. J. Kenney, and J. A. Richmond. Oxford 1966.

Xenophon
Kynegetikos: Xenophontis Opuscula, ed. E. C. Marchant. Oxford 1920.

Zenobios
Corpus Paroemiographorum Graecorum 1, ed. E. L. Leutsch and F. G. Schneidewin. Göttingen 1839.

Appendix C

Catalogue of Artistic Representations

Abbreviations

BF	Attic Black-Figure	MC	Middle Corinthian
EC	Early Corinthian	PA	Protoattic
LC	Late Corinthian	RF	Attic Red-Figure
LG	Late Geometric	WG	Attic White-Ground

ABL	C. H. E. Haspels, *Attic Black-Figured Lekythoi* (Paris 1936)
ABV	J. D. Beazley, *Attic Black-Figure Vase-Painters* (Oxford 1956)
ARV²	J. D. Beazley, *Attic Red-Figure Vase-Painters*, 2d ed. (Oxford 1963)
CH	J. M. Hemelrijk, *Caeretan Hydriae* (Mainz am Rhein 1984)
ChV	A. Rumpf, *Chalkidische Vasen* (Berlin 1927)
CorVP	D. A. Amyx, *Corinthian Vase-Painting of the Archaic Period* (Berkeley 1988)
DL 1	F. Brommer and A. Peschlow-Bindokat, *Denkmälerlisten zur griechischen Heldensage* 1 (Marburg 1971)
FS	K. Schefold, *Frühgriechische Sagenbilder* (Munich 1964)
LCS	A. D. Trendall, *The Red-Figured Vases of Lucania, Campania and Sicily* (Oxford 1967)
LIMC	*Lexicon Iconographicum Mythologiae Classicae* 1–5
LV	C. M. Stibbe, *Lakonische Vasenmaler des sechsten Jahrhunderts vor Chr.* (Amsterdam 1972)
OF II	E. Kunze, *Olympische Forschungen* II (Berlin 1950)
OF XVII	P. Bol, *Olympische Forschungen* XVII (Berlin 1989)
Para	J. D. Beazley, *Paralipomena* (Oxford 1971)
RVAp	A. D. Trendall and A. Cambitoglou, *The Red-Figured Vases of Apulia* 1–2 (Oxford 1978–82)
RVP	A. D. Trendall, *The Red-Figured Vases of Paestum* (Rome 1987)
SB II	K. Schefold, *Götter- und Heldensagen der Griechen in der spätarchaischen Kunst* (Munich 1978)
SB III	K. Schefold, *Die Göttersage in der klassichen und hellenistischen Kunst* (Munich 1981)
SB IV	K. Schefold and F. Jung, *Die Urkönige, Perseus, Bellerophon, Herakles und Theseus in der klassichen und hellenistischen Kunst* (Munich 1988)
SB V	K. Schefold and F. Jung, *Die Sagen von den Argonauten, von Theben und Troia in der klassichen und hellenistischen Kunst* (Munich 1989)
VL	F. Brommer, *Vasenlisten zur griechischen Heldensage* (Marburg 1973)

The catalogue is divided into six sections, as follows:

Vases:
> Painted
> Relief

Painted Clay Artifacts (other than vases)
Small Reliefs (ivories, terracottas, bronze fibulas, tripods, shield-bands, gems, etc.)
Architectural Sculpture
Free-standing Sculpture

Numbers in the bibliographic references refer to *page* numbers in the case of basic reference works (Beazley, Trendall, Amyx, Brommer, etc.), but *catalogue* numbers in Stibbe and *plate* numbers in Schefold's five *Sagenbilder* volumes (save where figures are specified). *LIMC* numbers refer to catalogue entries in the *Lexicon* articles cited; I follow that work's usage in appending an asterisk to those entries for which an illustration is included in the respective plate volume, and a bullet (°) for those in which a drawing accompanies the entry in the text volume. For references to the many illustrations of Attic Black- and Red-Figure vases published since Beazley's catalogue volumes the reader should consult the second edition of the *Beazley Addenda* (ed. T. H. Carpenter et al., Oxford 1989), using the page numbers to *ABV* and *ARV²* given below.

Vases

PAINTED

Adolphseck: Schloss Fasanerie

12	BF lekythos		Herakles and Geras
	ABV 491	*Para* 223	*LIMC:* Geras 3*

Agora Museum (Athens)

P334	BF dinos frr		"Silenos"
	ABV 23		Kalydonian Boar Hunt
			LIMC: Atalante 1*
P4885	LG oinochoe		Herakles and Moliones
		FS 7a	*LIMC:* Aktorione 3*
P10201a	LG fr		Death of Astyanax?
			LIMC: Astyanax I 26*°
P26228	RF cup fr		Ixion and wheel
	ARV² 110	SB III 203	*LIMC:* Ixion 8
P29612	RF bell krater fr		Danae on Seriphos
			LIMC: Danae 57

Aigina: Museum

566	PA oinochoe		Odysseus and ram
		FS 37	
no #	PC skyphos		Bellerophontes and Pegasos
		FS 22	

Aigina: Excavations

no #	BF tripod pyxis		Herakles and Kyknos

Amiens: Musée de Picardie

3057.225.47a	BF hydria		Herakles and Kerberos	
	ABV 384		LIMC: Hades 143	

Andreadis Collection (Thessalonike)

no #	MC column krater		Phineus
			LIMC: Iason 7*
			LIMC: Boreadai 4*

Arezzo: Museo Civico

1460	RF neck-amphora		Pelops and Hippodameia
	ARV² 1157	SB IV 9	LIMC: Hippoda-meia I 23*

Argos

no #	Argive krater		Odysseus and Polyphemos
		FS fig. 15	

Athens: National Museum

277	MC bottle		Ambush of Troilos
	CorVP 201		LIMC: Achilleus 251
354	Melian amphora		Hermes and Kalypso?
		FS fig. 45	LIMC: Hermes 689
397	BF lekythos		Sphinx
	ABV 505	ABL 19	
413	BF lekythos		Herakles on Olympos
	ABV 75	SB II 33–34	LIMC: Herakles 2848
	ABL 7		
488	WG lekythos		Death of Aktaion
	ABV 586	ABL 266	LIMC: Aktaion 3*
489	BF lekythos		Death of Aktaion
	ABV 500		LIMC: Aktaion 2*
513	BF lekythos		Herakles and Helios
	ABV 380	ABL 196	LIMC: Helios 95*
			LIMC: Herakles 2545°
664	MC amphoriskos		Return of Hephaistos?
			LIMC: Hephaistos 129*
1002	BF neck-amphora		Herakles and Nessos
	ABV 4		Gorgons
		FS 59	LIMC: Gorgo 313*
1061	BF lekythos		Labyrinth
	ABL 268		
1125	BF lekythos		Death of Amphiaraos
	ABL 266		LIMC: Amphiaraos 37*
1130	WG lekythos		Seirenes
	ABV 476	ABL 217	
1132	WG lekythos		Herakles and Atlas
	ABV 522	ABL 256	LIMC: Atlas 7*
1291	RF pyxis lid		Perseus and the Graiai
	VL 287	SB IV 119	LIMC: Graiai 2*

1607	RF lekythos *ARV*² 1172		Sphinx and youth
1926	WG lekythos *ARV*² 846		Charon *LIMC*: Charon I 5*
3961 (911)	Melian amphora	*FS* 10	Achilleus and Memnon? *LIMC*: Achilleus 846
9683	RF pelike *ARV*² 554	SB IV 214	Herakles and Bousiris *LIMC*: Aithiopes 13*
12821	BF lekythos *ABV* 505	*ABL* 198	Snakes and man
13910	Lakonian cup *LV* #103		Zeus and Kronos?
15113	RF neck-amphora *ARV*² 1411		Atalanta and Meleagros
15375	RF aryballos	SB III 258	Eros with whip *LIMC*: Eros 365a
15499	BF dinos frr *ABV* 39		Games for Patroklos *LIMC*: Achilleus 491*
16346	RF pelike *ARV*² 1113		Hades with cornucopia *LIMC*: Hades 25
16384	BF skyphos krater *ABV* 6	*FS* 57a	Herakles and Prometheus
18063	RF stamnos *ARV*² 1028	SB II 227	Helen and Phoibe *LIMC*: Helene 35*
19447	Lakonian olpe?		Leda and egg *LIMC*: Helene 4*
19765	BF lekythos		Hekate in Hades? *LIMC*: Erinys 7*
Akr 212	RF cup *VL* 384		Sack of Troy *LIMC*: Astyanax I 17*
Akr 288	RF cup frr *ARV*² 370		Herakles and Eurytos *LIMC*: Eurytos I 5*
Akr 587	BF dinos frr *ABV* 39		Wedding of Peleus and Thetis *LIMC*: Chariklo I 1*
Akr 590	BF dinos fr	*FS* 65	Games for Pelias *LIMC*: Alkestis 52* *LIMC*: Amphiaraos 2*
Akr 601	BF hydria frr *ABV* 80		Ikaros *LIMC*: Daidalos 14°
Akr 603	BF skyphos frr *VL* 488		Tydeus and Ismene *LIMC*: Ismene I 4*
Akr 607	BF dinos *ABV* 107	SB II 60–64	Gigantomachy *LIMC*: Gigantes 105
Akr 735	RF calyx krater *ARV*² 259	SB IV 46–47	Brothers of Aigeus Theseus and Minotaur *LIMC*: Ariadne 30
Akr 1280	BF skyphos *ABL* 249		Theseus and Skiron

Akr 1632	BF cup frr		Gigantomachy
	VL 65		*LIMC:* Ge 4*
Akr 2112	BF lekanis lid frr		Departure of Amphiaraos
	ABV 58		*LIMC:* Amphiaraos 8*
Akr 2134	BF kantharos frr		Gigantomachy
	ABV 347		*LIMC:* Gigantes 106*
no #	stand (Heraion)		Nessos and Deianeira
no #	PC pyxis lid fr		Herakles and Kentauroi
	VL 88		
no #	PC lekythos		Death of Achilleus?
		FS fig. 14	*LIMC:* Achilleus 848°
no #	RF cup		Boy on swan
	*ARV*² 17	SB II 53	*LIMC:* Hyakinthos 5

Bari: Museo Archeologico

1016	Apulian oinochoe		Kassiepeia?
	RVAp 874		*LIMC:* Andromeda I 16*
1535	Lucanian hydria		Makareus and Kanake
	LCS 45	SB IV 34	*LIMC:* Aiolos 1*

Basel: Antikenmuseum and Ludwig Collection

BS 403	RF calyx krater		Perseus and Andromeda
	Para 456	SB IV 132	*LIMC:* Andromeda I 6*
BS 404	RF !ekythos		Athena and Kekropid
	VL 258		*LIMC:* Aglauros 19*
BS 411	BF hydria		Sphinx on column
BS 425	MC aryballos		Odysseus and Seiren?
	CorVP 180	SB II 360	Herakles and Hydra
			LIMC: Herakles 1992*
BS 428	BF cup		Herakles and Kyknos
	ABV 60		Neleidai and cattle?
BS 481	RF hydria		Head of Orpheus
		SB IV 98	
BS 498	BF hydria		Herakles and Kyknos
	Para 119		Neoptolemos and Eurypylos
		SB II 339–40	*LIMC:* Eurypylos I 1*
Kä 404	RF bell krater		Aloadai and Artemis
	*ARV*² 1067	SB III 193	*LIMC:* Aloadai 1*
Kä 420	BF amphora		Silenoi making wine
	Para 65		*LIMC:* Dionysos 408*
Slg Ludwig	Lucanian bell krater		Laokoon
	LCS	SB III 202	*LIMC:* Apollon 273*
	Supp 154		
Loan (PrColl)	MC cup		Death of Aias
	CorVP 562	SB II 337	*LIMC:* Aias I 122*
Loan (PrColl)	RF lekythos		Death of Aias
			LIMC: Aias I 105*
Loan (PrColl)	BF hydria		Helen and Phoibe
		SB II 227	*LIMC:* Dioskouroi 180*

Berkeley: University of California

| 8.3316 | RF hydria | | Semele in child-birth |
| | *ARV²* 1343 | SB III 19 | *LIMC:* Dionysos 664* |

Berlin: Charlottenburg (Antikenmuseum)

A9	PA neck-amphora		Achilleus and Cheiron
		FS 29a	*LIMC:* Achilleus 21*
WS 4	Lakonian cup		Capture of Silenos
	LV #292		
F1704	BF amphora		Birth of Athena
	ABV 96	SB II 1	*LIMC:* Athena 346*
F1705	BF neck-amphora		Kalydonian Boar Hunt
	ABV 96		
F1722	BF column krater		Herakles and Prometheus
	ABV 104		
F1753	BF cup		Birth of Pegasos
	ABV 56		*LIMC:* Gorgo 319
F1775	BF cup		Eris
		SB II 246	*LIMC:* Eris 1*
F1837	BF amphora		Zeus and Pandora?
	ABV 509	SB II 21	*LIMC:* Artemis 1264*
			Peleus and Atalanta
			LIMC: Atalante 71*
F1862	BF neck-amphora		Aineias and Anchises
	Para 141		
F2163	RF amphora		Iris
	ARV² 409		*LIMC:* Iris I 27*
F2164	RF amphora		Herakles and Poseidon
	ARV² 183	SB III 150–51	*LIMC:* Herakles 3370*
F2278	RF cup		Herakles on Olympos
	ARV² 21	SB II 42–43	*LIMC:* Hestia 8*
			Achilleus and Patroklos
		SB II 277	*LIMC:* Achilleus 468*
F2279	RF cup		Peleus and Thetis
	ARV² 115	SB II 257	
F2288	RF cup		Theseus and Skiron
	ARV² 438		
F2291	RF cup		Paris and Helen
	ARV² 459		*LIMC:* Alexandros 63*
F2293	RF cup		Selene
	ARV² 370	SB III 121	*LIMC:* Astra 39*
			Gigantomachy
		SB III 122	*LIMC:* Gigantes 303*
F2403	RF volute krater		Wedding of Peirithoos
	ARV² 599		
F2455	WG lekythos		Hermes and Charon
	ARV² 846		*LIMC:* Charon I 7a*

Catalogue of Artistic
Representations

F2524	RF cup		Nyx?
	*ARV*² 931		*LIMC*: Astra 5*
F2537	RF cup		Gaia and Erichthonios
	*ARV*² 1268–69	SB III 65–66	*LIMC*: Ge 17
			Eos and Kephalos
		SB III 457	*LIMC*: Eos 274*
F3291	Apulian hydria		Omphale in love?
	RVAp 426		
F3296	Sicilian calyx krater		Amphion, Zethos, Lykos
	LCS 203		*LIMC*: Antiope I 6*
F3988	BF tripod kothon		Death of Priam
			LIMC: Astyanax I 10*
F4220	RF cup		Thetis and Cheiron
	*ARV*² 61		*LIMC*: Achilleus 39*
VI 3151	BF cup		Silenos captured
	ABV 79		
VI 3238	Campanian hydria		Perseus and Andromeda
	LCS 227		*LIMC*: Andromeda I 19*
VI 3283	BF skyphos		Seirenes
	Para 259		
VI 3317	RF pelike		Herakles and Geras?
		SB IV 212	*LIMC*: Geras 7
Inv 1966.1	BF neck-amphora		Three Silenoi
	ABV 285		
Inv 1966.18	RF hydria		Death of Pentheus
Inv 1968.12	Apulian bell krater		Laios and Chrysippos
	RVAp 501		*LIMC*: Chrysippos I 2*
Inv 1970.5	RF amphora		Theseus and Minotaur
			LIMC: Ariadne 29
Inv 1970.9	RF skyphos		Tydeus and Ismene?

Berlin: Pergamon-Museum

F336	PC aryballos		Herakles and Pholos
	CorVP 37	FS 24a	
F1147	MC krater		Achilleus and Memnon
	CorVP 234	FS 76c	*LIMC*: Achilleus 808*
F1652	LC amphora		Perseus and Andromeda
	CorVP 268	FS 44b	*LIMC*: Andromeda I 1*
F1685	BF amphora		Menelaos and Helen
	ABV 109		*LIMC*: Astyanax I 9*
F1697	BF amphora		Silenoi
	ABV 297		
F1732	BF oinochoe		Herakles and Kyknos
	ABV 110	SB II 176	*LIMC*: Ares 42*
F1895	BF hydria		Hermes and Iris
	ABV 268		*LIMC*: Iris I 127*
F2179	RF hydria		Dionysos and Ariadne
	*ARV*² 252	SB III 379	*LIMC*: Ariadne 93

F2184	RF stamnos		Death of Aigisthos
	ARV² 257		*LIMC*: Aigisthos 11*
F2264	RF cup		Iris
	ARV² 60	SB II 307	*LIMC*: Antilochos I 4*
F2588	RF skyphos		Odysseus and suitors
	ARV² 1300		*LIMC*: Amphialos II 1*
F2591	RF skyphos		Iris and Silenoi
	ARV² 888		*LIMC*: Iris I 113*
F3023	Campanian amphora		Ixion and wheel
	LCS 338	SB III 207	*LIMC*: Ixion 15*
VI 3261	BF lekythos		Herakles and Ophis
	ABV 472	*ABL* 198	*LIMC*: Herakles 2692*
VI 3289	RF cup		Phrixos and ram
	VL 502		
VI 3319	PC aryballos		Death of Aias
	VL 380		*LIMC*: Aias I 118
VI 3375	RF lekythos		Gigantomachy
		SB III 135	*LIMC*: Gigantes 389*
VI 3414	Boiotian skyphos		Omphale?
	VL 174		
VI 4841	BF amphora		Alkmaion and Eriphyle
	ABV 97	*FS* fig. 30	*LIMC*: Alkmaion 3*
Inv 30035	RF lekythos		Peirithoos in Hades
	ARV² 532	SB IV 224–25	*LIMC*: Herakles 3515
Inv 31094	RF bell krater		Herakles carries Hades?
	ARV² 1446		*LIMC*: Hades 71
Berlin: Lost or Unknown			
A32	PA krater		Death of Aigisthos?
	FS 36a		*LIMC*: Aigisthos 36*
F1655	LC krater		Departure of Amphiaraos
	CorVP 263		*LIMC*: Ainippe II 1*
			LIMC: Baton I 3*
			Funeral Games of Pelias
		SB II 233	*LIMC*: Amphiaraos 3*
			LIMC: Argeios II 1*
F1682	BF bowl		Perseus and Athena
	ABV 5	*FS* 44a	*LIMC*: Athena 6*
			Harpuiai
		FS 64a	*LIMC*: Harpyiai 1*
F1718	BF amphora		Aias and dead Achilleus
	ABV 144	SB II 334	*LIMC*: Achilleus 871
F1801	BF cup		Herakles and Hydra
	ABV 159		*LIMC*: Herakles 2029
F1904	BF hydria		Dionysos and Semele
	ABV 364		
F2000	BF lekythos		Aias and the arms
	ABL 258		*LIMC*: Aias I 75°

F2032	WG alabastron		Zeus and Ganymedes
	ABL 237	SB III 289–90	*LIMC:* Ganymedes 10
F2165	RF amphora		Boreas and Oreithuia
	*ARV*² 496		*LIMC:* Boreas 62a
F2186	RF stamnos		Boreas and Oreithuia
	*ARV*² 208		*LIMC:* Boreas 19
F2273	RF cup		Hephaistos in chariot
	*ARV*² 174	SB II 30	*LIMC:* Hephaistos 43*
F2634	RF hydria		Kadmos and snake
	*ARV*² 1187		*LIMC:* Kadmos I 19*
VI 3275	RF calyx krater		Persephone and Silenoi
	*ARV*² 1276		

Blatter Collection (Bollingen)

no #	BF dinos frr		Kalydonian Boar Hunt
			LIMC: Atalante 5*

Bochum: Ruhr Universität

S1060	RF pelike		Death of Achilleus
			LIMC: Alexandros 92*

Bologna: Museo Civico

230	RF column krater		Death of Aigisthos
	*ARV*² 504		*LIMC:* Aigisthos 12*
236	RF column krater		Hermes and Persephone?
	*ARV*² 532	SB III 435	or daughter of Dryops?
			LIMC: Hermes 886*
288 bis	RF calyx krater		Aphrodite and Phaon
	*ARV*² 1056	SB III 400–402	*LIMC:* Aphrodite 1549*
325	RF bell krater		Perseus and Polydektes
	*ARV*² 1069	SB IV 137	*LIMC:* Gorgo 337*
PU 195	BF neck-amphora		Herakles and Pholos
	ABV 288	SB II 159	

Bonn: Akademisches Kunstmuseum

39	BF neck-amphora		Death of Priam
	VL 394		*LIMC:* Astyanax I 13*
78	RF bell krater		Leda and the egg
	*ARV*² 1171	SB III 342	*LIMC:* Dioskouroi 185*
860	EC alabastron		Iason and serpent?
			LIMC: Iason 30*
2661	RF pelike		Erysichthon
	Para 448	SB III 251	*LIMC:* Erysichthon I 1*
2674	Ionian hydria		Wedding of Peirithoos
		SB II 206	*LIMC:* Kaineus 70*

Boston: Museum of Fine Arts

00.346	RF bell krater		Aktaion
	*ARV*² 1045	SB III 187	*LIMC:* Aktaion 81*
00.348	Apulian bell krater		Athena and Marsyas
	RVAp 267		*LIMC:* Athena 620*

00.349	Apulian stamnos		Bellerophontes and Proitos
	RVAp 24		
01.8027	BF neck-amphora		Herakles and Apollo
	ABV 152	SB II 189	*LIMC*: Hermes 538*
01.8100	LC aryballos		Seirenes
		FS fig. 46	
03.783	BF olpe		Herakles in Helios' cup
	ABV 378	*ABL* 197	*LIMC*: Herakles 2550*
03.792	RF hydria		Danae, Perseus, and chest
	ARV² 1076		*LIMC*: Akrisios 7*
03.804	Apulian volute krater		Death of Thersites
	RVAp 472		*LIMC*: Achilleus 794*
04.18	RF pyxis lid		Odysseus and Nausikaa
	ARV² 1177		
6.67	PA krater		Sacrifice of Iphigeneia?
	VL 413		*LIMC*: Iphigeneia 2°
08.30a	RF cup		Iris and Silenoi
	ARV² 135		*LIMC*: Iris I 110
08.417	RF hydria		Argos, Io, Hermes
	Para 391	SB III 135	*LIMC*: Hera 486*
10.177	RF stamnos		Hermes with scales
	ARV² 518		*LIMC*: Achilleus 800*
10.185	RF krater		Pan
	ARV² 550	SB III 436	*LIMC*: Daphnis 1*
10.221	RF psykter		Death of Pentheus
	ARV² 16	SB II 92	*LIMC*: Galene II 1*
13.186	RF cup		Paris and Helen
	ARV² 458		*LIMC*: Helene 166*
13.200	RF hydria		Danae, Perseus, and chest
	ARV² 247		*LIMC*: Akrisios 2*
13.206	Apulian fragment		Kallisto
	RVAp 166	SB III 322	*LIMC*: Kallisto 5*
34.79	RF pelike		Odysseus and Elpenor
	ARV² 1045		*LIMC*: Elpenor 6
63.420	LC krater		Herakles and Hesione
	CorVP 507		
63.952	BF amphora		Silenoi making wine
	Para 62	SB II 230	
63.1246	RF calyx krater		Death of Agamemnon
	Para 373		*LIMC*: Agamemnon 89*
			Death of Aigisthos
			LIMC: Aigisthos 10*
91.227a and			
91.226b	RF stamnos		Death of Aigisthos
	ARV² 208		*LIMC*: Aigisthos 13*
93.99	WG lekythos		Helios
	ABL 206		*LIMC*: Helios 2*
93.100			Pholos

95.10	PC aryballos		Bellerophontes and Pegasos
95.12	PC aryballos		Zeus and Typhoeus?
		FS fig. 4	
95.31	RF cup		Zephyros and Hyakinthos
	ARV² 443		LIMC: Hyakinthos 45*
95.39	RF lekythos		Birth of Dionysos
	ARV² 533	SB III 25	LIMC: Dionysos 666*
95.48	RF squat lekythos		Theseus and Hippolyte
	ARV² 1248		LIMC: Amazones 240*
97.374	lekythos (forgery)		Oidipous and Sphinx
98.916	BF neck-amphora		Telamon and Amazones
	ABV 98		LIMC: Amazones 9*
99.518	BF cup	SB II 354	Odysseus and Polyphemos
	ABV 198	SB II 359	Odysseus and Kirke
99.519	BF cup		Odysseus and Kirke
	ABV 69		Herakles and Acheloos
			LIMC: Acheloos 215*
99.539	RF cup		Peirithoos
	ARV² 1142		Leda and the egg
1960.302	LC aryballos		Telephos and Aleadai?
1970.237	Apulian bell krater		Perseus and Medousa
	RVAp 48		
1977.713	RF lekythos		Death of Aigisthos
			LIMC: Aigisthos 6a°
1979.40	RF pelike		Phineus and the Boreadai
			LIMC: Boreadai 17
1987.53	Apulian calyx krater		Birth of Aigisthos
Boulogne			
421	BF amphora		Herakles and the Hesperides
			LIMC: Herakles 2700*
558	BF amphora		Death of Aias
	ABV 145	SB II 338	LIMC: Aias I 104*
Breslau (now Wroclaw)			
lost	EC aryballos		Herakles and Hydra
	CorVP 557		LIMC: Herakles 1991°
Brommer Collection (Mainz)			
Mainz	BF lekythos		Herakles and Ophis
	ABV 499	SB II 155	LIMC: Herakles 2691
Brussels: Musées Royaux			
A4	LC olpe		Achilleus and Thetis
	CorVP 581	FS 73b	
A130	BF neck-amphora		Triptolemos
	ABV 308		
A1374	MC cup		Herakles and Acheloos
	CorVP 203	FS 58b	LIMC: Acheloos 246*
			Theseus and Minotaur

Cabinet des Médailles (Paris)

174	BF amphora		Theseus and Bull?
	ABV 315		*LIMC:* Aigeus 2*
190	Lakonian cup		Odysseus and Polyphemos
	LV #289	SB II 353	
202	Chalkidian neck-amphora		Herakles and Geryoneus
	ChV 8	SB II 146	*LIMC:* Herakles 2464*
219	BF neck-amphora		Birth of Dionysos?
	ABV 509	SB III 20	
222	BF neck-amphora		Dionysos and Mainades?
	ABV 152		*LIMC:* Dionysos 294*
223	BF neck-amphora		Herakles and Geryoneus
	ABV 308		*LIMC:* Herakles 2467
255	BF hydria		Herakles and Nereus
	ABV 361	SB II 168	
278	BF lekythos		Sphinx
298	BF lekythos		Persephone and Silenoi
	ABV 522	SB III 82	
	ABL 258		
306	WG lekythos		Apollo and Python
	ABV 572		*LIMC:* Apollon 993*
372	RF amphora		Euphorbos and Oidipous
	*ARV*² 987		
418	RF calyx krater		Theseus and Poseidon
	*ARV*² 260		
423	RF bell krater		Eos and Kephalos
	*ARV*² 1055		*LIMC:* Kallimachos 1*
442	Lucanian hydria		Amykos
	LCS 36		*LIMC:* Amykos 11*
536, 647 et al.	RF cup		Theseus' exploits
	*ARV*² 191	SB IV 294–96	*LIMC:* Athena 537*
542	RF cup		Hera and Prometheus
	*ARV*² 438	SB III 111	*LIMC:* Hera 347*
822	RF cup		Herakles carries Hades?
	*ARV*² 1521		*LIMC:* Herakles 3497*
846	RF skyphos		Eos and Tithonos
	*ARV*² 1050		*LIMC:* Eos 182*

Cahn Collection (Basel)

?	BF krater		Odysseus and ram
191	RF column krater frr		Capture of Silenos
		SB III 228	
541	RF skyphos		Ixion and wheel
		SB III 206	*LIMC:* Bia 1*
912	BF oinochoe frr		Abduction of Persephone?
		SB III 370	
921	BF amphora		Departure of Amphiaraos
			LIMC: Amphiaraos 10*

Catalogue of Artistic
Representations

1173	LC krater fr *CorVP* 582		Herakles and Nereus
Cambridge: Fitzwilliam Museum			
G100	BF lekythos *ABL* 120		Herakles and Helios *LIMC:* Helios 96*
no #	Pontic amphora		Herakles and Alkyoneus? *LIMC:* Alkyoneus 34*
Cerveteri: Museo Nazionale Cerite			
no #	BF neck-amphora		Herakles and Hind *LIMC:* Herakles 2181*
Chicago: University			
89.16	RF column krater *ARV²* 585	SB III 211	Salmoneus *LIMC:* Iris I 155*
Chiusi: Museo Civico			
1794	BF amphora *ABV* 330		Departure of Amphiaraos *LIMC:* Amphiaraos 13*
1831	RF skyphos *ARV²* 1300		Odysseus and Eurykleia *LIMC:* Antiphata I*
Cincinnati: Art Museum			
1959.1	BF amphora *Para* 134		Herakles and Bousiris *LIMC:* Bousiris 10*
1979.1	RF cup *ARV²* 416	SB IV 93–95	Death of Orpheus
Clairmont Collection (Princeton)			
no #	RF pyxis	SB IV 114–17	Diktys and Danae *LIMC:* Danae 57
Copenhagen: National Museum			
3293	RF stamnos *ARV²* 251		Herakles and Syleus
13567	Caeretan hydria *CH* 29		Atalanta and Boar *LIMC:* Atalante 12
14066	Pontic amphora *VL* 357		Death of Achilleus *LIMC:* Alexandros 97*
VIII 496	Pontic calyx krater *ChV* 15	SB II 240	Adrastos and suitors *LIMC:* Amphithea 1°
Cracow: Czartoryski Museum			
1225	RF hydria *ARV²* 1121	SB IV 247	Lykourgos
Cremona			
no #	Apulian calyx krater *RVAp* 263		Kallisto *LIMC:* Arkas 2*
Cyrene			
no #	Lakonian cup fr *LV* #221	SB II 244	Amphiaraos and Tydeus? *LIMC:* Amphiaraos 79

Delos
    B7263   RF krater fr   Perseus and the Graiai
                              *ARV*² 1019   SB IV 118   *LIMC*: Graiai 3*

Denman Collection (San Antonio)
    no #   RF column krater   Athena and Kekropides
                                                                   LIMC: Erechtheus 29*

Dresden: Albertinum
    350   RF calyx krater   Hermes and Persephone
                              *ARV*² 1056   *LIMC*: Hermes 639

Eleusis
    1231   BF sieve   Silenos captured
                                                                   LIMC: Hermes 887
    1804   RF skyphos   Hades and Persephone
                                             SB III 372   *LIMC*: Hades 110*
    no #   PA amphora   Odysseus and Polyphemos
                                                                  Gorgons
                                           FS 16   *LIMC*: Gorgo 312*

Erskine Collection (London)
    no #   Lakonian cup   Kerberos
                              LV #217   *LIMC*: Herakles 2605

Ferrara: Museo Nazionale di Spina
    818   RF cup   Danae, Perseus, and chest
                              *ARV*² 231   *LIMC*: Akrisios 4*
    2482   RF cup   Death of Kassandra
                              *ARV*² 1280   *LIMC*: Aias II 75
    2737   RF volute krater   Zeus and child Dionysos
                              *ARV*² 589   SB III 23   *LIMC*: Dionysos 702*
    2865   RF volute krater   Amykos
                              *ARV*² 1039   *LIMC*: Amykos 14*
    2890   RF calyx krater   Theseus and Antiope
                              *ARV*² 991   *LIMC*: Amazones 232*
    2893   RF volute krater   Atalanta and Hippomenes
    3031   RF volute krater   Persephone and Silenoi
                              *ARV*² 612   SB III 85–86
                                                                  Seven against Thebes
                                                                  LIMC: Amphiaraos 38*
    9351   RF cup   Zeus and Ganymedes
                              *ARV*² 880   SB III 297   *LIMC*: Ganymedes 44*
    44701   RF volute krater   Embassy to Skyros
                              *ARV*² 536

Florence: Museo Archeologico
    3790   BF hydria   Dionysos and Thyone
                              ABV 260   *LIMC*: Apollon 844*
    4209   BF volute krater   Wedding of Peleus and
                                                                  Thetis

	ABV 76		Ambush of Troilos
			LIMC: Achilleus 292*
			Return of Hephaistos
			LIMC: Hera 309*
			Wedding of Peirithoos
			LIMC: Kaineus 67*
			Games for Patroklos
			Theseus on Delos
			LIMC: Ariadne 48*
			Kalydonian Boar Hunt
			LIMC: Atalante 2*
4210	Chalkidian neck-amphora		Achilleus and Memnon
	ChV 7		*LIMC:* Achilleus 809
4218	RF skyphos		Iris and Kentauroi
	ARV² 191	SB III 157	*LIMC:* Iris I 167*
70993	BF amphora		Death of Troilos
	ABV 95		*LIMC:* Achilleus 360*
70995	BF neck-amphora		Judgment of Paris
	ABV 110		
76359	BF amphora		Herakles and Prometheus
	ABV 97		*LIMC:* Demeter 471*
81268 (3997)	RF column krater		Wedding of Peirithoos
	ARV² 541		
81600	RF cup		Hephaistos in chariot
			LIMC: Hephaistos 44*
81948	RF hydria		Aphrodite and Adonis
	ARV² 1312	SB III 399	*LIMC:* Adonis 10*
91456	RF cup		Theseus' exploits
	ARV² 108	SB III 255	
1 B 32	RF cup		Herakles and Mares
	ARV² 58		*LIMC:* Herakles 2415
4 B 19 et al.	RF cup frr		Death of Aigisthos
	ARV² 108		*LIMC:* Aigisthos 41
Fogg Museum (Cambridge, Mass.)			
1960.339	RF column krater		Theseus and Amphitrite
(60.339)	*ARV²* 274		*LIMC:* Amphitrite 78*
Foggia			
132723	Apulian amphora		Hera in throne
	RVAp 925		*LIMC:* Hephaistos 126*
Frankfurt: Liebieghaus			
560	BF eschara		Charon
			LIMC: Charon I 1*
ST V 7	RF cup		Kekropides
	ARV² 386	SB III 57–58	*LIMC:* Aglauros 15*

Gela: Museo Archeologico
125/B   WG lekythos   Herakles and the apples
               ABV 476   *ABL* 218   *LIMC*: Herakles 2716

Getty Museum (Malibu)
72.AE.128   Apulian oinochoe   Kallisto
               RVAp 167   SB III 319–21   *LIMC*: Kallisto 6*
77.AE.11   RF volute krater   Herakles and Ophis
               *ARV*² 186   *LIMC*: Herakles 1702*
77.AE.14   Apulian volute krater   Laios and Chrysippos
               RVAp 866   *LIMC*: Chrysippos I 4b*
77.AE.44.1   RF calyx krater fr   Athena and Philoktetes
                                                        LIMC: Herakles 2915*
77.AE.45   BF amphora   Omphale
81.AE.211   BF dinos   Gigantomachy
                                                        LIMC: Gigantes 171°
83.AE.346   Caeretan hydria   Herakles and Hydra
               CH 41   *LIMC*: Herakles 2016*
84.AE.569   RF cup   Eos and Kephalos
                                                        LIMC: Eos 48
85.AE.316   RF hydria   Phineus
                                                        LIMC: Harpyiai 9*
85.AE.377   RF cup   Sphinx and youth
86.AE.18.1–9   RF cup   Plouton
et al.
86.AE.286   RF calyx krater   Death of Aigisthos
88.AE.66   RF cup   Aias and the arms
(formerly NY   *Para* 367   *LIMC*: Aias I 72*, 83*
69.11.35 L)   Death of Aias
                                                        LIMC: Aias I 140*

Giessen: University
46   RF cup   Atalanta and Silenoi
               *ARV*² 768   *LIMC*: Atalante 96*

Göttingen: University
J14   BF neck-amphora   Triptolemos
               ABV 309   SB II 28
R23   BF oinochoe   Kadmos and Harmonia?
               Para 185   *LIMC*: Harmonia 10*

"H.A." Collection (Milan)
239   Apulian volute krater   Orestes and Neoptolemos
               RVAp 193   *LIMC*: Apollon 890*

Halle: University
214   Apulian amphora frr   Andromeda
               RVAp 504   *LIMC*: Andromeda I 12

Catalogue of Artistic
Representations

Hamburg: Museum für Kunst und Gewerbe
1960.1	BF amphora		Niobidai
	Para 40	*FS* 53	*LIMC:* Apollon 1077*
			LIMC: Artemis 1346*
1966.34	RF amphora		Argos
	Para 347	SB III 173	*LIMC:* Io I 4*

Hirschmann Collection (Zurich)
no #	Caeretan hydria		Perseus and *kêtos?*
	CH 45		

Hope Collection (Deepdene)
lost	BF cup		Herakles and Kerberos
	ABV 184		*LIMC:* Herakles 2606
lost	Chalkidian amph		Death of Achilleus
	ChV 9	SB II 297	*LIMC:* Achilleus 850*

Hunt Collection (Dallas)
no #	RF pelike		Theseus and Minotaur

Iraklion
no #	plate		Peleus and Thetis?
		FS figs. 11, 12	

Ithaka
no #	LG handle		Odysseus and Kirke?
		FS fig. 3	

Jena: University
137	MC cup		Herakles and Hydra
	CorVP 204		*LIMC:* Herakles 1995*

Jucker Collection (Bern)
no #	WG lekythos		Akrisios at tomb
		SB III 337	*LIMC:* Akrisios 10*

Kanellopoulos Collection (Athens)
1319	PC aryballos		Ambush of Troilos
	VL 364		*LIMC:* Chimaira 115°

Karlsruhe: Badisches Landesmuseum
167	BF krater		Odysseus and ram
	ABV 507	SB II 358	
B4	Apulian krater		Danaides?
	RVAp 431		*LIMC:* Danaides 8*
B2591	BF amphora		Herakles and Prometheus
	ABV 97		

Kassel: Staatliche Kunstsammlungen
S 49b (lost)	Lakonian cup frr		Sisyphos?
	LV #210		

Kavalla
A1086	Melian amphora		Peleus and Thetis

Kerameikos Museum (Athens)			
154	BF krater		Chimaira
	ABV 3		
658	BF amphora		Kentauroi
	ABV 3		
Kiel: University			
B555	RF lekythos		Sphinx
Kimbell Museum (Fort Worth)			
84.16	RF lekythos		Eros with bow
			LIMC: Eros 332*
Korinth			
C 72–149	LC krater		Achilleus and Memnon
	CorVP 582		*LIMC:* Achilleus 811
Kyrou Collection (Athens)			
no #	RF hydria		Hermes and child Dionysos
		SB III 31	*LIMC:* Ino 10*
Lecce: Museo Provinciale			
570	RF pelike		Polyneikes and Eriphyle
	ARV² 629		*LIMC:* Eriphyle I 2*
Leningrad/St. Petersburg: Hermitage Museum			
637 (St 1733)	RF calyx krater		Danae and golden rain
	ARV² 360		*LIMC:* Danae 1*
			Danae, Perseus, and chest
			LIMC: Danae 48*
640 (St 1641)	RF stamnos		Herakles on Olympos
	ARV² 639		*LIMC:* Herakles 2875
642 (St 1357)	RF stamnos		Danae, Perseus, and chest
	ARV² 228		*LIMC:* Danae 41*
649 (St 830)	RF cup		Theseus and Aithra
	ARV² 460		*LIMC:* Aithra I 25*
			Odysseus and Diomedes
			LIMC: Akamas 6*
			LIMC: Athena 104*
804 (St 1711)	RF stamnos		Theseus and Minotaur
	ARV² 484	SB IV 305	
988 (St 355)	Lucanian volute krater		Release of Hera
	LCS 161		*LIMC:* Hera 318*
St 426	Apulian volute krater		Danaides?
	RVAp 864		*LIMC:* Danaides 13*
St 427	Lucanian krater (forgery)		Bellerophontes and Stheneboia
St 1807	RF calyx krater		Eris and Themis
	ARV² 1185		*LIMC:* Eris 7*
St 1275	RF calyx krater		Achilleus and Telephos
	ARV² 23		*LIMC:* Diomedes I 7*

Catalogue of Artistic
Representations

Inv 9270	BF cup		Herakles and Mares
	ABV 294	SB II 130	LIMC: Herakles 2414*
London: British Museum			
A487	PC pyxis		Herakles and Geryoneus
	VL 63		LIMC: Geryoneus 11*
B57	Pontic amphora		Herakles and Hera?
			LIMC: Hercle 362*
B103.19	BF fragment		Seirenes?
B147	BF amphora		Birth of Athena
	ABV 135	SB II 6	LIMC: Athena 349*
B155	Chalkidian amphora		Perseus and Nymphai
	ChV 10	SB II 93	Herakles and Geryoneus
			LIMC: Herakles 2479*
B156	BF amphora		Herakles and Kyknos
	VL 103		
B163	BF belly amphora		Herakles and Birds
	ABV 134	SB II 126	LIMC: Herakles 2241*
B164	BF amphora		Argos, Io, Hermes
	ABV 148	SB II 20	LIMC: Hera 485*
B168	BF amphora		Dionysos and Ariadne?
	ABV 142		LIMC: Ariadne 156*
B197	BF amphora		Herakles and Kyknos
	ABV 296		LIMC: Ares 36*
B210	BF neck-amphora		Dionysos and Oinopion
	ABV 144	SB II 13	LIMC: Dionysos 785*
			Achilleus and Penthesileia
		SB II 320	LIMC: Achilleus 723*
B212	BF neck-amphora		Herakles and Kyknos
	ABV 297		
B213	BF neck-amphora		Herakles and Boar
	ABV 143		LIMC: Herakles 2115*
B215	BF neck-amphora		Peleus and Thetis
	ABV 286	SB II 255	
B221	BF neck-amphora		Medeia and ram
	ABV 321		
B226	BF neck-amphora		Herakles and Pholos
	ABV 273	SB II 158	LIMC: Hermes 545a*
B231	BF neck-amphora		Herakles and Hind
	ABV 139		LIMC: Athena 511*
B240	BF neck-amphora		Achilleus' psychê?
	VL 347	SB II 335	LIMC: Achilleus 901*
B261	BF neck-amphora		Hades, Persephone,
	ABV 373		Sisyphos
			LIMC: Hades 148*

B313	BF hydria *ABV* 360		Herakles and Acheloos *LIMC:* Acheloos 248*
B316	BF hydria *ABV* 268		Herakles and tripod *LIMC:* Apollon 1034*
B323	BF hydria *ABV* 362		Achilleus and Penthesileia *LIMC:* Achilleus 725*
B326	BF hydria *ABV* 363		Death of Troilos *LIMC:* Achilleus 363*
B328	BF hydria *ABV* 363		Medeia and ram
B379	BF cup *ABV* 60		Herakles on Olympos *LIMC:* Herakles 2847* Aias and Kassandra *LIMC:* Aias II 16*
B380	BF cup *ABV* 55		Birth of Pegasos *LIMC:* Gorgo 320*
B424	BF cup *ABV* 168–69	SB II 35	Herakles on Olympos *LIMC:* Athena 429*
B425	BF cup *ABV* 184		Dionysos and Semele?
B492	BF oinochoe *ABV* 256	SB II 119	Herakles and Boar *LIMC:* Herakles 2103*
B533	BF lekythos *ABV* 489		Herakles and Amazones *LIMC:* Amazones 70*
B639	WG lekythos *ABL* 227		Achilleus and Memnon *LIMC:* Achilleus 798
D4	WG cup *ARV²* 869	SB II 89	Anesidora *LIMC:* Anesidora 1*
D5	WG cup	SB IV 51	Polyidos and Glaukos *LIMC:* Glaukos II 1*
E3	RF cup *ARV²* 45, 70–71	SB II 74–75	Silenoi
E12	RF cup *ARV²* 126	SB II 329	Iris with corpse of Memnon *LIMC:* Iris I 146*
E36	RF cup *ARV²* 115	SB II 218–19	Theseus' exploits Theseus and Bull
E37	RF cup *ARV²* 72	SB II 202	Theseus and Minotaur
E41	RF amphora *ARV²* 58		Theseus and Antiope *LIMC:* Antiope II 8*
E45	RF cup *ARV²* 316		Herakles and Amazones *LIMC:* 67*
E48	RF cup *ARV²* 426, 431	SB II 198	Theseus and Sinis Theseus and Skiron
E64	RF cup *ARV²* 455	SB III 278	Apollo pursuing girl *LIMC:* Apollon 1085*

E65	RF cup		Iris and Silenoi
	*ARV*² 370	SB III 156	*LIMC:* Dromis 1*
			Hera and Silenoi
		SB III 155	*LIMC:* Babakchos 1*
E69	RF cup		Aias and the arms
	*ARV*² 369		*LIMC:* Aias I 73
E82	RF cup		Hades with cornucopia
	*ARV*² 1269	SB III 304	*LIMC:* Hades 44*
E84	RF cup		Theseus and Minotaur
	*ARV*² 1269	SB IV 301	Theseus' exploits
E140	RF skyphos		Triptolemos
	*ARV*² 459	SB III 71	*LIMC:* Demeter 344*
E155	RF kantharos		Laokoon and snake?
	*ARV*² 832	SB III 205	
			Ixion and wheel
		SB III 204	*LIMC:* Ares 86*
			LIMC: Ixion 1*
E163	RF hydria		Medeia and the ram
	*ARV*² 258		*LIMC:* Iason 62*
E178	RF hydria		Judgment of Paris
	*ARV*² 503		
E182	RF hydria		Gaia and Erichthonios
	*ARV*² 580		*LIMC:* Athena 477*
E224	RF hydria		Herakles and Hesperides
	*ARV*² 1313	SB IV 19	*LIMC:* Akamas 26*
			Leukippides
		SB IV 19	*LIMC:* Dioskouroi 201*
E257	RF amphora		Judgment of Paris
	*ARV*² 604		
E290	RF neck-amphora		Herakles and Geras
	*ARV*² 653		*LIMC:* Geras 1*
E291	RF neck-amphora		Phineus
	*ARV*² 662		
E313	RF neck-amphora		Zeus and Aigina
	*ARV*² 202		*LIMC:* Aigina 3*
E372	RF pelike		Erichthonios in the chest
	*ARV*² 1218		*LIMC:* Athena 480*
E382	RF pelike		Telephos and Orestes
	*ARV*² 632		*LIMC:* Agamemnon 11*
E440	RF stamnos		Seirenes
	*ARV*² 289		
E447	RF stamnos		Capture of Silenos
	*ARV*² 1035		
E458	RF calyx krater		Recovery of Aithra
	*ARV*² 239		*LIMC:* Aithra I 66*
E467	RF calyx krater		Pandora
	*ARV*² 601		*LIMC:* Anesidora 2*

E477	RF column krater ARV² 1114–15	SB IV 84	Prokris and Kephalos LIMC: Erechtheus 55*
E539	RF oinochoe ARV² 776		Satyros and Ophis
E696	RF lekythos ARV² 1325		Oidipous and Sphinx
E699	RF lekythos ARV² 1324		Aphrodite and Adonis
E773	RF pyxis ARV² 805–6		Iphigeneia LIMC: Helene 380*
E788	RF rhyton ARV² 764	SB IV 69	Kekrops LIMC: Aglauros 28*
F107	Apulian lekythos RVAp 395	SB IV 157	Hera nursing Herakles LIMC: Herakles 3344*
F149	Paestan bell krater RVP 139		Alkmene at the altar LIMC: Amphitryon 2*
F193	Campanian neck-amphora LCS 231		Alkmene at the altar LIMC: Alkmene 6*
F269	Apulian calyx krater RVAp 339	SB III 161	Hephaistos and Ares? LIMC: Ares 73*
F271	Apulian calyx krater RVAp 415		Lykourgos
H228	Etruscan hydria		Theseus and Minotaur LIMC: Ariatha 1°
1897.7–27.2	BF amphora ABV 97		Death of Polyxena LIMC: Amphilochos 3*
1898.7–16.5	RF stamnos ARV² 1027	SB IV 230	Herakles and Eurytion LIMC: Deianeira II 3*
1899.2–19.1	LG krater	FS 5c	Paris and Helen? LIMC: Alexandros 56°
1910.2–12.1	WG lekythos ABL 227		Capture of Silenos
1926.4–17.1	BF lekythos ABL 68		Medeia
1948.10–15.1	BF column krater ABV 108		Judgment of Paris LIMC: Hermes 455b*
1969.12–15.1	PC aryballos		Troilos?
1971.11–1.1	BF dinos Para 19		Wedding of Peleus and Thetis LIMC: Chariklo I 2*

Lost Vases (other than those once assigned to museums or collections)
From:

Argos	MC kotyle CorVP 185	FS fig. 23	Herakles and Hydra LIMC: Herakles 1990* Herakles and Kerberos LIMC: Athena 11°

Catalogue of Artistic
Representations

Bomarzo	BF cup		Aktaion
		FS fig. 19	*LIMC*: Aktaion 1°
Samos	Lakonian cup		Achilleus and snake
	LV #294		*LIMC*: Achilleus 264*
Samothrace	EC alabastron		Herakles and Amazones
	CorVP 557		*LIMC*: Amazones 1°
?	Apulian(?) amphora		Leto with children and snake
			LIMC: Apollon 995°
Louvre (Paris)			
A478	BF cup		Tantalos and Pandareos
	ABV 66	SB II 84	*LIMC*: Kameiro 2*
A519	LG krater		Herakles and the Moliones
CA 111	WG lekythos		Sphinx
	ABL 241		
CA 598	WG lekythos		Herakles and Hydra
	ABL 233		*LIMC*: Herakles 2004*
CA 616	BF pyxis		Birth of Athena
	ABV 58	SB II 2	*LIMC*: Athena 345*
			Judgment of Paris
CA 617	PC aryballos		Helen and Dioskouroi
	CorVP 23	*FS* fig. 9	*LIMC*: Helene 28*°
CA 823	BF lekythos		Herakles and Nereus
	ABL 1–2		
CA 1961	BF neck-amphora		Kadmos and Harmonia
	Para 248	SB IV 27	*LIMC*: Harmonia 9*
			LIMC: Kadmos 45*
CA 2569	BF plate		Peleus and Thetis
CA 3004	MC skyphos		Herakles and Hydra
	CorVP 190	*FS* 54c	*LIMC*: Iolaos 26*
CA 3837	Sicilian stamnos		Theseus and Minotaur
CA 6113	BF cup		Ambush of Troilos
			LIMC: Achilleus 310*
C10228	Caeretan hydria		Herakles and Nessos
	CH 31	SB II 197	
E635	EC column krater		Herakles and Eurytos
	CorVP 147	*FS* 60a	*LIMC*: Eurytos I 1*
			LIMC: Iole I 1*
			Death of Aias
		FS 78a	*LIMC*: Aias I 120*
E638 bis	MC column krater		Death of Troilos
	CorVP 567		*LIMC*: Hippichos 1°
E639	LC column krater		Peleus and Thetis
	CorVP 266	*FS* 70b	
E640	LC amphora		Tydeus and Ismene
	CorVP 270		*LIMC*: Ismene I 3*

E643	LC hydria		Thetis mourning
	CorVP 264		*LIMC:* Achilleus 897*
E662	Lakonian dinos		Herakles and Pholos
	LV #313	SB II 157	
E669	Lakonian cup		Kadmos and snake
	LV #303	SB II 91	*LIMC:* Gorgo 167*
E701	Caeretan hydria		Herakles and Kerberos
	CH 14	SB II 150	*LIMC:* Herakles 2616*
E703	Pontic neck-amphora		Death of Troilos
	VL 363		*LIMC:* Achle 17
E732	Caeretan amphora		Gigantomachy
			LIMC: Gigantes 170*
E812	Chalkidian? neck-amphora		Herakles and Lion
	ChV 162		*LIMC:* Herakles 1809*
E852	BF neck-amphora		Birth of Athena
	ABV 96		*LIMC:* Athena 334*
E857	BF neck-amphora		Birth of Chrysaor?
	ABV 97		
E864	BF neck-amphora		Tityos
	ABV 97	SB II 78	*LIMC:* Apollon 1066*
E874	BF dinos		Gorgons
	ABV 8	*FS* 45	*LIMC:* Gorgo 314*
E876	BF dinos		Silenoi
	ABV 90		*LIMC:* Hephaistos 138b*
F18	Chalkidian hydria		Theseus and Minotaur
	ChV 13		*LIMC:* Ariadne 25*
F29	BF amphora		Herakles and Kyknos
	ABV 109		Sack of Troy
		SB II 343	*LIMC:* Astyanax I 8*
F60	BF neck-amphora		Herakles and Alkestis?
	ABV 308	SB II 180	*LIMC:* Alkestis 58*
F122	BF cup		Aineias and Anchises
	ABV 231		*LIMC:* Aineias 60*
F204	RF amphora		Herakles and Kerberos
	*ARV*² 4	SB II 152	*LIMC:* Herakles 2554*
F208	BF amphora		Herakles and Alkyoneus
			LIMC: Alkyoneus 3*
F222	BF neck-amphora		Sack of Troy
	ABV 316		*LIMC:* Astyanax I 12*
F271	BF neck-amphora		Theseus and Bull
	*ARV*² 194		
F340	BF oinochoe		Aias and the arms
	ABV 176		*LIMC:* Aias I 77*
F342	BF oinochoe		Odysseus and Polyphemos
	ABV 433	SB II 355–56	
G18	RF cup		Death of Troilos
	*ARV*² 61		*LIMC:* Achilleus 369*

G42	RF amphora		Tityos
	ARV² 23	SB II 82	*LIMC:* Apollon 1069*
G104	RF cup		Theseus and Skiron
	ARV² 318		Theseus and Amphitrite
		SB IV 290	*LIMC:* Amphitrite 75*
G109	WG cup		Tydeus and Ismene?
		SB V 58	*LIMC:* Ismene I 6*
G115	RF cup		Eos and Memnon
	ARV² 434		*LIMC:* Eos 324*
G123	RF cup		Zeus and Ganymedes
	ARV² 435	SB III 296	*LIMC:* Ganymedes 52*
G147	RF cup		Prokne and Philomela
	ARV² 472	SB IV 79	
G152	RF cup		Sack of Troy
	ARV² 369		*LIMC:* Akamas 11*
			LIMC: Astyanax I 18*
G154	RF cup		Ambush of Troilos
	ARV² 369		*LIMC:* Achilleus 344*
G155	RF cup fr		Herakles in house of
	ARV² 347		Nereus
G164	RF calyx krater		Tityos
	ARV² 504	SB III 196	*LIMC:* Ge 44*
G192	RF stamnos		Herakles and snakes
	ARV² 208	SB IV 156	*LIMC:* Alkmene 8*
G197	RF amphora		Theseus and Antiope
	ARV² 238		*LIMC:* Antiope II 10*
G209	RF amphora		Hades with cornucopia
	ARV² 648		*LIMC:* Hades 20*
G210	RF amphora		Herakles and Syleus
	ARV² 647		
G228	RF pelike		Sphinx on column
	ARV² 250		
G234	RF pelike		Herakles and Geras
	ARV² 286		*LIMC:* Geras 4*
G263	RF cup		Herakles and Hind
	ARV² 341		*LIMC:* Herakles 2189*
G341	RF calyx krater		Niobidai
	ARV² 601	SB III 212	*LIMC:* Apollon 1079*
			Theseus and Peirithoos in
			Hades?
			LIMC: Herakles 3520*
G345	RF bell krater		Herakles and Eurytion
	ARV² 1108		*LIMC:* Deianeira II 1*
G364	RF column krater		Phineus
	ARV² 569		*LIMC:* Boreadai 18*
G365	RF column krater		Herakles and Acheloos
	VL 3	SB IV 227	*LIMC:* Acheloos 218*

G366	RF column krater *ARV*² 585		Kronos and Rheia
G372	RF skyphos *ARV*² 1300	SB III 116	Athena and Gigas *LIMC:* Athena 50*
G413	RF stamnos *ARV*² 484		Wounding of Philoktetes *LIMC:* Agamemnon 43*
G416	RF stamnos *ARV*² 484		Death of Orpheus
G423	RF bell krater *ARV*² 1064		Theseus and the rock
K36	Apulian oinochoe *RVAp* 206		Odysseus and Diomedes *LIMC:* Diomedes I 25*
K545	Lucanian pelike *LCS* 184		Omphale and spindle
MNC 675	Boiotian skyphos *VL* 242		Theseus and Minotaur *LIMC:* Ariadne 35*
MNC 677	MC kotyle *CorVP* 184		Herakles and Pholos
S1677	RF amphora *ARV*² 1344		Gigantomachy *LIMC:* Gigantes 322*

Lugt Collection (The Haag)

no #	BF lekythos *VL* 105		Herakles and Kyknos

Macinagrossa Collection (Bari)

26	Apulian hydria *RVAp* 871		Abduction of Persephone *LIMC:* Hades 113*

Madrid: Museo Arqueológico Nacional

10915	BF neck-amphora *ABV* 602		Herakles and Boar *LIMC:* Herakles 2098*
10916	BF amphora *ABV* 508	SB II 199	Herakles and Eurytos *LIMC:* Antiphonos 1*
11017	RF bell krater *ARV*² 1440		Hades with cornucopia *LIMC:* Hades 70
11094	Paestan calyx krater *RVP* 84	SB IV 162	Madness of Herakles *LIMC:* Herakles 1684°
11097	RF amphora *ARV*² 1043		Eos and Kephalos
11265	RF cup *ARV*² 1174		Theseus and Prokroustes Theseus and Sow

Matera: Museo Ridola

12538	Apulian calyx krater *RVAp* 501		Perseus and Andromeda *LIMC:* Andromeda I 64*

Metaponto

20145	RF column krater		Graiai *LIMC:* Graiai 1*

Milan (formerly Vidoni Collection)
no #   Herakles and Prometheus

Mormino Collection (Palermo)
769   WG lekythos   Gaia and Erichthonios
                                  SB IV 64–65   LIMC: Ge 13*

Moscow: State Historical Museum
70   BF amphora   Herakles and Kerberos
             ABV 255   LIMC: Herakles 2555

Munich: Antikensammlungen
585   Ionian amphora   Argos, Io, Hermes
                                  SB II 19   LIMC: Io I 31*
596   Chalkidian hydria   Zeus and Typhoeus
             ChV 12   FS 66

                                                     Peleus and Atalanta
                                                        LIMC: Atalante 74*
837   Pontic amphora   Judgment of Paris
                                  SB II 249   LIMC: Alexandros 14*
1379   BF amphora   Herakles and Kyknos
             ABV 303
1407   BF amphora   Herakles and Bull
             ABV 290   LIMC: Herakles 2329*
1411   BF amphora   Aias and the arms
             ABV 311   SB II 298   LIMC: Aias I 76*
1414   BF amphora   Theseus and Antiope
             ABV 367   LIMC: Antiope II 4*
1415   BF amphora   Peleus and Thetis
             VL 322, 376   Aias and dead Achilleus
                                                        LIMC: Achilleus 877*
1417   BF amphora   Herakles and Antaios
             ABV 367   LIMC: Antaios I 1*
1426   BF neck-amphora   Death of Troilos
             ABV 95   FS 73a   LIMC: Achilleus 364*
1470   BF neck-amphora   Aias and dead Achilleus
             ABV 144   LIMC: Achilleus 876*
1493   BF neck-amphora   Sisyphos
             ABV 316   LIMC: Amyetoi 2*
1494   BF neck-amphora   Sisyphos
             ABV 308   LIMC: Aias I 145*
1546   BF neck-amphora   Aineias and Anchises
             ABV 392 (as Munich   LIMC: Askanios 3*
             1554)
1549   BF neck-amphora   Sisyphos
             ABV 383   LIMC: Hades 121*
1615A   BF neck-amphora   Herakles and Cheiron
             ABV 484   LIMC: Herakles 1665°
1700   BF hydria   Sack of Troy
             ABV 362   SB II 285   LIMC: Astyanax I 29*

Appendix C

1708	BF hydria		Herakles and Antaios
	ABV 360	SB II 169	LIMC: Antaios I 5*
1784	BF oinochoe		Herakles and Alkyoneus
	Para 183		LIMC: Alkyoneus 10*
1842	BF lekythos		Herakles and Birds
	ABV 455		LIMC: Herakles 2275
2085	BF cup		Herakles and Lion
			LIMC: Herakles 1916*
2241	BF band cup		Peleus and Atalanta
2243	BF band cup		Sphinx
	ABV 163	SB II 238	Kalydonian Boar Hunt
			LIMC: Iason 76
			Theseus and Minotaur
			LIMC: Ariadne 28*
2304	RF amphora		Iris as cup-bearer
	ARV² 220		LIMC: Iris I 142*
2309	RF amphora		Theseus and Helen
	ARV² 27	SB II 209	LIMC: Helene 41*
2322	RF neck-amphora		Odysseus and Nausikaa
	ARV² 1107		LIMC: Athena 566
2345	RF amphora		Boreas and Oreithuia
	ARV² 496	SB III 461–62	LIMC: Boreas 62b*
			LIMC: Aglauros 30*
2408	RF stamnos		Medeia and ram
	ARV² 257		
2413	RF stamnos		Gaia and Erichthonios
	ARV² 495	SB III 63	LIMC: Hephaistos 217*
2417	RF psykter		Idas, Marpessa, Apollo
	ARV² 556	SB III 253–54	LIMC: Artemis 1433
2426	RF hydria		Iris and infant Hermes
	ARV² 189	SB III 54	LIMC: Hermes 734*
2618	RF cup		Achilleus and Priam
	ARV² 61	SB II 317	LIMC: Achilleus 656*
2620	RF cup		Herakles and Geryoneus
	ARV² 16	SB II 147–48	LIMC: Herakles 2501*
2638	RF cup		Aedon and Itys
	ARV² 456	SB IV 32	
2646	RF cup		Herakles and Linos
	ARV² 437		LIMC: Herakles 1671*
2670	RF cup		Theseus' exploits
	ARV² 861		
2686	WG cup		Europa and bull
		SB III 329	LIMC: Europe I 44*
2688	RF cup		Achilleus and Penthesileia
	ARV² 879		LIMC: Achilleus 733*
2777	WG lekythos		Hermes and Charon
	ARV² 1228		LIMC: Charon I 10*

Catalogue of Artistic
Representations

3185	Etruscan RF amphora VL 389		Aineias and Anchises LIMC: Aineias 94*
3268	Apulian volute krater RVAp 16	SB III 209	Laertes and Antikleia LIMC: Antikleia 1*
3296	Apulian volute krater RVAp 533		Medeia and Kreon's daughter LIMC: Hippotes 1*
3300	Apulian amphora RVAp 535		Lykourgos
8762	RF pelike ARV² 1638	SB IV 210	Herakles in house of Nereus
8771	RF cup	SB IV 287	Theseus and Sinis

Münster: University
673	Apulian dish RVAp 530		Phrixos and Helle

Naples: Museo Nazionale
("H" preceding numbers indicates vases included in Heydemann's 1872 catalogue of the museum [Heydemann 1872]; subsequent inventory numbers are given in parentheses. "Stg" indicates vases in the Niccola Santangelo collection, which is also included in that catalogue.)

H1767	Apulian krater		Daidalos and Ikaros LIMC: Daidalos 20
H2418 (82263)	Lucanian amphora LCS 44	SB IV 147	Bellerophontes and Proitos
H2422 (81669)	RF hydria ARV² 189		Sack of Troy LIMC: Aias II 44* LIMC: Astyanax I 19* LIMC: Andromache I 47*
H2883 (2045)	RF calyx krater ARV² 1338	SB III 132	Gigantomachy LIMC: Gigantes 316*
H3089	RF stamnos ARV² 1050	SB IV 229	Herakles and Eurytion? LIMC: Deianeira II 2°
H3091	RF amphora ARV² 647		Hades and Persephone LIMC: Hades 77*
H3222 (81666)	Apulian volute krater RVAp 431		Triptolemos in Hades Danaides? LIMC: Danaides 9*
H3237	Lucanian volute krater LCS 114		Lykourgos
H3241	Lucanian hydria LCS 36		Herakles and Amazones LIMC: Amazones 777*
H3358 (81038)	BF pelike ABV 338	SB II 336	Aias and the arms LIMC: Aias I 80*
H3412 (82411)	Paestan calyx krater RVAp 84		Phrixos and Helle

126053	RF amphora		Menelaos and Helen
	ARV² 202		LIMC: Helen 261
Stg 31	Apulian volute krater		Aktaion and Artemis
	RVAp 203		LIMC: Aktaion 110*
Stg 172	BF cup		Dionysos and Semele
	ABV 203	SB II 50	LIMC: Dionysos 55*
Stg 270	RF neck-amphora		Ino and Phrixos
	ARV² 1161		LIMC: Ino 13*
Stg 702	Apulian pelike		Aphrodite, Adonis, Persephone
	RVAp 490		LIMC: Adonis 5*
Stg 708	Apulian pelike		Andromeda
	RVAp 536		LIMC: Andromeda I 14
Stg 709	Apulian volute krater		Theseus and Peirithoos
	RVAp 533		in Hades
no #	BF lid		Sack of Troy
	ABV 58	FS 78b	LIMC: Astyanax I 28*

Nauplia
136	WG alabastron (forgery?)		Herakles and Hesperides
	VL 72		LIMC Vol. 5, p. 103

Naxos
no #	Cycladic amphora		Aphrodite and Ares
		FS 9	LIMC: Aphrodite 1285*

New York: Metropolitan Museum of Art
01.8.6	BF cup		Ambush of Troilos
	ABV 51	SB II 282	LIMC: Achilleus 307*
06.1021.48	BF hydria		Herakles and Triton
06.1021.144	RF pelike		Kronos, Rheia, and stone
	ARV² 1107	SB III 11	
06.1070	BF lekythos		Medousa and Pegasos
	ABV 702	ABL 235 SB IV 123	LIMC: Gorgo 309*
07.286.66	RF calyx krater		Kadmos and snake
	ARV² 617	SB IV 24	LIMC: Harmonia 1*
07.286.84	RF volute krater		Wedding of Peirithoos
	ARV² 613		
08.258.21	RF calyx krater		Peirithoos in Hades
	ARV² 1086	SB IV 223	LIMC: Hades 151*
11.210.1	PA amphora		Herakles and Nessos
		FS 23	
11.213.2	RF lekythos		Laios and Chrysippos
	ARV² 1324		LIMC: Chrysippos III 1*
12.198.3	RF hydria		Theseus and Antiope
			LIMC: Antiope II 6*
12.229.14	RF bell krater fr		Athena and Tydeus
	VL 489		LIMC: Athanasia 2*

12.231.2	RF cup		Herakles and Eurytos
	ARV² 319		LIMC: Iphitos I 2*
12.235.4	RF skyphos fr		Marsyas
		SB III 234	LIMC: Artemis 1430*
14.105.10	BF hydria		Herakles and Hebe
	ABV 261		LIMC: Apollon 840*
14.130.15	LG krater		Herakles and the Moliones
16.70	BF hydria		Herakles and Triton
22.139.11	RF bell krater		Kadmos and snake
	ARV² 1083		LIMC: Harmonia 4*
24.97.37	RF lekythos		Ikaros
	ARV² 696	ABL 270	LIMC: Daidalos 47*
27.116	MC krater		Paris and Helen
	CorVP 196	FS 70a	LIMC: Alexandros 67*
28.57.23	RF bell krater		Hekate and Persephone
	ARV² 1012		LIMC: Hermes 637*
31.11.11	BF krater		Return of Hephaistos
	ABV 108	SB II 23–24	LIMC: Dionysos 563*
34.11.7	RF column krater		Iason and serpent
	ARV² 524		LIMC: Iason 36*
41.83	RF calyx krater		Odysseus and Kirke
	ARV² 1012		
41.162.29	WG lekythos		Helios
	ABV 507	ABL 226	LIMC: Astra 3*
41.162.190	BF neck-amphora		Herakles and Boar
	ABV 287		
45.11.1	RF pelike		Perseus and Medousa
	ARV² 1032	SB IV 126	LIMC: Gorgo 301*
46.11.7	WG oinochoe		Peleus in a tree
	ABV 434	SB II 224	
49.11.1	BF pelike		Silenos
	ABV 384		
50.11.7	Lakonian bowl		Herakles going to Olympos
	LV #140	SB II 52	LIMC: Hera 459*
53.11.4	RF cup		Theseus and Amphitrite
	ARV² 406	SB IV 292	LIMC: Amphitrite 76*
56.171.33	BF lekythos		Herakles fishing
	ABL 54		LIMC: Herakles 3369
56.171.46	RF column krater		Theseus and Minotaur
59.15	Lakonian cup		Herakles and Bull?
	LV #300		LIMC: Herakles 2317*
59.64	BF neck-amphora		Herakles and Acheloos
	Para 31		LIMC: Acheloos 214*
88.AE.66	RF cup		Aias and the arms
	Para 367		LIMC: Aias I 72*, 83*
			Death of Aias
			LIMC: Aias I 140*

96.19.1	RF column krater		Zeus and Aigina
	ARV² 536		LIMC: Aigina 15*
98.8.11	BF neck-amphora		Judgment of Paris
	ABV 308		
1972.11.10	RF krater		Death of Sarpedon
		SB II 303	LIMC: Hermes 593*

Ortiz Collection (Geneva)

Orvieto: Museo Civico (Faina Collection)

78	BF amphora		Herakles on Olympos
	ABV 144	SB II 39	LIMC: Apollon 828*

Oxford: Ashmolean Musuem

G275 (525)	RF volute krater		Epimetheus and Pandora
	ARV² 1562	SB III 90	LIMC: Hermes 643
G291 (530)	RF hydria		Blinding of Thamyris
	ARV² 1061		LIMC: Argiope 1*
1912.1165	RF stamnos		Death of Pentheus
	ARV² 208	SB III 243	
1934.333	BF plate		Herakles and Hind
	ABV 115	SB II 123	LIMC: Artemis 1315*
1937.983	RF calyx krater		Theseus and Sinis
	ARV² 1153		
1943.79	RF skyphos		Herakles and Geras
	ARV² 889		LIMC: Geras 2*
1973.1032	RF cup frr		Death of Aigisthos
			LIMC: Aigisthos 23

Paestum

no #	RF amphora		Herakles and Kerberos
	ARV² 220		LIMC: Herakles 2564*

Palermo: Museo Nazionale

45	BF lekythos		Pholos
	ABL 208		
996	BF lekythos		Water-carriers
	ABL 66		LIMC: Amyetoi 3*
NI 1886	WG lekythos		Sacrifice of Iphigeneia
	ARV² 446		LIMC: Iphigeneia 3*°
P335	BF skyphos		Turtle-rider
V653	RF cup frr		Herakles and Eurytos
	ARV² 73		LIMC: Eurytos I 4*
V659	RF cup		Death of Troilos
	ARV² 480		LIMC: Achilleus 368*
no #	RF skyphos		Apollo and raven
		SB III 284	LIMC: Apollon 352*

Policoro

38462	Apulian hydria		Danaides?
	RVAp 407		LIMC: Danaides 7*

Private Collections (Unnamed)

Athens	BF amphora		Achilleus and Memnon
			LIMC: Achilleus 822*
Athens (lost?)	BF lekythos		Snake and tomb
	ABL 198		
Basel	WG lekythos		Phineus
			LIMC: Harpyiai 8*
Basel	BF cup		Death of Troilos
		SB II 278	LIMC: Achilleus 359a*
Basel	RF cup		Death of Pelias
			LIMC: Alkandre 2*
Basel (Market)	RF stamnos		Herakles and Eurytos
			LIMC: Eurytos I 7*
Bern	BF cup		Herakles and Atlas
			LIMC: Atlas 2*
Copenhagen	LG jug		Herakles and Birds?
		FS 5b	LIMC: Herakles 2275
Miami	Apulian krater		Daughters of Anios
New York	RF psykter		Herakles and Philoktetes
			LIMC: Herakles 2910
New York (Market)	RF cup		Iris with sacrifice
Rome (Market)	RF bell krater		Athena and Tydeus
	ARV² 1073		LIMC: Athanasia 1°
Zurich	RF lekythos		Poseidon and Amymone
	ARV² 656		LIMC: Amymone 17

Providence: Rhode Island School of Design

| 25.084 | RF lekythos | | Danae, Perseus, and chest |
| | ARV² 697 | | LIMC: Danae 53* |

Reading: University

| 47 VI 1 | Pontic amphora | | Abduction of Troilos |
| | | SB II 279–80 | LIMC: Achle 18* |

Reggio Calabria: Museo Nazionale

1027–28	Chalkidian lid		Leukippides
	ChV 14	SB II 225	LIMC: Dioskouroi 194*
4001	BF amphora		Triptolemos
	ABV 147	SB II 38	
no #	RF pyxis frr		Nemesis/Leda and egg
			LIMC: Helene 3*

Richmond, Va.: Virginia Museum of Fine Arts

62.1.1	RF hydria		Perseus and Medousa
	ARV² 1683		LIMC: Gorgo 299*
80.162	Apulian lekythos		Polydeukes and Idas
	RVAp	SB IV 20	LIMC: Dioskouroi 217
	Supp 1, 84		Leukippides
			LIMC: Dioskouroi 203*

Rome: Museo dei Conservatori			
no #	Italic krater		Odysseus and Polyphemos
Rome: Forum Antiquarium			
no #	RF cup fr		Ixion and wheel
	*ARV*² 178		*LIMC:* Ixion 11*
Ruvo: Museo Jatta			
1097	Apulian volute krater		Hesperides and snake
	RVAp 417		*LIMC:* Hesperides 2*
1501	RF volute krater		Talos
	*ARV*² 1338	SB V 17	*LIMC:* Argonautai 15*
no #	Apulian fr		Laokoon
	VL 533		
Samos: Excavations			
no #	Orientalizing krater		Herakles and Hebe
			LIMC: Herakles 3330
Samos: Vathy Museum			
1540	Lakonian cup		Boreadai and Harpuiai
	LV #119		
no #	Cor aryballos frr		Iason and serpent?
no #	BF hydria fr		Herakles and Nereus
	ABV 25	*FS* 55a	
Sciclounoff Collection (Geneva)			
no #	Apulian volute krater		Melanippe
		SB IV 36a	
Seillière Collection (Paris)			
no #	RF amphora		Artemis and Kallisto?
	*ARV*² 604	SB III 316	*LIMC:* Artemis 1347*
Stockholm: National Museum			
6	RF bell krater		Persephone and Silenoi
	*ARV*² 1053		*LIMC:* Erysichthon I 2*
1701	RF lekythos		Theseus and the rock
	*ARV*² 844		*LIMC:* Aithra I 19*
Stockholm: Medelhavsmuseum			
1963.1	RF amphora		Odysseus and Diomedes
	*ARV*² 1643		*LIMC:* Athena 103*
no #	BF oinochoe		Seirenes
	Para 183		
Stuttgart: Württembergisches Landesmuseum			
65/15	Chalkidian amphora		Oidipous and Sphinx
		SB II 104	
Syracuse: Museo Archeologico			
2408	RF column krater		Penelope and suitors
	*ARV*² 537		

12085	WG lekythos		Sphinx and youth
	ABL 241		
14569	BF lekythos		Herakles and Mares?
	ABV 487	*ABL* 222	*LIMC:* Herakles 2416*
21894	BF lekythos		Sack of Troy
	Para 201	*ABL* 15?	*LIMC:* Astyanax I 7*
23910	RF bell krater		Danae on Seriphos
			LIMC: Danae 55
25418	BF Siana cup		Sphinx and youths
	ABV 53	*FS* fig. 29	

Taranto: Museo Archeologico

I/96	Apulian amphora		Fall of Stheneboia
	RVAp 32		*LIMC:* Aphrodite 1531*
4545	RF lekythos		Theseus and Ariadne
	ARV² 560		*LIMC:* Ariadne 52*
4600	Sicilian calyx krater		Alkmene at the altar
	RVAp 36		*LIMC:* Amphitryon 1*
4991	Lakonian cup		Kyrene and lion
	LV #358	SB II 22	
7029	BF skyphos		Herakles and Helios
	ABV 518	*ABL* 120	*LIMC:* Herakles 2546*
		SB IV 197	
7030	BF skyphos		Herakles and Alkyoneus
	ABV 518		*LIMC:* Alkyoneus 17*
52155	BF cup		Herakles and Hesione
	VL 70	SB II 182	

Tarquinia: Museo Nazionale

RC 685	RF calyx krater		Alkandre and Pelias
	ARV² 864		LIMC: Alkandre 1*
RC 976	BF neck-amphora		Aineias and Anchises
	ABV 269		*LIMC:* Aineias 70
RC 1043	BF amphora		Tityos
	ABV 97	*Para* 37	*LIMC:* Ge 11
RC 1123	RF cup		Kadmos and snake?
	ARV² 120		*LIMC:* Kadmos I 56
RC 2070	BF cup		Herakles and Alkyoneus
	ABV 654		*LIMC:* Alkyoneus 16
RC 5291	RF cup		Theseus and Ariadne
	ARV² 405		*LIMC:* Ariadne 53*
RC 5564	BF neck-amphora		Telamon and Amazones
	ABV 84		*LIMC:* Amazones 5
RC 6848	RF cup		Assembly of gods
	ARV² 60	SB II 21	*LIMC:* Ganymedes 60*

Thasos

no #	plate		Bellerophontes and Pegasos

Thebes

31.166	BF lekythos *ABL* 68		Medeia
31.166a	BF lekythos *ABL* 68		Medeia

Toledo: Museum of Art

52.66	BF lekythos		Herakles and Alkyoneus *LIMC:* Alkyoneus 7*
69.369	RF lekythos		Danae, Perseus, and chest *LIMC:* Akrisios 5*
82.134	Etruscan BF kalpis		Men into dolphins

Tübingen: University

S/10 1605 (E120)	RF oinochoe		Eumaios *LIMC:* Eumaios 4*
S/10 1610	RF oinochoe	SB IV 334	Hippothoon *LIMC:* Alope 1*
S/12 2452 (D2)	BF amphora *ABV* 96		Kalydonian Boar Hunt

Vatican Museums

229	Ionian hydria		Herakles and Alkyoneus *LIMC:* Alkyoneus 31*
306	BF dinos		Kalydonian Boar Hunt *LIMC:* Atalante 4*
343	BF cup	SB II 330–31	Achilleus and Aias *LIMC:* Achilleus 398*
344	BF amphora *ABV* 145	SB II 332	Achilleus and Aias *LIMC:* Achilleus 397*
350	BF amphora *ABV* 140	SB II 328	Eos mourning *LIMC:* Eos 327*
372	BF amphora *ABV* 368	SB II 153	Herakles and Kerberos *LIMC:* Hades 137*
388	BF neck-amphora *ABV* 283		Herakles and Pholos
16541 (H569)	RF cup *ARV*² 451		Oidipous and Sphinx
16545	RF cup *ARV*² 437		Iason and serpent *LIMC:* Iason 32*
16554	RF hydria *ARV*² 252		Poseidon and Aithra *LIMC:* Aithra I 2*
16563 (H545)	RF cup *ARV*² 449	SB IV 198	Herakles in Helios' cup *LIMC:* Herakles 2552*
16592	Lakonian cup *LV* #196	SB II 56	Atlas and Prometheus? *LIMC:* Atlas 1*
K40099	LC krater *CorVP* 264	FS 72	Embassy to Troy *LIMC:* Harmatidas 1*

Vienna: Kunsthistorisches Museum

741	RF amphora *ARV*² 203		Menelaos and Helen *LIMC:* Helene 260*

1103	RF column krater *ARV²* 277		Death of Aigisthos
1773	RF skyphos *ARV²* 972	SB IV 342	Ariadne and children? *LIMC:* Akamas 1*
1841	WG lekythos *ABV* 522	*ABL* 256	Herakles and Birds *LIMC:* Herakles 2245*
3576	Caeretan hydria *CH* 50	SB II 171	Herakles and Bousiris *LIMC:* Bousiris 9*
3619	BF dinos *ABV* 140		Eos and Thetis *LIMC:* Achilleus 799*
3695	RF cup *ARV²* 429		Aias and the arms *LIMC:* Aias I 71*
3710	RF cup *ARV²* 380		Achilleus and Priam *LIMC:* Achilleus 659*
3725	RF pelike *ARV²* 204	SB II 351–52	Death of Aigisthos *LIMC:* Aigisthos 6*
3728	RF pelike		Sphinx and elders

Villa Giulia (Rome)

3579	RF column krater *ARV²* 514	SB IV 80	Tereus and the Pandionides
11688	RF bell krater frr		Herakles on pyre *LIMC:* Herakles 2909*
20760	RF cup *ARV²* 83	SB JI 216	Theseus and sow
20842	BF amphora *ABV* 381		Herakles and Poseidon
20846	RF pelike *ARV²* 494		Poseidon and Amymone *LIMC:* Amymone 20a
22679	PC olpe *CorVP* 32	FS 29b	Judgment of Paris *LIMC:* Alexandros 5*
24247	BF neck-amphora *VL* 318		Peleus in a tree *LIMC:* Cheiron 15*
48238	RF pelike *ARV²* 284	SB IV 211	Herakles and Geras *LIMC:* Geras 5*
48329	BF neck-amphora *ABV* 370		Herakles and Kerberos *LIMC:* Herakles 2560*
50279	Paestan calyx krater *RVP* 85		Aias and Kassandra *LIMC:* Aias II 107*
50406 (M472)	BF amphora *ABV* 291		Herakles and Lion *LIMC:* Herakles 1882*
50649	Caeretan hydria *CH* 23		Herakles and Kerberos
50626	BF neck-amphora *ABV* 270		Pholos
50683 (M430)	BF hydria *ABV* 108	SB II 142	Geryoneus *LIMC:* Herakles 2463*
57231	Lakonian cup *LV* #342		Capture of Silenos

57912	RF cup		Eos and Thetis
	ARV² 72	SB II 322	LIMC: Achilleus 804*
74989	BF amphora		Herakles and Hydra?
			LIMC: Herakles 2822*
106335	Lakonian cup		Boreadai and Harpuiai
	LV #122	SB II 231	LIMC: Boreadai 6*
106341	BF neck-amphora		Tityos
	ABV 121	FS 54b	LIMC: Ge 12*
106349	Lakonian cup		Achilleus and snake
	LV #291		LIMC: Achilleus 261*
106462	RF cup		Herakles and Nereus
	ARV² 1623		
106465	BF amphora		Herakles and Hydra
no #	MC aryballos		Herakles and Hebe
			LIMC: Herakles 3331°
no # (Ricci	Ionian hydria		Eos and Thetis
Hydria)	VL 166	SB II 324–25	LIMC: Achilleus 797
			Herakles going to Olympos
		SB II 44	LIMC: Herakles 2908*
no # (Stefani	Lakonian cup		Herakles and Amazones
Cup)	LV #193	SB II 131	LIMC: Amazones 2*
no #	RF pelike		Perseus and Polydektes

Vlastos Collection (Athens)

no #	RF chous		Ikaros
	ARV² 700	SB IV 55	

Walters Art Gallery (Baltimore)

48.198	BF exaleiptron		Odysseus and Nausikaa?

Weimar (once Preller Collection)

no #	RF cup		Herakles carries Hades?
	ARV² 1511		LIMC: Hades 71b

White-Levy Collection (New York)

no #	RF amphora		Herakles and Hydra

Würzburg: University (Martin von Wagner Museum)

164	Chalkidian cup		Silenoi
	ChV 15	SB II 17	LIMC: Dionysos 763
			Phineus
		SB II 232	LIMC: Boreadai 7*
			LIMC: Harpyiai 14*
199	BF neck-amphora		Herakles and Hind
	ABV 287		LIMC: Herakles 2177*
212	BF neck-amphora		Aineias and Anchises
	ABV 371		
218	BF neck-amphora		Aineias and Anchises
	ABV 316		LIMC: Aineias 69*
252	BF amphora		Silenoi
	ABV 315		

391	BF mastos cup		Dionysos and child
	ABV 262	SB II 12	*LIMC:* Ariadne 159*
452	BF cup		Achilleus and Cheiron
	ABV 63	SB II 262	*LIMC:* Achilleus 35*
474	RF cup		Silenos
	ARV² 173		
855	Apulian pelike fr		Andromeda
	RVAp 174		*LIMC:* Andromeda I 10*

Yale University

1913.111	BF lekythos		Admetos' chariot
	ABL 221		*LIMC:* Admetos I 15*

Zurich

ETH 4	LC amphora		Ambush of Troilos
	CorVP 268		*LIMC:* Achilleus 336

RELIEF

Athens: National Museum

2104	"Megarian" bowl		Theseus and Helen at Korinth
		SB IV 313	*LIMC:* Helene 37*°
5898	relief amphora		Leto in childbirth?
		FS 12	*LIMC:* Eileithyia 58*
11798	"Megarian" bowl		Zeus and Antiope
			LIMC: Antiope I 2*

Basel: Antikenmuseum and Ludwig Collection

BS 617	pithos		Minotaur and Athenians
		FS 25a	*LIMC:* Ariadne 36

Berlin: Pergamon-Museum

4996	"Megarian" bowl		Death of Agamemnon
			LIMC: Alkmeon 1°

Berlin: Lost or Unknown

3161a	"Megarian" bowl		Sisyphos and Autolykos
		SB III 210	*LIMC:* Antikleia 2°

Boston: Museum of Fine Arts

98.828	Arretine bowl		Death of Phaethon
		SB IV 42	
99.505	amphora		Agamemnon in bath?
			LIMC: Aigisthos 1*

Cabinet des Médailles (Paris)

3003	relief pithos		Europa and bull
		FS 11b	*LIMC:* Europe I 91*

Louvre (Paris)

CA 795	amphora		Medousa as Kentauros
		FS 15b	*LIMC:* Gorgo 290*

CA 937	amphora fr		Perseus
CA 4523	Cretan relief pithos		Fall of Bellerophontes
MNC 660	"Megarian" bowl		Oidipous as foundling

Mykonos

69	pithos		Trojan Horse
		FS 35a	LIMC: Equus Troianus 23*
			Death of Astyanax?
			LIMC: Astyanax I 27*
			Menelaos and Helen
		FS 35b	LIMC: Helene 225*

Tenos

no #	relief amphora		Birth of Athena
		FS 13	LIMC: Athena 360*

Painted Clay Artifacts (other than vases)

Berlin

F766	Corinthian pinax		Herakles and the Kerkopes
F767	Corinthian pinax		Herakles and the Kerkopes
	DL 97		
F768	Corinthian pinax		Gigantomachy
			LIMC: Gigantes 98

Eleusis

1398	pinax		Gigantomachy
		SB II 54	LIMC: Gigantes 99

Nauplia

4509	clay shield		Achilleus and Penthesileia?
		FS 7b	LIMC: Amazones 168*

London: British Museum

no #	Boccanera slab		Judgment of Paris

Small Reliefs (ivories, terracottas, bronze fibulas, tripods, shield-bands, gems, etc.)

Agrigento: Museo Civico

no #	terracotta arula		Achilleus and Memnon?
			LIMC: Achilleus 825*

Aigina: Museum

no #	shield-band		Death of Agamemnon

Athens: National Museum

4196	Melian relief		Phrixos and ram
11765	Kretan fibula		Herakles and the Moliones
		FS 6b	LIMC: Aktorione 7*
15350	ivory		Kentauros
15354	ivory		Prometheus and eagle
		FS 11a	

16368	ivory comb		Judgment of Paris
			LIMC: Alexandros 6*
no #	ivory seal		Aias and corpse of
			Achilleus
			LIMC: Achilleus 864
no #	bronze sheathing		Death of Kassandra
		FS 32c	

Basel: Antikenmuseum and Ludwig Collection

BS 318	terracotta frieze		Herakles and Alkyoneus
			LIMC: Hermes 537*
			Agamemnon in bath?
Lu 217	shield-band		Tityos
	Form CI: *OF* XVII		*LIMC:* Apollon 1076
	142	SB II 79	
			Herakles and Atlas
		SB II 154	*LIMC:* Atlas 3*

Berlin: Charlottenburg (Antikenmuseum)

GI 194	Etruscan gem		Seven against Thebes
			LIMC: Amphiaraos 29*
GI 332–36	gold plaques		Theseus and Minotaur
		FS fig. 7	*LIMC:* Ariadne 37

Berlin: Pergamon-Museum

TC 6281	Melian relief		Gaia and Erichthonios
			LIMC: Erechtheus 23

Boston: Museum of Fine Arts

99.494	Etruscan mirror		Suicide of Aias
			LIMC: Aias I 135*

Cabinet des Médailles (Paris)

276	Etruscan gem		Aineias and Anchises
			LIMC: Aineias 95
M5837	Cycladic sealstone		Kentauros

Delphi

4479	shield-band		Herakles and Geryoneus
	Form XXIV: *OF* II 25		*LIMC:* Geryoneus 9*
no #	ivory		Phineus and the Harpuiai
		FS 64b	*LIMC:* Boreadai 13*
no #	ivory		Departure of Amphiaraos
			LIMC: Amphiaraos 16*

Florence: Museo Archeologico

72740	Etruscan mirror		Hera nursing Herakles
			LIMC: Hercle 404*

Iraklion

11512	terracotta plaque		Death of Agamemnon?
		FS 33	*LIMC:* Agamemnon 91*

Lemnos
1205	terracotta mold		Aias and corpse of Achilleus *LIMC:* Achilleus 860*

London: British Museum
489	scarab		Herakles and Acheloos *LIMC:* Acheloos 222*
3204	Boiotian fibula		Man and lion *LIMC:* Herakles 1913 Man and birds *LIMC:* Herakles 2280
3205	Boiotian fibula	*FS* 6a	Herakles and Hydra *LIMC:* Herakles 2019* Trojan Horse *LIMC:* Equus Troianus 22*
B620	Etruscan mirror	SB IV 134	Perseus and Medousa
no #	Cretan gem (impression)		Prometheus

Munich: Antikensammlungen
A1293	seal *DL* 124	*FS* 6c	Nessos and Deianeira?
SL 66	tripod (Loeb B)		Peleus and Thetis (as lion) Achilleus and Troilos *LIMC:* Achle 63 *
SL 67	tripod (Loeb A)		Peleus and Thetis (as snake)
SL 68	tripod (Loeb C)		Peleus and Thetis (as lion)

Naples: Museo Nazionale
no #	terracotta	*FS* 32b	Aias and corpse of Achilleus *LIMC:* Achilleus 861°

New York: Metropolitan Museum of Art
17.190.73	ivory	*FS* 14	Proitides
42.11.1	steatite gem		Death of Agamemnon *LIMC:* Agamemnon 94*
42.11.13	steatite gem	*FS* 32a	Suicide of Aias *LIMC:* Aias I 110*
58.11.6	tripod leg (forgery?)		Peleus and Thetis

Olympia
B 103	bronze relief		Departure of Amphiaraos *LIMC:* Baton I 5°
B 112	shield-band Form V: *OF* II 11	*FS* fig. 38	Achilleus and Penthesileia *LIMC:* Amazones 171°

B 160	shield-band Form XXXV: *OF* II 35		Death of Priam
B 520	shield-band Form XXV: *OF* II 26		Herakles, Apollo, tripod *LIMC:* Herakles 2984
B 847	shield-band Form IX: *OF* II 14		Birth of Athena *LIMC:* Eileithyia 2e°
		FS fig. 40	Death of Polites? Troilos? *LIMC:* Astyanax I 34a°
B 975	shield-band Form XXIX: *OF* II 29		Aias and Kassandra Herakles and Kerkopes Perseus and Medousa *LIMC:* Athena 502°
B 984	shield-band Form XLVI: *OF* II 39		Herakles and Antaios? *LIMC:* Antaios I 33°
B 988	shield-band Form I: *OF* II 7	*FS* fig. 35	Death of Troilos *LIMC:* Achilleus 376*° Zeus and Typhoeus
		FS fig. 17	
		FS fig. 44	Death of Aigisthos *LIMC:* Aigisthos 2°
B 1010	shield-band Form III: *OF* II 9		Herakles and Alkyoneus Admetos and Mopsos boxing *LIMC:* Admetos I 8°
B 1555	shield-band Form XXXII: *OF* II 33		Achilleus and Penthesileia *LIMC:* Achilleus 721°
B 1636	shield-band Form XXVI: *OF* II 27		Zeus and Typhoeus Suicide of Aias *LIMC:* Aias I 127°
B 1643	shield-band Form VII: *OF* II 12		Zeus and Typhoeus Theseus and Minotaur *LIMC:* Ariadne 34°
B 1650	shield-band Form XXVIII: *OF* II 29		Herakles and Lion *LIMC:* Herakles 1847
B 1654	shield-band Form IV: *OF* II 10		Herakles and Lion *LIMC:* Herakles 1846° Theseus and Minotaur Amphiaraos and Lykourgos
		FS fig. 31	*LIMC:* Amphiaraos 33° Suicide of Aias Aias and Kassandra Death of Agamemnon
		FS fig. 43	*LIMC:* Agamemnon 92*

B 1687	shield-band		Medousa, Pegasos, Chrysaor
	Form XIV: *OF* II 18		*LIMC*: Gorgo 273°
			Birth of Athena
		FS fig. 20	*LIMC*: Athena 361°
B 1730	tripod leg		Herakles, Apollo, tripod
			LIMC: Apollon 1011
B 1801	shield-band		Herakles and Alkyoneus
	Form I: *OF* II 7		Aias and Kassandra
		FS fig. 42	*LIMC*: Aias II 48°
B 1881	shield-band		Herakles and Nereus?
	Form XXX: *OF* II 31		*LIMC*: Halios Geron 2°
B 1911	shield-band		Aias and corpse of Achilleus
	Form XIV: *OF* II 18		*LIMC*: Achilleus 862°
B 1912	shield-band		Death of Troilos
	Form XV: *OF* II 19	*FS* fig. 34	*LIMC*: Achilleus 377°
B 1921	shield-band		Aias and corpse of Achilleus
	Form XIII: *OF* II 17		*LIMC*: Achilleus 862°
B 1975	shield-band		Herakles and Geryoneus
	Form X: *OF* II 15	*FS* fig. 25	*LIMC*: Herakles 2478°
B 2198	shield-band		Theseus and Peirithoos in Hades
	Form XXIX bis: *OF* II 30	*FS* fig. 24	*LIMC*: Herakles 3519°
B 3600	tripod leg		Theseus and Ariadne?
		FS fig. 28	*LIMC*: Ariadne
			Death of Troilos
		FS fig. 28	*LIMC*: Achilleus 375°
B 4475	shield-band		Menelaos and Helen
	Form CXVIII: *OF* XVII 153		*LIMC*: Helena 69a*
B 4810	shield-band		Achilleus and Aias at dice
	Form CXXIX: *OF* XVII 156		Death of Priam
B 4836	shield-band		Herakles and Atlas
	Form CI: *OF* XVII 142		*LIMC*: Atlas 4
			Tityos
B 4900	mitra		Death of Klytaimestra?
			LIMC: Alexandros 52°
B 4964	shield-band		Man in cauldron
	Form CXXVII: *OF* XVII 155		
B 4992	shield-band		Prometheus and eagle
	Form XLV: *OF* XVII 149	*FS* 41a	

B 5800	tripod leg		Herakles and Hydra
			LIMC: Herakles 2025
B 8402	shield-band		Release of Hera
	Form CXX: OF XVII		LIMC: Hera 321
	154		
BE 11a	bronze plaque		Kaineus and Kentauroi
		FS 27c	LIMC: Kaineus 61*
E 161	shield-band (iron)		Herakles and Boar
	Form XXXVIII: OF II		LIMC: Herakles 2118
	36		
M 77	tripod leg		Theseus and Amazon?
		FS 80	LIMC: Antiope II 1*
			Death of Klytaimestra
		FS 80	LIMC: Aigisthos 19*
M 397	cuirass		Helen and the Dioskouroi
		FS 26	LIMC: Helene 58*

Philadelphia: University Museum

75-35-1	fibula	Herakles and Hydra
		LIMC: Herakles 2020
		Herakles and Hind
		LIMC: Herakles 2205

Reggio Calabria: Museo Nazionale

4337	terracotta plaque	Artemis and Aktaion
		LIMC: Aktaion 76*
no #	terracotta plaque	Persephone opening chest
		LIMC: Aphrodite
		1365b*

Samos: Vathy Museum

B 2518	bronze pectoral		Herakles and Geryoneus
			LIMC: Herakles 2476°
E 1	ivory		Perseus and Medousa
		FS 17	LIMC: Gorgo 291*
T 416	stamped clay		Aias carrying Achilleus
			LIMC: Achilleus 865

Sparta

1	grave relief		Menelaos and Helen
		FS 69	LIMC: Helene 230*

Villa Giulia

13199	Etruscan cista	Laios and Chrysippos
		LIMC: Chrysippos I 7*
24787	Etruscan cista	Amykos
	(Ficoroni Cista)	LIMC: Amykos 5*

Architectural Sculpture

Akropolis Museum (Athens)

1	pediment	Herakles and Hydra
		LIMC: Herakles 2021*

9	pediment		Herakles on Olympos
			LIMC: Hera 458*
35	pediment		Bluebeard group
52	pediment		Ambush of Troilos?
			LIMC: Achilleus 276*
55	pediment		Herakles on Olympos?
631	pediment		Athena and Gigantes
			LIMC: Athena 125°

Athens: National Museum

2870	metope fr		Sphinxes?
13401	Thermon metope		Perseus fleeing
		FS 18	
13410	Thermon metope		Aedon and Chelidon
		FS 20	
13413	Thermon metope		Proitides
		FS fig. 6	
no #	Kalydon metope		Herakles and Boar
			LIMC: Herakles 2135

Delphi (in museum)

Sikyonian Treasury

no #	metope		Europa and bull
			LIMC: Europe I 77*
no #	metope		Idas, Kastor, Polydeukes
		FS 63b	*LIMC:* Apharetidai 4*
no #	metope		Argo and crew
		FS 63a	*LIMC:* Argonautai 2*

Siphnian Treasury

no #	pediment		Apollo, Herakles, tripod
			LIMC: Herakles 3026*
no #	north frieze		Gigantomachy
		SB II 67–69	*LIMC:* Gigantes 2*°
no #	east frieze		Trojan War
		SB II 291–92	*LIMC:* Apollon 861a*
			LIMC: Hera 298*
no #	south frieze		Leukippides?
			LIMC: Dioskouroi 207*

Athenian Treasury

no #	pediment		Gigantomachy
no #	metopes		Theseus' exploits
no #	metope		Herakles and Hind
			LIMC: Herakles 1703°
no #	metopes		Herakles and Geryoneus
			LIMC: Herakles 1703°

Temple of Apollo

no #	pediment		Gigantomachy
		SB II 70	*LIMC:* Gigantes 3°

Glyptothek (Munich)			
no #	Aigina: East		Fall of Laomedon's Troy
		SB II 183–84	*LIMC:* Athena 129°
Hephaisteion (Athens: in situ)			
no #	metopes	SB IV 299	Theseus' exploits
no #	metope		Herakles and Boar
			LIMC: Herakles 1706*°
no #	metope		Herakles and Amazon
			LIMC: Herakles 1706*°
no #	metope		Herakles and Geryoneus
			LIMC: Herakles 1706*°
no #	pediment		Theseus and sons of Pallas
Kerkyra/Corfu			
no #	pediment		Medousa, Pegasos, Chrysaor
		FS fig. 16	*LIMC:* Gorgo 289*°
no #	pediment		Death of Aigisthos?
		FS 42	
Olympia (in museum)			
Temple of Zeus			
no #	east pediment	SB IV 2–5	Pelops and Oinomaos
no #	west pediment	SB IV 315	Wedding of Peirithoos
no #	metope		Herakles and Lion
			LIMC: Herakles 1705*°
no #	metope		Herakles and Boar
			LIMC: Herakles 1705*°
no #	metope		Herakles and the Stables
			LIMC: Herakles 1705*°
no #	metope		Herakles and Birds
			LIMC: Herakles 1705*°
no #	metope		Herakles and Bull
			LIMC: Herakles 1705*°
no #	metope		Herakles and Amazon
			LIMC: Herakles 1705*°
no #	metope		Herakles and Geryoneus
			LIMC: Herakles 1705*°
no #	metope		Herakles and Atlas
			LIMC: Herakles 1705*°
Megarian Treasury			
no #	pediment		Gigantomachy
			LIMC: Gigantes 6*°
Paestum (in museum)			
Foce del Sele temples			
no #	metope	SB II 350	Man and snake
no #	metope		Tityos
		SB II 76–77	*LIMC:* Apollon 1075*

no #	metope		Silenoi
		SB II 89	LIMC: Hera 328*
no #	metope		Herakles and Pholos
no #	metope	SB II 85	Sisyphos
no #	metope	SB II 226	Leukippides?
no #	metope		Man in cauldron
no #	metope		Herakles and Boar
			LIMC: Herakles 1698*
no #	metope		Herakles and Alkyoneus?
			LIMC: Herakles 1698*
no #	metope		Herakles and Deianeira (Hera?)
			LIMC: Herakles 1698*
no #	metope		Herakles, Apollo, tripod
		SB II 190	LIMC: Herakles 1698*
no #	metope		Herakles and the Kerkopes
		SB II 174	LIMC: Herakles 1698*
no #	metope		Achilleus at fountain house
			LIMC: Achilleus 279*
no #	metope		Achilleus and Troilos?
			Orestes and Aigisthos?
		SB II 349	LIMC: Aigisthos 20*
no #	metope	SB II 348	Klytaimestra
no #	metope	SB II 302	Hektor and Patroklos
no #	metope		Suicide of Aias
			LIMC: Aias I 128*
no #	metope	SB II 361	Man on turtle

Palermo: Museo Nazionale

Selinous Temple C

no #	pediment		Gorgon
			LIMC: Gorgo 61
3920B	metope		Perseus and Medousa
			LIMC: Athena 12*
3920C	metope		Herakles and the Kerkopes

Selinous Temple E

3921A	metope		Herakles and Amazon
			LIMC: Amazones 96*
3921C	metope		Death of Aktaion
			LIMC: Aktaion 31*

Selinous Temple F

3909A	metope		Gigantomachy
			LIMC: Gigantes 13*
3909B	metope		Gigantomachy
			LIMC: Gigantes 13*

Selinous Temple Y

3915	metope		Europa and bull
		SB II 15	LIMC: Europe I 78*

Parthenon (in situ)			
no #	metopes (east)		Gigantomachy *LIMC:* Gigantes 18*
Syracuse: Museo Archeologico			
no #	Gela pediment		Gorgon
Thermon			
no #	metope *DL* 140		Herakles and Kentauroi
Villa Giulia (Rome)			
Pyrgi Temple A			
no #	antepagmentum		Seven against Thebes *LIMC:* Athena/Menerva 239*

Free-standing Sculpture

Athens: National Museum			
6678	cauldron rim figure		Minotaur
7544	bronze statuette		Silenos
Lefkandi			
no #	terracotta		Kentauros
Louvre (Paris)			
C7286	cauldron rim figure		Minotaur
Naples: Museo Nazionale			
6351	marble		Ganymedes and eagle *LIMC:* Ganymedes 130*
New York: Metropolitan Museum of Art			
17.190.2072	bronze group		Man and Kentauros
		FS 4a	
Olympia			
T 2	terracotta		Zeus and Ganymedes
		SB III 295	*LIMC:* Ganymedes 56*

Appendix D

Genealogical Tables

TABLE 1: THE FIRST GODS

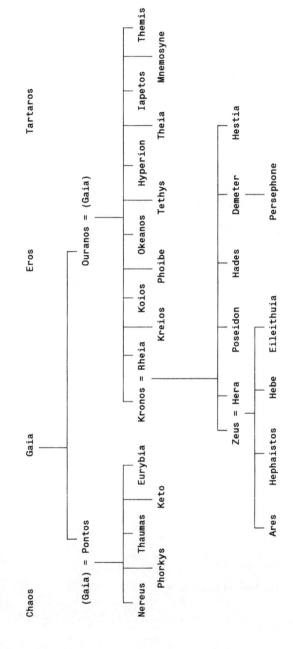

TABLE 2: THE CHILDREN OF PONTOS

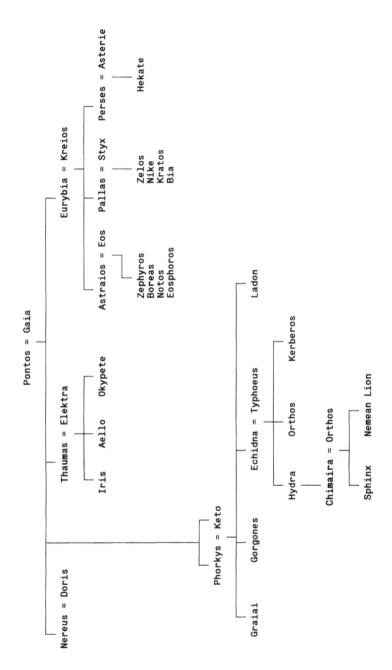

TABLE 3: THE LINE OF DEUKALION

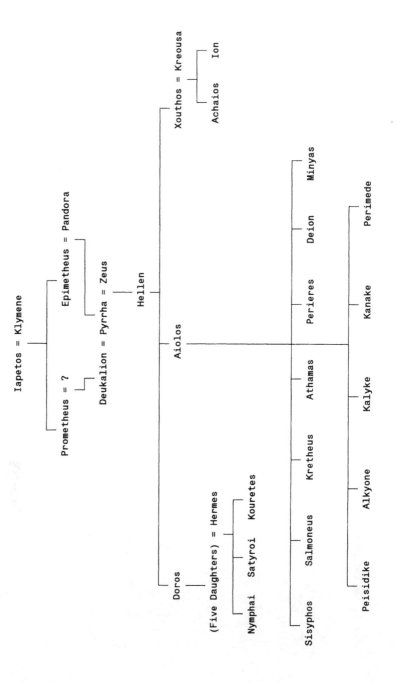

TABLE 4: THE DAUGHTERS OF AIOLOS

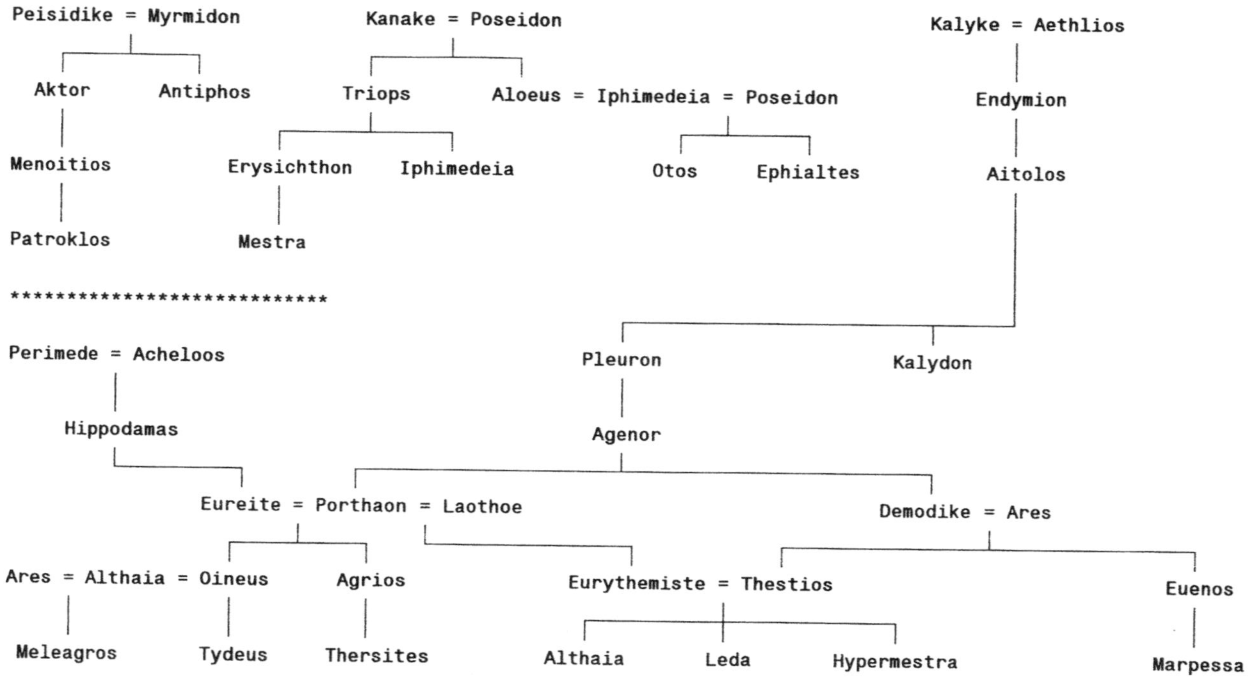

Peisidike = Myrmidon

Aktor   Antiphos

Menoitios

Patroklos

Kanake = Poseidon

Triops   Aloeus = Iphimedeia = Poseidon

Erysichthon   Iphimedeia   Otos   Ephialtes

Mestra

Kalyke = Aethlios

Endymion

Aitolos

Pleuron   Kalydon

Agenor

Porthaon = Laothoe   Demodike = Ares   Eurythemiste = Thestios

                                            Euenos

                                            Marpessa

Althaia   Leda   Hypermestra

****

Perimede = Acheloos

Hippodamas

Eureite = Porthaon = Laothoe

Oineus   Agrios

Ares = Althaia = Oineus   Thersites

Meleagros   Tydeus

807

TABLE 5: THE SONS OF AIOLOS I

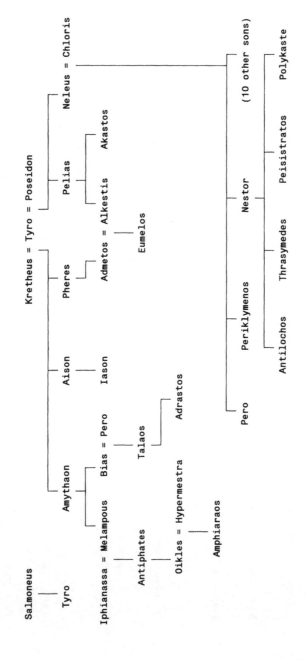

TABLE 6: THE SONS OF AIOLOS II

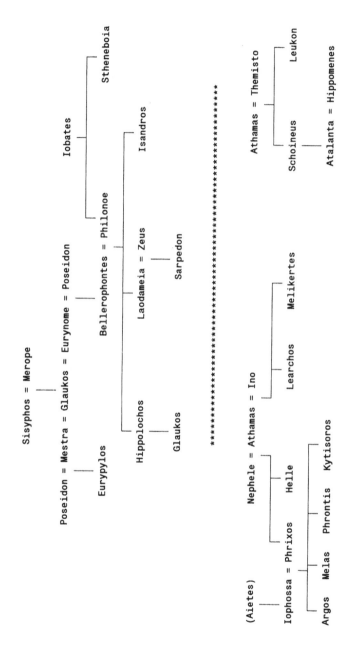

TABLE 7: THE SONS OF AIOLOS III

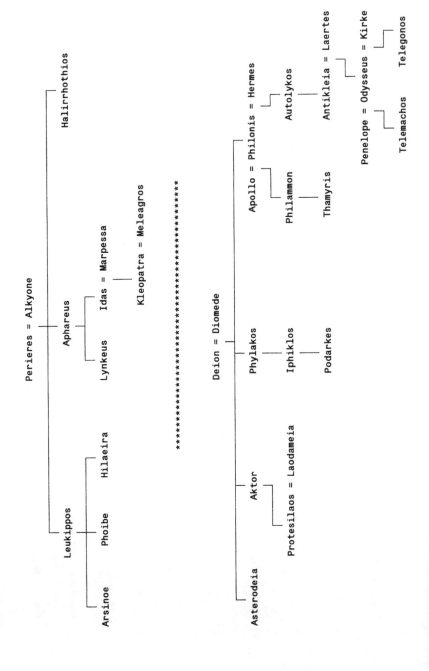

TABLE 8: THE LINE OF INACHOS

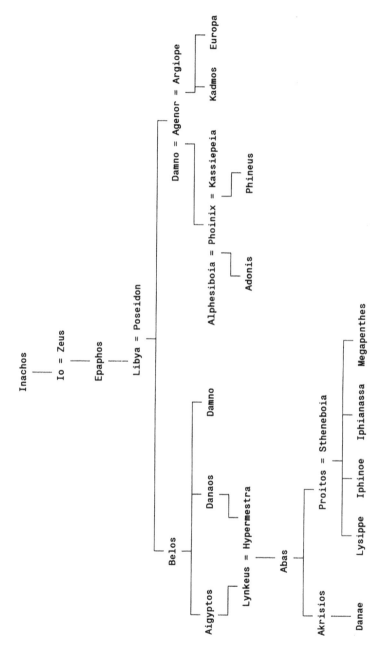

TABLE 9: THE DAUGHTERS OF ATLAS I

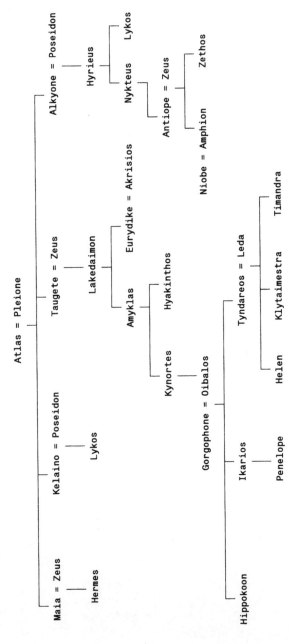

TABLE 10: THE DAUGHTERS OF ATLAS II

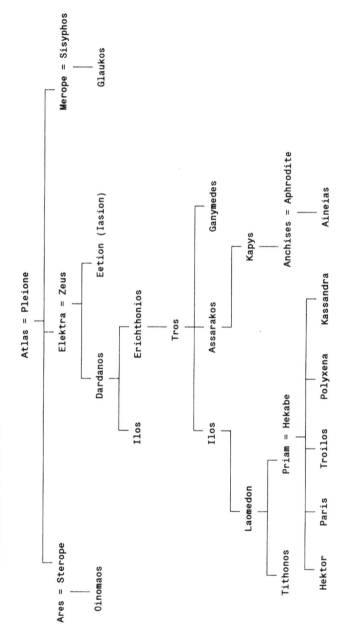

TABLE 11: THE DAUGHTERS OF ASOPOS

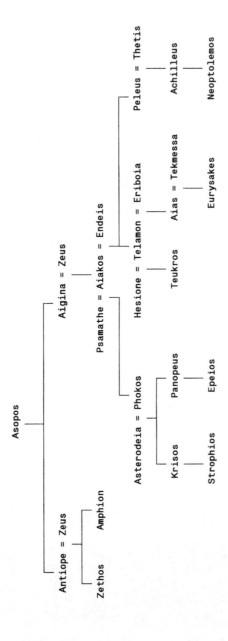

TABLE 12: THE HOUSE OF ATHENS

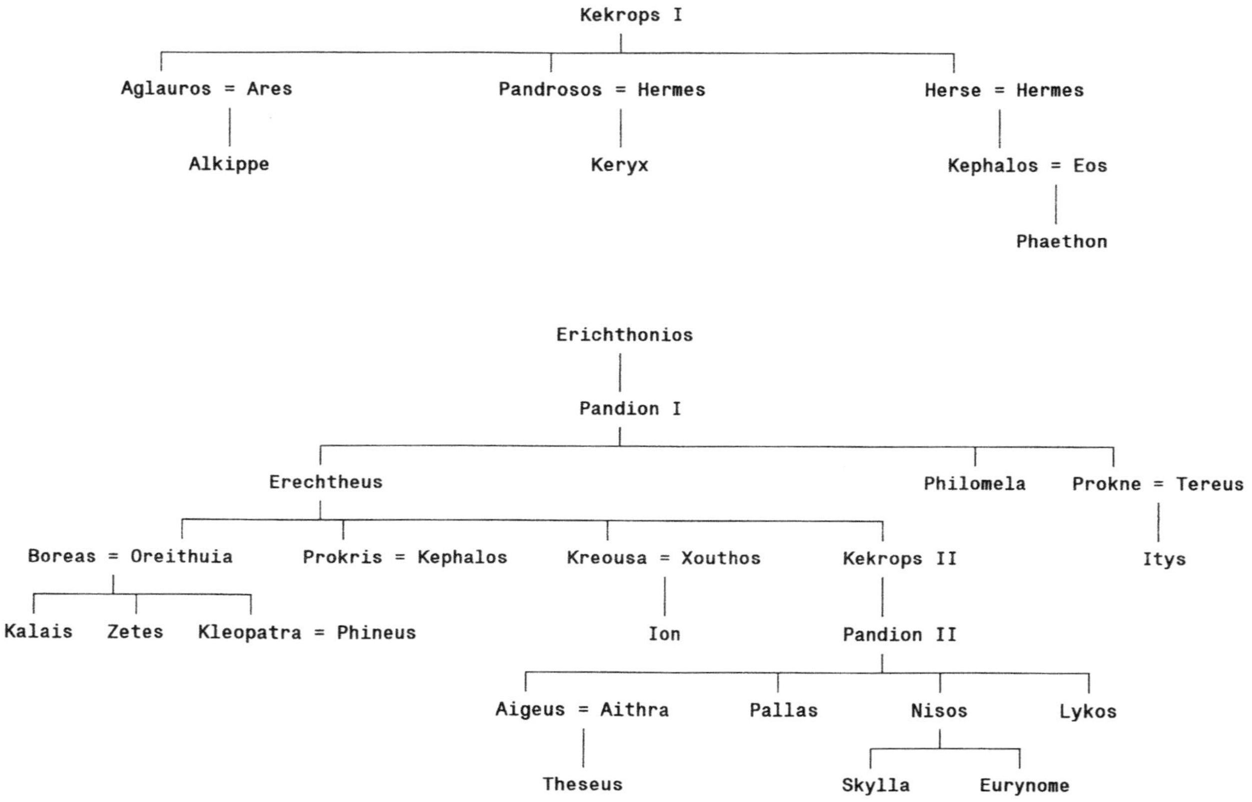

Kekrops I

Aglauros = Ares — Pandrosos = Hermes — Herse = Hermes

Alkippe

Keryx

Kephalos = Eos

Phaethon

Erichthonios

Pandion I

Erechtheus — Philomela — Prokne = Tereus

Itys

Boreas = Oreithuia — Prokris = Kephalos — Kreousa = Xouthos — Kekrops II — Aigeus = Aithra — Pallas — Nisos — Lykos

Kalais   Zetes   Kleopatra = Phineus

Ion

Pandion II

Theseus

Skylla   Eurynome

815

TABLE 13: THE LINE OF EUROPA

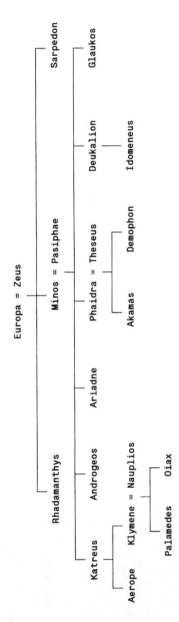

Europa = Zeus

Rhadamanthys   Minos = Pasiphae   Sarpedon

Katreus   Androgeos   Ariadne   Phaidra = Theseus   Deukalion   Glaukos

Aerope   Klymene = Nauplios   Akamas   Demophon   Idomeneus

Palamedes   Oiax

TABLE 14: THE LINE OF DANAE

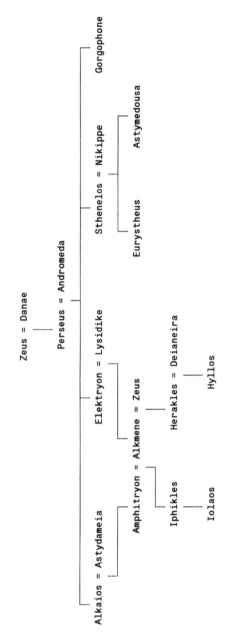

TABLE 15: THE LINE OF KADMOS

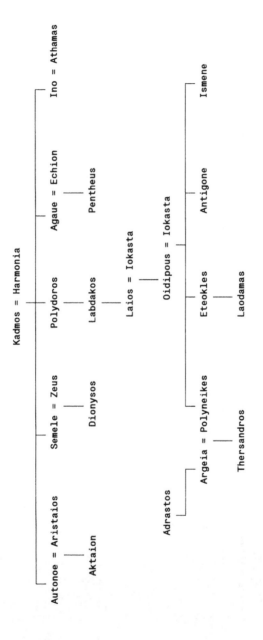

Kadmos = Harmonia

Autonoe = Aristaios   Semele = Zeus   Polydoros   Agaue = Echion   Ino = Athamas

Aktaion   Dionysos   Labdakos   Pentheus

Laios = Iokasta

Adrastos

Argeia = Polyneikes   Oidipous = Iokasta

Thersandros   Eteokles   Antigone   Ismene

Laodamas

TABLE 16: THE LINE OF TALAOS

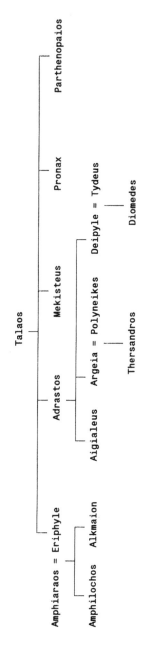

Talaos
├── Amphiaraos = Eriphyle
│   ├── Amphilochos
│   └── Alkmaion
├── Adrastos
│   ├── Aigialeus
│   └── Argeia = Polyneikes
│   └── Thersandros
├── Mekisteus
│   └── Deipyle = Tydeus
│   └── Diomedes
├── Pronax
└── Parthenopaios

TABLE 17: THE LINE OF TANTALOS

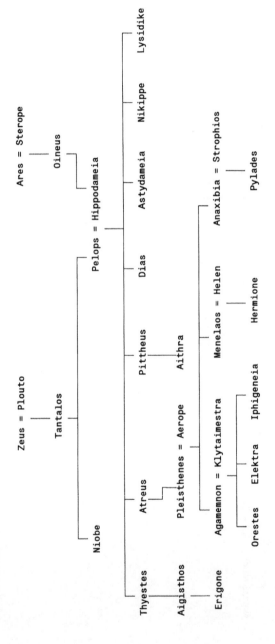

TABLE 18: THE LINE OF LYKAON

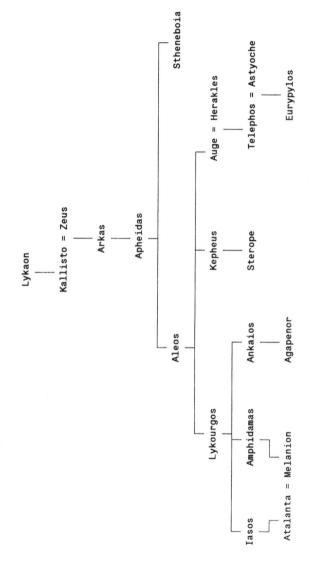

Abbreviations

A: *Hik*	Aischylos, *Hiketides (Supplices, Suppliants)*
AA	Ovid, *Ars Amatoria*
Ach	Statius, *Achilleis*
Ades	Adespota, that is, of uncertain authorship
AdvMath	Sextus Empiricus, *Pros Mathematikous (Adversus Mathematicos, Against the Scholars)*
Aen	Vergil, *Aeneid*
Ag	Aischylos, *Agamemnon*
Ai	Sophokles, *Aias*
Ais	Aischylos
Aith	*Aithiopis*
Akou	Akousilaos
Al	Alkaios
Alk	Euripides, *Alkestis*
Anab	Xenophon, *Anabasis*
And	Euripides, *Andromache*
Ant	Sophokles, *Antigone*
AntLib	Antoninus Liberalis
AP	*Palatine Anthology (Greek Anthology)*
Ap*B*	Apollodoros, *Bibliotheke (Library)*
Ap*E*	Apollodoros, *Epitome* (summary of last part of *Bibliotheke*)
Apl: *Met*	Apuleius, *Metamorphoses* (or *The Golden Ass*)
Apol	Plato, *Apologia*
Ap*Ty*	Flavius Philostratos, *Life of Apollonios of Tyana*
AR	Apollonios of Rhodes, *Argonautika*
Ar: *Lys*	Aristophanes, *Lysistrata*
Arat	Aratos, *Phainomena*
Arch	Isokrates, *Archidamos*

823

Aspis	*Aspis,* or *Shield of Herakles,* part of the Hesiodic Corpus
Astr	Hyginus, *De Astronomia*
Athen	Athenaios
AthPol	Aristotle, *Athenaion Politeia (Constitution of the Athenians)*
Aus	Recently discovered fragments of Euripides, cited according to Austin 1968
Ax	*Axiochos*
Bak	Bakchylides
Batr	Aristophanes, *Batrachoi (Ranae, Frogs)*
Bkch	Euripides, *Bakchai*
Bowra	Fragments of Pindar cited according to C. M. Bowra, *Pindari carmina* (Oxford 1947)
CarMin	Claudian, *Carmina Minora*
Cert	*Certamen Homeri et Hesiodi (The Contest between Homer and Hesiod)*
Chatzis	Fragments of Ptolemaios Chennos cited according to A. Chatzis, *Der Philosoph und Grammatiker Ptolemaios Chennos* (Paderborn 1914)
Cho	Aischylos, *Choephoroi*
Cl:*Pro*	Clement of Alexandria, *Protreptikos*
Coll	Collection
Cu	Vergil, *Culex*
Dar	Dares, *De Excidio Troiae Historia (Tale of the Fall of Troy)*
DD	Loukianos, *Dialogi Deorum (Dialogues of the Gods)*
Dem	Demosthenes
DH	Dionysios of Halikarnassos
Diehl	Fragments of Greek lyric poetry cited according to E. Diehl, *Anthologia Lyrica Graeca* 1–3 (Leipzig 1949–52)
Dik	Diktys, *Ephemeris Belli Troiani (Diary of the Trojan War)*
Div	Cicero, *De Divinatione*
DK	Testimonia and fragments of the Presocratic philosophers cited according to H. Diels and W. Kranz, *Die Fragmenta der Vorsokratiker* (6th ed., Berlin 1951)
DL	Diogenes Laertius
DMar	Loukianos, *Dialogi Marini (Dialogues of the Sea-gods)*
DMor	Loukianos, *Dialogi Mortuorum (Dialogues of the Dead)*
DP	Dion of Prusa
DS	Diodoros Siculus
E:*El*	Euripides, *Elektra*
E:*Hik*	Euripides, *Hiketides (Supplices, Suppliants)*
Ecl	Vergil, *Eclogues* (or *Bucolics*)
Epig	*Epigonoi*
Epitr	Menander, *Epitrepontes*

Eu-*Il*	Eustathios' commentary on the *Iliad*
Eu-*Od*	Eustathios' commentary on the *Odyssey*
Euag	Isokrates, *Euagoras*
Eum	Aischylos, *Eumenides*
Eum	Eumelos
Eur	Euripides
Fab	Hyginus, *Fabulae*
FGrH	Fragments of the Greek historians cited according to F. Jacoby, *Die Fragmente der griechischen Historiker* (Leiden 1923–58)
G	Vergil, *Georgics*
GLP	Fragments of more recent Greek literary papyri cited according to D. L. Page, *Select Papyri III* (London 1941)
Gomperz	Fragments of Philodemos cited according to T. Gomperz, *Herkulanische Studien* 2 (Leipzig 1866)
H	*Hymn*
HAp	*Homeric Hymn to Apollo*
HAph	*Homeric Hymn to Aphrodite*
HDem	*Homeric Hymn to Demeter*
Hdt	Herodotos
Hek	Euripides, *Hekabe (Hecuba)*
Hel	Euripides, *Helen*
Hell	Hellanikos
Hepta	Aischylos, *Hepta epi Thebas (Septem contra Thebas, Seven against Thebes)*
Her	Ovid, *Heroides*
Hes	Hesiod, or rather the corpus of "Hesiodic" fragments, most of them from the *Ehoiai*, cited according to the edition of R. Merkelbach and M. L. West, *Fragmenta Hesiodea* (Oxford 1967)
HF	Euripides, *Herakles Mainomenos (Hercules Furens)*
HHerm	*Homeric Hymn to Hermes*
Hipp	Euripides, *Hippolytos*
Hkld	Euripides, *Herakleidai*
HN	Pliny, *Historia Naturalis*
HomH	*Homeric Hymn*
Hyg	Hyginus
IA	Euripides, *Iphigeneia at Aulis*
IG	Inscriptiones Graecae
Il	Homer, *Iliad*
IlMik	*Ilias Mikra (Little Iliad)*
Is	Pindar, *Isthmian Odes*

IT	Euripides, *Iphigeneia among the Tauroi*
Kaibel	Fragments of Epicharmos cited according to G. Kaibel, *Comicorum Graecorum Fragmenta* 1 (Berlin 1899)
Katast	Ps-Eratosthenes, *Katasterismoi*
Kenyon	Fragments of Hypereides cited according to the edition of F. G. Kenyon, *Hyperidis Orationes et Fragmenta* (Oxford 1907)
Kern	Fragments of Orphic writers cited according to O. Kern, *Orphicorum Fragmenta* (Berlin 1922)
Kock	Fragments of Greek comedy cited according to T. Kock, *Comicorum Atticorum Fragmenta* (Leipzig 1880–88)
Kyn	Xenophon, *Kynegetikos*
Kyp	*Kypria*
LL	Varro, *De Lingua Latina*
LP	Fragments of Sappho and Alkaios cited according to E. Lobel and D. L. Page, *Poetarum Lesbiorum Fragmenta* (Oxford 1955)
Lyk	Lykophron, *Alexandra*
Lys	Plutarch, *Lysandros*
Med	Euripides, *Medeia*
Mem	Xenophon, *Memorabilia*
Met	Ovid, *Metamorphoses*
Mim	Mimnermos
Mir	Aristotle, *Peri Thaumasiôn Akousmatôn (Mirabilia, Concerning Wondrous Things)*
Mor	Plutarch, *Moralia*
MW	Fragments of the Hesiodic Corpus cited according to R. Merkelbach and M. L. West, *Fragmenta Hesiodea* (Oxford 1967)
N²	Fragments of Euripides cited according to A. Nauck, *Tragicorum Graecorum Fragmenta* (2d ed., Leipzig 1889)
NA	Aelianus, *De Natura Animalium*
Nau	*Naupaktia*
ND	Cicero, *De Natura Deorum*
Nem	Pindar, *Nemean Odes*
Neph	Aristophanes, *Nephelai (Nubes, Clouds)*
OA	*Orphic Argonautika*
OCT	*Oxford Classical Texts*
Od	Homer, *Odyssey*
Oed	Seneca, *Oedipus*
Oik	Loukianos, *Peri tou Oikou (De Domo, On the Hall)*
OK	Sophokles, *Oidipous at Kolonos*
Ol	Pindar, *Olympian Odes*

Or	Euripides, *Orestes*
OT	Sophokles, *Oidipous Tyrannos (Oedipus Rex, Oedipus the King)*
Pa	Pindar, *Paians*
Pac	Pacuvius
Pal	Palaiphatos
Panath	Isokrates, *Panathenaikos*
Par	Parthenios
Paus	Pausanias
PCG	Fragments of Greek comedy cited according to R. Kassel and C. Austin, *Poetae Comici Graeci* (Berlin 1983-)
PD	Aischylos, *Prometheus Desmotes (Prometheus Vinctus, Prometheus Bound)*
PEG	Fragments of early Greek epic cited according to the edition of A. Bernabé, *Poetae Epici Graeci* 1 (Leipzig 1987)
Per	Plutarch, *Perikles*
Pf	Fragments of Kallimachos cited according to Pfeiffer 1949
Ph	Sophokles, *Philoktetes*
Pher	Pherekydes of Athens
PHerc	Papyrus fragments from Herculaneum
Phil	Philochoros
Pho	Euripides, *Phoinissai (Phoinician Women)*
PMG	Fragments of the Greek lyric poets cited according to D. L. Page, *Poetae Melici Graeci* (Oxford 1962)
Poet	Aristotle, *Poetics*
Pol	Plato, *Politikos*
Pow	Fragments of Euphorion and other Hellenistic poets cited according to J. U. Powell, *Collectanea Alexandrina* (Oxford 1925)
POxy	Papyrus fragments from Oxyrhynchus in Egypt, as published in the *Oxyrhynchus Papyri* series (London 1898-)
Prop	Propertius
Prot	Plato, *Protagoras*
PRylands	Papyrus fragments in the John Rylands Library in Manchester
PSI	Papyrus fragments published in the Papiri Greci e Latini series (Pubblicazioni della Societa italiana, Florence 1912-)
Py	Pindar, *Pythian Odes*
QS	Quintus of Smyrna
R	Fragments of Aischylos' or Sophokles' lost plays, cited according to S. Radt's *Tragicorum Graecorum Fragmenta* editions (Göttingen 1985, 1977)
Rep	Plato, *Republic*
Rh	Euripides, *Rhesos*

Rhet	Aristotle, *Rhetoric*
Rib	Fragments of Roman tragedy cited according to O. Ribbeck, *Tragicorum Romanorum Fragmenta* (Leipzig 1897)
Rose	Fragments of Aristotle cited according to V. Rose, *Aristotelis qui ferebantur librorum fragmenta* (Stuttgart 1886)
RP	Claudian, *De raptu Proserpinae*
S: *El*	Sophokles, *Elektra*
Sal	Loukianos, *De Saltatione*
Sen: *Ag*	Seneca, *Agamemnon*
Sen: *Med*	Seneca, *Medea*
Sen: *Ph*	Seneca, *Phaedra*
Sen: *Tro*	Seneca, *Troades*
Sim	Simonides
SLG	Recently discovered fragments of the Greek lyric poets cited according to D. L. Page, *Supplementum Lyricis Graecis* (Oxford 1974)
SM	Fragments of Pindar or Bakchylides cited according to the Teubner editions of B. Snell and H. Maehler (Pindar: Leipzig 1975 [4th ed.]; Bakchylides: Leipzig 1970 [10th ed.])
Sn	Fragments of minor Greek tragedians cited according to B. Snell, *Tragicorum Graecorum Fragmenta* 1 (Göttingen 1971)
Sol	Plutarch, *Solon*
Soph	Sophokles
Sph	Aristophanes, *Sphekes (Vespae, Wasps)*
St: *Theb*	Statius, *Thebais*
Stes	Stesichoros
Str	Strabo
Sym	Plato, *Symposion*
TD	Cicero, *Tusculan Disputations*
Tel	*Telegoneia*
test	*testimonia*
Th	Hesiod, *Theogony*
Theb	*Thebais*
Theog	Theognis
Theok	Theokritos
Ther	Nikandros, *Theriaka*
Thes	Plutarch, *Theseus*
Thouk	Thoukydides
Tib	Suetonius, *Tiberius*
Tim	Plato, *Timaios*
Tit	*Titanomachia*

Tr	Sophokles, *Trachiniai (Women of Trachis)*
Tro	Euripides, *Troades (Trojan Women)*
VF	Valerius Flaccus, *Argonautica*
VH	Aelianus, *Varia Historia*
VM	Vatican Mythographer
W	Fragments of elegiac and iambic poets cited according to M. L. West, *Iambi et Elegi Graeci* (Oxford 1971)
Westermann	Mythological texts (assigned to Libanius and Nonnos) cited according to Westermann 1843
W&D	Hesiod, *Works & Days*

Notes to Volume Two

Chapter 14. Thebes

1. On the difficulties involved in this and other attributions to early mythographers see Vian 1963.21–26.

2. So Vian (ibid.), although he would exclude Kadmos' exile and servitude to Ares on the grounds that Zeus' resolution of the conflict between Kadmos and Ares precludes such exile. I confess I do not see why the two ideas are incompatible: on the scholiast's view Ares wants to destroy Kadmos, so that Zeus' resolution may well consist of letting the mortal off with a lighter sentence (certainly not inappropriate considering that Kadmos has dispossessed the original resident of the land). More skeptical on the question of Hellanikian origins are van der Valk (1963.305–6), who argues that the scholiast has simply attached Hellanikos' name to an Apollodoran account in order to look more scholarly, and Jacoby (commentary at 4F51).

3. So Vian (1963.44–45), pointing out armor, lack of pitcher, and lack of clear indication of fountain house. But these last two factors count against Achilleus as well; in favor of Kadmos (or at least a myth concentrating on the snake), see Stibbe 1972.170, Schefold 1978.79–80, and now Prag 1985.45–46 (arguing that the Rider Painter derived this scene from that of Achilleus in ambush).

4. Catalogue of these and other artistic representations in Vian 1963.35–44.

5. On scenes of Kadmos and Harmonia in art, see Schauenburg 1957, where in addition to the Louvre neck-amphora the author tentatively suggests Göttingen R23, a Black-Figure oinochoe with a boar, two lions, and a wolf drawing a chariot sometimes thought to be that of Admetos.

6. See E. R. Dodds' note ad loc. in his edition of the play (Oxford 1960).

7. Actually only the last twelve lines of the Hymn are preserved in manuscript; the beginning (presumably from the same poem) comes from a citation in Diodoros.

8. See Carpenter (1986.22–29), however, where it is argued that Aphrodite disappears from such scenes after about 540, leaving us unsure about the identity of the women who sometimes replace her.

9. See Gantz 1980.154–58.

10. See Gantz 1981.29–30.

11. See p. 220 above, and Kaempf-Dimitriadou 1979.23.

12. = PMich 1447: see T. Renner, *HSCP* 82 (1978) 282–87.

13. To this scant information on Aktaion in the *Ehoiai* should perhaps be added *POxy* 2509, as Lobel thought. The hexameter text describes some goddess (Athena? Artemis?) coming to the cave of Cheiron to tell him something about Dionysos, son of

Zeus and Semele, and about dogs, Aktaion, madness, and grief. Lobel supposed this to mean that Aktaion's death was prophesied, but subsequent scholars are surely right to think that Aktaion has just died, and that the goddess in question tells Cheiron that Dionysos himself will hunt with these dogs in future, until he goes up to Olympos. Either the goddess or Cheiron then removes the madness *(lussa)* from the dogs, and they are greatly upset to find their master dead (for this reconstruction see now R. Janko, *Phoenix* 38 [1984] 299–307). Much the same situation (without the goddess) appears in Apollodoros, where Artemis casts madness upon the dogs, and they do in fact come to Cheiron's cave after the slaying, to be mollified by an image of Aktaion which he makes for them (ApB 3.4.4). Whether this is sufficient to justify an attribution to the *Ehoiai* I do not know; the discursive tone, direct address, and concern for the future of the dogs might be thought to indicate epic proper rather than a catalogue poem.

14. On this version as perhaps earlier than we might have supposed (given that it appears only in Diodoros [and Hyginus]), see Lacy 1990.34–42. Among other arguments he suggests that Aktaion's intent to marry Artemis was suppressed by Kallimachos because such a circumstance gave Artemis more justification than was appropriate to a comparison with the "more merciful" Athena of *Hymn* 5.

15. The scene on an Apulian volute krater (Naples Stg 31), with Aktaion killing a deer in the presence of Artemis near a spring, has however been taken as an allusion to the goddess' bath: see ibid., 36–39.

16. For a very useful assessment that pulls together the different threads of Aktaion's story into a whole, see now Forbes-Irving 1990.80–90 together with 197–201.

17. See Radt 1985.116–17 for various other suggested possibilities. The (mistaken, I believe) notion of Asklepiades that Hera appeared in the *Xantriai* disguised as a temple priestess is discussed above, pp. 474–75.

18. For the following reconstruction see also Webster 1967.205–11.

19. Probably also on Athens 11798, a "Megarian" relief bowl with a representation of a Satyros and woman in a cave, as well as two other scenes that may be part of Euripides' play (or at least the story): see Sinn 1979.109 (MB 51) and pl. 21.1, 2.

20. So Jacoby, who includes this and other fragments of the presumed Peisandros under heading 16 in his edition of the lost Greek historians; see also his comments in the corresponding *Kommentar* volume, where the scholion is supposed to derive from a single account, itself patched together from various sources, including tragedy (1957.493–96). Earlier Bethe (1891.1–28) had argued that almost the entire scholion (including the Chrysippos section) was drawn from the epic *Oidipodeia*. But Robert (1915.149–67) has well shown the insuperable problems therein, especially regarding the attempt to link Hera's wrath against Laios with the Sphinx; he himself regards the scholion as a conflation of numerous different sources, only a few of which come from the Peisandros cited.

21. See Lloyd-Jones 1983.120–21 and Thalmann 1978.16. The latter argues that the naming of the Sphinx as a "reproach to Thebes" (*Hepta* 539: *poleôs oneidos*) means that the Thebans had for Aischylos done something to merit her depredations. But perhaps the reproach lay in their inability to deal with her until Oidipous arrived. Thalmann's further point, that in Aischylos' *Sphinx* someone sends the monster (fr 236 R), is dubious, since the word *pempei* at *Batr* 1287 almost certainly goes with the parody of the *Agamemnon*.

22. See Robert 1915.155–57, 396–414, supported by L. Deubner, *Abh Berlin* 4 (1942) 3–27; the latter regards the entire first half of the Peisandros scholion as drawn

from the *Chrysippos* (and culminating in Laios' death). More recently, K. Schefold (*Classica et Provincialia: Festschrift Erna Diez* [Graz 1978] 177–81) has returned to the theory of a Laios-Chrysippos tale in late Archaic epic, arguing that themes of transgression and hereditary atonement (by Laios and his descendants) are most appropriate to that period. Clearly much depends upon one's subjective reactions to the story and its place in Greek thought.

23. Conceivably this passage too allows Laios to avoid his fate by not begetting a child. But Iokaste's failure to mention that fact, plus the casual relegation of the birth to a subordinate clause, more naturally suggest that the child has already been conceived, so that exposure after its birth is Laios' only option.

24. See Sinn 1979.106 (MB 44) and pl. 21.3.

25. Robert (1915.94–97) cites in this connection the scholia at *Odyssey* 11.271, where the Sikyonian herdsmen care for Oidipous and he eventually sets out for Thebes (not Delphi) to find his parents, and postulates an Aischylean version in which Oidipous is not adopted by the king of any other land but knows from the beginning that he is a foundling, and knows as well the city where he may expect to find his parents, if not their identity. On this interpretation Laios himself is thought to be headed toward Kithairon in search of his son when the two meet and fail to recognize each other.

26. On this hydria's possible links to what we know as Chalkidian ware, see A. Collinge, *AA* (1988) 628–31.

27. Discussion in Robert 1915.48–58.

28. On the Sphinx of Thebes in art (with or without Oidipous) see the catalogue and discussion in Moret 1984. Two early items rightly (I think) discounted by him as generic man and Sphinx (if linked at all) are Thebes 50.265 (Boiotian kantharos) and Capua 183 (a Campanian amphora): see 81 n. 4.

29. On possible erotic motifs here see Vermeule 1979.171–73.

30. See M. L. West, *Greek Metre* (Oxford 1982) 98.

31. For other, less certain vases on which Oidipous defeating the Sphinx by force have been suspected, see Moret 1984.79–91. As he there notes (79), the painting on the Boston lekythos (97.374) which supported Robert's belief in the early existence of this version is probably modern. I omit here various other literary references that make Oidipous "destroy" or "kill" the Sphinx because such wording need mean no more than that the solving of the riddle caused the Sphinx to kill herself. But perhaps to be noted is Athenaios 6.253f, where as part of a song composed for Demetrios Poliorketes Oidipous is said to have thrown the Sphinx from a cliff.

32. See Webster's reconstruction (1967.242–46).

33. Published by P. Parsons (*ZPE* 26 [1977] 7–36) and now included by Malcolm Davies in volume 1 of his new edition of the melic poets (Oxford 1991) as Stesichoros 222b. The attribution to Stesichoros is not certain but seems very likely: on the metrics see M. Haslam, *GRBS* 19 (1978) 29–57.

34. See Severyns (1928.215), who believes that this can in fact be deduced (from the scholia and Eustathios at *Il* 23.681) as a conclusion of Aristarchos.

35. The T scholia at *Il* 23.679 seem in fact of the opinion that only in Homer and Hesiod (i.e., the *Ehoiai*) does Oidipous live on as king.

36. See n. 33 above.

37. Text uncertain, and *andrêlatên* has been emended to refer to Polyneikes (rather than Eteokles) as the future exiler of his brother. Even if the text is sound, we are probably dealing with a certain amount of emotional exaggeration.

38. Most notably F. Solmsen, *TAPA* 68 (1937) 197–211.

39. See A. Burnett, *GRBS* 14 (1973) 343–68.

40. Text not entirely certain, and one word (the corrupt *araias*) has been omitted; it is not certain with what it agreed. For an analysis of this passage with conclusions running counter to mine, see G. R. Manton, *BICS* 8 (1961) 81–83.

41. On a Tyrrhenian amphora in Basel, Eriphyle, Baton, and Oikles are all named as watching the departure (Cahn Coll 921). Other possible early representations of this scene include an ivory relief from the Halos deposit at Delphi and a bronze relief from Olympia (B 103).

42. The scholia at *Odyssey* 11.326 also state that Eriphyle received the necklace "from Polyneikes or Adrastos" but add no details. In Hyginus, surprisingly, Adrastos has the necklace made, and with it bribes Eriphyle to reveal the hiding place of her concealed husband (*Fab* 73). Bethe (1891.50–56) supposed from these accounts an epic version ("Der Amphiaraos Ausfahrt") in which Eriphyle had every right to prefer the necklace, not believing the predictions of her husband's death, and there was no matricide/revenge. Certainly this is a possible stage in the development of the story, but the evidence does not do much to support it. In Apollodoros, Polyneikes goes to Iphis, son of Alektor, who advises the necklace as a bribe to Eriphyle (Ap*B* 3.6.1).

43. Drachmann 1927.3.

44. The bulk of our information about this play derives from the text of a papyrus first published in 1908 and hence not included in Nauck. See Bond's edition of all this material, with commentary (Oxford 1963).

45. Kunze (1950.175) rather leans toward the view that this right-hand inscription does refer to an on-looker; he does not consider the possibility that the right-hand warrior was Tydeus.

46. The scene has also long been thought to represent Herakles killing Iphitos; if the victim could be male (the outline of a female breast seems the main point of contention) I would suggest too as a possibility Orestes and Aigisthos.

47. For this interpretation see R. Hampe, *AntK* 18 (1975) 10–16; the reverse of the skyphos may show the departure of Tydeus from Deipyle in Argos.

48. Robert, for example, argues (1915.121–29) that Ismene is a priestess of Athena seduced by Periklymenos, son of Poseidon, and punished by the goddess for that reason (in a context completely separate from the expedition); see in any case his discussion of the evidence from art.

49. For this gem see Krauskopf 1974.43, 108 and pl. 20.1; Hampe and Simon 1964.27–28 and fig. 5.

50. See R. Meiggs, *The Athenian Empire* (Oxford 1972) 469–72.

51. Just previously, Pausanias has noted the presence, near this group, of seven statues of the original attackers, although he names, alas, only Polyneikes. The wording of his description of the Epigonoi group may suggest that he did not think of (or see before him) Mekisteus as one of the Seven.

52. See Krauskopf 1974.43–45.

53. J. Nicole, *Les scolies genevoises de l'Iliade* (Geneva and Basel 1891) II 63–64.

54. *ARV²* 1073.4. For both these vases and their subject matter see Beazley, *JHS* 67 (1947) 1–7.

55. See now the assessment and bibliography in Hutchinson 1985.209–11, plus R. D. Dawe, *CQ* 17 (1967) 16–28 and *Dionysiaca* (ed. R. D. Dawe, J. Diggle, P. Easterling: Cambridge 1978) 87–103.

56. So Lloyd-Jones, *CQ* 9 (1959) 87–92, in the context of an interpretation in which he supposes the word *ateknous* to be corrupt or else to imply something closer to "ill-begotten" than "without children."

57. See the arguments of Hutchinson (1985.195–96), who discounts this last possibility and excises the line, probably rightly.

58. On this vase see F. Hauser, *JdI* 8 (1893) 93–103 (where the scene is interpreted as the sacrifice of Polyxena), H. Thiersch, *"Tyrrhenische Amphoren"* (Leipzig 1899) 55–58, and among more recent discussions of the problems, J. P. Small, *RM* 83 (1976) 124–26.

59. On this reconstruction see Webster 1967.265–68.

Chapter 15. The Line of Tantalos

1. Admittedly there is no hard evidence for this conclusion, merely the fact that a *Atreidōn Kathodos* is attested only here and at one other point in Athenaios, where a battle is in progress (9.399a). Either way, Tantalos' appearance in this poem is puzzling; Wilamowitz (1884.157) was surely right to stress that even if the work did include Agamemnon's descent to Hades, we ought not to expect to find Tantalos and his rock there.

2. The serving of Pelops will be attested already in the sixth century, if E. Simon (1967.281–87) is right in supposing the Foce del Sele *Dreifuss* metope to represent the child in the cauldron. But we have seen that there are many other possible interpretations, including the death of Minos: see p. 275.

3. Gerber (1982.55–59) well discusses these problems, although I am not in accord with his belief that the cauldron and ivory shoulder of the opening scene are part of what Pindar means to reject. My own views appear in *RivStCl* 26 (1978) 31–35.

4. So now Gerber 1982.99–103, with earlier bibliography and full discussion.

5. For the idea that Tantalos claimed (or revealed?) the sun to be a mass of hot metal (so Σ *Ol* 1.91, DL 2.8), plus a possible origin of Euripides' version in Anaxagoras' views on meteorites, see R. Scodel, *HSCP* 88 (1984) 13–24.

6. I am not convinced by Van Keuren's interpretation (1989.139–46) of the Turtle-rider Foce del Sele metope as Tantalos, but her arguments are intriguing and demonstrate how little we really know on this subject.

7. For the tradition that Minos was the one to kidnap Ganymedes, see p. 559 below.

8. Schefold suggests, however, that the two accounts are to be seen on a *terra sigillata* fragment in Bruges from the second century A.D. (1981.218 and fig.299): the wing of an eagle shows that he has flown off with Ganymedes as a distressed Tantalos (in Phrygian dress) and a small Eros look on. This is possible, although I would have thought Tros himself losing his son a more likely conjecture.

9. See Willcock 1964.141–42.

10. See, e.g., J. Th. Kakridis (*Homeric Researches* [Lund 1949] 96–103) for a reiteration of the ancient view that Niobe's metamorphosis here is an interpolation designed to bring Homer's innovations into line with the more familiar tradition.

11. On the identification of these at times disputed figures (and interpretation of Pausanias' account) see Säflund 1970.112–21.

12. On all phases of the story in the (mostly late) artistic tradition see Säflund 1970. 131–42.

13. For useful discussion and reconstruction of the play (assuming Myrtilos' par-

ticipation to have been central) see W. M. Calder, *Philologus* 118 (1974) 203–14, where it is argued that Myrtilos' betrayal of his master here is simply the carrying out of the will of Zeus against the murderous Oinomaos.

14. Calder (ibid.) supposes this motif to be the invention of Euripides.

15. For late Etruscan urns on which Myrtilos dies by some means other than falling from Pelops' chariot (but still at the hands of Oinomaos or Pelops), see Säflund 1970.142.

16. See Severyns 1928.231–34.

17. So Robert 1915.406–12, although he excludes the Dositheos version as plainly the invention of a later time. The evidence for a Sophoklean play of this name is a single quote by Stobaios (fr 472 R), who may intend by "Hippodameia" only the speaker of the lines (in the *Oinomaos?*), not the title of the work.

18. See p. 311 above.

19. On this scholion see n. 20 below.

20. From Wolfenbüttel Gudianus graec. 15, second hand (Gu). Not in Schwartz's edition of the scholia; text printed in Pearson 1917 1.92, Radt 1977.162. On the manuscript see A. Turyn, *The Byzantine Manuscript Tradition of the Tragedies of Euripides* (Urbana 1957) 20–21, 60–61.

21. Fraenkel, however, strongly defends the manuscript reading in his commentary (1950 3.758–60), arguing that the twelfth or thirteenth as saved is a folktale pattern on which our modern notions of seemliness should not be allowed to intrude.

22. In Hyginus' account something has fallen out, but both there and in Lactantius Placidus (who offers a fuller account drawn probably from the same source: Σ St: *Theb* 4.306) Pelopia seemingly knows her assistant and exposes the child for that reason; he is again suckled by goats, thus explaining his name.

23. Pelops' children here (which in fact match perfectly those reported by Σ *Or* 4) are in the part omitted by Merkelbach and West. For the form "Kleolla" actually reported by Tzetzes, see West 1985.111–12.

24. For this text see M. Papathomopoulos, *Nouveaux fragments d'auteurs anciens* (Ioannina 1980) 11–26.

Chapter 16. The Trojan War

1. So Robert 1920–26.388–89, arguing that a patronymic can in Homer go back to the grandfather at most, and then only exceptionally.

2. For these see Kaempf-Dimitriadou 1979.7–12, plus catalogue at 76–79.

3. Strabo, who gives a fuller account of this expedition (with the attack by mice) speaks only of Teukroi, and says that the elegiac poet Kallinos told their story (13.604). We find Teukros as a Kretan also in the second-century Hegesianax's *Troika* (45F4), and of course in Vergil (*Aen* 3.104–10).

4. Servius at *Aeneid* 3.167 suggests that Dardanos is the child of Zeus and Elektra, Iasion that of Korythos and Elektra. In this scholion Dardanos founds Dardania while Iasion takes possession of Samothrace. For Iasion there see also Diodoros 5.48.4–49.4, where his mating with Demeter is integrated into the local mysteries.

5. For this hypothesis and other fragments of Euripides' play, see R. A. Coles, *A New Oxyrhynchus Papyrus: The Hypothesis of Euripides' Alexandros* (London 1974).

6. See in addition to ibid. on the fragments the reconstruction of Scodel 1980. 20–42.

7. Some Alexandrian scholars did attempt to find references to such an oath in

several passages of the *Iliad* (e.g., 2.284–90, 2.337–41). But these clearly denote the boasts and promises warriors customarily make to each other when setting out for war.

8. In support of this point see now M. Davies, *JHS* 101 (1981) 56–62.

9. For the whole Greek artistic tradition of the Judgment see Raab 1972.

10. On the animals accompanying the goddesses (and the absence of the apple frequently assumed to have been held by Paris), see R. Hampe in *Neue Beiträge zur klassischen Altertumswissenschaft: Festschrift Bernhard Schweitzer* (Stuttgart 1954) 77–86.

11. So perhaps even earlier on NY 98.8.11, a Black-Figure neck-amphora by the Swing Painter on which the middle goddess of the procession holds up a very small round object. For these and other possible instances of the apple (and arguments against those [such as Clairmont 1951.102–4] who doubt its appearance in Attic art) see Raab 1972.49–60.

12. On this point see Stinton 1965.51–63.

13. On all these solutions, with bibliography, see Bernabé 1987.52–53 (*apparatus* to fr 14); he himself prefers the last-named possibility.

14. See the catalogue of Ghali-Kahil 1955.49–70.

15. For metrical arguments placing the *Elektra* in the 420s B.C., see G. Zuntz, *The Political Plays of Euripides* (Manchester 1955) 68–71. But even conceding the play's supposed link with Athens' Sicilian expedition, the work will date to 413, a year before the certain date of 412 for the *Helen*.

16. So in Apollodoros, and Tzetzes after correction; the *Odyssey* scholia (see below) have "Oinotropoi."

17. The text has the aorist of *peithô* here; presumably somewhere in transmission someone misconstrued a conative imperfect as representing a completed fact.

18. For the interpretation of the scene on this krater (there are no names) and a slightly later loutrophoros by the same painter in a private collection in Naples, see Trendall in Böhr and Martini 1986.165–68.

19. See Radt 1985.343–44.

20. See Severyns 1928.291–95.

21. On the interpretation see Bauchhenss-Thüriedl 1971.16–18.

22. The A (and in part T) scholia at *Iliad* 9.668 claim the existence of a town Skyros in Phrygia as well, perhaps simply to eliminate conflict between Homer and the tale of the concealment in Lykomedes' court. But whether they know of such a town or are just guessing, Homer certainly could have intended something local here.

23. So Severyns (1928.285–91), claiming that an epitomator of Proklos substituted the storm version for that of the concealment in Proklos' text so as to create agreement with the account of the *Little Iliad*. The *Iliad* scholion in question (Σb *Il* 19.326) is now printed by Bernabé in his edition as *Kyp* fr 19.

24. In contrast to Severyns (previous note) Robert suggests (1881.34) that Polygnotos in fact introduced this version into Athens as a variant designed to rescue Skyros from the humiliation of a military conquest.

25. For the text of the papyrus see Austin 1968.95–96; for the reconstruction of the play, Webster 1967.95–97.

26. So already the *Iliad* scholia (A at 9.145).

27. Solmsen 1981.353–58.

28. For this date see P. Von der Mühll 1958.141–46; for 454 B.C., the other possibility offered by the scholia, Bowra 1964.402–5.

29. For supporters of these opposing views see Gantz, *HSCP* 87 (1983) 71–78.

30. For this and other suggested trilogies see Radt 1985.115.

31. See Lesky 1972.481–82.

32. See Mette 1963.101–3.

33. See, for example, Strabo 13.1.35, where the precinct is located at the point where the Thymbraios River empties into the Skamandros.

34. On this problem see Kunze 1950.141–42.

35. Although the interpretation of this rare instance of Troilos defending himself is questioned by von Bothmer (1957.11) on the grounds that the rider is bearded.

36. On these and several other sixth-century Lakonian examples see Pipili 1987. 27–30.

37. So Zancani Montuoro and Zanotti-Bianco 1954.275–88; in support of the Troilos interpretation see now Van Keuren (1989.95–103), who offers among other arguments the belief that the victim here is unbearded.

38. Text not entirely certain: see Erbse ad loc. and Radt 1977.453.

39. That he was also conceived as a warrior in Vergil's *Aeneid* has sometimes been supposed, given the scene on the Carthage temple doors in Book 1 with Troilos dragged behind his chariot, still holding the reins, his "weapons having been lost," and his "reversed spear dragging in the dust" (*Aen* 1.474–78). Mention of this chariot and lost weapons has been thought to mean that Troilos has challenged Achilleus to battle and been struck by the latter's spear. But the emphasis throughout this section is on the brutality of the Greeks; Troilos has more likely "lost" his arms because he has taken them off, thinking himself safe, and the "reversed spear" seems proved by a later passage in the *Aeneid* to be his own, used as a goad for his horses (*Aen* 9.609–10): see R. D. Williams, *CQ* 10 (1960) 145–48.

40. Presumably to pass the time. In Polygnotos' Nekuia painting for the Knidian Lesche at Delphi, Pausanias reports seeing Palamedes and Thersites playing at dice (10.31.1); this might spring from an actual narrative or represent simply an artist's conceit.

41. For these sources (quoted in full) and very useful discussion see Scodel 1980. 43–54.

42. The Aischylean fragment 182 R is clearly an enumeration of Palamedes' accomplishments spoken by himself, and we know of no other play in which it could be placed. If it was part of the *Palamedes*, then Aischylos would seem to have staged both the execution (but probably not a trial) and Nauplios' protest in the same drama.

43. So Robert (1920–26.1134), who reminds us, however, that Oiax or even someone like Aias or Achilleus is also possible.

44. For this conclusion see Scodel 1980.51–54.

45. Virtually nothing survives of either play; the titles may well be two different appellations for the same drama.

46. Other such plays (about which nothing is known) include a *Priamos* by Philokles, a *Hektor* by Astydamas, son of Astydamas, and a *Ransoming of Hektor* by Dionysios I, tyrant of Syracuse.

47. See Webster 1967.84–85. The play is parodied as early as Aristophanes' *Acharnes* 421, where Euripides suggests to Dikaiopolis the rags of his blind Phoinix as a suitable costume.

48. For the arguments see W. Ritchie, *The Authenticity of the Rhesus of Euripides* (Cambridge 1964).

49. For a catalogue of such representations, with commentary, see K. Friis Johansen 1967.244–80.

50. Zancani Montuoro and Zanotti-Bianco 1954.250–59.

51. Ibid., 260–68.

52. Admittedly, Patroklos' tending has been taken by some to reflect a narrative moment from the *Kypria*, namely a wound sustained in the battle with Telephos (so Robert 1920–26.1148); there is really no evidence for or against this notion.

53. So Schefold 1964.42–43; K. Friis Johansen 1967.279–80, with bibliography.

54. For this (probably well-founded) skepticism, see Taplin 1977.431–33.

55. See Gantz 1980.220–21, 1981.146–48.

56. Adding probability to the interpretation of this scene as Achilleus and Paris is the fact that the other side almost certainly shows Achilleus, Hektor, and Athena.

57. Against this view Hampe (in Hampe and Simon 1964.47–49) argues that on the lost Chalkidian amphora Achilleus has been slain by the (much smaller) arrow in his side, the shot to the ankle having only incapacitated him. I would agree that Paris could make this shot, but Apollo should have no need for more than one arrow.

58. See P. Kakridis, *Hermes* 89 (1961) 288–97.

59. See Young 1979.12–17, in the context of an extremely valuable article on the transfer of motifs in myths.

60. The slaying of Achilleus with an arrow in the Thymbraion is also reported by Eustathios (Eu-*Il* p. 816), after which he notes that Hellanikos used the form "Dymbraios" of the god. Robert (1881.127) took this as proof that Achilleus' death in this fashion was actually related by Hellanikos, but that conclusion seems to me no more than possible.

61. What Homer meant by the term *paides Trôôn* was contested even in antiquity. Aristarchos supposed women of Troy, and thus athetised the line as contamination from the similar version of the *Little Iliad*. But probably these are Trojan prisoners, whether male or female, as in the scholia.

62. For what it is worth, the Geneva scholia at *Iliad* 14.406 (first hand) attribute the notion of Aias' invulnerability to the *neôteroi*.

63. Against this initial interpretation of D. von Bothmer and in favor of Aias' suicide, see B. B. Shefton, *RA* (1973) 203–18 and M. I. Davies, *AntK* 16 (1973) 60–70, the latter incorporating significant new fragments of the cup not originally available to von Bothmer; these last eliminate any possibility that the woman is removing a robe from the corpse rather than covering it with one. The odd position of this corpse may be due to nothing more than a desire to show Aias' dead body face up, but just possibly a reference to a single vulnerable spot (more toward the back than the ribs?) is also involved.

64. See D. L. Thompson, *ArchClass* 28 (1976) 30–39.

65. See Sadurska 1964.27–28; the entire left side of the relief, and with it the left half of this particular scene, is broken away, so that we do not know how Philoktetes was armed.

66. Athenaios 9.393d.

67. Conceivably she appeared in Bakchylides, if the letters *Oin*[. . .] in fragment 20D Sm refer to her (as wife of Paris) rather than to Althaia, wife of Oineus. On this point see Stinton (1965.40–50), who suggests that the papyrus' subsequent reference to Niobe could imply Oinone just as well as Althaia, since both women (like Niobe) bring

about the death of a loved one, Paris in the first case, Meleagros in the second. Stinton also interprets Paris' pre-Helen romantic attachment (minus Korythos) as very much a part of his shepherd *persona*, in contrast to his role as prince.

68. Admittedly, as Aristarchos noted, Deiphobos can be removed from the first of these scenes by the athetising of a single line. But in the second situation we must imagine that Menelaos' first thought will be to secure Helen, lest she escape or be killed by someone else; since he goes to Deiphobos' house, Homer surely means us to understand that she is there.

69. Earlier the plot of this play was taken to be the fetching of *Achilleus*, not Neoptolemos, from Skyros, as in the *Skyrioi* of Euripides, and the matter is not entirely certain, but see Pearson 1917 2.191–93 and Radt 1977.418–19.

70. For this papyrus fragment see A. S. Hunt, *Catalogue of the Greek Papyri in the John Rylands Library, Manchester* 1 (Manchester 1911) 40–42, and for the supplement Bernabé 1987.75. The papyrus relates three events as in the *Little Iliad*, although with the theft of the Palladion well out of the sequence Proklos reports; between the fetching of Neoptolemos (by Phoinix and someone) and the arrival of Eurypylos there is room for Achilleus' ghost, and some location seems to be specified.

71. Though note that Bernabé includes this among fragments he believes to come from a different *Little Iliad*. The *Iliad* scholia cite verses about the different medical skills of Machaon and his brother Podaleirios which they attribute to the *Iliou Persis* of Arktinos (ΣT *IL* 11.515); these *might* mean that the death of Machaon was also related in that poem.

72. Probably this last explanation is, as Severyns argues (1928.343–44), simply another Aristarchean attempt to separate Homer from what was to be found in later elaborations (i.e., the Cycle).

73. Aristotle (or an interpolation) mentions such a play, but without naming the author (*Poet* 23.1459b6). An *Oxyrhynchus papyrus* (POxy 1175 = frr 206a–222a R) apparently drawn from it now suggests Sophoklean authorship, given similarities to the papyrus of the same poet's *Ichneutai*.

74. Proklos' summary of the *Little Iliad* does not in fact say that Helenos counseled the theft of the Palladion, although it seems a reasonable assumption, and admittedly is the case in the PRylands 22 account perhaps drawn from the same epic: see n. 70 above. Helenos is likewise responsible in Apollodoros' account (ApE 5.10).

75. Severyns claims that Apollodoros here follows the version of Arktinos, contaminating it, however, with Odysseus' disguise as a beggar taken from Lesches (1928. 349–52). Certainly this is possible, but the inclusion of the theft of the Palladion in Arktinos' poem remains questionable (see p. 644 below), and if there is only one foray, then Odysseus' daytime visit as a beggar in the *Odyssey* stands unexplained. We will see, too, below that the curious anomaly of Odysseus disguising himself to infiltrate Troy at night appears already in Aristophanes and Antisthenes, however that story was concocted.

76. On the *Little Iliad* scenes from the *Tabula Iliaca Capitolina*, Diomedes exits from the city holding the Palladion, followed by Odysseus with a shield, if the names are correctly assigned: see Sadurska 1964.28, 30. Even if this does come from Lesches' poem, it is no more than we would expect from later versions.

77. Although of course Athena may not favor Odysseus in every account: see Severyns for the suggestion (1928.351–52, 354–55) that Lesches consciously minimizes Odysseus' roles and accomplishments, compared with Arktinos and the *Odyssey*.

78. On the evidence of Proklos, Arktinos' poem began only with the debate over the Horse, that is, with events belonging to the actual Sack of Troy. We cannot, however, be sure that a summary of earlier events has not been cut from our text to avoid overlap with the summary from Lesches, much as seems to have been done in making that latter summary end well before the *Little Iliad* does. Another possibility is that the reference to the Palladion occurred in the course of the description of the Sack, with no detailed narration of the attempted theft. Conceivably in that case Arktinos omitted any prophecy, motivated perhaps by a desire to have the Palladion remain in Troy until the Sack in the belief that this statue (not another) was required for the impiety against Kassandra.

79. For the various Roman explanations of how the true Palladion reached Italy (including some that recognize the difficulty of allowing the Trojans to keep the statue and make Diomedes bring it to Italy instead), see R. G. Austin, *Aeneidos Liber Secundus* (Oxford 1964) 84–85.

80. For discussion of this material (with illustrations), see Moret 1975 1.71–84.

81. Polyainos adds a version in which the statue is deposited with Demophon, who sends it to Athens while feigning a defense against Agamemnon, after which he fools the latter with a copy (1.5).

82. For the theory that two Palladia were needed (and *both* taken to Athens) because the Athenians had two such cult statues to explain, see Robert 1920–26.1235–37.

83. For what it is worth he does not appear in the *Little Iliad* scenes on the *Tabula Iliaca Capitolina:* see Sadurska 1964.28. But other events of the poem are also omitted (i.e., Odysseus' infiltration of Troy as a beggar) and then too the scenes in question conclude with the bringing of the Horse into the city; if Laokoon's tale appeared in Lesches where it does in Arktinos (i.e., only *after* the Horse is inside) we should not expect to find it here. The *Tabula* does show Sinon (bound) and Kassandra (agitated?) at the Skaian gates as the Horse enters; if this last detail is not interpolated from the *Aeneid* (see n. 90 below) it will constitute our first evidence of the seeress attempting to warn her people against the hidden Greeks.

84. Robert 1881.192–93.

85. One other artifact sometimes thought to represent the tale of Laokoon is a mid-fifth-century Red-Figure kantharos in London with a bearded figure at an altar being bitten by a snake and gazing with drawn sword at a just deceased youth (London E155). The bearded figure has been interpreted as Laokoon or the second of his sons (if he is not Ixion or Orestes), but either identification seems dubious (surely the man has slain the youth himself), and unless the winged figure holding the youth is a metamorphosed snake (rather than Thanatos) they offer in any case nothing noteworthy for our purposes. For arguments revising and bolstering earlier versions of this interpretation of the scene, see E. Buschor in A. Furtwängler, F. Hauser, and K. Reichhold, *Griechische Vasenmalerei*, Series 3 (Munich 1932) 274–76.

86. Severyns argues (*RBPh* 5 [1926] 317–21) that the original number was thirteen, although he also postulates that this was simply the number of Achaians (out of a larger total) actually *named* by the *Little Iliad*.

87. The improbability of Helen knowing the voices of the other Achaians' wives caused Aristarchos to athetise the line in question, but even without it Helen in tapping on the Horse is clearly aiming at the betrayal of those inside it.

88. Presumably Pausanias means that in Lesches Koroibos dies during the Sack by Diomedes' hand rather than Neoptolemos', but PRylands 22 has a Korybos, son of Myg-

842

don of Phrygia, slain during the theft of the Palladion, so that possibly both slayer and point in time were different in the *Little Iliad:* see n. 70 above.

89. See Sadurska 1964.28–30.

90. For the Vergilian contamination of material supposedly drawn from Greek epic, and the probable working methods of the artist (Theodoros) in crediting sources, see Horsfall 1979a.35–43.

91. But see n. 83 above on her possible appearance in this role in the *Little Iliad*.

92. See M. Ervin, *AD* 18 (1963) 37–75, for the full publication of this pithos.

93. Robert in fact argues (1920–26.1268 n. 2) that works such as the *Odyssey* and the *Nostoi*, where Kassandra is Agamemnon's prize, must reject this tradition of the rape.

94. On this scene as representing the death of Astyanax see E. T. H. Brann, *AntK* 2 (1959) 35–37.

95. See Payne 1931.136 n. 3; Hampe 1935/36.272–77; Kunze 1950.158. This view is by no means proved, but Dörig's attempt to return to the theory of a Titanomachy (with Poseidon threatening Rheia) is not likely to be right: see above, chap. 1, n. 55.

96. Catalogue of early representations in Ghali-Kahil 1955.71–112. Not included here is the Mykonos relief pithos, which was discovered only in 1961.

97. See R. Förster, *Hermes* 18 (1883) 475–78, where it is also proposed that the mention of Polyxena's death well in advance of the fact might have occurred as a remark of the poet, perhaps on the occasion of Troilos' death and her flight.

Chapter 17. The Return from Troy

1. See above, pp. 574–75.

2. See D. F. Sutton, *Philologus* 128 (1984) 127–30.

3. On the Homeric version of Agamemnon's death see now Prag 1985.68–73. Against his separation of the various accounts into "Aigisthos alone" and "Aigisthos and Klytaimestra" versions, I would argue that Homer stresses the complicity of each in accordance with the needs of the moment, but of course previous tellers of the tale may have themselves shifted responsibility one way or another as their tastes dictated. For an "Aigisthos alone" version much depends on how we understand *Odyssey* 3.269.

4. See S. West (1981.359–61) for objections to Agamemnon's unusual sea route and arguments that material has here been added.

5. Bowra 1961.112–14.

6. See Prag 1985.1–5.

7. In favor of these two points see Schefold (1964.44) and M. I. Davies (1969. 228–30), both of whom argue that Klytaimestra does hold a weapon in her right hand. More properly cautious, I think, are Fittschen, who doubts both net and weapon, supposing Aigisthos to commit the murder with his right hand (1969.189), and Prag, who does likewise but with Klytaimestra the assailant, operating with her left hand behind Agamemnon's back (1985.1–2).

8. See Kunze 1950.167–68.

9. In favor of this interpretation see Kunze 1950.168 and (with a new drawing) Prag 1985.2–3 and pl. 2b, c.

10. See Fittschen 1969.187; Prag 1985.58.

11. See Boardman 1963.128–29 and, for the interpretation of the scene as the death of Agamemnon, M. I. Davies 1969.224–28, 230–36.

12. See Schäfer 1957.75; Fittschen 1969.188, 191. Hampe (1936.71) argued that

the three figures shown could only be Hekabe, Priam, and Neoptolemos, but Kunze (1950.157 and n. 3) thought to see traces of a throne in the center and suggested the death of Aigisthos or Agamemnon; so too Fittschen (preferring Agamemnon) and now Van Keuren 1989.120–22 (Agamemnon in bath: see below).

13. See n. 12 above and Prag (1985.32–33), who favors Herakles and Apollo.

14. For the theory that relief vessel and Foce del Sele metope present Agamemnon's death in his bath, see Van Keuren 1989.120–22. The same scholar, following Schmidt (1977.269 n. 19), also argues that traces of a bath (i.e., a pitcher) can be seen on the New York steatite seal discussed above.

15. For discussion of both the metope and the Basel relief see p. 275 above.

16. See Fittschen 1969.186–87.

17. M. I. Davies 1969.252–56, interpreting at the same time the scene on the reverse (usually taken to show Apollo and Artemis) as the death of Aigisthos.

18. Sinn 1979.101 (MB 36); see also C. Robert, *JdI* 34 (1919) 72–76.

19. See E. Vermeule, *AJA* 70 (1966) 1–22.

20. On 474 B.C. as the more likely date of *Pythian* 11 see chap. 16, n. 28, above.

21. March (1987.86–98) argues that since in the *Kypria, Ehoiai*, and Stesichoros Iphigeneia is saved by Artemis, her fate cannot have served as motivation for Klytaimestra's deeds; probably that is reasonable, although Agamemnon did *intend* to sacrifice her, and she is thereby lost to her mother. March further suggests, based on the sudden spate of Attic vase-paintings with the killing, that Simonides is responsible for Klytaimestra's greater involvement.

22. Of these sources, the *Iliad* scholion specifically assigns the device of the chiton with no outlet at the neck to the tragedians; whether the scholiast knew of a play in which this was actually dramatized, as opposed to just the allusion in Euripides' *Orestes*, we do not know.

23. Although there was as well a recognition by means of a lock of Orestes' hair, as in Aischylos: 217 *PMG*.

24. This is the standard interpretation; for bibliography and other suggestions (apart from his own of the death of Agamemnon) see M. I. Davies 1969.252 n. 1 and 253 n. 1.

25. For the publication of this mitra see H. Bartels in E. Kunze et al., *VIII. Bericht über die Ausgrabungen in Olympia* (Berlin 1967) 198–205, where it is suggested that an already dead Aigisthos (on throne?) might have occupied the missing left half. Fittschen (1969.187–88, 191) likewise interprets the scene as the matricide.

26. So H. Hoffmann in H. Hoffmann and A. Raubitschek, *Early Cretan Armorers* (Mainz 1972) 26, 39.

27. Kunze 1950.168–69.

28. See above, chap. 1, n. 55, and p. 656.

29. See Fittschen 1969.188–89.

30. In support of this interpretation see Fittschen 1969.191; Schefold 1964.89. Against it Prag objects (1985.35–36) that Tydeus and Ismene might be intended (although he admits that the dress of the figures is wrong) or else that the relief has been reworked, the artist having originally intended a male figure in place of the female victim.

31. Zancani Montuoro and Zanotti-Bianco 1954.269–74 (Metope no. 24: "Laodameia and Klytaimestra").

32. Ibid., 141–45 (Metope no. 7: "Herakles and Hera"). The excavators as we saw

earlier associate this metope with two others showing attacking Silenoi; for the view that it represents Orestes and Elektra see Van Keuren 1989.57–64.

33. Zancani Montuoro and Zanotti-Bianco 1954.275–88 (Metope no. 25: "Orestes and Aigisthos").

34. For the identification of this metope as in fact Achilleus and Troilos see Van Keuren 1989.95–103.

35. So Zancani Montuoro and Zanotti-Bianco 1954.289–300, supported most recently by Van Keuren 1989.123–29.

36. See Prag 1985.47–48 and pls. 28d, 29a.

37. Against Simon's dubious opinion that Ixion could be portrayed (1955.25–26; 1967.280) there remains the difficult fact that no literary tradition records Ixion pursued by Erinyes; indeed, the crime he commits (killing his father-in-law) is not one that they properly punish, since the victim is not a real parent, or even a relative.

38. See most recently A. H. Somerstein in his commentary on the play (1989. 222–26), with argument that Athena votes as part of the jury and cogent discussion of previous views.

39. Discussion of these and other scenes of Aigisthos' death in Prag 1985.13–34.

40. See ibid., 106–7, and pl. 46.

41. Admittedly, Accius' *Erigona* does seem to have treated this figure (since Aigisthos and Orestes are mentioned), and presumably it had a Greek model. Pearson (1917.173–74) does suppose the subject of Sophokles' play the trial.

42. Stobaios is the sole source, citing a number of fragments (content of no help) from a play he calls *Aleites* and ascribes to Sophokles (see Pearson 1917.62–67). Modern opinion generally rejects the ascription (for the fragments in the new *Tragicorum Graecorum Fragmenta* see Ades fr 1b), and given Stobaios' spelling of the title even its link to the house of Atreus remains uncertain.

43. According to Pausanias, however, there was also such a statue, brought back by Iphigeneia when she left the Tauroi, at Brauron (1.33.1).

44. So H. Lloyd-Jones, *JHS* 103 (1983) 96.

45. We should remember that Aischylos' *Iphigeneia*—about which nothing whatever is known—could have dealt with these same events. Sophokles' *Iphigeneia* seems clearly to have dramatized the sacrifice at Aulis, but his *Chryses* has been suspected as a predecessor of Euripides' plot: see below.

46. The portent consists of finding a land where the houses have iron foundations, wooden walls, and roofs of wool; in Epeiros, Neoptolemos then encounters men who fix their spears in the ground and use their cloaks to form tents.

47. Schwartz in his edition of the *Orestes* scholia accepts the emendation to Machaireus; Jacoby in editing Pherekydes restricts it to the *apparatus*.

48. This conclusion will naturally be invalidated if, as some have thought, the controversial scene on London E155 (a Red-Figure kantharos of the early fifth century) does in fact represent Orestes with a just-slain Neoptolemos, rather than Laokoon and his sons, or Ixion. But the man on the altar (with snake and drawn sword) is bearded, while the dead person is not, and this is surely an impossible way in which to present the relationship between Orestes and a man his senior who has fought at Troy.

49. On the vexed question of what the contestant was supposed to shoot at after stringing the bow, see now the survey of views by Fernández-Galiano in Fernández-Galiano and Heubeck 1986.xviii–xxv.

50. See Gantz 1980.151–53.

51. Catalogue and discussion of the *Odyssey* in art in Touchefeu-Meynier 1968; see also the valuable compilation in Brommer 1983.56–109. For Polyphemos, Fellman (1972) now offers a separate study.

52. Against Schefold's view (1978.267–68) that this could be a non-Homeric version of the Odyssean tale see Amyx and Amandry 1982.113–15.

53. The eye of this rapidly falling Seiren seems clearly closed, leading to the suggestion that she is dead or dying, perhaps because in some accounts these creatures were fated to die when someone successfully resisted them: see Arafat 1990.1.

54. For this identification of the scene (cautiously advanced), see C. Weickert, *RM* 60/61 (1953–54) 56–61; he supposes the piece to be of Corinthian Late Geometric fabric.

55. Zancani Montuoro and Zanotti-Bianco 1954.301–15. The interpretation as Odysseus originates here (Zancani Montuoro). The same scholar argues her case in more detail in *PP* 14 (1959) 221–29.

56. For the theory (already noted in chapter 15) that the figure could be Tantalos, and a good discussion of other turtle riders in art, see Van Keuren 1989.139–46.

57. Earlier Pausanias also speculates that a scene on the topmost panel of the Chest—a man and woman on a couch in a grotto surrounded by attendants—represents Odysseus and Kirke (5.19.7); this he admits is wholly a guess on his part, and in this case at least we might think of numerous other possibilities.

58. So West (1966.433–36), arguing that this notion will derive from the sixth century, since before that time the Etruscans would not have been of sufficient interest to the Greeks, and after 510 b.c. Etruscans and Latins would have been more clearly differentiated. West also supposes the line mentioning Telegonos interpolated into this section, since it interrupts the link between the first two sons and their dominion.

59. According to the *Odyssey* scholia, Hephaistos makes this spear for Telegonos (at the request of Kirke) from a ray that Phorkys had slain; the shaft had parts of adamantine and gold.

60. H. Lloyd-Jones, in *CR* 14 (1964) 247, suggests that the words *ek toud'* in the third line of the quote might mean "after this" (the depositing of excrement) rather than "from this." The idea is attractive (and Sextus perhaps had no more evidence than we do), but in that case one must wonder that Aischylos would leave such an unfortunate ambiguity in his text.

61. See Sadurska 1964.24–37, in particular 29 (description of scenes in question), 30 (inscriptions), and 32–35 (survey of the [widely divergent] previous opinions and discussion of the problem). Her own conclusion, that the artist of the tablet has followed earlier pictorial models without introducing significant new elements, is not in my opinion compelling, nor does it take into account the fact that most (perhaps all) of the elements in question will be earlier than the *Aeneid*. A more properly skeptical analysis (on which many of the following arguments are based) appears in Horsfall 1979a.26–48; see also Galinsky, who suggests (1969.106–13) that Stesichoros may have left Aineias' westward goal quite vague, thus opening the door for later writers and artists to attribute an Italian (or Sicilian) landing to him. Most scholars seem now agreed that Stesichoros is not likely to have used the actual word *Hesperia*.

62. For these see S. Woodford and M. Loudon, *AJA* 84 (1980) 30–33, 38–39; K. Schauenburg, *Gymnasium* 67 (1960) 176–90.

63. In favor of the receptacle see Alföldi 1965.284–86; of the suitcase Horsfall 1979a.40.

64. Head 1911.214; M. Price and N. Waggoner, *Archaic Greek Coinage: The As-yut Hoard* (London 1975).

65. See Brommer 1967.220–21.

66. The problems in this passage are investigated at length by Horsfall (1979b. 377–83), although I am not sure I would agree that Aineias' arrival in Italy with Odysseus means that he left Troy as a captive. Horsfall's final judgment, that Aineias' link to Latium and Rome is probably no older than Timaios, remains the safest conclusion, although F. Solmsen (*HSCP* 90 [1985] 93–110) renews the arguments in favor of Hellanikos.

Chapter 18. Other Myths

1. See Gantz, *Hermes* 106 (1978) 14–26.

2. A fragmentary inscription from the Athenian Agora listing productions now increases the likelihood that Sophokles did write such a play (see B. Merritt, *Hesperia* 7 [1938] 116–18); the only other evidence is a one-word citation from the Apollonios scholia which some have thought might be in fact from Aischylos' version of the story.

3. For this interpretation see Robert 1881.210–12, subsequently supported by Simon 1955.5–14 and 1967.175–95. Both scholars concede that the victim cannot be Ixion's father-in-law, but argue that some other relative not known to us is intended.

4. See frr 293–96 Kern.

5. Sale (1962.122–31) argues, in fact, that nothing in this account after Kallisto's metamorphosis and the birth of Arkas is from "Hesiod," in part because Ps-Eratosthenes omits intervening material (the version of Amphis: see below) reported by our Latin derivatives of Eratosthenes. This cannot be certain, but Sale well points out the absurdities of a tale in which Arkas pursues his mother after they have grown up together. Originally they must have been separated after his birth, so that he might come in time to threaten her (in ignorance of her identity) and to endanger himself in so doing.

6. On this variant as Hesiodic (from the *Ehoiai*, in fact), see Sale, who argues (1965.14 plus 1962.140–41) that the evidence of Ps-Eratosthenes and Apollodoros indicates two retellings in the Hesiodic Corpus, one making Kallisto a Nymph, the other making her the daughter of Lykaon. Her role as Nymph slain by Artemis he sees as the earlier, local account, since it serves to explain her grave at Trikolonoi in Arkadia (Paus 8.35.8).

7. For the reconstruction see Webster 1967.147–50.

8. For the *Xantriai* as dramatizing this myth see Séchan 1926.102 n. 2 and Mette 1963.146–47; the suggestion was first made by Boeckh in the last century.

Appendix A. Some "Deviant" Cosmogonies

1. For what follows see, in particular, Schibli 1990.

Bibliography

As a rule, the following list includes only items that are cited more than once in the notes or were found to be generally useful in the writing of this book. Editions of ancient authors and scholia are cited in Appendix B; they reappear here only if the notes refer to them in some special connection. Reference works to Greek art are cited at the beginning of Appendix C.

Alföldi, A. 1965. *Early Rome and the Latins.* Ann Arbor, Mich.

Allen. T. 1912. *Homeri Opera 5.* Oxford.

Amyx, D. 1988. *Corinthian Vase-Painting of the Archaic Period.* 3 vols. Berkeley.

Amyx, D., and P. Amandry. 1982. "Héraclès et l'Hydre de Lerne dans la céramique corinthienne." *AntK* 25:102–16.

Arafat, K. W. 1990. *Classical Zeus.* Oxford.

Austin, C. 1968. *Nova Fragmenta Euripidea in papyris reperta.* Berlin.

Barrett, W. S. 1964. *Euripides: Hippolytos.* Oxford.

Barron, J. P. 1972. "New Light on Old Walls. The Murals of the Theseion." *JHS* 92:20–45.

Bauchhenss-Thüriedl, C. 1971. *Der Mythos von Telephos in der antiken Bildkunst.* Würzburg.

Beazley, J. 1951. *The Development of Attic Black-Figure.* Berkeley.

Beck, I. 1984. *Ares in Vasenmalerei, Relief und Rundplastik.* Frankfurt.

Beckel, G. 1961. *Götterbeistand in der Bildüberlieferung griechischer Heldensagen.* Stiftland.

Bérard, C. 1974. *Anodoi: Essai sur l'Imagerie des Passages chthoniens.* Rome.

Bernabé, A. 1987. *Poetae Epici Graeci 1.* Leipzig.

Bethe, E. 1891. *Thebanische Heldenlieder.* Leipzig.

Blome, P. 1978. "Das gestörte Mahl des Phineus auf einer Lekythos des Sapphomalers." *AntK* 21:70–75.

Boardman, J. 1963. *Island Gems: A Study of Greek Seals in the Geometric and Early Archaic Periods.* London.

———. 1968. *Archaic Greek Gems.* Evanston, Ill.

———. 1975. "Herakles, Peisistratos and Eleusis." *JHS* 95:1–12.

Böhr, E. 1982. *Der Schaukelmaler.* Mainz am Rhein.

Böhr, E., and W. Martini. 1986. *Studien zur Mythologie und Vasenmalerei: Konrad Schauenburg zum 65. Geburtstag am 16. April 1986.* Mainz am Rhein.

Bol, P. 1989. *Argivische Schilder (Olympische Forschungen XVII).* Berlin.

Bona Quaglia, L. 1973. *Gli "Erga" di Esiodo.* Turin.

Bond, G. W. 1963. *Euripides: Hypsipyle.* Oxford.

———. 1981. *Euripides: Heracles.* Oxford.

Bowra, C. M. 1961. *Greek Lyric Poetry: From Alkman to Simonides.* 2d ed. Oxford.

———. 1964. *Pindar.* Oxford.

Brize, P. 1980. *Die Geryoneis des Stesichoros und die frühe griechische Kunst.* Würzburg.

Brommer, F. 1937a. *Satyroi.* Würzburg.

———. 1937b. "Die Rückführung des Hephaistos." *JdI* 52:198–219.

———. 1942. "Herakles und die Hesperiden auf Vasenbildern." *JdI* 57:105–23.

———. 1944/45. "Herakles und Syleus." *JdI* 59/60:69–78.

———. 1957. "Attische Könige." In *Charites: Studien zur Altertumswissenschaft.* Bonn.

———. 1959. *Satyrspiele.* 2d ed. Berlin.

———. 1963. *Die Skulpturen der Parthenon-Giebel.* Mainz am Rhein.

———. 1967. *Die Metopen des Parthenon.* Mainz am Rhein.

———. 1972. *Herakles: Die zwölf Taten des Helden in antiker Kunst und Literatur.* Darmstadt.

———. 1973. *Vasenlisten zur griechischen Heldensage.* 3d ed. Marburg.

———. 1978. *Hephaistos: Der Schmiedegott in der antiken Kunst.* Mainz am Rhein.

———. 1982. *Theseus: Die Taten des griechischen Helden in der antiken Kunst und Literatur.* Darmstadt.

———. 1983. *Odysseus: Die Taten und Leiden des Helden in antiker Kunst und Literatur.* Darmstadt.

———. 1984. *Herakles II: Die unkanonischen Taten des Helden.* Darmstadt.

Burkert, W. 1985. *Greek Religion.* Cambridge, Mass.

Burow, J. 1989. *Der Antimenesmaler.* Mainz am Rhein.

Buschor, E. 1934. "Kentauren." *AJA* 38:128–32.

Carpenter, T. H. 1986. *Dionysian Imagery in Archaic Greek Art.* Oxford.

Clairmont, C. 1951. *Das Parisurteil in der antiken Kunst.* Zurich.

Conacher, D. J. 1967. *Euripidean Drama.* Toronto.

———. 1980. *Aeschylus' Prometheus Bound: A Literary Commentary.* Toronto.

Cook, A. B. 1914. *Zeus: A Study in Ancient Religion* 1. Cambridge.

———. 1925. *Zeus: A Study in Ancient Religion* 2. Cambridge.

Croiset, A. 1898. "Sur les origines du récit relatif à Méléagre dans l'ode V de Bacchylide," 73–80. In *Mélanges Henri Weil.* Paris.

Dale, A. M. 1967. *Euripides: Helen.* Oxford.

Davies, M. 1991. *Poetarum Melicorum Graecorum Fragmenta.* Oxford.

Davies, M. I. 1969. "Thoughts on the *Oresteia* before Aischylos." *BCH* 93:214–60.

de La Coste-Messelière, P. 1936. *Au Musée de Delphes.* Paris.

Diggle, J. 1970. *Euripides: Phaethon.* Cambridge.

Dörig, J., and O. Gigon. 1961. *Der Kampf der Götter und Titanen.* Olten and Lausanne.

Drachmann, A. B. 1927. *Scholia vetera in Pindarum* 3. Leipzig.

Dugas, C. 1944. "Le premier crime de Médée." *REA* 46:5–11.

Fellman, B. 1972. *Die antiken Darstellungen des Polyphemabenteuers.* Munich.

Felten, W. 1975. *Attische Unterweltsdarstellungen.* Munich.

Fernández-Galiano, M., and A. Heubeck. 1986. *Omero: Odissea 6.* Milan.

Fittschen, K. 1969. *Untersuchungen zum Beginn der Sagendarstellungen bei den Griechen.* Berlin.

Forbes-Irving, P. 1990. *Metamorphosis in Greek Myth*. Oxford.

Fraenkel, E. 1950. *Aeschylus: Agamemnon*. 3 vols. Oxford.

———. 1963. *Zu den Phoenissen des Euripides*. Munich.

Friis Johansen, H., and E. W. Whittle. 1980. *Aeschylus: The Suppliants*. 3 vols. Copenhagen.

Friis Johansen, K. 1923. *Les vases sicyoniens*. Paris and Copenhagen.

———. 1945. *Thésée et la danse à Délos (Det Kgl. Danske Videnskabernes Selskab: Arkeologisk-Kunsthistoriske Meddelelser)* 3, no. 3. Copenhagen.

———. 1967. *The Iliad in Early Greek Art*. Copenhagen.

Furtwängler, A. 1885. *Beschreibung der Vasensammlung im Antiquarium*. 2 vols. Berlin.

Galinsky, G. K. 1969. *Aeneas, Sicily, and Rome*. Princeton.

Gantz, T. 1980. "The Aischylean Tetralogy: Attested and Conjectured Groups." *AJPh* 101:133–64.

———. 1981. "Divine Guilt in Aischylos." *CQ* 31:16–32.

Garvie, A. F. 1969. *Aeschylus' Supplices: Play and Trilogy*. Cambridge.

Gerber, D. 1982. *Pindar's Olympian One: A Commentary*. Toronto.

Ghali-Kahil, L. 1955. *Les enlèvements et le retour d'Hélène dans les textes et les documents figurés*. Paris.

Glynn, R. 1981. "Herakles, Nereus and Triton." *AJA* 85:121–32.

Griffin, J. 1977. "The Epic Cycle and the Uniqueness of Homer." *JHS* 97:39–53.

Griffith, M. 1977. *The Authenticity of Prometheus Bound*. Cambridge.

———. 1983. *Aeschylus: Prometheus Bound*. Cambridge.

Grimal, P. 1951. *Dictionnaire de la Mythologie grecque et romaine*. Paris.

Hainsworth, J. B. 1982. *Omero: Odissea* 2. Milan.

Hampe, R. 1935/36. "Korfugiebel und frühe Perseusbilder." *AM* 60/61:271–99.

———. 1936. *Frühe griechische Sagenbilder in Böotien*. Athens.

Hampe, R., and E. Simon. 1964. *Griechische Sagen in der frühen etruskischen Kunst*. Mainz am Rhein.

Harrison, J. E. 1922. *Prolegomena to the Study of Greek Religion*. 3d ed. Cambridge.

Head, B. 1911. *Historia Numorum*. 2d ed. Oxford.

Helbig, W. 1969. *Führer durch die öffentlichen Sammlungen klassischer Altertümer in Rom*. 3: *Die staatlichen Sammlungen*. 4th ed. revised by H. Speier and others. Tübingen.

Hemelrijk, J. M. 1984. *Caeretan Hydriae*. Mainz am Rhein.

Heubeck, A. 1983. *Omero: Odissea* 3. Milan.

Heydemann, H. 1872. *Die Vasensammlungen des Museo Nazionale zu Neapel*. Berlin.

Horsfall, N. 1979a. "Stesichoros at Bovillae?" *JHS* 99:26–48.

———. 1979b. "Some Problems in the Aeneas Legend." *CQ* 29:372–90.

Howald, E. 1924. "Meleager und Achill." *RhM* 73:402–25.

Hutchinson, G. 1985. *Aeschylus: Septem contra Thebas*. Oxford.

Huxley, G. L. 1969. *Greek Epic Poetry: From Eumelos to Panyassis*. Cambridge, Mass.

Jacobsthal, P. 1931. *Die melischen Reliefs*. Berlin-Wilmersdorf.

Jacoby, F. 1949. *Atthis: The Local Chronicles of Ancient Athens*. Oxford.

———. 1957. *Die Fragmente der griechischen Historiker* 1. 2 vols. 2d ed. Leiden.

Janko, R. 1982. *Homer, Hesiod and the Hymns*. Cambridge.

Jucker, H. 1977. "Herakles und Atlas auf einer Schale des Nearchos in Bern." In *Festschrift für Frank Brommer*. Mainz am Rhein.

850

Bibliography

Kaempf-Dimitriadou, S. 1979. *Die Liebe der Götter in der attischen Kunst des 5. Jahrhunderts v. Chr. (AntK* Beiheft 11). Bern.

Kamerbeek, J. 1959. *The Plays of Sophokles* 4: *The Trachiniai.* Leiden.

Kerényi, K. 1951. *Die Mythologie der Griechen; die Götter- und Menschheitsgeschichten.* Zurich.

———. 1958. *Die Heroen der Griechen.* Zurich.

Keuls, E. C. 1974. *The Water Carriers in Hades.* Amsterdam.

Kirk, G., J. Raven, and M. Schofield. 1983. *The Presocratic Philosophers.* 2d ed. Cambridge.

Kirk, G. S. 1962. "The Structure and Aim of the *Theogony.*" In *Hésiode et son Influence (Entretiens sur l'Antiquité classique VII).* Geneva.

———. 1985. *The Iliad: A Commentary* 1: Books 1–4. Cambridge.

———. 1990. *The Iliad: A Commentary* 2: Books 5–8. Cambridge.

Kossatz-Deissmann, A. 1978. *Dramen des Aischylos auf westgriechischen Vasen.* Mainz am Rhein.

Kraus, T. 1960. *Hekate: Studien zu Wesen und Bild der Göttin in Kleinasien und Griechenland.* Heidelberg.

Krauskopf, I. 1974. *Der thebanische Sagenkreis und andere griechischen Sagen in der etruskischen Kunst.* Mainz am Rhein.

Krieger, X. 1975. *Der Kampf zwischen Peleus und Thetis in der griechischen Vasenmalerei.* Münster.

Kron, U. 1976. *Die zehn attischen Phylenheroen (AM* Beiheft 5). Berlin.

Kunze, E. 1950. *Archaische Schildbänder (Olympische Forschungen II).* Berlin.

Kurtz, D., and J. Boardman. 1971. *Greek Burial Customs.* Ithaca, N.Y.

Lacy, L. 1990. "Aktaion and a Lost 'Bath of Artemis.'" *JHS* 110:26–42.

Lasserre, F. 1950. *Les Épodes d'Archiloque.* Paris.

Lesky, A. 1972. *Die tragische Dichtung der Hellenen.* Göttingen.

Lindner, R. 1984. *Der Raub der Persephone in der antiken Kunst.* Würzburg.

Lloyd-Jones, H. 1957. *Aeschylus* 2:523–603. Loeb Library, Cambridge, Mass.

———. 1983. *The Justice of Zeus.* 2d ed. Berkeley.

March, J. 1987. *The Creative Poet.* London.

Mette, H. J. 1963. *Der verlorene Aischylos.* Berlin.

Metzger, H. 1951. *Les représentations dans la céramique attique du IVᵉ siècle.* 2 vols. Paris.

Meuli, K. 1921. *Odyssee und Argonautika.* Berlin.

Meyer, H. 1980. *Medeia und die Peliaden.* Rome.

Moon, W. 1983. *Ancient Greek Art and Iconography.* Madison, Wis.

Moret, J.-M. 1975. *L'Ilioupersis dans la céramique italiote.* 2 vols. Rome.

———. 1984. *Oedipe, la Sphinx et les Thébains.* 2 vols. Rome.

Nicolai, W. 1964. *Hesiods Erga.* Heidelberg.

Owens, A. S. 1939. *Euripides: Ion.* Oxford.

Page, D. L. 1941. *Select Papyri III.* Loeb Library, Cambridge, Mass.

———. 1951. *Alcman: The Partheneion.* Oxford.

———. 1955. *Sappho and Alcaeus.* Oxford.

Payne, H. 1931. *Necrocorinthia.* Oxford.

Pearson, A. C. 1917. *The Fragments of Sophocles.* 3 vols. Cambridge.

Pearson, L. 1942. *The Local Historians of Attica.* Philadelphia.

Peschlow-Bindokat, A. 1972. "Demeter und Persephone in der attischen Kunst des 6. bis 4. Jahrhunderts." *JdI* 87:60–149.

Pfeiffer, R. 1949. *Callimachus.* 2 vols. Oxford.

Phillips, K. M. 1968. "Perseus and Andromeda." *AJA* 72:1–23.

Pipili, M. 1987. *Laconian Iconography of the Sixth Century B.C.* Oxford.

Prag, A.J.N.W. 1985. *The Oresteia: Iconographic and Narrative Tradition.* Chicago.

Preller, L. and C. Robert. 1894. *Theogonie und Götter (Griechische Mythologie 1).* 4th ed. Berlin.

Raab, I. 1972. *Zu den Darstellungen des Parisurteils in der griechischen Kunst.* Frankfurt and Bern.

Radt, S. 1977. *Tragicorum Graecorum Fragmenta 4: Sophocles.* Göttingen.

———. 1985. *Tragicorum Graecorum Fragmenta 3: Aeschylus.* Göttingen.

Ribbeck, O. 1875. *Die römische Tragödie im Zeitalter der Republik.* Leipzig.

Richardson, N. J. 1974. *The Homeric Hymn to Demeter.* Oxford.

Ridgway, B. S. 1977. *The Archaic Style in Greek Sculpture.* Princeton.

Robert, C. 1881. *Bild und Lied.* Berlin.

———. 1914. "Pandora." *Hermes* 49:17–38.

———. 1915. *Oidipus.* Berlin.

———. 1916. "Tyro." *Hermes* 51:273–302.

———. 1920–26. *Die griechische Heldensage (Griechische Mythologie 2).* 3 vols. Berlin.

Russo, C. F. 1965. *Hesiodi Scutum.* Firenze.

Russo, J. 1985. *Omero: Odissea 5.* Milan.

Sadurska, A. 1964. *Les Tables Iliaques.* Warsaw.

Säflund, M. L. 1970. *The East Pediment of the Temple of Zeus at Olympia.* Gothenburg.

Sale, W. 1962. "The Story of Callisto in Hesiod." *RhM* 105:122–41.

———. 1965. "Callisto and the Virginity of Artemis." *RhM* 108:11–35.

Schäfer, J. 1957. *Studien zu den griechischen Reliefpithoi des 8.-6. Jahrhunderts v. Chr. aus Kreta, Rhodos, Tenos und Boiotien.* Kallmünz.

Schauenburg, K. 1953. "Pluton und Dionysos." *JdI* 68:38–72.

———. 1957. "Zu Darstellungen aus der Sage des Admet und des Kadmos." *Gymnasium* 64:210–30.

———. 1958. "Phrixos." *RhM* 101:41–50.

———. 1960a. *Perseus in der Kunst des Altertums.* Bonn.

———. 1960b. "Der Gürtel der Hippolyte." *Philologus* 104:1–13.

———. 1960c. "Herakles und Omphale." *RhM* 103:57–76.

Schefold, K. 1964. *Frühgriechische Sagenbilder.* Munich.

———. 1978. *Götter- und Heldensagen der Griechen in der spätarchaischen Kunst.* Munich.

———. 1981. *Die Göttersage in der klassischen und hellenistischen Kunst.* Munich.

Schefold, K., and F. Jung. 1988. *Die Urkönige, Perseus, Bellerophon, Herakles und Theseus in der klassischen und hellenistischen Kunst.* Munich.

———. 1990. *Die Sagen von den Argonauten, von Theben und Troja in der klassischen und hellenistischen Kunst.* Munich.

Schibli, H. 1990. *Pherekydes of Syros.* Oxford.

Schiffler, B. 1976. *Die Typologie des Kentauren in der antiken Kunst.* Frankfurt.

Schmidt, M. 1977. "Zur Deutung der Dreifuss-Metope Nr. 32 von Foce del Sele," 265–75. In *Festschrift für Frank Brommer.* Mainz am Rhein.

Scodel, R. 1980. *The Trojan Trilogy of Euripides*. Göttingen.
Séchan, L. 1926. *Études sur la tragédie grecque dans ses rapports avec la céramique*. Paris.
Severyns, A. 1928. *Le cycle épique dans l'école d'Aristarque*. Liège and Paris.
Simon, E. 1953. *Opfernde Götter*. Berlin.
———. 1955. "Ixion und die Schlangen." *JÖAI* 42:5–26.
———. 1967. "Die vier Büsser von Foce del Sele." *JdI* 82:275–95.
———. 1985. *Die Götter der Griechen*. 4th ed. Munich.
Simon, E., et. al. 1975. *Führer durch die Antikenabteilung des Martin von Wagner Museums der Universität Würzburg*. Mainz.
Sinn, U. 1979. *Die homerischen Becher*. Berlin.
Solmsen, F. 1981. "The Sacrifice of Agamemnon's Daughter in Hesiod's *Ehoeae*." *AJP* 102:353–58.
Somerstein, A. 1989. *Aischylos: Eumenides*. Cambridge.
Sourvinou-Inwood, C. 1979. *Theseus as Son and Stepson*. London.
Steingräber, S. 1984. *Catalogo Ragionato della Pittura Etrusca*. Milan.
Stibbe, C. M. 1972. *Lakonische Vasenmaler des sechsten Jahrhunderts v. Chr.* Amsterdam and London.
Stinton, T. C. W. 1965. *Euripides and the Judgement of Paris*. London.
Sutton, D. F. 1987. *Two Lost Plays of Euripides*. Frankfurt.
Taplin, O. 1977. *The Stagecraft of Aeschylus*. Oxford.
Thalmann, W. 1978. *Dramatic Art in Aeschylus's Seven against Thebes*. New Haven.
Thompson, H. A. 1962. "The Sculptural Adornment of the Hephaisteion." *AJA* 66:339–47.
Thomson, G. 1932. *Aeschylus: The Prometheus Bound*. Cambridge.
Thummer, E. 1969. *Pindar: Die isthmischen Gedichte*. 2 vols. Heidelberg.
Touchefeu-Meynier, O. 1968. *Thèmes Odysséens dans l'art antique*. Paris.
Trendall, A. D., and T.B.L. Webster. 1971. *Illustrations of Greek Drama*. London.
Tusa, V. 1983. *La scultura in pietra di Selinunte*. Palermo.
Unterberger, R. 1968. *Der gefesselte Prometheus des Aischylos*. Stuttgart.
van der Valk, M. 1963. *Researches on the Text and Scholia of the Iliad: Part One*. Leiden.
Van Keuren, F. 1989. *The Frieze from the Hera I Temple at Foce del Sele*. Rome.
Verdenius, W. J. 1985. *A Commentary on Hesiod: Works & Days, vv. 1–382*. Leiden.
Vermeule, E. 1979. *Aspects of Death in Early Greek Art and Poetry*. Berkeley.
Vian, F. 1945. "Le combat d'Héraclès et de Kyknos." *REA* 47:5–32.
———. 1951. *Répertoire des Gigantomachies figurées dans l'art grec et romain*. Paris.
———. 1952. *La guerre des Géants: Le mythe avant l'epoque hellénistique*. Paris.
———. 1963. *Les Origines de Thèbes: Cadmos et les Spartes*. Paris.
Vojatzi, M. 1982. *Frühe Argonautenbilder*. Würzburg.
von Bothmer, D. 1957. *Amazons in Greek Art*. Oxford.
Von der Mühll, P. 1958. "Wurde die elfte Pythie Pindars 474 oder 454 gedichtet?" *MH* 15:141–56.
von Steuben, H. 1968. *Frühe Sagendarstellungen in Korinth und Athen*. Berlin.
Webster, T.B.L. 1967. *The Tragedies of Euripides*. London.
Wendel, C. 1935. *Scholia in Apollonium Rhodium vetera*. Berlin.
West, M. L. 1966. *Hesiod: Theogony*. Oxford.

853

Bibliography

———. 1978. *Hesiod: Works and Days.* Oxford.

———. 1983. *The Orphic Poems.* Oxford.

———. 1985. *The Hesiodic Catalogue of Women.* Oxford.

West, S. 1981. *Omero: Odissea* 1. Milan.

Westermann, A. 1843. *Mythographoi: Scriptores poeticae historiae graeci.* Brunswick.

Wilamowitz-Moellendorff, U. von. 1884. *Homerische Untersuchungen.* Berlin.

———. 1914. *Aischylos Interpretationen.* Berlin.

Willcock, M. M. 1964. "Mythological Paradeigma in the *Iliad.*" *CQ* 14:141–54.

———. 1978. *The Iliad of Homer: Books I–XII.* London.

———. 1984. *The Iliad of Homer: Books XIII–XXIV.* London.

Young, D. C. 1979. "The Diachronic Study of Myth and Achilles' Heel." *Journal of the California Classical Association: Northern Section* 4:3–34.

Zancani Montuoro, P., and U. Zanotti-Bianco. 1954. *Heraion alla Foce del Sele II: Il primo thesauro.* Rome.

Index

868

Index

Lightning Source UK Ltd.
Milton Keynes UK
UKHW012048091222
413676UK00001B/5

9 780801 853623